M000206704

The Rhetoric of Saint Augustine of Hippo

Studies in Rhetoric and Religion 7

EDITORIAL BOARD

MARTIN J. MEDHURST
Editorial Board Chair
Baylor University

VANESSA B. BEASLEY
University of Georgia

RANDALL L. BYTWERK
Calvin College

JAMES M. FARRELL
University of New Hampshire

JAMES A. HERRICK
Hope College

MICHAEL J. HYDE
Wake Forest University

THOMAS M. LESSL
University of Georgia

The Rhetoric
of
Saint Augustine of Hippo

De Doctrina Christiana and the Search
for a Distinctly Christian Rhetoric

RICHARD LEO ENOS, ROGER THOMPSON,
AMY K. HERMANSON, DREW M. LOEWE,
KRISTI SCHWERTFEGER SERRANO, LISA MICHELLE
THOMAS, SARAH L. YODER, DAVID ELDER,
AND JOHN W. BURKETT
EDITORS

BAYLOR UNIVERSITY PRESS

© 2008 by Baylor University Press
Waco, Texas 76798

All Rights Reserved. No part of this publication may be reproduced, stored in
a retrieval system, or transmitted, in any form or by any means, electronic,
mechanical, photocopying, recording or otherwise, without the prior permission in writing of Baylor University Press.

Scripture quotations, where not an author's own translation, are from the
New Revised Standard Version Bible, copyright 1989, Division of Christian
Education of the National Council of the Churches of Christ in the United
States of America. Used by permission. All rights reserved.

Cover design by Stephanie Milanowski

Library of Congress Cataloging-in-Publication Data

The rhetoric of St. Augustine of Hippo : De Doctrina Christiana and the
search for a distinctly Christian rhetoric / Richard Leo Enos ... [et al.].
    p. cm. -- (Studies in rhetoric and religion ; 7)
  Includes bibliographical references and index.
  ISBN 978-1-60258-008-4 (pbk. : alk. paper)
  1. Augustine, Saint, Bishop of Hippo. De doctrina Christiana. 2. Bible--
Criticism, interpretation, etc.--History--Early church, ca. 30-600. 3. Theol-
ogy--History--Early church, ca. 30-600. I. Enos, Richard Leo.

  BR65.A6552R43 2008
  230'.14--dc22
                              2008010615

Printed in the United States of America on acid-free paper with a minimum
of 30% pcw content.

We fondly dedicate this work to two scholars who helped to begin the study of St. Augustine's rhetoric anew . . .

Sister Thérèse Sullivan
The Sisters of Notre Dame of Namur

and

James J. Murphy, Professor Emeritus
The University of California, Davis

CONTENTS

Part IV
Conclusion

ACKNOWLEDGMENTS

We wish to thank the following authors, editors, publishers, and literary executors for granting us permission to publish the following works:

Baldwin, Charles S. "St. Augustine on Preaching. (*De Doctrina Christiana*, IV)." In *Medieval Rhetoric and Poetic (to 1400): Interpreted from Representative Works*. Peter Smith, 1959; originally published Gloucester, 1928. 51–73. Reproduced by permission of Peter Smith Publisher.

Fortin, Ernest L. "Augustine and the Problem of Christian Rhetoric." *Augustine Studies* 5 (1974): 85–100. Reproduced by permission of George Leaman, Augustinian Studies, Villanova University.

Leff, Michael C. "St. Augustine and Martianus Cappella: Continuity and Change in Fifth-Century Latin Rhetorical Theory." *Communication Quarterly* 24 (1976): 2–9. Reproduced by permission of Danette Johnson, the Eastern Communication Association.

Murphy, James J. "Saint Augustine and the Debate about a Christian Rhetoric." *Quarterly Journal of Speech* 46 (1960): 400–410. Reproduced by permission of the Copyright Clearance Center.

Schaeffer, John D. "The Dialectic of Orality and Literacy: The Case of Book 4 of Augustine's *De Doctrina Christiana*." *PMLA* 111.5 (1996): 1133–45. Reproduced by permission of Marcia Henry, Modern Language Association of America.

Sullivan, (Sister) Thérèse. *S. Avreli Avgvstini Hipponiensis Episcopi De Doctrina Christiana, Liber Qvartvs: A Commentary, with a Revised Text, Introduction and Translation*. Patristic Studies Series, vol. 23. Washington, D.C.: Catholic University of America Press, 1930. Reproduced by permission of Melisa A. Darby of The Catholic University of America Press.

Tracy, David W. "Charity, Obscurity, Clarity: Augustine's Search for a True Rhetoric." In *Morphologies of Faith*. Edited by Mary Gerhart and Anthony C. Yu. Atlanta: Scholars Press, 1990. Reproduced by permission of Carey J. Gifford, director of Theological Programs, American Academy of Religion.

Watson, Gerard. "St. Augustine's Theory of Language." *Maynooth Review* 6.2 (1982): 4–20. Reproduced by permission of Monsignor Dermont Farrell, President, St. Patrick's College, Maynooth (Ireland).

We are very pleased to reproduce Sister Thérèse Sullivan's 1930 edition of St. Augustine's *De Doctrina Christiana*, book 4 in its original, complete, and unedited format. As discussed in our Introduction, there is no doubt that St. Augustine's work is one of the most heralded documents in the study of rhetoric and religion. Ironically, while Sister Sullivan's revised edition may well be the greatest scholarly edition of *DDC* IV, this is the first time that her work has been reproduced in its entirety. In fact, the force driving this project from its inception has been to provide scholars with this great scholarly work in its original form. Sister Sullivan's meticulous and detailed revision of St. Augustine's writings on rhetoric does more than revise the text. Specifically, her introduction and thorough commentary complement her textual criticism and philology. As a whole, Sullivan's translation captures nuances of meaning and insight that illuminate St. Augustine's theories on the relationship of rhetoric and religion. Her scholarship, as represented by this edition, is virtually unparalleled.

In addition, we wish to extend our appreciation to those who did so much—in so many different ways—to make this volume possible. James J. Murphy and the late Edward P. J. Corbett enthusiastically supported this project from the beginning. Roger Thompson did a monumental amount of work, particularly at the early phase of this project that provided an invaluable foundation. Stacia Dunn Neeley and D. B. Magee were more than generous in their contributions to the volume. Molly Marten, Nancy White, and Claudia Knott of the Texas Christian University English department provided help and expertise with the managerial and technological aspects of this work. We also thank our English department chair, Dan Williams, and our deans, Mary Volcansek and Andrew Schoolmaster, for their help, along with the gracious support of Texas Christian University and research funding from the Rupert Radford Estate Trust. Finally, we wish to thank Martin J. Medhurst, Diane Smith, and Carey C. Newman of Baylor University Press for the unwavering support that made this dream come true.

                                                          The Editors

FOREWORD

James J. Murphy

It is interesting to note that the first rhetorical work to be printed in the fifteenth century was not one of Aristotle or of Cicero, but rather book 4 of Saint Augustine's *De Doctrina Christiana* ([Strasbourg]: Johann Mentelin, [ca. 1466]). It appeared in print three years before any of Cicero's seven rhetorical works and nine years before any version of Aristotle's *Rhetoric*. Also, it is worth noting that hardly any of the three hundred preaching manuals composed during the Middle Ages have ever reached print at all; most remain in manuscript to this day.

Why this interest in a text that was then more than a thousand years old? Actually it was not a sudden interest. From its completion in A.D. 397, the *De Doctrina Christiana* had a continuous popularity throughout the Middle Ages. This is a largely undocumented history, but anyone who has read the medieval preaching manuals knows how much the ideas of Augustine permeate them. This tradition continues in the first original preaching rhetoric of the Renaissance, the *Margarita Eloquentia sive Rhetorica Nova of Laurentius Guilielmus Traversagnus* [Westminster: William Caxton, 1478], which combines Augustine with Cicero and contemporary rhetoricians to break new ground in the field. The scores of editions and translations since then are evidence of ongoing regard for the book.

Why should this be relevant to a modern reader? The answer may lie in the opening of book 4. Augustine says that the old rhetoric is not enough—it is not bad, or evil, and in fact he taught it for a time—but it is simply not enough. So he sets out to do his own thinking about the matter of "expressing" what is known. He cannot escape completely from his detailed knowledge of rhetoric, so his discussion includes many things laid out in the rule books. But they are woven into a personalized set of observations not unlike the way Quintilian handles so easily the blend of precept and common sense in his *Institutio Oratoria.*

The lesson for the modern reader is to think for oneself, to take up questions and to try answering them without relapsing into sterile systems or mechanisms. This approach makes Augustine's fourth book very readable for a modern thinker. If there is ever to be a "new rhetoric," it will come from going beyond the "rules" as Augustine does here. This is an ancient book, but it speaks to our modern world.

PART I

INTRODUCTION

SAINT AUGUSTINE AND THE CREATION
OF A DISTINCTLY CHRISTIAN RHETORIC

Amy K. Hermanson, Drew M. Loewe, Kristi Schwertfeger Serrano,
Lisa Michelle Thomas, and Sarah L. Yoder

The fourth and fifth Christian centuries were the most critical, transformative, and tumultuous periods in the history of rhetoric and
religion in the West. In the dawning decades of the fourth century
A.D., Rome still maintained elements of her long-established imperial power, although the glorious era of what historians call the "High
Empire" (69–180 A.D.) gave way to military assassinations of emperors, the warding off of barbarian invasions, and a crumbling of the
infrastructure of the Empire that had for so long been stable in her
government and state religion. During this time, Christians had a history of misery—hunted, tortured, and persecuted in almost every conceivable manner for their faith. Nevertheless, educational traditions
remained fairly consistent in their transmission of the classical curriculum. Sophists taught throughout the Roman Empire, instantiating the
importance of (pagan) rhetoric in the classical curriculum.

However, by the early decades of the fifth century A.D., Rome,
rhetoric, and the place of Christianity in the Empire had all changed
dramatically. Not only was Christianity allowed to function within the
Empire, but Christianity also irrevocably altered the very dynamics of
the Empire. Christian emperors frequently dismantled and crushed
remnants of "pagan" practices and idolatry, and Christianity became
the defining characteristic of what was showing signs of becoming
the *Holy* Roman Empire. It would be reasonable to believe that amid
these sweeping changes, "pagan" rhetoric also would be crushed—yet
the opposite happened. Just as a nascent version of the Holy Roman
Empire began to emerge from the ashes of a pagan culture, so too did
a Christian rhetoric. How do we account for this remarkable transformation, one that virtually ensured rhetoric a place in this new Christian world?

Among historians of rhetoric, there is little doubt that Saint Augustine of Hippo (354–430 A.D.) played a major part in nurturing the rise of Christian rhetoric during this tumultuous period, particularly with his eloquent statement of rhetoric in book 4 of *De Doctrina Christiana* (*DDC*).[1] While Augustine's significant contributions to rhetoric and religion have been acknowledged on a certain level, scholars in both of these fields still have a limited understanding of the nature of his contributions. In an effort to extend knowledge of this important period of rhetorical and religious history, the inextricable relationship between rhetoric and religion—and Augustine's role in facilitating this remarkable transformation—we offer this volume.

The cornerstone of this collection is a brilliant translation of book 4 of *DDC* by Thérèse Sullivan. We have selected this translation for two important reasons. First, on November 18, 1986, Edward P. J. Corbett sent fellow rhetorician Richard Leo Enos a copy of Sullivan's out-of-print translation and commentary of book 4 of *DDC*. In his accompanying letter to Enos, the late Professor Corbett wrote that he considered the Sullivan edition to be nothing less than "the greatest edition of a primary rhetoric text produced in the twentieth century." The fact that Corbett is widely regarded as one of the twentieth century's foremost scholars in the history of rhetoric itself carried great weight. Second, Corbett's opinion was confirmed indirectly by Patricia Bizzell and Bruce Herzberg, who included excerpts from Sullivan's work in both editions of their volume, *The Rhetorical Tradition: Readings from Classical Times to the Present* (1990, 2001). There is little doubt that Bizzell and Herzberg's collection is the single most widely read anthology on the history of rhetoric, and their choice to include excerpts from Sullivan's translation ensured that her work would be the basis for introducing book 4 of Augustine's *DDC* to scholars of rhetoric. In this volume, we provide Sullivan's unabridged English translation and commentary along with Augustine's complete Latin text of book 4. Presenting the complete text will enable scholars to study not only Sullivan's translation but also to access Augustine's writing in the original Latin. To be sure, the most common monograph edition of the full text of *DDC* is D. W. Robertson's 1958 translation. To provide readers with knowledge of all four books of *DDC*, this volume also includes a synopsis of the complete work, based on Robertson's translation.

In addition, other features of this volume are intended to facilitate a more thorough understanding and scholarly study of book 4 of *DDC*.

We include a detailed bibliography of research related to topics that Augustine discusses in book 4. Within this body of work, we have identified seven essays that offer strong introductions to the rhetorical concepts that Augustine discusses, as well as to the social contexts within which he developed these concepts. We have included these essays in this volume, along with headnotes that underscore the most important features of these foundational studies.

We can best appreciate *DDC* if, as indicated above, we view Augustine's work as a response to a series of changes and problems that were facing Christianity in the Roman Empire. By Augustine's time, the rhetoric of the Roman Republic, where proficiency in speaking and writing had tangible social power, had been replaced. Within the Empire, rhetorical functions still persisted in civic activities, but the powerful dynamism that characterized the oratory of speakers such as Marcus Tullius Cicero (106–43 B.C.) had shifted, making rhetoric into subject matter for higher education. The Empire provided governmental structures through which those skilled in oratory could affect public policy. Correspondingly, the Sophistic Movement responded to the need for proficiency in communication so effectively that, by the time of Augustine, arguing against the curriculum of the Sophists would have seemed like arguing against education itself. With these changes, there is good reason to conclude that Christianity and rhetoric would have nothing to do with each other. Yet, the growing strength of Christianity also posed a significant challenge to the traditional bonds between rhetoric and Roman public life. Constantine's accession to the imperial throne in 312–313 A.D., as well as his Edict of Religious Toleration in 313, began to provide Christians with legal protection and eventually with public patronage. Many church leaders, skeptical and suspicious of "pagan" rhetoric, used their new authority to confront what they believed were rhetoric's dangerous worldly aims and pragmatic perspectives.

Despite the close association of rhetoric with pagan culture, some church leaders such as Saint Ambrose recognized that rhetoric was necessary and even desirable. The Christian community faced internal problems that prompted rhetorical solutions. The Christian tradition fought to quell various schismatic and heretical alternatives regarding questions of doctrine and religious discipline. These alternatives to the Christian tradition demanded an ongoing, effective, and vigilant response. Moreover, the need to win souls for the Christian faith necessitated that clergy be able to reach audiences unfamiliar with Scripture and to move them toward Christ, making rhetoric attractive as an evangelical tool. At the same time, Christian leaders such as Cyprian, Titian, Gregory of Naziensus, and Basil of Caesarea still resisted what they believed was dangerous to their faith: the pagan practice of rhetoric.

These challenges to rhetoric, faith, and culture are at the heart of the ongoing scholarly discussions that the essays in this volume represent. We have sequenced the essays in this collection chronologically to provide a sense of growth in the rhetorical studies of Augustine, illustrating some of the shifts and trends in scholarly interest. Beginning with Charles Baldwin's 1928 essay, "Saint Augustine and the Debate about a Christian Rhetoric," and ending with John Schaeffer's 1996 essay, "The Dialectic of Orality and Literacy: The Case of Book 4 of Augustine's *De Doctrina Christiana*," the essays in this volume illustrate a progression of thought on Augustine and Christian rhetoric. These scholars engage in both macroscopic and microscopic discussions regarding Augustine's efforts to create a Christian rhetoric, reenvisioning the Greco-Roman model by consecrating its pagan elements.

For Baldwin, the main difference between Augustine and contemporary Sophists was one of ends sought. Whereas Sophists sought to please audiences through ornate wordplay, Augustine sought to lead souls to biblical Truth. However, for Augustine, in a fallen world, even Truth benefits from a leavening of pleasure. Augustine rehabilitates Ciceronian rhetoric to a *telos* that did not exist in Cicero's day and does not dismiss any means of spreading the Word effectively, even though some may misuse rhetoric. In this way, Baldwin argues that Augustine "begins rhetoric anew." Similarly, James J. Murphy, in "St. Augustine and the Debate about a Christian Rhetoric" (1960), contends that some scholars have undervalued Augustine's contribution to rhetorical history by a kind of myopia: that is, through an excessive focus on *DDC*'s significance to medieval homiletics at the expense of understanding how Augustine negotiated fourth-century challenges to the church. Murphy explores how Augustine's training in rhetoric led him to integrate Christian Truth with pagan-influenced educational and social institutions. Murphy concludes that, by arguing for the centrality of *modus proferendi* (that is, means of expression), Augustine intended book 4 to rebut any who would deny the church a useful means of saving sinners.

Ernest Fortin discusses other relationships between Augustine and classical rhetoric by examining the connections between Ciceronian rhetoric and *DDC*. In "Augustine and the Problem of Christian Rhetoric" (1974), Fortin argues that instead of simply adapting Ciceronian rhetoric for a new purpose, Augustine inverts Cicero's hierarchy of the rhetor's three *officia*, placing teaching at the top of a new, distinctly Christian hierarchy. Fortin contends that Augustine's use of the term *doctrina* to denote teaching—as opposed to Cicero's *docere*—underscores Augustine's commitment to a distinctly Christian perspective of carrying Truth to the human mind. This orientation is diametrically opposed to the Sophistic perspective of using language to shape contingent, social reality. Fortin does not attempt to establish that Augustine's rhetoric is wholly original, but he does build a case for Augustine's ability to derive the best from a pagan rhetorical tradition (one with its own epistemologies and ontologies) and to apply it to a new hierarchy of the rhetor's duties.

Fortin's efforts to examine *DDC* as a transitional work between classical ways of knowing and being to the new exigencies of Augustine's day are echoed in Michael Leff's essay, "St. Augustine and Martianus Capella: Continuity and Change in Fifth-Century Latin Rhetorical Theory" (1976). Unlike most scholars, who have considered the rhetorical treatises of Augustine and Martianus (*DDC* for Augustine and *On the Marriage of Philology and Mercury* for Martianus) to be incommensurable, Leff argues that Augustine the Christian and Martianus the pagan both wrote in response to the same exigence: the collapse of the Roman Empire and the rise of authoritarian autocracy. Leff argues that, in spite of the changing Roman political scene, both Augustine and Martianus held fast to the Ciceronian ideal of melding eloquence and wisdom. Leff maintains that to remain viable, rhetorical theory must be malleable and adapt to changing cultural conditions. However, the continuing influence of an iconic figure, such as Cicero, on two rhetorical theorists as different as Augustine and Martianus demonstrates that, while malleable, rhetoric is also a manifestation of durable traditions and conventions.

Augustine's own philosophy of language—particularly his concept of signs—has implications for his rhetorical theory, as classicist Gerard Watson suggests. In "St. Augustine's Theory of Language" (1982), Watson counters Wittgenstein's contention that Augustine's theory of language is essentialist. In *Philosophical Investigations*, Wittgenstein criticizes Augustine's view of language based on a single passage from the *Confessions*. Watson argues that Wittgenstein misread this passage, confusing Augustine's limited description of how a child learns language with a comprehensive theory of language that claims general explanatory power. Watson traces Augustine's grounding in the classical rhetorical tradition and analyzes Augustine's theory of language across a wider body of work than Wittgenstein. He concludes that Augustine's theory of language, which discusses "signs" as intrinsic to human communication, was far more nuanced than the simple word-object correspondence that Wittgenstein attributed to Augustine.

David Tracy also considers Augustine's theory of language in "Charity, Obscurity, Clarity: Augustine's Search for a True Rhetoric" (1990). Overall, Tracy challenges the conventional claim that Augustine's rhetorical theory lacks coherence. Some scholars have contended that *DDC* seems more like two separate texts than one coherent whole, in part because Augustine's *Confessions* intervened between the completion of books 3 and 4 of *DDC*. Tracy analyzes all four books of *DDC* and contends that, despite the hiatus between the writing of books 3 and 4, the work forms a coherent whole. Tracy argues that all four books of *DDC* share the goal of spreading Truth effectively through rhetorical invention. Augustine's distinctly Christian mode of invention involves a deep understanding of God, Scripture, and the material world, as well as sound judgments about the rhetorical styles used to teach, delight, and persuade.

Finally, in "The Dialectic of Orality and Literacy: The Case of Book 4 of St. Augustine's *De Doctrina Christiana*" (1996), John Schaeffer critiques twentieth-century scholarship by contending that book 4 often has been misread through a lens that privileges written composition—so much a part of present consciousness, but not necessarily widely applicable to Augustine's own time. In contrast to scholars such as Stanley Fish, who read book 4 as a treatise on writing sermons, Schaeffer contends that Augustine's purpose was to advise Christian preachers how to deliver extemporaneous oral sermons of the type that Augustine himself delivered. To create these extemporaneous sermons, the preacher draws on a uniquely Christian wellspring of rhetorical invention: his inner state as shaped by a close study of Scripture, prayer, and the inspiration of the Holy Spirit. Schaeffer resists drawing neat binaries between orality and literacy and examines how Augustine fashioned a rhetorical theory effective in spreading a textually based religion in circumstances of low literacy.

As these studies illustrate, Augustine's *DDC* lies at the intersection of rhetoric's persistent negotiations: communicative ethics; historiography; and the relationships between thought and expression, language and reality, and orality and literacy. This volume brings together some of the most important contributions to these ongoing inquiries about *DDC* and provides the reader with a contextual framework useful for understanding and contributing to these conversations. The seven essays reprinted here illuminate how Augustine refashioned rhetoric to remove its pagan associations while, at the same time, appropriated Greco-Roman rhetoric to serve the Christian's ultimate exigency: saving souls for Christ. In so doing, Augustine was sanctifying the pagan practice of rhetoric within the emerging Holy Roman Empire as well as by equipping preachers to redeem pagan souls through rhetorical skill.

The nature of Augustine's contribution to rhetoric and religion remains a vital area of inquiry; this volume offers some important insights into the depth of his contribution, even as it highlights significant tensions in Augustine's thought and its reception. In the pages of *DDC*, Augustine begins rhetoric anew within the tradition of Christian thought, but he simultaneously draws on the classical thought of Isocrates and Cicero in seeking to unite wisdom and eloquence. All told, Augustine may well be the first rhetorician to achieve this unification—specifically, doing so within the Christian tradition. He sought this unification not for personal gain but for the greater glory of God, yet his thought has undoubtedly influenced rhetorical and religious theory and practices that extend beyond the Christian tradition and the Roman Empire. Though Augustine recognized rhetoric as a valuable tool in Christian conversion, his body of work testifies to his recognition that rhetoric is more than a mere tool—namely, that rhetoric is a necessary and unavoidable context for lived religious practice. Rather than seeing rhetoric as an unfortunate liability, however, Augustine develops a theory for using language as a part of making full use of all God-given human gifts. In so doing, Augustine attempts to return his fullest efforts to God while also enabling others to do the same.

The tensions that emerge when reassessing Augustine's thought illustrate that it is impossible to discuss religion without discussing rhetoric. Rhetoric and religion have an endemic link, and Augustine's *DDC* exemplifies this connection. As suggested in this volume's conclusion, "Religion's Rhetoric," *DDC* may be the first significant exploration of the relationship between rhetoric and religion in that Augustine negotiates a union between two competing and seemingly irreconcilable ideologies (that is, religious fideism and rhetoric). Augustine's unlikely union of Christian wisdom and rhetorical eloquence is simultaneously a classical and a Christian success story and one with implications beyond its particular historical context. Specifically, Augustine's work demonstrates that socially situated religious practice must rely on a complex understanding of rhetoric and language and that religious thinkers can benefit greatly from rhetorical education.

While this volume emphasizes the *rhetoric* of Saint Augustine of Hippo and constitutes an important recovery of Augustine's rhetorical thought, as a whole, this collection also offers an important study in the vital relationship between rhetoric and religion. This relationship consumed Augustine throughout his life and will, without a doubt, preoccupy scholars for years to come.

PART II

DE DOCTRINA CHRISTIANA

2

SYNOPTIC OUTLINE OF SAINT AUGUSTINE'S
*DE DOCTRINA CHRISTIANA**

Stacia Dunn Neeley, D. B. Magee, and Lisa Michelle Thomas

PROLOGUE

I. Response to those who object to precepts for treating the Scriptures.

    a. Purpose Statement: Augustine reveals that "there are certain precepts for treating the Scriptures" (3).

    b. There are three kinds of detractors.

        i. Those who do not understand the precepts this work contains.

        ii. Those who are unable to "clarify and explain" (3) and who judge that Augustine has labored in vain.

        iii. Those who think they already are equipped to treat the Scriptures.

    c. Augustine is not to blame because readers do not understand; they should ask God to give them vision to help understand obscurities in the Scriptures.

    d. Augustine addresses "Christians who rejoice to know the Sacred Scriptures without human instruction" (4) so that he can convince them that human instruction can be worthwhile.

    e. Those things that can be learned by men should be communicated without pride or envy (5).

    f. It is God's intention that men should be taught by other men.

    g. Charity is important in building "a knot of unity" (6).

        i. "For charity itself, which holds men together in a knot of unity, would not have a means of infusing souls and

---

* This synoptic commentary is done for educational purposes and is based on the following work: Saint Augustine, *On Christian Doctrine*. Trans. D. W. Robertson Jr. (Upper Saddle River, N.J.: Prentice Hall, 1958). Parentheses pagination refers to the general location in the Robertson edition.

almost mixing them together if men could teach nothing to men" (6).

    ii. Importance of explanation in "human words and discourse" (6).

h. True counsel from men should always be attributed to God.

i. Our ability to discern obscurity is divinely given.

j. "For no one should consider anything his own, except perhaps a lie, since all truth is from Him who said, 'I am the truth'" (6).

BOOK 1—On enjoyment, use, interpretation, word as flesh, love, faith, hope, and charity.

I. Two items are necessary in the treatment of the Scriptures.

a. Discovery: "a way of discovering those things which are to be understood" (7).

b. Teaching: "a way of teaching what we have learned" (7).

II. Faith in future ability through God.

a. ". . . to those benevolently using that which they have received He will increase and heap up what He gives" (8).

b. We believe that the ideas here will be "multiplied by His inspiration" (8).

III. All doctrine concerns signs and things.

a. "[T]hings are learned by signs" (8).

    i. Strictly speaking, things are not used as signifiers (e.g., wood, stone, cattle).

b. However, some things can be signs of other things (e.g., Moses' wooden staff, the stone on Jacob's head, the beast that Abraham sacrificed in place of his son).

c. Words are signifiers.

d. "Thus every sign is also a thing . . . but not every thing is also a sign" (9).

IV. Some things are to be enjoyed, and others are to be used.

a. To enjoy is to appreciate; to use is to interpret.

b. "Using" helps us and sustains us.

c. If we mistakenly enjoy those things that are meant to be used, we are practicing an "inferior love," and "our course will be impeded and sometimes deflected" (9).

d. Enjoyment is to cling to something for its own sake.

e. To use something is to employ it in order to obtain what you love.

f. Illicit use, however, is both waste and abuse.

g. The act of interpretation is important in our relationship with the Trinity: ". . . we should use this world and not enjoy it, so that the 'invisible things' of God 'being understood by the things that are made' may be seen, that is, so that by means of corporal and temporal things we may comprehend the eternal and spiritual" (10).

h. The Trinity is to be enjoyed; i.e., the Father, Son, and Holy Ghost.

    i. Father = Unity.

    ii. Son = Equality.

    iii. Holy Ghost = Concord of unity and equality.

i. Words have been given power by God: "God . . . has accepted the tribute of the human voice and wished us to take joy in praising Him with our words" (11).

j. Men are moved by different motivations.

V. Different motivations vary with different people and in different ways.

a. There are appeals to the human body.

b. There are appeals to the mind.

c. "Those, however, who seek to know what God is through the understanding place Him above all things mutable, either visible and corporal or intelligible and spiritual" (11).

d. God is "life itself" (12).

e. Immutable truth is to be enjoyed, and "the mind should be cleansed so that it is able to see that light and to cling to it once it is seen" (13).

f. We come to God through "good endeavor and good habits" (13).

VI. Consider the power of the Word becoming flesh.

a. Our thoughts assume the form of words but remain thoughts in our heads.

b. Wisdom has a healing power that it brings to humanity.

    i. God uses His principle of contraries—e.g., curing pride by humility.

    ii. God uses His principle of similarities—e.g., "[I]n death He freed the dead" (15).

    c.   All such principles and acts contribute to God's plan: "He has given to each gifts proper to the building of His Church so that what He showed that we should do we may do, not only without murmuring, but also with delight" (16).

    d.   The Holy Church exists as God's body and bride.

    e.   The "health" of the Church is its bond of unity and charity.

    f.   Turning to God is a way for us to leave our past sins behind.

    g.   Salvation can be considered as healing "by that faith and correction" (17).

    h.   Belief is necessary in order to conform to the truth in salvation; lack of belief leads to desperation and disunity.

VII.   Man is made in God's image and likeness.

    a.   Man "excels the beasts in the dignity of a rational soul" (18).

    b.   Our existence begs a profound question: Should man enjoy himself, use himself, or both?

    c.   Man is to be used for something else (not just to be loved for his own sake).

    d.   Loving oneself means turning away from God and lapsing toward selfishness (19).

    e.   Heart, soul, and mind must be directed "into that channel into which the whole current of love flows" (19).

VIII. It is important to love only those things that are associated with God.

    a.   Four kinds of things may be loved.

       i.   That which is above us.

      ii.   That which constitutes ourselves.

     iii.   That which is equal to us.

     iv.   That which is below us.

    b.   The spirit cannot help but love itself, but the kind of self-love that aims to rule over others and receive the praise that belongs to God is rightly called "hate" (20).

    c.   Pride leads to corruption by endeavoring to dominate others.

    d.   No one hates himself or his body.

    e.   The body should be rendered subject to the spirit.

    f.   Man should be taught how to love himself profitably.

    g.   The whole law depends on loving God and loving neighbors.

    h.   The appropriateness of love is based on being able to assess intrinsic value.

      i.   We should love and try to help those "who are most closely bound to [us] by place, time, or opportunity, as if by chance" (24)—because we cannot help everyone.

      j.   We naturally try to convince others to love what we love.

      k.   Angels enjoy that which we desire to enjoy.

      l.   Anyone who is near and needs our mercy is our neighbor, even our enemies whom we should love and never fear.

      m. We may also expect this mercy from our neighbors.

      n.   "[W]e should enjoy anything only in so far as it makes us blessed, merely using everything else" (27).

IX. We have a special relationship with God.

      a.   God does not enjoy us; he uses us, but not as humans "use" (27).

      b.   "That use which God is said to make of us is made not to His utility but to ours, and in so far as He is concerned refers only to His goodness" (27–28).

      c.   "The greatest reward is that we enjoy Him and that all of us who enjoy Him may enjoy one another in Him" (28).

      d.   "When you enjoy a man in God, it is God rather than the man whom you enjoy" (28).

      e.   Our purpose is to achieve "the love of a Being which is to be enjoyed and of a being that can share that enjoyment with us" (30).

      f.   We can love the temporal only as an instrument that carries us along toward God.

X. We can appreciate God's love for us through the Scriptures, faith, and charity.

      a.   Understanding of the Scriptures builds a double love of God and of neighbors.

      b.   The goal of the Scriptures is to instill a sense of charity toward others.

      c.   Asserting a misinterpretation rashly leads to further misinterpretation and anger.

      d.   If faith fails, so will charity.

      e.   "Thus there are these three things for which all knowledge and prophecy struggle: faith, hope, and charity" (32); supported by these three, we do not even need the Scriptures except for instructing others.

    f.   We love temporal things before we have them and then lose that love once they are attained because they do not satisfy the soul; we love eternal things more when they are attained.

    g.   Faith and hope will fall away when we reach heaven, but charity will be multiplied.

    h.   Charity is the greatest of the three.

BOOK 2—On signs, ambiguities and obscurities, and methods for (and caveats about) seeking knowledge from the Scriptures.

I.   Signs.

    a.   "A sign is a thing which causes us to think of something beyond the impression the thing itself makes upon the senses" (34).

        i.   Natural signs are those things without intention (smoke signifies fire).

        ii.   Conventional signs are those things that humans show to one another to convey an understanding.

        iii. Augustine focuses on conventional signs here.

    b.   Senses related to signs; i.e., sight, hearing, and (very rarely) to other senses.

    c.   Verbal signs are the most common signs.

    d.   Writing preserves signs "because vibrations in the air soon pass away and remain no longer than they sound" (36). Words are shown to the eyes.

    e.   Scripture was written in one language, then translated and scattered worldwide.

II. Ambiguities and obscurities are many and varied, often deceiving those who are casual readers.

    a.   Augustine sees obscurities as God's design to motivate us: "I do not doubt that this situation was provided by God to conquer pride by work and to combat disdain in our minds, to which those things which are easily discovered seem frequently to become worthless" (37).

    b.   There exists a question of whether there is a difference in learning when one hears the same concept in plain words or with similitude.

    c.   This similitude gives pleasure to our minds.

    d.   It is important to understand "that things are perceived more readily through similitudes and that what is sought with difficulty is discovered with more pleasure" (38).

    e.   Scriptures offer "open places" (38) to avoid indifference in readers.

III. Steps toward knowledge proceed from fear to wisdom.

    a.   The first step is that we have to recognize and submit to God's will before we can gain knowledge.

    b.   The second step is that we have to "become meek through piety so that we do not contradict Divine Scripture" (38). We have to believe that what we read in the Scriptures is "better and more true than anything which we could think of by ourselves, even when it is obscure" (39).

    c.   The third step is the realization of our human predicament and fear of God's judgment; lamentation of the situation.

    d.   The fourth step is one of fortitude in hungering and thirsting for justice; a turning away from the temporal and toward the eternal.

    e.   The fifth step is attained after purging our minds of contamination and seeking the counsel of mercy.

    f.   The sixth step involves cleansing the eye so as to see God as clearly as possible in this world (which is still "'through a glass in a dark manner'" [40, from 1 Cor. 13:12]); simple and clean heart; loving God and neighbor.

    g.   The seventh step involves attaining a clean and simple heart that will not turn away from Truth; such a person ascends to wisdom and the enjoyment of peace and tranquility.

IV. It is important to elaborate on the third step: a canonical knowledge of the Scriptures through fear, piety, and seeking the will of God.

    a.   It is necessary first to read and have some knowledge of the canonical Scriptures.

    b.   Further, it is necessary to know these books even if we cannot understand them.

    c.   Memorizing is one way of gaining familiarity with the Scriptures.

V. We should have a method for approaching the Scriptures and their obscurities.

    a.   "Then, having become familiar with the language of the Divine Scriptures, we should turn to those obscure things which must be opened up and explained so that we may take examples from things which are manifest to illuminate those things which are obscure, bringing principles which are certain to bear on our doubts concerning those things which are uncertain" (42–43).

b. Obscurity is due to two kinds of signs.

   i. Literal signs, which designate the thing.

   ii. Figurative signs, which signify something else.

c. It is necessary to have a knowledge of languages in order to know literal signs (e.g., Latin, Hebrew, Greek).

d. Knowledge of other translations would help readers "avoid negligence" because obscure passages may become clear when we look at different translations (44).

e. Our goal is being a "discerning reader" (45).

f. Faith and a "cleansed understanding" unite us with Truth (45).

g. Ambiguity in the original language leads some to misread the writer's intention and to produce false translations that should be emended, not interpreted.

h. We must be careful in our choice of translators.

i. Integrity of expression is "the preservation of the customs of others, confirmed by the authority of ancient speakers" (47). Some examples include problems with solecisms and barbarisms.

j. We need to understand how to deal with unknown signs.

   i. To understand an unknown word or expression in a foreign language, we must find a translator or learn the language ourselves.

   ii. Learning and memorizing words in other languages is critical.

   iii. We must also be able to weigh and compare various translations.

k. Respect for past scholars is most helpful: ". . . it is not right or proper for any man, no matter how learned, to seek to emend the consensus of so many older and more learned men" (49).

l. Figurative signs should be studied.

   i. These signs should be studied partly with reference to knowledge of things and partly with knowledge of languages.

   ii. Knowledge of names and places helps in clarifying.

   iii. Knowledge of the way things are and behave is also

           important because they can be used to create similitudes (comparisons that will aid understanding).

    iv. Knowledge of the symbolism of numbers is also useful.

    v. Knowledge helps to untie the "knot" of figurative language in the Scriptures (51).

        1. Examples of animals and their ways.

        2. Examples of numbers and their meanings in the Scriptures.

        3. "[M]any other numbers and patterns of numbers are placed by way of similitudes in the sacred books as secrets which are often closed to readers because of ignorance of numbers" (52).

        4. Examples of music's relationship to language also clarify the point.

VI. Questioning the sources of knowledge is essential to our understanding of the Scriptures.

    a. When we are confronted with superstitions, "We must not listen to the superstition of pagans" (53).

    b. "[E]very good and true Christian should understand that wherever he may find truth, it is his Lord's" (54).

    c. Two doctrines of the pagans are worthy of note.

       i. Things that are instituted by humans (some of which are superstitious and some of which are not superstitious).

      ii. Things that are believed to be firmly established or divinely ordained.

    d. Examples of "vacuous observances" (55) include magic, augury, books of haruspicy, amulets, remedies, enchantments, secret signs, wearing of things occultic, wearing earrings.

    e. Saint Augustine's criticism of astrology illustrates the problem with sources of (pagan) wisdom.

       i. Astrology is "pernicious superstition" (56).

      ii. This kind of belief makes us servants of wrong ideas, "sell[s] unlearned men into a miserable servitude" (56).

     iii. Making astrological predictions from the positions of the stars at one's birth is "a great madness" that "may be altogether refuted" (57).

     iv. Examples of twins born under the same constellation but who are different illustrate the errors of human calculations.

  v. "[T]hose beliefs in certain signs of things instituted by human presumption are to be classed with those which result from certain pacts and contracts with demons" (58).

  vi. Illusion and deception are the rewards of this study.

 f. Diviners and omens also require our skepticism.

  i. Diviners may be right by coincidence, but they become more and more enmeshed in error.

  ii. Avoid making sacrifices to false idols that are not "publicly and divinely constituted for the love of God and of our neighbor" or do nothing but "debauch the hearts of the wretched through their love for temporal things" (59).

  iii. Omens have no innate validity; "they were made to have a validity through being noticed and pointed out" (60).

  iv. On consent, we should realize the following: "Therefore just as all of these significations move men's minds in accordance with the consent of their societies, and because this consent varies, they move them differently, nor do men agree upon them because of an innate value" (60–61).

 g. Warnings about human institutions should be taken to heart.

  i. Some human institutions "are superfluous and extravagant, others useful and necessary" (61).

  ii. "[S]igns are not valid among men except by common consent" (61).

  iii. Human society could not function without many of these signs.

  iv. These human institutions vary from nation to nation because they are human creations.

  v. If a human institution is helpful to the "necessary conduct of life" (62), Christians should not shun it. They should shun the extravagant and the superfluous.

  vi. We need to realize that human institutions are "imperfect reflections of natural institutions or are similar to them" (62).

  vii. These institutions may be useful as long as they do not interfere with putting God first.

 h. The corporal senses are important but imperfect and need to be judged accordingly.

      i.   Corporal senses are what we:
          1. believe when we hear them explained
          2. experience when they are demonstrated to us
          3. infer when we have experienced them.
      ii.   The importance of history is that it helps us to understand "the sacred books" (63). History is not a human institution; narrations of history should be written faithfully and usefully, not to show the audacity of the author but with faith as a guide (65).
      iii. Plato was influenced by theology, Augustine argues, not the other way around.
      iv. Descriptive narratives about the present also assist in solving "enigmas in the Scriptures" (65) if they are used in a Christian and logical way.
      v.   For example, we can study and learn about the stars in order to know about the stars, but not in order to make astrological predictions.
      vi. We also need knowledge of the three kinds of art (productive, active, and those arts, such as medicine and agriculture, that assist the word of God) because this knowledge will help us in interpreting "figurative locutions" in the Scriptures (67).

VII. There are institutions that pertain to reason.
    a. Disputation.
      i.   In disputation, "the love of controversy" and "ostentation in deceiving an adversary" are to be avoided (67).
      ii.   Sophisms are false conclusions of the reasoning process (67). Augustine believes "'He that speaketh sophistically is hateful'" (from Ecclus. 37:23).
      iii. Using verbal ornamentation to "inflate" is also a sophism.
    b. Valid processes of reasoning may have false conclusions that come from the error of the disputant.
    c. Correct inferences may be made concerning false as well as true propositions.
    d. "[T]he truth of valid inference was not instituted by men; rather it was observed by men and set down that they might learn or teach it"; discovery of the truth is the essence of invention (68).

e. Someone who describes does not describe anything instituted by himself or by other men; the order of things is instituted by God.

f. Describing is simply pointing out "an existing truth" (68).

g. "The principle that if the consequent is false the antecedent must also be false was not instituted by men, but discovered" (69).

h. "[T]he truth of a proposition is inherent in itself, but the truth of a consequent depends on the opinion or agreement of the disputant" (69).

i. Knowing the rules and knowing the truth are two very different things.

j. There is a problem with those who boast about knowing the rules as if they knew the truth.

k. Again, discovering the order of things is invention (e.g., discovering the science of definition, division, partition).

l. There are two kinds of falsehood.
    i.   That which is not possible.
    ii. That which is possible but does not exist.

VIII. We need to understand the nature of eloquence.

a. Precepts of eloquence may be true, but they may be used for good or for ill.

b. There is the possibility that eloquence will be used "to make falsehoods persuasive" (71).

c. Principles may be used for true or for false causes.

d. These principles are "discovered" rather than instituted by men.

e. These principles are to be used to express "those things which are understood" (72).

f. Practice and experience are the best ways to learn eloquence.

g. There is the potential for corruption: "[The precepts of rhetoric] may make men's discernment more alert, but they may also make men malign and proud so that they love to deceive with specious arguments and questions or to think themselves great because they have learned these things and therefore place themselves above good and innocent people" (72).

h. Our goal is to "turn all . . . knowledge toward the praise and love of one God from whom . . . everything is derived" (73).

     i.   False learning is exhibited by those who "seem" to be learned, but are not wise.

IX. Advice to studious youths.

     a.   Choose studies carefully, considering the effects of human institutions.

     b.   Repudiate and detest those that are extravagant or superfluous.

     c.   Involve yourselves in studies that are "helpful to social intercourse in the necessary pursuits of life" (74).

     d.   Learning history may necessitate knowledge of the pagans, but this study should be undertaken only to know the history.

     e.   Remember St. Augustine's maxim: "Nothing in excess" (74).

     f.   Become scholars who will interpret the scriptures with knowledge of the names, locations, animals, herbs, trees, stones, numbers, and so forth referenced.

     g.   Know that knowledge of disputation is "interwoven" throughout the Scriptures.

     h.   Do not fear learning about the philosophers; they have "said things which are indeed true and are well accommodated to our faith" (75).

     i.   Convert the knowledge of the ancients to Christian use.

     j.   Find in the philosophers not the pagan thoughts but the "liberal disciplines more suited to the uses of truth, and some most useful precepts concerning morals" (75).

     k.   Even some truths about worshiping God may be found among the philosophers' writings.

     l.   Take and use what is useful.

     m.   Always remember, "Knowledge puffs up; but charity edifies" (76, from 1 Cor 8:1).

     n.   Remove the impediments that hinder your study so that your work will be "'rooted and founded in charity'" (77, from Eph. 3:17-18).

     o.   The whole action of the Christian is described in the cross: "to perform good deeds in Christ, to cling to Him with perseverance, to hope for celestial things, to refrain from profaning the sacraments" (77).

     p.   Our end goal is to know the charity of God, which "'surpasseth all knowledge'" (77, from Eph 3:19).

q. Interpret the scriptures with a "meek and humble heart" and examine the "ambiguous signs in the Scriptures" (78).

BOOK III—methods of interpreting ambiguous signs and figures as a way to discover Truth.

I. Truth is found in scriptures.
   a. "A man fearing God diligently seeks His will in the Holy Scriptures" (78).
   b. Man is made gentle.
   c. A man must be "prepared with a knowledge of languages lest he be impeded by unknown words and locutions" (78).

II. Instruction on interpreting ambiguous signs is important for the study of the scriptures.
   a. Mispunctuated or misconstrued words in scripture should be noted.
      i. Our rule of faith is first to consult what is found in the Scriptures and the Church's authority.
      ii. If still ambiguous after "faith has been consulted, then it is necessary to examine the context of the preceding and following parts surrounding the ambiguous place" (79).
   b. Ambiguous constructions are:
      i. correct according to the rule of faith
      ii. correct according to the preceding and following passages, the same as for "ambiguous pointing" (81).
   c. Ambiguity in "doubtful sound of syllables" (82) should be studied.
      i. Look at the passage in an earlier language; if there is disagreement about, say, a Latin word or Scripture, consult the Greek.
      ii. Also, consult earlier languages for ambiguities that do not depend on punctuation or pronunciation (e.g., "Therefore we were comforted, brethren, in you"—question whether "brethren" should be read as a vocative or an accusative [83, from 1 Thess 3:7]).
   d. Ambiguity of figurative words.
      i. Be careful not to take such words literally. If you do, then they are understood "carnally" (84).
      ii. One has to refer to the things signified.

1. "[M]iserable servitude" results in taking signs for things literally (84).
2. Examples illustrate how Jewish people took signs for things but acted as if "they were pleasing the One God of All whom they did not see" (84).
3. "He is a slave to a sign who uses or worships a significant thing without knowing what it signifies" (86).
4. Those who use signs and understand their "signifying force" are "spiritual and free" (87).

e. Consider how to determine if a locution is literal or figurative.

   i. "[W]hatever appears in the divine Word that does not literally pertain to virtuous behavior or to the truth of faith you must take to be figurative" (88).
      1. Virtuous behavior pertains to love of God and one's neighbor.
      2. Truth of faith pertains to a knowledge of God and one's neighbor.

   ii. Men think in error when they think that whatever the scripture says contrary to their opinion is figurative.
      1. Yet, scripture "asserts nothing except the catholic faith as it pertains to things past, future, and present" (88).
      2. These points of faith "are of value in nourishing and supporting charity and in conquering and extirpating cupidity" (88).
         a. Charity is "the motion of the soul toward the enjoyment of God for his own sake, and the enjoyment of one's self and of one's neighbor for the sake of God" (88).
         b. "'[C]upidity' is a motion of the soul toward the enjoyment of one's self, one's neighbor, or any corporal thing for the sake of something other than God" (88).
         c. Vice is "that which uncontrolled cupidity does to corrupt the soul and its body" (88).
         d. Crime is what vice does when it harms someone.
         e. Utility is "what charity does to the charitable person" (89).

3. "Those things which seem almost shameful to the inexperienced, whether simply spoken or actually performed either by the person of God or by men whose sanctity is commended to us, are all figurative" (90).

4. "[W]hen the tyranny of cupidity has been over-thrown, charity reigns with its most just laws of love for God for the sake of God and of one's self and of one's neighbor for the sake of God" (93).

   a. "[W]hat is read should be subjected to diligent scrutiny until an interpretation contributing to the reign of charity is produced" (93).

   b. If a locution "commend[s] either vice or crime or . . . condemn[s] either utility or beneficence, it is not figurative" (93).

5. "It often happens that a person who is, or thinks he is, in a higher grade of spiritual life thinks that those things which are taught for those in lower grades are figurative" (94).

6. "[C]aution must be exercised lest anyone think that those things in the Scriptures which are neither vices nor crimes among the ancients because of the condition of their times, even when such things are taken literally rather than figuratively, may be transferred to our own times and put in practice" (94–95).

   a. Libidinous men do not think that "men of old" can use women "temperately" (96).

   b. King David, for example, did not lament his son's death when he was killed because of his carnality and impiety.

7. "[A]lthough all or almost all of the deeds which are contained in the Old Testament are to be taken figuratively as well as literally, nevertheless the reader may take as literal those performed by people who are praised, even though they would be abhorrent to the custom of the good who follow the divine precepts after the advent of the Lord" (98).

8. Of first importance is for us to decide whether or not a passage is figurative.

    a. If figurative, it is easy to examine.

    b. "[T]he words of which it is composed will be seen to be derived from similar things or related to such things by some association" (99).

    c. Things can signify many different things.

    d. Many meanings are acceptable, not dangerous, "if any of the meanings may be seen to be congruous with the truth taught in other passages of the Holy Scriptures" (102).

    e. When examining passages "obscured by figurative words . . . begin with a passage which is not controversial, or, if it is controversial, . . . conclude with testimonies applied from places wherever they are found in the same Scriptures" (102).

9. Understanding tropes will help us to understand the scriptures.

    a. Recognizing tropes will help in understanding.

    b. Do not teach tropes to the ignorant, "lest we seem to be teaching the art of grammar" (103). Learn tropes elsewhere.

    c. Irony relies on inflection; antiphrasis does not rely on inflection but uses its words, which come from the ordinary to imply the contrary.

10. Tyconius' seven rules in understanding the divine scriptures (from Tyconius' *Book of Rules* [*Liber Regularum*]).

    a. "Of the Lord and His Body" (106)—indicates one person, Christ and his Church.

    b. "Of the Bipartite Body of the Lord" (106)—indicates that the body of the Lord will not actually be with him in eternity, since hypocrites will not be with him.

    c. "Of Promises and the Law" (107)—refers to works given to us by God because of faith's merit; Tyconius inaccurately believes that faith originates in us.

    d. "Of Species and Genus" (108)—indicates the part and the whole.

e. "Of Times" (112)—makes discovery of hidden time intervals possible.
f. "Recapitulation" (113)—involves picking up on previous events that have been omitted from a chronological narrative.
g. "Of the Devil and his Body" (115)—portrays the devil as head of the impious (his body) "who will go with him to the tortures of eternal fire in the same way that Christ is the head of the Church" (116).

BOOK 4—rhetoric and the teaching of Scripture, the value of eloquence, and the *officia* of the speaker.
I. Repeats from prologue "'two things necessary to the treatment of the Scriptures'" (117).
   a. "[A] way of discovering those things which are to be understood" (117).
   b. "[A] way of teaching what we have learned" (117).
II. Augustine will not explain the rules of rhetoric here.
   a. Readers should know that the rules do have utility.
   b. However, their utility is better learned elsewhere, "if perhaps some good man has the opportunity to learn them" (118).
III. Eloquence should be understood in terms of truth and falsehood.
   a. Use eloquence for the good, because evil forces use it for the bad.
   b. Learn eloquence quickly or do not learn it at all.
   c. Learn eloquence by practicing writing, dictating, and speaking "what he has learned according to the rule of piety and faith" (119).
   d. Rules of rhetoric/eloquence are innate, ingrained; we cannot speak and think of rules at the same time.
   e. Men are made eloquent by reading and hearing expressions of the eloquent, not by teaching rules.
IV. Teaching the Scriptures should be done from an understanding of good and evil.
   a. We should "teach the good and extirpate the evil" (120).
   b. Exposition must be composed.
   c. Use whatever devices are necessary to move minds.

V. Wisdom should be emphasized over eloquence
   a. Just because something is eloquently said does not mean it is true or wise.
   b. Memorize the scriptures and understand them.
   c. "He shall give delight with his proofs when he cannot give delight with his own words" (122).
   d. "[A] pernicious sweetness" is to be avoided (123).
   e. There is a certain kind of eloquence that is fine for men of the "highest authority and clearly inspired by God" (123).
VI. Other points regarding eloquence should be considered.
   a. Note specific examples regarding digression about *membra*, *caesa*, and other devices of eloquence.
   b. Some may think he offers Paul as "our one eloquent speaker" (128), but Augustine says that if anything of Paul's is eloquent, we should go to the epistles for the best examples.
       i.   Eloquence of the prophets may be obscured by tropes, but the more obscurity "the sweeter they become when they are explained" (129).
       ii. Many examples from the prophets illustrate this point (129–32).
   c. In conclusion, eloquence ornaments wisdom.
   d. Eloquence is to be used in teaching.
       i.   One should not imitate eloquence that is cryptic, especially if the purpose is to exercise and sharpen skills.
       ii.   Speech should clarify, not confuse.
       iii. "He who teaches should thus avoid all words which do not teach" (134).
       iv.   Use less-correct words if you cannot find correct ones, as long as you teach.
       v.   Do not ramble, for "a speaker who insists on what is already known is burdensome" (135).
       vi.   The best teaching "method is that in accordance with which he who hears, hears the truth, and understands what he hears" (135).
       vii. If eloquence is used unpleasantly in teaching, "its fruits will come only to a few of the most studious who desire to learn what is to be taught no matter how abjectly and rudely it is presented" (135–36).

viii. A food metaphor illustrates the point: when students receive eloquence, they "feast delightedly on this truth" (136).

e. The eloquent man has the following traits.

   i. As a certain eloquent man (Cicero) said, he who is eloquent teaches, delights, and moves ("To teach is a necessity, to please is a sweetness, to persuade is a victory" [136, from Cicero's *Orator* 21:69]).

   ii. Sometimes persuasion is not necessary to produce action.

   iii. Sometimes eloquence is not brought into play.

f. Sometimes eloquence is a necessary evil, but be careful.

   i. It can become too sweet and "frothy" (139).

   ii. It can ornament trivial things (139).

VII. Divine inspiration is a force in understanding and expressing the truth found in the scriptures.

a. One should pray before speaking.

b. However, do not take divinity too far; teachers still need to be taught by men.

VIII. The value of teaching and eloquence should be realized.

a. He who wants to teach of goodness should pray that he be heard.

b. If he does those things well, he can be called eloquent.

   i. One "can speak of small things in a subdued manner"—to teach (143, from *Orator* 29:101).

      1. An example from Paul (146) reveals this point: most of Galatians is written in subdued style.

      2. An example from Cyprian, who discusses the sacrament of the chalice (153), illustrates this mode of speaking.

      3. Saint Ambrose speaking about the Holy Spirit (154) is worthy of note.

   ii. One "can speak of moderate things in a temperate manner"—to please (143, from *Orator* 29:101).

      1. An example from Paul (148) illustrates this ability.

      2. Examples from Cyprian and Ambrose, regarding the praises of virginity (155), underscore the value of this sort of presentation.

   iii. One "can speak of great things in a grand manner"—to persuade (143, from *Orator* 29:101).

1. That is, one can be "forceful with emotions of the spirit" (150).
2. Use what arms (of eloquence) you have and need, for why should one "seek them if it does not need them?" (150)
3. An example from Paul (150–51) reveals this point.
4. Examples from Cyprian and Ambrose about "women who color, or discolor, their features with paint . . . an attack on the divine work, a corruption of the truth" (157) reveal the importance of concern in the manner of speaking.
   a. "[W]hen she seeks to please others she reveals her own prior displeasure" (158).
   b. "If you are ugly, why do you lie in implying that you are beautiful, since you will have neither the reward of your own conscience nor that of another's deception?" (158).
   iv. One can and should mix styles, "[f]or when one style is maintained too long it loses the listener" (158).
   1. Decide which style works best with the other styles.
   2. Decide which style should be "employed in specific places" (159).
   v. The speaker may elicit applause from the audience, but this is not necessarily because he is speaking in the grand style.
   vi. Still the "universal office of eloquence, in any of these three styles, [is] to speak in a manner leading to persuasion" (161).
c. "The life of the speaker [or ethos] has greater weight in determining whether he is obediently heard than any grandness of eloquence" (164).
   i. Be a good, virtuous "example of the faithful in word, in conduct, in charity, in faith, in chastity" (165, from 1 Tim 4:12).
   ii. A teacher should not "serve the words" but let the words serve the teacher (165).
   iii. It is permissible to take something that is eloquent and memorize it, then offer it to the people "in the person of the author" (167).

iv. However, stealing words and giving false words (hypo-critical statements) is wrong.

v. Remember to pray before you speak.

vi. Augustine concludes by saying, "I nevertheless give thanks to God that in these four books I have discussed with whatever slight ability I could muster, not the kind of man I am, for I have many defects, but the kind of man he ought to be who seeks to labor in sound doctrine, which is Christian doctrine, not only for himself, but also for others" (169).

3

LATIN TEXT, TRANSLATION, AND COMMENTARY OF
BOOK IV OF *DE DOCTRINA CHRISTIANA*

Sister Thérèse Sullivan, M.A.
of the Sisters of Notre Dame of Namur

S. AVRELI AVGVSTINI
HIPPONIENSIS EPISCOPI
DE
DOCTRINA CHRISTIANA
LIBER QVARTVS

A Commentary, with a Revised Text,
Introduction, and Translation

SISTER THÉRÈSE SULLIVAN, SND

SIGLA

A — Codex Vaticanus Urbin. lat.	67, saec. xii
B — Codex Parisinus lat.	1595, " ix
C — Codex Parisinus lat.	1938, " x
D — Codex Parisinus lat.	2704, " x
E — Codex Parisinus lat.	1909, " xiv
F — Codex Vaticanus Palat. lat.	188, " ix–x
G — Codex Vaticanus Palat. lat.	189, " x
H — Codex Vaticanus Palat. lat.	190, " xiii
I — Codex Vaticanus lat.	657, " xiii

Maur. — Editio Maurina, t. III. Paris., 1680.
Mig. — Editio I. P. Migne, P.L., XXXIV. Paris., 1887.

S. AVRELI AVGVSTINI

HIPPONIENSIS EPISCOPI

DE

DOCTRINA CHRISTIANA

LIBER QVARTVS

1, 1. Hoc opus nostrum quod inscribitur *de doctria christiana*, in duo quaedam fueram prima distributione partitus. nam post prooemium, quo respondi eis qui hoc fuerant reprehensuri, *duo sunt res* inquam *quibus nititur omnis tractatio scripturarum: modus inueniendi quae intellegenda sunt, et modus proferendi quae intel-* 5 *lecta sunt. de inueniendo prius, de proferendo postea disseremus.* quia ergo de inueniendo multa iam diximus, et tria de hac una parte uolumina absoluimus. adiuuante Domino, de proferendo pauca dicemus, ut, si fieri potuerit, uno libro cuncta claudamus, totumque hoc opus quattuor uoluminibus terminetur.   10

2. Primo itaque exspectationem legentium, qui forte me putant

1 scribitur *B*.   2 quidem *F*.   fuerat *F*.   primo *om. B*; primum *F*.   6 sunt *om. C*.   7 ergo *om. B*.   8 absoluimus uolumina *A*.   domino adiuuante *Maur*. 9 de proferendo . . . uno libro *om. F*.   11 primum *B*.

1. *Introduction. Subject matter of Book IV: 'modus proferendi,' i.e., style. The book, however, is not intended as a treatise on rhetoric.*

1. **Doctrina** is used, of course, in the classical sense of 'teaching,' or 'instruction': cf. Cic. De Orat. 1, 48, 208: *illa non sunt aliqua mihi doctrina tradita, sed in rerum usu causisque tractata.*

4. **modus inueniendi . . . intellecta sunt**: Augustine reduces the traditional fivefold division of oratory (*inuentio, dispositio, elocutio, memoria, actio*) to a twofold division. *Inuentio* (*modus inueniendi*), he treats at length in the first three books of *De Doctrina Christiana*; *dispositio*, he omits; *elocutio, memoria*, and *actio* (*modus proferendi*), he develops in Book IV, analyzing fully the first, and giving a passing notice to the other two. His emphasis on *inuentio*, and *elocutio* is, however, only a

natural one, and is by no means peculiar to him alone. Aristotle divides oratory into εὕρεσις, λέξις, and τάξις (Rhet. 3, 1, 1403b), treating εὕρεσις (*inuentio*) in his first two books, and dividing his last book between the other two, giving the first twelve chapters to λέξις (*elocutio*), and the last six to τάξις (*dispositio*). Both Cicero and Quintilian also recognize the greater importance of *inuentio* and *elocutio*, and though they do not leave undeveloped the other parts as Augustine does, they give greater space to the discussion of these two. In De Orat., Cicero treats *inuentio, dispositio*, and *memoria* in Book II, and *elocutio* and *actio* in Book III; but in both these books more than two-thirds of the discussion is given to *inuentio* and *elocutio*, respectively. The Rhetorica ad Herennium, in four books, gives the first two, and a third of Book III to *inuentio*,

A TREATISE
BY
SAINT AURELIUS AUGUSTINE
BISHOP OF HIPPI
ON
CHRISTIAN TEACHING
BOOK IV

1, 1. This work of mine, entitled, "Christian Teaching," I had, according to my first arrangement, divided into a certain two parts. For after the introduction, in which I answered those who were likely to be critical, I said: "There are two things upon which every treatment of the Scriptures depends: the means of discovering what the thought may be, and the means of expressing what the thought is. We shall discuss first the discovery of the thought, then its expression." And so, because we have already spoken at length on the discovery of the thought, and have finished three books on this part alone, we shall, with the help of God, speak in brief on the expression of the thought, so as, if possible, to include all in one book, and to finish this whole work in four sections.

2. And so, first, in this introduction, I wish to put down the

---

the remainder of this book to *dispositio*, *pronuntiatio*, and *memoria*, and Book IV to *elocutio*. Quintilian devotes Books III through VI of De Instit. Orat. to *inuentio*, Book VII to *dispositio*, Books VIII and IX to *elocutio*.—Note the characteristically neat manner in which Augustine here states his twofold division, making use of common rhetorical figures in order to heighten his contrast: polyptoton, in *intellegenda . . . intellecta; homoioteleuton*, in *modus inueniendi . . . sunt, modus proferendi . . . sunt*; and parison, in the close agreement in number of syllables in the contrasted clauses. The expression is artificial, but it flows spontaneously from the writer's pen.

6. **disseremus**: a favorite word with Cicero: cf. De Repub. 1, 13; De Orat. 2, 157; De Fin. 2, 27; De Off. 3, 74, etc.: cf. Merguet (1) 206.

8. **de proferendo pauca dicemus**: cf.

Arist. Rhet. 3, 1, 1403b: οὐ γὰρ ἀπόχρη τὸ ἔχειν ἃ δεῖ λέγειν, ἀλλ' ἀνάγκη καὶ ταῦτα ὡς δεῖ εἰπεῖν.

9. **si . . . potuerit**: the future perfect for the simple future is Early, Poetic, and Silver. Cicero, however, also uses *potuero* and *uoluero* in this way, *e.g.* De Off. 3, 89: extorquebit, si potuerit; *ibid.* 3, 76: si uoluerit doceat. Cf. K.-Steg. II, 1, 151ff.; St.-Schm. 563. Note this below in 5, 8; 30, 63.

   cuncta = *totus* in plu.: cited for Afran., Cic., Sall.; Silver and Late writers: cf. T.L.L. IV, 1397, 77–1398, 6.

10. **terminetur**: Augustine prefers the passive to the active voice, seemingly to avoid the imperfect homoioteleuton: dicemus . . . claudamus . . . terminemus.

11. **forte** = *fortasse, forsitan*, belongs to Silver and Late Latin: cf. T.L.L. VI, 1131, 71–1132, 23; K.-Steg. II, 1, 812. See this below in 7, 15; 10, 25.

rhetorica daturum esse praecepta quae in scholis saecularibus et
didici et docui, ista praelocutione prohibeo, atque ut a me non
exspectentur, admoneo, non quod nihil habeant utilitatis, sed quod,
si quid habent, seorsum discendum est, si cui fortassis bono uiro
etiam haec uacat discere, non autem a me uel in hoc opere, uel in 5
aliquo alio requirendum.

2,   3. Nam cum per artem rhetoricam et uera suadeantur et falsa,
quis audeat dicere, adversus mendacium in defensoribus suis inermem debere consistere ueritatem, ut uidelicet illi qui res falsas
persuadere conantur, nouerint auditorem uel beneuolum uel inten- 10
tum uel docilem prooemio facere, isti autem non nouerint; illi
falsa breuiter, aperte, uerisimiliter, et isti uera sic narrent, ut
audire taedeat, intellegere non pateat, credere postremo non libeat;
illi fallacibus argumentis ueritatem oppugnent, asserant falsitatem,
isti nec uera defendere, nec falsa ualeant refutare; illi animos 15

---

1 *et om. C.*   2 cohibeo *A Maur.*   3 (sed) quod *om. ABD.*   4 si (quid) *om. D.*
habeant *BF.*   dicendum *B.*   5 discere *om. F.*   8 auderet *E.*   12 breuiter *om.*
E. narrant *E.*   14 isti *E.* falsis *E.*   15 neque falsa *A.*

---

2. **ista** = *hac*, as frequently throughout
this work: a characteristic usage of Late
Latin: cf. St.-Schm. 476-77.

   praelocutione, in the transferred
sense of 'preface,' is cited, besides for
this passage, only for Sen. excerpt. Con-
trov. 3 praef. 11; Frontin. 3 praef. in Aug.
Epist. 147, 5, 6, 11: cf. Georges s.v.

   a me non exspectentur: a Ciceronian expression: cf. Fam. 11, 5, 3: a te
hoc ciuitas uel omnes potius gentes non
exspectant solum sed etiam postulant;
ibid. 3, 12, 4: dixi Seruilio, ut omnia a
me maiora exspectaret; *ibid.* 3, 10, 1; De
Rep. 1, 4; *ibid.* 6, 19.

   4. **seorsum**: mostly Early; not in
Caes., Verg., or Hor.; once in Cic.: cf.
Benoist-Goelz and Georges s.v.

   si ciu fortassis . . . uacat discere:
the impersonal *uacat alicui* is Poetic
and Silver. The infinitive with *uacat*
occurs first in Cic. Fam. 12, 13, 2; in
poetry from Vergil on; and often in Silver Latin. Arts (85) notes one instance
in Augustine's Confessions (6, 11): non
uacat Ambrosio, non uacat legere. See
K.-Schm. s.v., St.-Schm. 582.

   fortassis: rare, almost entirely confined to Early, Silver, and Late Latin. Cf.
T.L.L. VI, 1143–1144; K.-Steg. II, 1,
812; Goelzer (2) 44. Arts (83) notes two
instances in the Conf. It occurs below
also in 20, 39.

   2. *The Christian orator should not
despise the skill afforded by rhetoric.*

   7. **nam cum . . . dormitent**: for an
estimate of the importance of this passage, cf. Norden 533–534. For a rhetorical analysis of it, see Introduction,
pp. 361–62. It would seem that Augustine, fired by enthusiasm for his subject,
makes use unconsciously, as it were, of
the devices common to Cicero and the
schools, in order to prove how rhetoric
may properly be used for strengthening
a good cause.

   per artem rhetoricam: A., in this
chapter, gives a digest of the classical
rules of procedure in the traditional six
parts of a speech: *exordium, narratio,
diuisio, confirmatio, confutatio,* and *conclusio.* He intends thereby to point out
the inequality between those who know
these rules and those who do not.

hopes of readers who, it may be, think that I am going to set forth the rules of rhetoric which I learned and taught in the public schools, and I wish to warn them not to look for this from me, not because such things have no utility, but because, if they have any, it must be got elsewhere if perchance a worthy person have time to learn even such things; but this must not be required of me, either in this work or in any other.

2,   3. For since through the art of rhetoric both truth and falsehood are pleaded, who would be so bold as to say that against falsehood, truth as regards its own defenders ought to stand unarmed, so that, forsooth, those who attempt to plead false causes know from the beginning how to make their audience well-disposed, attentive, and docile, while the others remain ignorant of it; so that the former utter their lies concisely, clearly, with the appearance of truth, and the latter state the truth in a way that is wearisome to listen to, not clear to understand, and finally, not pleasant to believe; so that one side, by fallacious arguments, attacks truth and propounds falsehood, the other has no skill either

per artem: a common equivalent in the later Latinity for the ablative of means. See also 7, 14; 12, 28; 20, 39. Cf. St.-Schm. 438.

suadeantur: this personal passive use of suadeo is Early and Late.

10. **nouerint**, meaning 'know how,' is Early, Poetic, and Late: see K.-Schm. s.v.

beneuolum . . . docilem: the traditional end of the *exordium*: cf. Ad Her. 1, 4, 6: exordiorum duo sunt genera: principium quod Graece προοίμιον appellatur, et insinuatio, quae ἔφοδος nominantur. principium est, cum statim animum auditoris nobis reddimus ad audiendum. id ita sumitur, ut *attentos*, ut *dociles*, ut *beneuolos* auditores habere possimus.

12. **breuiter, aperte, uerisimiliter**: the traditional qualities of the *narratio*: cf. Ad Her. 1, 9, 14: tres res conuenit habere narrationem, ut *breuis*, ut *dilucida*, ut *ueri similis* sit.

et, adversative, is used at times in classical prose, but becomes frequent in Tacitus, and Late writers: cf. St.-Schm. 660. Arts (66) notes several instances in the Confessions. See also 5, 7: et cor, etc.

14. **argumentis**: the weapons of the *confirmatio* and the *confutatio*: cf. Ad Her. 1, 10, 18: tota spes uincendi ratioque persuadendi posita est in confirmatione et in confutatione. nam cum *adiumenta nostra exposuerimus contrariaque dissoluerimus*, absolute nimirum munus oratorium confecerimus.

15. **ualeant** = *possint*: Poetic, Silver, and Late: cf. K.-Schm. s.v.; St.-Schm. 582. It occurs again in 7, 15.

animos audientium . . . exhortentur ardenter: the purpose of the conclusio: cf. Ad Her. 2, 30, 47–50: conclusiones, quae apud Graecos ἐπίλογοι nominantur, tripertitae sunt. nam constant ex enumeratione, amplificatione et commiseratione . . . misericordia commouebitur auditoribus, si uariam fortunarum commutationem dicemus, . . . si supplicabimus et nos sub eorum, quorum misericordiam captabimus, potestatem subiciemus: si, quid nostris parentibus, liberis, ceteris necessariis casurum sit propter nostras calamitates, aperiemus et simul ostendemus illorum nos solitudine et miseria, non nostris incommodis dolere, etc.

audientium in errorem mouentes impellentesque dicendo terreant, contristent, exhilarent, exhortentur ardenter, isti pro ueritate, lenti frigidique dormitent! quis ita desipiat, ut hoc sapiat? cum ergo sit in medio posita facultas eloquii, quae ad persuadenda seu praua seu recta ualet plurimum, cur non bonorum studio comparatur, 5 ut militet ueritati, si eam mali ad obtinendas peruersas uanasque causas in usus iniquitatis et erroris usurpant?

3, 4. Sed quaecumque sunt de hac re obseruationes atque praecepta, quibus cum accedit in uerbis plurimis ornamentisque uerborum exercitationis linguae solertissima consuetudo, fit illa quae facundia 10 uel eloquentia nominatur, extra istas litteras nostras, seposito ad hoc congruo temporis spatio, apta et conuenienti aetate discenda sunt eis qui hoc celeriter possunt. nam et ipsos Romanae principes eloquentiae non piguit dicere quod hanc artem nisi quis cito possit, numquam omnino possit perdiscere. quod utrum uerum sit, quid 15 est opus quaerere? non enim, etiam si possint haec a tardioribus

---

1 mouentes *in marg. B.* 3 -que *om. E.* 4 posita sit in medio *I.* persuadendum *A.* 5 seu recte seu praua *E.* comparetur *E.* 6 eam]iam *F.* 7 in usus *om. E*; in usu *A.* 9 accidit *B.* uerborum quod *CG.* 10 exercitationis *om. ABDF*; exercitationis uerborum linguae *H.* solertissimae *F.* 11 nostras *om. C*; nostras litteras *E.* 12 aetate *om. E*; aetati *B.* 14 artem hanc *D.* 15 utrumque *I.* uerum sit]est uerum *E.* 16 opus est *Maur.* si *om. I.*

---

3. **desipiat . . . sapiat**: a neat example of paronomasia. Augustine, in spite of his declared aversion for Sophistic, cannot always shake off his early training. The figure, here, however, is a moderate one, and is not in bad taste.

cum ergo sit . . . posita facultas eloquii, etc.: cf. Augustine's defense of eloquence in De Doctr. Chris. 2, 36, 54: sunt etiam quaedam praecepta uberioris disputationis, quae nihilominus uera sunt, quamuis eis possint etiam falsa persuaderi: sed quia et uera possunt, non est facultas ipsa culpabilis, sed ea male utentium peruersitas.—Compare Cicero's opinion of the value of rhetoric in the orator's training. It, too, is conservative, but fair: De Orat. 1, 32, 145: nam de actione et de memoria quaedam breuia, sed magna cum exercitatione praecepta gustaram. in his enim fere

rebus omnis istorum artificum doctrina uersatur, quam ego si nihil dicam adiuuare, mentiar. De Inuent. 1, 5, 7: ut [si] medicinae materiam dicamus morbos ac uulnera, quod in his omnis medicina uersetur, item, quibus in rebus uersatur ars et facultas oratoria, eas res materiam artis rhetoricae nominamus.

4. **in medio posita** = κείμενα ἐν μέσῳ: another common Ciceronia phrase; cf. De Orat. 1, 3, 12: dicendi ratio in medio posita: Verr. 2, 2, 42; De Nat. Deor. 1, 6, 14; Diu. in Caec. 11, 33, etc.

6. **ueritati**: dative of interest is employed by Late writers with considerable freedom. Note Ambrose's use of this construction, as pointed out by McGuire (29), and Buck (28–29).

3. *'Praecepta'* vs. *'imitatio': the place and importance of each.*

8. **obseruationes,** 'rules,' is Silver and Late.

in defending the true, or refuting the false; so that the one, moving and impelling the minds of the audience to error by the force of its oratory, now strikes them with terror, now saddens them, now enlivens them, now ardently arouses them, but the other in the cause of truth is sluggish and cold and falls asleep! Who is so foolish as to be thus wise? Since, therefore, there has been placed equally at our disposal the power of eloquence, which is so efficacious in pleading either for the erroneous cause or the right, why is it not zealously acquired by the good, so as to do service for the truth, if the unrighteous put it to the uses of iniquity and of error for the winning of false and groundless causes?

3,   4. But, whatever the rules and precepts are on this subject, which, with the addition of adroit oral practice in the use of a large vocabulary and rich diction, result in what we term eloquence, or oratory, they must be acquired by those who can do so quickly, outside of this treatise of ours, at a proper and fitting age, when a suitable amount of time has been set aside for them. For even the very masters of Roman eloquence themselves have not hesitated to say that no one can ever acquire this art at all unless he do so quickly. What need is there to question the truth of this? For even if these rules can at length finally be mastered by the

11. **istas litteras nostras**: note the Late combination of *iste* and *noster*. The classical sense of *iste* is here completely lost.

12. **congruo**: *congruus* is Early and Late, for classical *congruens*. It occurs again in 30, 63. See K.-Schm. s.v.; T.L.L. IV. 303–4.

13. **nam et . . . perdiscere**: cf. De Orat. 3, 36, 146: tum Caesar: unum inquit, me ex tuo sermone maxime, Crasse, commouit, quod eum negasti, qui non cito didicisset, umquam omino posse perdiscere.

et = *etiam*, 'even,' is frequent in Livy, Tacitus, and late writers: cf. K.-Schm. s.v.; St.-Schm. 661. Arts (66) notes the freedom with which Augustine uses *et* in the Confessions. For *et = etiam*, cf. below: 16, 33; 18, 35; 23, 52; 24, 54; 29, 62; 30, 63.

14. **dicere quod . . . possit**: the common Late equivalent for the infinitive and accusative of indirect course. Cf. St.-Schm. 720–21. This occurs also in 7, 11; 7, 13; 18, 37; 20, 41.

15. **quod utrum . . . sit**: *utrum* in a single indirect question is frequent in Late Latin: cf. Goel. (1) 430; *id.* (2) 686; St.-Schm. 651. It occurs frequently in De Ciu. Dei.: cf. Colbert 39–40.

16. **si possint**: the *si sit ,* . . *est* (*erit*) type of conditional sentence, for present general conditions, belongs to the later Latinity. Besides the present instance, this type occurs also in four other places in this chapter: si — adsit, adhaeret; etsi — non agat, . . . intentus sit, . . . imbuitur; si — desit, . . . capiuntur; si — capiantur, . . . prosunt; and in the following chapters: 4, 6; 7, 11; 7, 19; 7, 20; 7, 21; 10, 24; 12, 27; 12, 28; 16, 33; 17, 34; 19, 38; 20, 41; 23, 52; 25, 55; 29, 62. Cf. St.-Schm. 774.

tandem aliquando perdisci, nos ea tanti pendimus, ut eis discendis
iam maturas uel etiam graues hominum aetates uelimus impendi.
satis est ut adolescentulorum ista sit cura, nec ipsorum omnium quos
utilitati ecclesiasticae cupimus erudiri, sed eorum quos nondum
magis urgens et huic rei sine dubio praeponenda necessitas occu- 5
pauit. quoniam si acutum et feruens adsit ingenium, facilius
adhaeret eloquentia legentibus et audientibus eloquentes, quam
eloquentiae praecepta sectantibus. nec desunt ecclesiasticae litterae,
etiam praeter canonem in auctoritatis arce salubriter collocatum,
quas legendo homo capax, etsi id non agat, sed tantummodo rebus 10
quae ibi dicuntur, intentus sit, etiam eloquio quo dicuntur, dum
in his uersatur, imbuitur, accedente uel maxime exercitatione siue
scribendi, siue dictandi, postremo etiam dicendi, quae secundum
pietatis ac fidei regulam sentit. si autem tale desit ingenium, nec
illa rhetorica praecepta capiuntur, nec, si magno labore inculcata 15
quantulacumque ex parte capiantur, aliquid prosunt. quandoquidem etiam ipsi qui ea didicerunt et copiose ornateque dicunt, non
omnes ut secundum ipsa dicant, possunt ea cogitare cum dicunt,
si non de his disputant; imo uero uix ullos eorum esse existimo,

1 discendas *E.*   3 omnium]hominum *E.*   4 utilitatis *CFG.*   erudire *E.*
6 quoniam neque *F.*   11 etiam *om. I.*   quo]quod *F.*   12 hiis *E.*   induitur
BD. maxime et *F.*   17 copiose ornateque]copiosae ornatae quae *D*; copiose et
ornate *E.*   non omnes . . . possunt *om. H.*   18 cogitare ea *E.*   ea cogitare
cum dicunt *om. H.*   19 his]eis *DE.*   illos *F.*

1. **pendimus**, 'esteem,' is mostly Early and Poetic: cf. Ter. Heaut. 1, 1, 103: tu illum numquam ostendisti quanti penderes.

eis discendis: the ablative of the gerundive to express manner or circumstance is rare in Early Latin, and does not occur in Caesar or Cicero: cf. St.-Schm. 599-600; K.-Steg. II, 1, 752. Note this below in 4, 6.

3. **adolescentulorum ista sit cura**: cf. De Orat. 3, 31, 125: educatione doctrinaque *puerili.*

ipsorum: *ipse = is,* here, and many times below, as frequently in Late Latin.

4. **utilitati**: an extended use of the dative of purpose: Poetic, Tacitean, Late. See St.-Schm. 418–19. Buck (28) notes that this is a favorite construction with Ambrose.

ecclesiasticae: an attributive adjective to replace an objective or a subjective genitive became very common from the time of Augustus on. Compare the frequent use in Eccl. Latin of such adjectives in *-icus.* Several occur below: euangelicus, dominicus, apostolicus.

6. **quoniam . . . sectantibus**: Cicero says: vero ego hanc uim intellego esse in praeceptis omnibus, non ut ea secuti oratores eloquentiae laudem sint adepti, sed, quae sua sponte homines eloquentes facerent, ea quosdam obseruasse atque id egisse; sic esse non eloquentiam ex artificio, sed artificium ex eloquentia natum; quod tamen, ut ante dixi, non eicio; est enim, etiam si minus necessarium ad bene dicendum, tamen ad cognoscendum non illiberale. (De Orat. 1, 32, 146). But Cicero goes a step farther than Augustine

plodder, we do not consider them of such value that we wish the mature, or even the later years of life, to be spent in their acquisition. It is enough that this be the concern of the young, and not even of all whom we wish trained for service in the Church, but of those whose attention is not required by a more pressing duty, and one which ought unquestionably to take precedence of this study. For in the case of a keen and ardent nature, eloquence will come more readily through reading and hearing the eloquent, than through pursuing the rules of eloquence. Nor is the Church wanting in its own literature, even apart from the Canon which is with saving grace fixed in the place of supreme authority; and if a man of ability use this literature, although he has no further aim, but is occupied only with the matter which he finds there, even while he is attending to this alone, he becomes imbued with the eloquence of its diction. This is even especially the case if he adds practice in writing, or dictating, or too, even in speaking his views as guided by the rule of righteousness and faith. But if such ability be wanting, either the precepts of rhetoric will not be grasped, or if by dint of great labor they are grasped to some degree at least, they will be of no avail. For indeed even the very ones who have learned them, and express themselves fluently and elegantly, cannot all, when they are talking, think of these rules,

for he also says (*ibid*. 1, 34, 156): intuendi nobis sunt non solum oratores sed etiam actores, ne mala consuetudine ad aliquam deformitatem prauitatemque ueniamus.

7. **adhaeret** with dat.: Poetic, Silver, and Late. See T.L.L. I, 635, 77-84; 636, 1-19.

11. **intentus**: Cicero uses *intentus*, 'attentive to,' but with *ad* and the accusative: cf. Phil. 11, 9: intentus animus tuus est ad fortassimum uirum liberandum. Sall. and Livy use it, however, with the dative: cf. K.-Steg. II, 1, 316.

eloquio = *eloquentia*: Poetic and Silver.

12. **accedente . . . exercitatione . . . sentit**: cf. De Orat. 2, 23, 96: hanc igitur similitudinem qui imitatione adsequi uolet, quom exercitationibus crebris atque magnis tum scribendo maxume persequatur. See also *ibid*. 1, 33, 150.

uel maxime: *uel* with the superlative does not occur in prose before Cicero: cf. St.-Schm. 463. Note in De. Leg. 1, 52: in uoluptate spernenda et repudianda uirtus uel maxime cernitur.

16. **aliquid** = *quidquam*, as also in several other places in the Confessions: Late. See K. Schm. s.v.; St.-Schm. 483; Juret 36; Bonnet 304.

quandoquidem, causal, is often used by Plautus and Terence; sometimes by Cicero, though not in the orations; more often in Silver and Late Latin: cf. St.-Schm. 740.

17. **non omnes . . . dicunt** seems to imply the practice of extempore speaking: cf. Deferrari 111.

19. **si non** = *nisi*, first in the poets (Ov., Val. Fl., Juv.), and often in Late Lat., probably under the influence of the Greek εἰ μή. See St.-Schm. 777.

qui utrumque possint, et dicere bene, et ad hoc faciendum praecepta illa dicendi cogitare cum dicunt. cauendum est enim ne
fugiant ex animo quae dicenda sunt, dum attenditur ut arte dicantur. et tamen in sermonibus atque dictionibus eloquentium,
impleta reperiuntur praecepta eloquentiae, de quibus illi ut elo-   5
querentur uel cum eloquerentur, non cogitauerunt, siue illa didicissent siue ne attigissent quidem. implent quippe illa quia eloquentes sunt, non adhibent, ut sint eloquentes.

    5. Quapropter, cum ex infantibus loquentes non fiant nisi locu-
tiones discendo loquentium, cur eloquentes fieri non possint nulla   10
eloquendi arte tradita sed elocutiones eloquentium legendo et audi-
endo, et, quantum assequi conceditur, imitando? quid, quod ita
fieri ipsis quoque experimur exemplis? nam sine praeceptis rhetoricis nouimus plurimos eloquentiores plurimis qui illa didicerunt;
sine lectis uero et auditis eloquentium disputationibus uel dictioni-   15
bus, neminem. nam neque ipsa arte grammatica, qua discitur locutionis integritas, indigerent pueri, si eis inter homines, qui integre

---

1 possunt *E.*   et (ad) *om. Mig.*   hoc *om. E.*   2 si non de his . . . cum dicunt
om. I; utrumque . . . cum dicunt *om. sed add. in marg. F.*   4 atque]siue *E.*
5 ut eloquerentur]ut loquerentur *BE.*   6 uel cum eloquerentur *om. EI.*   9 non
fiant eloquentes *E.*   10 discendo loquentium]eloquentium discendo *B.*   possunt
ABCDEFI.   11 sed et *E.*   elocutiones eloquentium]elocutionum *CG*; eloquentium *om. H*; loquendo ergo *add. E.*   12 quid, quod]quod quidem *E.*   13 experi-
mur]ea perimus *F.*   14 plurimos]plures *DE.*   15 electis *D.*   16 nam neque]
namque *I.* elocutionis *A.*

---

    3. **attenditur ut**: T.L.L. cites *attendo*
(act.) with *ut* and the subj. for Plin.,
Porph. Hor., Verg. Vulg., Bened. The
impersonal use of *attendo* is not cited:
cf. T.L.L. II, 1122, 18-23.

    4. **et tamen** occurs from Plautus on:
cf. St.-Schm. 671; K.-Schm. s.v. Its use
is frequent in this treatise.

    dictionibus, 'declamations,' is used
by Cicero, then in Silver and Late writers: cf. T.L.L. V, 1006, 53–1007, 6.

    **eloquentium . . . eloquentiae . . .
eloquerentur**: note the figure of derivation: Paragmenon.

    6. **siue didicissent**: cf. De Orat. 1,
20, 91: eloquentissimos autem homines, qui ista nec didicissent nec omnino
scisse curassent, innumerabiles quosdam nominabat.

    7. **ne attigissent quidem**: cf. *ibid.* 1,

19, 87: quae isti rhetores ne primoribus
quidem labris attigissent.

    implent, . . . eloquentes: note
Cicero's expression of the same thought,
cited above (De Orat. 1, 32, 146): . . .
sic esse non eloquentiam ex artificio, sed
artificium ex eloquentia natum, etc.

    quippe = *enim*, in Plaut., Ter.; not
uncommonly in Cicero; in Sall., Livy;
often in Late writers: cf. St.-Schm. 681;
Arts 71. It occurs frequently below.

    9. **locutiones discendo**: the use of the
accusative after an ablative of the gerund
is found to some extent in Early Latin,
in the poets, and in Silver Latin, but it
becomes common in Late writers: cf.
St.-Schm. 596-7.

    10. **cur eloquentes . . . imitando**: cf.
De Orat. 2, 22, 90: ergo hoc sit primum
in praeceptis meis, ut demonstremus

in order to speak in accordance with them, unless the discussion be on the rules themselves. Nay more, I believe there are scarcely any who can do both things, viz., speak well, and in order to do so, think of the rules of oratory while speaking. For they have to be careful not to forget what they want to say, while they are attending to saying it according to theory. And yet, the rules of eloquence are found fully exemplified in the speeches and discourses of the eloquent, even though to arrive at that eloquence, or in the midst of that eloquence, these men did not think of them, whether indeed they had ever learned them, or whether perhaps they had not even slightly engaged in them. For they exemplify them because they are eloquent; they do not use them to become eloquent.

5. Wherefore, as children do not learn to talk except by listening to the talking of those who talk, why cannot men learn to be orators not by studying the rules of oratory, but by reading and listening to the orations of orators, and, in as far as it is possible, by imitating them? Is it not true that in actual experience we find that this is so? For we know many who are more eloquent without the rules of rhetoric than many who have learned them, but none who are eloquent without having read and heard the discussions and speeches of the eloquent. Children, for instance, would not even need the very rules of grammar, through which the purity of speech is attained, if they had the opportunity of growing up and living

---

quem imitetur atque ita ut, quae maxume excellent in eo. quem imitabitur, ea diligentissime persequatur.

14. **plurimos . . . plurimis**: superlatives, used merely with positive force.

15. **sine lectis . . . et auditis . . . disputationibus**, instead of the classical ablative absolute, evidently in order to balance by anaphora the preceding member of the antithesis, *sine praeceptis. Sine* with the past participle is used once by Seneca (Vit. Beat. 10, 1), four times by Livy, and is cited for Cyprian and Arnobius, among Late writers: cf. K.-Schm. s.v.; St.-Schm. 608.

16. **neque** = *non*, in Early Latin; in Cic. De Leg. 3, 9; occasionally in Vergil, Livy, Pliny, and frequently in Late writers: cf. K.-Steg. II, 1, 817; St.-Schm. 640. Arts (67) notes its frequent use in the Confessions. See also below: 7, 20; 12, 28; 15, 32; 18, 35; 24, 53; 26, 57; 28, 61.

arte: Cicero not infrequently uses the genitive with *indigeo*; but Augustan and Late writers often prefer the ablative. Adams (29) notes eight examples of this usage in the Letters of St. Ambrose. See also K.-Steg. II, 1, 468; St.-Schm. 408. Note this below in 23, 52; 25, 55.

loquerentur crescere daretur et uiuere. nescientes quippe ulla
nomina uitiorum, quidquid uitiosum cuiusquam ore loquentis audi-
rent, sana sua consuetudine reprehenderent et cauerent, sicut rus-
ticos urbani reprehendunt, etiam qui litteras nesciunt.

4, 6. Debet igitur diuinarum scripturarum tractator et doctor, 5
defensor rectae fidei ac debellator erroris, et bona docere et mala
dedocere, atque in hoc opere conciliare aduersos, remissos erigere,
nescientibus quod agitur, quid exspectare debeant intimare. ubi
autem beneuolos, intentos, dociles aut inuenerit aut ipse fecerit,
caetera peragenda sunt, sicut postulat causa. si docendi sunt qui 10
audiunt, narratione faciendum est, si tamen indigeat, ut res de qua

---

2 uitiorum *BCEFGHI* (*Bad. Am. Er. et septem MSS.* [*Maur.*]).   cuiusque
E.   7 docere *D.*   auersos *ABCFG.*   8 quod agitur]quid agatur *Maur.*   10 sicut
causa postulat *I.*

---

1. **crescere daretur**: the infinitive with *daretur* is not used in classical prose, but occurs in the best representatives of the Silver period: Tacitus, Pliny the Elder, Pliny the Younger, and Quintilian. See K.-Schm. s.v.; St.-Schm. 580, 583.

nescientes ... nomina: **nesciens** is Silver and Late Latin for class. *nescius.* See K.-Schm. s.v. *Nescire* with the accusative of a person or thing is mostly Poetic. This appears again in 4, 6; 5, 7.

2. **ore**: one would expect *ex ore*, but there is no authority for a preposition in my MSS., nor in the Benedictine text.

4. *An outline of the 'officia' — dialectical and rhetorical — of the Christian orator.*

5. **tractator**: Late. Cited for Sid., Hier., Spart., Sulp. Sev. See also Aug. Serm. 270, 3: scripturarum tractores dicimus: cf. For. s.v.

6. **defensor rectae fidei ac debellator erroris**: as will be seen below, the foundation of Augustine's offices is entirely classical; the spirit is wholly Christian; the result is a new rhetorical ideal.

debellator: rare, mostly Poetic and Late: cf. T.L.L. V, 83, 74-75; 84, 17.

et bona docere et mala dedocere: note again how naturally Augustine

falls into the figurative language of the schools: Paronomasia.

7. **conciliare . . . erigere . . . intimare**: the traditional *officia oratoris*, derived from Aristotle, and accepted by Cicero, Quintilian, etc.: cf. De Orat. 2, 28, 121: quibus ex locis ad eas tris res, quae ad fidem faciendam solae ualent, ducatur oratio, ut et concilientur animi, et doceantur, et moueantur. *Ibid.* 2, 77, 310: tribus rebus homines ad nostram sententiam perducimus, aut docendo aut conciliando aut permouendo. See also De. Orat. 2, 27, 115; Brut. 49, 185; De Opt. Gen. 1, 3; *ibid.* 5, 16.

8. **intimare** is Late. Augustine generally uses the common Ciceronian *docere. Intimare*, here, makes an interesting mingling of the old and the new.

10. **sicut postulat causa**: a favorite Ciceronian expression: cf. De Orat. 1, 42, 202: quemcumque in animis hominum motum res et causa postulet; Orat. 21, 70; *ibid.* 33, 117, etc.

si docendi sunt, etc.: the instruments of *docere* are exposition (*narratione*) and proof (*documentis adhibitis ratiocinandum est*), which are the matter, as Augustine will explain below, of the *genus submissum*, the 'plain style';

with men who talked correctly. For though ignorant of the names of mistakes in speech, they would recognize whatever was faulty in the language of another, and would, because of their own good usage, criticise it and guard against it; just as city people, even when unlettered, criticise country people.

4, 6. It is the duty, then, of the student and teacher of the Holy Scriptures, who is the defender of the true Faith, and the opponent of error, both to teach what is right, and to correct what is wrong; and in this function of discourse, to conciliate the hostile, to arouse the careless, and to inform those ignorant of the matter in hand, what they ought to expect. But when he finds his audience kindly disposed, attentive, and docile, or when he has himself made them so, the rest must be carried out as each case demands. If his hearers need information, the matter under discussion must be made clear by giving the history of the question, if indeed that is wanting. On the other hand, to make clear a doubtful matter, there is need of argument and the presentation of evidence. But if the audience

the instruments of *mouere* are entreaty, reproach, upbraiding (*obsecrationes*, etc.), and the style accommodated to these is *genus sublime,* 'grand.' Note the intended omission of *conciliare* as an object in oratory. The fact is that Augustine is here recognizing the time-honored conception of the means of persuasion, established by Aristotle: the pragmatic or dialectical (πίστεις ἐν αὐτῷ τῷ πράγματι = *docere* with its *narratio* and *documenta*), and the rhetorical, properly so-called, *i.e.*, those means which lie outside of the facts, and look especially to emotional effect on the hearers (πρὸς τὸν ἀκροατήν = *mouere* with its *obsecrationes*, etc.). *Conciliare*, in Aristotle, has a subordinate place under the means: πρὸς τὸν ἀκροατήν. This interpretation of persuasion as twofold was carried on by the Peripatetic school, and thence was accepted by Dionysius, Auct. ad Her., and Cicero, etc. Augustine recognizes it here, as also in Contr. Cresc. 1,

13, 16, and in De Dial. 7. In Contr. Cresc., however, he draws such a sharp distinction between these two aspects of persuasion as to make one feel that he is separating them not merely as different phases of rhetoric, but as different arts: dialectic (subtiliter arguteque disserere, hoc est dialectice), and rhetoric (copiose ornateque explicare, hoc est eloquenter). In reality they form, in his larger conception, the *officia oratoris,* including as was the custom of the schools somewhat before Cicero's time, and from his time on, a third, *conciliare,* recognized, especially by Augustine, as of vastly less importance than the other two, but a convenient middle ground between the extremes of dialectic and impassioned prose.

11. **si tamen** = 'if only' or 'if indeed': Poetic and Silver. The subjunctive is cited first for Columella: cf. St.-Schm. 782; K.-Steg. II, 2, 429, 12. *Si tamen* occurs also in 5, 8, but with the indicative.

agitur innotescat. ut autem quae dubia sunt certa fiant, documentis adhibitis ratiocinandum est. si uero qui audiunt mouendi sunt potius quam docendi, ut in eo quod iam sciunt, agendo non torpeant, et rebus assensum, quas ueras esse fatentur, accomodent, maioribus dicendi uiribus opus est. ibi obsecrationes et increpa- 5 tiones, concitationes et coercitiones, et quaecumque alia ualent ad commouendos animos, sunt necessaria, et haec quidem cuncta quae dixi, omnes fere homines in iis quae loquendo agunt, facere non quiescunt.

5, 7. Sed cum alii faciant obtuse, deformiter, frigide, alii acute, 10 ornate, uehementer, illum ad hoc opus unde agimus, iam oportet accedere, qui potest disputare uel dicere sapienter, etiamsi non potest eloquenter, ut prosit audientibus, etiamsi minus quam prodesset, si et eloquenter posset dicere. qui uero adfluit insipienti eloquentia, tanto magis cauendus est, quanto magis ab eo in iis 15

2 si]qui *G.*   4 et ut *A.*   5 maioribus uiribus dicendi *E.*   ubi *CEGHI.*   6 concinationes *E.*   ualent *om. E.*   7 sunt *om. E.*   haec *om. D.*   8 his *ABCDFGHI*; hiis *E.*   eloquendo *Maur.*   uel arguunt *supra* agunt *H*;   (quae loquendo arguunt *duo MSS.* [*Maur.*]).   10 faciant alii *EI.*   11 agimus oportet accedere iam *G.*   13 prosit]possit *AE.*   14 et si *E.*   possit *F.*   15 his *ABCDFGHI*; hiis *E.*

5. **increpationes**: Late.

6. **coercitiones**: Silver and Late: cf. Sen. Dial. 4, 28, 1: indignamur aliqua admonitione aut coercitione nos castigatos; Amb. exc. Sat. 1, 41, p. 1303 b; Aug. Epist. 155: cf. T.L.L. III, 1438, 16-75.

7. **cuncta** = *omnia*, became common in Silver and Late Latin: cf. T.L.L. IV, 1401, 34–1402, 43.

9. **quiescunt** = *desinunt*: very rare; used by Plaut. (cf. Most. 5, 2, 51: quiesce hanc rem modo petere) and then in Late Latin. See St.-Schm. 581.—For a definition of Cicero's ideal orator, see De Orat. 1, 15, 64; Orat. 2, 7-9; De Orat. 1, 8, 31; *ibid.* 2, 8, 34; and especially the following grand passage of De Orat. 1, 46, 202: sed eum uirum [conquirimus], qui primum sit eius artis antistes, cuius cum ipsa natura magnam homini facultatem daret, tamen esse deus putatur, ut id ipsum, quod erat hominis proprium, non partum per nos, sed diuinitus ad nos delatum uideretur; deinde, qui possit non tam caduceo quam nomine oratoris orna-

tus incolumis uel inter hostium tela uersari; tum, qui scelus fraudemque nocentis possit dicendo subicere odio ciuium supplicioque constringere; idemque ingenii praesidio innocentiam iudiciorum poena liberare; idemque languentem labentemque populum aut ad decus excitare aut ab errore deducere aut inflammare in improbos aut incitatum in bonos mitigare; qui denique, quemcumque in animis hominum motum res et causa postulet, eum dicendo uel excitare posset uel sedare.

5. *'Sapientia' vs. 'eloquentia': the acquisition of 'sapientia,' through a study of Holy Scripture; the acquisition of 'eloquentia,' through imitation of those who possess both eloquence and wisdom.*

10. **obtuse** = 'bluntly': besides for this passage, cited only for Schol. Pers. 5, 61: cf. Georges and Benoist-Goelz. s.v.

deformiter = 'inelegantly': used also by Quint., Apul., Aug. De Ciu. Dei 10, 17: cf. T.L.L. V, 369, 46-52.

11. **unde** = *de quo*: the pronomi-

needs to be aroused rather than to be informed, in order that they may not be slow in living up to what they already know, and that they may give their assent to what they are convinced is true, greater powers of oratory are required. In such a case, entreaties and reproaches, exhortations and compulsion, and every other means conductive to stirring the heart, are necessary. And indeed, every one of the methods which I have enumerated are continually made use of by nearly all men in their efforts in speaking.

5,   7. But as some do this bluntly, inelegantly, and coldly, while others, with tact, elegance, and force, the important thing now is that the instruction of which we speak, be made the business of one who, even though he has no powers of eloquence, does possess *wisdom* in arguing and speaking, so that he may do good to his audience, even though that be less than if he could at the same time use eloquence in speaking. But a man who has merely an

nal adverb in place of a pronoun in an oblique case occurs often in Early Latin, in legal speech, and generally in Late Latin and the Romance language. It seems to have belonged to the popular idiom, and thence to have passed into the literary languages: cf. St.-Schm. 491-92; Salonius 211. See this usage below in 7, 13; 18, 37; 20, 41; 21, 45.

14. **et** = 'also,' largely from Livy on. See also St.-Schm. 661–62. It occurs twenty or more times below.

qui . . . adfluit insipienti eloquentia: cf. De Orat. 1, 12, 50: haec autem oratio, si res non subest ab oratore percepta et cognita, aut nulla sit necesse est aut omnium irrisione ludatur. quid est enim tam furiosum quam uerborum uel optimorum atque ornatissimorum sonitus inanis, nulla subiecta sententia nec scientia? Also *ibid.* 1, 12, 53; and *ibid.* 1, 6, 20; et enim ex rerum cognitione ecflorescat et redundet oportet oratio; quae nisi subest res ab oratore percepta et cognita, inanem quandem habet elocutionem et paene puerilem. See also De. Orat. 1, 18, 83; 1, 20, 92; 3, 35, 142. Augustine—as also Cicero—is here harking back to Aristotle's distinction between pragmatic, or dialectical persua-

sion (*sapienter*), and emotional, or ornamental (*eloquenter*)—πίστεις ἐν αὐτῷ τῷ πράγματι and τὰ ἔξω τῶν πραγμάτων. Both Cicero and Augustine necessarily recognize with Aristotle that *res* (τὰ πράγματα)—dialectic—is fundamental and essential, without which eloquence is something empty and false. This was far from what was being accepted in practice, however, in Augustine's time. His fourth century readers had no trouble in recognizing, therefore, his attack, indirect as it is, on the Sophists, who from the earliest times were wont to dissociate *res* (philosophy, i.e., dialectic—*sapientia*) and *ornatus* (rhetoric—*eloquentia*): cf. Cicero's characterization of the Sophists (Orat. 19, 65): sophistarum de quibus supra dixi, magis distinguenda similitudo uidetur, qui omnes eosdem uolunt flores, quos adhibet orator in causis, persequi. sed hoc differunt quod, cum sit his propositum non perturbare animos, sed placare potius nec tam persuadere quam delectare, et apertius id faciunt quam nos et crebrius, *concinnas magis sententias exquirunt quam probabiles, a re saepe discedunt,* intextunt fabulas, uerba altius transferunt eaque ita disponunt ut pictores uarietatem colorum, paria paribus

quae audire inutile est, delectatur auditor, et eum quoniam diserte
dicere audit, etiam uere dicere existimat. haec autem sententia
nec illos fugit, qui artem rhetoricam docendam putarunt; fassi
sunt enim sapientiam sine eloquentia parum prodesse ciuitatibus,
eloquentiam uero sine sapientia nimium obesse plerumque, prodesse 5
numquam. si hoc ergo illi qui praecepta eloquentiae tradiderunt,
in eisdem libris in quibus id egerunt, ueritate instigante coacti
sunt confiteri, ueram, id est, supernam quae a Patre luminum
descendit, sapientiam nescientes, quanto magis nos non aliud sen-
tire debemus, qui huius sapientiae filii et ministri sumus? sapienter 10
autem dicit homo tanto magis uel minus, quanto in scripturis
sanctis magis minusue proficit. non dico in eis multum legendis
memoriaeque mandandis sed bene intellegendis et diligenter earum
sensibus indagandis, sunt enim qui eas legunt, et neglegunt; legunt
ut teneant, neglegunt ne intellegant. quibus longe sine dubio prae- 15
ferendi sunt qui uerba earum minus tenent, et cor earum sui cordis
oculis uident. sed utrisque ille melior, qui et cum uolet eas dicit,
et sicut oportet intellegit.

1 eum]cum *ABCDEI.*   quoniam]quem *H.*   deserti (disserte *in marg.*) *F.*
2 uera *B.*   3 fessi *B.*   4 enim]autem *E.*   (ciuibus *Lou.*; ciuitatibus *alii editi
et MSS.* [*Maur.*]).   6 hoc *om. E*; si ergo hoc *Maur.*   7 legerunt *D.*   10 huius
om. A.   11 homo dicit *I.*   quanto magis *A.*   12 magis]maius *A.*   proficit
DEG Maur.   14 et neglegunt legunt *om. E.*   15 ne]ut *E.*   16 cor eorum *F.*
17 uolet]uult et *A.*   eis *I.*

referunt, aduersa contrariis saepissim-
eque similiter extrema definiunt.

adfluit = 'to be rich in,' occurs frequently in Cicero, who even employs it
at times with a person as subject, *e.g.*,
Sest. 18: consul unguentis adfluens. This
use, however, seems to belong particularly to Early and Late Latin: cf. Plaut.
Pseud. 191: ut frumento adfluam. See
T.L.L. I, 1243, 37-52.

3. **nec** = *ne quidem*, does not appear in
Early Latin, is very rare in the classical
period, but is found in Livy, the Augustan
poets, in Silver Latin, and frequently in
Late Latin: cf. St.-Schm. 641; K.-Steg.
II, 2, 44. For this occurrence below, see
14, 31; 18, 35; 20, 40; 28, 61.

4. **sapientiam sine eloquentia, etc.**:
cf. De Inuent. 1, 1, 1: ac me quidem
diu cogitantem ratio ipsa in hanc potissimum sententiam ducit, ut existimem

*sapientiam sine eloquentia parum
prodesse ciuitatibus, eloquentiam uero
sine sapientia nimium obesse plerumque, prodesse nunquam.* quare si
quis omissis rectissimis atque honestis-
simis studiis rationis et officii consumit
omnem operam in exercitatione dicendi,
is inutilis sibi, perniciosus patriae ciuis
alitur; qui uero ita sese armat eloquentia, ut non oppugnare commoda patriae,
sed pro his propugnare possit, is mihi uir
et suis et publicis rationibus utilissimus
atque amicissimus ciuis fore uidetur.

8. **supernam** = 'supernal,' 'celestial,' is cited for Ovid, Lucan, and Late
writers.

a Patre luminum descendit: cf.
Iac. 1, 17: omne datum optimum . . .
desursum est, descendens a Patre luminum.

12. **magis . . . proficit**: *magis* for *plus*,

empty flow of eloquence, ought to be the more guarded against as he is the more pleasing to his audience in those matters which have no expedience, and as, since his audience hears him speak with fluency, it judges that he likewise speaks with truth. This view, indeed, did not escape even those who considered rhetorical training necessary, for they hold that wisdom without eloquence is of small avail to a country, but that eloquence without wisdom is generally a great hindrance, and never a help. If, therefore, those who have given us the rules of oratory, in the very books in which they have treated this subject are forced through the urgency of truth to make this confession, ignorant as they are of the true, that is, of the supernal wisdom which comes down from the Father of lights, how much more are we, who are the children and the ministers of this wisdom, under obligation to hold no other opinion! But a man speaks with more or less wisdom as he is the more or less versed in the Holy Scriptures—I do not mean in the very copious reading and memorizing of them, but in the true understanding and the careful investigation of their meaning. For there are some who read them, but indifferently; they read them in order to memorize them, but they are indifferent to understanding them. There can be no question but that they by far deserve the preference who know them less, word for word, but who look into the heart of the Scriptures, with the eyes of their own hearts. But he is better than either of these, who both quotes them at will, and understands them as he ought.

as often in the later Latinity: cf. Goel. (2) 683.

14. **sensibus**: *sensus = significatio*, is Poetic, Silver, and Late: cf. Quint. 8, 2: ambiguitas quae turbare potest sensum, etc.

sunt ... qui eas legunt: the indicative with *sunt qui*, most probably of vulgar origin, is found in Early Latin, *e.g.*, Plaut. Tru. 91: sunt quos scio esse amicos; in Cicero's early work and Letters; occasionally in the poets and Silver writers; and in Late Latin, especially in authors affecting the archaic (Apul., Gell., etc.) and in the grammarians; cf. St.-Schm. 712. It is used below in 9, 23; 29, 62.

15. **teneant** = 'remember': cf. Plaut. Pers. 2, 2, 1: satin' haec meministi et tenes? Verg. Ecl. 9, 45: numeros memini, si uerba tenerem. Cicero uses *tenere*, but with *memoriam*: cf. Cat. 3, 8; Fam. 6, 2. Horace, Quintilian, and Seneca the Younger, however, use *tenere* alone: cf. K.-Schm. s.v.

neglegunt ne: for *neglego ne = securus*, cf. Hor. Carm. 3, 8, 25: neglegens ne qua populus laboret.

16. **cor** = 'soul,' is Eccl.: cf. T.L.L. IV, 930, 17-25.

17. **cum uolet**: the future dependent on a present indicative is unusual in a clause of contemporaneous time: cf. K.-Steg. II, 2, 144-45.

8. Huic ergo qui sapienter debet dicere, etiam quod non potest
eloquenter, uerba scripturarum tenere maxime necessarium est.
quanto enim se pauperiorem cernit in suis, tanto eum oportet in
istis esse ditiorem, ut quod dixerit suis uerbis probet ex illis, et
qui propriis uerbis minor erat, magnorum testimonio quodammodo 5
crescat. probando enim delectat qui minus potest delectare dicendo.
porro qui non solum sapienter, uerum etiam eloquenter uult dicere,
quoniam profecto plus proderit, si utrumque potuerit, ad legendos
uel audiendos et exercitatione imitandos eloquentes eum mitto
libentius, quam magistris artis rhetoricae uacare praecipio: si 10
tamen ii qui leguntur et audiuntur, non solum eloquenter, sed
etiam sapienter dixisse uel dicere ueraci praedicatione laudantur.
qui enim eloquenter dicunt, suauiter; qui sapienter, salubriter
audiuntur. propter quod non ait scriptura, 'multitudo eloquen-
Sap. 6, 26 tium,' sed *multitudo sapientium sanitas est orbis terrarum.* sicut 15
autem seape sumenda sunt et amara salubria, ita semper uitanda
est perniciosa dulcedo. sed salubri suauitate uel suaui salubritate
quid melius? quanto enim magis illic appetitur suauitas, tanto
facilius salubritas prodest. sunt ergo ecclesiastici uiri qui diuina
eloquia non solum sapienter, sed eloquenter etiam tractauerunt,

1 huic etiam *E.*   quod]qui *E.*   2 maxime uerba scripturarum tenere necessarium *H.*   3 in suis cernit *E.*   4 oportet eum esse in istis *E.*   5 propriis]
ipsius *H.*   10 magistros *F.*   11 hii *ACEF;* hi *BDGHI.*   14 frustra *add. supra*
ait *alia m. F.*   15 multitudo eloquentium sed *om. F.*   16 autem]enim *E.*
17 salubri]salubria *A.*   suaui]suauia *A.*   18 quid quod *I.*   19 facilius *in marg.*
alia m. B.   prodest salubritas *E.*

4. **ex illis**: the idea of 'means' is strong
here, though linked with that of 'place
from which': whence the preposition.
The ablative with *ex*, to express means,
is a development of Late Latin: cf. K.-
Steg. II, 1, 505; St.-Schm. 437; 528–29.
See this use below in 23, 52; 27, 60.

8. **ad legendos . . . mitto libentius**:
cf. De Orat. 2, 20, 85: quare ego tibi
oratorem sic iam instituam, si potero, ut
quid efficere possit ante perspiciam. sit
enim mihi tinctus litteris; audierit aliquid, legerit, ista ipsa praecepta acceperit;
temptabo quid deceat, quid uoce, quid
uiribus, quid spiritu, quid lingua efficere
possit.

10. **magistris artis rhetoricae**: oratory degenerated into mere theatrical
declamation, after Tiberius by the aboli-
tion of the assemblies closed to the orator his proper field. Schools of rhetoric
became increasingly popular, but their
professors through the superficiality and
insincerity of their methods brought the
name of 'rhetorician' into ill-repute.
Though Quintilian and Tacitus did their
part to reclaim rhetoric from the excesses
to which it had passed in their day, their
influence was outweighed in the second
and succeeding centuries by that of the
Greek rhetors and sophists, so popular in
those years. It is no wonder, therefore, that

8. And so, for one who should speak with wisdom, even for the very reason that he cannot do so with eloquence, it is absolutely necessary that he remember the words of the Scriptures. For in as much as he sees himself poor in his own resources, in so much the more does it behoove him to be rich in those of the Scriptures, that what he says in his own words, he may prove by the Scriptures; and that he who was of little importance in his own words may gain, in some measure, from the authority of the great. For by his proofs he satisfies, even though he cannot satisfy by his bare statements. Furthermore, the man who wishes to speak not only with wisdom but also with eloquence, since indeed he will do more good if he be able to do both, I rather send to read or hear the eloquent, and to imitate them by practice, than advise to give his time to professors of rhetoric; on this condition, however, that those who are read and heard be recommended, in all truth, as men who have spoken and who speak not only with eloquence, but also with wisdom. For those who speak eloquently are listened to with pleasure; those who speak with wisdom are heard with profit. Wherefore, the Scripture does not say, "The multitude of the eloquent," but *The multitude of the wise is the welfare of the whole world.* But as often even bitter medicine must be taken, so always harmful sweets must be avoided. Still, what is better than wholesome sweets or sweet wholesomeness? For the greater the desire of sweets in such a case, the more readily does their wholesomeness prove beneficial. So there are churchmen who have expounded Sacred Scripture not only with wisdom, but also with eloquence;

Augustine, feeling the distrust with which his age regarded rhetoricians, should be on his guard to explain his meaning in regard to them. See Norden 351ff.; Lezat 11-12, 14, for a convenient summary of the conditions of oratory and rhetoric from Tiberius to Augustine. Cicero reflects the contempt of his time for *isti rhetores*, in the words which he ascribes to the Athenian Menedemus in De Orat. 1, 19, 87: ipsa uero praecepta sic illudere solebat, ut ostenderet non modo eos expertes esse illius prudentiae [*i.e.*, philosophiae], quam sibi ad sciscerent, sed ne hanc quidem ipsam dicendi rationem ac uiam nosse. *Ibid.* 1, 20, 91: nam primum quasi dedita opera neminem scriptorem artis ne medi-

ocriter quidem disertum fuisse dicebat, quom repeteret usque a Corace nescio quo et Tisia, quos artis illius inuentores et principes fuisse constaret; eloquentissimos autem homines, qui ista nec didicissent nec omnino scisse curassent, innumerabilis quosdam nominabat.

11. **eloquenter . . . sapienter . . . salubriter**: Augustine's fondness for adverbs is a characteristic of Late Latin: cf. Parsons 76.

17. **sed salubri suauitate, uel suaui salubritate**: notice how Augustine has enforced his figure of metathesis (*salubri suauitate . . . suaui salubritate*) by alliteration and assonance: *sed salubri . . . uel suaui.*

quibus legendis magis non sufficit tempus quam deesse ipsi studentibus et uacantibus possunt.

6,   9. Hic aliquis forsitan quaerit utrum auctores nostri, quorum
scripta diuinitus inspirata canonem nobis saluberrima auctoritate
fecerunt, sapientes tantummodo, an eloquentes etiam nuncupandi 5
sint. quae quidem quaestio apud meipsum et apud eos qui mecum
quod dico sentiunt, facillime soluitur. nam ubi eos intellego, non
solum nihil eis sapientius, uerum etiam nihil eloquentius mihi
uideri potest. et audeo dicere omnes qui recte intellegunt quod illi
loquuntur, simul intellegere non eos aliter loqui debuisee. sicut est 10
enim quaedam eloquentia quae magis aetatem iuuenilem decet, est
quae senilem, nec iam dicenda est eloquentia, si personae non con-
gruat eloquentis; ita est quaedam, quae uiros summa auctoritate
dignissimos planeque diuinos decet. hac illi locuti sunt, nec ipsos
decet alia, nec alios ipsa; ipsis enim congruit; alios autem, quanto, 15
uidetur humilior, tanto altius non uentositate, sed soliditate transcendit. ubi uero non eos intellego, minus quidem mihi apparet
eorum eloquentia, sed eam non dubito esse talem, qualis est ubi
intellego. ipsa quoque obscuritas diuinorum salubriumque dictorum
tali eloquentiae miscenda fuerat, in qua proficere noster intellectus, 20
non solum inuentione, ueram etiam exercitatione deberet.

10. Possem quidem, si uacaret, omnes uirtutes et ornamenta
eloquentiae, de quibus inflantur isti qui linguam suam nostrorum

1 quibus legendis non sufficit magis tempus *D*.   ipsis *ABCDEI*.   2
euacantibus *D*; baccantibus *E*.   ponunt *E*; possint *G*.   4 scripta]scriptura *E*.
canones *E*.   6 sunt *BCDEFGHI*.   8 etiam]et *E*.   9 nihil eis sapientius mihi
uideri potest, uerum etiam nihil eloquentius *A*.   10 loqui aliter *F*.   11 sicut
enim est *AE*; sicut autem est *CGHI*.   aetate *I*.   12 congruit *A*.   14 hanc *E*.
17 uere *F*.   18 eloquentiae *A*.   eam *om. C*; eam tamen *Maur*.   talis *E*.

1. **quibus legendis . . . possunt**: literally: and for the reading of these, time
no more suffices than their works can
possibly be exhausted by students and
those at leisure.

    studentibus: *studere* = 'to study,'
only from Silver Latin on. Cicero uses
litteris or *arti studere*.

    6. *'Sapientia,' in the sacred writers,
is aided by an 'eloquentia' all their own,
founded on that of the secular schools,
but superior to it, because adapted to
their character as 'sapientes,' and to the
'sapientia' of their discourse.*

3. **forsitan quaerit**: *forsitan* with the
indicative is Poetic and Late. It does
not become frequent until Min. Felix,
Jerome, Sulp. Sev., and other Eccl. writers: cf. K.-Steg. II, 1, 811; St.-Schm.
572; Arts 83.

    12. **nec iam dicenda est eloquen-
tia, etc.**: the principle of 'fittingness':
cf. Orat. 21, 71: est autem quid deceat
oratori uiendum non in sententiis solum
sed etiam in uerbis. non enim omnis for-
tuna, non omnis honos, non omnis auc-
toritas, non omnis aetas nec uero locus
aut tempus aut auditor omnis eodem

and for reading these, students and those at leisure have not sufficient time in which to exhaust them.

6,   9. Here, someone perhaps may ask whether our authors, whose divinely inspired writings, with saving authority, make up the Canon for us, should be ranked merely as wise, or also as eloquent men. For myself, and for those whose opinions are the same as mine, this question is, of course, easily settled. For when I understand them, it seems to me that nothing can have more wisdom or even more eloquence. And I venture to state this also, that all who rightly understand what these writers say, understand too that they could not have spoken otherwise. For as there is a certain eloquence which is more becoming to youth, and a certain one to old age; and as eloquence does not deserve the name, if it be not in accord with the person who speaks, so there is a certain eloquence suitable to men especially worthy of the highest authority, and who are clearly inspired. With such eloquence have our authors spoken. No other is fitting to them, nor is theirs, to others; for it perfectly accords with them; but as it seems the more lowly, so it the more highly transcends others, not by its inflation, but by its solidity. Where, however, I do not understand these writers, then indeed their eloquence is less apparent to me, but still I doubt not but that it is such as it is where I do understand them. Indeed, that very obscurity of the divine and saving writings had, of necessity, to be mingled with such eloquence whereby our minds should profit, not only through the working out of their meaning, but also through the practice of their art.

10. All the merits and beauties of eloquence, about which those

---

aut uerborum genere tractandus est aut sententiarum semperque in omni parte orationis ut uitae quid deceat est considerandum; quod et in re, de qua agitur, positum est et in personis *et eorum qui dicunt* et eorum qui audiunt.

14. **nec ipsos . . . alia, nec alios ipsa**: an effective metathesis, due to the brevity of the clauses, and to polysyndeton.

16. **uentositate**: one of Augustine's quiet insinuations directed against the Sophists: cf. Baldwin (2) 51-54.

   uentositate = *iactantia*, is Late: cf. Fulg. Myth. 2, 17; De Ciu. Dei 9, 20: cf. Georges and Benoist-Goelz. s.v.

transcendit = 'surpass': rare; not in Cic., but found in Silver Latin, *e.g.*, Sen. Troad. 702: transcendere ingenio; Sil. 3, 607: at tu transcendens, Germanice, facta tuorum: cf. Georges s.v.

19. **salubrium** = 'bringing salvation' is Eccl. Note how this meaning occurs in Augustine, side by side with the classical, 'healthful,' used *e.g.*, in 5, 8.

20. **intellectus** = 'comprehension': Silver.

23. **inflantur isti qui . . . praeponunt**: another quiet, but none the less obvious reference to Sophistic. See A.'s definition of this school, in De Doctr. Chris. 2, 31,

auctorum linguae, non magnitudine, sed tumore praeponunt, ostendere in istorum litteris sacris, quos nobis erudiendis, et ab hoc saeculo prauo in beatum saeculum transferendis, prouidentia diuina prouidit. sed non ipsa me plus quam dici potest in eloquentia delectant, quae sunt his uiris cum oratoribus gentilium poetisue 5 communia; illud magis admiror et stupeo, quod ista nostra eloquentia ita usi sunt per alteram quandam eloquentiam suam, ut nec deesset eis, nec emineret in eis, quia eam nec improbari ab illis, nec ostentari oportebat; quorum alterum fieret si uitaretur, alterum putari posset, si facile agnosceretur. et in quibus forte locis agnos- 10 citur a doctis, tales res dicuntur, ut uerba quibus dicuntur, non a dicente adhibita, sed ipsis rebus uelut sponte subiuncta uideantur, quasi sapientiam de domo sua, id est, pectore sapientis procedere intellegas, et tamquam inseparabilem famulam etiam non uocatam sequi eloquentiam. 15

3 in saeculum beatum *E.* 5 hiis *E.* gentibus *E.* 7 eloquentiam quandam *E.* suam *om. CEFI.* 8 meminerit (emineret *supra alia m.*) *F.* 9 uetaretur *F.* 13 id est de *B.* 14 intellegens *D.* famulam]causam *G.* uocata *I.*

48: quod genus captiosarum conclusionum scriptura, quantum existimo, detestatur illo loco, ubi dictum est: *qui sophistice loquitur, odibilis est* (Ecclus. 37, 23). quamquam etiam sermo non captiosus, sed tamen abundantius quam grauitatem decet, uerborum ornamenta consectans, sophisticus dicitur.

linguam = 'style,' is Poetic and Silver: cf. K.-Schm. s.v.

1. **tumore** = 'bombast': Silver. Concerning the inflation of the *declamatores*, cf. Petron. Satyr. 1: haec ipsa tolerabilia essent, si ad eloquentiam ituris uiam facerent: nunc et rerum tumore et sententiarum uanissimo strepitu hoc tantum proficiunt, ut cum in forum uenerint, putent se in alium terrarum orbem delatos.

ostendere in . . . litteris sacris: Augustine's tribute to the *style* of Holy Scripture. This is all the more remarkable as it was the custom of the day to disparage the literary value of the Sacred Writings. Augustine himself, in early life, had been driven from the study of the Bible by his aversion for its style; cf. Conf. 3, 5, 9: non enim sicut modo loquor, ita sensi cum attendi ad illam scripturam: sed uisa est mihi indigna quam Tullianae dignitati compararem. See Baldwin (2) 54, 59.

2. **nobis erudiendis**: dative of the gerundive to express purpose is not at all common in Early and Class. Latin. Its use gained ground after Livy, and was greatly widened by Tacitus: cf. K.-Steg. II, 1, 746, 749; St.-Schm. 598. It occurs again in 7, 15.

ab hoc saeculo prauo in beatum saeculum: chiasmus, followed in the next line by the figure of derivation, paragmenon: prouidentia diuina prouidit.

4. **plus** = *magis*, as often in Late Latin. See also 20, 41. Cf. note on *magis = plus* in 5, 7.

7. **per alteram . . . eloquentiam**: *alter* for *alius* occurs often in Late writers, due to the influence of the colloquial language. Note it below in 8, 22; 25, 55. See

critics are puffed up, who, not because of its real greatness, but because of its bombast, prefer their own language to the language of our writers, I could, if there were time, point out in the Sacred Writings of those whom Divine Providence has provided to instruct us, and to bring us from this corrupt world to the world of the blessed. But it is not the points which they have in common with the pagan orators and poets that please me more than I can say, in their eloquence; what I admire and wonder at more, is that they so use our eloquence, through another kind of eloquence, as it were, of their own, that ours is not wanting to them, and still is not conspicuous in them, for it would not be fitting for them either to reject it, or to flaunt it. The former would be the case if they avoided it, the latter might be imputed to them if they made it too noticeable. And in those places where it happens to be recognized by scholars, the subject-matter is such that the words in which it is expressed seem not to have been sought out by the writer, but seem to belong naturally to the matter itself, as if, to express a comparison, wisdom came forth from its own dwelling-place, that is, from the heart of the wise man, and eloquence, its inseparable handmaid, followed, even though uninvited.

St.-Schm. 491; Juret 37; Gabarrou 160; Bonnet 278; Goel. (1) 416, (2) 673; etc.

8. **improbari ... agnosceretur**: notice the predominantly passive construction throughout this passage, quite in keeping with the increase in the use of the passive in Late Latin. See also 10, 25, and *passim*.

12. **uelut** = *quasi*, does not occur in Cic., but from Livy on: cf. K.-Steg. II, 2, 718; St.-Schm. 783. Note the use of the classical *quasi* (1.13), side by side with this. *Velut* is thus used also in 7, 12; 7, 16; 20, 39; 20, 41. It occurs with a noun in 7, 20.

13. **sapientiam de domo sua**: cf. Orat. 21, 70: sed est eloquentiae sicut reli-

quarum rerum fundamentum sapientia.

de domo: *de* for *ex* with the abl., to express separation, occurs frequently in Augustine and in Late Latin: cf. St.-Schm. 526; Arts 29; Bonnet 607. For the distinction between *de* and *ex*, cf. T.L.L. V, 43, 47–66. The use of *de* with *procedere* is cited for Ulp. and Apul.: cf. T.L.L. V, 48. 70-71.

14. **tamquam** with a substantive is used by Cic.; but an adverb as an attribute of a substantive is at all times rare: cf. St.-Schm. 733. See below, *tamquam* with a noun: 7, 15: 7, 17; 20, 40; 23, 52; with a phrase: 18, 37; 21, 48; with an adjective: 7, 16; 26, 56.

inseparabilem: Silver and Late.

7, 11. Quis enim non uideat quid uoluerit dicere, et quam sapienter
dixerit apostolus: *gloriamur in tribulationibus, scientes quia tri-*
bulatio patientiam operatur, patientia autem probationem, probatio
autem spem, spes autem non confundit; quia charitas Dei diffusa
est in cordibus nostris per Spiritum sanctum qui datus est nobis? 5
hic si quis, ut ita dixerim, imperite peritus, artis eloquentiae praecepta apostolum secutum fuisse contendat, nonne a christianis
doctis indoctisque ridebitur? et tamen agnoscitur hic figura, quae
κλίμαξ graece, latine uero a quibusdam est appellata *gradatio*, quoniam *scalam* dicere noluerunt, cum uerba uel sensa conectuntur 10
alterum ex altero; sicut hic, ex *tribulatione patientiam*, ex *pati-*
entia probationem, ex probatione spem conexam uidemus. agnoscitur et aliud decus, quoniam post aliqua pronuntiationis uoce
singula finita, quae nostri *membra* et *caesa*, Graeci autem κῶλα et

Rom. 5, 3-5

---

1 quid]quod *E.*   dicere uoluerit *EI.*   2 quod *EH Ver.An. Vulg.*   3 patien-
tiam] patientia *B.*   autem] uero *E.*   4 spes autem]spes uero *E Ver.An.*   Dei
om. A.   5 datis in *G.*   6 hoc *E.*   7 secundum (secutum *supra alia m.*) *F.*
9 est *om. E*; autem *add. I.*   10 uoluerunt *A.*   12 uideamus *E.*   13 post aliqua
... uoce]post aliquam ... uocem *A*; post aliquam ... uoce *EI*; post alia qua ... uoce *D.*

---

7. *Analysis of the 'compositio' of St.*
Paul and of the Prophet Amos, by way
of proof of the rhetorical, as well as of
the spiritual excellence of the inspired
writers.

2. **gloriamur, etc.**: note in Introduction, page 19 [now p. 342], that the
Old Version and the Vulgate practically
coincide in this passage. Augustine follows the Old Version, however, in the
one word wherein they differ: probatio
autem spem.

6. **hic si quis . . . contendat, etc.**:
Norden (503), however, rightly observes
that St. Paul knows well the figures of
rhetoric, and half consciously, half
unconsciously uses them as the occasion
demands. An analysis of the preceding
passage proves this. For a graphic study
of Augustine's analysis which follows in
this chapter, cf. Eskridge 30–36; Baldwin (2) 61–64.

   imperite peritus: Oxymoron: A.
falls as naturally into figurative terms as
does St. Paul, in the passage just quoted.

8. **figura . . . κλίμαξ . . . gradatio**: cf.

Ad Her. 4, 25, 34: gradatio est, in qua non
ante ad consequens uerbum descenditur,
quam ad superius conscensum est, hoc
modo: 'nam quae reliqua spes manet libertatis, si illis et quod libet, licet et quod
licet, possunt, et quod possunt, audent,
et quod audent, faciunt, et quod faciunt,
uobis molestum non est?' . . . habet in
se quendam leporem superioris cuiusque
crebra repetitio uerbi, quae propria est
huius exornationis. Also Quint. 9, 3,
55: gradatio, quae dicitur κλίμαξ, aper-
tiorem habet artem et magis affectatam,
ideoque esse rarior debet. est autem ipsa
quoque adiectionis; repetit enim, quae
dicta sunt, et priusquam ad aliud descen-
dat, in prioribus resistit.

10. **scalam** = 'ladder': used only in
the plural in Caesar and Cicero; found in
the sing. in Cels. 8, 15, and frequently
in Late Latin: cf. K.-Schm. s.v.; Neue-
Wagener 1, 687.

   sensa = 'ideas,' 'thought': used
only twice by Cicero: De Orat. 1, 8, 32:
exprimere dicendo sensa possumus; *ibid.*
3, 14, 55: sensa mentis et consilia expli-

7,   11. For who cannot but see what the Apostle wished to say and with what wisdom he has said it, in the following: *We glory in tribulations, knowing that tribulation worketh patience; and patience trial; and trial hope; and hope confoundeth not: because the charity of God is poured forth in our hearts by the Holy Ghost, who is given to us?* Here if anyone, unlearnedly learned, so to speak, contend that the Apostle has followed the rules of rhetoric, will he not be laughed at by Christians, cultured and uncultured alike? And still we recognize here the figure called in Greek, κλίμαξ, in Latin, by some, *gradatio*—a name which they prefer to *scala*, ladder—for the words or the thoughts are connected one with another, as, for example, here we see *patience* connected with *tribulation*, *trial* with *patience*, *hope* with *trial*. Another ornament, too, is recognized here, for after several elements marked off by an unbroken utterance in delivery, which we call *membra* and *caesa*, and the Greeks, κῶλα and κόμματα, there

care; in Silver Latin by Quint., *e.g.*, 8, 5, 1; more often in Late Latin, *e.g.*, Macr. Sat. 7, 5, 4: sensa et inuenta Disarii: cf. K.-Schm. s.v.; For. s.v.

14. **singula**: *singuli*, in the singular, is found only once—in Plautus—in Early and Class. usage, but frequently in Late Latin: cf. K.-Schm. s.v. Note this again in 26, 56.

   membra: cf. Ad Her. 4, 19, 26: membrum orationis appellatur res breuiter absoluta sine totius sententia demonstratione, quae denuo alio membro orationis excipitur, hoc modo: 'et inimico proderas.' id est unum, quod appellamus membrum; deinde hoc excipiatur oportet altero: 'et amicum laedebas.' ex duobus membris suis haec exornatio potest constare; sed commodissima et absolutissima est, quae ex tribus constat, hoc pacto: 'et inimico proderas et amicum laedebas et tibi non consulemus.' Quint. 9, 4, 123: membrum autem est sensus numeris conclusus sed a toto corpore abruptus et per se nihil efficiens. 'o callidos homines,' perfectum est sed remotum a ceteris uim non habet, ut per se manus et pes et caput; et 'o rem excogitatam.' quando ergo incipit corpus esse? cum uenit extrema conclusio: 'quem, quaeso, nostrum fefellit, id uos ita esse facturos?'

   caesa: Cicero and Quintilian use *incisum* in place of *caesum*: cf. Orat. 62, 211: transferenda tota dictio est ad illa quae nescio cur, cum Graeci κόμματα et κῶλα nominent, nos non recte incisa et membra dicamus. Quint. 9, 4, 22: incisa, quae κόμματα dicuntur, membra, quae κῶλα, etc. Quintilian's definition is as follows: incisum (quantum mea fert opinio) erit sensus non expleto numero conclusus, plerisque pars membri. tale est enim, quo Cicero utitur: 'domus tibi deerat? at habebas. pecunia superabat? at egebas.' fiunt autem etiam, singulis uerbis incisa: 'diximus, testis dare uolumus'; incisum est 'dicimus' (Quint. 9, 4, 122). Among Late commentators, Aquila, Rhet. 18, says: caesum . . . est pars orationis ex duobus aut ex pluribus uerbis, non quicquam absolute significans. This agrees with Quintilians's definition of *incisum*, and Aquila does in fact mean the same, for he explains: ambitus constat ex membris . . . et ex caesis, quae κόμματα Graeci appellant. *Caesum* is also called *comma*, a 'pause' or 'stop': cf. T.L.L. III, 58, 37-49. Modern scholars are by no means agreed as to an explanation of the distinction made by the ancients in the meaning of *membra* and *caesa*. To some the difference lies in the length of the clause, *i.e.*, they consider

κόμματα uocant, sequitur ambitus siue circuitus, quem περίοδον illi appellant, cuius membra suspenduntur uoce dicentis, donec ultimo finiantur. nam eorum quae praecedunt circuitum, membrum illud est primum, *quoniam tribulatio patientiam operatur;* secundum, *patientia autem probationem;* tertium, *probatio uero spem.* deinde 5 subiungitur ipse circuitus, qui tribus peragitur membris, quorum primum est, *spes autem non confundit;* secundum, *quia charitas Dei diffusa est in cordibus nostris;* tertium, *per Spiritum sanctum qui datus est nobis.* at haec atque huiusmodi in elocutionis arte traduntur. sicut ergo apostolum praecepta eloquentiae secutum 10 fuisse non dicimus, ita quod eius sapientiam secuta sit eloquentia, non negamus.

12. Scribens ad Corinthios, in secunda epistola redarguit quosdam qui erant ex Iudaeis pseudoapostoli, eique detrahebant; et quoniam seipsum praedicare compellitur, hanc sibi uelut insipi- 15 entiam tribuens, quam sapienter dicit, quamque eloquenter; sed comes sapientiae, dux eloquentiae, illam sequens, istam praecedens

3 finiatur *AD Maur.*   4 est illud primum *EI.*   operatur *om. C.*   5 tertium *om. G;* tertia *F.*   7 quoniam *ABC.*   8 est *om. E.*   9 at haec atque]atque haec ac *E;* aiunt haec atque *I.*   huiuscemodi *Maur.;* huius *I.*   11 eloquentiam *A.* 14 eique]neque *E.*   15 hanc]ac *F.*   uel *E.*   17 illam]illa *A.*

that the number of syllables contained in a clause determines whether it should be called a *membrum* or a *caesum.* Du Mesnil (Begriff der drei Kunstformen der Rede, etc.: Zum zweihundertjährigen Jubiläum des Gymnasiums zu Frankfort, Frankfort, 1894, 32–121) holds that a *caesum* should have from one to seven syllables, a *membrum*, from eight to seventeen. This theory is at once too rigid and too superficial, and has not gained acceptance. It would seem better to base the difference, with Quintilian (9, 4, 122–24), on finished and unfinished rhythm. A satisfactory translation of these terms is likewise wanting. Since the distinction which they conveyed to the ancients is no longer regarded, they have no equivalent in modern English. The terms *clauses, phrases, commas, pauses, members, sections* express in some part the proper meaning, but they also differ, each one, in some fundamental point. It has seemed better, therefore, to attempt no translation of *membra* and *caesa*, but rather to hold merely to the ancient expression for what belongs wholly to ancient thought.

1. **ambitus:** for synonyms cf. Orat. 61, 204: in quo quaesitum est in totone circumitu illo orationis, quem Graeci περίδον, nos tum ambitum, tum circumitum, tum comprehensionem aut continuationem aut circumscriptionem dicimus, an in principiis solum an in extremis an in utraque parte numerus tenendus sit; deinde cum aliud uideatur esse numerus aliud numerosum, quid intersit. Quintilian quotes Cicero, in his definition (9, 4, 124), but characteristically analyzes the period into its kinds: periodo plurima nomina dat Cicero, 'ambitum, circuitum, comprehensionem, continuationem, circumscriptionem.' genera eius duo sunt: alterum simplex, cum sensus unus longiore ambitu circumducitur; alterum,

follows a rounded sentence, or period, which the latter call περίοδος, whose *membra* are held suspended by the voice of the speaker, until completed by the last one. For, of the *membra* preceding the period, the first one is, *since tribulation worketh patience*; the second, *and patience trial*; the third, *and trial, hope*. Then the period itself follows, which is completed in three *membra*, the first of which being, *and hope confoundeth not*; the second, *because the charity of God is poured forth in our hearts*; the third, *by the Holy Ghost, who is given to us*. But this, and things of this kind are set forth in the art of oratory. So, though we do not say that the Apostle followed the rules of eloquence, still, we do not deny that eloquence followed close upon his wisdom.

12. Writing to the Corinthians, in the second Epistle, he refutes certain false apostles from among the Jews, who were maligning him, and being obliged to speak of himself—granting it a kind of folly in himself—how wisely and how eloquently does he speak! But he is the attendant of wisdom, the master of eloquence; he follows the one, taking precedence of the other, and yet not

quod constat membris et incisis, quae plures sensus habent: 'aderat ianitor carceris et carnifex praetoris,' reliqua. Mart. Cap. (5, 527) uses practically the same terms: περίοδος multis constat ex membris quae κῶλα Graeci dicunt et caesis quae κόμματα appellant. For further references on the period, cf. T.L.L. I, 1860, 46–79.

2. cuius membra . . . finiantur: Baldwin (2, 64) notes how A. by this observation throws the emphasis on *delivery*, in his definition of the period. This, however, Cicero also does, *e.g.*, Brut. 8, 34: ipsa enim natura circumscriptione quadam uerborum comprehendit concluditque sententiam, quae cum aptis constricta uerbis est, cadit etiam plerumque numerose. nam et aures ipsae quid plenum, quid inane sit iudicant et spiritu quasi necessitate aliqua uerborum comprehensio terminatur; in quo non modo defici, sed etiam laborare turpe est.

suspenduntur = 'suspended,' is Poetic, Silver, Late.

3. praecedunt = 'go before': Poetic, Silver.

6. subiungitur = 'added': not frequent in Cicero, but often used by Pliny and Quint. It is related, in this meaning to *subnectere*, which, too, is scarcely ever used by Cic. and Caes., but often by Quint., Val. Max., Just., Hier.: cf. K.-Schm. s.v. It occurs again in 7, 13.

9. at haec . . . in elocutionis arte traduntur: as for instance in Ad. Her. 4; De Orat. 3; Quint. 9.

11. quod . . . secuta sit . . . negamus: note again the use of the Late *quod* clause in place of the regular infinitive and accusative of indirect discourse. In this instance it is in obvious contrast with the preceding *secutum fuisse*, used in an analogous clause with *dicimus*.

15. praedicare compellitur: the infinitive with *compellere* is used first by the poets, then in Silver Latin and frequently in Late writers. See Colbert (58) for its common use in De Ciu. Dei. See also St.-Schm. 580; T.L.L. IV, 2034, 12.

2 Cor. 11, 16-30 et sequentem non respuens. *iterum dico* inquit *ne quis me existimet insipientem esse; alioquin uelut insipientem suscipite me, ut et ego modicum quid glorier. quod loquor, non loquor secundum Deum, sed quasi in stultitia, in hac substantia gloriae. quoniam quidem multi gloriantur secundum carnem, et ego gloriabor.* 5 *libenter enim sustinetis insipientes, cum sitis ipsi sapientes. toleratis enim si quis uos in seruitutem redigit, si quis deuorat, si quis accipit, si quis extollitur, si quis in faciem uos caedit. secundum ignobilitatem dico, quasi nos infirmati simus. in quo autem quis audet (in insipientia dico), audeo et ego. Hebraei sunt? et ego.* 10 *Israelitae sunt? et ego. semen Abrahae sunt? et ego. ministri Christi sunt? (insipiens dico) super ego. in laboribus plurimum, in carceribus abundantius, in plagis supra modum, in mortibus saepius. a Iudaeis quinquies, quadraginta una minus accepi. ter uirgis caesus sum, semel lapidatus sum, ter naufragium feci; nocte* 15 *et die in profundo maris fui; in itineribus saepe, periculis fluminum, periculis latronum, periculis ex genere, periculis ex gentibus, periculis in ciuitate, periculis in deserto, periculis in mari, periculis in falsis fratribus; in labore et aerumna, in uigiliis saepius, in fame et siti, in ieiuniis saepius, in frigore et nuditate; praeter* 20 *illa quae extrinsecus sunt, incursus in me quotidianus, sollicitudo omnium ecclesiarum. quis infirmatur, et ego non infirmor? quis scandalizatur, et ego non uror? si gloriari oportet, in iis quae infirmitatis meae sunt, gloriabor.* quanta sapientia ista sint dicta, uigilantes uident. quanto uero etiam eloquentiae cucurrerint flu- 25 mine, et qui stertit aduertit.

13. Porro autem qui nouit, agnoscit quod ea caesa quae κόμματα Graeci uocant, et membra et circuitus, de quibus paulo ante disserui, cum decentissima uarietate interponerentur, totam istam speciem dictionis, et quasi eius uultum, quo etiam indocti delec- 30

---

2 et *om. I Ver.An.* 4 Dominum *A Vulg.* substantiam *I.* 5 multi quidem *I.* 6 ipsi *om. ACEFGHI Ver.An.* 7 si quis deuorat *om. E.* 9 ignorantiam *E.* quasi . . . simus *om. E*; simus] sumus *D*; infirmati simus]infirmi fuerimus *F Ver.An. Vulg.* 10 in quo . . . dico *om. E.* 11 semen Abrahae sunt et ego *om. I.* 12 sunt et ego *BE*; sunt ut *C.* plus ego *F Vulg (MSS. duo*; super ego *alii omnes cum editis;* ὑπὲρ ἐγώ *Graece [Maur.])*. plurimum *F Ver.An.* 14 saepius]saepe *E*; frequentur *I Ver.An. Vulg.* quadragenas *EFHI Vulg.* 15 semel lapidatus sum *om. E.* 16 profundum *AEGHI.* 18 ciuitatibus *F.* 19 in falsis]ex falsis *F.* fratribus falsis *F.* saepius] multis *AE Ver.An.Vulg.* 20 saepius]multis *FI.* 22 ego *om. D.* qui *F.* 23 non ego *C Ver. An.* in *om. E.* his *ABCDFGHI*; hiis *E.* 25 uideant *D.* etiam *om. CH.* eloquentia *F.* concurrerint *ABG Mig.*; cucurrerunt *F.* fluminis *F.* 26 auerit *AE.* 28 disseruimus *F.* 30 etiam *om. E.*

---

1. **iterum dico, etc.**: cf. Introduction p. 347, for a comparison of this quota- tion with the Old Version and the Vulgate; cf. Eskridge 31–35, for a graphic

spurning it as it follows him. *I say again* he says (*let no man think me to be foolish, otherwise, take me as one foolish, that I also may glory a little.) That which I speak, I speak not according to God, but as it were in foolishness, in the matter of glorying. Seeing that many glory according to the flesh, I will glory also. For you gladly suffer the foolish; whereas yourselves are wise. For you suffer if a man bring you into bondage, if a man devour you, if a man take from you, if a man be lifted up, if a man strike you on the face. I speak according to dishonor, as if we had been weak. Wherein if any man dare (I speak foolishly), I dare also. They are Hebrews? So am I. They are Israelites? So am I. They are the seed of Abraham? So am I. They are the ministers of Christ? (I speak as one foolish); I am more; in labors, very often, in prisons more frequently, in stripes above measure, in deaths, many times. Of the Jews five times did I receive forty stripes, save one. Thrice was I beaten with rods, once I was stoned, thrice I suffered shipwreck, a night and a day I was in the depth of the sea. In journeyings often, in perils of water, in perils of robbers, in perils from my own nation, in perils from the Gentiles, in perils in the city, in perils in the wilderness, in perils in the sea, in perils from false brethren. In labors and painfulness, in watchings many times, in hunger and thirst, in fastings very often, in cold and nakedness. Besides those things which are without: my daily care, the solicitude for all the churches. Who is weak, and I am not weak? Who is scandalized, and I am not on fire? If I must needs glory, I will glory in the things that concern my infirmity.* The great wisdom with which this is expressed, those who have their eyes open can see. But too, the mighty torrent of eloquence with which these words rush on, even one snoring in sleep must notice.

13. Furthermore, the scholar recognizes that it is the *caesa* called by the Greeks, κόμματα, and the *membra* and periods mentioned a little above, which interspersed as they are in the most fitting variety, have here produced the whole form and feature, so to speak, of the diction, whereby even the unlettered are pleased and moved. For from the beginning of the preceding quotation, periods are used. The first is the shortest, that is, it has only two

analysis of its *membra* and *caesa*.

29. **cum decentissima uarietate**: cf. De Orat. 1, 32, 144: apte et quasi decore; Orat. 29, 103: at haec interdum temperanda et uarianda sunt.

decentissima: *decens*, in the superlative, is cited for Silver Latin, and for frequent use in Late writers: cf. T.L.L. IV, 135, 41–136, 11.

tantur mouenturque, fecerunt. nam unde coepimus hunc locum
inserere, circuitus sunt; primus minimus, hoc est bimembris—
minus enim quam duo membra circuitus habere non possunt, plura
uero possunt—ergo ille primus est: *iterum dico, ne quis me existi-*
met insipientem esse. sequitur alius trimembris: *alioquin uelut* 5
insipientem suscipite me, ut et ego modicum quid glorier. tertius
qui sequitur membra habet quattuor: *quod loquor, non loquor*
secundum Deum, sed quasi in stultitia, in hac substantia gloriae.
quartus duo habet: *quoniamquidem multi gloriantur secundum*
carnem, et ego gloriabor. et quintus habet duo: *libenter enim sus-* 10
tinetis insipientes, cum sitis ipsi sapientes. etiam sextus bimembris
est: *toleratis enim, si quis uos in seruitutem redigit.* Sequuntur
tria caesa: *si quis deuorat, si quis accipit, si quis extollitur.* deinde
tria membra: *si quis in faciem uos caedit, secundum ignobilitatem*
dico, quasi nos infirmati simus. additur trimembris circuitus: *in* 15
quo autem quis audet (in insipientia dico), audeo et ego. hinc iam
singulis quibusque caesis interrogando positis, singula itidem caesa
responsione redduntur, tria tribus: *Hebraei sunt? et ego. Israe-*
litae sunt? et ego. semen Abrahae sunt? et ego. quarto autem caeso
simili interrogatione posito, non alterius caesi, sed membri oppo- 20

---

1 fecerunt]ceperunt *E.*   2 minimus]minor *C, (supra) G*; minus *D.*   4 est *om.*
E.   6 et *om. C Ver.An.*   quid modicum *A.*   7 habet membra *E.*   8 Dominum *AC Vulg.*   9 quandoquidem *Maur.*; quia *Ver.An.*; quoniam *Vulg.*   10 et
(quintus) *om. E.*   habet *om. CFGH.*   duo habet *I.*   11 ipsi *om. MSS Ver.An.*
13 tria *om. D.*   15 infirmi *EH Ver.An. Vulg.*   16 autem]eius *E.*   in *om. I.*   17
-que *om. D.*   18 tria *om. D.*   19 Israelitae sunt . . . Abrahae sunt et ego   *om.*
I.   20 positi *D.*   ulterius *E.*   bimembri *A.*

---

1. **delectantur mouenturque**: *delec-*
tare and *mouere*, the objects of the temperate and grand styles respectively,
are shown therefore to be attained by a
fitting use of *caesa, membra*, and *cir-*
cuitus.

   unde = *a quo*: cf. 5, 7, and below:
18, 37; 20, 41; 21, 45.

2. **hoc est**: a parallel use of *id est*
and *hoc est* is noted in Latin from
Cicero down to the seventh century
A.D. Cicero himself, in his later writings, abandoned *hoc est* for *id est. Id est*
remained thereafter the normal phrase,
though *hoc est* continued to be used, and
finally triumphed in Italian: cioè < ecce

+ hoc est: cf. Meader 53ff. In De Doct.
Christ. 4, *hoc est* occurs five times, *id*
est seven times. For Ambrose's use of
these phrases, see McGuire 22, Adams
54, Buck 20.

   bimembris . . . trimembris: Silver
and Late.

3. **minus enim . . . plura possunt**:
cf. Ad Her. 4, 19, 26: ex duobus membris suis haec exornatio potest constare;
sed commodissima et absolutissima est,
quae ex tribus constat, hoc pacto 'et
inimico proderas et amicum laedebas et
tibi non consulebas.' Orat. 66, 221–22:
constat enim ille ambitus et plena comprehensio e quattuor fere partibus, quae

membra—periods cannot have less than this, though they may have more—so the first is: *I say again, let no man think me to be foolish.* Another, made up of three *membra*, follows: *Otherwise, take me as one foolish, that I also may glory a little.* The third in order has four *membra*: *That which I speak, I speak not according to God, but as it were in foolishness, in this matter of glorying.* The fourth has two: *Seeing that many glory according to the flesh, I will glory also.* And the fifth has two: *For you gladly suffer the foolish; whereas yourselves are wise.* In like manner the sixth has two: *For you suffer if a man bring you into bondage.* Three *caesa* follow: *If a man devour you, if a man take from you, if a man be lifted up.* Then three *membra*: *If a man strike you on the face. I speak according to dishonor, as if we had been weak.* A period of three *membra* then follows: *Wherein if any man dare (I speak foolishly), I dare also.* Then several distinct *caesa* are put in question form, and as many distinct *caesa* are returned in answer, three against three: *They are Hebrews? So am I. They are Israelites? So am I. They are the seed of Abraham? So am I.* But the fourth, put likewise as a question, is answered not by the balance of another *caesum*, but of a *membrum*: *They are the ministers of Christ? (I speak as one foolish), I am more.* Then the question form being fittingly dropped, the four following *caesa* pour

membra dicimus, ut et aures impleat et neque breuior sit quam satis sit neque longior. . . . (e quattuor igitur quasi hexametrorum instar uersuum quod sit constat fere plena comprehensio.) Quint. 9, 4, 125: habet periodus membra minimum duo. medius numerus uidentur quattuor, sed recipit frequenter et plura. Aug. Mus. 4, 17, 36: circuitus ergo minor esse non potest, quam qui duobus membris constat. . . . licet igitur minimum bimembrem, medium trimembrem, ultimum quadrimembrem uocare.

17. **singulis quibusque**: *quisque* restricted to use with (1) a pronoun, relative, interrogative, or reflexive, (2) a superlative, (3) an ordinal, was not adhered to even by Cicero himself, who in his rhetorical and philosophical works used *quisque* freely, regarding only the rule of not beginning a sentence with this pronoun. Later writers used *quisque* with the same freedom, *e.g.*, with the positive and comparative of adjectives, and with *singuli* in place of an ordinal numeral: cf. Hor. De Arte Poet. 92: singula quaeque; Vopisc. Sat. 11, 4: singuli quique; Hier. Contr. Pelag. 2, 20: in singulis quibusque sanctorum. See K.-Schm. s.v. Lebreton 106–8; Goel. (1) 410. See the singular use of this combination, below in 26, 56: singulo quoque.

18. **responsione**: *responsio = responsum*, is rare, but classical: cf. K.-Schm. s.v. The figure of rhetoric, *responsio*, called also *subiectio*, is mentioned by Auct. ad Her., Cicero, and Quintilian. This passage is a good example of it. Cicero refers to this figure in Orat. 40, 137: ut interrogando urgeat; ut rursus quasi ad interrogata sibi ipse respondeat; and in De Orat. 3, 54, 207, in an enumeration of figures: et dissupatio et continuatum et interruptum et imago et sibi ipsi *responsio*.

sitione respondet: *ministri Christi sunt? (insipiens dico) super ego.* iam quattuor sequentia, remota decentissime interrogatione funduntur: *in laboribus plurimum, in carceribus abundantius, in plagis supra modum, in mortibus saepius.* deinde interponitur breuis circuitus, quoniam suspensa pronuntiatione distinguendum 5 est, *a Iudaeis quinquies,* ut hoc sit unum membrum, cui conectitur alterum, *quadraginta una minus accepi.* inde reditur ad caesa, et ponuntur tria: *ter uirgis caesus sum, semel lapidatus sum, ter naufragium feci.* sequitur membrum: *nocte ac die in profundo fui.* deinde quattuordecim caesa decentissimo impetu profluunt: *in* 10 *itineribus saepe, periculis fluminum, periculis latronum, periculis ex genere, periculis ex gentibus, periculis in ciuitate, periculis in deserto, periculis in mari, periculis in falsis fratribus; in labore et aerumna, in uigiliis saepius, in fame et siti, in ieiuniis saepius, in frigore et nuditate.* post haec interponit trimembrem circuitum: *in* 15 *praeter illa quae extrinsecus sunt, incursus in me quotidianus, solli-citudo omnium ecclesiarum.* et huic duo membra percontatione subiungit: *quis infirmatur, et ego non infirmor? quis scandali-zatur, et ego non uror?* postremo totus iste quasi anhelans locus, bimembri circuitu terminatur: *si gloriari oportet, in iis quae* 20 *infirmitatis meae sunt gloriabor.* quod vero post hunc impetum interposita narratiuncula quodammodo requiescit et requiescere auditorem facit, quid decoris et delectationis habeat, satis dici non potest, sequitur enim dicens: *Deus et Pater Domini nostri Iesu Christi scit, qui est benedictus in saecula, quod non mentior.* ac 25 deinde quomodo periclitatus fuerit, et quomodo euaserit, breuissime narrat.

2 Cor. 11, 31

1 respondit *F.*   sunt et ego *DEF.*   2 decentissima *BF.*   3 plurimus *I Ver.An.* abundanti *D.* 4 saepius]frequenter *DF Ver.An. Vulg.*   5 (qui suspensa pronuntiatione distinguendus est *MSS* quattuor [*Maur.*]).   7 et]ut *D.*   9 et *EFG Ver.An. Vulg.*   profundum *AEG.*   14 uigiliis sae-pius]uigliis multis *AF Ver.An. Vulg.*   15 interponet *G.*   16 in me incursus *A.*   18 perconta-tione subiungit]per percontationes ibi iungit *I*; percontatione]percontationis (*sic em.*) *B.* 20 bimembri circuitu]bimembris in circuitu *E.*   20 his *ABCDFGHI*; hiis *E.*   22 et *om. I.* 23 facit auditorem *Maur.*   et]quid *Maur.*   dilectionis *E.*   habet *E.*   25 Pater Domini nostri Iesu Christi] Pater Domini Iesu *BCFG.*   et requiescere auditorem . . . scit *om. I.*

5. **distinguendum**: *distinguere* = 'separate,' is common to Late Latin. though found in Cicero and Quintil-ian: cf. Quint. 1, 8, 1: quo loco uersum distinguere debeat puer, ubi claudatur sensus, unde incipiat: cf. T.L.L. V, 1528, 8-59. It occurs again in 7, 19.

6. **cui conectitur**: *cum* with the abl. is the usual construction with *conectere*; the dative is sometimes used, however, as in De Orat. 2, 80, 325: conexum autem ita sit principium consequenti orationi: cf. K.-Steg. I, 1, 330; T.L.L. IV, 165ff.

forth: *In labors, very often, in prisons more frequently, in stripes above measure, in deaths many times.* Next a short period is inserted, for by keeping the voice raised in delivery, *Of the Jews five times* is to be set off as one *membrum*, with which is connected a second, *did I receive forty stripes save one.* Then the *caesa* are taken up again, and three are given: *Thrice was I beaten with rods, once I was stoned, thrice I suffered shipwreck.* A *membrum* follows: *A night and a day, I was in the depth of the sea.* Then fourteen *caesa* stream forth with most appropriate force: *In journeyings often, in perils of water, in perils of robbers, in perils from my own nation, in perils from the Gentiles, in perils in the city, in perils in the wilderness, in perils in the sea, in perils from false brethren. In labor and painfulness, in watchings many times, in hunger and thirst, in fastings very often, in cold and nakedness.* After this he inserts a period of three *membra*: *Besides those things which are without: my daily care, the solicitude for the churches.* And to this he adds two *membra* in question form: *Who is weak, and I am not weak? Who is scandalized, and I am not on fire?* Finally the whole passage, as though panting for breath, ends with a period of two *membra*: *If I must needs glory, I will glory in the things that concern my infirmity.* But because after this outburst, by inserting a bit of narrative he calms down after a fashion, and makes his reader calm down, it is impossible to express what a fine and pleasing effect he attains. For he continues with the words: *The God and Father of our Lord Jesus Christ, who is blessed forever, knoweth that I lie not.* And then he proceeds to tell in short how he has been in danger, and how he has escaped.

---

19. **anhelans** = 'panting,' is Poetic, Silver, and Late: cf. Hier. Epis. 125, 12: stridentia anhelantiaque uerba: cf. T.L.L. II, 66, 18.

22. **narratiuncula**: cited for Quint. 1, 9, 6; Plin. Epis. 6, 33, 8.

requiescere . . . facit: *facere* with the infinitive was a popular idiom of the *sermo plebeus*, though used at times in the literary languages of Early, Class., and Silver writers. It became frequent in Late Latin as a colloquial idiom, but also through the influence of the Bible, where it is often found as a translation of Greek and Hebrew causatives: *e.g.*, Exod. 23, 11: dimittes eam et requiescere facies.

Augustine uses it in the Confessions, and frequently in De Ciu. Dei: cf. St.-Schm. 580; K.-Steg. II, 1, 694; T.L.L. VI, 115–16; Rönsch 366–67; Arts 90; Colbert 58; McGuire 192. It appears again below in 7, 20.

24. **sequitur**: *sequi* = 'continue,' is rare, but occurs in Lucr. 5, 529: sequor disponere causas.

dicens: a stereotyped introduction to biblical quotations, often used by ecclesiastical writers, and found frequently below. *Dico* in all forms with direct quotations is common to this treatise, as to all Late Latin: cf. St.-Schm. 606; T.L.L. V, 982, 33–983, 33.

14. Longum est caetera persequi, uel in aliis sanctarum scripturarum locis ista monstrare. quid, si etiam figuras locutionis quae
illa arte traduntur, in iis saltem quae de apostoli eloquio commemoraui, ostendere uoluissem? nonne facilius graues homines me
nimium, quam quisquam studiosorum sibi sufficientem putaret? 5
haec omnia quando a magistris docentur pro magno habentur,
magno emuntur pretio, magna iactatione uenduntur. quam iactan-
tionem etiam ego redolere uereor, dum ista sic dissero. sed male
doctis hominibus respondendum fuit, qui nostros auctores con-
temnendos putant, non quia non habent, sed quia non ostentant, 10
quam nimis isti diligunt, eloquentiam.

15. Sed forte quis putat, tamquam eloquentem nostrum elegisse
2 Cor. 11, 6 mea apostolum Paulum. uidetur enim ubi ait, *etsi imperitus ser-*
mone, sed non scientia, quasi concedendo obtrectatoribus sic locutus, non tamquam id uerum agnosceret, confitendo. si autem dix- 15
isset, 'imperitus quidem sermone, sed non scientia,' nullo modo
aliud posset intellegi. scientiam plane non cunctatus est profiteri,
sine qua esse doctor gentium non ualeret. certe si quid eius pro-
ferimus ad exemplum eloquentiae, ex illis epistolis utique proferi-
2 Cor. 10, 10 mus, quas etiam ipsi obtrectatores, eius qui sermonem praesentis 20
contemptibilem putari uolebant, graves et fortes esse confessi sunt.

---

2 demonstrare *D*.   quod *EH*.   locutiones *G*.   3 his *ABCDFGHI*; hiis *E*.
saltem]autem *D*.   de . . . eloquio] ad . . . eloquium *D*.   5 sufficientem sibi *A*.
putarent *AE Maur*.   6 a *om. E*.   7 pretio *om. ADEFGHI*; pretio emuntur *C*.
pretio . . . uenduntur *in marg. alia m. B*.   8 ego *om. A*.; ego etiam *F*.   reco-
lere *A*.   10 habeant (*sic em.*) *B*.   ostendunt *F*.   12 putant *G*.   nostrorum *A*.
15 id *om. E*.   uero *I*. autem] uero *E*.   16 sermone et non addidisset *C*.
scientia (*sic Bad. Am. Er. et MSS*; et non addidisset sed non scientia *Lou.*
[*Maur*.]).   quasi concedendo . . . non scientia *rep. F*.   18 non ualeret] nequaquam esse ualeret *E*.   si quid certe eius *G*.   20 praesente *B*.   21 parere *C*;
pari (parere *supra*) *G*. nolebant *E*.

---

3. **eloquio** = *eloquentia*, in Aug. poets
and Silver prose.

5. **studiosorum** = 'students,' belongs
particularly to Silver Latin, but already
occurs in Cic. De Opt. Gen 5, 13: putaui
mihi suscipiendum laborem utilem stu-
diosis. Cf. K.-Schm. s.v.; For. s.v.

sufficientem: the present participle
is used predicatively with verbs denot-
ing mental action, by Cic., Sall., Hor.,
Nepos., Vitr., and Livy: cf. St.-Schm.

605; K.-Steg. II, 1, 763.

6. **haec omnia . . . eloquentiam**: A.,
while quietly denouncing the excesses
of Sophistic, is here led to express one
of the principal aims of the present treatise: to prove the value of Holy Scripture
as a model of style: cf. Norden 526-28;
Baldwin (2) 53.

quando: temporal, was popular
in colloquial Latin, but avoided in the
polished literary language, *e.g.*, of Ter.,

14. It would be tedious to follow out other points, or to indicate such features in other places of the Holy Scriptures. What, if in the passages at least which I have quoted illustrative of the Apostle's eloquence, I had also wished to point out the figures of speech taught in rhetoric? Would not serious-minded men consider that I was going too far, rather than any student, that I was satisfactory to him? All these things, when taught by professors, are esteemed of great value; they are bought at a great price, and sold with great display. Such display, even I fear to smack of, as I thus discuss these matters; but it has seemed necessary to answer the ill-informed who think that our writers deserve contempt, not because they do not possess, but because they do not make display of the eloquence which the former too highly esteem.

15. But some perhaps may think that I have chosen the Apostle Paul as *the* example of our eloquence. For when he says, *Although I be rude in speech, yet not in knowledge*, he seems to have spoken thus merely by way of giving in to his detractors, not of confessing it as if he recognized it to be true. If, however, he had said, "I, indeed, rude in speech, but not in knowledge," no other meaning could possibly be taken from his words. Clearly, he did not hesitate to profess knowledge, without which he could not succeed as the teacher of the Gentiles. And, indeed, if we point out any thing of his as an example of eloquence, we assuredly point it out from those Epistles which even his detractors, themselves, who wanted his spoken word to be thought contemptible, admitted to be weighty and strong. And so I see that I must say something also of the eloquence of the Prophets, greatly cloaked as it is in a metaphorical style. The more, however, that they seem obscure by the use of

Caes., Varro., Sall., Plin. Min., Tac. Cicero used it only occasionally; as also the poets. It became common in Late Latin; and in the Romance languages entirely replaced cum (cf. Ital. *quando*, and French *quand*). It is frequently used in the Confessions, as also in this treatise: cf. chapters 10, 25; 12, 28; 13, 29; 18, 37; 22, 51; 23, 52; 24, 54; 26, 56; 26, 58; 29, 63; See K.-Steg. II, 2, 365; St.-Schm. 740; Arts 101.

10. **non quia non habent**: the indicative here is classical, as expressing an excluded fact, but the use of *non quia* for *non quod*, though it occurs in Early Latin,

is rare in the Class. period, becoming, however, more common from Livy on: cf. St.-Schm. 727; Gildersleeve 340.

12. **sed forte quis putat . . . Paulum**: of modern critics, this seems to be the opinion of Norden (528), who holds that outside of St. Paul, the Scriptures have no intrinsic claim to be reckoned rhetorical.

forte quis putat: for *forte = forsitan*, see 1, 2, and 10, 25.

19. **epistolis . . . fortes esse**: cf. 2 Cor. 10, 10: quoniam quidem epistolae, inquiunt, graues sunt et fortes, praesentia autem corporis infirma, et sermo contemptibilis.

dicendum ergo mihi aliquid esse uideo et de eloquentia prophe-
tarum, ubi per tropologiam multa obteguntur. quae quanto magis
translatis uerbis uidentur operiri, tanto magis cum fuerint aperta
dulcescunt. sed hoc loco tale aliquid commemorare debeo, ubi quae
dicta sunt non cogar exponere, sed commendem tantum quomodo 5
_{Amos 7, 14-15} dicta sint. et ex illius prophetae libro potissimum hoc faciam qui
se pastorem uel armentarium fuisse dicit, atque inde diuinitus
ablatum atque missum, ut Dei populo prophetaret: non autem
secundum septuaginta interpretes, qui etiam ipsi diuino Spiritu
interpretati, ob hoc aliter uidentur nonnulla dixisse, ut ad spiri- 10
tualem sensum scrutandum magis admoneretur lectoris intentio—
unde etiam obscuriora nonnulla, quia magis tropica, sunt eorum—
sed sicut ex hebraeo in latinum eloquium, presbytero Hieronymo
utriusque linguae perito interpretante, translata sunt.
   16. Cum igitur argueret impios, superbos, luxuriosos, et frater- 15

4 ubi ea *F*.   5 sint *G*.   tantummodo *E*.   sunt non cogar . . . quomodo dicta
om. D.   6 sunt *EH*.   et ex *om. A*.   potissimum libro *E*.   haec *F*.   10 ab *H*.
12 obscuriora *om. C*.   nonnulla obscuriora *E*.   sunt *om. F*.   15 impios et *F*.

---

2. **tropologiam**: Late Latin.

3. **cum fuerint aperta**: in Late Latin
the future perfect with *si, ubi, cum*, and
relatives occurs with the meaning of the
simple future or present, to correspond
to the present of the main clause. This
usage occurs below in 7, 15; 10, 25; 11,
26; 20, 39; 22, 51; 23, 52; 30, 63. See
St.-Schm. 564.

6. **qui se . . . prophetaret**: cf. Amos
7, 14-15: responditque Amos, et dixit
ad Amasiam: non sum propheta, et non
sum filius prophetae, sed armentarius
ego sum, uellicans sycomoros. et tulit
me Dominus, cum sequerer gregem; et
dixit Dominus ad me: uade, propheta ad
populum meum Israel.

7. **armentarium**: cited for Varro, the
poets, Silver and Late Latin: cf. T.L.L.
II, 610, 43-55: cf. Verg. Georg. 3, 244:
omnia secum armentarius Afer agit.

8. **non autem, etc.**: this is treated as a
separate sentence by the Benedictine editors, but there is no need of considering it
thus, as elliptical, since it clearly follows
closely upon *hoc faciam*, etc., above.

10. **spiritualem** = 'spiritual,' is Late
Latin.

11. **sensum** = 'meaning,' is Poetic,
Silver, and Late.

   magis = *potius*, as also in 10, 24;
15, 32; 20, 41: common to Late Latin: cf.
St.-Schm. 464, 672.

   intentio = 'attention': found three
times in Cicero, once in Livy, more frequently in Silver and Late Latin.

12. **unde**, as a conclusive particle, is
Late: cf. K.-Schm. s.v.; Goel. (1) 424;
and for its use in Augustine: Arts 62,
Colbert 36. It occurs below in 10, 24; 16,
33; 26, 58; 29, 62; 27, 59.

   tropica: Late Latin for *per transla-
tionem*: cf. K.-Schm. s.v.; Goel. (1) 220.

13. **hebraeo**: *hebraeus* is generally
only a substantive, but it appears in place
of *hebraicus*, not only in Stat. Silv. 5, 1,
213, but also in Tacitus, Pliny, and then
in Late writers.

   Hieronymo . . . interpretante: the
redundant use of the participle changes
the ablative from that of agent, as would
normally be expected, to ablative abso-

figurative expressions, the more pleasing they are when their meaning has been made clear. But I must here quote some passage wherein I may not have to explain what is said, but may merely commend the manner in which it is said. Wherefore, I shall draw especially from the book of that Prophet, who says that having been shepherd and herdsman, he was by divine appointment taken and sent to prophesy to the people of God: but not according to the Septuagint translators, who even themselves, working under the inspiration of the Holy Ghost, seem for this very reason to have expressed some things in a different way, in order that the attention of the reader might be rather directed to a study of the spiritual sense—and thus some of their passages are even more obscure because more figurative—but rather as the translation has been made from the Hebrew into the Latin language, done by the presbyter, Jerome, himself a skillful expounder of both tongues.

16. And so, when he was inveighing against the wicked, the proud, the luxurious, and those, therefore, who were totally indiffer-

lute, a construction used with ever greater freedom in Late Latin.—In 383 Jerome began his work on what later developed into the Vulgate. In 390 he revised a part of the Old Testament by direct comparison with the Hebrew; another part he corrected from the Aramaic. His work did not meet with immediate favor, but it gradually gained recognition, until it supplanted the Old Latin Versions. As for Augustine's opinion of Jerome's work, his letter of 403 A.D. leaves no doubt of his acceptance of the Gospels, which had been revised after the completion of part of the books of the Old Testament. He says: proinde paruas Deo gratias agimus de opere tuo quod euangelium ex Graeco interpretatus es, quia paene in omnibus nulla offensio est (Epist. 71, 4, 6). Moreover, the text used in his critical work, *De Consensu Euang.* (400 A.D.), is clearly that of Jerome's Gospel. As for the Old Testament, in De Ciu. Dei 18, 43 Augustine, while giving the preference to the Septuagint translators, speaks in terms of no small praise of his learned contemporary: quamuis

non defuerit temporibus nostris presbyter Hieronymus, homo doctissimus, et omnium trium linguarum peritus, qui non ex Graeco, sed ex Hebraeo in Latinum eloquium easdem scripturas comuerterit. sed eius tam litteratum laborem quamuis Iudaei fateantur esse ueracem, Septuaginta, uero interpretes in multis errasse contendant, tamen ecclesiae Christie tot hominum auctoritati, ab Eleazaro tunc pontifice ad hoc tantum opus electorum, neminem iudicant praeferendum. Besides this, his open preference for the Vulgate over the Septuagint, in the present selection from Amos, is proof of his respect for, and appreciation of the later work: cf. Burkitt 55ff.

15. et with only the last member of a series in coordination is not found in the best classical prose. When Cicero connects three or more substantives, either all are left without conjunctions, or conjunctions occur with each member, or *-que* is put with the last. *Et* in Cicero with the final member draws attention to an effect or a result: cf. K.-Schm. s.v.; Dräger II, 3; Gildersleeve 303.

70 SULLIVAN

nae ideo negligentissimos charitatis, rusticus uel ex rustico iste
Amos 6, 1-6 propheta exclamauit, dicens: *uae qui opulenti estis in Sion, et
confiditis in monte Samariae, optimates capita populorum, ingredientes pompatice domum Israel! transite in Chalanne, et uidete,
et ite inde in Emath magnam, et descendite in Geth Palaestinorum,* 5
*et ad optima quaeque regna horum, si latior terminus eorum ter-
mino uestro est. qui separati estis in diem malum, et appropinquatis solio iniquitatis. qui dormitis in lectis eburneis, et lasciuitis
in stratis uestris; qui comeditis agnum de grege, et uitulos de
medio armenti; qui canitis ad uocem psalterii. sicut Dauid puta-* 10
*uerunt se habere uasa cantici; bibentes in phialis uinum, et optimo
unguento delibuti; et nihil patiebantur super contritione Ioseph.*
nunquidnam isti, qui prophetas nostros tamquam ineruditos et
elocutionis ignaros uelut docti disertique contemnunt, si aliquid eis
tale uel in tales dicendum fuisset, aliter se uoluissent dicere qui 15
tamen eorum insanire noluissent?

17. Quid enim est quod isto eloquio aures sobriae plus desi-
derent? primo ipsa inuectio, quasi sopitis sensibus ut euigilarent,
quo fremitu illisa est: *uae uobis qui opulenti estis in Sion, et confiditis in monte Samariae, optimates capita populorum, ingredi-* 20
entes pompatice domum Israel. deinde ut beneficiis Dei, qui eis
ampla spatia regni dedit, ostendat ingratos, quoniam confidebant
in monte Samariae, ubi utique idola colebantur, *transite* inquit *in*

---

1 rusticus uel ex *om. E.*   3 montes *H*; montem *I.*   5 in (Emath) *om. C.*
6 ad *om. E Ver.An.*   10 armento *I.*   14 uel *E*; ueluti *Maur.*   15 fuisset]nolu-
issent *E.*   uoluissent]uoluerunt *E.*   16 uoluissent *FH.*   19 uobis *om. Maur.*
21 domus *G Ver.An.*   transite in Chalanne . . . domum Israel *om. A.*   23
montes *H.*

---

1. **ex rustico**: *ex* meaning a change of
state or profession, is a natural extension
of the use in which it marks source or
origin: cf. K.-Steg. II, 1, 505; Goel. (2)
195: ex interfectore, medicus; martyr,
ex fure; sit uerax sacerdos ex laico, qui
fieri laicus ex fallace sacerdote contentus est; cf. also the phrases so frequent
in the Late period: ex consule (Eutr.); ex
corniculario (Cod. Theod.); ex comite
largitionum (Amm.).

2. **uae qui opulenti, etc.**: cf. Baldwin
(2) 62-64, Eskridge 35-36, for an analysis of this passage in graphic form.

13. **numquidnam**: *numquid* is especially common in Early Latin, and in
the Vulgate, where it is used indiscrimi-
nately for a question requiring a positive
or a negative answer. It occurs to some
extent also in Class. and Silver Latin: cf.
St.-Schm. 649, 696; Salonius 316; Bonnet 324; McGuire 117. It is used below
in 16, 33, and 24, 53.

**tamquam ineruditos . . . uelut
docti**: *tamquam* with a participle is cited
first for Cic. Verr. 2, 5, 28; *uelut* with a
participle, for Livy. After Livy the use
of *tamquam* or *uelut* with a participle
increased until it became frequent in
Tacitus and Late writers. Cf. St.-Schm.

ent to brotherly love, this peasant, or rather peasant become prophet, cried out, saying: *Woe to you that are wealthy in Sion, and to you that have confidence in the mountain of Samaria, ye great men, heads of the people, that go in with much state into the house of Israel. Pass ye over into Chalane, and see, and go from thence into Emath the great: and go down into Geth of the Philistines, and to all the best kingdoms of these: if their border be larger than your border. You that are separated unto the evil day: and that approach to the throne of iniquity: you that sleep upon beds of ivory, and are wanton on your couches: that eat the lambs of the flock, and the calves out of the midst of the herd: you that sing to the sound of psaltery: they have thought themselves to have instruments of music like David: that drink wine in bowls, and anoint themselves with the best ointments: and they are not concerned for the affliction of Joseph.* Tell me pray, would those very men who, as though themselves learned and eloquent, condemn our Prophet as unlettered and unskilled in speech, would they, if they had had to address some such rebuke to such people, have wanted to express themselves in any other way—those of them, of course, who would not have wanted to appear mad?

17. For what more could the sober ear desire in this passage? First of all, with what a clash does the mere denunciation beat against senses deadened, as it were, in order to arouse them: *Woe to you that are wealthy in Sion, and to you that have confidence in the mountain of Samaria: ye great men, heads of the people, that go in with state into the house of Israel!* Then in regard to the gifts of God who had bestowed on them wide regions for their kingdom, to show them how ungrateful they were, since they were

---

603; Gildersleeve 427. See below: 7, 16.

18. inuectio = 'invective,' is cited for Cic. Verr. 2, 10; De Inuent. 2, 54, 164; and Late writers.

19. illisa est: mostly Poetic and Silver.

22. ampla: the forms *amplus* and *amplior* are very rare in Early Latin, and are uncommon in all periods. *Amplius* is frequent in Early and Class. Latin, and very frequent in the Silver and Late writers. *Amplus*, used of places, is mostly Silver and Late: cf. T.L.L. I, 2007, 7-17.

   spatia regni: the genitive of definition, restricted in Class. prose, was gradually extended in the Silver and Late

periods. Note examples below: inter opera misericordiae uel beneficientiae (16, 30); commotionis affectum (21, 46); exempli forma (21, 48); toris ornamentorum (23, 52). See St.-Schm. 394-95.

23. in monte: the use of *in* with the ablative construed with *confido* is Eccl., due to the influence of the Hebrew and Greek idioms which passed into the Latin versions of the Bible. cf. T.L.L. IV, 208, 39ff.; Rönsch 397. Augustine merely echoes the text of Amos.

   idola = 'idols,' is found often in Eccl. Latin, from Tertullian on: cf. K.-Schm. s.v.

Chalanne, et uidete, et ite in Emath magnam, et descendite in
Geth Palaestinorum, et ad optima quaeque regna horum, si latior
terminus eorum termino uestro est. simul etiam cum ista dicuntur,
locorum nominibus tamquam luminibus ornatur eloquium, quae
sunt *Sion, Samaria, Chalanne, Emath magna,* et *Geth Palaesti-* 5
norum. deinde uerba quae his adiunguntur locis, decentissime uari-
antur: *opulenti estis, confiditis, transite, ite, descendite.*

18. Consequenter denuntiatur futura sub iniquo rege appropinquare captiuitas, cum adiungitur: *qui separati estis in diem*
malum, et appropinquatis solio iniquitatis. tunc subiciuntur merita 10
luxuriae: *qui dormitis in lectis eburneis, et lasciuitis in stratis*
uestris; qui comeditis agnum de grege, et uitulos de medio armenti.
ista sex membra tres bimembres circuitus ediderunt. non enim ait,
'qui separati estis in diem malum, qui appropinquatis solio iniquitatis, qui dormitis in lectis eburneis, qui lasciuitis in stratis 15
uestris, qui comeditis agnum de grege, et uitulos de medio armenti.'
quod si ita diceretur, esset quidem et hoc pulchrum, ut ab uno
pronomine repetito omnia sex membra decurrerent, et pronuntiantis uoce singula finirentur; sed pulchrius factum est, ut eidem
pronomini essent bina subnexa, quae tres sententias explicarent: 20
unam ad captiuitatis praenuntiationem: *qui separati estis in diem*
malum, et appropinquatis solio iniquitatis, alteram ad libidinem:
qui dormitis in lectis eburneis, et lasciuitis in stratis uestris, ad
uoracitatem uero tertiam pertinentem: *qui comeditis agnum de*
grege, et uitulos de medio armenti: ut in potestate sit pronunti- 25
antis, utrum singula finiat, et membra sint sex, an primum et
tertium et quintum uoce suspendat, et secundum primo, quartum

2 horum regna *I.*   5 sunt *om. E.*   6 hiis *E.*   7 estis et *E.*   ite transite *D.*
8 futura denuntiatur *EI.*   appropinquare *om. D*; propinquare *BI.*   9 separati
estis] separatis *B.*   13 reddiderunt *EI.*   16 et] qui *H.*   17 quod *om. Maur.* pul-
crum quidem et hoc esset *E.*   18 omnia] singula *Maur.*   et] ut (*sic em.*) *B.*
20 explicarunt *CDFG.*   23 uestris *om. D.*   24 comeditis inquit *BCDEFGH.*

3. **simul etiam**: *simul etiam, simul*
uero (autem) etiam, for simple *simul* or
simulque, is of doubtful Class. usage,
but is found in Celsus 2, 1: nocturnis
atque matutinis, simulque etiam ues-
pertinis (temporibus) frigus est: cf. K.-
Schm. s.v.

4. **tamquam luminibus**: cf. De Orat.
3, 54, 205: his fere luminibus inlustrant
orationem sententiae.

6. **decentissime**: this superlative is
used from Seneca on, especially in Late
writers: cf. T.L.L. V, 136, 58-60.

8. **consequenter** = *deinde*, is Late
Latin: cf. Aug. Epist. 185, 49: consequenter adiungit apostolus: cf. T.L.L. III,
412, 74–85.

13. **ista sex membra . . . monstretur**:
Augustine gives only passing notice to
pronuntiatio. His remarks, however, as

then putting their confidence in the mountain of Samaria, where, in truth, idols were worshipped, he says: *Pass ye over to Chalane, and see, and go from thence into Emath the great: and go down into Geth of the Philistines, and to all the best kingdoms of these; if their border be larger than your border.* Moreover, also, in this passage the language is adorned by the names of places, as though by lights, to wit, *Sion, Samaria, Chalane, Emath the great,* and *Geth of the Philistines.* Then too, the words used in connection with these places are very fittingly varied, *you that are wealthy—have confidence—pass ye over—go—go down.*

18. Next, announcement is made that a future captivity under a cruel king is approaching, in the words: *You that are separated unto the evil day: and that approach to the throne of iniquity.* Then the evils of luxury are summed up: *You that sleep upon beds of ivory, and are wanton on your couches: that eat the lambs out of the flock, and the calves out of the midst of the herd.* These six *membra* make three periods of two *membra* each. For the writer does not say: "You that are separated unto the evil day, that approach to the throne of iniquity, that sleep upon beds of ivory, that are wanton on your couches, that eat the lambs out of the flock, and the calves out of the midst of the herd." If he had so put it, it would, to be sure, be well expressed also, so that with the repetition of the same pronoun each of the six *membra* would be introduced, and each would be finished off by the fall of the speaker's voice. But it is finer as it is written, with each two *membra* depending on one pronoun, in order to explain three ideas: one pertaining to the announcement of captivity: *You that are separated unto the evil day: and that approach to the throne of iniquity*; the second, to unlawful pleasures: *You that sleep upon beds of ivory, and are wanton on your couches*; and the third, to gluttony: *that eat the lambs out of the flock, and the calves out of the midst of the herd*; so that the speaker is free either to complete each separately, and have six clauses, or to suspend by his

---

here, are full of suggestion: cf. Baldwin (2) 64.

20. **subnexa**: Poetic and Silver.

21. **praenuntiationem** = 'prediction,'

is Eccl.: cf. Tert. Anim. 46; Aug. Serm. 101, 1.

24. **uoracitatem** = 'gluttony,' is Late Latin: cf. Benoist-Goelz. and Georges s.v.

tertio, sextum quinto conectendo, tres bimembres circuitus decentissime faciat: unum quo calamitas imminens, alterum quo lectus impurus, tertium quo prodiga mensa monstretur.

19. Deinde luxuriosam remordet aurium uoluptatem. ubi cum dixisset, *qui canitis ad uocem psalterii*, quoniam potest exerceri 5 sapienter a sapientibus musica, mirabili decore dicendi, inuectionis impetu relaxato, et non ad illos, sed de illis iam loquens, ut nos musicam sapientis a musica luxuriantis distinguere commoneret, non ait 'qui canitis ad uocem psalterii, et sicut Dauid putatis uos habere uasa cantici'; sed cum illud ad illos dixisset, quod luxu- 10 riosi audire deberent, *qui canitis ad uocem psalterii*, imperitiam quoque eorum aliis quodammodo indicauit, adiungens, *sicut Dauid putauerunt se habere uasa cantici, bibentes in phialis uinum, et optimo unguento delibuti.* tria haec melius pronuntiantur, si suspensis duobus prioribus membris circuitus, tertio finiantur. 15

20. Iam uero quod his omnibus adicitur, *et nihil patiebantur super contritione Ioseph*, siue continuatim dicatur ut unum sit membrum, sius decentius suspendatur, *et nihil patiebantur*, et post hanc distinctionem inferatur, *super contritione Ioseph*, atque sit bimembris circuitus, miro decore non dictum est, 'nihil patieban- 20 tur super contritione fratris,' sed positus est pro 'fratre,' 'Ioseph,' ut quicumque frater proprio significaretur eius nomine,

---

2 quo lectus] collectus *DF*.   6 a *om I*.   9 ait] dicit *H*.   10 illud *om. E*. 12 quoque] quorum *H*.   13 se habere *om. E*.   cantici uasa *E*.   habentes *D*.   et ad *F*.   15 circuitu *CDF*.   finiatur *B*; firmatur *D*.   16 hiis *E*.   17 continuatum *DF*. ut] sit *D*; nec *E*.   19 super *om. F*.   contritionem *F*.   20 et post hanc . . . patiebantur *in marg. F*.   21 super contritionem fratritionem fratris *D*.   pro fratre Ioseph positus est *I*.

4. **remordet** = 'attacks,' is not cited in the Lexica, though its development from the usual meaning 'vex' can be seen from the following examples: Lucr. 4, 1135: animus se forte remordet; Liv. 8, 4, 3: sin tandem libertatis desiderium remordet animos; Pelag. Epist. ad Demetr. 4: quid est, quod . . . conscientia remordemur?

7. **impetu relaxato, et . . . loquens**: the ablative absolute in Late Latin came to be looked upon as a real clause, and as such was often connected by a conjunction with a following verb: cf. Bonnet 559: nullam poterat uocem emittere

sensu integro sed multatus uocis officio (having the use of his reason but being deprived of the use of his voice). See also St.-Schm. 448.

8. **distinguere commoneret**: *commonere* with the infinitive of command is Late, being used by Rufinus, Augustine, and Gregory the Great: cf. T.L.L. III, 1931, 63–70.

10. **ad illos**, in place of the dative, is common in Eccl. Latin, due to the influence of the Hebrew and the Greek: cf. T.L.L. I, 512, 30ff.

11. **imperitiam**: not found in Caes. or Cic.; occurs in Sall. Iug. 38, and in Silver

voice the first, third, and fifth, and by connecting the second with the first, the fourth with the third, the sixth with the fifth, to make, very appropriately, three periods of two clauses each: one, to point out the impending calamity; the second, the unchaste couch; the third, the luxurious table.

19. Then he attacks the inordinate pleasure of the ears. And here having said, *You that sing to the sound of psaltery*, since the wise can use music wisely, he with admirable propriety checks his flow of invective, and now speaking not to them, but of them, in order to warn us to distinguish between the music of the wise, and the music of the licentious, he does not say, "You that sing to the sound of psaltery, and think you have instruments of music like David"; but when he has said to them what it behooves the licentious to hear, *You that sing to the sound of the psaltery*, he, after a manner, points out their ignorance to others, by adding, *They have thought themselves to have instruments of music like David; that drink wine in bowls, and anoint themselves with the best ointments.* These three *membra* are delivered in the best way, by holding suspended the first two members of the period, and rounding them out by the third.

20. But now as to what follows all this, *And they are not concerned for the affliction of Joseph*, whether it be read straight through as one *membrum*, or whether more fittingly the words, *And they are not concerned*, be held suspended, and then after setting them off, *for the affliction of Joseph* be introduced, thus making a period of two *membra*, it is with rare propriety that the wording does not read thus, "And they are not concerned for the affliction of their brother," but in the place of 'brother,' 'Joseph' is put, that brotherhood in general may be expressed by the proper name of one whose fame stands out from among brothers whether as regards the evil which he suffered, or the good which he paid in re-

---

and Late Latin: cf. K.-Schm. s.v.

12. **indicauit, adiungens**: another form of the Eccl. stereotyped *dicens*, used to introduce a direct Biblical quotation: cf. St.-Schm. 606; 450.

14. **tria haec . . . finiantur**: another suggestion in regard to delivery, as also below, lines 16–20.

17. **continuatim**: Late. Augustine explains the word in Quaest. Hept. 2, 133: quod continuatim fieret, id est nullo die praetermitteretur: cf .T.L.L. IV, 725, 29-45.

18. **decentius**: this comparative is mostly Silver and Late: cf. T.L.L. V, 136, 55-58. Used again below in 22, 51.

cuius ex fratribus fama praeclara est, uel in malis quae pendit, uel in bonis quae rependit. iste certe tropus ubi Ioseph quemcumque fratrem facit intellegi, nescio utrum illa quam didicimus et docuimus, arte tradatur. quam sit tamen pulcher, et quemadmodum afficiat legentes atque intellegentes, non opus est cuiquam dici, si 5 ipse non sentit.

21. Et plura quidem, quae pertineant ad praecepta eloquentiae, in hoc ipso loco, quem pro exemplo posuimus, possunt reperiri. sed bonum auditorem, non tam si diligenter discutiatur, instruit, quam si ardenter pronuntietur, accendit. neque enim haec humana indus- 10 tria composita, sed diuina mente sunt fusa et sapienter et eloquenter, non intenta in eloquentiam sapientia, sed a sapientia non recedente eloquentia. si enim, sicut quidam disertissimi atque acutissimi uiri uidere ac dicere potuerunt, ea quae oratoria uelut arte discuntur, non obseruarentur et notarentur, et in hanc doctri- 15 nam non redigerentur, nisi prius in oratorum inuenirentur ingeniis, quid mirum si et in istis inueniuntur, quos ille misit qui facit ingenia? quapropter et eloquentes quidem, non solum sapientes, canonicos nostros auctores doctoresque fateamur, tali eloquentia qualis personis eiusmodi congruebat.   20

8,   22. Sed nos etsi de litteris eorum, quae sine difficultate intel-

1 ex *om. E.*   pendit id est pertulit *E.*   2 pendit uel in bonis quae *B.*   certe] ergo *A.*
3 illa *om. DG.*   4 traditur *E.*   qua *G.*   5 efficiat *F.*   7 pertinent *Maur.*   9 quam si] quasi *I.*
11 industria composita sed diuina *in marg. alia m. B.*   fusa sunt]sunt infusa *C.*   14 uiri *om. I.*
ac dicere] accendere *D.*   uelut oratoria *EI Maur.*   15 dicuntur *C Mig.*   16 non *om. BC.*   17
fecit *BI.*   18 et *om. F.*   19 tali] dei *E; talia F.*   eloquentia usos *CEGHI (Bad. Am. Et. et
MSS septem [Maur.]).*   20 persona *E.*   huiusmodi (*sic em.) B.*   21 etsi *om. E.*

1. ex fratribus fama praeclara est: Cicero uses *inter* and the acc., in a somewhat equivalent expression: Acad. 1, 4 16: suos inter aequales longe praestitit. Doubtless *ex* and the abl. is used here because the idea of 'place from which' is so strong ('from among brothers'). For the same reason *ex* and the abl. in Late Latin is often used for the partitive genitive: cf. K.-Steg. II, 1, 425; Salonius 89.

uel in malis quae pendit, uel in bonis quae rependit: antithesis, enforced by parallel structure and paronomasia.

2. **rependit** = 'repay,' is Poetic, Silver, and Late.

tropus, the Greek technical term for 'figure,' was introduced by Cicero into Latin, although in general he himself employed *translatio* or *immutatio uerborum* in this sense. *Tropus* came into common use only in Silver Latin. Quint. (8, 6, 1) thus defines it: tropus est uerbi uel sermonis a propria significatione in aliam cum uirtute mutatio: cf. K.-Schm. s.v.

3. **nescio utrum**: for utrum in a simple question, see 3, 4. With nescio, Cicero uses -ne, *e.g.*, Fam. 2, 5. 2: sed haec ipsa nescio rectene sint litteris commissa: cf. K.-Schm. s.v.

turn. Really, I do not know whether that figure whereby 'Joseph' is made to express brotherhood in general is explained in that art which we have studied and taught. But what its beauty is, and how affecting it is to readers and men of thought, there is no need of telling a person if he does not feel it himself.

21. And indeed many more things which pertain to the rules of eloquence can be discovered in this same passage which we have taken as an example. But its value lies not so much in the instruction it affords a good audience if it be analyzed carefully, as in the sentiment it enkindles if it be read with feeling. For these words were not written by human industry, but were poured forth by Divine Intelligence, with wisdom and eloquence — wisdom not being intent on eloquence, but eloquence not deserting wisdom. For as certain very able and discerning orators have been able to perceive and state, if what is laid down in the so-called art of oratory could not be observed and noted and reduced to this discipline unless it were first found in the natural genius of orators, what wonder is there that it is found likewise in those men whom He has sent who fashions natural genius? Wherefore, let us claim that our canonical writers and doctors possessed eloquence too as well as wisdom — eloquence of such a kind as was fitting to men of their character.

8, 22. But though we take some examples from their writings which can without difficulty be understood, still we ought by no

---

7. **et plura . . . accendit**: Augustine's method is one of suggestion rather than of exhaustive analysis. It is thus that he shows the real teacher's power to enliven his matter and to stimulate his hearers. Note how here again he lays stress on *pronuntiatio*. See Baldwin (2) 63-64.

9. **discutiatur** = 'analyzed,' is Late, being used by Macrob. Som. Scip. 1, 5, 1; Tert.; Hier.; Aug.: cf. T.L.L. V, 1374, 67–1375, 8.

13. **sicut quidam . . . ingeniis**: cf. De Orat. 1, 32, 146: uerum ego hanc uim intellego esse in praeceptis omnibus non ut ea secuti oratores eloquentiae laudem sint adepti, sed, quae sua sponte homines eloquentes facerent, ea quosdam obseruasse atque egisse. Quint. 2, 17, 9: illud enim admonere satis est, omnia, quae ars consummauerit, a natura initia duxisse. De Doctr. Chris. 2, 36, 54: *nam neque*

hoc ab hominibus institutum est, ut charitatis expressio conciliet auditorem, aut ut facile quod intendit, insinuet breuis et aperta narratio, et uarietas eius sine fastidio teneat intentos; et ceterae huiusmodi obseruationes, quae siue in falsis siue in ueris causis, uerae sunt tamen, in quantum uel sciri uel credi aliquid faciunt, aut ad expetendum fugiendumue animos mouent, *et inuentae potius quod ita se habeant, quam ut ita se haberent institutae.*

8. *The obscurity of the sacred writers accounted for, but not offered for imitation to the Christian teacher. Clearness, the first requisite of all oratory.*

21. **de litteris**: *de* in the local figurative sense is often substituted for *ex* or *ab*: cf. T.L.L. V, 50, 33ff. For its frequent use with *sumere* in this sense, cf. T.L.L. V, 51, 39-40. See also 6, 9 for *de = ex*.

leguntur nonnulla sumimus elocutionis exempla, nequaquam tamen
putare debemus imitandos nobis eos esse in iis quae ad exercendas
et elimandas quodammodo mentes legentium, et ad rumpenda fastidia atque acuenda studia discere uolentium, celandos quoque, siue
ut ad pietatem conuertantur, siue ut a mysteriis secludantur, ani- 5
mos impiorum, utili ac sulubri obscuritate dixerunt. sic quippe
illi locuti sunt, ut posteriores qui eos recte intellegerent et exponerent, alteram gratiam, disparem quidem, uerumtamen subsequentem in Dei ecclesia reperirent. non ergo expositores eorum ita
loqui debent, tamquam se ipsi exponendos simili auctoritate pro- 10
ponant; sed in omnibus sermonibus suis primitus ac maxime ut
intellegantur elaborent, ea quantum possunt perspicuitate dicendi,
ut aut multum tardus sit qui non intellegat, aut in rerum quas
explicare atque ostendere uolumus difficultate ac subtilitate non in
nostra locutione sit causa qua minus tardiusue quod dicimus possit 15
intellegi.

9, 23. Sunt enim quaedam quae ui sua non intelleguntur, aut uix
intelleguntur, quantolibet et quantumlibet, quamuis planissime,
dicentis uersentur eloquio; quae in populi audientiam, uel raro,

1 tamen *om. AB.*   2 eos nobis *I Maur.*   his *ABCDFGHI*; hiis *E.*   exercitandos *A.*   4 studio *D.*   celandos] (zelandos *MSS tres*; *sic etiam Bad. Am. et Er.* [*Maur.*]).   5 animi *B.*   7
eos recte intellegerent et exponerent] eos intellegentes exponerent *D.*   9 in Dei ecclesia
subsequentem *E.*   ecclesiam *A.*   10 debent ut *E.*   se ipsi] se et ipsi *AB*; si et ipsi *D*; se
ipsos *EI.*   proponunt *D.*   12 ea] et *BD*; et haec *A.*   quanta (*sic em.*) *E.*   13 intellegit
BDI.   14 atque]at quas *D*; siue *E*; aut *F.*   15 quo *CGH Maur.*   17 ui] in *H.*   19 uersentur
in marg. alia m. E; uersetur *A.* audientia *D.*

4. **siue ut . . . siue ut** occurs in Cicero,
e.g., De Orat. 3, 6, 23: siue ut impellat
homines siue ut doceat siue ut deterreat
siue ut concitet siue ut reflectat siue
ut incendat siue ut leniat . . . riuis est
diducta oratio, non fontibus. Isolated
examples of *siue quod* (*quia*) . . . *siue
quod* (*quia*) likewise appear in Caesar
and Livy: cf. St.-Schm. 780; K.-Steg.
II, 2, 436. An example of *siue quia . . .
siue quia* occurs in 10, 24.

7. **posteriores** is used in its true
comparative sense, not as often in Late
Latin as the unclassical equivalent of
posteri.

9. **expositores**: Late: cf. K.-Schm. s.v.

11. **primitus**: used in Early, Poetic,
Silver, and Late Latin, but avoided by

Class. writers who preferred *primum* or
primo: cf. St.-Schm. 214; For. s.v.

12. **ut intellegantur elaborent**: cf.
Arist. Rhet. 3, 5, 1407b: ὅλως δὲ δεῖ
εὐανάγνωστον εἶναι τὸ γεγραμμένον
καὶ εὔφραστον.

ea . . . perspicuitate: cf. Arist.
Rhet. 3, 2, 1404b: ὡρίσθω λέξεως ἀρετὴ
σαφῆ εἶναι· σημεῖον γὰρ ὅτι ὁ λόγος,
ὡς ἐὰν μὴ δηλοῖ οὐ ποιήσει τὸ ἑαυτοῦ
ἔργον. Quint. 8, 2, 1: perspicuitas in
uerbis praecipuam habet proprietatem.
Augustine treats 'clearness' at some
length below, in chapter 10.

13. **multum tardus**: *multum* with a
positive adjectiue, to replace the elative
superlative, belongs to the colloquial
speech: cf. St.-Schm. 462.

means to think that our authors are to be imitated by us in those places where they speak with useful and helpful obscurity, either to exercise and, as it were, to refine the minds of their readers, or to break down the prejudices and to whet the zeal of those who are willing to learn, or, too, to keep in the dark the minds of the wicked, either that they may be converted to a good life, or be excluded from the mysteries. Such, indeed, has been their manner of expressing themselves, that those following them, who have understood and expounded them aright have acquired distinction also in the Church of God, not in the same degree, of course, but next in order. Their interpreters, therefore, ought not to express themselves in such a way as if putting themselves forward to be interpreted with like authority; but in all their discourses they should labor, first and foremost, to be understood through their clearness of expression, in as far as this is possible, so that either he who does not understand is very slow of wit, or in the difficulty and subtlety of the matters which we wish to unfold and make clear, not in our manner of expressing them, lies the reason why what we say is not understood, or is understood but slowly.

9,   23. There are some matters, which in their true force are not intelligible, or scarcely intelligible, no matter how great the eloquence, nor how extended nor how clear the speaker's explanation. Such matters should be put before a popular assembly either rarely, if necessity urges, or not at all. In books, however, which are so written that they, so to speak, hold the reader to themselves, when

---

9. *Matters difficult of understanding, when necessary to be handled, should be presented with care for clearness, rather than for eloquence: 'plane' vs. 'ornate.'*

18. **quamuis planissime**: *quamuis* with the superlative is Silver Latin, though Cicero uses *quiuis* with the superlative: cf. De Orat. 3, 26, 103: quiuis uitiosissimus orator. See K.-Schm. s.v.; Gildersleeve 393. This appears again below on p. 90, 1. 5: quamuis difficillima.

19. **quae . . . nunquam . . . mittenda sunt**: Augustine decidedly separates himself from the camp of the Sophists, known to Aristotle, to Quintilian, and no less to his own day: cf. Arist. Rhet. 3, 5, 1407a: ταῦτα δέ, ἄν μὴ τἀναντία προαιρῆται, ὅ περ ποιοῦσιν ὅταν μηθὲν μὲν ἔχωσι λέγειν προσποιῶνται δέ τι λέγειν. Quint.

8, 2, 18: in hoc malum a quibusdam etiam laboratur; neque id nouum uitium est, cum iam apud Titum Liuium inueniam, fuisse praeceptorem aliquem, qui discipulos obscurare, quae dicerent, iuberet, Graeco uerbo utens σκότισον. unde illa scilicet egregia laudatio: *tanto melior; ne ego quidem intellexi.*

audientiam = 'a hearing,' in the Class. period: cf. De Orat. 2, 80, 325: nam nonnulli, quom illud meditati ediderunt, sic ad reliqua transeunt, ut *audientiam* fieri sibi uelle non uideantur. Liv. 43, 16, 8: *audientiam* facere praeconem iussit. *Audientia* became increasingly concrete, until in Late Latin it meant 'audience,' *e.g.*, Salv. Epist. 4, 26: nec audientia humanior nec gratior fuit: cf. T.L.L. II, 1260, 19–1261, 33; K.-Schm. s.v.

si aliquid urget, uel numquam omnino mittenda sunt. in libris
autem, qui ita scribuntur ut ipsi sibi quodammodo lectorem tene-
aut cum intelleguntur, cum autem non intelleguntur molesti non
sint nolentibus legere, et in aliquorum collocutionibus, non est hoc
officium deserendum, ut uera, quamuis ad intellegendum difficil- 5
lima, quae ipsi iam percepimus, cum quantocumque labore disputa-
tationis ad aliorum intellegentiam perducamus, si tenet auditorem
uel collocutorem discendi cupiditas, nec mentis capacitas desit,
quae quoquo modo intimata possit accipere, non curante illo qui
docet, quanta eloquentia doceat, sed quanta euidentia.   10

10,   24. Cuius euidentiae diligens appetitus aliquando neglegit uerba
cultiora, nec curat quid bene sonet, sed quid bene indicet atque
intimet quod ostendere intendit. unde ait quidam, cum de tali

---

3 non (intelleguntur) *om. F.*   cum autem non intelleguntur *in marg. alia
m. B.*   4 molentibus *Mig.*; uolentibus *DF.*   (cum intelleguntur molesti non
sint uolentibus legere: cum autem non intelleguntur molesti non sint nolentibus legere *in prius editis* [*Maur.*]).   et iam *E.*   hoc *om. EG.*   5 ad *om. I.*
difficillima ad intellegendum *Maur.*   7 perducantur *E.*   9 quoquo]quo *CE.*
10 docet]doceat *F.*   11 diligentes *G.*   12 sonat *I.*   13 intimet et *E.*

---

4. **collocutionibus**: very rare, but
Ciceronian: cf. T.L.L. III, 1649, 12–50.

non est . . . perducamus: cf. Aug.
Contr. Cres. 1, 15, 19: qui autem uerus
disputator est, id est, ueritatis a falsitate
discretor, primo id apud se ipsum agit,
ne non recte discernens ipse fallatur;
quod nisi diuinitus adiutus peragere non
potest: deinde, cum id quod apud se
egit ad alios docendos profert, intuetur
primitus quid iam certi nouerint, ut ex
his eos adducat ad ea quae non nouerant
uel credere nolebant, ostendens ea con-
sequentia his quae iam scientia uel fide
retinebant: ut per ea uera de quibus se
perspiciunt consentire, cogantur alia uera
quae negauerant approbare: et sic uerum
quod falsum antea putabatur, discernatur
a falso, cum inuenitur consentaneum illi
uero quod iam antea tenebatur.

8. **collocutorem**: it is interesting to
note this Late formation side by side
with the preceding Class. noun of the
same root. *Collocutor* is used by Tert.,
Aug., and other Late writers: cf. T.L.L.

III, 1649, 69-75. For the frequent use of
nouns in *-tor* in Late Latin, cf. St.-Schm.
790; Parsons 43.

capacitas mentis = 'comprehension,' in Late Latin: cf. Ps. Aug. Serm.
223, 2: capacitatem intellegentiae meae:
cf. T.L.L. III, 299, 72-300, 28. Classical
Latin uses *uis percipiendi, indoles*, or
ingenium: cf. K.-Schm. s.v.

9. **intimata** = 'things explained': cf.
4, 6. *Intimare* is used again below in 10,
24.

non curante . . . quanta euidentia:
cf. Cicero's and Quintilian's regard for
clearness: De Orat. 3, 10, 37-39: quinam
igitur dicendi est modus melior—nam de
actione post uidero—, quam ut Latine, ut
plane, ut ornate, ut ad id, quodcumque
agetur, apte congruenterque dicamus?
Atque eorum quidem, quae duo prima
dixi, rationem non arbitror exspectari
a me puri dilucidique sermonis. neque
enim conamur docere eum dicere, qui
loqui nesciat; nec sperare, qui Latine
non possit, hunc ornate esse dicturum;

they are intelligible, or when they are not intelligible are still not a burden to those who do not wish to read them, and in conversations with others, the duty ought not to be neglected of bringing the truth—though it may be most difficult to understand, which we, however, have already grasped—to the understanding of others, no matter what the labor of discussion, provided that the listener or interlocutor have the desire to be informed, and that mental capacity be not wanting to enable him to receive the information in whatever manner presented, the instructor attending not to the degree of eloquence with which he teaches, but to the degree of clearness.

10,   24. A studied leaning toward such clearness, at times neglects the more elegant expression, and has no concern for what sounds well, but for what tells and explains well what one aims to point out. And so it is that a certain authority says, in treating of such kind of speech, that it possesses a kind of careful negligence. Still,

---

neque uero, qui non dicat quod intellegamus, hunc posse quod admiremur dicere. linguamus igitur haec, quae cognitionem habent facilem usum necessarium. nam alterum traditur litteris doctrinaque puerili, alterum adhibetur ob eam causam, *ut intellegatur quid quisque dicat, quod uidemus ita esse necessarium, ut tamen eo minus nihil esse possit.* Quint. 8, 2, 22: nobis prima sit uirtus perspicuitas, propria uerba, rectus ordo, non in longum dilata conclusio; nihil neque desit neque superfluat. ita sermo et doctis probabilis et planus imperitis erit. haec eloquendi obseruatio . . . quare non, ut intellegere possit, sed, ne omnino possit non intellegere, curandum.

10. *'Elegantia' interpreted in its true sense, i.e. purity of language as governed by clearness, in the expression of truth: a repudiation of Sophistic.*

11. **appetitus** = *studium*, is Late: cf. Vulg. Ezech. 21, 16: uade . . . quocumque faciei tuae est appetitus; Sidon. Epist. 3, 14, 2; 4, 22, 4: cf. T.L.L. II, 282, 47–50.

13. **ostendere intendit**: the infinitive with intendo is cited for Caesar, Sallust, and Livy: cf. St.-Schm. 581; K.-Steg. II, 1, 667; For. s.v.

unde . . . quidam . . . neglegentiam: cf. Orat. 23, 77ff.: solutum quiddam sit [orator submissus] nec uagum tamen, ut ingredi libere, non ut licenter uideatur errare. uerba etiam uerbis quasi coagmentare neglegat. habet enim ille tanquam hiatus et concursus uocalium molle quiddam et quod indicet non ingratam neglegentiam de re hominis magis quam de uerbis laborantis. sed erit uidendum de reliquis, cum haec duo ei liberiora fuerint, circuitus conglutinatioque uerborum. illa enim ipsa contracta et minuta non neglegentur tractanda sunt, sed *quaedam etiam neglegentia est diligens. . . .* tum remouebitur omnis insignis ornatus quasi margaritarum, ne calamistri quidem adhibebuntur; fucati uero medicamenta candoris et ruboris omnia repellentur; elegantia modo et munditia remanebit. sermo purus erit et Latinus, *dilucide planeque* dicetur, quid deceat circumspicietur; unum aberit, quod quartum numerat Theophrastus in orationis laudibus: ornatum illud, suaue et afluens. acutae crebraeque sententiae ponentur et nescio unde ex abdito erutae; ac—quod in hoc oratore dominabitur—uerecundus erit usus oratoriae quasi supellectilis.

genere elocutionis ageret, esse in ea quandam diligentem neglegentiam. haec tamen sic detrahit ornatum, ut sordes non contrahat.
quamuis in bonis doctoribus tanta docendi cura sit, uel esse debeat,
ut uerbum quod nisi obscurum sit uel ambiguum, latinum esse non
potest, uulgi autem more sic dicitur ut ambiguitas obscuritasque 5
uitetur, non sic dicatur ut a doctis, sed potius ut ab indoctis dici
Psal. 15, 4 solet. si enim non piguit dicere interpretes nostros, *non congregabo
conuenticula eorum de sanguinibus*, quoniam senserunt ad rem
pertinere, ut eo loco pluraliter enuntiaretur hoc nomen, quod in
latina lingua singulariter tantummodo dicitur, cur pietatis doctorem 10
pigeat imperitis loquentem, *ossum* potius quam *os* dicere, ne ista
syllaba non ab eo quod sunt *ossa*, sed ab eo quod sunt *ora* intelle-

---

1 genere tali *BDFI*; genere talis *E*.   locutionis *A Maur*.   eam *A*. 2 detra-
hit]trahit *A*.   4 ut]nec *I*.   6 uidetur *DE*.   7 enim]ergo *BF*.   10 tantummodo
singulariter *Maur*.   11 dicere os *EI*.   12 ab eo]habeo *DG*.   quod sunt ossa sed
ab eo *om. G*.

2. haec detrahit . . . contrahit: this admonition is most important in view of the radical concession made below as to the sacrifice of *Latinitas* (*i.e.*, purity of phrase), if that be necessary, in order to secure clearness of expression. Augustine may depart from the classical norm in regard to the admission even of barbarism in speech, but he will not countenance *common* expressions.

sordes = 'vulgarities of speech,' is Silver and Late Latin: cf. Tac. Dial. de Orat. 21: sordes uerborum et hians compositio et inconditi sensus redolent antiquitatem. An equivalent term is 'sordida verba,' *e.g.*, Quint. 8, 3, 17: nec sordidis uerbis in oratione erudita locus.

3. quamuis . . . dicatur: *quamuis* as a corrective appears in the poets from Propertius on, and in prose from Celsus on into Late Latin: cf. Juret (1) 165.

4. latinum esse: the traditional requisites of an orator's language were *elegantia, compositio*, and *dignitas*. For an explantaion of the meaning of *elegantia*, cf. Ad Her. 4, 12, 17: elegantia est, quae facit, ut unum quidque *pure* et aperte dici uideatur. haec tribuitur in Latinitatem et explanationem. Latinitas est, quae sermonem *purum* conseruat ab omni uitio remotum. uitia in sermone, quo minus is Latinus sit, duo possunt esse: soloecismus et barbarismus. Cicero also identifies *Latinitas* and integrity of speech: cf. Orat. 23, 79: sermo purus erit et Latinus, dilucide planeque dicetur; De Orat. 3, 11, 40: atque ut Latine loquamur, non solum uidendum est, ut et uerba efferamus ea, quae nemo iure reprehendat, et ea sic et casibus et temporibus et genere et numero conseruemus, ut ne quid perturbatum ac discrepans aut praeposterum sit, sed etiam lingua et spiritus et uocis

while this discountenances florid expressions, it does not countenance vulgar ones. And yet good teachers have, or ought to have such care in teaching that a word which cannot be expressed in good Latin except obscurely and ambiguously, but which as given in the common idiom, has neither ambiguity nor obscurity, should be expressed not as the cultured, but rather as the uncultured are wont to express it. For if our translators have not hesitated to say, *I will not gather together their meetings for blood offerings*, since they consider that the subject matter called for the plural use of the noun in this place, though in good Latin this word is used only in the singular, then why should a teacher of righteousness when addressing the unlettered, hesitate to use *ossum* for *os* for fear lest this word might be understood as coming not from the same form as *ossa*, but from the same form as *ora*, since the African ear does not distinguish between short and long vowels? For what is the good of correctness of speech if the understanding of the hearer does not follow it, since there is absolutely no reason for

sonus est ipse moderandus. Augustine, therefore, departs from the strict classical norm, in what he teaches below: uulgi—dici solet, and in his following vindication of the use of *ossum* for *os*. Quintilian also advocates the use of ordinary, everyday expressions (*e.g.*, 8, 2, 24: quae causa utique nostra culpa dicta obscurius est: ab planiora et communia magis uerba descendimus) but he wholly repudiates whatever is offensive to purity of speech: cf. 1, 5, 5: prima barbarismi ac soloecismi foeditas absit.

9. **ut eo loco . . . dicitur**: Quintilian would class this as a barbarism. He gives a similar example in 1, 5, 16: *scala* tamen et *scopa* contraque *hordea* et *mulsa*, . . . non alio uitiosa sunt, quam quod pluralia singulariter et singularia pluraliter efferunter.

pluraliter = 'in the plural'; a technical term, in Cicero.

enuntiaretur = 'express': used for the most part only in Cic. and Quint., in rhetorical and grammatical explanations.

10. **singulariter** = 'in the singular,' only in Quintilian and Late writers. In classical usage it means 'especially,' *e.g.*, Cic. Verr. 2, 117: singulariter diligere.

11. **ossum potius quam os**: an example such as this is catalogued as a barbarism by Quintilian (1, 5, 10): tertium est illud uitium barbarismi, cuius exempla uulgo sunt plurima . . . ut uerbo, cui libebit, adiiciat litteram syllabamue uel detrahat. Augustine, therefore, here lays himself open to Cicero's stinging words: nemo enim unquam est oratorem, quod Latine loqueretur, admiratus. *si est aliter, irrident, neque eum oratorem tantummodo sed hominem non putant* (De Orat. 3, 14, 52).

12. **non ab eo**: derivation (origin), expressed by *ab* is cited for Cic., Sall., Varro, etc.: cf. T.L.L. I, 25, 59–26, 43.

gatur, ubi Afrae aures de correptione uocalium uel productione non iudicant? quid enim prodest locutionis integritas, quam non sequitur intellectus audientis, cum loquendi omnino nulla sit causa, si quod loquimur non intellegunt, propter quos ut intellegant loquimur? qui ergo docet, uitabit uerba omnia quae non docent; et si 5 pro eis alia, quae intellegantur integra, potest dicere, id magis eliget; si autem non potest, siue quia non sunt, siue quia in praesentia non occurrunt, utetur etiam uerbis minus integris dum tamen res ipsa doceatur atque discatur integre.

2 inducant (indicant *supra*) *F*.   3 loquendis *F*.   4 quos]quod (*sic em.*) *B*. 5 omnia uerba *Maur*.   decent *I*.   6 integra quae intellegantur *Maur*.   7 eligat *B* (*sic em.*), *EFH*; eligit *I*.   8 utatur *B* (*sio em.*), *E*; utitur *I*.   9 integrem *D*.

1. ubi Afrae aures . . . non iudicant: Reynolds (6) points out that the reference here is only to the masses. In Augustine's own studied use of classical clausulae in *De Ciuitate Dei*, sufficient proof can be found that in his case and in that of the cultured reading public in Africa, the provincial ear had been trained to Roman appreciation of long and short syllables. North Africa at the time, however, was a country of numerous nationalities and languages. Augustine confessed (De Ord. 2, 17, 45) that he himself spoke Latin with a provincial accent, since Punic was his native tongue. The precautions, therefore, that he here takes in order to reach his audience do not seem strange. On the medley of races and customs in Africa at the time, cf. Bertrand 106-107: 'Pourtant, cette unité romaine ne doit pas nous faire illusion. Derrière la façade imposante qu'elle offrait d'un bout à l'autre de la Méditerranée, la diversité des peuples avec leurs moeurs, leurs traditions, leur religion particulière, subsistait toujours, en Afrique plus qu'ailleurs. La population de Carthage était étonnement mélangée. La caractère hybride de ce pays sans unité s'y reflétait dans la bigarrure des foules carthaginoises. Tous les échantillons des races africaines s'y coudoyaient dans les rues, depuis le nègre amené de son Soudan natal par les marchands d'esclaves, jusqu'au Numide romanisé. L'affux sans cesse renouvelé des trafiquants et des aventuriers cosmopolites augmentait encore cette confusion. Et ainsi Carthage était une Babel de races, de coutumes, de croyances, et d'idées.'

ubi: the use of *ubi* as a true casual participle is cited once for Cic. (Quinct. 71), but otherwise belongs to Late Latin: cf. St.-Schm. 767; Gildersleeve 362.

correptione: *correptio*, opposed to *productio*, is used by Vitruvius, and thence often by grammarians, Silver and Late: cf. Quint. 9, 3, 69: uoces . . . aut productione tantum uel correptione mutatae: cf. T.L.L. IV, 1030, 50-71.

2. quid . . . prodest locutionis integritas, etc.: in De Catech. Rud. 9, 13, also, Augustine gives purity of diction second place—there, to integrity of character: discant non contemnere quos cognouerint morum uitia quam uerborum amplius deuitare, et cordi casto linguam exercitatam nec conferre audeant. He excuses barbarisms and solecisms in a preacher, if the latter has love of God: nouerint etiam non esse uocem ad aures dei nisi animi affectum; ita enim non irridebunt, si aliquos antistites et ministros ecclesiae forte animaduerterint *uel barbarismis et soloecismis deum inuocare*, uel eadem

speaking if they for whose instruction we speak are not instructed by our speaking. And so, one who teaches will avoid all words which do not teach; and if in place of them he can use other correct expressions which are intelligible, he will choose them by preference, but if he cannot, either because they do not exist, or because they do not occur to him at the moment, he will use words even less correct, provided, however, that the matter itself be taught and learned correctly.

uerba quae pronuntiant non intellegere perturbateque distinguere. Again, in Conf. 1, 18, 29, he says: uide quomodo diligenter obseruent filii hominum pacta litterarum et syllabarum . . . et aeterna pacta perpetuae salutis neglegant. And in Contr. Adu. Leg. 1, 24, 52: Deus magis morum quam uerborum pulchritudinem quaerens atque munditiam.

3. **intellectus audientis**: Cicero in De Orat. 3, 13, 48ff. sums up the means considered sufficient by the classical orator in order to reach his audience: neque uero in illo altero diutius commoraremur, ut disputemus quibus rebus assequi possimus, ut ea quae dicamus intellegantur: *Latine scilicet dicendo*, uerbis usitatis ac proprie demonstrantibus ea quae significari ac declarari uolemus, sine ambiguo uerbo aut sermone, non nimis longa continuatione uerborum, non ualde productis iis quae similitudinis causa ex aliis rebus transferuntur, non discerptis sententiis, non praeposteris temporibus, non confusis personis, non perturbato ordine. But Augustine would go further!

4. **si quod . . . loquimur**: to make oneself understood is of course also with Cicero the *sine qua non* of good oratory: cf. De Orat. 3, 14, 52: nemo extulit eum uerbis, qui ita dixisset, ut qui adessent intellegerent quid diceret, *sed contempsit eum, qui minus id facere potuisset.*

5. **uitabit uerba omnia quae non docent**: Augustine refers to the second quality of *elegantia*, named above, viz. *explanatio*, defined thus in Ad Her. 4, 12, 17: explanatio est, quae reddit apertam et dilucidam orationem. ea comparatur duabus rebus, usitatis uerbis et propriis. usitata sunt ea quae uersantur in ser-

monis consuetudine cotidiana; propria, quae eius rei uerba sunt aut esse possunt, qua de loquemur. Cicero (Orat. 24, 80) explains the matter in like terms, coupling, however, *ornatus* with *explanatio*: simplex probatur in propriis usitatisque uerbis, quod aut optime sonat aut rem explanat.

6. **integra**, the adjective, is not used until Late Latin with the meaning 'grammatically correct,' though its corresponding noun and adverb are classical in this meaning. For *integritas*, cf. Cic. Brut. 35, 132: incorrupta quaedam Latini sermonis integritas; for *integre*, cf. Cic. Opt. Gen. 4, 12, and Gell. 13, 6: pure atque integre locuti sunt. Augustine is here reiterating his acceptance of that which is unacceptable to classical *Latinitas*.

7. **si autem . . . siue quia non sunt, . . . integris**: but Quintilian (1, 5, 71) says: usitatis tutius utimur, noua non sine quodam periculo fingimus.

8. **dum tamen res ipse doceatur . . . integre**: cf. Aug. De Catech. Rud. 9, 13: his enim maxime utile est nosse, ita esse praeponendas uerbis sententias ut praeponitur animus corpori. As for Augustine's own practice, cf. Bertrand 162-63: 'Enfin sa phrase écrite ou parlée était dépourvue du brillant, des ingénieuses recherches d'expression qui plaisaient dans les cercles lettrés et mondains. Cet écrivain d'une fécondité inépuisable n'est point du tout un styliste. A cet égard, il est inférieur à un Apulée, à un Tertullien, s'il les laisse bien loin derrière lui *pour la sincérité* et la profondeur du sentiment, le lyrisme, la couleur, l'emportement des métaphores, et, avec cela, l'onction, la suavité de l'accent.'

25. Et hoc quidem non solum in collocutionibus, siue fiant cum aliquo uno, siue cum pluribus, uerum etiam multo magis in populis quando sermo promitur, ut intellegamur instandum est. quia in collocutionibus est cuique interrogandi potestas, ubi autem omnes tacent ut audiatur unus, et in eum intenta ora conuertunt, ibi ut 5 requirat quisque quod non intellexerit, nec moris est nec decoris; ac per hoc debet maxime tacenti subuenire cura dicentis. solet autem motu suo significare utrum intellexerit cognoscendi auida multitudo; quod donec significet, uersandum est quod agitur, multimoda uarietate dicendi, quod in potestate non habent, qui prae- 10 parata et ad uerbum memoriter retenta pronuntiant. mox autem ut intellectum esse constiterit, aut sermo finiendus, ant in alia transeundum est, sicut enim gratus est qui cognoscenda enubilat, sic onerosus qui cognita inculcat, eis duntaxat quorum tota ex-

1 locutionibus *A*.   2 uno *om. E.*   etiam et *AB*.   3 proditur *C*.   intellegatur *BCF* (*sic em.*) *EI*.   5 ut (audiatur) *om. D*.   6 quisquis *E*.   8 autem]enim *BDF*.   10 non *om. A*.   12 ut autem *AD*.   constituerit *F*.   13 est gratus *D*. 14 onerosus est *Maur*.

1. **non solum in collocutionibus . . . quando promitur**: again in De Catech. Rud. 15, 23, Augustine differentiates between instruction given to a few in private and after a fashion familiarly, and a sermon properly so called, delivered to a congregation. With true pedagogical instinct, he recognizes wherein these are to be handled alike, wherein differently.

2. **populis** = 'throngs': Poetic, Silver, and Late Latin.

3. **ut intellegamur instandum est**: this was Augustine's own practice: cf. Serm. 131, 9: paucos intellexisse uideo, plures non intellexisse, quos ego nequaquam tacendo fraudabo. *Ibid.* 23, 8: iam multos uestrum intellexisse non dubito. non uideo, sed ex colloccutione, quia loquimini ad alterutrum, sentio eos qui intellexerunt, uelle exponere iis qui nondum intellexerunt. *ergo planius aliquanto dicam, ut ad omnes peruieniat.*

4. **ubi . . . omnes tacent . . . conuertunt**: cf. De Catech. Rud. 15, 23: cum populus tacens unum de loco superiore dicturum suspensus intuetur. That this attention however was not always usual,

is proved by the frequent reproofs and exhortations to silence found in the Sermons of Augustine: cf. Deferrari 205–7.

7. **per hoc** = 'therefore,' is frequent in Late Latin: cf. St.-Schm. 521; Bonnet 591; Goel. (2) 171; Adams 36; Arts 25. It occurs many times below.

debet maxime . . . cura dicentis: *e.g.*, in Tract. XI in Euang. S. Ioan. VIII, Augustine repeats a statement entire in order to bring it home to his hearers: in omnibus enim christianis, fratres intendite, aut per malos nascuntur boni, aut per bonos nascuntur mali, aut per bonos boni, aut per malos mali: amplius istis quattuor generibus non potestis inuenire. quare iterum repetam, aduertite, retinete; excutite corda uestra, nolite pigri esse: capite, ne capiamini, quomodo quattuor genera sunt omnium christianorum *aut per bonos nascuntur boni, aut per malos nascuntur mali, aut per bonos mali, aut per malos boni. puto quia planum est.* Quintilian (8, 2, 23) likewise advocates such clearness in discourse as to impose one's conclusions upon the mind of the judge with the same blinding force as that of sun in the eyes: nam si neque pau-

25. And this indeed must be insisted upon, that we may be understood, not only in conversations with one person or with several, but also much more when a sermon is being delivered before assemblies. For in conversations, each one has the opportunity of questioning; but when all are quiet, that one may be heard, and all are turned toward him with fixed attention, then it is neither customary nor proper for any one to ask about what he has not understood, and for this reason it should be the special concern of the speaker to assist the silent listener. But an assembly eager to learn generally shows by some movement whether it has understood, and until it does show this, the matter in hand ought to be presented in many different forms; but this they have not the power of doing who deliver word for word what they have prepared and committed to memory. However, as soon as it is clear that the matter has been understood, the discourse ought to be ended, or to pass on to other

ciora, quam oportet, neque plura neque inordinata aut indistincta dixerimus: erunt dilucida et neglegenter quoque audientibus aperta; quod et ipsum in consilio est habendum, non semper tam esse acrem iudicis intentionem, ut obscuritatem apud se ipse discutiat et tenebris orationis inferat quoddam intellegentiae suae lumen, sed multis eum frequenter cogitationibus auocari, nisi tam clara fuerint, quae dicemus, ut in animum eius oratio, ut sol in oculos, etiamsi in eam non intendatur, incurrat.

9. **uersandum est . . . uarietate dicendi**: cf. Quint. 8, 2, 24: propter quod etiam repetimus saepe, quae non satis percepisse eos, qui cognoscunt, putamus. Augustine himself expresses the same thought in De Catech. Rud. 13, 18: sed re uera multum est perdurare in loquendo usque ad terminum praestitutum, cum moueri non uidemus audientem; quod siue non audeat, religionis timore constrictus, uoce aut aliquo motu corporis significare approbationem suam, siue humana uerecundia reprimatur: siue dicta non intellegat, siue contemnat; quando quidem nobis non cernentibus animum eius incertum est, *omnia sermone tentanda sunt, quae ad eum excitandum* et tanquam de latebris eruendum possint ualere.

multimoda: Late Latin: cf. K.-

Schm. s.v.; Goel. (1) 169.

10. **quod in potestate . . . pronuntiant**: Augustine is clearly advocating extempore address. That this was the method of preaching used by such renowned speakers as Origen, Cyril of Jerusalem, John Chrysostom, Pope Faustus, Jerome, and especially Augustine himself, is shown by Deferrari 97-123; 193–211.

11. **mox ut . . . constiterit . . . finiendus**, as was Augustine's own custom: cf. Deferrari 207-208.

mox ut = 'as soon as,' is Late: cf. St.-Schm. 759; K.-Steg. II, 2, 365. It occurs several times in the Confessions: cf. Arts 102.

13. **enubilat** = 'makes clear,' is Late: cf. Tert. Anim. 3: ea erunt christianis enubilanda.

14. **sic onerosus . . . inculcat**: cf. De Catech. Rud. 13, 18: quaerendum etiam de illo utrum haec aliquando iam audierit, *et fortassis eum tamquam nota et peruulgata non moueant*; et agendum pro eius responsione, ut aut planius et enodatius loquamur, aut opinionem contrariam refellamus, aut ea quae illa nota sunt non explicemus latius, sed breuius complicemus. For Augustine's own practice, cf. Enarrat. 2, 1, 12 in Psalm. 32: quamuis ergo, fratres, psalmi plura restent consulendum est tamen uiribus et

spectatio in dissoluenda eorum, quae panduntur, difficultate pen-
debat. nam delectandi gratia etiam nota dicuntur, ubi non ipsa
sed modus quo dicuntur attenditur. quod si et ipse iam notus est,
atque auditoribus placet, pene nihil interest utrum is qui dicit,
dictor an lector sit. solent enim et ea quae commode scripta sunt,   5
non solum ab iis quibus primitus innotescunt, iucunde legi;
uerum ab iis etiam quibus iam nota sunt, neque adhuc illa de
memoria deleuit obliuio, non sine iucunditate relegi, uel ab utrisque libenter audiri. quae autem quisque iam oblitus est, cum com-
moneretur, docetur. sed de modo delectandi nunc non ago; de   10
modo quo docendi sunt qui discere desiderant, loquor. is est autem
optimus, quo fit ut qui audit, uerum audiat, et quod audit intellegat. ad quem finem cum uentum fuerit, nihil tunc amplius de
ipsa re tamquam diutius docenda laborandum est, sed forte de
commendanda ut in corde figatur; quod es faciendum uidebitur,   15
ita modeste faciendum est, ne perueniatur ad taedium.

1 penduntur *G*; pandantur *Mig.*   3 motus *F.*   quod si et ipse]quod et si
ipse *E*; quod si et ipsi *F.*   4 his *A.*   5 an]uel *El Maur.*   et *om. CEHI*; et]ut
G.   6 his *ABCDFGHI*; hiis *E.*   7 ab *om. E.*   his *ABCDFGHI*; hiis *E.*   etiam
om. E.   9 oblitus est iam *A.*   10 non *om. E.*   11 autem est *I Maur.*   12 uero *I.*
quod] qui *E.*   14 docendo *D.*

animae et corporis propter uarietatem
audientium. Serm. 343, 4: de quo latius
dicerem, nisi sermo iam longior et meis
senilibus viribus, et uestrae fortasse sati-
etati parcere cogeret.

onerosus = *molestus*, is Poetic and
Silver.

2. **nam delectandi . . . dicuntur**: cf.
De Orat. 3, 30, 121: non enim solum
acuenda nobis neque procudenda lingua
est, sed onerandum complendumque
pectus maximarum rerum et pluri-
marum suauitate, copia, uarietate. *Ibid.*
3, 31, 125: rerum enim copia uerborum
copiam gignit; et, si est honestas in rebus
ipsis de quibus dicitur, existit ex re natu-
ralis quidam splendor in uerbis.

3. **modus**, *i.e.* in the middle style,
whose aim is to please.

5. **dictor**: another formation in *-tor,*
belonging to Late Latin: cf. T.L.L. V,
1014, 48-64.

commode = 'pleasingly,' is used in
early Latin, though also by Cicero (cf.
Verr. 5, 95; De Orat. 2, 83, 240), then in

Late Latin: cf. T.L.L. III, 1926, 3–18.

6. **innotescunt**, used absolutely, is
Silver and Late.

8. **relegi** = 'reread,' is mostly Poetic.

11. **discere desiderant**: *desidero* with
the infinitive, though found in Cicero and
occasionally in Silver Latin, becomes
common only in the Late period: cf.
T.L.L. V, 707, 9–42; K.-Steg. II, 1, 676.
It occurs again in 11, 26.

is est . . . intellegat: this thought is
developed below in chapters 23 and 25.
With St. Augustine, the *genus temperatum* has no justification for existence by
itself alone. Augustine stands severely
apart from the Sophists.

15. **corde**: *cor* as the seat of feeling or
of thought, occurs generally in the poets,
and in the language of the people, but is
avoided in prose up to the time of Fronto.
In Eccl. Latin it is often used also for
anima: cf. K.-Schm. s.v.; T.L.L. IV, 930,
17-25. It occurs several times below: 15,
32; 24, 53; 26, 58; 27, 59.

16. **ne perueniat**: *ne* for *ut non* is

things. For though one gives pleasure when he clears up matters that need to be made understood, he becomes wearisome when he keeps hammering at things which are already understood, at least to those men whose whole expectation was centered in the solution of the difficulty in the matter under discussion. It is true that for the sake of giving pleasure, even well-known things are talked over; when, not the facts themselves, but the manner in which they are expressed, holds the attention. And if this itself also is now well known, and is popular with the audience, it makes almost no difference whether the man talking be a speaker or a reader. For generally, things which are attractively written are also read with pleasure, not only by those who come to know them for the first time; but even by those who have already made their acquaintance, and from whose memory they have not yet been effaced, are they reread not without pleasure; or they are listened to willingly by both classes. On the other hand, what a person has forgotten, when it is recalled to him, he learns again. But I am not now treating of how to please; I am speaking of how they are to be taught who desire instruction. That, indeed, is the best method, which results in the listener hearing the truth, and understanding what he hears. When this end has been attained, then there should be no further effort toward expounding the matter longer, as it were, but perhaps toward commending it, so that it may be fixed deep in the heart; but if it seem that this ought to be done, it must be done with such moderation as not to lead to weariness.

sometimes used in a result clause when the result implies an effect intended, *e.g.*, Cic. Fam. 6, 7, 6: ita corrigas ne mihi noceat.

taedium: not frequent until after the classical period. — In comparison with classical rigidity in the matter of *integritas*, Augustine's views would seem at first radical and dangerous, as admitting of extravagant deviation from the standards of the best Latin. Lezat (35-36) sees in Augustine's disregard of the classical norm on the question of *Latinitas* an important cause of the degeneration of the language in the hands of succeeding generations. A study, however, of the Latinity of Augustine and of the great contemporary writers reveals that on the whole these writers, far from going to the extreme in admitting nonclassical forms and con-

structions, are in reality dominated by classical standards, and that where, as in the case of Augustine, the influence of the prevalent usage caused a tendency toward archaism, colloquialism, and neologism, these uses still form but a very conservative part of the writer's language. The studies on St. Augustine's syntax made in the Catholic University Patristic series show that in the *De Ciuitate Dei* and in the Confessions, Augustine's deviations from Ciceronian Latin are on the whole but little more marked than those of the writers of the Silver Age. Arts states that in the Confessions, Augustine's language contains little or nothing of what we understand by 'Vulgar Latin' in the strict sense of the term (cf. Colbert 99–101; Arts 120–27). A study of Augustine's Letters shows the importance of the colloquial

11, 26. Prorsus haec est in docendo eloquentia, qua fit dicendo, non ut libeat quod horrebat, aut ut fiat quod pigebat, sed ut appareat quod latebat. quod tamen si fiat insuauiter, ad paucos quidem studiosissimos suus peruenit fructus, qui ea quae discenda sunt, quamuis abiecte inculteque dicantur, scire desiderant. quod cum 5 adepti fuerint, ipsa delectabiliter ueritate pascuntur; bonorumque ingeniorum insignis est indoles, in uerbis uerum amare, non uerba. quid enim prodest clauis aurea, si aperire quod uolumus non potest? aut quid obest lignea si hoc potest? quando nihil quaerimus nisi patere quod clausum est. sed quoniam inter se habent nonnullam 10 similitudinem uescentes atque discentes, propter fastidia plurimorum, etiam ipsa sine quibus uiui non potest, alimenta condienda sunt.

1 in *om. E.* quae *D.* dicendum *A*; docendo *E.* 4 suus peruenit] superuenit *G.* dicenda *H.* 5 inculteque]inculte qui *B.* 7 indolis *CDF.* 8 enim]si *E.* 9 nihil est *F.* 11 dicentes *D.*

element, and in matter of neologisms reveals a great freedom of derivation; still it likewise proves that Augustine is decidedly classical, since in nearly every word-category used in the Letters the classical forms exceed the Late words (cf. Parsons 269-77). A comparison of the classical and non-classical words in the present treatise leads to a similar conclusion. It seems safe, therefore, to state that Augustine's opposition to the classical norm appears more radical in his statement of it than it was in his own practice. He realized that language to remain living must change; but by making good usage, as influenced by popular expression and the exigencies of the popular understanding, the arbiter of that change, he advocated a language strong in its classical traditions, and at the same time vital in its reflection of the living thought of the day. Moreover, the present avowal of his preference for clearness before *integritas* was occasioned, as Baldwin (2, 65) suggests, by his desire to offset the boasted correctness of the Sophists, which was carried by them to the extreme of over-refining the language by a rigid maintenance of

the ideals of the past. The middle ground taken by Augustine shows the sanity of his views. In *De Ordine* 2, 17, 45, he says: soloecismos autem quos dicimus, fortasse quisque doctus diligenter attendens in oratione mea reperiet. non enim defuit qui mihi nonnulla huiusmodi uitia ipsum Ciceronem fecisse peritissime persuaserit. He is obviously slurring the Sophists and their correctness, which could not only find faults in contemporaries, but even in Cicero himself. To combat this ultraclassical correctness, he makes the statements above, which at first sight appear radical and unclassical. That he is not so in reality is proved by his actual practice.

11. *A concession, because of popular taste, of a moderate use of 'ornatus' to the office of 'docere.'*

1. **prorsus haec . . . latebat**: cf. Arist. Rhet. 3, 1, 1404a: τό γε δίκαιον μηδὲν πλείω ζητεῖν περιτὸν λόγον, ἢ ὡς μήτε λυπεῖν μήτ' εὐφραίωειν. δίκαιον γὰρ αὐτοῖς ἀγωνίζεσθαι τοῖς πράγμασιν, ὥστε τἆλλα ἔξω τοῦ ἀποδεῖξαι περίεργα ἐστίν. The Stoics, following Aristotle's emphasis on the pragmatic, elaborated the dialectical aspect of rhetorical

11,   26. This, of course, is eloquence in teaching, whereby the result is attained in speaking, not that what was distasteful becomes pleasing, nor that what one was unwilling to do is done, but that what was obscure becomes clear. Still, if this be done in an unpleasing manner, its fruit falls to the very few zealous persons, forsooth, who are eager for the knowledge which is proposed for instruction, no matter how meanly and inelegantly it be explained. When they have once gained this end, they feast upon the truth itself with delight; and it is the fine characteristic of great minds that they love the truth in words, not just the words. For what is the use of a golden key if it cannot open what we want it to? Or what is the objection to a wooden one if it can do so, since we are asking nothing save that what is closed be opened? But as eating and learning have a certain similarity one to the other, because of the natural fastidiousness of most people, even the very food which is necessary for life's sustenance must have seasoning.

proof, but unlike Aristotle, due to their general doctrine of ἀπάθεια, excluded in large measure that phase of rhetoric which has to do with emotional appeal. See De Orat. 1, 53, 229, for an instance of the Stoic ideal, Rutilius Rufus, of whom Cicero says: ne ornatius quidem aut liberius causam dici suam, quam simplex ratio ueritatis ferebat. This describes of course the plain style: ut probemus uera esse quae defendimus (De Orat. 2, 27, 115).

2. **horrebat** = 'was distasteful,' is rare, being mostly Poetic.

3. **si fiat . . . peruenit fructus**: cf. De Orat. 3, 11, 41: nolo uerba exiliter exanimata exire. Ad Her. 4, 11, 16: qui non possunt in illa *facetissima* uerborum *attenuatione* commode uersari, ueniunt ad aridum et exsangue genus orationis, quod non alienum est exile nominari. *Ornatus* and the middle style (*ad delectandum*) find their proper use in aiding the plain style (*ad docendum*). Augustine develops

this point in 25, 55.

6. **delectabiliter**: Late: cf. T.L.L. V, 418, 59.

pascuntur: largely Poetic, but used by Cicero, *e.g.*, De Off. 2, 11: ne illi quidem, qui maleficio et scelere pascuntur, possint sine ulla particula iustitiae uiuere.

bonorum . . . non uerba: a subtle thrust at the Sophists.

9. **quaerimus . . . patere**: *quaerere* with the infinitive occurs in the poets and in Silver Latin: cf. K.-Steg. II, 1, 667.

10. **sed quoniam . . . condienda sunt**: cf. Cicero's concession of *suauitas* to the plain style: et contra tenues acuti, omnia docentes et dilucidiora, non ampliora facientes, subtili quadam et pressa oratione limati; in eodemque genere alii callidi, sed impoliti et consulto rudium similes et imperitorum, *alii in eadem ieiunitate concinniores id est faceti, florentes etiam et leuiter ornati* (Orat. 6, 21).

12, 27. Dixit ergo quidam eloquens, et uerum dixit, ita dicere
debere eloquentem, ut doceat, ut delectet, ut flectat. deinde addidit,
docere necessitatis est, delectare suauitatis, flectere uictoriae. horum
trium quod primo loco positum est, hoc est docendi necessitas, in
rebus est constituta quas dicimus; reliqua duo, in modo quo dici- 5
mus. qui ergo dicit cum docere uult, quamdiu non intellegitur,
nondum se existimet dixisse quod uult ei quem uult docere. quia
etsi dixit quod ipse intellegit, nondum illi dixisse putandus est, a
quo intellectus non est; si uero intellectus est, quocumque modo
dixerit, dixit. quod si etiam delectare uult eum cui dicit, aut 10

1 ergo]enim *BDF.*   2 delectat *E.*   flectet *B.*   3 suauitatis est *CE.*   4 obposi-
tum *F.*   5 quo]quod *D.*   dicimus docendi *I.*   6 intellegetur *Mig.*   7 ei] ille *B.*
8 intellexit *BDE.*   ei *E.*   9 si uero intellectus est *om. I.*   10 eum]ei *E.*   dixit *I.*

12. The *'officia'* of the orator:
'docere,' 'delectare,' 'flectere': their
meaning, relation, and culmination.
  1. **dixit . . . uictoriae**: cf. Orat. 21,
69: erit igitur eloquens—hunc enim auc-
tore Antonio quaerimus—is qui in foro
causisque ciuilibus ita dicet, *ut probet,*
ut delectet, ut flectat. probare neces-
sitatis est, delectare suauitatis, flectere
uictoriae: nam id unum ex omnibus ad
optinendas causas potest plurimum. See
also De Orat. 2, 27, 115. Though Augustine substitutes *doceat* for *probet,* he
does not in reality misquote the thought
of Cicero, as is shown by the fact that
in very many of the other places where
Cicero explains these functions, he himself uses *docere* for *probare, e.g.,* De
Orat. 2, 28, 121: quibus ex locis ad eas
tris res, quae ad fidem faciendam solae
ualent, ducatur oratio, *ut et concilientur*
animi et doceantur et mouentur; *ibid.* 2,
77, 310: tribus rebus homines ad nostrum
sententiam perducimus, *aut docendo aut*
conciliando aut permouendo; Brut. 49,
185: tria sunt enim, ut quidem ego sentio,
quae sint efficienda dicendo: *ut doceatur*
is, apud quem dicetur, ut delectetur, ut
moueatur uehementius; De Opt. Gen. 1,
3: optumus est enim orator qui dicendo
animos audientium *et docet et delec-*
tate et permouet. docere debitum est,
delectare honorarium, permouere nec-

essarium; *ibid.* 5, 16: necesse est tamen
oratori, quem quaerimus, controuersias
explicare forenses dicendi genere apto *ad*
docendum, ad delectandum, ad permou-
endum. These three *officia oratoris* are
derived from the Aristotelian division of
πίστεις, which in spite of Stoic elaboration of the pragmatic aspect of rhetoric at
the expense of the emotional, continued
for centuries to the prevailing one. Aristotle (Rhet. 1, 2, 1355b) regards means
of persuasion as (1) those contained in
the subject matter itself (ἐν αὐτῷ τῷ
πράγματι), and (2) those outside it (τὰ
ἔξω τῶν πραγμάτων). The latter he sub-
divides into (a) persuasion through the
speaker's character (ἤθη) and (b) persuasion through the stirring of the emotions of the hearers (πάθη). Compare De
Orat. 2, 27, 115: ita omnis ratio dicendi
tribus ad persuadendum rebus est nixa:
(1) ut probemus uera esse quae defendimus, (2a) ut conciliemus eos nobis qui
audient, (2b) ut animos eorum ad quem-
quomque causa postulabit motum uocemus. The first, (1) ut probemus uera esse
quae defendimus, corresponds to πίστεις
ἐν αὐτῷ τῷ πράγματι; the second, (2a)
ut conciliemus . . . audient, to τὰ ἔξω
τῶν πραγμάτων, *i.e.* ἤθη; the third, (2b)
ut animos . . . uocemus, to τὰ ἔξω τῶν
πραγμάτων, i.e., πάθη. Hendrickson
(2) 260 considers De Orat. 2, 27, 115 as

12, 27. And so, a well-known orator has said, and has said truly that an orator ought to speak in such a way as to instruct, to please, and to persuade. Then he adds, "Instructing belongs to necessity; pleasing, to interest; persuading, to victory." Of these three, that which is given first place, the necessity of instructing, depends upon the things we say; the other two, upon our manner of saying them. Therefore, the man who speaks with the view to instructing, as long as he is not intelligible, should consider he has not yet said what he wishes to say to the one whom he wishes to instruct. Because, though he has said what he himself understands, he should not be thought yet to have said it to him by whom

the earliest recorded Latin formulation of the Peripatetic conception of the orator's *officia*, afterward to be followed by Quintilian and all later Roman rhetoric. For a discussion of the development of *docere, delectare, flectere* from Aristotle and his school, cf. Hendrickson (2) 249–60.

3. **horum trium . . . in modo quo dicimus**: this twofold division is that which is followed by Augustine in Contr. Cresc. 1, 13, 16: uideo te quaedam copiose ornateque explicare, hoc est eloquenter; quaedam uero subtiliter arguteque disserere, hoc est dialectice. It also follows from his conception of the nature of words as twofold, discussed in De Dial. 7: duplex hic ex consideratione sensus nascitur: partim propter explicandum ueritatem, partim propter seruandum decorem, quorum primum ad dialecticum, secundum ad oratorem maxime pertinet. Aristotle's conception, of course, of the aspects of proof admits of interpretation as being either twofold or threefold. The interpretation as threefold was shown above as developing into the *docere, delectare, flectere* of the schools, but the twofold division, *viz.* merely (1) πίστεις ἐν τῷ πράγματι, and (2) τὰ ἔξω τῶν πραγμάτων is the more logical one, and is of earlier date and wider diffusion. Cicero himself often conceives of the usual threefold *officia* as being, in strict analysis, only twofold: cf. De Orat. 2, 77, 310: et quoniam, quod saepe iam dixi, tribus rebus homines ad nostram sententiam

perducimus, aut docendo aut conciliando aut permouendo, una ex tribus his rebus res prae nobis est ferenda, ut nihil aliud nisi docere uelle uideamur; reliquae duae, sicuti sanguis in corporibus, sic illae in perpetuis orationibus fusae esse debebunt; Brut. 23, 89: duae summae sint in oratore laudes una subtiliter disputandi ad docendum, altera grauiter agendi ad animos audientium permouendos. As was seen in the first chapter of the present treatise, the natural division of *res* and *modus quo* was accepted by Augustine in place of the traditional fivefold division of oratory; here, in speaking of the functions of the orator, he sees its bearing again, but recognizes how it easily resolves itself into the more usual threefold division, and this he follows, in view of his subsequent treatment of the three traditional styles: plain, temperate, and grand, discussed in chapter 17, and the succeeding chapters.

6. **qui ergo . . . dixerit, dixit**: here the point in question is that of *res*, the method used is the dialectic of Contr. Cresc. (cf. 1, 13, 16: dialecticus ille appellandus est, qui non solum subtiliter, sed ueraciter etiam disserit), the function is *ad docendum*, and the style, as will be explained in chapter 17, is plain.

10. **quod si etiam delectare . . . ut faciat**: here the question is that of *modus quo*, the method is the rhetoric of Contr. Cresc. (cf. 1, 13, 16: eloquens ille appellandus est, qui non solum copiose et ornate, sed etiam ueraciter dicit), the func-

flectere non quocumque modo dixerit, faciet; sed interest quomodo
dicat, ut faciat. sicut est autem, ut teneatur ad audiendum, delectandus auditor, ita flectendus, ut moueatur ad agendum. et sicut
delectatur, si suauiter loquaris, ita flectitur, si amet quod polliceris,
timeat quod minaris, oderit quod arguis, quod commendas amplec-   5
tatur, quod dolendum exaggeras doleat, cum quid laetandum prae-
dicas gaudeat, misereatur eorum quos miserandos ante oculos dicendo constituis, fugiat eos quos cauendos terrendo proponis—et
quidquid aliud grandi eloquentia fieri potest ad commouendos animos auditorum, non quid agendum sit ut sciant, sed ut agant quod   10
agendum esse iam sciunt.

28. Si autem adhuc nesciunt, prius utique docendi sunt quam
mouendi. et fortasse rebus ipsis cognitis ita mouebuntur, ut eos
non opus sit maioribus eloquentiae uiribus iam moueri. quod
tamen cum opus est, faciendum est; tunc autem opus est, quando   15
cum scierint quid agendum sit, non agunt. ac per hoc docere neces-

---

1 faciet] facienti *A*; faciat *BF*.   2 ut]aut *BF*.   est autem ut *om*. *E*.   delectandus est *E*.   4 loqueris *ABDFI*, flectetur *C*.   5 odiat *E*. commendas]
connolenda sunt *A*.   6 laetandum]dolendum *E*.   9 aliud *om*. *A*.   eloquentiae *A*.
10 agendum sit . . . quod *om*. *F*.   13 et]etsi *C*.   ipsis *om*. *E*.   14 iam *om*. *B*.
admoueri *B*.   15 est faciendum *E*.   16 scierunt *C*; scirent *F*.

---

tions are *ad delectandum* and *ad flecten-*
dum, and the styles are the moderate and
grand, Augustine's language in these
two sentences is meant to illustrate the
subject in hand. His purpose is first of all
ad docendum, and so he uses the plain-
est words only, and only those absolutely
necessary; but these he repeats either
outright, or by polyptoton, so that the
result is a very clear explanation of the
matter, but one put in such a neat, succinct way as also to please and convince
(*ad delectandum* and *ad flectendum*), his
further purposes.

3. **et sicut . . . sciunt**: an obvious use
of the grand style, in illustration of the
subject under discussion.—Note the use
of the accusative with intransitive verbs,
in this sentence. Though this construction is found to some extent in Cicero,
and later in Silver Latin, it does not
become common until Late Latin: cf.
K.-Steg. II, 1, 275, 277.

5. **arguis** takes the accusative of the
thing (object of censure) in Cic., Liv.,
the poets, and Silver and Late writers:
cf. T.L.L. II, 553, 61–554, 17.

6. **exaggeras** is here used as a *verbum*
dicendi, meaning 'emphasize.' Its usual
transferred meaning is 'exaggerate': cf.
Orat. 3, 55: oratione exaggerare aliquid.
With the accusative and the gerundive,
its use seems peculiar to Augustine in
this place, and is certainly Late.

quid: indefinite, is classical: cf.
Lane 435.

laetandum: cited as used transitively by Cic. (with neuter pronoun),
Verg., Sall., Fronto, Aug.: cf. K.-Steg. II,
1, 261.

7. **misereatur . . . miserandos**: Festus
thus distinguishes between *miserari* and
misereri: ut miseretur is, qui conqueritur
aliena incommode; *misereatur* is, qui
miserum subleuat (Fest. apud Paul. Diac.
123). Pompeius and others, however, say

he has not been understood; if, however, he has been understood, whatever the manner of his having said it, he has said it. But if his aim is also to please the one to whom he speaks, or to persuade him, he will not accomplish it by any manner of speaking whatsoever, but it is of [the] moment how he speaks, in order to accomplish it. Moreover, as a listener must be pleased if his attention is to be held, so he must be persuaded if he is to be moved to action. And as he is pleased if you speak attractively, so he is persuaded if he likes what you promise, fears what you threaten, hates what you censure, embraces what you command, grieves over what you emphasize as deserving of grief, rejoices when you say something should gladden, sympathizes with those whom you by your words set before his eyes as objects of pity, shuns those whom you with threats consider ought to be avoided — and so on in regard to whatever else in the way of moving the hearts of an audience is possible through powerful eloquence, not that they may know what they must do, but that they may do what they already know they ought to do.

28. But if they do not yet know this, instruction must, of course, precede persuasion. And perhaps, when the facts themselves have been learned, they will be so far moved, that there will be no longer need that they be moved by greater powers of eloquence. However, when there is need, this must be used; but there is then need when, although they know what they ought to do, they do not do it. And for this reason, instruction is of necessity. For men have the liberty of doing or not doing the things they know. But who would

that these verbs differ in syntax only, not in sense: *miserari* takes the accusative, *misereri* takes the genitive.

quos miserandos . . . constituis: *constituo* with an accusative gerundive was admitted from the time of Vitruvius on. This construction, or *ut* and the subjunctive became then the ordinary usage with this verb to express a dependent noun clause with subject differing from *constituo*: cf. St.-Schm. 595; K.-Schm. s.v.

8. **fugiat**: transitive at times in Cicero, Caesar, Livy, and Quintilian, though the construction is largely poetical: cf. T.L.L. VI, 1485, 31ff.; K.-Steg. II, 1, 257.

terrendo: used absolutely, is found in Livy: cf. 28, 26: ut ultro territuri succlamationibus, concurrunt. Classical Latin, on the whole, restricted the absolute use of verbs. On the extension of this usage in Late Latin, cf. St.-Schm. 376-78; K.-Steg. II, 1, 95; Arts 80. Note this use below in 13, 29 (instruat); 15, 32 (praeferentem); 16, 33 (largiente); 18, 36 (indignari . . . corripere . . . exprobare . . . increpare . . . minari); 20, 42 (rimanti); 20, 39 (incidentibus).

sitatis est. possunt enim homines et agere et non agere quod sciunt. quis autem dixerit eos agere debere quod nesciunt? et ideo flectere necessitatis non est, quia non semper opus est, si tantum docenti uel etiam delectanti consentit auditor. ideo autem uictoriae est flectere, quia fieri potest ut doceatur et delectetur et non assen- 5 tiatur. quid autem illa duo proderunt, si desit hoc tertium? sed neque delectare necessitatis est; quandoquidem cum dicendo uera monstrantur—quod ad officium docendi pertinet—non eloquio agitur, neque hoc attenditur, ut uel ipsa uel ipsum delectet eloquium, sed per seipsa, quoniam uera sunt, manifestata delectant. unde 10 plerumque delectant, etiam falsa patefacta atque conuicta. neque enim delectant, quia falsa sunt, sed quia falsa esse uerum est, delectat et dictio, qua hoc uerum esse monstratum est.

13, 29. Propter eos autem quibus fastidientibus non placet ueritas, si alio quocumque modo, nisi eo modo dicatur, ut placeat et sermo 15 dicentis, datus est in eloquentia non paruus etiam delectationi locus. quae tamen addita non sufficit duris, quos nec intellexisse,

2 dixit *DF.* 3 non necessitatis *E.* si]sed *E.* tantum]tamen *F.* 4 delectati *I.* consentiat *BDF.* 5 flectere *om. ABCDFG;* flectere uictoriae est *I.* ut et *ACDF.* 7 delectari *B.* necessitas *B.* 8 nec *E.* eloquium *F.* 10 quando *E.* 11 unde plerumque delectant *om. D.* unde plerumque etiam falsa . . . conuicta delectant *B.* 12 falsa esse] falsum esse *G.* 13 qua] quia *CF.* 14 autem]a *E.* 15 si] sed *EI.* aliquocumque *CD;* aliquid quocumque *E;* aliquo quocumque *I.* sed si eo modo *ACGI;* sed si in eo modo *BDF.* ut]et *D.* 16 dicenti *DF.* 17 quae et *BF.* duris] illis *B.* quos ut quibus *E.* non *E.*

6. **quid autem illa . . . tertium:** granting that persuasion is the end of oratory (cf. Arist. Rhet. 1, 2, 1355b: ἔστω δὴ ῥητορικὴ δύναμις περὶ ἕκαστον τοῦ θεωρῆσαι τὸ ἐνδεχόμενον πιθανόν), *docere* and *delectare* are merely steps in a sort of geometrical progression, as Baldwin (2, 66) puts it, leading up to *flectere;* the one, *docere,* a necessary groundwork (*necessitatis*), the second, *delectare,* of use for the purpose of interesting (*suauitatis*), the third, *flectere,* the culminating point whose function is to win (*uictoriae*). The mutual dependence, yet individuality, of these offices is brought out even more clearly in the next chapter.

10. **manifestata:** *manifestare* for *manifestum facere* or *patefacere,* appears first in Ovid, Met. 13, 106, then in Late Latin in Just., Commod., Hier., Lucif. Cal., and in the jurists: cf. K.-Schm. s.v. Note, however, the use of the classical *patefacta* below.

13. *A further explanation of the meaning and relation of the offices of the orator. Their culmination in 'flectere.'*

14. **propte eos . . . locus:** in the preceding chapter, *docere* was shown to be of necessity (*necessitatis*); *flectere,* not of necessity (*non necessitatis*), but of victory (*uictoriae*); and *delectare,* not of necessity (*non necessitatis*). Here *delectare* is shown to be for interest

say that they ought to do what they do not know? And so it is that persuasion is not of necessity, because there is not always need of it if only the listener is in agreement with the one who is instructing, or also pleasing. But so it is that persuasion is of victory, because there is the possibility that a person may be instructed, and pleased, and still not give his assent. But what will the two former things avail if the third be lacking. For too, pleasing is not of necessity, since, indeed, when in a speech the truth is pointed out—a thing which belongs to instruction to do—it is not done by using eloquence, nor indeed is attention given to this, to please by the matter or the style itself, but the mere exposition of the truth gives pleasure through its very nature, since it is the truth. Whence it is that many times, even falsehood, when exposed and refuted, is a source of pleasure. For it does not please because it is falsehood, but because it is true that it is falsehood, the very explanation which shows that this is true, is a matter of pleasure.

13, 29. But because of those whom by reason of their prejudice truth does not satisfy if it is put in any other way than that whereby the speaker's words also are attractive, no small place has been given in oratory even to the art of pleasing. And still, when this is added, it is not enough for hardened natures who reap no profit from having understood and having enjoyed the

---

(*suauitatis*). For the place conceded to *delectatio* in rhetoric, cf. Arist. Rhet. 3, 1, 1404a: δίκαιον γὰρ αὐτοῖς ἀγωνίζεσθαι τοῖς πράγμασιν, ὥστε τἆλλα ἔξω τοῦ ἀποδεῖξαι περίεργα ἐστιν· ἀλλ' ὅμως μέγα δύναται, καθάπερ εἴρηται, διὰ τὴν τοῦ ἀκροατοῦ μοχθηρίαν. τὸ μὲν οὖν τῆς λέξεως ὅμως ἔχει τι μικρὸν ἀναγκαῖον ἐν πάσῃ διδασκαλίᾳ· διαφέρει γὰρ τι πρὸς τὸ δηλῶσαι ὡδὶ ἢ ὡδὶ εἰπεῖν, οὐ μέντοι τοσοῦτον, ἀλλ' ἅπαντα φαντασία ταῦτ' ἐστὶ καὶ πρὸς τὸν ἀκροατήν. Hence as Cicero also admits, even in the plain style some attractiveness of manner is permitted: cf. Orat. 6, 20: alii in eadem ieiunitate concinniores, id est faceti, florentes etiam et leuiter ornati. *Ibid.* 25, 83: illam autem concinnitatem, quae uerborum conlocationem inluminat iis luminibus quae Graeci quasi aliquos gestus orationis σχήματα appellant, quod idem uerbum ab iis etiam in sententiarum ornamenta transfertur, adhibet quidem hic subtilis,—nam sic ut in epularum apparatu a magnificentia recedens non se parcum solum sed etiam elegantem uideri uolet, eliget quibus utatur. De Orat 3, 25, 97: genus igitur dicendi est eligendum, quod maxime teneat eos, qui audiant, et quod non solum delectet, sed etiam sine satietate delectet.

14. **fastidientibus**: not frequent until Silver Latin: cf. T.L.L. VI, 309, 5–31.

17. **quos nec intellexisse ... profuerit**: the accusative and the infinitive with *prosum* is not found before Cic. Verr. 1, 39, 102. It occurs thereafter in Varro, in the poets, and often in Pliny and Late writers. Goelzer cites the following striking example from Avitus: quos contempores mundi amatoresque sapientiae, . . . quia fides defuit, non profuit operatos (esse): cf. K.-Steg. II, 1, 695; Goel. (2) 252.

nec docentis elocutione delectatos esse profuerit. quid enim haec
duo conferunt homini, qui et confitetur uerum, et collaudat eloquium, nec inclinat assensum, propter quem solum, cum aliquid
suadetur, rebus quae dicuntur inuigilat dicentis intentio? si enim
talia docentur quae credere uel nosse sufficiat, nihil est aliud eis 5
consentire, nisi confiteri uera esse. cum uero id docetur quod agendum est, et ideo docetur ut agatur, frustra persuadetur uerum esse
quod dicitur, frustra placet modus ipse quo dicitur si non ita discitur ut agatur. oportet igitur eloquentem ecclesiasticum, quando
suadet aliquid quod agendum est, non solum docere ut instruat, 10
et delectare ut teneat, uerum etiam flectere ut uincat. ille quippe
iam remanet ad consensionem flectendus eloquentiae granditate,
in quo id non egit usque ad eius confessionem demonstrata ueritas,
adiuncta etiam suauitate dictionis.

14, 30. Cui suauitati tantum operae impensum est ab hominibus, 15

1 docentes *F.* delectatus *G.*   profuerint *F.*   haec enim *A.*   haec] hoc *D.*
2 duo *om. I.*   conferunt]profuerunt *G.*   5 dicentur *CFG.*   uel]et *E.*   sifficiant
D.   6 consentire eis *A.*   uero] ergo *H.*   8 discitur] dicitur *DEH.*   10 aliquid
suadet *H.*   11 ipse *Maur.*   15 qui *E.*   opere *ACDG.*   impensus *D.*

1. **quid . . . intentio**: a restatement of the conclusion reached in chapter 12; but it is by such repetitions that Augustine hopes to drive home his point. *Flectere*, persuasion, is the final and most important stage in the 'rhetorical progression'; it is the end of oratory: cf. Arist. Rhet. 1, 1, 1354a: αἱ γὰρ πίστεις ἔντεχνόν ἐστι μόνον, τὰ δ'ἄλλα προσθῆκαι. Cic. De Inuent. 1, 5, 6: officium autem eius facultatis [oratoriae] uidetur esse dicere apposite ad persuasionem; finis persuadere dictione; De Orat. 1, 61, 260; *ibid.* 1, 31, 138: primum oratoris officium esse dicere ad persuadendum accommodate; *ibid.* 1, 49, 213: eum puto esse [oratorem], qui et uerbis ad audiendum iucundis et sententiis ad probandum accommodatis uti posit.

4. **rebus . . . inuigilat**: the dative with *inuigilo* is mostly Poetic, though it is found in Cicero.

si enim talia . . . discitur ut agatur: *docere* may at times end with itself; *i.e.*, to inculcate a truth may be the end of persuasion. Generally, how-
ever, *action* is the end of persuasion, and then not only *docere* and *delectare*, but also *flectere* must be used if the speaker expects *victoria*. Augustine returns again in chapter 25 to *docere* as an end.

9. **oportet . . . ut uincat**: a 'linking summary,' almost like a refrain; given in order to make sure that the 'rhetorical progression' is understood. With the doctrine of the *officia oratoris* thus inculcated, Augustine can safely pass on to a discussion of the styles, which flow from the *officia*.

quando suadet aliquid: the indefinite *quid* is generally used in Class. Latin after *si, ne, num, an, quo,* or *quando*, in preference to *aliquid*, which is employed only when a special emphatic force is desired. *Aliquid* is used with these particles in Late Latin, without this force: cf. St.-Schm. 482–83.

11. **ille . . . dictionis**: a final statement of the importance of *flectere*. Augustine finds the climax of his chapter in the culminating point of the *officia*.

12. **remanet . . . flectendus**: Late

instructor's speech. For what do these two things avail a person who both owns the truth and praises eloquence, but who does not give his assent, although it is for this alone that the speaker in an argument gives close attention to the matter which he is treating? For if the matters taught are such that knowledge of and belief in them are sufficient, agreement with them is nothing more than confessing their truth. But when a line of action is the matter of instruction, and that this be followed is the reason for the instruction, in vain is conviction that the words are true, in vain is the style of the speech pleasing, if action does not follow upon understanding. It is necessary, therefore, that the sacred orator, when urging that something be done, should not only teach in order to instruct, and please in order to hold, but also move in order to win. For indeed, it is only by the heights of eloquence that that man is to be moved to agreement who has not been brought to it by truth, though demonstrated to his own acknowledgment, even when joined with a charming style.

14,   30. And for the sake of this charm, such an amount of trouble

Latin; an extension of the use of classical *curo, trado, do, mitto*, etc., with the accusative of the gerundive (or nominative with passive verbs), to express purpose. Augustine makes use of *remanere* in the same construction in the Confessions (9, 2, 4): et ego premendus remanseram, nisi patientia succederet: cf. K.-Steg. II, 1, 731; Arts 115.

granditate = 'sublimity': as a technical term in rhetoric, very rare, but used by Cicero (Brut. 31, 121), and Pliny (Epist. 6, 21, 5): cf. Georges s.v.

14. *The Sophists' false conception and use of 'delectare.' Its legitimate place in Christian oratory is dependent on moderation in its use.*

15. **cui . . . lectitentur:** having explained the right order of 'rhetorical progression,' Augustine, in this chapter, forces his reader to conclude for himself the false basis of sophistic teaching, even from the standpoint of art, since contrary to the theory just explained, the principal aim of the Sophists, by their own acknowledgement, is to please. *Delectare*, he insists, is only the middle stage; it cannot be made the end. This is proved here,

and is concluded with finality in chapter 25. Concerning the character of Sophistic, Augustine says in Contr. Cresc. 1, 2, 3: quaedam sophistica et maligna professio, quae sibi proponit, *non ex animo, sed ex contentione uel commodo*, pro omnibus et contra omnia dicere. de hoc ait sancta scriptura: *qui sophistice loquitur odibilis est* (Ecclus. 37, 23). The Sophists' method, he describes in the same work (1, 1, 2), in explaining Prou. 10, 19: *ex multiloquio non effugies peccatum.* He says: multiloquium autem est superflua locutio, uitium scilicet loquendi amore contractum. plerumque autem loqui amant, etiam qui nesciunt quid loquantur, siue ad sanitatem sententiarum, siue ad ipsum qui arte grammatica discitur, integrum sonum ordinemque uerborum. It is of such as these that he speaks in Conf. 1, 18, 28: quid autem mirum quod in uanitates ita ferebar, et a te, Deus meus, ibam foras, quando mihi imitandi proponebantur homines, qui aliqua facta sua non mala, si cum barbarismo aut soloesismo enuntiarent, reprehensi confundebantur; *si autem libidines suas integris et rite consequentibus uerbis copiose ornateque narrarent,*

ut non solum non facienda, uerum etiam fugienda ac detestanda
tot et tanta mala atque turpia, quae malis et turpibus disertissime
persuasa sunt, non ut eis consentiatur, sed sola delectationis gratia,
lectitentur, auertat autem Deus ab ecclesia sua quod de synagoga
Iudaeorum Ieremias propheta commemorat dicens: *pauor et hor-* 5
renda facta sunt super terram; prophetae prophetabant iniqua, et
sacerdotes plausum dederunt manibus suis, et plebs mea dilexit sic.
et quid facietis in futurum? o eloquentia tanto terribilior, quanto
purior; et quanto solidior, tanto uehementior! o uere securis concidens petras! huic enim rei simile esse uerbum suum, quod per 10
sanctos prophetas fecit, per hunc ipsum prophetam Deus ipse dixit.
absit itaque, absit a nobis, ut sacerdotes plaudant iniqua dicentibus,
et plebs Dei diligat sic. absit a nobis, inquam, tanta dementia, nam
quid faciemus in futurum? et certe minus intellegantur, minus
placeant, minus moueant quae dicuntur; uerumtamen dicantur; 15
et iusta, non iniqua libenter audiantur; quod utique non fieret, nisi
suauiter dicerentur.

Psal. 34, 18   31. In populo autem graui, de quo dictum est Deo, *in populo*

Ier. 5, 30-31 (margin line 5) *Ier. 23, 29* (margin line 9)

---

7 fecerunt *H.*   9 plurior *CG* (uel purior *supra*) *H.*   10 esse]est *EH.*
11 fecit . . . prophetam *om. F.*   13 Dei plebs *E.*   diligat Dei *A.*   sic *om. EF.*
absit inquam a nobis *E.*   inquam]iniquum *D.*   14 futuro *E.*   15 uera
tamen *AC*; ueram tamen *I.*   16 iusta (*sic MSS melioris notae*; uera tamen dicantur
et iusta *editi* [*Maur.*]); iusta et *A.*   18 Deo *om. I*; Domino *BD*; in populo . . .
est Deo *om. E.*

---

laudati gloriabantur. Cicero also gives a discriminating characterization of the Sophists when he says: uerbi enim controuersia iam diu torquet Graeculos homines *contentionis cupidiores quam ueritatis* (De Orat. 1, 11, 47). For a brief account of the character of the Second Sophistic, cf. Norden 351ff.; Meridier 11ff.; Campbell 14–19; Lezat 11–19.

   cui suauitati . . . impensum est: Cicero uses in (*ad*) and the accusative with *impendo*. The dative appears first in Quintilian and Tacitus, in Silver Latin.

   1. non solum . . . uerum etiam: Cicero uses *uerum etiam* in his earlier, but *sed etiam* in his later works. The same preference is shown by Auct. ad Her., Caes., Varro, Sall., Nep., Liv., Curt., the two Senecas, Tac.; but Val.

Max., the two Plinys, Quint., Suet., and Late writers, as Arnobius and Augustine particularly, return to *uerum etiam*: cf. St.-Schm. 684. See *uerum etiam* also in 21, 45; 26, 57; 28, 61.

   2. quae persuasa sunt: *persuadere*, used transitively, is found in Seneca and in Late Latin: cf. K.-Schm. s.v.

   4. auertat autem Deus, etc.: in itself, because it is false, and has brought rhetoric into ill-repute, Sophistic deserves to be repudiated. Still, where it alone is concerned, Augustine's mode of attack is quiet, and at times even indirect. Here however, since the danger of its influence upon the sacred orator is felt, the writer in his indignation falls into the grand style.

   5. pauor . . . futurum: see Intro-

has been taken by men, that not only must we not follow, but even we must shun and detest the many abominably wicked and shameful deeds which are urged in this most elegant way by the evil and unjust, not to gain assent for them, but that they may be read eagerly for the mere sake of the pleasure in them. But may God keep from the Church what the prophet Jeremias relates of the synagogue, saying: *Fearful and dreadful things have been done in the land. The prophets prophesied falsehoods, and the priests clapped their hands; and my people loved such things: and what will you do in the future?* O eloquence, so much the more terrible as it is so unadorned; and as it is so genuine, so much the more powerful! O truly, an axe hewing the rock! For it was in this similitude that God Himself through this same prophet spoke of His own word, which He has uttered through the holy prophets. Far be it, then, far be it from us, that priests should applaud evil-speakers, and that the people of God should be pleased thereat! Far be such great madness from us, I say, for what shall we do in the future? And assuredly let what is said be less understood, less pleasing, less moving, but still let it be said; and let righteousness, not evil, gain a willing hearing! But this undoubtedly would not be possible unless it possess charm.

    31. But in a strong people, such as are spoken of by God—*I will*

---

duction, pp. 340–41, for the difference between the Old Version and the Vulgate, in this verse. The Old Version is followed here.

9. **o uere . . . ipse dixit**: Augustine echoes the Old Version rendering of Ier. 23, 29, which varies considerably from that of the Vulgate. The Old Version reads: nonne uerba mea sicut ignis, dicit Dominus, et sicut securis concidens petram? The Vulgate is: numquid non uerba mea sunt quasi ignis, dicit Dominus, et quasi malleus conterens petram?

12. **absit . . . ut**: in Eccl. Latin *absit* is commonly used either absolutely, or with an infinitive or dependent clause: cf. T.L.L. I, 210, 65–211, 18. See Parsons (178) and Arts (82) for its frequent use in Augustine's Letters, and the Confessions. It marks passages of impassioned expression. Note its absolute use below (1. 13), and also in 18, 36.

14. **et certe . . . suauiter dicerentur**: Augustine is claiming for the sacred orator a lower place than that of the Sophist in popular favor, if that must be, but a definite place, where truth may gain a willing hearing over falsehood. He sees the necessity of the concession that to make this hearing a willing one, the eloquence of the Church must also use, to a moderate degree, the quality of *delectatio*.

18. **in populo . . . ornarentur**: a caution, in consequence of the concession just granted. Even where legitimately used, *i.e.*, where charm is not employed to cloak falsehood, *delectatio* must in the speech of an ecclesiastic be used *in moderation*. The excess in St. Cyprian's Epistle, quoted below, not only proves this point, but also shows that ecclesiastics have equal ability with Sophists in the use of ornament, though because of their good taste, they generally prefer a restrained diction.

gravi laudabo te, nec illa suauitas delectabilis est, qua non quidem iniqua dicuntur, sed exigua et fragilia bona spumeo uerborum ambitu ornantur, quali nec magna atque stabilia decenter et grauiter ornarentur. est tale aliquid in epistola beatissimi Cypriani, quod ideo puto uel accidisse uel consulto factum esse, ut sciretur a posteris, quam linguam doctrinae christianae sanitas ab ista redundantia reuocauerit, et ad eloquentiam grauiorem modestioremque restrinxerit, qualis in eius consequentibus litteris secure amatur, religiose appetitur, sed difficilime impletur, ait ergo quodam loco: *petamus hanc sedem: dant secessum uicina secreta, ubi dum erratici palmitum lapsus pendulis nexibus per harundines baiulas repunt, uiteam porticum frondea tecta fecerunt.* non dicuntur ista nisi mirabiliter adfluentissima fecunditate facundiae, sed profusione nimia grauitati displicent. qui uero haec amant, profecto eos qui non ita dicunt, sed castigatius eloquuntur, non posse ita eloqui existimant, non iudicio ista uitare. quapropter iste uir sanctus et posse se ostendit dicere, quia dixit alicubi, et nolle, quoniam postmodum nusquam.

5

10

15

---

1 quia *D.*   2 diliguntur *CEFGHI.*   3 quo *E.*   4 oriuntur *C*; ornentur *FH*; orientur *G.*   aliquid] quid *B.*   5 puto] dico *E.*   consuete *C.*   6 sanitatis *D.* redundatione *F.*   7 uocauerit *F.*   9 religioseque *B.*   adimpletur *E.*   10 errati *D.*   11 pensulis *A*; nexibus pendulis *Cyp.* (*C. S. E. L.*).   12 uiteam *om. E.* 13 fecunditate *om. BDF.*   facundia *BDF.*   14 gratuitate *C.*   displicent grauitati *A.*   15 loqui *C.*   16 deuitare *E Maur.*   17 et posse sic dicere se ostendit *E.* quoniam et *E.*

---

1. **delectabilis**: Silver and Late Latin for *iucundus*: cf. Gell. 1, 4, 1: doctrina . . . utiliore ac delectabili: cf. T.L.L. V, 417, 65.

2. **ambitu** = περιόδῳ: cf. 7, 11.

3. **beatissimi**: beatus (class. 'happy'), through its frequent application to the dead, in such contexts as Apoc. 14, 13: beati mortui qui in domino moriuntur, came in Late Latin to take on the meaning of 'blessed': cf. K.-Schm. s.v.; T.L.L. II, 1914, 9-52.

5. **sciretur . . . reuocauerit**: an indirect question sometimes appears in its original tense, present or perfect, with a main secondary tense: cf. Lane 298; K.-Steg. II, 2, 191. See below 28, 61: ostenderet qualis . . . debeat.

6. **linguam** = 'style' (as in 7, 10), is Poetic and Silver Latin: cf. K.-Schm. s.v.

9. **quodam loco**: Epist. 1 ad Donatum 1.

13. **mirabiliter adfluentissima fecunditate, etc.**: Augustine's explanation itself imitates Cyprian's style. He is justified in appreciating the rhythm of this Epistle, while at the same time recognizing its profuseness. Norden (621, 944) quotes this passage as representative of Cyprian's care in the use of clausulae. Each least phrase is worked out with great precision, in perfect accordance with the laws of rhythm. For an analysis of the clausulae in this Epistle, cf. Norden (Nachträge 6).

praise thee in a strong people — that charm of style is not pleasing in which, though indeed falsehood is not involved, still, slight and unimportant truths are adorned with a foamy redundancy of expression, such as even great and enduring matters would not fittingly and worthily be adorned with. There is such an instance in one of the letters of the blessed Cyprian, which, I think, so fell out, or was thus done on purpose, in order that succeeding ages might know from what redundancy the soundness of the Christian teaching has recalled his style, and to what more dignified and reticent eloquence it has restricted him; which is such in his succeeding letters that he is safely admired, scrupulously copied, but with difficulty imitated. So he says in a certain passage: "Let us seek for that spot; the neighboring solitudes offer a retreat, where, as the wandering tendrils of the vine-shoots with overhanging interlacings creep along the trellis supports, the covering leaves have formed an arbor of vines." This is certainly expressed with marvellously flowing exuberance of language, but because of its excessive profuseness, it is not pleasing to the serious reader. However, those who admire this style think that of a certainty those who do not express themselves after this manner, but rather keep their eloquence within bounds, cannot thus be eloquent, and not that they avoid such language by preference. For this reason, this holy man shows that he *can* thus express himself, since he has done in this place, but that he does not *wish* to do so, for nowhere does he do so afterward.

adfluentissima: *adfluens* is frequent in Cicero, though not found in Caesar. Its superlative use, however, is confined to Late Latin: cf. Hier. in Iob. 38: adfluentissimam adfluitatem largitatemque diuinae gratiae: cf. K.-Schm. s.v.; T.L.L. I, 1244, 48-52.

profusione: *profusio* = 'profusion,' for Class. *effusio*, is Silver and Late: cf. K.-Schm. s.v.

14. **qui uero . . . uitare**: the Sophists' contempt for all that is not sophistic.

15. **castigatius**: the comparative of *castigate* is cited only for Late writers: Amm., Aug., Macr., Boeth.: cf. T.L.L. III, 537, 26-29.

16. **iudicio** is used as an ablative of manner from the time of Cicero on: cf. St.-Schm. 431.

17. **quia . . . quoniam**: A. here varies his casual particles, but on the whole in this treatise, as generally in Late Latin, *quia* is used preferably to classical *quod*, or *quoniam*: cf. St.-Schm. 725; 753. For this use in the Confessions, cf. Arts 95.

15, 32. Agit itaque noster iste eloquens, cum et iusta et sancta
et bona dicit—neque enim alia debet dicere—agit ergo quantum
potest cum ista dicit, ut intellegenter, ut libenter, ut obedienter
audiatur; et haec se posse, si potuerit, et in quantum potuerit,
pietate magis orationum, quam oratorum facultate non dubitet, 5
ut orando pro se, ac pro illis quos est allocuturus, sit orator antequam dictor. ipsa hora iam ut dicat accedens, priusquam exserat
proferentem linguam, ad Deum levet [*sic*] animam sitientem, ut eructet
quod biberit, uel quod impleverit [*sic*] fundat. cum enim de unaquaque
re, quae secundum fidem dilectionemque tractanda sunt, multa 10
sint quae dicantur, et multi modi quibus dicantur ab eis qui haec
sciunt, quis nouit quid ad praesens tempus, uel nobis dicere, uel
per nos expediat audiri, nisi qui corda omnium uideat; et quis
facit ut quod oportet et quemadmodum oportet, dicatur a nobis,
_{Sap. 7, 16} nisi in cuius manu sunt et nos et sermones nostri? ac per hoc, 15
discat quidem omnia quae docenda sunt, qui et nosse uult et docere,

---

1 egit itaque *ABDF*; age it itaque *G;* aget itaque *HI.*   iste noster *E*; iste
om. I. et (iusta) *om. ABCDFGHI.*   2 et bona et sancta *BEI.*   debet alia *B.*
aget *AGH.*   4 audiantur *F.*   7 doctor (*sic em.*) *F.*   accendens (*sic. em.*)
G. 8 ructet *ABDGH.*   10 delectationem *BCEFGHI*; delectatione *D*; (dilectatio-
nemque *editi* [*Maur.*]); -que]quae *D.*   sint *B.*   11 moda *A.*   12 uel]et *F.*
13 audire *F.*   omnium]hominum *E.*   14 quid *D.*   15 manus *G.*

---

15. *The place of prayer and of confidence in God, in Christian oratory.*

1. **agit . . . audiatur**: thus far there
is perfect agreement between Christian
and pagan orator.

3. **ut intellegenter . . . audiatur**:
intellegenter is used by Cicero only in
Part. Orat. 8, 28, and 29: ut amice, ut
intellegenter, ut attente audiamur. *Obedienter* is a favorite word with Livy, but
elsewhere is very rare. Classical Latin,
in this place, would most probably have
used a more concrete form of expression: a predicate adjective with *facere*
or *habere*: cf. De Orat. 2, 79, 323: nam
[et] attentum monent Graeci ut principio
faciamus iudicem et docilem; Auct. ad
Her. 1, 4, 6: ut attentos, ut dociles, ut
beneuolos auditores habere possimus.
This difference in expression is quite
in keeping with the great fondness for
adverbs found in Late writers. Adverbs

in -*ter* are especially favored by Augustine. Their use is a noticeable point of
style in his Letters (cf. Parsons 76–78),
as also in the present treatise. The preceding group appears again and again. It
pleases him because of its similarly ending syllables (homoioteleuton).

5. **pietate . . . orationum**: this is the
great mark of distinction between pagan
and Christian orator. As it is developed
in the remainder of this chapter, it shows
the Saint's intense realization of, and
faith in the existence and power of the
supernatural. Quite in keeping with his
style, however, Augustine does not disdain a play on words even here, though
his purpose in doing so—to mark more
clearly his antithesis—is plainly evident.
Note paragmenon coupled with chiasmus in *pietate magis orationum, quam
oratorum facultate*, and paronomasia in
sit orator antequam doctor. This light-

15,   32. And so, that orator of ours, in speaking of justice, holiness, and a good life, the subjects on which alone he should speak, strives, in as far as possible, when speaking on such subjects, to make his words understood, enjoyed, and persuasive; and this he should not doubt but that he can do if it is possible, and in so far as it is possible, more through the piety of his prayers than through his orator's skill, so that by praying for himself and for those whom he is going to address, he is a petitioner before a speaker. At the very time, then, when he is going to preach, before he loosens his tongue to speak, he should lift up his thirsting soul to God, in order to give forth what he will drink in, and to pour out what he will be filled with. For although on every topic which can be treated according to faith and love, there is much that may be said, and many ways in which it may be said by those versed therein, who knows either what is best for us on a special occasion to say, or what is best that others should hear from us, if it be not He who sees the hearts of all? And who can make us say what we ought, and in the manner we ought to say it, if not He in whose

---

ness of treatment, because of its restraint, and because of the writer's evident sincerity and earnestness, does not detract from the authority of the explanation.

se posse . . . non dubitet: *non dubitare* with the accusative and infinitive is rare in Classical Latin (except in Nepos), but becomes general in Silver and Late Latin. It is frequently used in De Ciu. Dei: cf. St.-Schm. 586; K.-Schm. s.v.; Colbert 59.

non: for *ne* in prohibitions is found once in Cicero (Att. 11, 9, 3), but becomes more common in the poets and in Silver Latin. It belongs properly to colloquial speech and grows frequent only in Late Latin: cf. St. Schm. 573-74.

7. **exserat** = 'puts out,' is mostly Poetic and Silver. Livy (7, 10) writes: Gallus linguam ab irrisu exserens.

8. **proferentem**: though redundant, this participle emphasizes the idea of 'speaking,' and serves also to balance *sitientem* in the following clause. Its absolute use is unusual, not being cited in the Lexica.

eructet: rare but classical.

9. **de unaquaque re**: cf. Cic. Font. 10, 21: unaquaque de re.

10. **dilectionem**: an Eccl. Word, found first in Tertullian: cf. T.L.L. V, 1166, 69–1167, 34.

12. **ad praesens tempus**: *in praesens*, 'for the present,' occurs often in Livy, Silver, and Late writers; *ad praesens* is found in Tacitus, Pliny the Elder, Suetonius, and Late Latin: cf. K.-Schm. s.v.

16. **discat quidem . . . in uobis**: the ecclesiastical orator must prepare himself with as great thoroughness as the pagan orator, but he must pass beyond the pagan in his belief that in reality all his power comes from God. Cicero himself, however, also advocates self-diffidence, as an essential to success in speaking. His lines are interesting as proving that humility is a natural, as well as a supernatural virtue. Cicero realizes that man cannot rely upon himself; Augustine knows that man not only cannot rely upon himself, but must rely wholly upon God. Cf. De Orat. 1, 26, 119: ac, si quaeritis, plane quid sentiam enuntiabo apud homines familiarissumos, quod adhuc semper tacui et tacendum putaui, mihi, etiam qui optime dicunt quique id facillime atque ornatissime facere possunt, tamen, nisi timido

facultatemque dicendi, ut decet uirum ecclesiasticum, comparet;
ad horam uero ipsius dictionis, illud potius bonae menti cogitet
_{Matt. 10, 19-20} conuenire quod Dominus ait, *nolite cogitare quomodo aut quid lo-*
quamini, dabitur enim uobis in illa hora quid loquamini; non enim
uos estis qui loquimini, sed Spiritus Patris uestri qui loquitur in 5
uobis. si ergo loquitur in eis Spiritus sanctus, qui persequentibus
traduntur pro Christo, cur non et in eis qui tradunt discentibus
Christum?

16, 33. Quisquis autem dicit non esse hominibus praecipiendum
quid uel quemamodum doceant, si doctores sanctus efficit Spiritus, 10
_{Matt. 6, 8} potest dicere nec orandum nobis esse, quia Dominus ait, *scit pater*
uester quid uobis necessarium sit, prius quam petatis ab eo, aut
apostolum Paulum Timotheo et Tito non debuisse praecipere quid
uel quemadmodum praeciperent aliis. quas tres epistolas ante
oculos habere debet, cui est in ecclesia persona doctoris imposita. 15
_{1 Tim. 4, 11} nonne in prima ad Timotheum legitur: *annuntia haec et doce?* quae
_{1 Tim. 5, 1} autem sint, supra dictum est. nonne ibi est: *seniorem ne incre-*
_{2 Tim. 1, 13} *paueris sed obsecra ut patrem?* nonne in secunda ei dicitur: *formam*
habe uerborum sanorum, quae a me audisti? nonne ibi ei dicitur:
_{2 Tim. 2, 15} *satis age, teipsum probabilem operarium exhibens Deo, non eru-* 20
bescentem, uerbum ueritatis recte tractantem? ibi est et illud:
_{2 Tim. 4, 2} *praedica uerbum, insta opportune, importune, argue, obsecra, in-*
crepa in omni longanimitate et doctrina. itemque at Titum, nonne

---

2 cogitat *B.*   4 in illa hora *om. I.*   6 sanctus Spiritus *C.*   7 et]est *E.*
9 quisquis]qui *C.*   non esse *om. E.*   10 docent *A.*   11 non *E.*   Dominus nobis
E.   pater]dominus *E.*   14 uel *om. B;* quid uel *om. D.*   15 habere debet *om. D.*
doctoris persona *Maur.*   16 legitur ad Timotheum *CGH.*   17 sunt *BD.*   dictum
est *supra E.*   ne]non *E.*   19 habe formam *E.*   sanorum uerborum *C Ver.An.*
Vulg.   audisti a me *A.*   nonne et *F.*   dicit *H.*   20 agens *F.*   22 importune
om. E.   obsecra]hortare *ABCDFGH*; exhortare *Ver.An.*

---

ad dicendum accidunt et in ordienda
oratione perturbantur, paene impudentes
uidentur. *Ibid.* 1, 26, 121: quidem et in
uobis animum aduertere soleo et in me
ipso saepissime experior, ut et exalbes-
cam in principiis dicendi et tota mente
atque artubus omnibus contremescam.
adulescentulus uero sic initio accusa-
tionis exanimatus sum, ut hoc summum
beneficium Q. Maximo debuerim, quod
continuo consilium dimiserit simul ac
me fractum ac debilitatum metu uiderit.

2. ad horam . . . dictionis: *ad* with
the accusative in place of the ablative
of time was used by Pac., Cato, Caes.,
Cic., Varro, and Silver and Late Writers:
cf. T.L.L. I, 556, 48ff. The formula *ad*
horam is cited for Sen., Quint., and Late
Latin: cf. T.L.L. I, 557, 1-5.

6. persequentibus: *persequor* = 'persecute,' is Eccl. Latin.

16. *The compatibility of ardent prepa-*
ration and total reliance on God. Proofs
from Scripture of the divine economy,

hands are both ourselves and our words? And for this reason the one who would both know and teach should learn, of course, all that he has to teach, and should acquire such skill in speaking as becomes an ecclesiastic; but indeed at the time of the sermon itself he should consider that admonition rather as befitting a good disposition, which the Lord utters: *Take no thought how or what to speak: for it shall be given you in that hour what to speak. For it is not you that speak, but the Spirit of your Father that speaketh in you.* And so, if the Holy Spirit speaks in those who are given over to persecution for the sake of Christ, why will He not do so also in those who give Christ to their disciples?

16,   33. But if any one says there is no need to lay down rules as to what and how men should teach, since it is the Holy Spirit who forms the teacher, he can say likewise that we do not need to pray, since the Lord says: *Your Father knoweth what is needful for you, before you ask Him,* or that the Apostle Paul ought not to have given instructions to Timothy and to Titus as to what or how to instruct others. Nay, he who has been given the role of teacher in the Church ought to have before his eyes three of the Apostle's Epistles. In the first Epistle to Timothy, do we not read: *These things announce, and teach,* that is the things which he explained above? Do we not read there too: *An ancient man rebuke not, but entreat him as a father*? In the Second Epistle does he not say: *Hold the form of sound words, which thou hast heard of me*? And does he not say to him in the same place: *Carefully labor to present thyself approved unto God, a workman that needeth not to be ashamed, rightfully handling the word of truth*? There too is this: *Preach the word: be instant in season, out of season: reprove, entreat, rebuke in all patience and doctrine.* And so too

---

i.e., the seeming interdependence of the natural and the supernatural, though in reality on God depends all.

For comparison of the Old Version and Vulgate readings of the verses in this chapter, and in the longer Scriptural quotations in the succeeding chapters, cf. introduction, biblical quotations.

23. **itemque** = *item*: in Late Latin *-que*, attached to introductory words, loses its own force, *e.g., utinamque = utinam;*

ideoque = *ideo*: cf. St.-Schm. 657. See this usage also in 16, 33; 20, 39; 20, 43.

ad Titum . . . dicit: the use of *dico, aio*, etc. with *ad* and the acc. of a person is cited first for Apul. Met. 2, 15. Due to its common use in the *Versio Antiqua* and in the Vulgate, it became widespread in Eccl. writers: cf. T.L.L. I, 1459, 67–72; K.-Schm. s.v.; Goel. (1) 329. Note this use below, again in this chapter, and in 18, 37; 19, 38; 28, 61; 7, 19.

dicit episcopum iuxta doctrinam fidelis uerbi perseuerantem esse

Tit. 1, 9 debere, *ut potens sit in doctrina sana et contradicentes redarguere?*

Tit. 2, 1-2 ibi etiam dicit: *tu uero loquere quae decent sanam doctrinam, senes*

Tit. 2, 15 *sobrios esse,* et quae sequuntur, ibi et illud: *haec loquere, et exhor-*

Tit. 3, 1 *tare, et increpa cum omni imperio. nemo te contemnat. admone* 5

illos principibus et potestatibus subditos esse, etc. quid ergo puta-

mus? numquid contra seipsum sentit apostolus, qui cum dicat

doctores operatione fieri Spiritus sancti, ipse illis praecipit quid

et quemadmodum doceant? an intellegendum est, et hominum

officia ipso sancto Spiritu largiente, in docendis etiam ipsis doc- 10

1 Cor. 3, 7 toribus non debere cessare; et tamen *neque qui plantat est aliquid,*

neque qui rigat, sed Deus qui incrementum dat? unde ipsis quoque

ministris sanctis hominibus, uel etiam sanctis angelis operantibus,

nemo recte discit quae pertinet ad uiuendum cum Deo, nisi fiat a

Psal. 142, 10 Deo docilis Deo, cui dicitur in psalmo: *doce me facere uoluntatem* 15

tuam, quoniam tu es Deus meus. unde et ipsi Timotheo idem dicit

2 Tim. 3, 14 apostolus loquens utique ad discipulum doctor: *tu autem perseuera*

in iis quae didicisti, et credita sunt tibi, sciens a quo didiceris.

sicut enim corporis medicamenta, quae hominibus ab hominibus

adhibentur, nonnisi eis prosunt quibus Deus operatur salutem, qui 20

et sine illis mederi potest, cum sine ipso illa non prosint, et tamen

adhibentur—et si hoc officiose fiat, inter opera misericordiae uel

---

3 decet *BFGHI Ver.An.*   5 condempnat *E.*   8 doctores *om. D.*   fieri *om C.*
aliquid *E.*   10 docentis *F.*   11 est esse *El Maur.*   12 neque qui plantat neque
qui rigat esse aliquid *E.*   Deum *El Maur.*   sed qui . . . dat Deus *DGH Ver.An.*
Vulg.   14 nemo]ne *E.*   dicit *E.*   pertineant *A.*   Domino *B.*   15 Deo (cui)
om. EH, del. B.   facere] ut faciam *A.*   16 quia *CEF et om. F.*   18 his
ABCDFGHI Ver.An.; his *E.*   tradita *BDEF.*   19 hominibus (ab) *om. AF.*
21 prosint] possunt *AE;* possint *CFI.*   22 fiant *E.*

---

1. **episcopum . . . debere esse**: cf. Vulg. Tit. 1, 7-9: oportet enim epis-copum sine crimine esse . . . amplect-entem eum, qui secundum doctrinam est, fidelem sermonem ut potens sit, etc. The Old Version, differing in the ninth verse reads: adplectentem id, quod secundum doctrinam est fidelis uerbi, ut potens sit, etc. The replacement of *secundum* by *iuxta* is Late: cf. St.-Schm. 503. While *perseuerantem esse* in place of *perseuerare* is obviously an echo of

the scriptural language above, it should be noted that such an analytical form of expression is a characteristic of the later Latinity in general: cf. St.-Schm. 606.

6. **quid . . . putamus**: the indicative in deliberative questions occurs in Early Latin, in the poets, in Cicero's early works and letters, and in Late Latin: cf. Lane 257.

7. **numquid** = *num*: the negative force is not lost here, as often in Late Latin: cf. St.-Schm. 649.

to Titus, does he not say that a bishop ought to be persevering *in that faithful word which is according to doctrine, that he may be able in sound doctrine to convince the gainsayers*? There again he says: *But speak thou the things that become sound doctrine, that the aged men are sober*, and so on. There, too, we read: *These things speak, and exhort, and rebuke with all authority. Let no man despise thee. Admonish them to be subject to princes and powers*. What then should we think? Can it be that the Apostle holds contrary opinions to himself, since though he says that teachers are formed by the action of the Holy Spirit, he himself gives others instructions as to what and how they should teach? Or are we to understand that even with the outpourings of the Holy Spirit, man's help too is not to be dispensed with in the instructing of even the instructors themselves, and still, *neither he that planteth is anything, nor he that watereth, but God that giveth the increase*? And so it is that though, too, holy men themselves should help, or even the holy Angels should lend their aid, no one learns aright the things which pertain to life with God, if he becomes not through God, docile to God, to whom it is said in the Psalms: *Teach me to do thy will, for Thou art my God*. And therefore the Apostle says the like also to the same Timothy, speaking certainly as the master to his disciple: *But continue thou in those things which thou hast learned, and which have been committed to thee: knowing of whom thou hast learned them*. For as the medicine of the body, which is administered to men by men is of no avail except to those to whom God restores health, since He can cure even without it, though without Him, it cannot, and

8. **operatione**: not in Cic. or Caes.; used by Vitr., Plin., Late writers; frequently found in Vulg.: cf. Benoist-Goelz.

9. **an intellegendum est**: sometimes the thought in the first part of a disjunctive question is involved. The second part, introduced by an, serves to force the acceptance of the positive or negative proposition, urged in the first question. Here *numquid* suggests our refusal of the first statement. This is enforced by the alternative an question, which as is evident to the reader, possesses the truth of the matter: cf. Gildersleeve 292.

10. **largiente** is used absolutely also by Plaut., Just., and later writers. For this usage in Ambrose, for instance, cf.

McGuire 24–25.

13. **operantibus** = 'administer' is Eccl. Latin.

14. **nemo . . . docilis Deo**: St. Augustine has the power of expressing truths of the deepest faith and spiritual penetration with such simplicity that the average reader is liable to see only the surface, and to miss the depth of meaning hidden within. This short sentence possesses the very key to all asceticism.

20. **operatur salutem**: *operari*, used transitively, is Eccl. Latin, being common to Vulg., Lact., Hier., Ambr., Aug., etc. Note the use of *operari* below, with a clause as object: cf. Benoist-Goelz. and Georges s.v.

beneficentiae deputatur—ita et adiumenta doctrinae tunc prosunt
animae adhibita per hominem, cum Deus operatur ut prosint, qui
potuit euangelium dare homini, etiam non ab hominibus, neque
per hominem.

17, 34. Qui ergo dicendo nititur persuadere quod bonum est, nihil 5
horum trium spernens, ut scilicet doceat, ut delectet, ut flectat, oret
atque agat, ut quemadmodum supra diximus, intellegenter, libenter, obedienterque audiatur. quod cum apte et conuenienter facit,
non immerito eloquens dici potest, etsi non eum sequatur auditoris
assensus. ad haec enim tria, id est ut doceat, ut delectet, ut flectat, 10
etiam illa tria uidetur pertinere uoluisse idem ipse Romani auctor
eloquii, cum itidem dixit: *is erit igitur eloquens, qui poterit parua*

3 etiam] et *E.*   5 qui ergo persuadere nititur dicendo *A*; qui ergo nititur
dicendo persuadere *Maur.*   6 illorum *ABEFGH.*   oret *om. F.*   8 -que *om.*
DGH.   9 loquens *I.*   eum] enim *E.*   assequatur *E*; sequitur *I.*   11 tria illa
Maur.   12 idem *E.*   is] iste *C.*   igitur erit *E. Maur*; erit *om. C.*   potuerit *F.*

1. **deputatur** = 'numbered among,'
is Late Latin: cf. Aug. Epist. 13, 16:
deputare inter poenas: cf. K.-Schm. s.v.;
T.L.L. V, 622, 77–623, 14.
17. *The development of the three
styles from the three functions of the
orator.*
5. *qui ergo . . . audiatur*: cf. Arist. Rhet.
1, 2, 1355b; 1356a: ἔστω δὴ ῥητορικὴ
δύναμις περὶ ἕκαστον τοῦ θεωρῆσαι τὸ
ἐνδεχόμενον πιθανόν. . . . τῶν δὲ διὰ
τοῦ λόγου ποριζομένων πίστεων τρία
εἴδη ἐστίν· αἱ μὲν γὰρ εἰσιν ἐν τῷ ἤθει
τοῦ λέγοντος (= *ut delectet*), αἱ δὲ ἐν
τῷ τὸν ἀκροατὴν διαθεῖναί πως (= *ut
flectat*), αἱ δὲ ἐν αὐτῷ τῷ λόγῳ διὰ τοῦ
δεικνύναι ἢ φαίνεσθαι δεικνύναι (= *ut
doceat*). διὰ μὲν οὖν τοῦ ἤθους, ὅταν
οὕτω λεχθῇ ὁ λόγος ὥστε ἀξιόπιστον
ποιῆσαι τὸν λέγοντα (= *libenter*). . . . διὰ
δὲ τῶν ἀκροατῶν, ὅταν εἰς πάθος ὑπὸ
τοῦ λόγου προαχθῶσιν (= *obedienter*).
. . . διὰ δὲ τοῦ λόγου πιστεύουσιν, ὅταν
ἀληθὲς ἢ φαινόμενον δείξωμεν ἐκ τῶν
περὶ ἕκαστα πιθανῶν (= *intelligenter*).
nititur . . . persuadere: *nitor* with
the infinitive is cited for Caes. (B.G. 6,
37, 10), Sisenn., Sall., Nep., Ov., Liv.,
before Silver and Late Latin: cf. K.-
Steg. II, 1, 667.

7. **quemadmodum**, 'as,' particularly
in answer to *sic, ita, eodem modo*, etc.
was used in colloquial speech from
Cicero's time on, and is often found in
Cicero's Letters. Quintilian advances
the usage a step farther, and employs it
to mean 'as for instance,' to introduce
examples: cf. St.-Schm. 765.
8. **quod apte . . . facit . . . potest**: a
formulation of the Peripatetic *mean* of
style. To Aristotle, and to all who with
him are governed by taste and reason,
rhetorical excellence depends on adherence to the 'appropriate': cf. Arist. Rhet.
3, 2, 1404b: 3, 2, 1404b: ὡρίσθω λέξεως
ἀρετὴ σαφῆ εἶναι· σημεῖον γὰρ ὅτι ὁ
λόγος, ὡς ἐὰν μὴ δηλοῖ, οὐ ποιήσει τὸ
ἑαυτοῦ ἔργον· καὶ μήτε ταπεινὴν μήτε
ὑπὲρ τὸ ἀξίωμα, ἀλλὰ πρέπουσαν.
Cicero sums up the doctrine of 'fitting-
ness,' among other places, in Orat. 35,
123: is erit ergo eloquens, *qui ad id
quodcumque decebit poterit accommodare orationem.* quod cum statuerit, tum
ut quidque erit dicendum ita dicet, nec
satura ieiune nec grandia minute nec item
contra, et erit rebus ipsis par et aequalis
oratio. In De Orat. 1, 61, 260, he speaks
concisely as Augustine: sit orator nobis
is qui . . . accommodate ad persuaden-

yet it is administered—and if this be done in kindliness, it is counted among the works of mercy or charity—so, also, aids to learning, when given by men, are of help to the soul when God makes them of help, who could have given his Gospel to man even without man's agency or help.

17,   34. He, therefore, who strives in speaking, to convince of what is good, since he is concerned with the threefold aim, viz., instructing, pleasing, and persuading, should pray and labor, as we have said above, to make himself understood, enjoyed, and persuasive. And when he accomplishes this rightly and fitly, he is not unworthily called eloquent, even though the agreement of his hearer does not follow him. For it is to these three points, viz., instructing, pleasing, and persuading, that the great authority on Roman eloquence himself seems to wish to apply those other three points in

dum possit dicere. In De Orat. 1, 32, 144, the conventional adverbs appear, echoed here and elsewhere by Augustine: audieram etiam quae de orationis ornamentis traderentur: in quo praecipitur primum, ut pure et Latine loquamur, deinde ut plane et dilucide, tum ut ornate, post *ad rerum dignitatem apte et quasi decore.* It should be observed that Augustine has followed much the same order in discussing these *praecepta* as Cicero, in enumerating them: *pure et Latine, plane et dilucide* were treated in chapter 10, *ornate* was touched on in chapters 11 and 14; *apte et decore*, the cardinal virtue of the orator, is here given its rightful place as essential to the offices and styles, and will receive due treatment as the styles are developed.

12. **is igitur, etc.**: Orat. 29, 101.

is erit igitur, etc.: Augustine's ingenious linking of Cicero's separate explanations of the styles and the offices makes a statement even more telling than Cicero's own expression of the relation between the two: cf. Orat. 21, 69: erit igitur eloquens ... is qui in foro causisque ciuilibus ita dicet, ut probet, ut delectet, ut flectat. ... sed quot officia oratoris, tot sunt genera dicendi: subtile in probando, modicum in delectando, uehemens in flectendo. Thus we have developed the three traditional styles: the plain (*genus submissum*), the

middle (*genus temperatum*, or *moderatum*), the grand (*genus grande*, or *sublime*). As the *officia oratoris* were found traceable to the Peripatetic School, so the styles grow out of Aristotle's conception of the two-fold aspect of persuasion, since as Cicero and Augustine show, the styles are merely an outflowing from the offices. Their history can quickly be summarized. Following the distinction of his master, Theophrastus took a step nearer to the definition of styles by applying Aristotle's division of πίστεις to language, speaking of λόγος πρὸς τὰ πράγματα and λόγος πρὸς τούς ἀκροωμένους (cf. fragment cited by Ammonius in Aristotelis De Interpretatione Comm. 65, 31). Of these parts the Stoics in the succeeding centuries, when they gained widespread influence, developed only the dialectical, and formulated a stylistic doctrine corresponding to pragmatic argument. Meanwhile, the Peripatetic School held to Aristotle's division of πίστεις, and in consequence must also early have developed a doctrine of style in accordance with it, though the actual record of this is not preserved. In *De Inuentione*, we find the first record of a tacit or implied recognition of two styles corresponding to Aristotle's two aspects of argument. It must be recognized, however, that there is a long break in the tra-

submisse, modica temperate, magna granditer dicere, tamquam si adderet illa etiam tria, et sic explicaret unam eandemque sententiam dicens: 'is erit igitur eloquens, qui ut doceat, poterit parua submisse; ut delectet, modica temperate; ut flectat, magna granditer dicere.' 5

18, 35. Haec autem tria ille, sicut ab eo dicta sunt, in causis forensibus posset ostendere, non autem hic, hoc est in ecclesiasticis quaestionibus, in quibus huius, quem uolumus informare, sermo uersatur. in illis enim ea parua dicuntur, ubi de rebus pecuniariis iudicandum est; ea magna, ubi de salute et de capite hominum; 10 ea uero ubi nihil horum iudicandum est, nihilque agitur ut agat siue decernat, sed tantummodo ut delectetur auditor, inter utrumque quasi media, et ob hoc modica, hoc est moderata dixerunt. modicis enim modus nomen imposuit; nam modica pro paruis abusiue, non proprie dicimus, in istis autem nostris, quandoquidem 15 omnia, maxime quae de loco superiore populis dicimus, ad homi-

1 temperata *E.*   granditer magna *A.*   2 illa tria etiam *E.*   -que *om. E.*
3 igitur *om. E.*   4 flectet *E.*   6 sicut]sic *D*; sic ab eo ut (*supra*) *B.*   7 possit *A.*   hic *om. ABDF.*   hoc est] etiam *E.*   8 in quibus *om. E.*   huius modi *H Maur.*   9 enim *om. E.*   11 uero modica *G.*   nihil]in *D.*   12 decernat]discet *E.*   13 hoc est] id est *E.*   16 ab *D*; ob *E.*

dition. Cicero merely echoes what was the traditional stylistic theory of his day. The same is, of course, true of the definition of the styles found in Ad. Her. 4, 8, 11 (sunt igitur tria genera, quae genera nos figuras appellamus, in quibus omnis oratio non uitiosa consumitur: unam grauem, alteram modiocrem, tertiam extenuatam uocamus). This latter, however, is the earliest extant occurrence of the threefold division of style. Our next mention of the three styles is found in De Orat. 3, 45, 177; 3, 52, 199; 3, 55, 212. These reference are mere allusions. Cicero gives his first clear explanation of the three styles and their development in Orat. 21, 69, quoted above. For a brief history of the origin and meaning of the characters of style, cf. Hendrickson (2) 249ff.

18. *The subject matter of the Christian orator is always great.*

6. **haec tria . . . forensibus posset ostendere:** Augustine uses *forensis* in its broadest sense, not to mean that kind of oratory (primarily forensic) called *genus iudicale* (δικανικόν) as distinct from *genus deliberatiuum* (συμβουλευτικόν) and *genus demonstratiuum* (ἐπιδεικτικόν), but to express 'legal' in the sense of that which is opposite to 'ecclesiastical.' —As a matter of fact, Cicero *does* exemplify the styles by reference to three of his own speeches wherein they are respectively outstanding. The plain style, he says, is used in *Pro Caecina* (an example of *genus iudicale*), the middle style in *Pro Manilia Lege* (*genus deliberatiuum*), and the grand style in *Pro Rabirio* (*genus demonstratiuum*): cf. Orat. 29, 102: tota mihi causa pro Caecina de uerbis interdicti: res inuolutas definiendo explicauimus, ius ciuile laudauimus,

that place where he has said, "He therefore will be eloquent, who can speak in a subdued manner on unimportant matters, in a moderate style on things of greater importance, and in a grand style on great matters," as if he would add also those other three points given above, and would express one and the same idea, thus: "He, therefore, will be eloquent who, in order to instruct, can speak in a subdued manner on unimportant matters; in order to please, in a moderate style on things of greater importance; and in order to persuade, in a grand style on great subjects."

18,   35. Now our authority could have illustrated these three points, explained by him, in legal cases; but he could not have done so here, *i.e.*, in the instance of ecclesiastical questions, the type with which that form of discourse is concerned which we wish to describe. For in the former, those matters can be called unimportant where money questions are concerned; those are great where it is a question of the welfare and life of man; but where neither of these is concerned, and it is not a matter of pleading or judging, but merely of pleasing the listener, such questions are midway between the two, and for that reason are called "middling," that is "moderate." For "moderate" gets its name from *modus*, "measure," so we do not apply the term properly, but misuse it, when we say

---

uerba ambigua distinximus. fuit orandus in Manilia lege Pompeius: temperata oratione ornandi copiam persecuti sumus. ius omne retinendae maiestatis Rabiri causa continebatur: ergo in ea omni genere amplificationis exarsimus.

8. **huius** = *eius*: *hic qui* for *is qui* appears first in the Silver period. For the encroachment of *hic* on *is*, cf. Meader 35; St.-Schm. 475; K.-Steg. II, 1, 621.

11. **ea uero . . . dixerunt**: Augustine, with Auct. ad Her., Cicero, and Quintilian, accepts as the origin of the middle style its rise as a *tertium quid* between the plain and the grand styles. See Ad Her. 4, 8, 11: grauis est, quae constat ex uerborum grauium et leui et ornata constructione. *mediocris est, quae constat ex humiliore neque tamen ex infima et peruulgatissima uerborum dignitate.* attenuata est, quae demissa est usque ad usitatissimam puri consuetudinem sermonis. De Orat. 3, 52, 199: est et plena quaedam, sed tamen teres; et tenuis, non sine neruis ac uiribus; *et ea, quae particeps utriusque generis quadam mediocritate laudatur. Ibid.* 3, 55, 212: figuram orationis plenioris et tenuioris *et item illius mediocris.* See also Orat. 26, 91; Quint. 12, 10, 58: *tertium . . . medium ex duobus.*

ut agat siue decernat: the employment of *siue* = *aut* is Late Latin: cf. St.-Schm. 676; Goel. (2) 319-20; Bonnet 315. See this usage in 26, 57.

15. **abusiue**: used by Quintilian, and Late writers: cf. T.L.L. I, 239, 17-30.

in istis . . . pecunia: one of the telling differences between ecclesiastical and the legal orator: the ecclesiastic's theme is always 'great'.

16. **populis**: *populus* in the plural, meaning 'people', is Poetic, Silver, and Late.

num salutem, nec temporariam, sed aeternam referre debemus, ubi etiam cauendus est aeternus interitus, omnia magna sunt quae dicimus, usque adeo ut nec de ipsis pecuniariis rebus uel acquirendis uel amittendis, parua uideri debeant, quae doctor ecclesiasticus dicit, siue sit illa magna, siue parua pecunia. neque enim 5 parua est iustitia, quam profecto et in parua pecunia custodire

Luc. 16, 10 debemus, dicente Domino, *qui in minimo fidelis est, et in magno fidelis est.* quod ergo minimum est, minimum est, sed in minimo fidelem esse, magnum est. nam sicut ratio rotunditatis, id est ut a puncto medio omnes lineae pares in extrema ducantur, eadem est 10 in magno disco, quae in nummulo exiguo, ita ubi parua iuste geruntur, non minuitur iustitiae magnitudo.

36. De iudiciis denique saecularibus (quibus utique nisi pecu-

1 Cor. 6, 1-9 niariis?) cum loqueretur apostolus, *audet quisquam uestrum* iniquit *aduersus alterum negotium habens, iudicare ab iniquis, et non* 15 *apud sanctos? an nescitis quia sancti mundum iudicabunt? et si in uobis iudicabitur mundus, indigni estis qui de minimis iudicetis? nescitis quoniam angelos iudicabimus, nedum saecularia? saecularia igitur iudicia si habueritis, eos qui contemptibiles sunt in ecclesia, hos collocate ad iudicandum. ad reuerentiam uobis dico.* 20 *sic non est inter uos, quisquam sapiens, qui possit inter fratrem suum iudicare? sed frater cum fratre iudicatur, et hoc apud infideles. iam quidem omnino delictum est, quia iudicia habetis uobiscum. quare non magis iniquitatem patimini? quare non potius fraudamini? sed uos iniquitatem facitis, et fraudatis, et hoc fratres.* 25 *an nescitis quia iniusti regnum Dei non haereditabunt?* quid est quod sic indignatur apostolus, sic corripit, sic exprobrat, sic incre-

1 salute *D*. 2 cauendum *G*. omnia sunt magna *ABGH*. 3 acquirendis rebus *E*. 4 admitendis *B*. 8 minimum est (sed) *om. F*; *est om. A*. minimo]minimis *B*. 9 id *om. C*. ut *om. I*. a puncto[ab cuncto *D*; a pucto *A*. 10 partes *A*. est et *H*. 11 mago in disco *B* ubi]ut *D*; ut (ibi *supra alia m.) B*. 13 quibus *om. D*. 14 dum *A*. 15 habens negotium *Maur. Vulg.* iudicati *E*. apud iniquos *A Vulg*.; apud iniustos *Ver.An* 17 iudicatur *ADEFGHI*. iudicatis *E*. 18 quia *EFI*. necdum *BDFGI*. 20 collocate]constituite *E. Maur. Ver.An. Vulg*.; conlaudate *A*. iudicandum et *E;* ad iudicandum *om. ACG Ver.An. (prope omnes MSS; quod etiam abest a graeco textu Apostoli [Maur*.]). 21 sapiens quisquam *ACGH Vulg*. 24 patimini iniquitatem *E*. 25 sed *om. E*. fratribus *BFH Ver.An. Vulg*.; (et hoc apud fratres *MSS quinque*; et hoc fratribus *alii tres [Maur*.]). 26 iniqui *A Ver.An. Vulg*. haereditabunt]possidebunt *H. Ver.An. Vulg*. 27 sic improbat increpat *E*.

9. **rotunditatis**: Silver and Late Latin. Frequent in Plin. Mai.: cf. 37, 73, 3: gemma rotunditatis absolutae.

26. **quid est quod . . . indignatur**: *quid est quod*, 'why is it that,' is found largely in Early Latin, but occurs also in Cicero, generally however with the hypothetical subjunctive, *e.g.* Clu. 22, 59: quid est quod plura dicamus? The indicative as expressive of a fact—as

"moderate" for "small." However, in these discourses of ours, since indeed everything, especially all which we address to the people from our high position, we must direct to man's welfare—and that not his temporal but his eternal welfare—where, besides, we must warn against eternal destruction, all that we say is of great importance, even to the extent that even money matters themselves, whether in regard to gain or loss, when put forth by the ecclesiastical teacher ought not seem of small importance, let the amount be great or little. For the matter of justice is not of small importance, and this surely we must safeguard even as regards a small amount of money, since the Lord says: *He that is faithful in that which is least, is faithful also in that which is greater.* And so a little thing is a little thing, but to be faithful in a little thing is a great thing. For as it is the nature of a circle that all the lines drawn from a point in the middle to the circumference are equal, and this principle is the same in a large disk and in a small coin, so when justice is administered even in a small matter, the greatness of justice is not diminished.

36. Therefore, when the Apostle spoke of worldly trials (and with what, truly, were these concerned unless with money matters?), he said: *Dare any of you, having a matter against another, go to be judged before the unjust, and not before the saints? Know you not that the saints shall judge this world? And if the world shall be judged by you, are you unworthy to judge the smallest matters? Know you not that we shall judge angels, not to speak of things of this world? If therefore you have judgments of things pertaining to this world, set them to judge, who are the most despised in the Church. I speak to your shame. Is it so that there is not among you one wise man, that is able to judge between his brethren? But brother goeth to law with brother, and that before unbelievers. Already indeed there is plainly a fault among you, that you have lawsuits one with another. Why do you not rather suffer wrong? Why do you not rather suffer yourselves to be defrauded? But you do wrong and defraud, and that to your brethren. Know you not that the unjust shall not possess the kingdom of God?* Why is it that the Apostle is so indignant, that he so upbraids, so reproaches, so rebukes, so threatens? Why is it that he calls the

here in Augustine—occurs in Verr. 4, 20, 43: cf. Lebreton 318; Lane 312; Gilder-sleeve 328.

27. **indignatur**: this absolute use of the verb begins in Silver Latin.

corripit = 'upraids,' though it occurs in Caes. B. G. 1, 2; Cael. ap. Cic. 8, 21; Ov. Met. 5, 565; and Hor. Sat. 2, 3, 257, is not frequent until Silver and Late Latin. Its absolute use belongs to Silver writers:

pat, sic minatur? quid est quod sui animi affectum tam crebra et
tam aspera mutatione testatur? quid est postremo quod de rebus
minimis tam granditer dicit? tantumne de illo negotia saecularia
meruerunt? absit. sed hoc facit propter iustitiam, charitatem, pietatem, quae, nulla sobria mente dubitante, etiam in rebus quam- 5
libet paruulis magna sunt.

37. Sane si moneremus homines quemadmodum ipsa negotia
saecularia uel pro se uel pro suis apud ecclesiasticos iudices agere
deberent, recte admoneremus ut agerent tamquam parua submisse;
cum uero de illius uiri disseramus eloquio, quem uolumus earum 10
rerum esse doctorem, quibus liberamur ab aeternis malis, atque ad
aeterna peruenimus bona, ubicumque agantur haec, siue ad populum siue priuatim, siue ad unum siue ad plures, siue ad amicos
siue ad inimicos, siue in perpetua dictione siue in collocutione, siue
in tractatibus siue in libris, siue in epistolis uel longissimos uel 15
breuissimis, magna sunt, nisi forte quoniam calix aquae frigidae
res minima atque uilissima est, ideo minimum aliquid atque uilissi-

Matt. 10, 42 mum Dominus ait quod eum qui dederit discipulo eius, non perdet
mercedem suam, aut uero quando iste doctor in ecclesia facit inde
sermonem, paruum aliquid debet existimare se dicere, et ideo non 20
temperate, non granditer, sed submisse sibi esse dicendum. nonne
quando accidit ut de hac re loqueremur ad populum, et Deus adfuit

2 Mach. 1, 32 ut non incongrue diceremus, tamquam de illa aqua frigida quaedam

1 anima *D.*   tam *om. MSS.*   3 illo]bello *E.*   4 pietatem quae]pietatemque
D. 5 mente sobria *G.*   dubitant *D.*   quamlibet *om. A.*   7 homines]omnes *D.*
8 uel (pro se) *om. C.*   ecclesiastico *D.*   9 paruula *E.*   11 rerum *om. B*;
uolumus *add. B.*   12 agatur *A*; aguntur *H.*   ad]apud *ADI.*   13 siue ad
(amicos) *om. D.*   14 siue ad inimicos *om. D.*   siue ad imperpetua et continua dictione *E.*   18 discipulis *I.*   19 aut]at *BD.*   20 paruum aliquid existimare debere se dicere *E.*   et]ut *I.*   21 esse *om. E.*   22 accidit . . . ad
populum *om. E.*   affuit *BCDE.*   23 non incongrue]congrue *MSS.*

cf. Mart. 11, 39, 9: corripis, obseruas,
quereris, suspiria ducis. Cf. T.L.L. IV,
1045, 9—1046, 43; K.-Schm. s.v.

exprobrat is used as an absolute
verb in Early, Silver, and Late Latin.

increpat and *minatur* are first used
absolutely by Vergil.

12. **ubicumque agantur**: *ubicumque*
is used from the time of Horace, Propertius, and Ovid: cf. St.-Schm. 487–88.
The subjective in iterative sentences

become increasingly common in Silver
and Late Latin. *Ubi* as an iterative with
the subj. is used by Liv., then by Vell.,
Tac., Justin.: cf. St.-Schm. 767; Gildersleeve 364.

**agantur ... ad populum ... inimi-
cos**: *agere ad populum* means 'to bring a
proposition before the people.' A technical expression is here extended to admit
of general application.

15. **tractatibus** = 'tracts' is Late

emotion of his soul to witness, with such numerous and harsh expressions? Why is it, finally, that he speaks in such a lofty strain on trivial matters? Is it that mere worldly questions deserved so much from him? Far from it! But he does so because of justice, charity, and righteousness, which no one in a sane mind can doubt but are great, even in things however insignificant.

37. Certainly, if we were to advise men how they ought to plead such worldly cases before ecclesiastical judges either for themselves or for their friends, we should be right in advising them to plead in a subdued manner, as of matters of small importance. But since it is a question of the eloquence of one whom we wish to be a teacher of those matters through which we are freed from eternal pains and brought to eternal happiness, it makes no difference where such things are treated, whether before the people or privately, whether with one person or with more, whether with friends or with enemies, whether in an unbroken speech or in a conversation, whether in tracts or in books, whether in letters, long or short, they are great; except perhaps that because a cup of cold water is a very little and unimportant thing, so what the Lord says is very little and unimportant, viz., that whosoever shall give one to his disciple shall not lose his reward; or, indeed, that when a preacher in the Church develops a sermon from this text, he ought to consider that he is talking on something of little weight, and so should express himself not in the moderate or in the grand style, but in the subdued style. Is it not true that when we chance to speak to the people on this text, and God's Presence is with us so that we speak not unfittingly, that a kind of a flame darts forth, as it were, from that cold water, which inflames men's cold hearts to the

---

Latin: cf. Hier. Epist. 54, 11: post scripturas sanctas doctorum hominum tractatus lege: cf. K.-Schm s.v.

16. **calix ... mercedem suam**: cf. Vulg. Matt. 10, 42: et quicumque potum dederit uni ex minimis istis calicem aquae frigidae tantum in nomine discipuli: amen, dico uobis: non perdet mercedem suam.

20. **et ideo**, as a conclusive participle connecting coördinate sentences, is rare in Classical writers, but is found more frequently in Late Latin: cf. K.-Steg. II, 2, 146. McGuire (43) notes its common occurrence in Ambrose. See this usage again in 22, 51.

23. **incongrue**: Late Latin: cf. Macr. S. 513; Aug. Epist. 17: cf. K.-Schm. s.v.

de illa . . . surrexit: cf. Vulg. 2 Mach. 1, 31–32: cum autem consumptum esset sacrificium, ex residua aqua Nehemias iussit lapides maiores perfundi. quod ut factum est, ex eis flamma accensa est.

flamma surrexit, quae etiam frigida hominum pectora, ad misericordiae opera facienda, spe coelestis mercedis accenderet?

19, 38. Et tamen cum doctor iste debeat rerum dictor esse magna-
rum, non semper eas debet granditer dicere, sed submisse cum aliquid docetur; temperate cum aliquid uituperatur siue laudatur; 5
cum uero aliquid agendum est, et ad eos loquimur, qui hoc agere
debent, nec tamen uolunt, tunc ea quae magna sunt, dicenda sunt
granditer, et ad flectendos animos congruenter. et aliquando de
una eademque re magna, et submisse dicitur, si docetur; et temperate, si praedicatur; et granditer, si auersus inde animus ut con- 10
uertatur impellitur. quid enim Deo ipso maius est? numquid ideo
non discitur? aut qui docet unitatem Trinitatis, debet nisi submissa disputatione agere, ut res ad dignoscendum difficilis, quantum datur, possit intellegi? numquid hic ornamenta, et non documenta quaeruntur? numquid ut aliquid agat est flectendus audi- 15

1 hominum corda uel *E.*   2 spe *om. F.* faciendas . . . coelestis mercedes *F.*
3 dictor]doctor *H*; doctor rerum *E.*   4 debet eas *E.*   10 aduersus *BDFH* ut
om. I.   12 non]cum *H.*   dicitur *EH* (*editi;* discitur *concinnius MSS* [*Maur.*]).
aut]at (*sic em.*) *B.*   15 numquid hic ornamenta . . . quaeruntur *om. H.*

19. *The purpose of the discourse must
be the ecclesiastic's guide to the use of
the styles.*

3. **et tamen . . . congruenter**: though
the ecclesiastical orator cannot be guided,
as the legal orator can, by difference in
matter (*parua, modica,* or *magna*), he
can, with the legal orator, take as norm
for the use of the styles the *officia oratoris*: cf. Orat. 21, 70: magni igitur iudicii,
summae etiam facultatis esse debebit
moderator ille et quasi temperator huius
tripertitae uarietatis; nam et iudicabit
quid cuique et poterit quocumque modo
postulabit causa dicere. It is again the
case of *apte et decore* (τὸ πρέπον): is erit
ergo eloquens, qui ad id quodcumque
decebit, poterit accommodare orationem
(Orat. 35, 123).

4. **submisse cum aliquid docetur**:
as an example of the plain style, Auct.
ad Her. gives a *narratio*, marked by a
free, unconstrained, conversational
tone; Cicero give *Pro Caecina*, a piece
of close reasoning; Augustine (Contr.

Cresc. 1, 16, 20) cites St. Paul on circumcision, or the distinction between
the law and grace, and (De Doctr. 4,
20, 39) the 3rd and 4th chapters of the
Epistle to the Galatians, all strictly dialectical. These models represent the two
aspects of *docere* and the plain style:
(1) its familiar, conversational side,
and (2) its argumentative side: both,
originally connoted in the Greek term
διαλέγεσθαι.

5. **temperate . . . laudatur**: Auct.
ad Her. gives as example of the middle
style, what seems to correspond to a
rationis confirmatio, i.e., the elaboration
of a proof; Cicero, the ornamental *De
Manilia Lege*, with its praise of Pompey;
Augustine, Cyprian's praise of virginity.
This style is that most fitting for the panegyric. It depends on sound and rhythm
for much of its pleasing effect.

6. **cum uero . . . congruenter**: to
exemplify the grand style a peroration,
highly figurative and elaborate, is given
by Auct. ad Her.; the impassioned *Pro*

accomplishment of works of mercy, through the hope of heavenly reward?

19, 38. And still, although our teacher is necessarily the spokesman of great subjects, he need not necessarily always speak in the grand style, but in a subdued manner when something is being explained, moderately when a thing is being criticised or commended; but when something ought to be done, and we are speaking to those who ought to do it, although they do not wish to, then the matter which is an important one, should be stated in the grand style, and in a manner adapted to move their hearts. But sometimes one and the same great matter is treated in a subdued way, if information is given; moderately, if commendation is made; and in the grand style, if adverse opinion is forced to change. For what is greater than God Himself? But is that a reason why He should not be studied? Or should one who teaches about the unity of the Trinity use other than subdued language if he wishes to make a matter difficult of distinction understood, in as far as it is possible? In such a case, are embellishments demanded rather than proofs? Is the listener to be persuaded to do something, and not rather to be instructed so as to learn something? But when God is being

Rabirio by Cicero; and 2 Cor. 6, 2-11 (ecce nunc tempus acceptabile, etc.) by Augustine. As the examples of the plain style represent the Peripatetic conception of λόγος πρὸς τὰ πράγματα, so this with the middle style represents λόγος πρὸς τοὺς ἀκροωμένους (ἔξω τῶν πραγμάτων).

8. **congruenter**: found twice in Cic.: De Fin. 3, 7, 26, and De Orat. 3, 10, 37: apte congruenterque dicamus; very rare in Class. Latin, but more frequent in Late writers: cf. T.L.L. III, 303, 1-33.

et aliquando . . . impellitur: the Auct. ad Her. (4, 8, 11ff.) exemplifies this by choosing a *narratio*, a *rationis confirmatio* and a *peroratio* to illustrate the different styles. All might belong to a single speech. Augustine proves the same possibility by showing, below, that the mysteries of God must be treated in the plain style, the praise of God in the middle style, the overthrowing of idols for the true worship of God, in the grand style.

11. **numquid ideo . . . instruendus**:

the *officium* here is *docere*, hence the style should be *submissum*.

ideo, used absolutely, occurs in Early, Silver, and Late writers: cf. St.-Schm. 684; K-Steg. II, 2, 146.

12. **unitatem**: Silver and Late: cf. Gell. 19, 8: singularis numeri unitas.

13. **disputatione**: the frequent use, throughout this chapter, of *disputatio*, *disputare, disserere*, to describe the plain style, shows the importance, in Augustine's eyes, of its dialectical aspect. In Contr. Cresc. 1, 13, 16, also, he says: quaedam uero subtiliter arguteque disserere, hoc est, dialectice, and in *ibid*. 1, 16, 20: si autem presse atque constricte, magis eum disputatorem quam dictorem appellare consueuerunt. The examples of this style which he cites below (20, 39) show even more clearly that he regards it not as something essentially simple and plain, but rather as the instrument of intricate argument.

14. **documenta**: the argumentative quality further emphasized.

tor, et non potius ut discat instruendus? porro cum laudatur Deus
siue de seipso, siue de operibus suis, quanta facies pulchrae ac
splendidae dictionis oboritur ei qui potest quantum potest laudare,
quem nemo conuenienter laudat, nemo quomodocumque non laudat! at si non colatur, aut cum illo uel etiam prae illo colantur 5
idola, siue daemonia, siue quaecumque creatura, quantum hoc
malum sit, atque ut ab hoc malo auertantur homines, debet utique
granditur dici.

20, 39. Submissae dictionis exemplum est apud apostolum Paulum,
Gal. 4, 21-26 ut planius aliquid commemorem, ubi ait: *dicite mihi, sub lege* 10
uolentes esse, legem non audistis? scriptum est enim, quod Abra-
ham duos filios habuit, unum de ancilla, et unum de libera, sed ille
quidem qui de ancilla, secundum carnem natus est; qui autem de
libera, per repromissionem; quae sunt in allegoria. haec enim sunt
duo testamenta: unum quidem in monte Sina in seruitutem gene- 15
rans, quae est Agar. Sina enim mons est in Arabia, qui coniunctus
est huic quae nunc est Ierusalem, et seruit cum filiis suis. quae
autem sursum est Ierusalem, libera est, quae est mater nostra, etc.

---

1 et non ut discat potius *CGH.*   instruendus est *E.*   2 ipso *H.*   3 qui potest
laudare *E.*   4 conuenienter non *E.*   quocumque *E.*   non *om. G.*   5 at si]at
siue (*sic em.*) *B*; ac si *I.*   7 ut *om. C.*   9 apud *om. D.*   11 audistis]legistis
CGHI Ver.An. Vulg.; egistis *E.*   enim *om. D.*   quoniam *E.*   12 et unum]
unumque *E.*   13 quidem *om. EI Maur. Vulg.*   14 in allegoriam *AF*; per allegoriam *Vulg.*; dicta *add. F. Vulg.*   15 quidem *om. E.*   a monte *ABC Ver.An.*
16 quae]quod *BCDGH.*   enim *om. E.*   quae coniuncta *ACDFG* (*MSS fere*
omnes [*Maur.*]); quae consonat *Ver.An.*   17 huic]ei *E.* quae nunc est *om. CF.*

---

1. **cum laudatur . . . laudat**: the
officium here is *praedicare* (*delectare*);
hence the style must be *temperatum*.
    2. **pulchrae . . . dictionis**: the mid-
dle style is distinguished by its beauty,
effected through figures, particularly
those of words and of rhythm (σχήματα
τῆς λέξεως): cf. Orat. 27, 96: est enim
quoddam etiam insigne et florens orationis pictum et expolitum genus, in quo
omnes uerborum, omnes sententiarum
illigantur lepores.
    5. **at si . . . dici**: the *officium* here is
flectere; the style, *grande*.
    6. **daemonia** = 'demons' is Eccl.: cf.
T.L.L. s.v.
        creatura: Late: cf. T.L.L. IV, 1116,
44–1117, 50.

20. *Examples of the three styles, taken
from St. Paul.*
    9. **submissae . . . exemplum**: see
Introduction, pp. 350–51, for a comparison of this and the following selections
with the Old Version and the Vulgate.
See Eskridge 37–49, for a graphic rhetorical analysis of these, as well as the
quotations from the Fathers, given
in chapter 21. St. Augustine chooses
as examples of the plain style, first, a
passage which, while being didactic,
shows a certain amount of attractiveness
through its incorporation of a narrative
element—an allegory; next, a selection
purely dialectical in its use of argument
and refutation. This choice is in strict
accordance with the conventional rhe-

praised either for Himself or for His works, what a glory of beautiful and splendid language wells forth for one who can go to the very lengths of praise of Him whom no one fittingly praises, but whom no one fails to praise in one way or another. But if He be not worshipped, or if with Him or even before Him idols be worshipped, either demons or some other creature, the grievousness of this offense, and the exhortation to men to be converted from it, ought certainly be expressed in the grand style.

20,   39. To speak more explicitly, we have an example of the subdued style in the Apostle Paul, where he says: *Tell me, you that desire to be under the law, have you not heard the law? For it is written that Abraham had two sons: the one by a bondwoman, and the other by a freewoman. But he indeed who was of the bondwoman, was born according to the flesh: but he of the free woman, was by promise. Which things are said by an allegory. For these are the two testaments. The one from Mount Sinai, engendering to bondage; which is Agar. For Sinai is a mountain in Arabia, which hath affinity to that Jerusalem which now is, and is in bondage with her children. But that Jerusalem, which is*

torical theory, as explained above. The best classical authorities bear witness to the plain style as being the instrument of both the ordinary conversational narrative, and of strict logical demonstration: cf. Quint. 12, 10, 59: itaque illo subtili praecipue *ratio narrandi probandique* consistet, sed quod etiam detractis ceteris uirtutibus suo genere plenum; Auct. ad Her. 4, 10, 14 (considering especially the colloquial quality): id quod ad infimum et cotidianum demissum est; Orat. 23, 76; 24, 79; 28, 99 (recognizing both, but emphasizing the dialectical): summissus est et humilis, consuetudinem imitans . . . ; acutae crebraeque sententiae ponentur et nescio unde ex abdito erutae; . . . ille enim summissus quod *acute* et *ueratorie* dicit, sapiens iam . . . qui potest tranquille . . . partite definite distincte . . . dicere. Cicero's choice, however, of *Pro Caecina* as his own example of this style is an even stronger proof of the importance he attaches to the dialectical element in the plain style.

10. **dicite . . . nostra**: Auct. ad Her. (4, 11, 16) warns against this style becoming, in the extreme, dry and lifeless: qui non possunt in illa facetissima uerborum attenuatione commode uersari, ueniunt ad aridum et exsangue genus orationis quod non alienum est exile nominari. This distinction, Augustine recognizes for he takes care to choose as his first example of the plain style this passage of real literary merit. Cicero himself admits the legitimate use of restrained figures in this style (as the allegory, used in this instance): cf. Orat. 25, 85: utatur uerbis quam usitatissimis, *tralationibus quam molissimis*; etiam illa sententiarum lumina adsumat, quae non erunt uehementer inlustria. In Orat. 33, 117, he explains the difference between the plain style in the hands of the orator, and in the hands of the dialectician proper: erit igitur haec facultas in eo quem uolumus esse eloquentem ut definire rem possit nec id faciat *tam* presse et anguste, quam in illis eruditissimis *disputationibus* fieri solet, sed cum explanatius tum etiam uberius et ad commune iudicium popularemque intellegentiam accommodatius. From his practice, it is clear that St. Paul also recognized this difference.

Gal. 3, 15-22 itemque ubi ratiocinatur, et dicit: *fratres, secundum hominem dico, tamen hominis confirmatum testamentum nemo irritum facit, aut surperordinat. Abrahae dictae sunt promissiones et semini eius. non dicit, 'et seminibus,' tamquam in multis, sed tamquam in uno, 'et semini tuo,' quod est Christus.* hoc autem dico, testamentum con- 5 firmatum a Deo, quae post quadringentos et triginta annos facta est lex, non infirmat ad euacuandas promissiones. si enim ex lege haereditas, iam non ex promissione. Abrahae autem per repromissionem donauit Deus. et quia occurrere poterat audientis cogitationi, 'utquid ergo lex data est, si ex illa non est haereditas?' 10 ipse sibi hoc obiecit atque ait uelut interrogans, *quid ergo lex?* deinde respondit, *transgressionis gratia posita est, donec ueniret semen cui promissum est, disposita per angelos in manu mediatoris. mediator autem unius non est, Deus uero unus est.* et hic occurrebat, quod sibi ipse proposuit, *lex ergo aduersus promissa Dei?* 15 et respondit, *absit,* redditque rationem dicens: *si enim data est lex quae posset uiuificare, omnino ex lege esset iustitia. sed conclusit scriptura omnia sub peccato, ut promissio ex fide Iesu Christi daretur credentibus,* etc.; uel si quid eius modi est. pertinet ergo ad docendi curam non solum aperire clausa, et nodos soluere quaes- 20 tionum, sed etiam dum hoc agitur aliis quaestionibus, quae fortassis inciderint, ne id quod dicimus improbetur per illas aut refellatur, occurrere, si tamen et ipsa earum solutio pariter occurrerit, ne moueamus quod auferre non possumus. fit autem ut cum inci-

1 itaque *E.* ibi *CEFGHI.* dicit enim *E.* 3 eius quod est Christus *I.* 6 quae *om. ABCG;* quod *D.* et *om. ABD.* annos quae *C,* (alia m.) *G* 7 est *om. F.* infirmat]infirma *A;* inritum facit *F;* irritum facit *Vulg.;* irritam facit *Ver.An.* euacuandas]infirmandas *C.* promissiones patrum *F.* 8 repromissionem]promissionem *ABCDFG.* 9 cogitatione *A.* 10 lex *om. F.* illa data *E.* 11 hoc *om. D.* 12 proposita *CFGH Maur.* 13 dispositum *BDF Ver. An.* (*MSS plerique* [*Maur.*]). 14 unius]unus *BE.* uero]autem *E Ver.An. Vulg.* 15 ergo] autem *E.* Dei est *F.* 16 et *om. E.* respondet *D.* redditque rationem]respondet rationemque *E.* 17 omnino]uere *I Vulg.* 18 omnia esse *E.* 19 eius modi]ex huius *E.* 20 nodosa *BDF.* quaestiones *H.* 21 haec *E.* agitur *om. E.* 22 incederint *D;* inciderunt *H.* refellantur (*sic em.*) *B.* 23 et *om. EHI.*

1. **ratiocinator:** Augustine thus advises us as to the quality of his second example. It is, in fact, a piece, plain and unadorned, thoroughly in keeping with its argumentative nature. One is reminded by it of Cicero's characterization of the plain style: et contra tenues acuti, omnia docentes et dilucidiora non ampliora facientes, subtili quadam et pressa ora-

tione limati (Orat. 5, 20). Cf. also Quint. 12, 10, 59: in docendo autem acumen. In Contr. Cresc. 1, 16, 20, Augustine again points out this passage of St. Paul as an example of dialectic, which he there, and in chapter 13 of the same treatise, characterizes by the adverbs *presse, constricte, subtiliter argute.*

10. **utquid** = *cur,* was probably used

above, is free: which is our mother. So too, where he reasons, saying: *Brethren (I speak after the manner of a man) yet a man's testament, if it be confirmed, no one rendereth void, nor addeth to it. To Abraham were the promises made, and to his seed. He saith not, "And to his seeds," as to many, but as to one, "And to thy seed," which is Christ. Now this I say, that the testament which was confirmed by God, the law which was made after four hundred and thirty years, doth not weaken, to make the promises of no effect. For if the inheritance be of the law, it is no more of promise. But God gave it to Abraham by promise.* And because it might occur to the mind of the listener, "But why, therefore, was the law given if there is no inheritance of the law?" he put this objection to himself, as if raising a question: *What then was the law? Then he answered: It was set for the sake of transgression, until the seed should come, to whom he made the promise, being ordained by angels in the hand of a mediator. Now a mediator is not of one: but God is one.* And here arose an objection, which he put to himself: *Was the law then against the promises of God?* And he answered, *God forbid*, and gave his reason, saying: *For if there had been a law given which could give life, verily justice should have been by the law. But the Scripture hath concluded all under sin, that the promise by the faith of Jesus Christ might be given to them that believe* — or something to that effect. It belongs, therefore, to the duty of the teacher not only to make clear obscure matters, and to solve the difficulties in questions, but also while this is being done, to anticipate other questions, which perchance may come up, so that our words may not be disproved or refuted by them, provided of course that the solution itself, also, of these occur along with them, lest we bring up what we cannot

in the colloquial speech even of Cicero's time, but did not become common in the literary language until its free use by Eccl. writers, who were influenced by its frequent usage in the Latin versions of the Scripture, where it renders ἵνα τί: cf. Rönsch 253–54; Goel. (1) 431; (2) 687; St.-Schm. 647; McGuire 148.

19. **pertinet, etc.**: Augustine's conclusion as to the most important function of the plain style. He concerns himself here only with its argumentative side: exposition, proof, refutation. See Cicero's characterization of *Pro Caecina* (Orat.

29, 102): res inuolutas definiendo explicauimus, . . . uerba ambigua distinximus; also 33, 116: explicanda est saepe uerbis mens nostra de quaque re atque inuoluta rei notitia definiendo aperienda est; and his description of the *narratio* and *confirmatio* in Orat. 35, 122: rem breuiter exponere et probaliter et aperte, ut quid agatur intellegi possit; sua confirmare, aduersaria euertere, eaque efficere non perturbate, sed singulis argumentationibus ita concludendis, ut efficiatur quod sit consequens iis quae sumentur ad quamque rem confirmandam.

dentes quaestioni aliae quaestiones, et aliae rursus incidentibus
incidentes pertractantur atque soluuntur, in eam longitudinem
ratiocinationis extendatur intentio, ut nisi memoria plurimum
ualeat atque uigeat, ad caput unde agebatur disputator redire non
possit. ualde autem bonum est, ut quidquid contradici potest, si 5
occurrerit, refutetur, ne ibi occurrat, ubi non erit qui respondeat,
aut praesenti quidem, sed tacenti occurrat, et minus sanatus
abscedat.

1 Tim. 5, 1-2   40. In illis autem apostolicis uerbis dictio temperata est: *seni-
orem ne increpaueris, sed obsecra ut patrem, iuniores, ut fratres,* 10
Rom. 12, 1 *anus ut matres, adolescentulas ut sorores.* et in illis: *obsecro autem
uos, fratres, per miserationem Dei, ut exhibeatis corpora uestra,
hostiam uiuam, sanctam, Deo placentem.* et totus fere ipsius exhortationis locus temperatum habet elocutionis genus, ubi illa pul-

---

1 rursus]quidem *E.*   2 incidentes principes *A.*   soluantur *F*; ut *add. EI.*
12 misericordiam *CFGH Ver.An. Vulg.*   uos per miserationem fratres Dei *I.*
13 uiuentem *A Ver.An. Vulg.*   ipsius *om. E.*   14 locutionis *H.*

---

3. **memoria**: Augustine refers not to
verbal memory such as he discusses in
chapter 29, but to that which, as Cicero
says, is proper to orators: memory of
things: cf. De Orat. 2, 88, 359: sed uerborum *memoria,* quae minus est nobis
necessaria, maiore imaginum uarietate
distinguitur. . . . *rerum memoria propria
est oratoris*; eam singulis personis bene
positis notare possimus, ut sententias
imaginibus ordinem locis comprehen-
damus.

5. **ualde . . . bonum**: *ualde* with a
positive adjective to express a superlative, belongs to the *sermo plebeius.* It
was introduced into the written language
by Cicero, being frequently used in his
Letters. Found occasionally in Silver
Latin, this usage becomes common in
Late, especially in Eccl. writers, due to
its frequent occurrence in the Scriptures:
cf. K.-Schm. s.v.; Bonnet 308. Augustine makes use of this idiom rather frequently in the Confessions: cf. Arts 43.

contradici, as one word, occurs
first in Silver Latin, beginning with Sen.

Rhet., in whose writings, moreover, first
appears *contradictio*: cf. T.L.L. IV, 753,
71–81.

9. **dictio temperata**, viewed negatively, is that style which is neither plain
nor grand, but something between: cf.
Auct. ad Her. 4, 9, 13: in mediocri figura
uersabitur oratio, si haec, ut ante dixi,
aliquantulum demiserimus neque tamen
ad infimum descenderimus. Orat. 6, 21:
est autem quidam interiectus inter hos
medius et quasi temperatus nec acumine
posteriorum nec fulmine utens superio-
rum, uicinus amborum, in neutro excel-
lens, utriusque particeps uel utriusque,
si uerum quaerimus, potius expers. *Ibid.*
26, 91: uberius est aliud aliquantoque
robustius quam hoc humile, de quo dictum est, summissius autem quam illud,
de quo iam dicetur, amplissimum. . . .
est enim plenius quam hoc enucleatum,
quam autem illud ornatum copiosumque
summissius. But the middle style has
also a positive side, an individuality all
its own, viewed as a γένος ἀνθηρόν: cf.
Quint. 12, 10, 58: tertium alii medium

remove. On the other hand, it happens sometimes in the handling and solving of certain questions coming out of a first question, and of others coming out of these, that the strain of reasoning is drawn out to such an extent, that unless the disputant's memory be very strong and vigorous, he is not able to go back to the original question. But it is a very good thing to answer whatever objection can be raised, as it occurs, for fear lest it occur at a time when there will be no one to answer it, or lest it occur to someone present indeed, but silent, and he go away unhelped.

40. But in the following words from the Apostle we have an example of the moderate style: *An ancient man rebuke not, but entreat him as a father: young men, as brethren: old women, as mothers: young women, as sisters.* And in these words: *I beseech you therefore, brethren, by the mercy of God, that you present your bodies a living sacrifice, holy, pleasing unto God.* And almost the whole passage containing this exhortation is in the moderate style, but it is particularly fine in those places where, as with debts

ex duobus alii floridum (namque id ἀνθηρόν appellant) addiderunt. This quality he explains in 12, 10, 60: medius hic modus et translationibus crebrior et figuris erit iucundior, egressionibus amoenus, compositione aptus, sententiis dulcis, lenior tamen ut amnis lucidus quidem sed uirentibus utrinque sepibus inumbratus. Cicero describes the positive side of the middle style by the term *suauitas*: cf. Orat. 26, 91ff.: hoc in genere neruorum uel minimum, suauitatis autem est uel plurimum. . . . huic omnia dicendi ornamenta conueniunt plurimumque est in hac orationis forma suauitatis; *ibid.* 27, 96: est enim quoddam etiam insigne et florens orationis pictum et expolitum genus in quo omnes uerborum, omnes sententiarum illigantur lepores. The identification, however, of γένος ἀνθηρόν and *genus medium* was recognized, even in antiquity, as a distortion. The florid style is not in reality a stage intermediate between the plain and the grand style. It

is in essence merely one *aspect* of that division of language called by Theophrastus λόγος πρὸς τοὺς ἀκροωμένους, of which the grand style is another; and λόγος πρὸς τοὺς ἀκροωμένους is set over against λόγος πρός τὰ πράγματα (the plain style). The distinction between the grand and the middle style was apparently brought about at a time subsequent to Theophrastus, when the fame of Demosthenes was beginning to encroach upon that of Isocrates. It is certain that at a later period the doctrine of figures helped toward distinguishing between the two types, the *figurae uerborum* (σχήματα λέξεως) characterizing the florid style, the *figurae sententiarum* (σχήματα διανοίας), the grand style. The reason for calling the florid style middle is still a matter of discussion with scholars: cf. Hendrickson (2) 286–88.

13. **exhortationis**: not in Cicero; often in Silver and Late Latin, especially in Eccl. writers: cf. K.-Schm. s.v.

chriora sunt, in quibus propria propriis tamquam debita reddita

Rom. 12, 6-16 decenter excurrunt, sicuti est: *habentes dona diuersa secundum gratiam quae data est nobis; siue prophetiam, secundum regulam fidei; siue ministerium, in ministrando; siue qui docet, in doctrina; siue qui exhortatur, in exhortatione; qui tribuit, in simplicitate;* 5 *qui praeest, in sollicitudine; qui miseretur, in hilaritate. dilectio sine simulatione; odio habentes malum, adhaerentes bono; charitate fraternitatis inuicem diligentes, honore mutuo praeuenientes, studio non pigri, spiritu feruentes, Domino seruientes, spe gaudentes, in tribulatione patientes, orationi instantes, necessariis sanc-* 10 *torum communicantes, hospitalitatem sectantes. benedicite persequentes uos; benedicite, et nolite maledicere. gaudere cum gaudentibus, flere cum flentibus; idipsum inuicem scientes.* et quam pulchre ista omnia sic effusa, bimembri circuitu terminantur, *non alta*

Rom. 13, 6-8 *sapientes, sed humilibus consentientes!* et aliquanto post: *in hoc* 15 *ipso* inquit *perseuerantes, reddite omnibus debita; cui tributum, tributum; cui uectigal, uectigal; cui timorem, timorem; cui honorem, honorem.* quae membratim fusa clauduntur etiam ipsa cir-

1 in quibus]ubi *CG*.   reddidit *DF*; reddita debita *E*.   5 siue *om. EI Ver.An. Vulg.*   7 simulatio *D*.   odio habentes malum]odientes malum *D Ver.An. Vulg.* bonum *D*.   charitatem *F*.   8 mutuo]inuicem *I Ver.An. Vulg.*   10 necessitatibus *EHI Ver.An. Vulg. Maur.*   11 persequentibus *FGHI Maur. Vulg. Ver.An.* 12 benedicite *om. E Ver.An.*   gaudentibus et *I*.   16 ipsum *CFGH Ver.An. Vulg.* 18 ipso *ACDE*, (*supra*) *G, H*.

1. **propria . . . excurrunt**: parallelism, particularly antithetical, and often emphasized by similar endings in clauses, amounting at times to rhymes (*homoioteleuton*), is a most important feature in the middle style, which differs from the grand style in its use of *figurae uerborum* (σχήματα λέξεως) rather than of *figurae sententiarum* (σχήματα διανοίας), and in the importance which it attaches to sound and rhythm rather than to vehemence of feelings and emotion. It traces its sources to Gorgias and the first Sophists; it reached perfection in Isocrates: cf. Orat. 12, 38: datur etiam uenia concinnitati sententiarum et arguti certique et cirumscripti uerborum ambitus concenduntur, de industriaque non insidiis sed aperte ac palam elaboratur,

ut uerba uerbis quasi demensa et paria respondeant, ut crebro conferantur pugnantia comparenturque contraria et ut pariter extrema terminentur eundemque referrant in cadendo sonum; quae in ueritate causarum et rarius multo facimus et certe occultius. in Panathenaico autem Isocrates ea studiose consectatum fatetur; non enim ad iudiciorum certamen, *sed ad uoluptatem aurium* scripserat, haec tractasse Thrasymachum Calchedonium primum et Leontinum ferunt Gorgiam, Theodorum inde Byzantium multosque alios, quos λογοδαιδάλους appellat in Phaedro Socrates. Cicero later (Orat. 49, 163) distinguishes beween the two elements here involved, sound and rhythm, and gives them more detailed treatment. He says: duae sunt igitur res, quae per-

and payments, like things stand out with like, thus: *And having different gifts, according to the grace that is given us, either prophecy, to be used according to the rules of faith, or ministry in ministering; or he that teacheth, in doctrine; he that exhorteth, in exhorting; he that giveth, with simplicity; he that ruleth, with carefulness; he that showeth mercy, with cheerfulness. Let love be without dissimulation, hating that which is evil, cleaving to that which is good. Loving one another with the charity of brotherhood, with honor preventing one another. In carefulness, not slothful. In spirit fervent. Serving the Lord. Rejoicing in hope. Patient in tribulation. Instant in prayer. Communicating to the necessities of the saints. Pursuing hospitality. Bless them that persecute you: bless, and curse not. Rejoice with them that rejoice: weep with them that weep. Being of one mind one toward another.* And how beautifully is all this, flowing forth as it does, brought to a conclusion in a period of two *membra*: *Not minding high things, but consenting to the humble.* And a little below: *Persevering in this, render to all men their dues. Tribute, to whom tribute is due: custom, to whom custom: fear, to whom fear: honor to whom honor.* And this, flowing forth in *membra*, likewise

mulceant aures, sonus et numerus. de numero mox, nunc de sono quaerimus, ... finiuntur [uerba] aut ipsa compositione aut quasi sua sponte, ut quaedam genera uerborum, in quibus ipsis concinnitas inest; *quae siue casus habent in exitu similes siue paribus paria redduntur* siue opponuntur contraria, suapte natura numerosa sunt, etiam si nihil est factum de industria. in huius concinnitatis consectatione Gorgiam fuisse principem accepimus. —For the importance of this parallelism of structure in the syle of Christian Latin literature, cf. Norden 616ff.

2. **decenter**: Poetic, Silver, and Late: cf. T.L.L. V, 136, 53—137, 33.

habentes dona, etc.: cf. Eskridge (47): "It would be difficult to find in Sacred literature a specimen of oratory illustrating more perfectly the temperate style than the above extract from the Epistle of the Romans. A very high degree of art is employed in a very delicate and inconspicuous fashion. The passage is worthy of a great religious teacher, and

unquestionably has the right to stand as a model of sacred eloquence."Analysis of its sentence structure, or *compositio* shows the reason for this. It is most carefully constructed both in matter of sound and of rhythm, parallelism and homoioteleuton being most meticulously, but at the same time most artistically worked out. Its *compositio* is as follows: three introductory *caesa*, seven pairs of balanced *caesa*, a period of six *caesa* and seven *membra* interlocked, a period of two pairs of balanced *membra* closed by a single *membrum*, a closing period of two balanced *membra* (cf. Eskridge 46–47).

14. **sic effusa**: rhythm: the middle style is commonly likened to a gently flowing river: cf. Quint. 12, 10, 60: lenior tamen ut amnis lucidus quidem sed uirentibus utrinque sepibus inumbratus. Orat. 6, 21: isque uno tenore, ut aiunt, in dicendo *fluit* nihil afferens praeter facilitatem et aequabilitatem. *Ibid.* 27, 96: hoc totum e sophistarum fontibus defluxit in forum.

cuitu, quem duo membra contexunt, *nemini quidquam debeatis,* Rom. 13, 12-14 *nisi ut inuicem diligatis.* et post paululum, *nox praecessit* inquit *dies autem appropinquauit. abiciamus itaque opera tenebrarum, et induamus nos arma lucis; sicut in die honeste ambulemus; non in comessationibus et ebrietatibus, non in cubilibus et impudicitiis, non in contentione et aemulatione; sed induite Dominum Iesum Christum, et carnis prouidentiam ne feceritis in concupiscentiis.* quod si quisquam ita diceret: 'et carnis prouidentiam ne in concupiscentiis feceritis,' sine dubio aures clausula numerosiore mulceret; sed grauior interpres etiam ordinem maluit tenere uerborum. quomodo autem hoc in graeco eloquio sonet, quo est locutus apos-

2 inquit *om. EI.* 3 appropinquabit *DI.* itaque]ergo *EFI Ver.An. Vulg.* 4 induamur *EI Ver.An. Vulg.* 6 induimini *AEI Vulg.* 7 prouidentiam]curam *F Ver.An. Vulg.* concupiscentias *A*; desideriis *F.* 8 concupiscentias *ACDFH*; concupiscentiam *G*; concupiscentia (*sic em.*) *B.* 9 quod si quis . . . feceritis *om. I.* 11 quo]quod *ADEFHI.*

1. **contexunt**: Poetic, Silver, and Late: cf. Quint. 9, 4, 19: oratio alla uincta atque contexta, soluta alia: cf. T.L.L. IV, 692, 38–85. *Contexo*, meaning in its literal sense 'interweave', is well chosen, expressive of the care as to sound and rhythm, of rhetorical sentence structure, where *caesa* and *membra* form the material, as it were, for an elaborate oratorical tapestry.

8. **quod si . . . currere numerose**: having treated, at least suggestively, St. Paul's handling of sound (i.e. his use of parallelism), Augustine turns to the question of rhythm (cf. Orat. 49, 163: duae sunt . . . res quae permulceant aures, sonus et numerus), and though his treatment here is a summary one, it is broad and suggestive. The ancients believed in prose rhythm, and used it, though they were unable to give an accurate account of its nature. Cicero states that prose rhythm is something that belongs to nature, and that the art of rhythm is merely the formulation of laws established by nature: cf. Orat. 55, 183: esse ergo in oratione numerum quendam non est difficile cognoscere. iudicat enim sensus; in quo est iniquum quod accidat non agnoscere, si cur id accidat reperire nequeamus. neque enim ipse uersus ratione est cognitus, sed natura atque sensu, quem dimensa ratio docuit quid acciderit. ita notatio naturae et animaduersio peperit artem. In 20, 67, he defines rhythm in its broadest sense: quicquid est enim, quod sub aurium mensuram aliquam cadit, etiam si abest a uersu—nam id quidem orationis est uitium—numeros uocatur, qui Graece ῥυθμός dicitur. —Rhythm must have place in the whole body of the oration, but especial care is demanded by the close of *membra* and periods, *i.e.* by the clausulae: cf. Quint. 9, 4, 61: et in omni quidem corpore totoque (ut ita dixerim) tractu numerus insertus. . . . magis tamen et desideratur in clausulis et apparet: primum quia sensus omnis habet suum finem possitque naturale interuallum, quo a sequentis initio diudatur; deinde quod aures continuam uocem secutae ductaeque uelut prono decurrentis orationis flumine tum magis iudicant, cum ille impetus stetit et intuendi tempus dedit. non igitur durum sit neque abruptum, quo animi uelut respirant ac reficiuntur. haec est sedes orationis, hoc auditor expectat, hic laus omnis declamat. For a study of Cicero's use of clausulae, cf. especially Zielinski

is concluded by a period made up of two *membra*: *Owe no man any-thing, but to love one another.* And a little afterward: *The night is passed, and the day is at hand. Let us therefore cast off the works of darkness, and put on the armour of light. Let us walk honestly, as in the day: not in rioting and drunkenness, not in chambering and impuri-ties, not in contention and envy: But put you on the Lord Jesus Christ, and make not provision for the flesh in its concupiscences.* If this were written: "And provision for the flesh in its concupiscences, make not," it would doubtless please the ear with a more rhythmic close, but the stricter translator has preferred to keep even the exact word order. How this sounds in Greek, the language in which the Apostle spoke, I leave

(1); Laurand 165ff.; De Groot (1) 119–31; (2) 9–11.

si . . . diceret . . . concupiscentiis feceritis: the Latin rendering, following the Greek, which has the cadence in *con-cupiscentiis*, gives a clausula perfect in quantity and perhaps in accent, made up of two cretics ($| - \smile - | - \smile - |$), which accord-ing to De Groot (2, 9) forms the clausula most favored by Cicero, and which according to Reynolds (7) is the one used to terminate one-tenth of the sentences of De Ciu. Dei. A word of several syllables should not be used as a cadence, however, (cf. Quint. 9, 4, 66: quare hoc quoque uitandum est, ne plurium syllaborum his uerbis utamur in fine). *Concupiscentiis* is, therefore, a poor cadence through its want of a caesura, but also probably from the point of view of accent, for if, as is pos-sible, the secondary accent fell on the sec-ond syllable of this word in Augustine's time, there would also be a difference here between word accent and metrical ictus. That accent as well as quantity was a matter of consideration in clausulae, at this time, and one of no small importance, see Norden 948, Laurand 356. Lack of caesura, and clash of accent and ictus, therefore, were doubtless the reasons for Augustine's preference for *concupiscen-tiis feceritis*, which gives a clausula made up of a cretic followed by a dichoreus ($| - \smile - | - \smile | - \smile |$), the best and most sonorous of all the clausulae, perfect in quantity and accent (since *feceritis* was

here doubtless acceptably accented on the penult, cf. St.-Schm. 340), and one show-ing the usual caesura. See Norden (948) for his discussion of this passage. In the Nachträge (19) to his latest edition (1923), he corrects his former interpretation of the clausula in question.

si quisquam: *quisquam* in place of the more usual *quis*, is sometimes used with *si* for emphasis, in Classical Latin. In Late writers this is done where no particular emphasis is intended: cf. K.-Schm. s.v.; St.-Schm. 483. *Quisquam* with *si* occurs frequently in the Confessions and De Ciu. Dei: cf. Arts 56; Colbert 31. Note this use also in 20, 41.

9. **mulceret**: mostly Poetic, Silver, and Late: cf. Gell. 20, 9: delectari, mulcerique aureo figmentis uerborum nouis. Cicero prefers *permulcere*, cf. Orat. 49, 163, quoted above (p. 136) in note on *propria . . . excurrunt*.

10. **sed grauior . . . uerborum**: Bald-win (2) 69 adds that logical emphasis is also secured by the given word order. Note (Intro. p. 345) that both the Old Ver-sion and the Vulgate also use this order, though they differ in choice of words.

11. **quomodo . . . ad ista doctiores**: Augustine confesses to his youthful abhorrence of Greek (cf. Conf. 1, 14, 23), and admits his deficiency in it even in his maturer years: cf. De Trin. 3, 1, 1: Graecae . . . linguae non sit nobis tantus habitus, ut talium rerum [*s.c.* de Trinitate] libris legendis et intellegendis ullo modo

tolus, uiderint eius eloquii usque ad ista doctiores; mihi tamen
quod nobis eodem uerborum ordine interpretatum est, nec ibi uidetur currere numerose.

41. Sane hunc elocutionis ornatum, qui numerosis fit clausulis,
deesse fatendum est auctoribus nostris. quod utrum per interpretes   5
factum sit, an—quod magis arbitror—consulto illi haec plausibilia
deuitauerint, affirmare non audeo, quoniam me fateor ignorare.
illud tamen scio, quod si quisquam huius numerositatis peritus
illorum clausulas eorundem numerorum lege componat, quod facillime fit mutatis quibusdam uerbis, quae tantundem significatione   10
ualent, uel mutato eorum quae inuenerit ordine, nihil illorum quae
uelut magna in scholis grammaticorum aut rhetorum didicit, illis
diuinis uiris defuisse cognoscet, et multa reperiet locutionis genera

1 dictiones *D*.   tamen]autem *EH*.   2 quod]qui *E*; quo *F*.   uerborum eodem
E.   6 an *om. D*.   9 clausulas eorundem]clausulae ordinem *CFGHI*; clausulam
D.   12 didicit in *EFH*.   13 reperiet et *D*.

reperiamur idonei. It is not from the
standpoint of the professional scholar,
therefore, that he makes his next assertion; he speaks merely as one who ven-
tures his opinion, dictated by the general
norm of taste. On the whole, however, it
should be noted that Augustine's knowledge of Greek was not inconsiderable:
cf. Angus, S., The Sources of the First
Ten Books of the De Civitate Dei of St.
Augustine (Princeton, 1906), 236ff.;
De Labriolle 528. The Greek rendering
of the passage in question (ποιεῖσθε εἰς
ἐπιθυμίας [˘ ˘ – ˘ –]) gives a clausula
not uncommon in Greek (cf. De Groot
(1) 26, 61). The word accent and metrical ictus do not tally, however, hence
doubtless Augustine's criticism. That
is his own practice, Augustine used
clausulae at once metrical and rhythmical, *i.e.* such as show the distribution of
quantities and the position of accents
regulated by constant and consistent
laws, is pointed out by Reynolds (10ff.)
in his study of De Ciu. Dei. That A. was
the first to consider accent as well as
quantity in clausulae, as Norden (948)
suggests, seems too bold an assertion:
cf. Laurand 356 and footnote.

4. **sane ... auctoribus nostris**: Augustine's criticism of Paul's rhythm in the
preceding paragraph, and his admission
here and below of the deficiency of the
inspired writers in the use of the clausulae, even though rhythm, and especially
cadences form such an important element of the middle style, is an indirect
answer to sophistic criticism of Christian style. Augustine has shown above,
Paul's artistry in the use of words, but
he desires to prove that in Paul as in all
the inspired writers, verbal beauty is not
of paramount importance as it is in the
Sophists, but that in the Christian writer,
the ornaments of the middle style, when
they occur, are always made subservient
to the matter they embellish.

6. **plausibilia**: the 'clap-traps' of the
Sophists, called by Cicero in Orat. 12,
39, *deliciis uel ineptiis*, since their aim is
nec tam persuadere quam delectare. In
Orat. 69, 230ff., there is a description of
Asianism and its subservience of thought
to sound and rhythm, which equally
applies to the applause-seeking Sophists
of the fourth century: apud alios autem
et Asiaticos *maxume numero seruientes*
inculcata reperias inania quaedam uerba

to those to explain who are more versed in that tongue even to these technicalities; but to me, it seems that the word order—and it is the same as in our translations—does not even there run musically.

41. We must confess, certainly, that our writers are faulty in that elegance of style marked by rhythmic closings. Whether this is the fault of translators, or, as I rather believe, they themselves purposely avoided such claptraps, I dare not say, since I confess I do not know. But this I do know, that if some one who understands this rhythm, arrange the endings of these writings in accordance with the law of the said rhythms, as can easily be done by replacing certain words by others of the same meaning, or by changing the existing order of words, he will recognize that none of those points which he has learned to consider important in the schools of the grammarians or rhetoricians are missing in these

quasi complementa numerorum. sunt etiam qui illo uitio . . . infringendis concidendisque numeris in quoddam genus abiectum incidant uersiculorum simillimum. Cicero then proceeds to sum up the chief excesses to which rhythmic prose is open (Orat. 69, 231): sed apud eos uarietas non erat, quod omnia fere concludebantur uno modo. quae uitia qui fugerit ut neque uerbum ita traiciat ut id de industria factum intellegatur, neque inferciens uerba quasi rimas expleat, nec minutos numeros sequens concidat delumbetque sententias, nec sine ulla commutatione in eodem semper uersetur genere numerorum, is omnia fere uitia uitauerit. It is such excesses as these that Augustine likewise decries, claiming that the inspired writers purposely seek to avoid such pitfalls.

8. **numerositatis** = 'rhythm,' is noted by Harper as occurring in De Doctr. 4, 20, 41; but the citation, *id. ib.* 55, 109, is incorrectly added. Forcellini, B.-Goelzer, and Georges, all inaccurately cite De Doctr. Chris. 4, 20, 41 under *numerositas,* as meaning 'great number.'

11. **mutato . . . ordine**: Cicero, however, claims that the same result follows the rhythmic ordering of *any* unformed writers: cf. Orat. 70, 233: aut si alicuius inconditi arripias dissupatam aliquam sententiam eamque ordine uerborum pau-

lulum commutato in quadrum redigas, efficiatur aptum illud, quod fuerit antea diffluens ac solutum. age sume de Gracchi apud censores illud: 'abesse non potest quin eiusdem hominis sit probos improbare qui improbos probet;' quanto aptius, si ita dixisset: 'quin eiusdem hominis sit qui improbos probet probos improbare'! And in the same paragraph, he claims that if the rhythm of a well-ordered passage is broken up, *corrumpatur . . . tota res.* It must be understood, however, that the discussion is here of extremes. The sacred writers, on the other hand, while not making rhythm their purpose and concern, certainly express themselves in a style far from meriting the terms *exilis, arida, exsanguis, hirsuta*, etc. They possess rather a rhythm natural and unsought for, inherent in the subject itself, to use Augustine's own terms (4, 26, 56).

13. **multa reperiet locutionis genera, etc.**: cf. De Doctr. Chris. 3, 37, 56: proinde sicut in uerbia propriis, de quibus superius disputauimus, ubi res dicuntur intellegendae sunt, sic in translatis quae faciunt tropicas locutiones, ubi aliud ex alio intellegendum est, de quibus huc usque quantum uisum est, satis egimus, non solum admonendi sunt studiosi uenerabilium litterarum ut in scripturis sanctis *genera locutionum* sciant, et quomodo apud eos

tanti decoris, quae quidem et in nostra, sed maxime in sua lingua decora sunt, quorum nullum in eis, quibus isti inflantur, litteris inuenitur. sed cauendum est ne diuinis grauibusque sententiis, dum additur numeros, pondus detrahatur. nam illa musica disciplina, ubi numerus iste plenissime discitur, usque adeo non defuit 5 prophetis nostris, ut uir doctissimus Hieronymus quorundam etiam metra commemoret, in hebraea duntaxat lingua, cuius ut ueritatem seruaret in uerbis, haec inde non transtulit. ego autem ut de sensu meo loquar, qui mihi quam aliis et quam aliorum est utique notior, sicut in meo eloquio, quantum modeste fieri arbitror, non praeter- 10 mitto istos numeros clausularum, ita in auctoribus nostris hoc mihi plus placet, quod ibi eos rarissime inuenio.

---

2 decorata *E.*   quibus]quorum *F.*   litteris]numeris *CFI.*   3 -que *om. G.* 4 detrahat *D.*   5 usque *om. E.*   6 doctus *DHI.*   7 metra]membra *E.*   commoraret *BFH.*   cuius ut]sicut *DF;* sed ut *B, (supra alia m.) F.*   uerita *D.* 8 hoc *E.*   ut]ne *E.*   9 loquor *F.*   10 meo]medio *E.*

---

aliquid dici soleat, uigilanter aduertant, memoriterque retineant, uerum etiam . . . orent ut intellegant. And in chapter 29, 40, of the same book, Augustine speaks even more plainly of the figurative style of Holy Scripture: sciant autem litterati, modis omnibus locutionis, quos grammatici graeco nomine tropos uocant, auctores nostros usos fuisse, et multiplicius atque copiosius, quam possunt existimare uel credere qui nesciunt eos, et in aliis ista didicerunt. quos tamen tropos qui nouerunt, agnoscunt in litteris sanctis, eorumque scientia ad eas intellegendas aliquantum adiuuantur.

3. **sed cauendum . . . detrahatur**: Cicero's ideal is much the same, but expressed from the standpoint of one claiming the necessity of rhythm. He holds that that rhythm is best which is so unobtrusive as not to be noticed by the listener. Weighty matter makes this all the more possible. The audience is pleased by the beauty of the *thought* in the words, not realizing that technique has a great part to play in the accomplishment of the effect: cf. Orat. 58, 197: itaque in uaria et perpetua oratione

hi sunt inter se miscendi et temperandi. sic minime animaduertetur delectationis aucupium et quadrandae orationis industria; quae latebit eo magis, si et uerborum et sententiarum ponderibus utemur, nam qui audiunt haec duo animaduertunt et iucunda sibi censent, uerba dico et sententias, eaque dum animis attentis admirantes excipiunt, fugit eos et praeteruolat numerus; qui tamen si abesset, illa ipsa delectarent minus. St. Augustine judges from the viewpoint of one whose first thought is for the weightiness of the matter, for whom rhythm while not to be condemned, is always of secondary consideration. Both these views are sane ones, in comparison with the extreme tenets of the Sophists.

7. **metra**: Silver Latin: cf. Quint. 9, 4, 46: nam rhythmi, id est numeri, spatio temporum constant, metra etiam ordine, ideoque alterum esse quantitatis uidetur, alterum qualitatis.

ut ueritatem . . . transtulit: the Christian ideal: truth has first place; beauty, second.

8. **ego autem . . . numeros clausularum**: De Ciu. Dei may be taken as an

divinely inspired authors; and he will find many kinds of expressions of great beauty—beautiful indeed also in our own language, but especially so in theirs, none of which are to be found in that literature of which they are so vain. But care must be taken not to detract from the weight of the divine and authoritative utterances, while adding rhythm to them. For that musical training in which rhythm is thoroughly learned is so far from being lacking in our Prophets that the learned Jerome even makes mention of the meters used by some, in the Hebrew only however, for in order to keep the true meaning of the words he has not translated them metrically. But as for myself, to speak of my own tastes—better known to me, of course, than to others, and than those of others—although in my own language, as far as I think it reasonable, I do not neglect these rhythmic endings, still, in our authors I am better pleased to find them used very rarely.

example of Augustine's own practice in the use of clausulae. It shows first of all that he was not unmindful of the rhythmic precepts of his day, but that in using them he preferred to return, as in other matters, to classical standards rather than to follow the formalism of the third and fourth centuries. His language is simple and natural, not violent and strained, the thought governing the rhythm, not the rhythm the thought. Because of the importance that accent had gained in his day, his clausulae pass beyond Cicero's in being at once metrical and rhythmical. How thoroughly he was dominated, however, by the classical ideal, can readily be seen by a comparison of the following resumé of his accomplishment in clausulae, with the Ciceronian standard expressed in the quotation from the *Orator* given above. Reynolds (63) draws the following conclusions from his study of the cadences of De Ciu. Dei: 'Both the metrical system and the rhythmical system here employed embrace a wide variety of possible and allowed forms.

There is no monotony in the wearisome repetition of a few excessively palpable metres. The art of concealing art is practiced by means, first of the large number of forms used, second by the variation of these forms through resolution, and third by the large percentage of weak and poor forms admitted, which while they do not grate upon the ear, at the same time do not weary it by a too obvious perfection. And another purpose is at the same time served, namely that of allowing greater ease and freedom to the writer, to the advantage of the naturalness and forcefulness of his style.'

10. **non praetermitto ... clausularum**: Reynolds offers his belief that A. here is not limiting the frequency of his own use of clausulae in general, but merely of his use of the few forms recommended by the schools. Augustine's aversion is not to the tempered use of the rhythmic prose of the classical period, but to the formalism and excess of Sophistic.

12. **rarissime**: this superlative belongs to Silver Latin.

42. Grande autem dicendi genus hoc maxime distat ab isto genere temperato, quod non tam uerborum ornatibus comptum est, quam uiolentum animi affectibus. nam capit etiam illa ornamenta pene omnia; sed ea si non habuerit, non requirit. fertur quippe impetu suo, et elocutionis pulchritudinem, si occurrerit, ui rerum 5 rapit, non cura decoris assumit. satis enim est ei propter quod agitur ut uerba congruentia non oris eligantur industria, sed pectoris sequantur ardorem. nam si aurato gemmatoque ferro uir fortis armetur, intentissimus pugnae, agit quidem illis armis quod agit, non quia pretiosa, sed quia arma sunt; idem ipse est tamen, 10 et ualet plurimum, etiam cum rimanti telum ira facit. agit apostolus, ut pro euangelico ministerio patienter mala huius temporis,

1 isto *om. E.*   2 compositum *BDF*; acceptum *E*; coeptum *CG*; aptum *I.*
3 quam]quod *A.*   uiolentis *E.*   illa *om.D.*   5 puchritudine *B.*   ui *om.F*;
ui]ut *A*; eorum *add.E.*   uerum *F.*   6 capit *I*; rapit rerum *E.*   enim *om.D.*
7 uerbis *E.*   cordis *E.*   9 quidem agit *E.*   armis illis *H.*   10 tamen est *E.*
11 et *om.I.*   etiam *om.H.*   uibranti *C.*   telum ira]tela mira *A*; telam ira *G*;
telo mira *EHI (Lou. [Maur.]).*

1. **grande . . . affectibus**: the grand style and the temperate spring from the same source, the λόγος πρὸς τοὺς ἀϰροωμένους of Theophrastus, representing rhetoric proper *vs.* λόγος πρὸς τὰ πράγματα, dialectic. It is of importance to distinguish between the two styles properly called rhetorical. The middle style is characterized by the ornaments of figures of words (σχήματα λέξεως), the grand by the emotion of figures of thought (σχήματα διανοίας). It was when these figures were themselves definitely distinguished that these two styles found their proper differentiation. The figures of words belong particularly to the middle style because they most readily bring about its end, *delectare*, the office as seen above, developed from Aristotle's conception of the personal character of the speaker (ἦθος) as a means of persuasion; the figures of thought belong particularly to the grand style as being most adapted to its end, *flectere*, that office conceived of by Aristotle as especially dealing with the emotions (πάθη). These traditional distinctions, Cicero takes over, explain-

ing in Orat. 37, 128 the character of the two styles, which may together be called eloquence in the true sense of the word: duae res sunt enim, quae bene tractatae ab oratore admirabilem eloquentiam faciant. quorum alterum est, quod Graeci ἠθιϰὸν uocant, ad naturam et ad mores et ad omnem uitae consuetudinem accommodatum; alterum, quod idem παθητιϰὸν nominant, quo perturbantur animi et concitantur, in quo regnat oratio. illud superius come iucundum, ad beneuolentiam conciliandam paratum; hoc uehemens incensum incitatum, quo causae eripiuntur: quod cum rapide fertur, sustineri nullo pacto potest.
3. **quam uiolentum animi affectibus**: cf. Quint. 12, 10, 61: at ille [modus dicendi] qui saxa deuoluat et pontem indignetur et ripas sibi faciat, multus et torrens iudicem uel nitentem contra feret cogetque ire, qua rapiet. Orat. 28, 97: sed hanc eloquentiam, quae cursu magno sonituque ferretur. *Ibid.* 5, 20: nam et grandiloqui, . . . uehementes copiosi graues, ad permouendos et conuertendos animos instructi et parati.
nam capit . . . omnia: cf. Auct. ad

42. The grand style of speaking differs from this moderate style especially in this that it is not so much adorned by ornate expressions, as rendered passionate by the heart's emotions. For it uses, indeed, almost all of the ornaments of the other, but if it does not have them at hand, it does not seek them out. It is borne on, in fact, by its own vehemence, and catches up any beauty of style, which may occur, through the very force of the matter, but it does not put on any such through care of ornament. It is enough for its purpose, not that fitting terms be chosen with thought of the expression, but that they be governed by the ardor of the heart. For if a brave man be armed with weapons adorned with gold and jewels, being fully intent on battle, he accomplishes indeed what he does with these very arms, not because they are precious, but because they are arms; and still he himself is the same, and very formidable even when but anger furnishes a weapon for him at his seeking. The Apostle urges that for the sake of the ministry of the Gospel all the evils of this life be suffered through the help of

Her. 4, 8, 11: in graui consumetur oratio figura, si, quae cuiusque rei poterunt ornatissima uerba reperiri siue propria siue extranea, ad unam quamque rem adcommodabuntur, et si graues sententiae, quae in amplificatione et commiseratione tractantur, eligentur, et si exornationes sententiarum aut uerborum, quae grauitatem habebunt, . . . adhibebuntur. Orat. 39, 134: ex omni genere frequentissimae tralationes erunt, quod eae propter similitudinem transferunt animos et referunt ac mouent huc et illuc.

4. sed ea si non . . . ardorem: Augustine is again warning the Christian orator against sophistic methods, and is making a plea for the πρέπον, *decorum*, of classical standards: cf. Orat. 35, 123ff.: nam nec semper nec apud omnis nec contra omnis nec pro omnibus nec cum omnibus eodem modo dicendum arbitror. is erit ergo eloquens, qui ad id quodcumque decebit poterit accommodare orationem. . . . cum uero causa ea *inciderit*, in qua uis eloquentiae posit expromi, tum se latius fundet orator, tum reget et flectet animos et sic afficiet, ut uolet, *id est ut causae natura et ratio temporis postulabit.*

8. nam si . . . ira facit: a comparison

that cannot but bring home *the* quality of the grand style that is all essential: ψυχαγωγία, cf. Plato, Phaedrus 271d: ἐπειδὴ λόγου δύναμις τυγχάνει ψυχαγωγία οὖσα.

aurato: mostly Poetic and Silver, but used by Cicero three times: cf. T.L.L. II, 1520, 17–27.

gemmato: Poetic and Silver.

11. rimanti . . . ira facit: cf. Verg. Aen. 7, 507: quod cuique repertum rimanti telum ira facit.

agit . . . tolerentur: to prove that the essential of the grand style is emotional appeal, whether made with the help of ornaments of speech or not, A. proceeds to give three examples of this style, all of which are grand by reason of the emotion with which they throb, but all of which attain this end by different means: the first from 2 Cor. 6, 2-11, making use of figures of thought; the second from Rom. 8, 28-39, using the lesser ornaments, figures of words, but raising them above mere floridness of style by the ardor with which they are expressed; the third from Gal. 4, 10-20, wanting in embellishments, but grand by reason of its moving force.

cum solatio donorum Dei, omnia tolerentur. magna res est, et
graniter agitur, nec desunt ornamenta dicendi. *ecce* inquit *nunc
tempus acceptabile, ecce nunc dies salutis. nullam in quoquam
dantes offensionem, ut non reprehendatur ministerium nostrum;
sed in omnibus commendantes nosmetipsos ut Dei ministros, in* 5
*multa patientia, in tribulationibus, in necessitatibus, in angustiis,
in plagis, in carceribus, in seditionibus, in laboribus, in uigiliis,
in ieiuniis, in castitate, in scientia, in longanimitate, in benignitate,
in Spiritu sancto, in charitate non ficta, in uerbo ueritatis, in uirtute Dei; per arma iustitiae dextra et sinistra, per gloriam et igno-* 10
*bilitatem, per infamiam et bonam famam; ut seductores et ueraces;
ut qui ignoramur et cognoscimur; quasi morientes, et ecce uiuimus,
ut coerciti, et non mortificati; ut tristes, semper autem gaudentes;
sicut egeni, multos autem ditantes; tamquam nihil habentes, et
omnia possidentes.* uide adhuc ardentem, *os nostrum patet ad uos,* 15
o Corinthii, cor nostrum dilatatum est, et caetera, quae persequi
longum est.

43. Itemque ad Romanos agit, ut persecutiones huius mundi
charitate uincantur, spe certa in adiutorio Dei. agit autem granditer et ornate. *scimus* inquit *quoniam diligentibus Deum omnia* 20
*cooperantur in bonum, iis qui secundum propositum uocati sunt.
quoniam quos ante praesciuit, et praedestinauit conformes imaginis*

2 Cor. 6, 2-11

Rom. 8, 28-39

1 cum solatio]consolatio *D;* consolatione *H;* cum *om. EI.*   2 ecce nunc inquit tempus
acceptabile *D.*   3 nunc *om. E.* quodam *H.*   4 nostrum *om. ABDI.*   10 a dextris et a sinistris
El Maur. Vulg.; a dextris et sinistris *Ver.An.;* a dextra et sinistra *D;* dextrae et sinistrae *G.*
13 ut (coerciti) *om. Ver.An.Mig.*   14 egentes *AC Ver.An. Vulg.*   autem *om. I.*   15 uide]
unde *A.*   20 inquit]enim *E.*   21 cooperatur *B.*   his *ABCDFGHI Ver.An.;* hiis *E.*   uocat *E.*
uocati sunt sancti *ACEFHI Vulg.*   22 conformis *D;* fieri *add. A (supra alia* m.). *B (supra),*
EHI Ver.An. Vulg. (editi; at MSS carent uocibus sancti *et* fieri, *quae praetermitti solent ab*
Aug., et a Graeco textu absunt [Maur.]).   imagines *GI.*

1. magna res ... ornamenta dicendi:
in Orat. 39, 136, Cicero after summarizing figures of words says: *sed senten-*
tiarum ornamenta maiora sunt. These
are the figures proper to the grand style
(σχήματα διανοίας). In 40, 137, he
describes them. It is interesting to find
many exemplified in the passage from
the Second Corinthians, *e.g.* the following: sic igitur dicet ille, quem expetimus,
ut uerset saepe multis eadem et una in
re haereat in eademque commoretur
sententia; . . . ut quid dixit iteret, . . . ut
contra ac dicat accipi et sentiri uelit; . .

ut hominum sermones moresque descri-
bat; . . . ut comparet similitudines; . . .
ut deprecetur, ut supplicet, ut medeatur;
. . . ut optet, ut execretur; ut fiat iis apud
quos dicet familiaris.

2. ecce ... dilatatum est: Augustine
quotes verses 4-10 of this chapter, in
Contr. Cresc. 1, 16, 20, in his differentiation, there, between rhetoric and dialectic. He says: hoc ille uerus disputator
si late diffuseque faciat eloquenter facit,
alioque tunc censetur augetur uocabulo,
ut dictor potius quam disputator uocetur;
sicut illum locum apostolus copiose

the consolation accompanying God's gifts. Great is the theme, and grandly it is treated, though still not without ornaments of style. *Behold* says he *now is the acceptable time; behold now is the day of salvation. Giving no offense to any man, that our ministry be not blamed. But in all things commending ourselves as the ministers of God, in much patience, in tribulations, in necessities, in trials, in stripes, in prisons, in seditions, in labors, in watchings, in fastings, in chastity, in knowledge, in long-suffering, in kindness, in the Holy Ghost, in charity unfeigned, in the word of truth, in the power of God; by the armour of justice on the right hand and on the left; by honour and dishonour; by evil report and good report; as deceivers and yet true; as unknown, and yet known; as dying and behold we live; as chastised, and not killed; as sorrowful, yet always rejoicing; as needy, yet enriching many; as having nothing, yet possessing all things.* Behold him still on fire: *Our mouth is open to you, O ye Corinthians, our heart is enlarged*, and so on, but it would take long to pursue it further.

43. And so, too, he urges upon the Romans that the sufferings of this world be overcome by charity, with certain hope in the help of God. His exhortation is in the grand style, and at the same time figurative. *We know* he says *that to them that love God, all things work together unto good, to such as, according to His purpose, are called. For whom He foreknew, he also predestinated to be made*

dilatat atque diffundit. Then after giving the quotation, he concludes: quid enim hoc stilo apostolico uberius et ornatius, id est *eloquentius*, facile inuenis?

15. **uide . . . dilatatum est**: note the discrimination of the teacher. *Ardens* expresses the very essence of the grand style, and the part of this quotation which most *ardently* throbs and glows is precisely this concluding apostrophe: *os nostrum*, etc.

18. **ad Romanos agit**: the Epistle to the Romans is largely plain in style, being especially expository and argumentative. It rises, however, at times to the grand style, as here.

ad . . . agit . . . ut = 'urge upon that,' is limited, in Class. Latin, to a formal proposal of a measure before the people. *Cum* and the ablative with a following *ut*, is the usual construction with *ago* used informally: cf. Ad Fam. 5, 2: egi cum

Claudia et cum uestra sorore Mucia ut eum ad illa iniuria deterrerent: cf. T.L.L. I, 1391, 21–56; 1393, 20–32.

19. **spe . . . in**: cf. De Inuent. 1, 39, 71: summa amentia est in eorum fide spem habere. The usual classical construction, however, with *spes* is either an objective genitive or *ad* and the accusative. *In* and the ablative, here, may be a development of the colloquial language, but the influence of the Hebrew and Greek idioms on the Latin Bible is also responsible for the extension of this usage in Late Latin: cf. Rönsch 397; McGuire 37; Arts 36.

adiutorio: rare, mostly Silver and Late: cf. Sen. Contr. 1, 2, 18: sine deorum immortalium adiutorio. Vulg. Psalm. 7, 11: adiutorium meum a Domino. Cf. T.L.L. I, 717, 2–4.

granditer et ornate: Cicero enumerates the principal *figurae uerborum* in Orat. 39, 135. It should be noted how Paul

Filii sui, ut sit ipse primogenitus in multis fratribus. quos autem
praedestinauit, illos et uocauit; et quos uocauit, ipsos et iustifi-
cauit quos autem iustificauit, illos et glorificauit. quid ergo dice-
mus ad haec? si Deus pro nobis, quis contra nos? qui Filio proprio
non perpercit, sed pro nobis omnibus tradidit eum, quomodo non 5
et cum illo omnia nobis donauit? quis accusabit aduersus electos
Dei? Deus qui iustificat? quis est qui condemnet? Christus Iesus
qui mortuus est, magis autem qui resurrexit, qui est in dextera Dei,
qui et interpellat pro nobis? quis nos separabit a charitate Christi?
tribulatio?an angustia an persecutio? an fames? an nuditas? an 10
Psal. 43, 22 *periculum? an gladius? sicut scriptum est, quia propter te morti-*
ficamur, toto die, aestimati sumus ut oues occisionis. sed in his
omnibus superuincimus per eum qui dilexit nos. certus sum enim
quia neque mors, neque uita, neque angelus, neque principatus,
neque praesentia, neque futura, neque uirtus, neque altitudo, neque 15
profundum, neque creatura alia poterit nos separare a charitate Dei,
quae est in Christo Iesu Domino nostro.

44. Ad Galatas autem quamuis tota ipsa epistola submisso dicendi genere scripta sit, nisi in extremis partibus ubi est eloquium
temperatum, tamen interponit quendam locum eo motu animi, ut 20
sine ullis quidem talibus ornamentis, qualia sunt in iis quae modo
Gal. 4, 10-20 posuimus, non posset tamen nisi granditer dici. *dies* inquit *obser-*
uatis, et menses, et annos, et tempora. timeo uos, ne forte sine
causa laborauerim in uobis. estote sicut et ego, quoniam et ego sicut
uos; fratres, precor uos; nihil me laesistis. scitis quia per infirmi- 25
tatem carnis iampridem euangelizaui uobis, et tentationem uestram

2 ipsos]illos *HE*.   3 illos]ipsos *ABDEF*.   dicimus *H*.   4 proprio Filio *EI Maur*.; Filio
suo proprio *F*.   5 illum *AEI Ver.An. Vulg. Maur*.   6 et]etiam *Ver.An. Vulg. Maur*.; et *om. EI*.
nobis omnia *Maur*.   accusauit *F*; excussauit *Ver.An*.   7 est *om. C Ver.An*.   qui *om. F Ver.
An*. condemnat *BDG*.   8 qui et est *B Ver.An*.   in dextera]ad dexteram *F Ver.An*.   10 an
(angustia) *om. D*; an]et *E*.   11 quoniam *G (sic em.), Maur*.   12 hiis *E*.   13 superamus *EF*
(superuincimus *supra alia m.*), *Ver.An*.   per]in *E*.   14 angeli *AEI Maur. Vulg*.   16 aliqua *E*.
nos poterit separare *BF*.   18 ipsa *om. E*; illa *BDH*.   19 in *om. EI*.   20 eo *om B*.   21 his
ABCDFGH; illis *I*.   22 possit *CH*.   23 uos *om. E*.   24 in uos *DFH Maur*. (*MSS iuxta
Graecum* εἰς ὑμᾶς [*Maur*.]).   (sicut) et *om. CE Vulg*.   25 sciatis *F*.   26 euangelizaui uobis
iampridem *F Ver.An. Vulg*.   tentationes uestras *EI Maur*.

makes use of many of these in the passage given below, although he couples
with them some of the greater *figurae*
sententiarum (for enumeration, see note
above on p. 136, *magna res*, to which
add: ut interrogando urgeat, ut rursus
quasi ad interrogata sibi ipse respondeat

[Orat. 40, 137]). The σχήματα λέξεως,
described by Cicero are: cum aut dupli-
cantur iteranturque uerba aut breuiter
commutata ponuntur, aut ab eodem
uerbo ducitur saepius oratio . . . aut idem
ad extremum refertur; . . . aut cum similiter uel cadunt uerba uel desinunt; aut

comformable to the image of His Son; that He might be the First-
born among many brethren. And whom He predestinated, them He
also called. And whom [H]e called, them He also justified. And whom
He justified, them He also glorified. What shall we say then to these
things? If God be for us, who is against us? He that spared not His
own Son, but delivered Him up for us all, hath He not also, with Him,
given us all things? Who shall accuse against the elect of God? God
that justifieth? Who is he that shall condemn? Jesus Christ that died,
but more, that is risen again; who is at the right hand of God, who
also maketh intercession for us? Who then shall separate us from the
love of Christ? Shall tribulation? or distress? or persecution? or fam-
ine? or nakedness? or danger? or the sword? As it is written: "For
thy sake we are put to death all the day long. We are counted sheep
for the slaughter." But in all these things we overcome, because of
Him that hath loved us. For I am sure that neither death, nor life, nor
might nor height, nor depth, nor any other creature, shall be able to
separate us from the love of God, which is in Jesus Christ our Lord.

44. And in writing to the Galatians, although the whole Epistle is written in the subdued style, except at the very end where
the moderate style is used, nevertheless he inserts one passage of
such emotion, that destitute as it is of such ornament as we see in
the selection just quoted, still it could not but be expressed in the
grand style. *You observe days* he says *and months, and years, and*
times. I am afraid of you, lest perhaps I have labored in vain for
you. Be ye as I, because I also am as you: brethren, I beseech you:
you have not injured me at all. And you know, how through infir-
mity of the flesh, I preached the Gospel unto you heretofore: and
your temptation in my flesh, you despised not, nor rejected: but
received me as an angel of God, even as Christ Jesus. Where then

cum sunt contrariis relata contraria; . . .
aut cum corrigimus nosmet ipsos quasi
reprehendentes (Orat. 39, 135).

18. **ad Galatas . . . dici**: this Epistle, as
a whole, exemplifies the blending of the
three styles in one composition, though
with the predominance of one—the ideal
in writing or speaking, which Augustine
will treat of in chapters 22, 23, and 26.

20. **tamen**, for greater emphasis, at
times is found at the beginning of a

clause: cf. Cic. Marc. 4; Liv. 21, 55, 10:
cf. K.-Schm. s.v.

22. **dies . . . obseruatis, etc.**: an example of the unadorned grand style. The
emotion of the writer is sufficient in itself
without ornaments, to lift the listener to
the higher levels of grandeur of speech.
Augustine expresses this succinctly
below: non tepuit grandis *affectus*, quo
eloquium *feruere* sentimus.

in carne mea non spreuistis, neque respuistis; sed sicut angelum
Dei excepistis me, sicut Christum Iesum. quae ergo fuit beatitudo
uestra? testimonium uobis perhibeo, quoniam si fieri posset, oculos
uestros eruissetis et dedissetis mihi. ergo inimicus factus sum uobis
uerum praedicans? aemulantur uos non bene, sed excludere uos 5
uolunt, ut eos aemulemini. bonum est autem aemulari in bono
semper, et non solum cum praesens sum apud uos. filioli mei, quos
iterum parturio donec Christus formetur in uobis. uellem autem
nunc adesse apud nos, et mutare uocem meam, quia confundor in
uobis. numquid hic aut contraria contrariis uerba sunt reddita, 10
aut aliqua gradatione sibi subnexa sunt, aut caesa et membra cir-
cuitusque sonuerunt? et tamen non ideo tepuit grandis affectus,
quo eloquium feruere sentimus.

21, 45. Sed apostolica ista sic clara sunt, ut et profunda sint, atque
ita conscripta memoriaeque mandata, ut non solum lectore uel 15
auditore, uerum etiam expositore opus habeant, si quis in eis non
superficie contentus altitudinem quaerat, quapropter uideamus ista
genera dicendi in eis qui istorum lectione ad rerum diuinarum
atque salubrium scientiam profecerunt, eamque ecclesiae ministrarunt. beatus Cyprianus submisso dicendi genere utitur in eo libro 20
ubi de sacramento calicis disputat. soluitur quippe ibi quaestio, in
qua quaeritur utrum calix dominicus aquam solam, an eam uino
mixtam debeat habere. sed exempli gratia aliquid inde ponendum

---

1 non]si *A.*   2 me *om. CGH.*   Iesum Christum *EH*; Christum Dominum *F.*
8 uobis *om. D.*   4 sum *om. E.*   6 ut]ne (ut *supra*) *G.*   est *om. C Vulg.* in
bono aemulari *Maur.*; aemulamini in bono *C Vulg.*   7 uos *om. E.*   8 formetur
Christus *EI Maur. Ver.An. Vulg.*   9 esse *CGH*; et esse *E.*   immature *E;* mutarem
G.   12 non *om. D.*   13 quod *E.*   eloquiorum *I.*   sentiamus *E.*   14 et *om. D.*
sint *om. E.*   15 ita *om. A.*   conscripta sint *E.* commendata *B.*   18 ad]in *E;* at *G.*
19 esque *CG*; eademque *EI.*   ministrantur ecclesiae *E.*   20 eodem *E.*   22 eam
uino]etiam uino *B (sic em.), I*; uino etiam *E*; eam in uino *H.*   23 mixtum *D.*

---

11. **sibi**: the use of the reflexive pronoun to express reciprocal relation is
found especially in the language of the
people: cf. St. –Schm. 471.

12. **tepuit** = 'cooled off,' is found in
Silver and Late Latin: cf. Lucan 4, 284:
paulatim cadit ira ferox, mentesque
tepescunt.

13. **feruere**, in the transferred sense,
is used only for great emotion, otherwise
uigere is employed, *e.g.* studium litterarum uiget. Cf. K.-Schm. s.v.

21. *Examples of the three styles,*
drawn from SS. Cyprian and Ambrose.

15. **conscripta memoriaeque mandata**: cf. De Catech. Rud. 4, 8: quaecumque posterius salubriter conscripta
sunt memoriaeque mandata diuinarum
uolumina litterarum. *Memoriae mandata* (= class. *memoriae prodita*) means
'handed down as tradition' in Late Latin,
though in classical times it meant only
'impressed on the memory'. For an
example of the latter usage in Augustine,

is your blessedness? For I bear you witness, that if it could be done, you would have plucked out your own eyes, and would have given them to me. Am I then become your enemy, because I tell you the truth? They are zealous in your regard not well: but they would exclude you, that you might be zealous for them. But to be zealous in good always, is good: and not only when I am present with you. My little children, of whom I am in labour again, until Christ be formed in you. And I would willingly be present with you now, and change my voice: because I am ashamed for you. Here have we examples of antithesis, or climax, or the resonance of *caesa* and *membra* or periods? And yet, notwithstanding, there is no flagging in the deep emotion with which we feel that the language of the passage is aglow.

21,   45. But these writings of the Apostle, though clear, are nevertheless also deep, and are so written and handed down, that they not only require to be read and heard, but also to be explained, if anyone, not content with superficial knowledge of them, inquire also into their depths. Therefore, let us examine these kinds of style in the writings of those men who through their reading of the Scriptures have attained knowledge of the divine and saving truths, and have ministered it unto the Church. The blessed Cyprian uses the subdued style of speech in his book on the Sacrament of the chalice. For there he answers the question as to whether the chalice of the Lord should contain water only, or water mixed with wine. But we must give a passage therefrom by way of illustration. After

---

cf. Conf. 5, 3, 3: et quoniam multa philosophorum legeram memoriaeque mandata retinebam.

16. **opus habeant**: *opus habere* is found in Columella 9, 1, 5, then only in Late Latin. There are three examples of it in the Confessions: cf. K.-Schm. s.v.; St.-Schm. 436; Salonius 263; Arts 78.

17. **superficie**, in the transferred sense, is Late: cf. Tert. ad Nat. 1, 5; Prosp. Aquit. in Psalm. 147, v. 16; Aug. in Psalm. 107, 2: ubi significatur ad unum aliquid concurrere utrumque, non superficie historiae, sed altitudine prophetiae.

altitudinem = 'depth.' 'profundity.'

is found particularly in Silver and Late Latin: cf. K-Schm. s.v.; T.L.L. I, 1769, 34–50.

19. **ministrarunt**, 'presented.' is mostly Silver and Late Latin.

20. **beatus . . . disputat**: the following examples of the plain style from Cyprian and Ambrose, are purely dialectical in character. They again prove that to Augustine the plain style was essentially an argumentative one. Note the dialectical terms used: *disputat . . soluitur quaestio . . . quaeritur . . . demonstrat . . . rerum documenta desiderat.*

est. post principium ergo epistolae, iam soluere incipiens proposi-
tam quaestionem, *admonitos autem nos scias* inquit *ut in calice
offerendo dominica traditio seruetur neque aliud fiat a nobis quam
quod pro nobis Dominus prior facit, ut calix qui in commemora-
tionem eius offertur, mixtus uino offeratur. nam cum dicat Chris-* 5

Ioan. 15, 5 *tus, 'ego sum uitis uera,' sanguis Christi non aqua est utique, sed
uinum; nec potest uideri sanguis eius, quo redempti et uiuificati
sumus, esse in calice, quando uinum desit calici, quo Christi san-
quis ostenditur, qui scripturarum omnium sacramento ac testimonio
praedicatur. inuenimus enim in Genesi circa sacramentum Noe* 10
hoc idem praecucurisse et figuram dominicae passionis illic exti-

Gen. 9, 21-23 *tisse quod uinum bibit, quod inebriatus est, quod in domo sua
nudatus est, quod fuit recubans nudis et patentibus femoribus, quod
nuditas illa patris a medio filio denotata est, a maiore uero et
minore contecta, et caetera quae necesse non est exsequi, cum satis* 15
*sit hoc solum complecti quod Noe typum futurae ueritatis osten-
dens, non aquam sed uinum biberit et sic imaginem dominicae
passionis expresserit. item in sacerdote Melchisedech dominicum
sacramentum praefiguratum uidemus secundum quod scriptura*

Gen. 14, 18-19 *diuina testatur et dicit, 'et Melchisedech rex Salem protulit panem* 20
*et uinum. fuit autem sacerdos Dei summi, et benedixit Abraham.'
quod autem Melchisedech typum Christi portaret, declarat in psalmis*

Psal. 109, 4 *Spiritus sanctus, ex persona Patris ad Filium dicens: 'ante
Luciferum genui te. tu es sacerdos in aeternum secundum ordinem
Melchisedech.'* haec et alia quae sequuntur huius epistolae sub- 25
missae dictionis modum seruant, quod facile est explorare legentibus.

46. Sanctus quoque Ambrosius cum agat rem magnam de Spiritu sancto, ut eum Patri et Filio demonstret aequalem, submisso
tamen dicendi genere utitur, quoniam res suscepta non ornamenta 30
uerborum, aut ad flectendos animos commotionis affectum, sed rerum documenta desiderat. ergo inter caetera, in principio huius

---

1 ergo epistolae]ergo eius epistolae *B*; eius epistolae *D*.   2 ut *om. F.* 3 traditio seruetur]obseruetur traditio
E.   4 Dominus pro nobis *C.*   in commemoratione *ABCDEFG Cyp (C. S. E. L.).*   5 uino mixtus *Maur.*
7 uideri *om. E.*   8 in calice esse *E.*   quo]quod *Cyp. (C. S. E. L.).*   9 ostenditur]effunditur *D.*   omnium]
nominum *D.*   10 praedicetur *ACD. (sic em.) F, G Cyp. (C. S. E. L.).*   enim et *D.*   11 praecurrisse *AE.*
12 est et *E.*   13 nudus *C.*   14 illa patris nuditas *E.*   denotata est]denudata est *H, (sic em.) G*; et foras
nuntiata *add. D*; sed et foras, etc. *add. Cyp. (C. S. E. L.).*   a (maiore) *om. D.*   15 a duobus uero maiore
et minore *Cyp. (C. S. E. L.).*   16 *ueritatis futurae C.*   18 dominicum sacramentum]sacrificii dominici
sacramenti *DG*; sacrificii dominici sacramentum *Cyp. (C. S. E. L.).*   19 uidemus mysterium *CFGH*;
(dominici sacramenti praefiguratum uidemus mysterium *prius editi* [*Maur.*]). divina scriptura *E.*   20 Salem
om. E.   22 portarit *A.*   24 generaui te et *A.*   25 haec *om. DF.* talia *D.*   submisse *AD.*   26 dictionis]
dicimus (dicendi *in marg. alia m.*) *D.*   28 quoque]uero *E.*   29 demonstraret *BD.*   30 genere dicendi *E.*
re *FI.*   31 ad]de *E.* commotionis affectum] commotioni affectum *D*; commotio affectuum *B.*

the introduction, therefore, to his letter, already beginning his answer to the question proposed, he says: "But you should know that we have been taught in offering the chalice, to observe the tradition of the Lord, and not to do anything other than what the Lord first did for us, namely, to offer water mixed with wine in the chalice which is offered in commemoration of Him. For since Christ says, *I am the true vine*, the Blood of Christ is certainly not water, but wine; and so His Blood, by which we are redeemed and vivified, cannot possibly be held to be in the chalice when the chalice does not contain wine, for in the wine is Christ's Blood manifested as foretold by the mystical testimony of all the Scriptures. For we find in the book of Genesis in regard to the sacrament, that Noe has foreshadowed it and has stood out as a type of our Lord's Passion, in that he drank wine and was inebriated therewith, and that in his own house he lay uncovered, with limbs bare; and that this nakedness of his father was exposed by his second son, but that by his elder and his younger it was covered up—but there is no need to carry the account further, since it is sufficient to explain this one point, that Noe, showing himself a type of the future reality, drank not water, but wine, and thus set forth a figure of our Lord's Passion. In like manner we see the Sacrament of the Lord prefigured in the priest Melchisedech, according to what Holy Scripture testifies in these words: *But Melchisedech, the King of Salem, brought forth bread and wine. For he was the priest of the most high God, and he blessed Abraham.* And that Melchisedech was a figure of Christ, is declared in the Psalms, by the Holy Spirit, where in the person of the Father addressing the Son, He says: *Before the day star I begot Thee. Thou art a priest forever according to the order of Melchisedech."* This and the remainder of the letter maintained the subdued style of speech, as is easy for readers to ascertain.

46. St. Ambrose, too, though treating a subject of great importance, to prove that the Holy Spirit is equal to the Father and the Son, uses, none the less, the subdued style, for the matter in hand calls not for embellishment in words, nor for the stirring of the emotions to move hearts, but for the proof of facts. And so, among other things in the introduction to this work he says: "Gedeon,

---

2. **admonitos autem nos, etc.**: Cypr. Epist. ad Caecil. 63, 2-4.

32. **desiderat** = 'wants': cf. Caes. B. G. 2, 32, 12: nulla omnino naue desiderata.

Iud. 6, 11-21 operis ait, *quo motus oraculo Gedeon, cum audisset quod deficien-*
tibus licet populorum milibus, in uno uiro Dominus plebem suam
ab hostibus liberaret, obtulit haedum caprarum, cuius carnem
secundum praeceptum angeli, et azyma supra petram posuit, et ea
iure perfudit; quae simul ut uirgae cacumine, quam gerebat, an- 5
gelus Dei contigit, de petra ignis erupit, atque ita sacrificium quod
offerebatur absumptum est. quo indicio declaratum uidetur, quod
petra illa typum habuerit corporis Christi; quia scriptum est,
1 Cor. 10, 4 *'bibebant de consequenti petra, petra autem erat Christus.' quod*
utique non ad diuinitatem eius, sed ad carnem relatum est, quae 10
sitientium corda populorum perenni riuo sui sanguinis inundauit.
iam tunc igitur in mysterio declaratum est, quia Dominus Iesus
in carne sua, totius mundi peccata crucifixus aboleret, nec solum
delicta factorum, sed etiam cupiditates animorum, caro enim haedi
ad culpam facti refertur, ius ad illecebras cupiditatum, sicut scrip- 15
Num. 11, 4 *tum est, 'quia concupiuit populus cupiditatem pessimam, et dixe-*
runt, 'quis nos cibabit carne?' quod igitur extendit angelus
uirgam, et tetigit petram, de qua ignis exiit, ostendit quod caro
Domini Spiritu repleta diuino, peccata omnia humanae conditionis
Luc. 12, 49 *exureret, unde et Dominus ait, 'ignem ueni mittere in terram,'* 20
et caetera, in quibus rei docendae ac probandae maxime incumbit.

47. De genere temperato est apud Cyprianum uirginitatis illa
laudatio: *nunc nobis ad uirgines sermo est, quarum quo sublimior*
gloria est maior et cura. flos est ille ecclesiastici germinis, decus
atque ornamentum gratiae spiritualis, laeta indoles, laudis et hono- 25
ris opus integrum atque incorruptum, Dei imago respondens ad
sanctimoniam Domini, illustrior portio gregis Christi. gaudet per
ipsas atque in illis largiter floret ecclesiae matris gloriosa fecun-
ditas, quantoque plus gloriosa uirginitas numero suo addit, gau-

---

1 ait. *om. I.*   quo motus]commotus *ADEHI Maur.; non tamen BCFG Ambr.-Mig. (uet. et*
MSS longe plurimi [Ambr.-Mig.]).   2 militibus *D.*   3 carne *D.*   4 praecepta *EG.*   azymi
D. 5 iuge *A;* iusse (*supra*) *F.*   et ea iure perfudit] (et super eam ius effudit *MSS aliquot;* et ea
thure effudit *Albin. [Ambr.-Mig.]).*   ut]et *EG.*   angeli *A.*   6 ita *om. E.*   7 assumptum *F.*
8 habuerint *E.*   9 consequente *B Vulg.;* eos *add. AF Ambr.-Mig.;* se *add. Ver.An.*   11 mun-
dauit *B.*   12 Iesus his *H.*   15 facti *om. CG.*   refertur facti *E.*   16 cupiditate pessima *F.*
17 cibabit carne]cibauit carnem *D;* cibauit carnes *F;* cubabit carne *G.*   quid *E.*   18 exit *F.*
19 omnia diuine *E.*   conditionis humanae *E.*   20 in]super *GH.*   21 in quibus]cuius *CG.*
23 uobis *I.*   qua *F;* et *add. F.*   24 cura est *Cyp. (C. S. E. L.).*   illi *F.*   25 indoles atque *E.*
28 ipsas]illas *Cyp. (C. S. E. L.).*   floret largiter *E.*   generosa *C.*   29 copiosa *Cyp. (C. S. E.*
L.); generosa *Floriacensi [Maur.]).*   addit tanto plus *Maur.*

1. **quo motus oraculo, etc.**: Ambr. De   23. **nunc nobis, etc.**: Cypr. De Habitu
Spir. Sanct. 1, prol. 2-3.   Virg. 3. This, as well as the example

being troubled when he heard through the oracle of God that though thousands of people would fail, still through one man God would save his people from the enemy, took a goat's kid, and in accordance with the instruction of the angel, placed the flesh thereof with unleavened bread upon a rock, and sprinkled them with broth; and as soon as the angel of God touched them with the tip of the rod which he carried, a flame burst forth from the rock, and thus was consumed the sacrifice which was offered. By this sign it seems to be indicated that the rock was a type of Christ, for it is written: *They drank of the rock that followed them, and the rock was Christ.* This of course refers not to His Divinity, but to His Flesh which waters the hearts of His thirsting people with the ever-flowing tide of His Blood. It was therefore declared mystically that the Lord Jesus in His Flesh would be crucified and would wash away the sins of the whole world, and not only the sinful deeds, but also the evil desires of their hearts. For the flesh of the kid refers to sinful deeds; the broth to the allurements of the passions, as it is written: *For the people gave way to the worst passions, saying:—'Who will feed us with flesh?'* And so the angel stretching forth his rod and touching the rock from which a flame came forth, signified that the Flesh of the Lord, filled with the Holy Spirit, would burn away all the sins of man's condition. And so it is that the Lord says: *I am come to cast fire on the earth,*" and so on, wherein he particularly devotes himself to setting forth and proving the matter.

47. The well-known encomium of virginity in Cyprian is an example of the moderate style: "Now our discourse directs itself to the virgins, who as their honor is higher, are therefore our greater care. They are the flower of the tree of the Church, the beauty and ornament of spiritual grace, its bright natural virtue: of its praise and honor, a work pure and untarnished, the image of God, answering to the sanctity of the Lord, the brighter portion of the flock of Christ. The glorious fruitfulness of their Mother the Church rejoices through them, and in them richly flowers; and in proportion as glorious virginity adds to her numbers, in so much does the Mother's joy increase." And in another place, at the end of the letter, he says: *"As we have borne the image of the earthly, let us*

---

cited from Ambrose in illustration of the middle style, is distinguished by its figures of parallelism and especially by its homoioteleuton (clauses or phrases ending in similar sounds): cf. Norden 617–18.

1 Cor. 15, 49 *dium matris augescit.* et in alio loco in fine epistolae, *'quomodo*
portauimus inquit imaginem eius qui de limo est, sic portemus et
imaginem eius qui de caelo est.' hanc imaginem uirginitas portat,
portat integritas, sanctitas portat et ueritas, portant disciplinae Dei
memores, iustitiam cum religione retinentes, stabiles in fide, hu- 5
miles in timore, ad omnem tolerantiam fortes, ad sustinendas iniu-
rias mites, ad faciendam misericordiam faciles, fraterna pace unani-
mes atque concordes. quae uos singula, o bonae uirgines, obseruare,
diligere, implere debetis, quae Deo et Christo uacantes, ad Domi-
num cui uos dicastis, maiore et meliore parte praeceditis. prouectae 10
annis, iunioribus facite magisterium; minores natu, praebete maio-
ribus ministerium, comparibus incitamentum. hortamentis uos
mutuis excitate; aemulis de uirtute documentis ad gloriam prouo-
cate. durate fortiter, spiritualiter pergite, peruenite feliciter, tan-
tum mementote tunc nostri, cum incipiet in uobis uirginitas 15
honorari.

48. Ambrosius etiam genere dicendi temperato et ornato professis uirginibus proponit, tamquam sub exempli forma, quod moribus imitentur, et dicit: *uirgo erat, non solum corpore, sed etiam*
mente, quae nullo doli ambitu sincerum adulteraret affectum; corde 20
humilis, uerbis grauis, animi prudens, loquendi parcior, legendi
studiosior; non in incerto diuitiarum, sed in prece pauperis spem
reponens; intenta operi, uerecunda sermoni; arbitrum mentis solita
non hominem, sed Deum quaerere; nullum laedere, bene uelle om-
nibus; assurgere maioribus natu, aequalibus non inuidere; fugere 25
iactantiam, rationem sequi, amare uirtutem. quando ista uel uultu
laesit parentes? quando dissensit a propinquis? quando fastidiuit
humilem? quando risit debilem? quando uitauit inopem? eos solos
solita coetus uirorum inuisere, quos misericordia non erubesceret,

---

2 est *om. E.* sic *om. El Cyp.* (*C. S. E. L.*) *Ver.An. Vulg.* et *om. BCDH.* 8 uirginitas *om. I*;
uirginitatis *D.* uirginitas portat *om. E.* 5 iustitiam Dei *E.* religionem *I.* retinentes et *A.*
6 omnem tolerantiam]omnes tolerantias *El.* ad sustinendam iniuriam *Cyp.* (*C. S. E. L.*).
7 ad misericordiam faciendam *A.* faciles et *A.* 8 uos *om. E.* singulae *ABDEFGI.* o *om.*
ABF. 9 uocantes *F.* 10 dicastis et *Cyp.* (*C. S. E. L.*). praecedatis *C.* 11 iunioribus]
minoribus *E.* 12 paribus *El.* ornamentis *El.* uos *om. E.* 13 prouocate *G.* 15 nobis *E.*
uirginitas *om. E.* 20 ambitus *BF.* 22 pauperum *Ambr.-Mig.* 23 sermonibus *A;* sermone
CE. Ambr.-Mig. solita *om. MSS; non tamen Maur. et Ambr.-Mig.* 24 hominum *F.*
nullum laedere]nulli laedere os *AD*; nullum laedere os *BF.* 25 natis *E.* aequalibus]et
qualibus *H.* 26 uirtutes *D.* 27 dissens sit *B.* 29 solita]sollicita *MSS; non tamen Maur.*
et Ambr.-Mig. uirorum coetus *E.*

bear also the image of the heavenly. This image does virginity bear, righteousness bears it, holiness bears it, and truth; they bear it who are mindful of God's law, who observe justice with the fear of God, who are firm in faith, humble in fear, strong in every suffering, meek in sustaining injuries, ready to grant mercy, of one mind and heart in brotherly concord. And each one of these things, O holy virgins, ought you to keep, to love, to fulfill, for you with hearts free for God and for Christ, lead the way through your greater and better part, to the Lord to whom you have dedicated yourselves. You who are advanced in years, be the teachers of the younger; you who are younger, minister to the older, and be an inspiration to those of your own age; urge on one another by mutual encouragement; rouse one another to glory by rivaling each other in acts of virtue; endure valiantly, proceed in the spiritual life, attain your goal gloriously; only, be mindful of us then when your virginity will begin to be in honor."

48. Ambrose also uses the moderate, adorned style of speech when, as though in illustration, he holds up to virgins who have made their profession a model for their imitation. He says: "She was a virgin, not only in appearance, but in heart, who sullied not upright sentiments with any leanings toward deceit; humble of heart, dignified in speech, prudent in spirit, sparing of words, devoted to study, placing her hope not in the uncertainty of riches, but in the prayers of the poor, attentive to duty, respectful to discourse; one wont to seek God, not man, as the guide of her judgment; harming no one, but wishing well to all; rising to her elders, not envying her equals; avoiding boastfulness, following reason, loving virtue. When did she wound her parents even by a look? When did she disagree with her relatives? When did she condemn the humble? When did she mock the weak? When did she shun the needy? She was wont to go only into those gatherings of men which charity would not be shamed by, and which modesty would

---

1. **quomodo, etc.:** *id. ib.* 23–24.

17. **professis** = 'having made religious profession,' belongs to Eccl. Latin.

18. **sub . . . forma:** *sub* with the ablative to express condition or circumstance is cited in prose first for Livy: cf. St.- Schm. 539; K.-Steg. II, I, 570–71. T.L.L. for the phrase *sub forma* cites only Test. Optati (Corp. II, 4514) 35: cf. T.L.L. VI, 1076, 26–27.

19. **virgo erat, etc.:** Ambr. De Virg. 2, 1, 7–8.

neque praeteriret uerecundia. nihil toruum in oculis, nihil in uerbis procax, nihil in actu inuerecundum; non gestus fractior, non incessus solutior, non uox petulantior, ut ipsa corporis species simulacrum fuerit mentis, et figura probitatis. bona quippe domus in ipso uestibulo debet agnosci, ac primo praetendat ingressu nihil 5
intus latere tenebrarum, tamquam lucernae lux intus posita, foris luceat. quid ego exsequar ciborum parsimoniam, officiorum redundantiam; alterum ultra naturam superfuisse, alterum paene ipsi naturae defuisse? illic nulla intermissa tempora, hic congeminati ieiunio dies; et si quando reficiendi successisset uoluntas, cibus 10
plerumque obuius qui mortem arceret, non delicias ministraret.
haec autem propterea in exemplo huius temperati generis posui, quia non hic agit ut uirginitatem uoueant quae nondum uouerunt, sed quales esse debeant quae iam uotae sunt. nam ut aggrediatur animus tantum ac tale propositum, grandi utique dicendi genere 15
debet excitari et accendi. sed martyr Cyprianus de habitu uirginum, non de suscipiendo uirginitatis proposito scripsit. iste uero episcopus etiam ad hoc eas magno accendit eloquio.

49. Verum ex eo quod ambo egerunt, dictionis grandis exempla memorabo. ambo quippe inuecti sunt in eas quae formam pig- 20
mentis colorant, uel potius decolorant; quorum prior ille cum hoc ageret, ait inter caetera: *si quis pingendi artifex uultum alicuius et speciem et corporis qualitatem aemulo colore signasset, et signato iam consummatoque simulacro manus alius inferret, ut iam formata, iam picta, quasi peritior reformaret, grauis prioris arti-* 25

4 fuerit]fieret *E.*   5 praetentat *AF.*   7 ego]ergo *BCD.*   8 fuisse *C.*   alterum ipsi naturae pene *El Maur.*; ipsi *om. D.*   9 nulla fuisse *H.*   intermissa uel praemissa (*supra alia m.*) *H.* tempora intermissa *E.*   congeminat *A*; congeminatus *E*; congeminatos *Ambr.-Mig.*   11 plerumque sumebatur *E.*   obuius]ob huius *D*; obuios *F.*   12 propterea *om. E.*   13 uirginem *F.* moueant *E.*   nondum uouerunt]non nouerunt *E.*   14 aggrediatur]hac grediatur *D.*   17 scribit *I.* 18 ad hoc etiam *EI.*   20 pigmento *A.*   21 quorum *om. A.*   24 ut *om. Cyp.* (*C. S. E. L.*). 25 peritior *del. E.*

14. **uotae sunt** = 'consecrated themselves': the passive here has a middle sense: an Eccl. usage.

16. **debet excitari et accendi**: Augustine's discrimination between the temperate and grand style by examples drawn from a common subject, made different by different circumstances, shows the teacher's instinct for clearness and force.

debet: *debere* was used by the poets as a synonym of *necesse esse.* This became frequent in Late Latin: cf. Goel. (1) 418; K.-Schm. s.v.; Georges s.v. Note this below in 24, 54, where the analogy has been carried so far as to cause the use of an impersonal *debet*: debet granditer dici. While impersonal *debet* already occurs in Cicero, it is confined in most part to Late Latin: cf. St.-

not permit her to pass by. There was nothing sharp in her glance, nothing bold in her words, nothing unseemly in her conduct; her bearing was not sensuous, nor her gait too free, nor her voice petulant, so that her outward appearance was an image of her soul, and was a picture of purity. For a fine house ought to be recognized as such at its very vestibule, and ought at the first step inside to show that no darkness lurks within, as though the light from the lamp inside were illuminating the parts without. What need to mention her abstemiousness in food, her superabundance in duties — the one exceeding the powers of nature, the other almost falling below nature's needs; in the one case, no intermissions in time; in the other, the days doubled for fasting! But when the want of refection did arise, it was answered generally with such food as would prevent starvation, not with such as would afford pleasure." This passage I have chosen to illustrate the temperate style for this reason, that here the author does not urge those who have not yet consecrated themselves to virginity to do so, but treats of what the character of those should be who have thus consecrated themselves. For, that the heart be led to make so important and so serious a decision, it must certainly be aroused and set on fire by the grand style of oratory. Cyprian, the martyr, has written on the dress of virgins, not on embracing the profession of virginity. And still this bishop inflames women even as to this, with great eloquence.

49. But I shall draw illustrations of the grand style from a subject which both have treated. For both have inveighed against those women who color, or rather discolor their faces with paint. The first, in his condemnation of this, says among other things: "If some artist had painted the features, form, and outward appearance of a certain person in colors rivaling nature's, and when the picture had been painted and finished, another hand, as if being more skilled, should set about doing over what had already been conceived and painted, the insult to the first artist would seem to be a serious one, and his indignation just. And you, do you think

Schm. 622; T.L.L. V, 102, 43–59.

18. **ad hoc . . . accendit**: *accendo* with *ad* is cited for Cic. Tusc. 1, 4; Sall. Jug. 31, 16, and for Silver writers: cf. T. L. L. I, 276, 48–75.

21. **decolorant**: mostly Poetic, Silver, and Late: cf. T.L.L. V, 199, 71–200.

22. **inter caetera**: this phrase is cited first for Livy 3, 10, 7, and then with increasing frequency for Silver and Late Latin: cf. T.L.L. III, 968, 32–42.

si quis pingendi, etc.: Cypr. De Habitu Virg. 15.

ficis iniuria et iusta indignatio uideretur. tu te existimas impune laturam tam improbae temeritatis audacium, Dei artificis offensam? ut enim impudica circa homines, et incesta fucis lenocinantibus non sis, corruptis uiolatisque quae Dei sunt, peior adultera detineris. quod ornari te putas, quod putas comi, impugnatio est ista divini 5
1 Cor. 5, 7-8 *operis, praeuaricatio est ueritatis. monentis apostoli uox est: 'expurgate uetus fermentum, ut sitis noua conspersio, sicut estis azymi: nam pascha nostrum immolatus est Christus. itaque festa celebremus non in fermento ueteri neque in fermento malitiae et nequitiae sed in azymis sinceritatis et ueritatis.' num sinceritas* 10
perseuerat et ueritas, quando quae sincera sunt polluuntur, et colorum adulteriis et medicaminum fucis in mendacium uera mutan-
Matt. 5, 36 *tur? Dominus tuus dicit, 'non potes facere capillum unum album aut nigrum,' et tu ad uincendam Domini tui uocem uis te esse potiorem. audaci conatu et sacrilego contemptu crines tuos inficis;* 15
malo praesagio futurorum capillos iam tibi flammeos auspicaris. longum est inserere omnia quae sequuntur.

50. Ille uero posterior ut in tales diceret, *hinc illa* inquit *nascuntur incentiua uitiorum, ut quaesitis coloribus ora depingant, dum uiris displicere formidant, et de adulterio uultus meditentur* 20
adulterium castitatis. quanta hic amentia, effigiem mutare naturae, picturam quaerere, et dum uerentur maritale iudicium, prodere suum? prior enim de se pronuntiat, quae cupit mutare quod nata est; ita dum alii studet placere, prius ipsa sibi displicet. quem iudicem, mulier, ueriorem requirimus deformitatis tuae, quam teip- 25
sam, quae uideri times? si pulchra es, quid absconderis? si deformis, cur te formosam esse mentiris, nec tuae conscientiae, nec alieni gratiam erroris habitura? ille enim alteram diligit, tu alteri uis placere; et irasceris si amet alteram, qui adulterare in te docetur. mala magistra es iniuriae tuae. lenocinari enim refugit, etiam quae 30
est passa lenonem, ac licet uilis mulier, non alteri tamen, sed sibi peccat. tolerabiliora propemodum in adulterio crimina sunt; ibi

2 latura *D.* tam *om. B.* 3 enim *om. Cyp. (C. S. E. L.).* fuscis *E.* 4 retineris *DF.* 5 ornare *CH.* putas (comi) *om. BD.* comi impugnatio]comum pugnatio *F.* est *om. E.* ista *om. I.* 7 consparsio *DFG Cyp. (C. S. E. L.).* 8 nam]etenim *Maur. Ver. An. Vulg.;* et *add. Cyp. (C. S. E. L.).* 9 celebremus festa *H.* et]uel *E.* 10 et nequitiae *om. I.* num] nam *DEF.* non *add. supra* sinceritas *alia m. F.* 11 quae]-que *E.* et *om. Cyp. (C. S. E. L.)* color *E.* 12 adulterinis *BCDEFGHI; non tamen Maur. et Cyp. (C. S. E. L.);* (et cotorum adulterinis medicaminum *editi et MSS* [*Maur.*]), et *om. MSS et Cyp. (C. S. E. L.),* in mendacium *om. I.* 13 unum *om. A;* unum capillum *E Ver. An. Vulg.* 15 tuas *F.* 18 ut in tales diceret *om. E.* hinc inquit illa nascuntur *H.* 20 meditantur *BH Ambr.-Mig.* 21 haec *Maur.* naturae mutare *E.* 22 uenerentur *D.* perdere *ADF;* perdidere *BCG (quidam MSS*

that you can carry through such shameless and daring insolence, an offence against God, the great Artist, without being punished? For although toward man you are not unchaste, nor are you corrupted in heart through your meretricious adornments, yet in spoiling and violating what is God's, you are a worse adulteress. That you consider yourself adorned and beautified, this is an insult to the divine work, a violation of truth. The Apostle's word of admonition is: *Purge out the old leaven that you may be a new paste, as you are unleavened. For Christ our Pasch is sacrificed. Therefore, let us feast, not with the old leaven, nor with the leaven of malice and wrongdoing; but with the unleavened bread of sincerity and truth.* But can sincerity and truth remain when what is sincere is polluted, and when what is true is turned into a lie by immodest coloring and deceitful cosmetics? Your Lord says: *Thou canst not make one hair white or black*, and do you wish to be more powerful, so as to set at naught the words of your Lord? With insolent daring and sacrilegious contempt, do you dye your hair; with evil presage of the future, do you make your locks flame-colored." It would take long to quote all that follows.

50. And the later writer, speaking against such women, says: "Hence arise those allurements to sin, that they seek color with which to paint their cheeks, fearing to lose the good opinion of men; and from adultery of their faces, they consider adultery of their chastity. What folly is this to change the appearance of nature, and to seek merely for its likeness, and while fearing a husband's disapproval, to betray one's own! For that woman is the first to pronounce against herself who wishes to change what nature has made; and so, while she studies to make herself pleasing to another, she is already not pleasing to herself. What truer judge shall we ask, oh woman, of your want of beauty, than yourself, since you fear to be seen? If you are beautiful, why do you hide it? If ugly, why do you pretend to be beautiful, enjoying neither peace in your own conscience, nor satisfaction in misleading others? For he loves another; you wish to please another; and you are angry if he loves another, being taught adultery by you. You are the evil teacher of your own wrong. For a woman who has been the victim of the panderer, still herself refuses to pander, and bad

[*Ambr.-Mig.*]); prodidere *H*; prodicerunt *E*; perdiderunt *I*.   23 quae]qui *D*.   24 aliis *B Ambr.-Mig.*   25 meliorem *D*.   requiremus *Maur.*   27 te *om. E*.   28 diligit tu alterum diligis *E*.   29 aliam   *BDEFI Ambr.-Mig.*   qui]quia *E*; quae *H*.   docere *G*.   30 male *ABCDFGHI*.   enim *om. ABDEFHI*.   30 refugit enim *CG*; refugi *D*.   etiam *om. CEG*.   31 est ipsa *H*; quae passa est *Ambr.-Mig.*   32 adulterio]altero *Ambr.-Mig.*

18. **hinc illa, etc.**: Ambr. De Virg. 1, 6, 28.

enim pudicitia, hic natura adulteratur. satis ut existimo, apparet feminas ne suam fucis adulterent formam et, ad pudorem et ad timorem hac facundia uehementer impelli. proinde neque submissum neque temperatum, sed grande omnino genus hoc elocutionis agnoscimus. et in his autem quos duos ex omnibus proponere uolui, 5 et in aliis ecclesiasticis uiris et bona, et bene — id est sicut res postulat — acute, ornate, ardenterque dicentibus, per multa eorum scripta uel dicta possunt haec tria genera reperiri, et assidua lectione uel auditione, admixta etiam exercitatione, studentibus inolescere. 10

22, 51. Nec quisquam praeter disciplinam esse existimet ista miscere; immo quantum congrue fieri potest, omnibus generibus dictio uarianda est. nam quando prolixa est in uno genere, minus detinet auditorem. cum uero fit in aliud ab alio transitus, etiamsi longius eat, decentius procedit oratio; quamuis habeant et singula genera 15 uarietates suas in sermone eloquentiam, quibus non sinuntur in eorum qui audiunt, frigescere uel tepescere sensibus. uerumtamen facilius submissum solum, quam solum grande diutius tolerari potest. commotio quippe animi quanto magis excitanda est, ut nobis assentiatur auditor, tanto minus in ea diu teneri potest, cum 20 fuerit quantum satis est excitata. et ideo cauendum est, ne dum

1 adulterat *B*.　2 ne fucis suam *H*.　formas *A*.　4 hic *C*. locutionis *E*.　5 et in his]ex his *CI;* ex hiis *E*.　6 et (bona) *om. A*.　7 ornate acute ardenterque *A*. 8 uel]et *F*. genera *om. E*.　9 uel auditione *om. AD*.　11 nec]haec *E*.　esse *om. E*.　ista]ita *Mig*.　12 potest de *BF*.　13 (uarianda) est *om. A*.　14 longus *I*.　15 detentius *B*.　17 audiant *D*; qui audiunt *om. E*.　18 diutius *om. E*.　diutius]huius *C*.　21 quanto *I*.

2. **fucis** = 'coloring for the face or hair,' is mostly Poetic and Eccl.: cf. T.L.L. VI, 1461, 62–73.

9. **inolescere** = 'to be fixed in mind': Late.

22. *Variation in the use of the styles.*

11. **nec . . . uarianda est**: cf. Auct. ad Her. 4, 11, 16: sed figuram in dicendo commutare oportet, ut grauem mediocris, mediocrem excipiat attenuata, deinde identidem commutentur, ut facile satietas uarietate uitetur. Orat. 29, 103: at haec [genera] interdum temperanda et uarianda sunt. Quint. 12, 10, 71: dicet idem grauiter, seuere, acriter, uehementer, concitate, copiose, amare, comiter, remisse, subtiliter, blande, leniter, dulciter, breuiter, urbane; non ubique similis sed ubique par sibi.

12. **congrue**: Early and Late Latin for *congruenter*: cf. T.L.L. III, 305, 1–30.

13. **prolixa** = 'long drawn out': Late: cf. K.-Schm. s.v.

14. **transitus** = 'change': mostly Poetic and Silver: cf. Benoist-Goelz. and Georges s.v.

15. **quamuis habeant . . . eloquentium**: cf. Quint. 12, 10, 67: ac sic prope innumerabiles species reperiuntur, quae utique aliquo momento inter se differant: sicut quattuor uentos generaliter a totidem mundi cardinibus accepimus flare, cum interim plurimi medii et eorum uaria nomina quidem etiam regionum ac

woman as she is, still she sins not so much against another as against herself. The sin of adultery is almost more tolerable than yours, for in the first instance modesty is corrupted; in the second, nature." It is certainly clear, I think, that here women are eloquently and passionately dissuaded from spoiling their faces by paint, and are urged to modesty and fear of self. We recognize, therefore, not the subdued style of oratory here, but the grand style throughout. But in these two authors whom out of many I have chosen in illustration, and in the other ecclesiastical writers who speak on worthy subjects, and in a worthy way, that is, as the matter demands, to the point, eloquently, and passionately, these three styles can be found scattered through their many writings and treatises, and can, through abundant reading and hearing, with the addition of practice, become engrafted in students' minds.

22,   51. No one should suppose that it is against the rule to mingle these three styles. On the contrary, as far as it can properly be done, one should vary his diction by using all three. For when a speech is surfeited with one style, it does not keep the listener's attention. But when a change is made from one to another, even if the discourse is stretched out to some length, it proceeds in a more pleasing fashion; although each style, too, has variations of its own in the language of the eloquent, which do not allow the attention of the audience to grow languid or to cool off. However, we can more readily bear the subdued style alone for a longer

fluminum proprii, deprehenduntur.

16. **quibus . . . sensibus**: cf. De Doctr. Chris. 2, 36, 54: et uarietas eius sine fastidio teneat intentos.

17. **uerumtamen . . . potest**: it is easier to maintain the level of the plain style than the heights of the grand; there is less danger of slipping and falling: cf. Orat. 28, 98: qui in illo subtili et acuto elaborauit, ut callide arguteque diceret, nec quicquam altius cogitaret, hoc uno perfecto magnus orator est, sed non maximus. *minimeque in lubrico uersabitur et, si semel constiterit, numquam cadit.*

19. **commotio . . . excitata**: cf. Orat. 28, 99: at uero hic noster, quem principem ponimus, grauis acer ardens, si ad hoc unum est natus aut in solo se exercuit aut huic generi studuit uni nec suam copiam

cum illis duobus generibus temperauit, maxime est contemnendus. ille enim summissus, quod acute et ueratorie dicit, sapiens iam, medius suauis, hic autem copiosissimus, si nihil aliud est, uix satis sanus uideri solet.

21. **et ideo . . . perductum**: Cicero implies this in speaking of the middle style which he contrasts with the grand style in just this very point: cf. Orat. 28, 98: medius ille autem, quem modicum et temperatum uoco, si modo suum illud satis instruxerit, non extimescet ancipites dicendi incertosque casus; *etiam si quando minus succedet, ut saepe fit, magnum tamen periculum non adibit: alte enim cadere non potest.*

et ideo: for *et ideo* as a conclusive particle, cf. 18, 37.

uolumus altius erigere quod erectum est, etiam inde decidat, quo
fuerat excitatione perductum. interpositis uero quae sunt dicenda
submissius, bene reditur ad ea quae opus est granditer dici, ut
dictionis impetus sicut maris aestus alternet. ex quo fit ut grande
dicendi genus, si diutius est dicendum, non debeat esse solum, sed 5
aliorum generum interpositione uarietur. ei tamen generi dictio
tota tribuitur, cuius copia praeualuerit.

23,   52. Interest enim quod genus cui generi interponatur, uel adhi-
beatur certis et necessariis locis. nam et in grandi genere semper
aut pene semper temperata decet principia. et in potestate est 10
eloquentis ut dicantur nonnulla submisse, etiam quae possent granditer dici, ut ea quae dicuntur granditer, ex illorum fiant comparatione grandiore, et eorum tamquam umbris luminosiora reddantur.

1 quo]quod *E.*   2 fuerit *D.*   3 est *om. E.*   dici granditer *E.*   6 generum]
genere *E.*   tamen ei *H.*   generi]genere *Maur.*   dictionis *E.*   7 tota *om. I.* at-
tribuitur *E.*   praeualuerit]tribuitur *A.*   8 enim *om. E.*   generi]genere *B.*
10 aut]ac *E.*   decet]debent *E.*   est *om. F.*   11 eloquentiae *E.*   nonnullae *E.*
12 ut]inde *E.*   granditer dicuntur *E.*   fiant comparatione]comparatione
fiunt *E.*

2. **excitatione**: Late.

interpositis ... alternet: Augustine
insists on the importance of this, also in
Contr. Cresc. 1, 16, 20, in speaking of
rhetoric and dialectic: siue autem sit dictor, siue disputator, nec dictio sine disputatione est cum et in ipsa eloquentiae
latitudine ueritas a falsitate discernitur;
nec disputatio potest esse sine dictione,
quando utique uerbis et lingua ipsa con-
strictio sermonis exprimitur.

4. **alternet**: Poetic, Silver, and
Late: cf. K.-Schm. s.v.; T.L.L. I, 1753,
67-1754, 26.

ex quo fit ... praeualuerit: Augustine brings out the necessity of rhetoric
to dialectic, and *vice versa*, in De Dial. 7.
The dialectician must, at times, borrow
some of the graces of rhetoric if he sees
the need of attracting his audience; the
orator, on the other hand, must strengthen
his cause by making dialectic the bones
and sinews, as it were, of his persuasion:
manifestum est et disputatorem, si qua
ei delectandi cura est, rhetorico colore
aspergendum; et oratorem, si ueritatem

persuadere uult, dialecticis quasi neruis
atque ossibus esse roborandum, quae
ipsa natura corporibus nostris, nec firmi-
tati uirium subtrahere potuit, nec oculo-
rum offensioni patere permisit.

7. **praeualuerit**: mostly Silver Latin.

23. *How the styles are to be inter-
mingled.*

8. **interest ... locus**: the various purposes of a discourse, as differentiated in
the offices, *docere, delectare, flectere,*
are the criteria for the intermingling of
the styles; the different kinds of speeches
and the different parts of a speech are
the means, in general, for determining
the necessary places for each style: cf.
Quint. 12, 10, 69: utetur enim, *ut res
exiget,* omnibus, nec pro causa modo sed
pro partibus causae, nam ut non eodem
modo pro reo capitis et in certamine
hereditatis et de interdictis ac sponsioni-
bus et de certa credita dicet, sententiarum
quoque in senatu et contionum et priua-
torum consiliorum seruabit discrimina,
multa ex differentia personarum, locorum temporumque mutabit: ita in eadem

time, than the grand style alone. For the higher the pitch to which the feelings are to be excited in order to gain the assent of the audience, the shorter the time that this can be maintained once they have been sufficiently excited. And so we must take care lest desiring to lift higher what is already lifted high, there be rather a fall from the pitch of excitement already attained. But by interspersing matter which requires rather the subdued style, a pleasing return can then be made to the subject calling for grand expression, so that the flow of diction comes and goes like the tides of the sea. Hence it is that the grand style of diction, if it has to be continued for some time, must not be used alone, but must be varied by the interspersion of the other styles. The whole discourse, however, is attributed in kind to the style which predominates.

23,   52. It is, therefore, a matter of importance to know what style should be interspersed with what other style, and what kind should be used in definite, necessary places. For even in the grand style, properly the introduction should always, or nearly always be moderate. And the orator has the right in some places to speak in the subdued style, even when the grand style could have been used, so that what he expresses in the grand style may by comparison

oratione aliter conciliabit, non ex iisdem haustibus iram et misericordiam petet, alias ad docendum alias ad mouendum adhibebit artes. Cicero in summing up the various parts of an oration, applies to each the manner of presentation it requires, and thus implies the proper use and intermingling of the styles: cf. Orat. 35, 122: tractatio igitur rerum efficit admirabilem orationem; nam ipsae quidem res in perfacili cognitione uersantur. quid enim iam sequitur, quod quidem artis sit, nisi ordiri orationem, in quo aut concilietur auditor aut erigatur aut paret se ad discendum; rem breuiter exponere et probaliter et aperte, ut quid agatur intellegi possit; sua confirmare, aduersaria euertere, eaque efficere non perturbate, sed singulis argumentationibus ita concludendis, ut efficiatur quod sit consequens iis quae sumentur ad quamque rem confirmandam; post

omnia perorationem inflammantem restinguentemue concludere?

9. **nam et . . . principia**: cf. Orat. 36, 124: principia uerecunda, nondum elatis incensa uerbis, sed acuta sententiis uel ad offensionem aduersarii uel ad commendationem sui.

10. **et in potestate . . . reddantur**: though certain places call for the grand style, there is no violation of principle to use a lesser style in part, in order by contrast to enhance the grand style when used.

in potestate est . . . ut: uncommon but classical: cf. Cic. Ad Fam. 13, 39: est in tua potestate, ut ille . . . putet: cf. K.-Steg. II, 2, 245.

12. **ex comparatione**: this phrase is cited first for Cic. Part. Orat. 19, 66: quaeritur . . . ex comparatione quid utile, quid aequum: cf. T.L.L. III, 2006, 41ff.

in quocumque autem genere aliqua quaestionum uincula soluenda
sunt, acumine opus est. quod sibi submissum genus proprie uindicat. ac per hoc eo genere utendum est et in aliis duobus generibus, quando eis ista incidunt, sicut laudandum aliquid uel uitu-
perandum, ubi nec damnatio cuiusquam nec liberatio, nec ad acti- 5
onem quamlibet assensio requiritur, in quocumque alio genere
occurrerit, genus adhibendum et interponendum est temperatum.
in grandi ergo genere inueniunt locos suos duo caetera, et in submisso similiter. temperatum autem genus non quidem semper, sed
tamen aliquando submisso indiget, si, ut dixi, quaestio cuius nodus 10
est soluendus, incurrat, uel quando nonnulla quae ornari possent,
ideo non ornantur, sed submisso sermone dicuntur, ut quibusdam
quasi toris ornamentorum praebeant eminentiorem locum. grande

1 uincla *BF.*   2 propriae *DFG.*   3 generibus *om. A.*   4 ista]ita *C.*   5 ad
om. A.   7 occurit *DH.*   adhibendum genus *E.*   9 non quidem]in quid est *D.*
10 si ut dixi]sicut dixi *ABF;* sicut dixi si *DE.*   nodus *in marg. alia m. F.*
11 est *om. F.*   somuendus est *EI.*   occurrat *D.*   possunt *A.*   13 toribus
sic em. alia m. AB; choris *E.*

1. **in quocumque . . . uindicat**:
another identification of the plain style
and dialectic. To Cicero, *uincula quaestionum* would mean the *confirmatio* and
confutatio of a speech. These parts, as
well as the *narratio*, he assigns to the
plain style: cf. Orat. 36, 124ff.: narrationes credibiles nec historico sed prope
cotidiano sermone explicatae dilucide.
dein si tenuis causa est, tum etiam argu-
mentandi tenue filum et in docendo et in
referendo, idque ita tenebitur, ut quanta
ad rem tanta ad orationem fiat accensio.

quaestionum uincula: genitive,
in place of a noun and adjective, for
emphasis and stylistic effect. Even outside of figurative expressions, as here,
this usage is increasingly common in
Late Latin, especially with abstact nouns
of dependence: cf. St.-Schm. 395, 823;
Gabarrou 185–86; McGuire 30–31. See
this below in 25, 55 (bona morum).

4. **sicut laudandum . . . temperatum**:
as the plain style accomplishes the *officium* of *docere*, and is used particularly
in judicial oratory (considering classical
genus; dialectic, considering Augus-

tine's conception of kind of speech), and
in the *narratio, confirmatio, confutatio*
(considering parts of a speech), so the
moderate style accomplishes the *officium*
of *delectare*, and is used particularly in
deliberative oratory (considering classical *genus*; panegyric in Augustine's conception), and in the *exordium* (aiming
to make the audience *attentos, dociles,
beneuolos*) and *rationis confirmatio*, or
elaboration of the proof (considering
parts of a speech).

**laudandum aliquid uel uituper-
andum**: the attributive use of the gerundive is relatively restricted before the
Silver and Late writers. The attributive
use of *laudandus*, however, is classical,
and the use of *uituperandus* is modelled
closely also on the Ciceronian *contemnendus*: cf. St.-Schm. 595.

5. **damnatio cuiusquam . . . liberatio**
would demand the grand style.

8. **in grandi . . . similiter**: in a speech
preponderatingly grand, the plain style
has place (1) where *docere* is the object,
i.e. clearly to define a position, or to
prove or refute an argument. (2) in more

become even grander, and as it were, through the shadows of the other appear even more luminous. But whatever the style, if some knotty question demands solution, acumen is called for, and this the subdued style claims as its own. And for this reason, this style must be used even in the other two, when such questions arise in them; just as when something requires praise or censure, and it is not the question of the condemnation or the acquittal of anyone, nor of a person's assent to some course of action, no matter what the kind of style used when this occurs, the moderate style must then be taken up and interposed. And so in the grand style and in the subdued also, the other two find place. The temperate style, on the other hand, not indeed always, but still sometimes requires the subdued style if, as I have said, some question occurs whose difficulty demands solution, or when something which could be embellished is not embellished, but expressed in subdued language that it may furnish a more conspicuous place for certain

elevated thought, in order to enhance the grand by contrast. In a speech outstandingly grand, the moderate style has place (1) where *delectare* is the aim, *i.e.* to conciliate the audience in the *principium*, and to please in the amplification of the proof, (2) in oratory leaning to the panegyric, where violence of feeling is not called into play. Considering, on the other hand, a speech preponderatingly plain, or dialectical, the moderate style has place where the circumstances just mentioned are evident, and the grand style has place where, as Augustine will emphasize below, the audience needs to be persuaded, by the moving of their emotions, to do that which, through reasoning, they realize is right. Cicero expresses this last relation in the conclusion to the quotation given above (in note: *in quocumque . . . uindicat*) where he speaks of the styles in their connection with the various parts of a speech (Orat. 36, 125): cum uero causa ea inciderit, in qua uis eloquentiae possit expromi, tum se latius fundet orator, tum reget et flectet animos et sic afficiet, ut uolet, id est, ut causa et ratio temporis postulabit.

9. **temperatum . . . requirit**: there is a difference in regard to the temperate style.

It, at times, uses the plain style, when the circumstances are such as explained above, where the plain was found necessary to the *genus grande*. But it has no need of the grand style, from the very nature of its purpose, *delectare*, which does not seek to rise to *flectere*, as *docere* often does, but is rather an aim in itself. Augustine, though he maintains the threefold division traditional and popular in Roman rhetoric, still often recognizes, as here, that style is fundamentally twofold, as the Peripatetics conceived it, λόγος πρὸς τὰ πράγματα and λόγος πρὸς τοὺς ἀκροωμένους, and that the grand and the temperate styles are connected in being merely phases of the latter.

10. **submisso indigent**: for *indigeo* with the abl. cf. 3, 5.

13. **toris ornamentorum**: Augustine borrows his figure from Cicero. A *torus* was a raised ornament, a knot on the garland: cf. Orat. 6, 21: isque [modus mediocris] uno tenore . . . fluit . . . aut addit aliquos *ut in corona toros* omnemque orationem ornamentis modicis uerborum sententiarumque distinguit.

ornamentorum: a so-called genitive of identity, which belongs almost entirely to Late Latin: cf. St.-Schm. 395.

autem genus temperata dictio non requirit; ad delectandos quippe animos, non ad mouendos ipsa suscipitur.

24, 53. Non sane si dicenti crebrius et uehementius acclametur, ideo granditer putandus est dicere; hoc enim et acumina submissi generis et ornamenta faciunt temperati. grande autem genus plerumque 5 pondere suo uoces premit, sed lacrimas exprimit. denique cum apud Caesaream Mauritaniae populo dissuaderem pugnam ciuilem,

1 autem]ergo *E.*   dicta *E.*   3 dicenti]dicendi *CEF.*   acclamatur *I.*   4 dicendi (dicere *supra alia m.*) *F.*   5 plerumque *om. E.*   6 suo pondere *E.*   lacrimas *om. E.*   7 suaderem *F.*

1. **ad delectandos . . . suscipitur**: the purposes of the middle and the grand style remain distinct. That of the middle does not merge into that of the grand, as is often the case with the purposes of the plain and the grand. The reason, as given above, is clear. They do not deal separately with *res* and *modus quo*, but both with *modus quo*, though each in a different way, because of different ends.

24. *The effects wrought by the various styles.*

3. **non sane . . . exprimit**: the grand style appeals not merely to the mind; it touches the heart. Therefore, though the plain and the temperate styles may receive great applause, the grand style is heard rather in hushed silence, or with tears. Augustine must have frequently experienced this himself. He gives one example of it below, in the instance of the effect of his address at Caesarea. Another interesting one is found in Retract. 2, 51, where he describes the utter silence with which Emeritus, the Donatist bishop, heard the discourse delivered in answer to the charges he had brought against the church: ubi non inueniens quid responderet, totum sermonem meum quem de solis Maximianistis in auribus eius et omnium qui aderant explicaui tamquam mutus audiuit. Turning to the *De Gestis cum Emerito*, to examine the speech itself for evidence of its power, while one recognizes that the force of its dialectic must have had a strong effect in silencing Augustine's opponent, still it is evident that the moving eloquence of its final words, spoken in the unadorned grand style, could not but have helped powerfully not only to hold silent the Donatist bishop himself, but also to move to tears the Catholic bishops who were also present at the conference: cf. De Gest. Emer. 12: et tamen, fratres mei, non inuidemus concordiae ipsorum . . . sed hoc dico: si ramus fractus quaesiuit uirgultum a se fractum, qua diligentia debet arbor ipsa quaerere ramum ex se fractum? ideo sudamus, ideo laboramus, ideo inter eorum arma et cruentas furias Circumcellionum periclitati sumus, et adhuc qualiacumque donata a Deo patientia toleramus, dum arbor quaerit ramum, dum grex et ouili Christi ouem perditam quaerit. si pastoralibus uisceribus praediti sumus, per sepes et spinas non coarctare debemus. membris lacertis ouem quaeramus, et pastori principique omnium cum laetitia reportemus. multa diximus etiam fatigati, et tamen, frater noster, propter quem ista dicimus uobis, et cui partier dicimus, et pro quo tanta agimus, adhuc pertinax constitit. constantem se putat fortitudo crudelis. non adhuc de uana et falsa fortitudine glorietur. audiat apostolum dicentem: *uirtus in infirmitate perficitur.* oremus pro illo. unde scimus quid uelit Deus? *multae cogitationes*, sicut scriptum est, *in corde uiri; consilium autem Domini manet in aeternum.*

bows as it were, of embellishment. But moderate diction does not need the grand style, for it is used to please the mind, not to move it. **24,**   53. If a speaker get frequent and loud applause, it should not on that account be imagined that he is talking in the grand style, for this is the effect of the acumen of the subdued style, and of the ornament of the temperate. But the grand style does generally silence all voices by its impressiveness, and calls forth tears. In fact, when at Caesarea in Mauritania, I was urging the people against civil strife or worse than civil strife, which they called

acclametur: *acclamare*, as also *acclamatio*, in classical Latin (especially in Cic.) expresses disapprobation. Not until Livy, Silver, and Late Latin does *acclamare* express approbation and applause: cf. K.-Schm. s.v.; T.L.L. I, 325, 80–326, 40. Note this later use also in 26, 56.

6. **cum apud Caesaream Mauritaniae**: the dating of this trip to Caesarea is of importance, since in connection with the statement made below (iam ferme octo uel amplius anni sunt, etc.), it serves to fix the date of the present book, *i.e.* 426 A.D. A trip to Caesarea is recorded by Augustine in the following places: (1) in letter 190, 1, 1, written to Optatus in 418 A.D., where Augustine says: quamuis tuae sanctitatis nullas ad me ipsum datas acceperim litteras; tamen quia illae quas ad Mauritaniam Caesariensem misisti, me apud Caesaream praesente uenerunt, quo nos iniuncta nobis a uenerabili papa Zosimo apostolicae sedis episcopo ecclesiastica necessitas traxerat; (2) in the Retractions 2, 51, which in giving the occasion of the *Gesta cum Emerito Donatista*, speak also of Augustine's having been urged by necessity to go to Caesarea: aliquanto post collationem quam cum haereticis Donatistis habuimus, orta est nobis necessitas pergendi in Mauritaniam Caesariensem. ibi apud ipsam Caesaream Emeritum Donatistarum episcopum uidimus, etc. The very opening words of the De. Gest. cum Emer. fix definitely the date of the last mentioned journey: gloriosissimis imperatoribus, Honorio duodecim, et Theodosio octauum consulibus (*i.e.* 418 A.D.), duodecimo calendas octobris, Caesareae in ecclesia maiori, cum . . . adesset etiam Emeritus partis Donati episcopus, Augustinus episcopus ecclesiae catholicae dixit, etc. Possidius (14) connects these two events, *i.e.* Augustine's visit to Caesarea due to letters from the Pope, and his speaking before Emeritus (Sept. 418 A.D.): tamen omnipotens Dei praestitit auxilium, ut postea in Caesariensi Mauritaniae ciuitate constitutus uernerabilis memoriae Augustinus, quo eum uenire cum aliis coepiscopis sedis apostolicae litterae compulerant, ob terminandas uidelicet alias ecclesiae necessitates: hoc ergo occasione prouenit, ut Emeritum eiusdem loci Donatistarum episcopum, quem suae sectae praecipuum in illa collatione habuerunt defensorem uideret . . . et prouocaret gestis ecclesiasticis, etc. It seems most probable, therefore, that this important trip, recorded so especially by Augustine and his biographer, is identical with the one mentioned in the present instance, since Augustine's mention of his trip here is as of something about which his readers are already informed. If this is so, it, too, should be dated September 418. The Benedictine editors also accept this view: cf. Aug. Epist. 193, n. 1; De Doctr. Chris. 4, 24, 53, n. 1. For a full and critical account of Augustine's meeting with Emeritus the Donatist, cf. Monceaux, P., Histoire littéraire de l'Afrique chrétienne, VI, 145–89. Paris, 1922.

uel potius plus quam ciuilem, quam cateruam uocabant, neque enim
ciues tantummodo, uerum etiam propinqui, fratres, postremo parentes ac filii lapidibus inter se in duas partes diuisi, per aliquot
dies continuos, certo tempore anni solemniter dimicabant, et quisque ut quemque poterat occidebat, egi quidem granditer, quantum 5
ualui, ut tam crudele atque inueteratum malum de cordibus et
moribus eorum auellerem pelleremque dicendo; non tamen egisse
aliquid me putaui, cum eos audirem acclamantes, sed cum flentes
uiderem. acclamationibus quippe se doceri et delectari, flecti autem
lacrimis indicabant. quas ubi aspexi, immanem illam consuetu- 10
dinem a patribus et auis longeque a maioribus traditam. quae
pectora eorum hostiliter obsidebat, uel potius possidebat, uictam,
antequam re ipsa id ostenderent, credidi. moxque sermone finito
ad agendas Deo gratias corda atque ora conuerti. et ecce iam ferme
octo uel amplius anni sunt, propitio Christo, ex quo illic nihil tale 15
tentatum est. sunt et alia multa experimenta quibus didicimus,
homines, quid in eis fecerit sapientis granditas dictionis, non clamore potius quam gemitu, aliquando etiam lacrimis, postremo uitae
mutatione monstrasse.

1 uel potius quam ciuilem *om. A.*   enim *om. D.*   2 uerum]sed *E.*   propinqui
et *H.*   3 in *om. E.*   4 dies]tempus *E.*   continuo *D.*   5 poterant *F.*   occidebant
FG.   egi]ego *C;* eici *D;* ei *F.*   6 crudelem *A.*   et]ac *E.*   8 me aliquid *BF.*
10 ubi]ut *E.*   12 obsidebant *B.*   possidebat *om. G.*   deuictam *C Maur.;* uitam
G.   13 ostenderunt *E*; ostenderem *G.*   credi *DF.*   -que *om. E.*   14 atque]et *E.*
et *om. A.*   15 uel eo *B.*   16 dicimus *DG*; discimus *H.*

apud Caesaream: *apud* with
proper names of places is found in Early
Latin (comedy), Sall., Tac., Suet., and in
Late writers: cf. St.-Schm. 499; T.L.L.
II, 337, 61–79.

1. **cateruam**: Augustine refers to a
very turbulent celebration held in honor
of the god Mars, the festival of the Octo-
ber horse: cf. Wissowa, G.: Religion
und Kultus der Römer, 2d ed., Munich,
1912, p. 145; also, Usener, H.: Kleine
Schriften, IV, 435-37, Leipzig-Berlin,
1914.

4. **solemniter** = 'regularly,' in Silver
and Late Latin.

6. **de cordibus . . . auellerem**: *auellere* though used by Cicero, occurs
mostly in Poetic, Silver, and Late Latin.

Cicero seems to use *de* with this verb in
the sense of 'out of,' *ab* or *ex* as 'away
from': cf. Font. 21, 46: aliquem de matris
complexu auellere atque abstrahere; De
Orat. 3, 5, 20: nullum est enim genus
rerum, quod aut auulsum a ceteris per se
ipsum constare; De Sen. 19, 71: poma ex
arboribus, si cruda sunt, uix auelluntur.
Augustine here uses de in the same sense
as Cicero, but he does not observe the
same distinction in De Ciu. Dei 18, 47:
quibus Iudaeis auulsis de sedibus propriis et . . . toto orbe dispersis. *De* with
avellere is rare until Late Latin, being
used by Cic. (Font. 21, 46), Sil., Tert.,
Hier., Aug. In Late Latin, *de* came to
replace *ab* and *ex* in many of their uses:
cf. T.L.L. II, 1305ff.; V, 51, 82–83.

caterva—for not only fellow-citizens, but also relatives, brothers, even fathers and sons, setting themselves into two divisions, fought each other with stones for several days at a time regularly each year at a certain season, and each killed whomever he could—I pleaded indeed in the grand style to the best of my power, to root out and dispel by my words so cruel and inveterate an evil from their hearts and lives; still, it was not when I heard their applause, but when I saw their tears, that I felt I had gained something. For by their applause they showed that they understood and were pleased, but that they were won, they made evident by their tears. When I saw these, I knew, even before they proved it by the actual fact, that that barbarous custom, handed down from fathers, grandfathers, and far back from their ancestors, which had obsessed, or rather possessed their hearts in so savage a manner, was conquered. And directly my discourse was ended, I turned their hearts and lips to offering thanksgiving to God. And behold, it is now almost eight or more years since, through the grace of Christ, anything of that kind has been attempted there. And there are also many other experiences through which I have found out that men manifest the effect of the grandeur of grave eloquence not by shouting, but rather by groans, sometimes by tears, finally by change of life.

14. **ecce iam ferme octo . . . sunt**: fixing the date of Augustine's visit to Caesarea as 418 A.D., as shown above, this statement serves to determine, at least approximately, the date of writing of the fourth book of *De Doctrina Christiana*. That this book was written some time later than the first three, Augustine himself states in Retract. 2, 4, 1: libros de doctr. chris., cum imperfectos comperissem, perficere malui quam eis relictis ad alia retractanda transire. . . . compleui ergo tertium, . . . addidi etiam nouissimum librum, et quattuor libris opus illud impleui. From internal evidence, the first three books are to be dated 397 A.D. Considering the words in this passage (iam ferme octo . . . anni), and their reference

to the trip to Caesarea which occurred in 418 A.D., it is reasonably certain that the fourth book was written in 426.

16. **experimenta** = 'experiences,' is used very seldom in Class. Latin, but is found in the Silver and Late period: cf. K.-Schm. s.v.

17. **granditas dictionis**: for *granditas*, meaning 'sublimity', cf. 13, 29; for the use of the genitive phrase instead of noun and adj. (*dictio grandis*), cf. 23, 52.

non clamore . . . mutatione: the effect of the grand style, when successful, is the touching of the heart and the moving of the will, revealed immediately by the restraint of the audience rather than by a demonstration, and ultimately by conversion of life.

54. Submisso etiam dicendi genere sunt plerique mutati, sed ut quod nesciebant, scirent, aut quod eis uidebatur incredibile crederent, non autem ut agerent quod agendum iam nouerant, et agere nolebant. ad huius modi namque duritiam flectendam, debet granditer dici. nam et laudes et uituperationes quando eloquenter di- 5 cuntur, cum sint in genere temperato sic afficiunt quosdam, ut non solum in laudibus et uituperationibus eloquentia delectentur, uerum et ipsi laudabiliter appetant fugiantque uituperabiliter uiuere. sed numquid omnes qui delectantur, imitantur, sicut in grandi genere omnes qui flectuntur, agunt, et in submisso genere omnes qui do- 10 centur, sciunt aut credunt uerum esse quod nesciunt?

25,   55. Unde colligitur illa duo genera quod efficere intendunt, hoc eis esse maxime necessarium, qui sapienter et eloquenter uolunt dicere. illud uero quod agitur genere temperato, id est, ut eloquentia ipsa delectet, non est propter seipsum usurpandum, sed ut 15 rebus quae utiliter honesteque dicuntur, si nec docente indigent eloquio nec mouente, quia et scientes et fauentes auditores habent,

1 etiam]itaque *E.*   plerumque *DF.*   2 non sciebant *E.*   eis *om. F.*   3 agere] geri *D*; agendum *E.*   4 uolebant *AE.*   modi *om. I.*   5 laudes ac *BDGH.* 7 eloquentiae *EI.*   8 et *om. A.*   9 imitantur]mutantur *Maur.*   13 esse *om. E.* 15 est genere dictionum *FH.*   ipsum *A.*   16 honeste utiliterque *CGH.*   indiget *I.*   17 facientes *B.*

1. **submisso . . . nolebant**: the effect of the plain style is upon the mind, not upon the heart and will. It involves a mental change, not necessarily a moral one. Note the dialectical cast of Augustine's thought, an illustrative explanation of his subject.

4. **debet . . . dici**: for impersonal *debet*, cf. 21, 48.

5. **nam et laudes, etc.**: the temperate style, aiming primarily to please, may however, through its aptness to praise or blame, influence its audience to change of life in accordance with this censure or praise. But unlike the other two styles, the middle style does not directly set out to effect change in its hearers, and does so only at times, not as a rule. Augustine's language here is also in imitation of the style under discussion. His use of the figure of derivation, paragmenon (laudibus: laudabiliter : : uituperationibus: uituperabiliter), accompanied by chias-

mus (laudabiliter appetant fugiantque uituperabiliter) is more ornate and pleasing than the simpler figure of polyptoton used in the sentence above, explaining the plain style, since the latter implies only the more usual difference of mood and tense in the repetition of a word (agerent . . . agendum . . . agere), though this too is accompanied by paronomasia (nesciebant: scirent; incredibile: crederent), used however not to please the fancy, but to clarify the thought.

7. **uerum et**: *et = etiam*, is used by Cicero after *uerum, nam, simul*, and at times before substantives, in the sense of 'also'. Livy and later writers carry on and increase this usage: cf. St.-Schm. 661; K.-Steg. II, 2, 8–9.

8. **laudabiliter**: adverbs in *-iter* gained wide use in Late Latin. This formation is found, however, in Tusc. 5, 5, 12, in Val. Max. 5, 1, and in Gell. 7, 3. But uituperabiliter is Late.

54. But even by the subdued style many have been changed, but only to know what they were ignorant of, or to believe what seemed unbelievable to them, not, however, to do what they already knew they should do, and did not wish to do. For truly to bend stubbornness of this kind, the grand style is necessary. For even when praise and censure are expressed eloquently, though merely in the moderate style, some people are so affected that they are not only pleased by the eloquence with which the praise or censure are expressed, but they seek to live in a manner deserving praise, and they avoid living in one deserving censure. But who will claim that all who are pleased by a speech, model themselves on it, as all who are moved by the grand style act in accordance with it, and all who are instructed by the subdued style understand or believe the truth of which they are ignorant?

25, 55. From this we may conclude that the end which the two last named styles aim to bring about is very important to those who desire to speak with wisdom and eloquence. But the end in view in the moderate style, namely, to please by eloquence, is not in itself worthy of being used, except, through the very pleasing quality of the expression, to gain a somewhat more willing assent or a firmer hold for a matter which is useful and good but which

fugiantque . . . uiuiere: *fugere* with the infinitive is cited for Cicero, but is mostly confined to Augustan poets and later writers: cf. St.-Schm. 581; T.L.L. VI, 1491, 64–77.

25. *The end for which the moderate style should be used.*

12. **unde colligitur, etc.**: all of Augustine's teaching in regard to the temperate style tends toward, and finds its conclusion in this chapter. He here differentiates definitely between Christian ideals and Sophistic, in regard to that all important tenet of sophistic teaching, 'art for art's sake.'

colligitur = 'it is concluded,' is Silver and Late Latin. The accusative and infinitive with this verb is cited for Cels., Sen., Tac., Gell., Ulp., Mela, Apul., Hier.: cf. T.L.L. III, 1617, 75–1618, 23.

intendunt: *intendo* with the infinitive is first cited for Sallust and Livy.

14. **illud . . . assensus**: Augustine's expression of this fundamental truth of

Christian oratory could not be clearer or more concise. He has been preparing for it in all he has taught above, especially in chapters 13 and 14, so that he can afford here to state his ground in the most succinct, decisive terms: 'Art for art's sake' has no place in Christian oratory; 'art for truth's sake' should have, and has. This can be illustrated from almost any of Augustines' own sermons. An interesting example is found in Serm. 52, 14. There, being assured that he has made his point as to *docere* in regard to the mystery of the Blessed Trinity, he concludes by a summary of the doctrine, but in order to gain a prompter and firmer hold on the audience (ut promptius . . . uel tenacius . . . adherescat assensus) he clothes his reasoning in an attractive style (delectare): exsoluimus quae promisimus: propositiones nostras firmissimis, ut arbitror, testimoniorum documentis probauimus. tenete quod audistis. breuiter replico, et rem utilissimam, quantum existimo,

aliquanto promptius ex delectatione ipsa elocutionis, accedat uel
tenacius adherescat assensus. nam cum eloquentiae sit uniuersale
officium, in quocumque istorum trium genere, dicere apte ad persuasionem; finis autem, id quod intenderis, persuadere dicendo: in
quocumque istorum trium genere dicit quidem eloquens apte ad 5
persuasionem, sed nisi persuadeat, ad finem non peruenit eloquentiae. persuadet autem in submisso genere uera esse quae dicit;
persuadet in grandi, ut agantur quae agenda esse iam sciuntur nec
aguntur; persuadet in genere temperato, pulchre ornateque se
dicere: quo fine nobis quid opus est? appetant eum qui lingua 10
gloriantur, et se in panegyricis talibusque dictionibus iactant, ubi
nec docendus nec ad aliquid agendum mouendus, sed tantummodo
est delectandus auditor. nos uero istum finem referamus ad alterum
finem, ut scilicet quod efficere uolumus, cum granditer dicimus,
hoc etiam isto uelimus, id est, ut bona morum diligantur, uel deui- 15
tentur mala, si ab hac actione non sic alieni sunt homines, ut ad
eam grandi genere dictionis uideantur urgendi, aut, si iam id
agunt, ut agant studiosius atque in eo firmiter perseuerent. ita fit
ut etiam temperati generis ornatu, non iactanter, sed prudenter
utamur, non eius fine contenti, quo tantummodo delectatur audi- 20
tor, sed hoc potius agentes, ut etiam ipso ad bonum quod persuadere uolumus, adiuuetur.

1 ipsa elocutionis]ipsius locutionis *F.*   3 generum *Maur.*   5 generum *Maur.*
eloquentes *A.*   6 suadent *F.*   uenit *C.*   10 quid]quod *E.*   qui in *A.*   11 iactent
ACDGI.   12 ne *I.*   ad *om. DEF.*   13 delectandus est *E.*   fine *D.*   15 id]hoc
G.   17 urgendi uideantur *Maur.* aut si iam]ut suam *A.*   18 ut *om. AE;* si *add. G.*
ut agant *om. D.*   studiose *E.*   in eo]nec *C.*   19 ornatum *A*; ornamenta *C.*   non
om. AD.   20 contempti *AG.*   21 hic *E.* ut etiam *om. D.* ad bonum quod]ad bona
quae *D.*   22 adiuuemur *EH.*

mentibus uestris collocandam com-
mendo. Pater non est natus de uirgine:
natiuitatem tamen istam Filii et Pater
et Filius operatus est ex uirgine. Pater
non est passus in cruce: passionem
tamen Filii et Pater et Filius operatus est. non resurrexit Pater a mortuis:
resurrectionem tamen Filii et Pater et
Filius operatus est. habetis personarum
distinctionem, et operationis insepara-
bilitatem . . . *haec quae diximus plana
erant, tantum dicenda erant: non laborandum ut intellegerentur, sed curandum ut commemorarentur.*

1. **promptius**: the comparative is
cited for Hirt., Tac., Cels., Juv., and Late
Latin.

2. **tenacius**: both positive and comparative of the adverb are Late: cf. K.-
Schm. s.v.

nam cum . . . eloquentiae: Augustine has in mind the general classical
teaching: cf. again the standard authorities quoted above in chapter 13: Arist.
Rhet. 1, 1, 1354a; De Inuent. 1, 5, 6; De
Orat. 1, 61, 260; *ibid.* 1, 31, 138; *ibid.*
1, 49, 213, etc. Since persuasion is the
end of oratory, it is likewise the end of

does not require explanation or persuasive eloquence, since it already has its audience well-informed or favorably disposed. For since the function of all eloquence, no matter in which of these three styles, is to speak in a way adapted to persuasion, and the end, that is, what you aim at, is to persuade by speaking, so, in whatever of the three styles indeed an orator speaks in a manner adapted to persuasion, unless he does persuade, he does not attain the end of eloquence. For instance, in the subdued style he persuades his audience that what he says is true; he persuades them in the grand style, to do what they now know they ought to do, but are not doing; he persuades them in the moderate style that he is expressing himself in beautiful and elegant language. But of what use to us is this end? Let them aim at it who glory in fine language, and who show off in panegyrics and such like modes of speech, in which the aim is not to instruct the audience, nor to move them to some course of action, but merely to please them. But as for us, let us turn this end to another end; for instance, to aim to bring about, even by this style, what we aim to effect in a speech in the grand style, that is, to make good morals esteemed or evil morals avoided, if the audience are not so hostile to this course of action as to seem to need urging to it by the grand style, or if they are now following it, to make them follow it with greater zest and to persevere in it with constancy. Thus it is that we use even the ornament of the moderate style not ostentatiously, but wisely, not content with its own purpose, namely, merely to please the audience, but rather striving for this, to help them even thereby to the good toward which our persuasion aims.

each and all of the styles; and unless one succeeds in persuading, he does not attain the end of oratory. Augustine wants to prove that the middle style also aims at persuasion—in its case, merely this: that it is persuading well—a wholly unlawful end, and therefore to be rejected, or rather turned into something useful and fitting, by the Christian orator.

uniuersale: Silver Latin.

10. **appetent . . . gloriantur**: the insinuation is unmistakable: let Sophists vaunt themselves in the middle style; the Christian orator must turn *delectatio* to a nobler end.

11. **panegyricis** = 'eulogies': Silver and Late Latin.

13. **nos . . . ad alterum finem**: Augustine's conclusion: The ornament of the middle style is to be used as an aid to the other styles, and in order to insure [sic] the accomplishment of their ends.—Note how well Augustine recognizes this in practice, as for instance in the sermon quoted above. See also Norden 617.

19. **iactanter**: Late.

26, 56. Illa itaque tria, quae supra posuimus, eum qui sapienter
dicit, si etiam eloquenter uult dicere, id agere debere, ut intellegenter, ut libenter, ut obedienter audiatur, non sic accipienda sunt
tamquam singula illis tribus dicendi generibus ita tribuantur, ut
ad submissum intellegenter, ad temperatum libenter, ad grande 5
pertineat obedienter audiri; sed sic potius ut haec tria semper in-
tendat, et quantum potest agat, etiam cum in illorum singulo
quoque uersatur. nolumus enim fastidiri, etiam quod submisse
dicimus, ac per hoc uolumus non solum intellegenter, uerum etiam
libenter audiri. quid autem agimus diuinis testimoniis docendo 10
quod dicimus, nisi ut obedienter audiamur, id est, ut credatur eis,
_{Psal. 92, 5} opitulante illo cui dictum est, *testimonia tua credita facta sunt*
ualde? quid etiam cupit nisi credi, qui aliquid, licet submisso eloquio, discentibus narrat? et quis eum uelit audire, nisi auditorem
nonnulla etiam suauitate detineat? nam si non intellegatur, quis 15
nesciat nec libenter eum posse, nec obedienter audiri? plerumque
autem dictio ipsa submissa, dum soluit difficillimas quaestiones et
inopinata manifestatione demonstrat; dum sententias acutissimas
de nescio quibus quasi cauernis, unde non sperabatur, eruit et os-

1 eum]cum *B (sic em.), Mig.*   qui]quis *(sic. em.) B.*   3 audiantur *CD.*   4 ita]ista *(sic em.) B.*
6 obedienter pertineant *E.*   audire *H.*   7 singulorum *DF.*   10 quod *H.*   docendo testimoniis *G.*   11 audiamus *B*; audiatur *HI.*   12 credibilis *CEFGHI Ver. An. Vulg.* facta *om. E.*
13 cupit]quaerit *ABDFI (editi, non tamen MSS [Maur.]).*   quid etiam nisi credi cupit *H.*
aliquid]aliud *BCI.*   14 dicentibus *I.*   et *om. CEGH.*   quis etiam *E.*   audire et *A.*   16 eum]
cum *I.*   17 dum soluit]dissoluit *CGI (in uulgatis [Maur.])*; dum soluit *om. E.*   19 quibus
nescio *E.*   quasi *om. C.*   aperabuntur *D.*   et]ut *I.*

26. *How all three 'officia' — 'docere,'*
'delectare,' and 'flectere' — are the object
of each style individually.

1. **illa itaque tria . . . uersatur**: in
chapter 12, Augustine discussed the
three *officia oratoris*; in chapter 17, he
showed their relation to the three styles,
i.e. how they give rise to the plain, the
middle, and the grand styles respectively
(is erit igitur eloquens, etc.), *docere* being
the end of the plain style, *delectare*, of
the middle, *flectere*, of the grand. But
viewing the styles in a broader way, *viz.*
as all being the vehicles of persuasion,
and as all having, in reality, this one end,
namely, to persuade, the conclusion is
here drawn that each style while aiming

particularly at its own special *officium*,
must necessarily include the other *officia*
also, in order to reach the general end,
persuadere. — Augustine thus logically
proves how the individuality of each
style merges into a unity, perfect in its
interlocked relation of part to whole, and
part to part.

8. **nolumus . . . audiri**: the plain style
aims at *docere*, but without tedium,
hence it includes also *delectare*.

10. **quid . . . ualde**: the plain style
aims to teach, but when scriptural proofs
are adduced, it aims to teach so as to
persuade, hence it involves *docere* and
flectere.

11. **nisi ut**, used with a negative

26, 56. And so those three points which we named above as ends to be striven for by everyone who desires to speak with wisdom and with eloquence, namely, to make one's words understood, enjoyed, and persuasive, are not to be so taken as to be applied only respectively to the three styles of speaking: being understood, to the subdued style; being enjoyed, to the moderate style; and being persuasive to the grand style; but rather in such a way that the orator ever aims at all three, and employs them all, in so far as it is possible, even when he is concerned with each one of them separately. For it is not our desire that even what we say in the subdued style be tiresome, but through this style we wish not only to make ourselves understood, but even enjoyed. And why do we enforce what we have to say in teaching, by quotations from Holy Scripture, but to make ourselves persuasive, that is, to make our audience believe us, with the assistance of Him to whom it is said, *Thy testimonies are become exceedingly credible?* What too does he desire except to be believed, who tells a story to an audience even though in the subdued style? But who would wish to give one his attention unless the latter could hold his listener by some charm of style? For who does not know that one who is not understood cannot make himself either pleasing or persuasive? For as to this subdued style, many times when it unravels very difficult questions, and proves them by an unexpected explanation, when it unearths and displays the most penetrating observations from obscure caverns, as it were, whence they were not expected, when it

(expressed or implied) in the main clause to produce an affirmative, belongs to Silver and Late Latin: cf. St.-Schm. 761; K.-Steg. II, 2, 417.

13. **quid . . . detineat**: a narration belongs to the plain style, but it exhibits this style in its most attractive form, hence it belongs both to necessity and to charm, involving *docere* and *delectare* (docere necessitatis est, delectare suauitatis).

15. **nam si . . . audiri**: the conclusion is that since *docere* is of necessity, *suauitas* (through *delectare*) and the consequent *uictoria* (through *flectere*)—i.e. persuasion accomplished—are impossible without *docere*.

16. **plerumque . . . dictio ipsa submissa**: the plain style, even of the *argumentative* type, when it is accompanied

by a natural grace (*decus naturale*), and a rhythm of cadences (*numerositas clausularum*), inherent in the subject itself, often accomplishes, because of its unadorned simplicity and its evident strength and truth, all three ends, *docere, delectare*, and *flectere*, just as well as does the *narrative* plain style. The conclusion is that the plain style is *naturally* apt to the accomplishment of the three *officia*.

17. **dum soluit . . . demonstrat**: note the terms expressive of strict dialectic, the second aspect of the plain style, as narration is considered the first.

18. **manifestatione**: a Late formation in *–io*: cf. K.-Schm. s.v.

dum sententias . . . ostendit: cf. Orat. 24, 79: acutae crebraeque sententiae ponentur et nescio unde ex abdito erutae.

tendit; dum aduersarii conuincit errorem et docet falsum esse quod
ab illo dici uidebatur inuictum; maxime quando adest ei quoddam
decus non appetitum sed quodammodo naturale, et nonnulla, non
iactanticula, sed quasi necessaria, atque, ut ita dicam, ipsis rebus
extorta numerositas clausularum, tantas acclamationes excitat, ut 5
uix intellegatur esse submissa. non enim quia neque incedit ornata
neque armata, sed tamquam nuda congreditur, ideo non aduersa-
rium neruis lacertisque collidit, et obsistentem subruit ac destruit
membris fortissimis falsitatem. unde autem crebro et multum
acclamatur ita dicentibus, nisi quia ueritas sic demonstrata, sic 10
defensa, sic inuicta delectat? et in hoc igitur genere submisso iste
noster doctor et dictor id agere debet, ut non solum intellegenter,
uerum etiam libenter et obedienter audiatur.

57. Illa quoque eloquentia generis temperati apud eloquentem
ecclesiasticum, nec inornata relinquitur, nec indecenter ornatur, 15
nec solum hoc appetit ut delectet, quod solum apud alios profitetur,
uerum etiam in iis quae laudat siue uituperat, istis appetendis uel
firmius tenendis, illis autem deuitandis uel respuendis, uult utique

2 ei]eius *DFG*.   3 decus quoddam *E*.   naturalem *D*.   et quod *CEG*; et quando
H; et]quod *I*.   ulla *E*.   4 iactanticida *C*; iactanti uincula *EI*.   atque]et *CG*.   5
exorta *AE* (*MSS plures [Maur.]*).   6 esse *om. H*.   8 ac]sed *B*.   10 ita]ista *E*.   sic
(demonstrata) *om. E*.   15 inornata]in ornamenta *E*.   indecenter]decenter *D*.   17
iis]hiis *ABCDFGHI*; hits *E*.   18 uel firmius tenendis *om. G*.

3. **decus non appetitum**: figures resident in the matter itself.

nonnulla . . . numerositas: cf. Reynold's (65) characterization of the cadences of De Ciu. Dei: 'They are constantly in evidence, but they are rather the natural turns of a style that is vigorous and orderly, than the labored devices of a meticulous artificer.'

5. **tantas acclamatones excitat**: Augustine's sermons bear witness to the applause which he himself called forth: cf. Tract. III in Euang. Ioan. XXI: fratres mei, unde clamatis, unde exsultatis, unde amatis, nisi quia ibi est scintilla huius charitatis? Tract. VI in Epist. Ioan. VII: rogasti, clamasti, ter clamasti, etc. Serm. 151, 8: unde omnes acclamastis, nisi quia omnes agnouis-

tis? Almost any of the sermons could be taken to illustrate what he claims, here, in theory for the plain style. Sermon 288, 1, for instance, delivered on the Feast of St. John the Baptist, illustrates well strength of thought, accompanied by an ever present natural grace of expression and rhythm of clausulae: Ioannes ergo praeco Domini missus ante illum, sed factus per illum, *omnia enim per ipsum facta sunt, et sine ipso factum est nihil*. missus homo ante hominem Deum, agnoscens Dominum suum, annuntians Creatorem suum; iam in terra praesentem mente discernens, digito ostendens. ipsius enim uerba sunt ostendentis Dominum et testimonium perhibentis, *ecce Agnus Dei, ecce qui tollit peccatum mundi*.

proves an opponent's error, and shows that to be false which seemed to have been stated as unassailable by him, especially if a certain grace accompanies it, not aimed at, but, in a certain measure natural, and some use of rhythm in clausulae, not obtrusive, but, as it were, necessary, and, so to speak, drawn out of the subject itself, it excites such applause that one would scarcely believe it to be the subdued style. For from the very fact that it does not come forth adorned and armed, but stalks out stripped bare, as it were, for that very reason it does not fail to crush its opponent by its very sinew and muscle, and to overwhelm and destroy the resistance of falsehood by its own strong arm. But whence comes it that such speakers are so frequently and greatly applauded except that truth thus set forth, thus defended, thus rendered unassailable, gives pleasure? And, therefore, in this subdued style, that teacher and speaker of ours ought to strive not only to make his discourse understood, but also to make it enjoyable and persuasive.

57. The eloquence of the moderate type, too, in the case of the ecclesiastical orator is not left unadorned, and yet it is not unbecomingly adorned, nor does it only aim at giving pleasure, the sole end that it professes in the hands of others, but in holding up those things which it praises or censures, on the one hand as matters worthy of being sought for and firmly maintained, on the other, as deserving to be avoided and rejected, it also certainly aims at

8. **neruis lacertisque**: cf. Aug. De Dial. 7: et oratorem, si ueritatem persuadere uult, dialecticis quasi neruis atque ossibus esse roborandum.

collidit: rare, mostly Silver and Late; most frequent in Quint.: cf. T.L.L. III, 1602, 1–57.

destruit: *destruere = infringere*, is mostly Silver and Late: cf. T.L.L. V, 774, 14–52.

10. **nisi quia** = 'except that,' occurs in Plautus, rarely in Class. Latin, but frequently in Late Latin, especially in Eccl. writers, due to the influence of the Old Version and Vulgate. *Nisi quod* is a more literary form, though it differs also from nisi quia by its more restrictive meaning of 'apart from the fact that.' *Nisi quod* is the regular usage in Cic., Sall., Liv., Tac.: cf. St.-Schm. 727.

14. **illa . . . ornatur**: the temperate style calls for ornament, but ornament in moderation. Note how Augustine, in his final summary of the styles, repeats the points he has made above as essentials. *Moderation* in the use of the florid style was insisted on in chapter 14, where the excess of the Sophists was decried. Consideration so far is only of *delectare* in the middle style.

15. **indecenter**: Poetic and Silver.

16. **nec solum . . . audiri**: here the middle style is shown to have not only *delectare* as aim, but also the purpose of being an aid to *flectere*. This second point was the matter of discussion of chapter 25. The middle style, in Augustine's theory, is lawfully used only as a supplement to *docere* or *flectere*.

17. **siue** = *aut*: cf. 18, 35.

obedienter audiri. si autem non auditur intellegenter, nec libenter
potest. proinde illa tria, ut intellegant qui audiunt, ut delectentur,
ut obediant, etiam in hoc genere agendum est, ubi tenet delectatio
principatum.

58. Iam uero ubi mouere et flectere grandi genere opus est audi- 5
torem—quod tunc est opus, quando et ueraciter dici et suauiter
confitetur, et tamen non uult facere quod dicitur—dicendum est
procul dubio granditer. sed quis mouetur, si nescit quod dicitur?
aut quis tenetur ut audiat, si non delectatur? unde et in isto
genere, ubi ad obedientiam cor duram dictionis granditate flec- 10
tendum est, nisi et intellegenter et libenter qui dicit audiatur, non
potest obedienter audiri.

27, 59. Habet autem ut obedienter audiatur, quantacumque granditate dictionis maius pondus uita dicentis. nam qui sapienter et
eloquenter dicit, uiuit autem nequiter, erudit quidem multos dis- 15

1 audiatur *F.*   nec]uel *A.*   2 tria illa *A.*   6 opus est *AI.*   et (ueraciter)
om. D.   dicit *CE.*   suauiter dicit *E.*   8 sed]uel *G*; si *I.*   9 et *om. A.* in
om. C.   ipso *E.*   10 ubi]nisi *E.*   cur *E.*   granditate dictionis *E.*   11 et (intellegenter) *om. E.*   quae *B.*   13 ut]et *F.*   audiamus *BDEI*; audiamur *CG*
(audiri *supra*) *F.*   quantumcumque *H.*   14 dicentis]dicendis *D.*   15 autem
uiuit *A.*   quidem]autem *B.*

1. **si . . . potest**: since *docere* is of necessity, it too must be aimed at by the middle style, along with *delectare* and *flectere*. This point is rendered more emphatic by the fact that it has just been concluded in regard to the plain style.

nec = *non*, as in Early and Late Latin: cf. St.-Schm. 640.

2. **proinde . . . principatum**: a restatement for clearness and emphasis, just as in the preceding paragraph.

illa tria . . . agendum est: the impersonal gerundive with an object in the accusative belongs especially to Early Latin, appearing only rarely in the classical period (though frequently in Varro), and coming into common use in the later jurists: cf. K.-Steg. II, 1, 743–45; St.-Schm. 596.

5. **iam ... granditer**: *flectere, i.e.* persuasion apt to move the will to action, is the proper object of the grand style.

6. **ueraciter**: found only in Late Latin,

though Priscian claims that Plautus used it.

8. **procul dubio**: cited for Liv. 39, 40, 10; Plin. Nat. 9, 184; Suet., Quint., and Late writers: cf. K.-Schm. s.v.

sed quis . . . delectatur: Augustine, at this third repetition, does not have to prove that *docere necessitatis est, delectare suauitatis*; he can link the two together, and express them in mere question form, which has weight because of the logical sequence of the thoughts.

9. **unde et . . . audiri**: a final summarizing sentence. This chapter is a good example of Augustine's admirable power as a teacher and a dialectician. Every link in his chain of reasoning is perfectly welded and connected with what precedes and with what follows, so that the conclusion is accepted by the reader as a simple matter of course. Such paragraphs represent Augustine's power of expressing clearly, simply, and suc-

being persuasive. But if it is not understood, neither can it give pleasure. And so all three ends, viz., that the audience should understand,
be pleased, and be persuaded, must be striven for even in this one
style, where giving pleasure holds first place.

58. But when it is necessary to move and convince a listener by
the grand style—as it is when one's opponent grants the truth and
attractiveness of what is said, but is unwilling to act upon it—one
must without doubt express himself *grandly*. But who is moved if
he does not understand what is said, or whose attention is held if he
is not pleased? Wherefore, in this style also, when an obdurate heart
has to be bent by the grand manner of speech, unless the speaker
makes himself both understood and enjoyed, he cannot make himself
persuasive.

27, 59. But the life of the speaker has greater force to make him
persuasive than the grandeur of his eloquence, however great that
may be. For the man who speaks wisely and eloquently, but lives
evilly, instructs indeed many who are eager to learn, though *he is*

---

cinctly the relation of part to part, of his
subject, and by linking-summaries, the
connection between part to whole. Such
treatment is only possible to a mind at
once lucid and penetrating, and as simple
as profound.

27. *A good life is the orator's best
asset.*

13. **habet . . . dicentis**: this is also the
teaching of pagan rhetoricians: cf. Arist.
Rhet. 1, 2, 1356 a: τοῖς γὰρ ἐπιεικέσι
πιστεύομεν μᾶλλον καὶ θᾶττον. *Ibid.*
2, 1, 1377 b: ἀνάγκη μὴ μόνον πρὸς
τὸν λόγον ὁρᾶν, ὅπως ἀποδεικτικὸς
ἔσται καὶ πιστός, ἀλλὰ καὶ αὐτὸν ποιόν
τινα. *Ibid.* 2, 1, 1378 a: τοῦ μὲν οὖν
αὐτοὺς εἶναι πιστοὺς τοὺς λέγοντας
τρία ἐστὶ τὰ αἴτια· τοσαῦτα γάρ ἐστι
δι' ἃ πιστεύομεν ἔξω τῶν ἀποδείξεων.
ἔστι δὲ ταῦτα φρόνησις καὶ ἀρετὴ καὶ
εὔνοια. De Orat. 2, 43, 182: ualet igitur
multum ad uincendum probari mores
et instituta (et facta et uitam) eorum,
qui agent causas, et eorum pro quibus;
et item improbari aduersariorum ani-
mosque eorum, apud quos agetur, con-
ciliari quam maxime ad beneuolentiam
quom erga oratorem tum erga illum,

pro quo dicet orator. conciliantur autem
animi dignitate hominis rebus gestis exis-
timatione uitae; quae facilius ornari possunt, si modo sunt, quam fingi, si nulla
sunt. Quint. 12, 1, 1: sit ergo nobis orator,
quem constituimus, is qui a M. Catone
finitur, *uir bonus dicendi peritus*; uerum,
id quod et ille posuit prius, et ipsa natura
potius ac maius est, utique uir bonus. See
also De Orat. 2, 20, 85; *ibid.* 3, 14, 5.

14. **nam . . . studiosus**: the classical
student may be struck by the fact that here
Augustine's views seem less strict, and
more compromising than Quintilian's.
Cf. Quint. 12, 1, 2-3: mutos enim nasci
et egere omni ratione satius fuisset, quam
prouidentiae munera in mutuam per-
niciem conuertere…neque enim tantum
id dico, eum qui sit orator, uirum bonum
esse oportere, sed ne futurum quidem oratorem nisi uirum bonum. In reality, Quintilian and Augustine deal with different
circumstances, in their respective discussions. Quintilian has to do with the legal
orator whose ideals are not set for him, but
who is guided wholly by the case in hand,
and the attitude which he himself brings to
bear upon it. Such a one when evil minded,

Ecclus. 37, 21 cendi studiosos, quamuis *animae suae sit inutilis*, sicut scriptum
Philipp. 1, 18 est. unde ait apostolus, *siue occasione, siue ueritate, Christus an-
nuntietur.* Christus autem ueritas est, et tamen etiam non ueritate
annuntiari ueritas potest, id est, ut prauo et fallaci corde, quae
recta et uera sunt, praedicentur. sic quippe annuntiatur Iesus 5
Christus ab eis qui sua quaerunt, non quae Iesu Christi. sed quoniam boni fideles non quemlibet hominum, sed ipsum Dominum
Matt. 23, 3 obedienter audiunt, qui ait, *quae dicunt, facite, quae autem faciunt, facere nolite; dicunt enim, et non faciunt,* ideo audiuntur
utiliter, qui etiam utiliter non agunt. sua enim quaerere student, 10
sed sua docere non audent, de loco scilicet superiore sedis ecclesiasticae, quam sana doctrina constituit. propter quod ipse Dominus
priusquam de talibus, quod commemoraui, diceret, praemisit, *super*
Matt. 23, 3 *cathedram Moysi sederunt.* illa ergo cathedra, non eorum sed
Moysi, cogebat eos bona dicere, etiam non bona facientes. agebant 15
ergo sua in uita sua; docere autem sua, cathedra illos non permittebat aliena.

60. Multis itaque prosunt dicendo quae non faciunt, sed longe
pluribus prodessent faciendo quae dicunt. abundant enim qui ma-
lae uitae suae defensionem ex ipsis praepositis et doctoribus quae- 20

1 studiosus *G.*   2 scriptum est scribae et pharisaei in cathedra Moysi sederunt quae dicunt
facite, quae autem faciunt facere nolite dicunt enim et non faciunt *CEFGHI (editi; abest ab
omnibus MSS [Maur.]).* unde ait apostolus]unde apostolus ait *A;* unde et apostolus ait *CH;*
unde ait et apostolus *G Maur.;* unde et ait apostolus *B.*   3 autem]enim *E.*   tamen etiam]
tamen et *E.*   4 potest *om. D.*   prauo et fallaci corde]a prauo et a fallaci corde *E.*   5. id
est … uera sunt *om. D.*   quae recta et uera sunt]quae recte uera sunt *A;* quae recta sunt et
uera *I.*   6 Christi Iesu *A.*   7 Dominum *om. E.*   8 obedienter Deum *E.*   10 etiam qui *E.*
utiliter (non) *om. E.*   12 instituit *A.*   13 super *om. ABCDFGI.*   14 sedent *MSS; non tamen
Maur. Ver. An. Vulg.*   ergo]uero *E.*   illorum *D.*   16 non eorum . . . cathedra *om. I.*   illos
om. C.   18 multi *I.*   20 quaerunt *C.*

Quintilian can not but consider a menace
to the public. Augustine realizes that
the ecclesiastical orator, dealing as he
does with the Word of God, possesses
an instrument which will effect its end,
even though the speaker himself is not
exemplary of life. The Christian in his
possession of Truth can meet and combat error in a way of which the pagan is
wholly incapable. Moreover, Quintilian
in his discussion is expressing his ideal
of a *perfect* orator; Augustine, speaking from a more practical standpoint,
explains the ideal, *i.e.* eloquence cou-

pled with nobility of character, but he
also has to recognize the truth, *viz.* that
Holy Scripture, explained eloquently,
even without a corresponding integrity
in the speaker, is necessarily effective,
since it is the Word of God.

4. **annuntiari**: *annuntio* = 'preach,' is
mostly Late and Eccl.; here, an echo of
the preceding Scriptural verse.

ut . . . praedicentur: *ut*, temporal, with the subjunctive in an iterative
clause, at first mostly with the imperfect, then with the present, perfect, and
pluperfect, appears to have belonged to

unprofitable to his own soul, as it is written. And so the Apostle says: *Whether by occasion, or by truth, Christ be preached.* Now Christ is truth and still, truth can be preached, even though not with truth, that is when by a mean and deceiving heart righteousness and truth are preached. Thus, indeed, Jesus Christ is preached by those who seek their own ends, not those of Jesus Christ. But since good Christians obey not any man whatsoever, but the Lord Himself, who says: *Whatsoever they say to you, do: but according to their works, do you not, for they say and do not,* therefore are they heard with profit, even though they themselves do not lead profitable lives. For they are zealous in seeking their own ends, but they dare not teach their own from the high place, forsooth, of ecclesiastical authority, which sound doctrine has established. For this reason the Lord Himself, before saying what I have just quoted about men of this kind, declared: *They have sitten on the chair of Moses.* That chair, therefore, which was not theirs but Moses', forced them to say what was good, even though they were not doing what was good. And so they pursued their own ends in their lives, but to teach their own, that, the chair which belonged to another did not allow them to do.

60. And so they do good to many by preaching even what they do not live up to; but far more would they do good to by practising what they preached. For there are many who seek to defend their own evil lives by their very superiors and teachers answering in their hearts, or even if they go so far, saying with their

the Early colloquial language. It occurs frequently in the Late period, after *ut* and *quod* had gained such extended usage. Cf. Enn. Sat. 22 ap. Gell. 2, 29, 4 (where the wording however is Gellius'): nidulantur in segetibus id ferme temporis ut appetat messis: cf. St.-Schm. 758–59; Salonius 318–19; McGuire 128.

5. **praedicentur**: *praedico* = 'preach,' is Eccl. So used also in 27, 59; 27, 60; 29, 62.

13. **praemisit** = 'said first': cf. Suet. Calig. 58: ceruicem gladio caesim grauiter percussit, praemissa uoce: 'hoc age'. Tac. Ann. 12, 6: postquam haec fauorabili oratione praemisit. Then Late Latin. See K.-Schm. s.v.

16. **docere . . . permittebat**: *permittere* with the accusative and infinitive occurs in Early Latin, in Livy and Tacitus, and in Late Latin: cf. St.-Schm. 580.

18. **multis . . . dicunt**: cf. Quint. 12, 1, 29: quae certe melius persuadebit aliis, qui prius persuaserit sibi.

longe pluribus: *longe* in place of *multo*, with a comparative is Poetic, Silver, and Late: cf. St.-Schm. 463; K.-Schm. s.v.; Lane 247; Arts 45.

19. **abundant . . . facis**: Quintilian likewise acknowledges that a bad life must betray itself in a speaker: cf. 12, 1, 29: prodit enim se, quamlibet custodiantur, simulation nec unquam tanta fuerit loquendi facultas, ut non titubet atque haereat, quotiens ab animo uerba dissentiunt. In this moral influence Augustine sees the real danger of a preacher whose life is not in conformity with his words.

rant, respondentes corde suo, aut etiam si ad hoc erumpunt, ore
suo, atque dicentes: 'quod mihi praecipis, cur ipse non facis?' ita
fit ut eum non obedienter audiant, qui se ipse non audit, et Dei
uerbum quod eis praedicatur, simul cum ipso praedicatore contemnant. denique apostolus scribens ad Timotheum, cum dixisset, 5

1 Tim. 4, 12 *nemo adolescentiam tuam contemnat*, subiecit unde non contem-
neretur, atque ait, *sed forma esto fidelium in sermone, in conuer-
satione, in dilectione, in fide, in castitate.*

28, 61. Talis doctor ut obedienter audiatur, non impudenter non
solum submisse ac temperate, uerum etiam granditer dicit, quia 10
non contemptibiliter uiuit. sic namque eligit bonam uitam, ut

2 Cor. 8, 21 etiam bonam non neglegat famam, sed prouideat bona coram Deo
et hominibus, quantum potest, illum timendo, his consulendo. in
ipso etiam sermone malit rebus placere quam uerbis, nec aestimet
dici melius, nisi quod dicitur uerius, nec doctor uerbis seruiat, sed 15

1 Cor. 1, 17 uerba doctori. hoc est enim quod apostolus ait: *non in sapientia
uerbi, ne euacuetur crux Christi.* ad hoc ualet etiam quod ait ad

2 Tim. 2, 14 Timotheum: *noli uerbis contendere, ad nihil enim utile est, nisi
ad subuersionem audientium.* neque enim hoc ideo dictum est, ut
aduersariis oppugnantibus ueritatem, nihil nos pro ueritate dica- 20
mus. et ubi erit quod cum ostenderet qualis esse episcopus debeat,

Tit. 1, 9 ait inter caetera: *ut potens sit in doctrina sana et contradicentes*

1 cordi *BF.* erumpant *EI.* 3 obedienter non *AH.* 5 cum]enim *H.* 7 at-
que]et *I.* fidelibus *B Ver. An.* 8 delectatione *B.* 10 dicit quia non contemptibiliter dicit *DF.* 11 elegit *F.* 12 bona]uitam bonam *B.* 13 illum]illud *A.*
hiis *E.* 14 alit *D.* ne *BDH.* 16 ait apostolus *DFGH.* 17 etiam *om. E.*
18 contendere *om. D.* 19 non *E.* est *om. BD.* ut *om. I.* 20 repugnantibus
B; pugnantibus *F;* impugnantibus *H.* nos *om. A.* 21 ostendit *D.* episcopus
esse *E.*

2. **ita fit . . . contemnant**: cf. the
pagan's realization of a similar loss
accruing, in his case, to eloquence:
Quint. 12, 1, 32: facultas dicendi, si
in malos incidit, et ipsa iudicanda est
malum. The harm done by the Christian
is incomparably greater, since it involves
contempt for the Word of God.

4. **praedicatore** = 'a preacher': Eccl.
Used also in 29, 62.

6. **unde** = *quomodo*: though this
idiom is used by Terence and Ovid (cf.
Georges s.v.), it becomes common only
in Late Latin. Colbert (36) notes its fre-

quent use in De Ciu. Dei. Cf. St.-Schm.
492; Salonius 212.

28. *How truth should dominate in
oratory: Truth in matter, truth in treatment (τὸ πρέπον), truth in life.*

9. **impudenter . . . contemptibiliter**:
note how the force and flavor of this passage lies in these two adverbs.

11. **contemptibiliter**: very rare; cited
only for Schol. Hor. 26, 87, and Pallad.
hist. mon. II, 13, besides the present passage: cf. T.L.L. IV, 654, 44–50.

sic namque, etc.: sincerity should
be dominant in the Christian orator, and

lips, "What you tell me to do, why do you not do yourself?" And so it comes about that they do not follow one who does not follow his own preaching, and they condemn the word of God which is preached to them, along with the preacher himself. Accordingly, the Apostle, in writing to Timothy, after saying, *Let no man despise thy youth*, adds how he would avoid being despised, saying, *Be thou an example of the faithful in word, in conversation, in charity, in faith, in chastity.*

28,   61. Such a teacher, to render himself persuasive, may without presumption express himself not only in the subdued and in the moderate style, but also in the grand style, because his life is beyond reproach. For truly he so chooses to live a good life as not indeed to neglect a good reputation, but especially so as to forecast what is good before God and man, in as far as possible, by fearing God and by caring for man. Even in his very speech he should prefer to please through his matter rather than through his words, and he should consider that a thing is not well said unless it be truthfully said; nor should the teacher serve words, but words, the teacher. For this is what the Apostle says: *Not in wisdom of speech lest the cross of Christ be made void.* Of the same purport, too, is what he says to Timothy: *Contend not in words, for it is to no profit, but to the subverting of the hearers.* This, however, is not said to the end that we should say nothing in defense of truth whenever opponents attack it. And where will be what, among other things, he said when he was showing of what character a bishop ought to be: *That he may be able in sound doctrine,*

---

a singleness of purpose that aims first at pleasing God, then, as a necessary consequnence, at pleasing men. A good reputation naturally follows, but is not primarily sought for. Augustine, of course, is guarding his disciples against the pitfalls of Sophistic. This, his next words make clear.

12. **sed prouideat . . . homnibus**: cf. Vulg. 2 Cor. 8, 21: prouidemus enim bona non solum coram Deo, sed etiam coram hominibus; also, Rom. 12, 17.

13. **in ipso . . . doctori**: Augustine crystallizes in a brief sentence what he has tried to inculcate throughout the entire treatise. With the Christian orator, matter is of first importance, style is secondary;

truth is the grand object, ornament must be subservient to it. As shown above in chapter 5, in quotations from Cicero, this was recognized and practised by the best speakers of classical times, but the prevalent formalism of the third and fourth centuries was, in Augustine's time, a factor that had to be combatted, and this is done here by a trenchant restatement of old ideals.

17. **ad hoc ualet**: *ualere = significare*, also in Class. Latin, but it usually takes *idem*, not *ad hoc*: cf. De Fin. 2, 4: quaerimus uerbum latinum par graeco, et quod idem ualeat; Quint. 10, 1, 13: et intellego et sentio et uideo saepe idem ualent quod scio.

redarguere? uerbis enim contendere, est non curare quomodo error
ueritate uincatur, sed quomodo tua dictio dictioni praeferatur alterius. porro qui non uerbis contendit, siue submisse, siue temperate,
siue granditer dicat, id agit uerbis ut ueritas pateat, ueritas placeat,
ueritas moueat; quoniam nec ipsa, quae praecepti finis et plenitudo   5
legis est charitas, ullo modo recta esse potest, si ea quae diliguntur,
non uera sed falsa sunt. sicut autem cuius pulchrum corpus et
deformis est animus, magis dolendus est quam si deforme haberet
et corpus, ita qui eloquenter ea quae falsa sunt dicunt, magis miserandi quam si talia deformiter dicerent. quid est ergo non solum   10
eloquenter, uerum etiam sapienter dicere, nisi uerba in submisso
genere sufficientia, in temperato splendentia, in grandi uehementia,
ueris tamen rebus, quas audiri oportet, adhibere? sed qui utrumque

1 Tim. 1, 5

Rom. 13, 10

1 redarguere]se arguere *A*.   5 praecepit *A*.   6 nullo *E*.   esse recta *BEDH*.
potest *om. D*.   diliguntur]dicuntur *C*. 7   corpus pulchrum *AE*.   8 colendus *I*.
si]se *H*.   9 et *om. B*.   miserandi sunt *C Maur*.   13 quos *G*. audire *CF*.

1. **uerbis . . . alterius**: a definition of
Sophistic practice: cf. Orat. 19, 65: sed
hoc differunt quod, cum sit his propositum non perturbare animos, sed placare
potius nec tam persuadere quam delectare et apertius id faciunt quam nos et
crebrius, concinnas magis sententias
exquirunt quam probabiles.

3. **porro . . . moueat**: this is Augustine's culminating statement in regard
to the three styles and the three *officia*.
Having carefully explained their nature,
relation, and effects, their striking individuality, and their yet grander unity, he
here shows that in the highest oratory,
they find their most complete *one-ness*
in the singleness of their matter, *i.e.* in
ueritas.

5. **finis . . . charitas**: cf. 1 Tim. 1, 5:
finis autem praecepti est caritas; Rom.
13, 10: plenitudo ergo legis est dilectio.
plenitudo, thus used figuratively,
belongs to Late Latin: cf. K.-Schm. s.v.

7. **sicut . . . dicerent**: this expresses,
in its proper connection with *ueritas*
as the dominating factor of eloquence,
the contrary practice of the Sophists, of
clothing falsehood in fine language. See
chapter 14 for Augustine's full treatment
of this point.

10. **quid est . . . adhibere**: Augustine
again looks back to his earlier discussion (cf. chapter 5), and connects with
the styles and their common subject-
matter, *ueritas*, the eloquence and wisdom there differentiated and explained.
He now states that the orator who would
speak *eloquently* must use the styles,
but that if he would also speak *with
wisdom* he must (1) make the subject
of these, *truth*, and (2) apply the styles
to this subject in such a way as to be
adequate in the plain style, attractive in
the temperate, and moving in the grand.
This second point is nothing else than
the application of the old classical ideal
of τὸ πρέπον, *decorum*, 'fitting-ness'.
It is characteristic of Augustine thus to
lead up to the orator's supreme quality,
which though hinted at, wherever it was
fitting to do so, throughout the treatise,
is here given its proper importance.
Because of the unanimous agreement
of classical authors as to the dominating place of τὸ πρέπον in eloquence,
it is interesting to compare the following summary of their opinions: Arist.
Rhet. 3, 2, 1404 b: σημεῖον γὰρ ὅτι ὁ

also to convince the gainsayers? For to contend in words is not to care how error may be overcome by truth, but how your style may be preferred to another's. However, the man who does not contend in words, whether he expresses himself in the subdued, or in the moderate, or in the grand style, has this aim in speaking, that truth be made clear, that truth be made pleasing, that truth be made convincing; for not even love itself, which is the end of the commandment and the fulfilling of the law, can in any way be right if the objects of love are not true but false. For as one whose body is comely, but whose heart is depraved is more to be pitied than if his body also were deformed, so those who express falsehood with eloquence are more to be deplored than if they should express the same in an unseemly way. And so what is it to speak not only with eloquence but also with wisdom, except to employ words which are adequate, in the subdued style; striking, in the temperate style; and strong, in the grand style—in regard to truth, of course, which

λόγος, ὡς ἐὰν μὴ δηλοῖ, οὐ ποιήσει τὸ ἑαυτοῦ ἔργον· καὶ μήτε ταπεινὴν μήτε ὑπὲρ τὸ ἄξίωμα, ἀλλὰ πρέπουσαν· ἡ γὰρ ποιητικὴ ἴσως οὐ ταπεινή, ἀλλ' οὐ πρέπουσα λόγῳ. Orat. 21, 70 and 73: magni igitur iudicii, summae etiam facultatis esse debebit moderator ille et quasi temperator huius tripertitae uarietatis; nam et iudicabit quid cuique opus sit et poterit quocumque modo postulabit causa dicere. sed est eloquentiae sicut reliquarum rerum fundamentum sapientia. ut enim in uita sic in oratione nihil est difficilius quam quid deceat uidere. πρέπον appellant hoc Graeci, nos dicamus sane *decorum*; de quo praeclare et multa praecipiuntur et res est cogitatione dignissima; huius ignoratione non modo in uita sed saepissime et in poematis et in oratione peccatur... in omnibusque rebus uidendum est quatenus; etsi enim suus cuique modus est, tamen magis offendit nimium quam parum; in quo Apelles pictores quoque eos peccare dicebat qui non sentiret quid esset satis. magnus est locus hic, Brute, quod te non fugit, et magnum uolumen aliud desiderat; sed ad id quod agitur illud satis. cum hoc decere—quod semper usurpamus in omnibus dictis et factis, minimis et maximis—cum hoc, inquam, decere dicimus, illud non decere, et id usquequaque quantum sit appareat in alioque ponatur aliudque totum sit, utrum *decere* an *oportere* dicas;—oportere enim perfectionem declarat officii, quo et semper utendum est et omnibus, decere quasi aptum esse consentaneumque tempori et personae. Quint. 12, 10, 79–80: sed et copia habet modum, sine quo nihil nec laudabile nec salutare est, et nitor ille cultum uirilem et inuentio iudicium. sic erunt magna, non nimia; sublimia, non abrupta; fortia, non temeraria; seuera, non tristia; grauia, non tarda; laeta, non luxuriosa; iucunda, non dissoluta; grandia, non tumida. similis in ceteris ratio est ac tutissima fere per medium uia, quia utriusque ultimum uitium est.

12. **sufficientia** = 'adequate': Silver and Late: cf. K.-Schm. s.v.

splendentia: in transferred sense, Poetic and Late.

13. **sed qui ... insipienter**: this was the conclusion of chapter 5.

non potest, dicat sapienter quod non dicit eloquenter, potius quam
dicat eloquenter quod dicit insipienter. si autem ne hoc quidem
potest, ita conuersetur, ut non solum sibi praemium comparet sed
etiam praebeat aliis exemplum, et sit eius quasi copia dicendi forma
uiuendi.   5

**29, ** 62. Sunt sane quidam qui bene pronuntiare possunt, quid autem
pronuntient, excogitare non possunt. quod si ab aliis sumant eloquenter sapienterque conscriptum, memoriaeque commendent atque,
ad populum proferant, si eam personam gerunt, non improbe faciunt. etiam sic enim, quod profecto utile est, multi praedicatores   10
1 Cor. 1, 10 ueritatis fiunt, nec multi magistri, si unius ueri magistri idipsum
dicant omnes, et non sint in eis schismata. nec deterrendi sunt isti
Ier. 23, 30 uoce Ieremiae prophetae, per quem Deus arguit eos qui furantur
uerba eius, unusquisque a proximo suo. qui enim furantur, alienum
auferunt; uerbum autem Dei non est ab eis alienum qui obtem-   15
perant ei; potiusque ille dicit aliena, qui cum dicat bene, uiuit
male. quaecumque enim bona dicit, eius excogitari uidentur ingenio, sed ab eius moribus aliena sunt. eos itaque dixit Deus furari
uerba sua, qui boni uolunt uideri, loquendo quae Dei sunt, cum
mali sint, faciendo quae sua sunt. nec ipsi dicunt bona quae dicunt,   20
si diligenter attendas. quomodo enim dicunt uerbis, quod negant
Tit. 1, 16 factis? non enim frustra de talibus ait apostolus: *confitentur se
nosse Deum, factis autem negant.* modo ergo quodam ipsi dicunt,

2 potius quam dicat eloquenter *om. F.*   nec *A.*   3 non *om. A.*   sibi]si *D.*
praemium sibi *A.*   4 etiam]et *D.*   exemplum aliis *A.*   et]ut *AE.*   eius]eis *EH.*
6 quidam]quippe *E.*   8 atque]esque (atque *supra*) *B*; ea quae *D.*   9 gerant *E.*   10
etiam *om. E Maur.; del. B.*   sic enim]si enim *B*; si *I.*   profecto]ad profectum *F.*   11
ueritatis praedicatores *A.*   multo *D.*   si]sed (*sic. em.*) *B.*   ipsum *D.*   12 perdicant
I.   13 Deus]Dominus *A.*   14 eius]eorum *E.*   15 Dei *om. EI.*   16 ei *om. A*; eis
F.   -que]quae *F.*   dicat bene dicit bona *D.*   17 quicumque *E.*   excogitare *H*;
excogitari eius *A.*   uidetur *H.*   18 alieni *G.*   19 eloquendo *D.*   22 de talibus
ait apostolus]quod ait apostolus de alibus *G.*   confitentur enim *A.*   23 dicunt
Deum *I.*

2. **ai autem . . . uiuenda**: a spiritual
point of view, showing how the Christian
standard transcends the pagan. Cicero
concedes that eloquence without wisdom is of small avail, but the idea that
wisdom (particularly that, expressed by
integrity of life) without eloquence can
effect anything in oratory, is something
quite beyond his conception.

3. **conuersetur** = 'lives,' is cited in
its absolute sense, for Seneca, and Late
Latin.

4. **forma** = 'beauty', used of things, is
mostly Late, though cited once for Cic.:
cf. T.L.L. VI, 1073, 62–71.

29. *That it is permissible for one to
memorize a sermon, not his own, and to
deliver it.*

7. **quod si . . . faciunt**: this in no
wise proves that Augustine himself
was accustomed first to write his sermons and then to memorize them, nor

it is fitting should be heard? But if a person cannot do both, let him speak with wisdom, even though he cannot with eloquence, rather than with eloquence without wisdom. But if even this is impossible, let him so conduct himself as not only to deserve a reward for himself, but also to offer an example to others; and in his case, let his manner of life be, as it were, a flowing speech.

29, 62. But there are, indeed, some men who can deliver a sermon well, but who cannot think out its matter. Now if they take what has been eloquently and wisely written by others, and commit it to memory, and deliver it before the people, if they assume this character, they do no wrong. For thus, as is certainly profitable, many become preachers of truth, though not many, teachers, if they all speak the same thing of one true teacher, and there are no schisms among them. Nor need they be frightened by the word of Jeremiah the Prophet, through whom God rebukes those who steal His words, everyone from his neighbor. For those who steal take what belongs to another, but the word of God belongs to those who obey it; and that man rather speaks the words of another, who speaks well but lives badly. For whatever good sentiments he expresses seem to proceed from his own thought on them, but they do not belong to his way of living. And so God has said that those men steal His words who wish to appear good by speaking God's word, though they are evil in following a course of their own. And indeed it is not they themselves who speak the good that they speak, if you study the matter closely. For how can they express in words what they do not express in deeds? Truly not for nought does the Apostle say of such: *They profess that they know God: but in their*

---

that he in any way rejects extempore address either for himself or for others. On the contrary, as expressed above, in chapters 3, 4, 5, 10, Augustine inculcates the doctrine of adaptation to one's matter and audience—a thing which is only perfectly attainable in speeches that are extemporaneous. What he says here in regard to memorizing a set speech is clearly by way of concession, for one of mean abilities. On the whole question of Augustine and extempore sermons, cf. Deferrari 97ff.

8. **memoriae commendent**: for this *uerborum memoria*, see also chapter 10. Note the difference between it and the

rerum memoria, mentioned in chapter 20.

11. **idipsum . . . schismata**: cf. Vulg. 1 Cor. 1, 10: obsecro autem uos, fratres, per nomen Domini nostri Iesu Christi, ut idipsum dicatis omnes, et non sint in uobis schismata.

12. **schismata** (σχίσματα) = *scissurae*, is Eccl. Latin. However, the Old Version uses *scissurae* in 1 Cor. 1, 10.

19. **loquendo . . . faicendo**: the ablative of the gerund in Classical Latin expresses means, rarely manner, and very rarely cause. The causal use is found here, and also below in: non ipsi dicunt uoluntate . . . negando, etc. Cf. K.-Steg. II, 1, 751–53; St.-Schm. 599–600.

et rursus alio modo ipsi non dicunt, quoniam utrumque uerum est
quod ueritas ait. de talibus enim lequens, *quae dicunt* inquit *facite,*
Matt. 23, 3 *quae autem faciunt, facere nolite*, hoc est, 'quod ex ore illorum
auditis, facite; quod in opere uidetis, facere nolite.' *dicunt enim*
inquit *et non faciunt*. ergo quamuis non faciant, dicunt tamen. 5
Matt. 12, 34 sed alio loco tales arguens, *hypocritae* inquit *quomodo potestis bona
loqui, cum sitis mali?* ac per hoc et ea quae dicunt, quando bona
dicunt, non ipsi dicunt, uoluntate scilicet atque opere negando quod
dicunt. unde contingit ut homo disertus et malus, sermonem quo
ueritas praedicetur, dicendum ab alio non diserto sed bono, ipse 10
componat. quod cum fit, ipse a seipso tradit alienum, ille ab alieno
accipit suum. cum uero boni fideles bonis fidelibus hanc operam
commodant, utrique sua dicunt, quia et Deus ipsorum est, cuius
sunt illa quae dicunt, et ea sua faciunt, quae non ipsi componere
potuerunt, qui secundum illa composite uiuunt. 15

30, 63. Siue autem apud populum uel apud quoslibet iamiamque dicturus, siue quod apud populum dicendum uel ab eis qui uoluerint
Esther 14, 13 aut potuerint legendum est dictaturus, oret ut Deus congruum
sermonem daret in os eius. si enim regina orauit Esther, pro suae
gentis temporaria salute locutura apud regem, ut in os eius Deus 20
congruum sermonem daret, quanto magis orare debet, ut tale munus
accipiat, qui pro aeterna hominum salute in uerbo et doctrina la-
borat? illi uero qui ea dicturi sunt quae ab aliis acceperunt, et
antequam accipiant, orent pro eis a quibus accipiunt, ut eis detur
quod per eos accipere uolunt; et cum acceperint, orent ut bene et 25

1 non ipsi *CH Maur.* et rursus . . . dicunt *om.* G. quoniam]quod *E.* uerum]ueritas *A.*
2 ait ueritas *EI.* 3 nolite dicunt enim inquit et non faciunt *E.* 5 dicunt . . . non faciunt *om.*
E. tamen dicunt *ACGH.* 6 quomodo]modo *D.* 8 quando bona dicunt *om. E.* 9 ut]quod *E.*
quo]quod *D.* 10 dicendum ab alio]dicendo alii *A*; dicendum non ab alio *EI.* ipse]ipso *D.*
11 componat]contemnat *A.* quod cum fit ipse a seipso tradit]quod ipse cum fit a semetipso
trahit *F.* ille autem *E.* 12 boni uiri *A.* 13 commendat *E.* suam *E.* 14 ipso *D.* 16 apud
(populum)]ad *D.* iamiamque dicturus]iam quaedam dicturus aliquis *C*; iamque dicturus *A.*
18 oret *om. A.* 19 Hester orauit *A.* sua *D.* 20 temporali *EI*; sermone *add. E.* 21 quanto
magis orare debet *om. I* ; debet]debent *A.* 22 accipiant *A.* salutem *D.* uerbo et in uerbo *E.*
laborant *A.* 23 ea dicturi]edicturi *D.* et *om. A.* 24 pro eis]pro ipsis *A.* 25 et (cum) *om. H.*

10. **dicendum . . . componat**: the
predicate use of the gerundive in connection with an accusative object is
restricted in classical Latin to a relatively small number of verbs. In Silver
and Late Latin, however, we note an
ever increasing number of verbs admitting of this construction: cf. St.-Schm.

595; K.-Steg. II, 1, 731.

12. **cum uero . . . uiuunt**: another
evidence of that dependence on faith
which distinguishes Christian from
pagan oratory.

30. *Prayer should hold first place in
the esteem of the Christian orator.*

18. **dictaturus**: *dictare* = 'dictate to a

works they deny Him. And so in a certain sense they speak, and again in another sense they do not, since both these verses are true, because Truth itself utters them. For, again, speaking of such as these, He says: *What they shall say to you, do; but according to their words, do ye not.* That is, "What from their lips you hear, that do, but what in their works you see, that do not do." *For they say,* he continues, *and do not.* And so though they *do* not, still they *say.* But in another place, rebuking such men, He says: *Hypocrites, how can you speak good things, whereas you are evil?* And from this it would seem that even what they say when they speak good things, they do not themselves say, since forsooth in will and in deed, they gainsay what they say. And so it may happen that an eloquent man, though bad, may himself compose a sermon in which truth is set forth to be delivered by another who, though not eloquent, is good. And when this is done, the former gives as from himself what belongs to another, while the latter receives from another what is really his own. But when good Christians render this service to good Christians, both speak what is their own, because God is theirs, and to Him belong the words which they speak; and they make these, too, their own, though they were not able to compose them, if they compose their lives in accordance with them.

30, 63. But whether a person is now making ready to speak before the people or before any other group whatever, or to compose something either to be delivered before the people or read by those who wish or can do so, he should pray God to put a fitting discourse upon his lips. For if Queen Esther prayed when she was about to address the king in regard to the temporal affairs of her people, that God might give her a well-ordered speech in her mouth, how much more ought he to pray to receive such a gift who labors in word and teaching for the eternal welfare of mankind? Those, too, who are to deliver what they receive from others, even before they receive it, ought to pray for those from whom they receive it, that what they wish to receive, may be given to them; and when

---

stenographer,' often from the end of the Republic after the *notarii* had become so important an adjunct to men of letters. From this meaning of expressing oneself in written language by dictating, *dictare* in Silver and Late Latin came also to mean, as here, simply 'to compose,' not necessarily by dictating: cf. T.L.L. V,

1009, 75–1012, 40.

Deus . . . os eius: an echo of Esther 14, 13: tribue sermonem compositum in ore meo. A somewhat closer rendering is given on lines 20–21.

20. **temporaria** = 'that which is not eternal,' 'transitory,' is Eccl. Latin: cf. K.-Schm. s.v.

ipsi proferant, et illi ad quos proferunt sumant; et de prospero
exitu dictionis eidem gratias agant, a quo id se accepisse non dubi-
^{Sap.7, 16} tant, ut qui gloriatur, in illo glorietur, in cuius manu sunt et nos
et sermones nostri.

31, 64. Longior euasit liber hic quam uolebam, quamque puta- 5
ueram. sed legenti uel audienti, cui gratus est, longus non est;
cui autem longus est, per partes eum legat, qui habere uult cognitum; quem uero cognitionis eius piget, de longitudine non queratur. ego tamen Deo nostro ago gratias, quod in his quattuor
libris non qualis ego essem, cui multa desunt, sed qualis esse debeat, 10
qui in doctrina sana, id est christiana, non solum sibi, sed aliis
etiam laborare studet, quantulacumque potui facultate disserui.

1 ut bene et ipsi]ut ipsi et bene *E*. et illi]ut illi (*sic em.*) *B*.   prospere *D*.   2 id
se]ipsi *A*; se *om. E*.   5 -que *om. D*.   6 non erit *C*.   8 queretur *D*.   9 Domino
A; Domino Iesu Christo *EI*.   gratias ago *Maur.;* gratias ago Domino Iesu Christo
EI.   quod]quo *D*.   eis *A*; hiis *E*.   11 id est christiana *om. E*.   12 etiam aliis *A*
Maur.   quantulamcumque *E*.

1. **de . . . exitu**: *de* with the ablative, to express cause, is particularly a colloquial usage, sometimes found in the poets, and of increasing frequency in Late Latin: cf. K.-Steg. II, 1, 498; St.-Schm. 526; T.L.L. VI, 611, 17.

31. *Conclusion.*

6. **sed legenti . . . queratur**: Augustine can never entirely rid himself of his training as a dialectician. Here, even in his words of apology for a long work, he is not able to refrain from getting the better of his reader by this clever turn of a dilemma, which is all the more characteristic of him by being expressed in the order of the figure of *climax*: gratus est, . . . longus non est: longus est, . . . habere cognitum: cognitionis piget, . . . non queratur.

7. **per partes**: *per* with the accusative to express manner is used occasionally by Plautus, Cicero, Sallust, Livy, but more frequently in Silver and Late Latin: cf. St.-Schm. 438; K.-Steg.

they have received it, they should pray that they themselves may deliver it well, and that those to whom they speak may take it; and for the successful issue of their discourse, they should give thanks to Him from whom they cannot doubt but that they have received it, that he who glories may glory in Him in whose hand are both we and our words.

31,   64. This work has turned out longer than I had wished, and than I had planned. But if it is interesting to one who reads it or listens to it, it will not be long; if, however, anyone finds it long, he should read it in parts if he still wishes to become acquainted with it; on the other hand, one who is not interested in making its acquaintance should not complain of its length. But for my part, I give thanks to God that in these four books, I have treated with whatever little ability I have, not of such a one as I myself am, for I have many deficiencies, but of such a person as he should be who in sound teaching, that is in Christian teaching, strives to labor not only for himself, but also for others.

II, 1, 557. The present phrase is cited for Colum. 1, 4, 5; Plin. Epist. 2, 5, 10; Dig. 12, 1, 13.

11. **doctrina sana . . . christiana**: Augustine ends on the note which he has tried to keep dominant throughout this book, viz., that the instruction aimed at by the Christian speaker is, unlike that prevalent in the schools of the Sophists, a thoroughly sound and wholly natural one. It is for this reason that passing over the popular rhetorical precepts of the fourth century, he returns to the sane theory of classical times. This, vivified by the Christian spirit, he puts forward as a new-old ideal.

PART III

THE RHETORIC OF SAINT AUGUSTINE

4

ST. AUGUSTINE ON PREACHING
(*DE DOCTRINA CHRISTIANA*, IV)*

Charles Sears Baldwin

Charles Sears Baldwin argues that Augustine "begins rhetoric anew" with De
Doctrina Christiana. *Baldwin substantiates this claim through an examination
of book 4, where he argues that Augustine rejects Sophistic rhetoric and revives the
true spirit of Ciceronian rhetoric in the service of Christian preaching. Baldwin notes
that the primary difference between Augustine and contemporary Sophists was the
value Augustine placed on teaching biblical wisdom versus pleasing the audience.
This is not to suggest that Augustine did not seek to please his audience but, rather,
that pleasing the audience was viewed as secondary to teaching and persuading the
audience of divine truths. In addition to rejecting Sophistic rhetoric, Baldwin argues
that Augustine's volume is significant for the way in which he adapts Ciceronian
rhetorical principles to Christian ends. In book 4 Augustine adopts Cicero's three*
officia—*to teach, to delight, and to persuade—and three divisions of style—the
subdued, the moderate, and the grand. Baldwin argues Augustine's view to be that
all three* officia *and all three styles are integrated in the service of what Augustine
perceives as the greatest* officium, *to teach, as practical in the context of Christian preaching. Augustine begins rhetoric anew not only by drawing on Ciceronian
rhetoric, thereby resurrecting it for future generations of rhetors, but also by tailoring
Cicero's rhetoric to new Christian ends.*

With this elaborate pedagogical tradition [that of the Sophists] a
clean break is made by St. Augustine. The fourth book of his *De Doctrina Christiana*[1] has historical significance in the early years of the fifth
century out of all proportion to its size; for it begins rhetoric anew. It
not only ignores sophistic; it goes back over centuries of the lore of

* Originally published in *Medieval Rhetoric and Poetic (to 1400): Interpreted from Representative Works.* Gloucester, Mass.: Peter Smith, 1959 (rpt. of 1928 original). 51–73.
Reprinted by courteous permission from vol. 22 (April, 1925) of *Proceedings of the (British) Classical Association*, to which it was presented under the title "St. Augustine and the
Rhetoric of Cicero." Headnote by Amy K. Hermanson.

personal triumph to the ancient idea of moving men to truth; and it gives to the vital counsels of Cicero a new emphasis for the urgent tasks of preaching the word of God.

Abstractly and in retrospect the very character of Christian preaching seems necessarily to reject sophistic. But at the time this seemed anything but inevitable. Sophistic was almost the only lore of public speaking then active. It dominated criticism and education. The Greek fathers Gregory of Nyssa and Gregory Nazianzen might expose its falsity of conception; but they could not escape it. It had brought them up. Its stylistic habits were ingrained in their expression. Augustine too had been brought up on sophistic. Nor could he escape it. Again and again his style rings with its tradition.[2] Not only had he learned it for good; he had taught it. He had been himself, in Plutarch's sense and Strabo's, a sophist. We must hasten to add that the great Christians of the fourth century, if they could not escape sophistic, at least redeemed it by curbing its extravagance and turning it to nobler uses. But Augustine did much more. He set about recovering for the new generation of Christian orators the true ancient rhetoric. He saw that for Christian preaching sophistic must not only be curbed; it must be supplanted. Against the background of his day his quiet, simple book, renouncing the balances and figures of his other works without renouncing their fervor, is seen to be a startling innovation.

Not the least striking trait of the innovation is its reserve. Augustine does not attack sophistic as the Gregorys do; he ignores it. In chapter 31 of book 2 he had, indeed, mentioned it. Discussing there not style, but matter, he had contrasted the necessary training in argument with sophistic quibbling, and had then added, forecasting book 4, that superfluous stylistic ornament also is sophistic.

> But training in argument on questions of all such kinds as are to be investigated and resolved in sacred literature is of the highest value; only we must beware of the lust for quarrelling, and of the puerile display of skill in disappointing an opponent. . . . This sort of quibbling conclusion Scripture execrates, I think, in the text *Qui sophistice loquitur odibilis est*.[3] Even though not quibbling, a speech seeking verbal ornament beyond the bounds of responsibility to subject matter (*gravitas*) is called sophistic. (II.xxxi)

But an uninformed modern reader of book 4 would hardly be aware that sophistic existed. No denunciation could be more scathing than this silence. In Augustine's view of Christian preaching sophistic simply has no place. A good debater, instead of parrying he counters. He spends his time on his own case. A good teacher, he tells his neophytes not what to avoid, but what to do. He has so far renounced sophistic that he has no concern to triumph. He wishes simply to teach sound rhetorical doctrine. He achieves an extraordinary conciseness not so much by compression as by undeviating straightforwardness.

A reader familiar with the times, however, will be reminded of sophistic by many allusions. Single phrases or sentences some of them, a few more extended, they all serve to illuminate by contrast the true rhetoric.

> All these things, when they are taught by rhetors, are thought great, bought at a great price, sold with great boasting. Such boasting, I fear, I may suggest myself in speaking so; but I had to answer those ill-educated men who think that our authors are to be despised, not because they lack the eloquence which such critics love too much, but because they do not use it for display. (vii)
>
> [But an audience of Christian sobriety] will not be pleased with that suave style in which though no wrong things are said, right things slight and frail are adorned with foamy circumlocution. (xiv)
>
> I think I have accomplished something not when I hear them applauding, but when I see them weeping. (xxiv)[4]

Display, inflation, thirst for applause—every reader of Augustine's time would recognize in these allusions a repudiation of sophistic.

For Augustine thinks that Christian preaching is to be learned best from Christian preachers. As if in reply to Julian's scornful "Let them elucidate their Matthew and Luke,"[5] he recommends not only for doctrine, but for rhetoric, the Epistles, the Prophets, and the Fathers, and proceeds to analyze their style. The analysis, though based on the current Latin version, is generally transferable to the Greek, since it is much simpler than the classification set forth by sophistic. It exhibits sentence movement simply in climax, period, balance—those devices which are most easily appropriated and most useful. The general ancient counsels of aptness and variety are applied specifically to preaching. As to cadence (*clausula*), Augustine dispenses with all subdivisions, and even makes bold to assert that it must sometimes be sacrificed. Similarly omitting all classification of figures, he manages to suggest in a few words what figures are for. In a word, he shows how to learn from the Canon and the Fathers the rhetoric that is vital to homiletic.

This rhetoric, not only simpler than sophistic, but quite different in emphasis, is set forth in the terms of Cicero. Augustine has gone back four and a half centuries to the days before *declamatio*. The instruction that he draws from his analysis of Christian literature is planned upon the "instruct, win, move" (*docere, delectare, movere*) of *De oratore* and upon the corresponding three typical styles (*genus tenue—medium—grande*) of *Orator*.[6] Evidently Augustine had the greater Cicero, not the lesser that sufficed for the Middle Age. He neither quotes nor cites any other rhetorician; and though his doctrine of aptness and of variety is common throughout the older rhetoric, for this too he had no need to go beyond the master's two great works. Nor have any others been more persuasive as to imitation,[7] which is Augustine's controlling idea. This first Ciceronianism, too immediately aware of the perverted imitation of style taught by sophists to fall into the archaism and redundancy of later worship of Cicero, is a penetrative recovery of Cicero's larger meaning. Augustine's application of the three typical styles is more just and more practically distinct than Cicero's own. Would that all Ciceronians had been equally discerning!

TABULAR VIEW OF ST. AUGUSTINE'S
DE DOCTRINA CHRISTIANA IV

A. For learning to preach, models are more fruitful than rules (i–v)
B. Eminent models are offered by the literature of Christian eloquence (vi–viii)
    1. Christian eloquence not merely comparable with pagan, but distinctive.
    2. Analysis of Romans 5 especially of climax, period, clauses, etc.
    3. Analysis of 2 Corinthians 11:16, especially of variety.
    4. Analysis of Amos 6, especially of figures.
C. Christian preaching must fulfill all three typical tasks of oratory summarized in Cicero's *docere, delectare, movere* (ix–xix)
    1. *docere*, subordinating even *integritas* to clearness (ix–xi)
    2. *delectare*, necessary as a means, never an end (xii–xvii)
    3. *movere*, to carry assent into action (xviii, xix)
D. The three corresponding styles of oratory, Cicero's *tenue, medium, grande*, are exemplified in the Canon (xx)

1. *genus tenue (submissum)* in Galatians 4:21 and 3:15 as demanding trained reasoning and memory.
2. *genus medium (temperatum)* in 1 Timothy 5, Romans 12, 13, as rhythmical, but with cadence often sacrificed.
3. *genus grande* in 2 Corinthians 6:2, Romans 8:28, Galatians 4:10, the last without the usual stylistic means.

E. They are also exemplified in St. Cyprian *Ad Cæcilium and De habitu virginum,* St. Ambrose *De Spiritu and De virginibus* (xxii)
F. No one of the three can effectively be constant. (xxii, xxiii)
G. Constancy is rather in the aim, which is always persuasion (xxiv–xxvi)
   1. The speaker's life is the greater means of persuasion in the third style (xxvii–xxviii)

(Appended Note) The recital of borrowed sermons is permissible (xxix)

Conclusion, with reminder of prayer, in thanksgiving (xxx, xxxi)

The fourth book of the *De Doctrina Christiana* is specifically linked by its proem to the preceding three as setting forth presentation (*modus proferendi*). Books 1–3 have dealt with study of the subject matter (*inventio*); book 4 is to deal with expression. Augustine thus makes the traditional fivefold division twofold. *Inventio*, which under sophistic had lapsed, he restores to its rightful place and gives it a new application to the exegesis of Scripture. Of the remaining four left to his second heading he discusses only style (*elocutio*). Delivery and memory are mentioned incidentally; plan is omitted. The omission is not negligent. The first chapter warns us not to expect a manual of rhetoric. Nevertheless a modern student cannot help wishing that so suggestive a treatise had both applied to preaching the ancient counsels as to plan and exhibited the New Testament in this aspect. Thus to analyze for imitation not only the style of the Pauline epistles, but their cogency of order, would doubtless have made the work unduly extensive. One hopes that seminarians of the fifth century were stimulated, and that seminarians of the twentieth century will be stimulated, by the example of the treatise itself to study Romans not only for appeal, but for cogency. Meantime Augustine's fourth book remains one of the most fruitful of all discussions of style in preaching.

Who dare say that the defenders of truth should be unarmed against falsehood? While the proponents of error know the art of winning an audience to good will, attention, and open mind,[8] shall the proponents of truth remain ignorant? While the [sophist] states facts concisely, clearly, plausibly,[9] shall the preacher state them so that they are tedious to hear, hard to understand, hard to believe? While the one attacks truth and insinuates falsehood by fallacious argument, shall the other have too little skill either to defend the true or to refute the false? Shall the one, stirring his hearers to error, urging them by the force of oratory, move them by terror, by pity, by joy, by encouragement, and the other slowly and coldly drowse for truth?(ii).

But to learn such skill from rules, he goes on, is the way rather for boys than for men who have immediately before them the urgent tasks of preaching.

For eloquence will stick to such men, if they have the talent of keenness and ardor, more easily through their reading and hearing of the eloquent than through their following of the rules of eloquence. Nor does the Church lack literature, even outside the Canon established in the citadel of authority, to imbue a capable man with its eloquence, even though his mind be not on the manner but on the matter, provided he add practice in writing, in dictating, finally also in composing orally[10] what he feels according to the rule of piety and faith. Besides, if such talent be lacking, either the rules of rhetoric will not be grasped, or if by great labor some few of them are partially grasped, they will be of no avail. . . . [Young preachers] must beware of letting slip what they have to say while they attend to saying it in good form. (iii)

They must, indeed, know the principles of adaptation (iv) and develop their expression as far as they can; but they will do so best by imitation.

Whoever wishes to speak not only with wisdom, but with eloquence. . . . I rather direct to read or hear the eloquent and to imitate them by practice than advise to spend his time on teachers of the art of rhetoric. (v)

Expressed in modern terms, Augustine's position is that rhetoric as a classified body of doctrine is properly an undergraduate study. It is not the best approach for seminarians because its method is analytical. The young preacher, needing rather promotion than revision, will advance more rapidly by imitation.

Starting from this principle, that the more fruitful study for learning to preach is imitation of Christian eloquence, Augustine proceeds to show (vi–viii) how distinctive is the eminence of such models and how repaying to analysis. His vindication should be pondered by those who still permit themselves to disparage without distinction the literary value of the New Testament, and by those who, granting poetic to Ambrose, remain unaware of his rhetoric.

At this point the question, perhaps, arises whether our authors, whose divinely inspired writings constitute for us a canon of most salutary authority, are to be called philosophers[11] only, or also orators. To me and to those who agree with what I am saying, the question is very easily answered. For where I comprehend them, nothing can seem to me either more philosophical or more eloquent. And all, I venture to say, who rightly comprehend what they speak, comprehend at the same time that they could not have spoken otherwise. For as there is an eloquence becoming to youth, another to age, nor can that be called eloquence which does not befit the character of the speaker, so there is an eloquence becoming to men most worthy of the highest authority and evidently inspired. Our authors have spoken with such eloquence. No other is becoming to them, nor theirs to others. For it is like themselves; and, the more it rejects display, the more it ranges above others not by inflation, but by cogency. Where on the other hand I do not comprehend them, though their eloquence is less apparent to me, I have no doubt that it is such as I find it where I do comprehend. The very obscurity of inspired and salutary utterances has been tinged with such eloquence that our minds should be stimulated not only in study [of their meaning], but in practice [of their art]. Indeed, if there were leisure, all the virtues and graces of eloquence with which those are inflated who put their style ahead of the style of our authors not by greatness, but by distension, could be exhibited in the sacred literature of those whom divine Providence has sent to instruct us and to draw us from this corrupt world to the world of happiness. But what delights me more than I can say in their eloquence is not what it has in common with pagan orators and poets. What I rather admire, what fills me with amazement, is that the eloquence which we hear around us has so been used, as it were through another eloquence of their own, as to be neither deficient nor conspicuous. For it should be neither condemned nor displayed; and they would have seemed to do the one if they shunned it, the other if it became noticeable. Even in those places where perhaps it is noticeable to experts, such is the message that the words in which it is expressed seem not to be sought by the speaker, but to subserve that message naturally, as if one saw philosophy issuing from her own home in the heart of the philosopher, and eloquence following as an inseparable servant even when not called.[12] (vi)

The vindication of an eloquence distinctly Christian has the more weight because its doctrine of form and substance echoes from Cicero the best ancient tradition. The older tradition had in Augustine's time been so overlaid that he could do no better service to rhetoric than to recall it. In fact, Christian eloquence redeemed public speaking by reviving the true persuasion.

The insistence on the Ciceronian doctrine that style is not separable has a bearing more than historical. Not only for Augustine's time, but for any time, the truism must be reasserted. His iteration is more than preoccupation with Cicero, more than repudiation of sophistic. It springs from the cardinal importance of the truism for homiletic. In the pulpit the sophistic heresy of art for art's sake becomes intolerable.

Augustine's next step (vii) is to support his general claims for Christian eloquence, and to show how it may be studied, by analyzing briefly three typical passages. In the first, Romans 5:3-5, he analyzes prose rhythm under the familiar heads of classical sentence movement (*compositio*): phrases and subordinate clauses (*cæsa*), coordinate clauses (*membra*), period (*circuitus*), climax (*gradatio*), adding the equivalent Greek terms.[13]

RHYTHMICAL ANALYSIS OF ROMANS 5:3, 4, 5

(1) καυχώμεθα ἐν ταῖς θλίψεσιν, (1) Gloriamur in tribulationibus,

(2) εἰδότες ὅτι ἡ θλῖψις ὑπομονὴν κατεργάζεται, (2) scientes quod tribulatio patientiam operatur,

(3) ἡ δὲ ὑπομονὴ δοκιμήν,   (3) patientiam autem probationem,

(4) ἡ δὲ δοκιμὴ ἐλπίδα, (4) probatio vero spem,

(5) ἡ δὲ ἐλπὶς οὐ καταισχύνει, (5) spes autem non confundit,

(6) ὅτι ἡ ἀγάπη τοῦ θεοῦ ἐκκέχυται ἐν ταῖς καρδίαις ἡμῶν, (6) quia caritas Dei diffusa est in cordibus nostris,

(7) διὰ πνεύματος ἁγίου τοῦ δοθέντος ἡμῖν, (7) per Spiritum sanctum qui datus est nobis.

The passage is short enough, and the sentence movement simple enough, to be grasped readily. Its balance is striking without being monotonous and is reinforced by a linking iteration that leads to a climax.[14] He is a wise teacher who begins with an instance so memorable. It must have seized even more quickly a generation familiar with both the terms and the method.

The next example, 2 Corinthians 11:16-31, shows the same sentence devices carried through a much longer reach, and is therefore used both to reinforce the first and to add the importance of rhythmical variety. The counsel of variety, though a commonplace of the older rhetoric, had especial point by contrast with the sophistic fondness for trimming and prolonging balances. Incidental to the exhibition of variety is a reminder of aptness; and the analysis concludes:

> Finally all this breathless passage is closed with a period of two members. . . . But how after this impetus the brief statement interposed comes to rest, and rests the reader, how apt it is and how charming, can hardly be said. (vii)

The analysis of the third example, Amos 6:1-6, leads the study to longer and more sustained rhythmical reaches. Lest it seem the more difficult in the more figurative version of the Septuagint, Augustine quotes it "as translated from the Hebrew into Latin style through the interpretation of the priest Jerome, expert in both languages."

ANALYSIS OF AMOS 6:1-6

(1) Woe to them that are at ease in Zion and trust in the mountains of Samaria, which are named chief of the nations, to whom the house of Israel came!

(1) Væ qui opulenti estis in Sion et confiditis in monte Samariæ, optimates, capita populorum, ingredientes pompatice domum Israel;

(2) Pass ye unto Calneh, and see; and from thence go ye

(2) transite in Chalanne et videte, et ite inde in Emath magnam,

to Hamath the great: then go down to Gath of the Philistines: be they better than these kingdoms? or their border greater than your border?

et descendite in Geth Palæstinorum, et ad optima quæque regna horum, si latior terminus eorum termino vestro est:

(3) Ye that put away the evil day, and cause the seat of violence to come near;

(3) qui separati estis in diem malum, et adpropinquatis solio iniquitatis;

(4) That lie upon beds of ivory, and stretch themselves upon their couches, and eat the lambs out of the flock, and the calves out of the midst of the stall;

(4) qui dormitis in lectis eburneis, et lascivitis in stratis vestris; qui comeditis agnum de grege, et vitulos de medio armenti;

(5) That chant to the sound of the viol,

(5) qui canitis ad vocem psalterii:

(6) and invent to themselves instruments of musick, like David; that drink wine in bowls, and anoint themselves with the chief ointments:

(6) sicut David putaverunt se habere vasa cantici, bibentes in phialis vinum, et optimo unguento delibuti;

(7) but they are not grieved for the affliction of Joseph.

(7) et nihil patiebantur super contritione Joseph.

Much more urgent, leaping to attack, rising, prolonging, varying, subsiding to a pregnant close, the prophecy widens the conception of rhythmical range. Marking the rhythms briefly, Augustine uses it also to show the oratorical force of figures.[15] Thus a few pages of analysis are made to yield wide and definite suggestion. This, perhaps, is their outstanding merit; while they show the student what to look for, they invite him to go on for himself. But the pedagogical achievement does not stop there. The professor of rhetoric has seen that rhetorical analysis must be simplified, and that it must be made progressive. Where else shall we find so much drawn from three analyses? The first reduces the complicated lore of rhythm to its essentials. The second, reinforcing and extending these, dwells upon aptness as a corrective of rhetorical zeal, and as a constructive principle. The third, quoting rhythms still more urgent with emotion, passes to the emotional value of concrete words. To bring the overclassified lore of sophistic back to the simplicity of Aristotle was a service not only to homiletic, but to all rhetoric. A greater service was to substitute for the static and formalized pedagogy of the day a vital order. Augustine had been doubtless a popular professor; Christianity made him a great teacher.

Pedagogically, therefore, even his incidental definitions are worth noticing. That the function of grammar is traditionally to impart correctness of speech (iii) is used to support the contention that even this elementary skill comes best in fact from imitation. The period (vii) is defined so as to throw the emphasis on delivery. Its "clauses are suspended by the speaker's voice until it is concluded at the end." Therefore it "cannot have fewer than two clauses." So he points out in the passage above from Amos that the rhythm is available for delivery (*in potestate pronuntiantis*) either as a series of six or as three pairs, and that the latter is more beautiful. So he suggests limiting analysis to give room for oral interpretation.

> This same passage which we have set as an example can be used to show other things relevant to the rules of eloquence. But a good hearer is not so much instructed by discussion in detail as he is kindled by ardent delivery. (vii)

The next and longest section (ix–xix) is based on Cicero's "inform, please, move" (*docere, delectare, movere*). Distinguishing each of these tasks clearly, Augustine is at the same time careful to unite them, by progressively iterative transitions, in the single and constant task of persuasion. In exposition (*docere*) clearness may demand the use of popular expressions. What avails correctness in a diction that is not understood?

> He who teaches will rather avoid all words that do not teach. If he can find correct words that are understood, he will choose those; if he cannot, whether because they do not exist or because they do not occur to him at the time, he will use even words that are less correct, provided only the thing itself be taught and learned correctly. (ix)

The correctness (*integritas*) of diction boasted by the sophists, and carried by them even to the pedantry of archaism, is here faced squarely. The assertion that it must sometimes be sacrificed, the making of clearness absolutely paramount, is the bolder at a time when Christian preaching was not yet recognized as having secure command of elegance. Unmistakable clearness, Augustine goes on, is so much more important in preaching than in discussions permitting question and answer that the speaker must be quick to help unspoken difficulties.

> For a crowd eager to grasp will show by its movement whether it has understood; and until it has given this signal the subject must be turned over and over by various ways of expressing it—a resource beyond the power of those who deliver speeches written out and memorized.[16] (x)

No warrant here, he adds (xi), for dilation beyond the demands of clearness, but good warrant for making instruction pleasant and appealing in order to hold attention. Passing thus to the two other tasks of oratory, he quotes (xii) Cicero's "to instruct is of necessity, to please is for interest, to move is for victory."[17] The three are then both carefully distinguished and shown to be a sort of geometrical progression. The first is first of necessity. It must be mastered; but it is rarely sufficient. To supply the lack, the second demands more rhetoric by demanding further adaptation to the audience; but it too must remain insufficient. So the third task, to move, is not merely the third item in a classification; it is the final stage in a progress. That progress is increasingly emotional. The last stage demands not only all the rhetoric of the preceding, but also the art of vivid imagery[18] and of urgent application. So Augustine arrives at one of those linking summaries which constitute almost a refrain.

> Therefore the eloquence of the Church, when it seeks to have something done, must not only explain to instruct and please to hold, but also move to win. (xiii)

The next chapter (xiv) warns against resting in the second stage.[19] To make the pleasing of the audience an end in itself is the typical vice of sophistic. If preaching tolerates it, "the time will come when they will not endure sound doctrine; but after their own lusts shall they heap to themselves teachers, having itching ears." Augustine quotes, not these words of Saint Paul, but Jeremiah, and rises to denunciation of mere pleasing. "Far from us be that madness." One of Cyprian's rare descriptive passages is adduced to show how "the wholesome-ness of Christian preaching has recalled his diction from [sophistic] redundancy and held it to a graver eloquence of less display." As the ultimate objection to the sophistic ideal is moral, so is the preacher's ultimate resource. Since his strength is derived from a source deeper than human skill, his best preparation is prayer. Augustine is not above enforcing this reminder by playing upon the words *orare, orator, oratio*. Nevertheless human skill is to be cultivated. Prayer itself proves the folly (xvi) of making no other preparation. He who abjures human lore of preaching because God gives us our messages might equally well abjure prayer because God knows us and our needs. The Pauline counsels specify how Timothy should preach. As God heals through doctors and medicines, so he gives the gospel to men by men and through man.

The transition (xvii) to the final task of moving men to action is another full and explicit iteration of all three, and at the same time a preparation for the next section on the corresponding three typical styles. Since the subject matter of preaching is always great, at least in implication (xviii), does it not always demand a great style? No; for a great matter (xix) may at the time rather demand exposition; and this in turn demands a restrained style. Again, a great matter may at the time rather demand praise or blame; and here enters the second task of so adapting the style as to win sympathy.

> But when something ought to be done, and we are talking to those who ought to do it and will not, then the great subject is to be expressed greatly and in such wise as to bend their minds. . . . What subject is greater than God? Is it therefore not a subject for instruction? Or how can any one expounding the unity of the Trinity do it except by con-fining himself to exposition, that so difficult a distinction may as far as is possible be understood? Is ornament demanded here, and not rather argument?[20] Is there here something that the audience is to be moved to do, and not rather something that it is to be taught to learn? Again, when God is praised in himself or in his works, what a vision of beautiful and splendid diction rises before anyone praising as well as he can him whom no one praises aright and no one fails to praise in some way or other! But if God be not worshipped, or if idols be worshipped with him or even in his stead, whether dæmons or any other created being, then to meet so great an evil, and from this evil to save men, the preaching too must be great. (xix)

Augustine has passed (xvii–xix) from Cicero's three tasks of oratory to his three typical styles by applying to the preacher Cicero's
definition of the orator: "He, then, shall be called eloquent who can
speak small things quietly, larger things proportionally, great things
greatly."[21] Thus the three styles are *genus submissum* (or *tenue*), *genus temperatum* (or *medium*), and *genus grande*. As in Cicero, these correspond to
docere, delectare, movere, and the second is connected with panegyric.

Augustine now proceeds to exemplify the first style (xx) from Galatians as calling for skill in reasoning and for a memory trained to bring
in objections and difficulties where they can best be met. This debater's memory is precisely the ancient *memoria*, the fifth of the traditional
parts of rhetoric. It seems to have fallen into abeyance under sophistic. What the sophists boasted was verbal memory, which Augustine
merely mentions in his appendix as something quite different.[22]

The same chapter (xx) exemplifies the second, or median style
from Timothy and Romans as having the charm of aptness. Here
Augustine confronts squarely the sophistic habit of making rhythmical
beauty paramount and the pagan disparagement of Christian style.
Some one may find the cadence of Romans 13:14 defective. Certainly
it would soothe the ear more rhythmically if the verb came last.

> But a graver translator has preferred to keep the usual word-order [and,
> he might have added, the logical emphasis]. How this sounds in the
> Greek used by the apostle they may see whose expertness in that lan-
> guage goes so far. To me at least, the word-order, which is the same as in
> our version, does not seem there either to run rhythmically. Indeed, the
> stylistic beauty (*ornatum*) which consists of rhythmical cadences is defec-
> tive, we must confess, in our authors. Whether this is due to our versions,
> or whether, as I incline to think, the authors deliberately avoided these
> occasions for applause, I do not venture to affirm, since I confess that I
> do not know. But this I know, that anyone who shall make their cadences
> regular in the same rhythms—and this is done very easily by shifting
> certain words that have equal force of meaning in the new order—will
> recognize that these inspired men lacked none of those things which he
> learned as great matters in the schools of the grammarians or rhetors.
> Moreover, he will discover many sorts of diction of so great beauty as to
> be beautiful even in our customary language, much more in theirs, and
> never found in the literature with which [the sophists] are inflated. But
> we must beware lest the addition of rhythm detract from the weight of
> inspired and grave sentences. Most learned Jerome does not carry over

into his translation the musical skill in which rhythm is learned most fully, though our prophets did not lack even that, as he shows in the Hebrew meters of some of them; [and he gave this up] in order to keep truth to their words. . . . As in my own style, so far as I think I may do so modestly, I do not neglect rhythmical cadences,[23] so in our authors they please me the more because I find them there so rarely. (xx)

The third, or great style, whether it be elegant or not, has for its distinguishing quality the force of emotional appeal. The instances are from 2 Corinthians 6 and Romans 8. Romans is a long epistle, not a sermon. Though it was read aloud, of course, it is essentially a treatise, a philosophy of history. It is largely expository and argumentative. Since it is addressed primarily to reflection and reason, its main artistic reliance is on cogency of order. But even here presentation does not remain purely logical. For persuasion it must rise also emotionally. As we read in Acts 17 the outline of the apostle's Areopagus speech, we discern beyond the logical chain of propositions an expanding conception of the Life-giver. Who can doubt that the style too, as in Romans, rose to *grande*? The traditional doctrine of the peroration, easily as it may be abused, is only the expression in rhetoric of the audience's final demand and the speaker's final answer. That demand and that answer are emotional.

Adding Galatians 4, Augustine says of it:

Although the whole epistle, except in the elegant last part, is written in the plain style, nevertheless the apostle inserts a certain passage of such moving force that it must be called great even though it has no such embellishments as those just cited. . . . Is there here either antithesis, or subordination for climax, or rhythm in phrase, clause, or period? None the less for that there is no cooling of the great emotion with which we feel the style to glow. (xx)

After quoting without further comment examples from Cyprian and Ambrose, Augustine shows (xxii, xxiii) the need of variety. More even than other forms of oratory, preaching seems to suffer from a stylistic level. No one of the three styles, least of all the third, can effectively be prolonged; the change from style to style gives relief; and subordination of what might be heightened may enhance the emotion of what must be. What must be heightened is what is to rouse the audience to action. So the test of achievement in the third style is not applause, but tears and change of life (xxiv). So also the end of all eloquence, in whatever style, is persuasion (xxv).

> In the restrained style the orator persuades of truth. In the great style he persuades to action. In the elegant style is he to persuade himself that he is speaking beautifully? With such an end what have we to do? Let them seek it who glory in language, who display themselves in panegyrics and such exercises, in which the hearer is neither to be instructed nor to be moved to any action, but merely to be pleased. But let us judge this end by another end. (xxv)

Thus Augustine is more explicit than Cicero in showing that the three typical styles are but three ways (xxvi) of achieving a single end, even as the three corresponding tasks, though one of them absorbs attention at a time, are but three aspects of the single task. Nor can persuasion dispense with a means beyond art, the appeal of the speaker's life[24] (xxvii). Though the Church speaks not merely through a man, but through his office, persuasion needs for full effect his whole influence. Because his life is without shame, the preacher speaks not shamelessly (xxviii), not only with restraint and charm, but with power, to win obedience to the truth.

The historical significance of the *De Doctrina Christiana*, important as it is, should not obscure its value as a contribution to homiletic. The first homiletic, though one of the briefest, remains one of the most suggestive. It omits no essential; while it reminds us of the general principles of rhetoric, it emphasizes those applications to preaching which are distinctive; and it proceeds pedagogically. Though the *doctrina* of the title refers strictly to exposition, and this is amplified and iterated as a constant necessity, Augustine includes specifically and from the start both charm and appeal, and concludes by showing emotional appeal to be the final stage of the comprehensive task of persuasion. Homiletic is an application of rhetoric long established as permanent, consistent, and in both materials and conditions fairly constant. That it is also comprehensive, demanding all three typical styles, including argument in its exposition, winning sympathy in order to urge action, varying its art[25] while holding to its single aim, is most suggestively established here in its first great monument.

Not only does Augustine forbid the arid and the tedious, not only does he insist on emotional appeal; he also vindicates for Christian eloquence the importance of charm. This was the more delicate because charm was both abused by contemporary sophists and still suspected by contemporary preachers. Augustine presents it at once frankly and with just discrimination. To make it an end in itself, he is careful to show, is indeed sophistic; but to ignore it is to forget that preaching is a form of the oratory of occasion.[26] The Areopagus speech of Saint Paul,[27] though it is only summarized in Acts 17, is evidently occasional and has clear indications of that adaptation to win sympathy which is Augustine's interpretation of Cicero's *delectare*. The speech on occasion, favorite form of oratory in Augustine's time, had been conventionalized to the point of recipe. The recipes, though he knew them all, Augustine simply ignores; the field he redeems. He shows Christian preaching how to cultivate it for real harvest. History has shown no other direction of rhetoric to be so peculiarly homiletic.

Already Christian eloquence had reached conspicuous achievement in panegyric and more widely in the field of occasional oratory. The pagan sophist must look to his laurels. But these very triumphs had brought the danger of lapsing into too familiar conventions. What in pagan oratory might be no worse than pretty or merely exciting, in Christian oratory would be meretricious. To hold his difficult course, the preacher, as Augustine reminds him again and again, must at every moment steer for his message. He must never deviate. Though sophistic lost its dominance centuries ago, it has never been quite dead, and it always besets preaching. Therefore a constant concern of homiletic is to exorcise it by a valid rhetoric; and no book has ever revealed this more succinctly, more practically, or more suggestively than the *De Doctrina Christiana*.

5

ST. AUGUSTINE AND THE DEBATE ABOUT
A CHRISTIAN RHETORIC*

James J. Murphy

James J. Murphy asserts that prior scholarship regarding Augustine's De Doctrina Christiana *frequently skews Augustine's contribution to rhetorical history by limiting its focus to the* DDC*'s significance for medieval homiletics. To fully recognize the importance of Augustine and* DDC, *Murphy suggests scholarship must dilate its scope to include how Augustine assessed and negotiated the internal and external difficulties facing the Christian Church during its fourth-century rise to social and political prominence. Murphy discusses the complexities that the Christian leaders grappled with as they determined whether—and in what ways—Christianity could adapt the highly secular, pagan-based ideologies and education practices of Greco-Roman culture to a Christian purpose. Augustine's rhetorical training provided him the means to resolve the church's conflicts by recognizing content independently from expression. By referencing several biblical texts, Augustine argues in book 4 that the Bible inherently engages style and demonstrates how ecclesiastical orators could apply the three Ciceronian modes of style to their own sermons. Moreover, Augustine reminds his contemporaries in book 4 that* materia *alone is not enough to communicate biblical and spiritual truths; he claims that by using plain homiletics, Christians would mirror the pagans' error of adhering to* forma *only. Through his arguments in book 4, Augustine constructs a bridge that allows Christian ministers the means to appropriate a purified Greco-Roman rhetoric. By discussing the twenty-five year span between Augustine's publication of books 1–3 and book 4, coupled with the shift in content from doctrine to style, Murphy concludes that Augustine intended book 4 to rebut critics who would deny the Christian church a "useful tool" for spiritual salvation.*

The importance of Saint Augustine's *De Doctrina Christiana* to rhetorical history has long been recognized. Charles Sears Baldwin asserts

* Originally from James J. Murphy. "St. Augustine and the Debate About a Christian Rhetoric." *Quarterly Journal of Speech* 46 (1960): 400–10. Headnote by Kristi Schwertfeger Serrano.

205

the book "begins rhetoric anew" after centuries of sophistry.[1] Sister
Thérése Sullivan applauds it for returning to the *doctrina sana* of Cicero
as a base for Christian preaching.[2] More recent studies find in the work
"a Christian theory of literature"[3] or a foundation of medieval preaching theory.[4] Its influence is clearly visible, being copied or quoted by
such writers as Rhabanus Maurus in the ninth century, Alain de Lille
in the twelfth, Humbert of Romans in the thirteenth, and Robert of
Basevorn in the fourteenth.[5]

Since Augustine's attitude toward the Second Sophistic is so clearly
expressed,[6] there has been some tendency to regard his work as a mere
attempt to rescue rhetoric from the taint of the sophistic. Indeed his
firm espousal of a union between meaning and expression marks his
rejection of the sophistic, as Baldwin has pointed out.

Nevertheless the attention paid to his later influence and to his
rejection of the Second Sophistic may obscure Saint Augustine's role
in providing an answer to a Christian dilemma of the fourth century. A
brief survey of the Church's position during this period may illustrate
the nature of the dilemma, and of Augustine's solution of it.

The Emperor Theodosius formally abolished paganism by decree
in A.D. 342, seventeen years after the first ecumenical council at Nicea
had outlined twenty canons for the government of the Church. With
the exception of such lapses as that under Julian, the fourth century was
marked by such gains that the converter of Saint Augustine, Ambrose
of Milan (340–397), could refer to his age as Christian times, *christiana
tempora*. As one historian says:

> Until the peace of the Church, the hostility of the public powers had
> weighed heavily on the life of the Christian community. On the day
> when it had definitely been removed we see the church coming forth, as
> it were, from a long winter, consolidating and developing her ranks, dis-
> cussing her hierarchal powers, defining the lines of her doctrines, draw-
> ing up the formulae of her faith, regulating her worship, surrounding the
> holy places with public marks of veneration, providing holy retreats for
> souls desirous of perfection, and giving to the Latin half of the Church
> a more faithful version of the Bible. All these fruits are the harvest of the
> fourth century.[7]

The century was therefore one for many decisions. During the
lifetime of Augustine, for instance, the Church faced the heresies of

Manichæans, Pelagians, Donatists, and Priscillianists. But besides the problems of defining Christian doctrines in reply to heretical attacks, the Christian community faced another problem of almost equal magnitude—the problem of defining the intellectual base for a culture which would permit the Church to perform its duty of leading men to salvation. This was a matter of the greatest moment, for upon its success depended the training of future apologists to defend doctrine against heresy, the formation of future poets to carry the Word of God to the people through literature, and the very education of the people themselves.

The basic issue was whether the Church should adopt *in toto* the contemporary culture which Rome had taken over from Greece. The fate of rhetoric, as a part of the Greco-Roman culture, was involved not only in the debate over the larger issue, but in more limited controversies about its own merits. Indeed, the contrast between *Verbum* (Word of God) and *verbum* (word of man) was stressed from the very beginnings of the Church,[8] long before the broader cultural issue was joined.

Ecclesiastical leaders of the fourth century continued the debate begun more than a century earlier when the conversion of many writers, poets, orators, and other public figures had at last given the Church a corps of well-equipped apologists. From the first, some individuals reacted violently to their former pagan culture; Lactantius speaks of pagan literature as "sweets which contain poison";[9] Arnobius, converted in his old age, tried to show his new fervor by writing a book which among other things tried to show that even the old grammar was no longer necessary:

> Or how is the truth of a statement diminished if an error is made in number or case, in preposition, particle, or conjunction?[10]

Cyprian, who had been a teacher of rhetoric at Carthage when he was converted, renounced profane letters completely and for the rest of his life never again quoted a pagan poet, rhetorician, or orator.[11]

Titian rails against literature in general and rhetoric in particular:

> You have invented rhetoric for injustice and calumny . . . you have invented poetry to sing of battles, the loves of the gods, of everything which corrupts the spirit.[12]

Justin warns against venerating unduly words (i.e., literature) which are not from God.[13] Clement of Alexandria points out that this revulsion against the old order was not limited to the intellectual classes: "The common herd fear Greek philosophy just as children fear goblins."[14]

Tertullian directs an attack against Greek philosophy and other pagan writings. "Where is there any likeness between the Christian and the philosopher?" he asks in his defense of pure faith, and terms philosophers "patriarchs of heresy." In a famous passage in his *De præscriptione hæerecticorum* he outlines the problem as many of his contemporaries saw it:

> What indeed has Athens to do with Jerusalem? What concord is there between the Academy and the church? What between heretics and Christians?[15]

The necessity for education posed a dilemma to Tertullian, who realized that it would be foolhardy to espouse ignorance, but who declared also that it was not licit for Christians to teach literature because it dealt with false gods.[16]

Similar remarks may be found in the writings of Justin Martyr, Clement of Alexandria, Synesius of Cyrene, and the historian Socrates. As Labriolle observes: "There emerges, therefore, the fact that we can state that during the first centuries of the Empire there is hardly a Christian writer in whose case there does not intrude or show itself more or less sincerely, more or less diplomatically, a hostility in some regard to the different forms of pagan learning."[17] Nor was this antipathy short-lived, for even while Augustine was engaged in writing the first books of *De Doctrina*, the fourth Council of Carthage (398) forbade bishops to read *libros gentilium* unless necessary.

From the Christian point of view there were many reasons for such attitudes. Even if Rome had not been the Rome of persecutions with their awful memories, its literature was studded with man-like gods parading what some Christian writers saw as a virtual gallery of sins. What is the use of decrees against sin, Augustine asks, when the adulteries of even Jove are portrayed by actors, painters, writers, reciters, and singers?[18] Referring in scathing tones to the fables of the pagan gods, Minucius Felix points out that men even study how to improve on such tales, "especially in the works of the poets, who have had such fatal influence in injuring the cause of truth." He adds that

Plato was wise to exclude Homer from his ideal republic, for giving the gods a place in the affairs of men, and then asks: "Why should I mention Mars and Venus caught in adultery, or Jupiter's passion for Ganymedes, hallowed in Heaven? Such stories are but precedents and sanctions for men's vices."[19] At best, secular education would divert the attention of the devout toward earthly things rather than spiritual matters. And since heretics often used logical argument to attack the doctrines of the Church, there was a corresponding tendency to fall back upon fideism (e.g., Tertullian: *regula fidei*) and decry reasoning itself. Hilary of Poitiers, for instance, states that truth is impervious to "marvelous devices of perverted ingenuity" in Arian logic.[20]

Another aspect of Greco-Roman culture which drew fire was the rhetorical excess of the Second Sophistic. Moreover, the rhetorician Fronto had been an early opponent of the Church, Minucius Felix notes. Although attacks upon rhetoric had an ancient tradition, the Christian writer often saw in rhetoric of his time the taint of a worldly, pagan culture which could lead men away from God. It is in this light that Gregory Naziensus reproves Gregory of Nyssa for abandoning Christian books to take up the trade of rhetorician.[21] Augustine himself was, in a certain sense, converted from rhetoric to Christianity.

"Our writers do not waste their time in polishing periods," declares Basil of Cæsarea, "we prefer clarity of expression to mere euphony." And again, "The school of God does not recognize the laws of the encomium," nor does it deal in "sophistic vanities."[22]

The most extreme Christian viewpoint seemed to be that rhetorical forms might be dispensed with altogether. In the middle of the third century Cyprian had posed the problem as follows:

> In courts of law, in public meetings, in political discussions, a full eloquence may be the pride of vocal ambition, but in speaking of the Lord God, a pure simplicity of expression (*vocis pura sinceritas non eloquentiae*) which is convincing depends upon the substance of the argument rather than upon the forcefulness of eloquence.[23]

Both Ambrose and Jerome decry rhetorical excesses in their fellow preachers, calling for adherence to Paul's advice. The Donatist Cresconium went so far as to quote Proverbs 10:19 as proof that eloquence was sinful; although this drew a sharp reply from Augustine,[24] the incident may serve as an illustration of the temper of the times.

This is not to say, of course, that opinion was completely aligned in one direction. A true debate took place among the leaders of the Church as official persecution faded into the background and the exigencies of ecclesiastical organization forced new decisions upon its leaders. Some of the most vehement opponents of pagan literature admitted the necessity of education, while others (like Saint Cyprian) resolutely turned their backs upon the old order.

Saint Basil and Saint Ambrose, for example, illustrate the mixed feelings of the Fathers of the Church as they faced a cultural dilemma. Basil recommends gathering roses among the thorns of pagan literature, on one hand, yet warns students not to abandon themselves to their pagan professors' ideas as they would their course to a navigator on a ship.[25] He also feels constrained to defend the Bible even though it is written in "a barbarian tongue." This points up still another cultural problem for the educated ecclesiastic of the fourth century, the apparently unliterary style of the Scriptures. Basil concludes that "although their style is unlearned, their content is true and they are the thoughts to which we give utterance."[26]

Ambrose also has mixed feelings. Although he emphasizes the distinction between *sapientia sæculi* and *sapientia spiritualis*, he recognizes the need for training of preachers and condemns not rhetoric itself but its sophistic abuses. His defense of the Scriptures is based on his approval of their simple style in contrast with the "showy" language of philosophers and orators. Saint Luke, he asserts, excels, in *stilus historicus*. Nevertheless he admits that rhetorical ornament may sometimes be useful and, indeed, sometimes occurs in the Scriptures themselves.[27]

His ingenious solution to the problem of pagan philosophy, on the other hand, was one which did not win general approval. The pagans, Ambrose states, originally got their wisdom from Scriptures; Plato went to Egypt to "know the deeds of Moses, the oracles of the law, the worthy sayings of the prophets."[28] As Laistner observes, this was an attractive way out of a dilemma—one which even attracted Augustine for a time—but one which could not long withstand further inquiry.[29] Ambrose was sufficiently impressed with Roman learning, however, that he modeled his instruction book for priests upon Cicero's *De officiis*.[30] Hilary of Poitiers condemns Arian verbal display, yet prays for a good style in his own sermons. Honor, he says, is given to the word of God by one who speaks with beauty of expression.

But Saint Jerome, contemporary and friend of Augustine, may perhaps illustrate best the inner conflict faced by many Christian leaders in the fourth century. In his famous letter of advice to the virgin Eustochium, he warns:

> What communion hath light with darkness? What concord hath Christ with Belial? What has Horace to do with the Psalter, Vergil with the Gospels and Cicero with the Apostle [Paul]? . . . we ought not to drink the cup of Christ and the cup of devils at the same time.[31]

Later in the same epistle he relates a dream which came to him after he had been wrestling with the question of whether a Christian could legitimately enjoy the Greek and Roman classics:

> Miserable man that I am! I was fasting and then I began to read Cicero; after many nights spent in watching, after many tears, which the remembrance of my faults of not so long ago drew forth from the depths of my heart, I took Plautus in my hands. If by chance, on recollecting myself, I started reading the Prophets, their unadorned style awoke in me feelings of revulsion. My eyes, blinded, no longer saw the light, and it was not on my eyes that I laid the blame, it was on heaven.
>
> While the old serpent thus misused me, a violent fever penetrated the marrow of my worn-out body towards the middle of Lent, without any respite, in an incredible manner, it so consumed my poor members that I had scarcely any flesh on my bones. Already people were thinking of my funeral. My body felt quite frozen; a remnant of vital heat no longer palpitated save in the lukewarmness of my poor breast.
>
> Suddenly I felt myself ravished away in ecstacy and transported before the tribunal of the Judge. Such a dazzling light emanated from those present that, crouched on the ground, I dared not lift up my eyes. On being asked my profession, I replied, "I am a Christian." Whereupon He who presided, thundered: "Thou dost lie—thou art not a Christian, but a Ciceronian. Where thy treasure is, there is thy heart also."

Then Jerome relates that he swore an oath in his dream: "Lord, if it ever happens to me to possess or read profane books, I shall have denied Thee." From that moment the dreamer betook himself "to the reading of the divine books with as much passion as I had formerly given to reading the books of men."[32]

Interpretations of this dream have been many and varied, and it is generally wise to refrain from taking too literally a work designed to point up a moral. Nevertheless, Pease points out, Jerome did refrain from using classical quotations in his works for about fifteen years following the time at which the dream is supposed to have occurred. The very fact that Jerome felt it necessary to reply to Rufinus in A.D. 402 may be another indication of the state of the times, and possibly of his contemporaries' views of his so-called oath.[33]

His basic dilemma reveals itself elsewhere too. At one point he is concerned because heathen sources are used to attack the doctrine of resurrection of the body, and enjoins Christians to "lay aside the weapons of the heathens" in their replies; it is better to have a just unlearnedness than an evil wisdom.[34] In another place:

> We do not wish for the field of rhetorical eloquence, nor the snares of
> dialecticians, nor do we seek the subtleties of Aristotle, but the very words
> of Scripture must be set down.[35]

He refers often to his desire for a simple, clear style which will avoid "pomp . . . structures of words," yet he was a student of the famous grammarian Donatus and in later life recommended Demosthenes and Cicero to his students as models.[36]

Jerome employs the figure of the "captive woman" at one point to illustrate his desire to take from the old what was useful for the new order. The figure occurs in Deuteronomy 21:10-13.

> If thou go to fight against thy enemies, and the Lord thy God deliver
> them to thy hand, and thou lead them away captives, and seest in the
> number of the captives a beautiful woman, and lovest her, and wilt have
> her to wife, thou shalt bring her into thy house: and she shall shave her
> hair, and pare her nails and shall put off the raiment, wherein she was
> taken: and shall remain in thy house, and mourn for her father and her
> mother one month: and after that thou shalt go unto her, and shalt sleep
> with her, and she shall be thy wife.[37]

The captive woman, of course, is secular wisdom, to be purged of its falsities and dangers. The metaphor clarifies the desire of Jerome, but does not specify what is to be sheared away and what is to be kept whole.

In the case at hand—the matter of the worth of rhetoric—his feelings are ambivalent. "Saint Jerome's attitude toward rhetoric," concludes Ellspermann, "cannot be summed up in one bald statement. In the texts considered there is indeed unfeigned favor of the rhetorical art, but there are also sentiments of mixed approval and disapproval, and even of evident disapproval."[38]

Even so, it might be argued at this point that the bulk of these Christian statements might be attributed to a reluctance to acknowledge publicly the worth of the Roman cultural heritage, while at the same time taking advantage of it. The Church Fathers were trained in Roman rhetorical schools, and many had actually taught rhetoric themselves. It might be expected that they would readily avail themselves of their training.

Nevertheless, two factors must be appreciated. The first is that the few citations offered above could be multiplied many times, the abundance of Christian comment offering clear indication that this issue was one of real concern up to and including the fourth century.[39]

A second point is that, despite the rhetorical training of the major ecclesiastical orators, the fourth century marks a high point of popularity for the simple "homily" style of preaching. Students of such preachers as Chrysostom and Basil have generally concluded that their sermons show less of the contemporary sophistic than might ordinarily be expected from men of their educational background. Coupled with the many utterances denouncing the sophistic, the comparative simplicity of the homilies might be seen as further indication of the dilemma of the times.[40] The reader's attention is directed, for example, to Chrysostom's first homily on the Statues: the sermon has no proper beginning or end, and might satisfactorily be ended at any point without damaging the speaker's point; the use of figures is comparatively restrained, and there is virtually no repetition for emphasis.

Whatever the modern critic may decide about the intrinsic merit of the homily form of the fourth century, its very appearance in a highly sophisticated age might well argue a deliberate choice on the part of preachers. It was an age, after all, when the same man who delivered the eulogy for the archsophist Prohæresius could castigate a friend for forsaking Christian books for the rhetorician's trade.[41] It was an age also in which former teachers of rhetoric—Jerome, Basil, and Augustine, among others—felt that they must decide whether their former profession deserved a place in the new order.

The resolution of this question was demanded at a critical period in the history of Western culture, for the barbarian erosion of the Roman Empire was already well under way. Alaric swept into Rome itself in 410, and Augustine's episcopal seat of Hippo was under Vandal siege as he lay on his deathbed in 430. The homogeneous Roman culture had already begun to suffer from the questionings of the new Christian element within it, and at the same time it faced annihilation from without. From the Christian point of view, it was an age of selection, a time to examine the *sapientia sæculi* to extract from a thousand-year-old heritage whatever would aid in the work of the Lord. The decisions made would influence Western culture for another thousand years.

The historian is often tempted into a feeling of inevitability about events, a feeling that since events took a certain turn they could have taken no other. But it has been noted that some of the most influential Christians were at least undecided about the role of rhetoric and indeed about Roman culture in many aspects. When it is recalled that Greco-Roman culture was largely transmitted to the early Middle Ages through the very narrow funnel of the encyclopedists like Isidore and Cassiodorus, it might well be wondered what might have occurred if a spokesman as influential as Augustine had denied rhetoric a place in Christian culture.[42]

It was perhaps inevitable that Augustine's opinions would have a strong influence on the future development of rhetoric—if for no other reason than his general influence in a number of fields which gave added weight to his rhetorical ideas. Moreover, the *De Doctrina* provided the basic statement of a Christian homiletic until the emergence of the highly formalized "thematic" or "University Style" sermon about the beginning of the thirteenth century.[43] In light of these factors, then, it would seem useful not only to identify Augustine's contribution to the debate, but to determine his own assessment of the problems presented in it.

Augustine composed the four books of *De Doctrina Christiana*[44] between 396 and 426, the first three books being completed almost a quarter of a century before he decided to resume work on the volume by adding book 4. His goal was a treatise which would give the preacher both the substance and the form for sermons:

> There are two things necessary to the treatment of the Scriptures: a way of discovering (*modus inveniendi*) those things which are to be under-

stood, and a way of expressing to others (*modus proferendi*) what we have learned.[45]

The first three books deal with the *materia* of the sermons—that is, with the ways in which the words of Scripture may be understood. Book 1 deals with signs of realities, book 2 with words as conventional signs, and book 3 with the problem of ambiguity. Throughout the three books he is concerned with the uses of words and points out that the preacher needs a knowledge of language to equip himself with the tools of understanding. Thus he treats both ambiguities growing out of words used literally, and ambiguities deriving from words used figuratively.

It is plain throughout that he intends the student of this subject to master the ordinary things taught in the schools. Although Augustine severely limits the number of things which a student might profitably learn from the profane culture, he is equally quick to point out that the young should pursue "those human institutions helpful to social intercourse in the necessary pursuits of life."[46]

But it is the fourth book which contains an outspoken plea for the use of *eloquentia* in Christian oratory, making the volume what has been called "the first manual of Christian rhetoric." His basic principle is presented in an *a fortiori* argument early in the book:

> But a man who has merely an empty flow of eloquence ought the more to be guarded against as he is the more pleasing to those in his audience in those matters which have no expedience, and, as his audience hears him speak with fluency, it judges likewise that he speaks with truth. This view, indeed, did not escape even those who considered rhetorical training necessary, for they hold that wisdom without eloquence is of small avail to a country but that eloquence without wisdom is generally a great hindrance, and never a help. If, therefore, those who have given us the rules of oratory, in the very books in which they have treated this subject are forced through the urgency of truth to make this confession, ignorant as they are of the true, the supernal wisdom which comes down from the Father of Lights, how much more so are we, the ministers and children of this wisdom, under obligation to hold no other opinion?[47]

In an effort to combat the point of view represented by such writers as Cyprian and Cresconium, he restates the point in another place:

For since through the art of rhetoric both truth and falsehood are pleaded, who would be so bold as to say that against falsehood, truth as regards its own defenders ought to stand unarmed, so that, forsooth, those who attempt to plead false causes know from the beginning how to make their audience well-disposed, attentive, and docile . . . so that the one, moving and impelling the minds of the audience to error by the force of its oratory, now strikes them with terror, now saddens them, now enlivens them, now ardently arouses them; but the other, in the cause of truth, is sluggish and cold and falls asleep! Who is so foolish to be thus wise?[48]

Augustine takes his stand, therefore, in the great debate about the use to which the new Christian society is to put the *sapientia mundi*. He declares that the art of eloquence should be put into active service, and not rejected out of hand because it is tainted with paganism. To those who might reply that rhetoric is the tool of the wicked, he responds with the Aristotelian dictum that the art can serve both truth and falsehood:

Since, therefore, there has been placed equally at our disposal the power of eloquence, which is so efficacious in pleading either for the erroneous cause or the right, why is it not zealously acquired by the good, so as to do service for the truth?[49]

Still another concern to ecclesiastical authorities in the fourth century was the matter of examples to be used in literary education. Almost every writer from Paul to Jerome had warned of the dangers inherent in sending Christians to schools which taught through *imitatio* of Homer and Vergil. Augustine's proposal is to look at the Scriptures themselves for examples of style, and the bulk of book 4 is taken up with an attempt to demonstrate how this could be done. Indeed, Augustine postulates the existence of a new type of eloquence:

Thus there is a kind of eloquence fitting for men most worthy of the highest authority and clearly inspired by God. Our authors speak with an eloquence of this kind, nor does any other kind become them.[50]

Since Ciceronian rhetorical doctrine insisted that three levels of style must be employed, however, Augustine is careful to show that all three levels exist in the Scripture.

It should be noted also that Augustine is unwilling to relegate rhetoric to the position of a mere preliminary study. Instead he wishes to use it in the active service of the ministry. Jerome and Ambrose were apparently somewhat willing to accord rhetoric a place in primary education, but were unsure of the extent to which it should be allowed elsewhere. Augustine insists upon the homiletic utility of the subject, whether its study followed *præcepta* or *imitatio*.[51]

Moreover, it will be recalled, he begins the *De Doctrina* with the statement that the *modus inveniendi*, or means of discovery, is distinct from the *modus proferendi*, or means of expression. The structure of the whole work therefore becomes an argument for the necessity of studying the "means of expression" with the same care given to the study of the Scriptures themselves. The disproportionate amount of space accorded each of the two subjects is due to the fact that he is in a sense creating the first, while merely arguing for the use of the second. It is for this reason that he begins book 4 with the statement that he does not intend to supply the rules of rhetoric which can be found elsewhere. Book 4 is intended as a *ratio eloquentiæ Christianæ*.

It would therefore seem to be misleading to imply, as do Baldwin and Sister Thérèse Sullivan, that Augustine intended the fourth book of *De Doctrina* as a mere rejection of the Second Sophistic. Certainly his attitude toward the "empty eloquence" of the sophistic is clear enough, but this was an attitude which was shared after all by every one of his Christian contemporaries and thus one which needed little proof.

Instead it might be more nearly accurate to say that he saw the dangers of an opposite rhetorical heresy. The sin of the sophist is that he denies the necessity of subject matter and believes that *forma* alone is desirable. An opposite vice, one to which historians of rhetoric have never given a name, depends upon the belief that the man possessed of truth will *ipso facto* be able to communicate the truth to others. It is a dependence upon *materia* alone. Its chief proponent in ancient times was the young Plato, and it would seem fair to label it the "Platonic rhetorical heresy" just as we apply the term "sophistry" to its opposite theory. This is not to say that the ecclesiastical writers of the fourth century looked to the *Gorgias* and *Protagoras* for a theory of communication, but rather that their reactions to the pagan culture of Rome led many of them to take up a somewhat similar attitude toward the rhetoric which was a part of that culture. Augustine apparently recognized a danger in this aspect of the cultural debate of his times, and used the *De Doctrina* to urge a union of both matter and form in Christian preaching.

Only if one views the book as a part of the great debate of the fourth century, therefore, does its historical importance emerge clearly. The reader is struck by the author's insistence upon the folly of abandoning a useful tool to the enemy. For this is a book written, not for enemies, but for other Christians. It can only be his own fellows in the Church whom he describes as "dull and cold" (*lenti fridique*) when they try to speak as if the mere utterance of God's Word would by itself move the minds of men. Augustine appreciates the role of God's grace in preaching, but he warns that the preacher must do his work well too.[52]

The *De Doctrina Christiana* emerges, consequently, as a book written as a rebuttal to those who would deprive the Church of a useful tool in the work of winning souls. Significantly, the debate ends with its appearance. Marie Comeau states the conclusion well:

> *Il était indispensable qu' Augustin abordât dans ce traité la question de la légitimité de la rhétorique, question constamment agitée depuis Platon, et que le christianisme présentait sous un jour nouveau. Il semble avoir dit le dernier mot sur le problème.*[53]

6

AUGUSTINE AND THE PROBLEM OF
CHRISTIAN RHETORIC*

Ernest L. Fortin

Ernest Fortin refutes the claim that Augustine's rhetoric closely mirrors the rhetoric of Cicero, rendering the rhetorical theories outlined in De Doctrina Christiana (DDC) *mere copies of the more widely circulated works of Cicero. Instead of imitating Cicero, Fortin argues that Augustine's rhetoric is actually an inverse of Ciceronian rhetoric. Cicero, Fortin argues, valued persuasion and pleasing the audience over teaching, but Augustine viewed teaching as the most valuable duty of Christian rhetoric. Augustine did more than just value teaching: he uses a term for teaching,* doctrina, *that would not have had much significance for the secular orator. Fortin further contends that Cicero's teaching (*docere*) was understood to describe a type of manipulation, whereas Augustine's teaching (*doctrina*) is a more altruistic conveyance of truth that Augustine believed to be more in line with Christianity. Augustine viewed rhetoric as a means to reach Truth, which meant no persuasion should be necessary—just good teaching. However, the audience would not accept the teaching without a speech that was pleasing to the ear. Thus, according to Fortin, Augustine's call for a Christian rhetoric required both an application of style as well as doctrinal instruction based on church teachings.* DDC *is a text in conversation with Cicero and, ultimately, an adjustment of Ciceronian rhetoric. Fortin does not attempt to prove Augustine's rhetoric as wholly original; he points to the obvious parallels between the Augustinian and Roman traditions of rhetoric. The rhetorical theory Augustine sets forth in* DDC *illustrates that Augustine was connected with his rhetorical roots, but his homage to the classical tradition was not as simple as many scholars believe—Augustine provided Christian orators an alternative rhetoric specifically designed for Christianity.*

It is surprising, particularly when one considers the importance which the Church Fathers attached to the transmission of the Word of God, that so little should have been written on the art of preaching during

---

* Originally published as Ernest L. Fortin. "Augustine and the Problem of Christian Rhetoric." *Augustinian Studies* 5 (1974): 85–100. Headnote by David Elder.

the early Christian centuries. The one notable exception is, of course, book 4 of Augustine's *De Doctrina Christiana*, which has long been acclaimed as the first handbook of Christian rhetoric.[1] While no one to my knowledge has ever questioned the uniqueness of Augustine's treatise, the novelty of the views contained therein has been the subject of a good deal of discussion in recent years. With few dissenting voices, the trend among scholars has been to minimize Augustine's originality in favor of the once commonly held opinion that the core of his teaching is simply derived from Cicero's rhetorical works.

There are, to be sure, a number of features that set Augustine's treatise apart from those of his illustrious predecessor, not the least obvious of which is that the content of Christian rhetoric, which is drawn for the most part from Sacred Scripture, differs significantly from that of pagan rhetoric. It is also true that Augustine regards the rules of the rhetorical art as being less important to the Christian orator than to the statesman or the lawyer in a civil court and even goes so far as to propose that they may be dispensed with altogether if the preacher has reached the age beyond which they can no longer be profitably acquired.[2] A greater simplicity would likewise seem to be required of the Christian orator than would normally be the case with his pagan counterpart, although it is not clear in this instance whether Augustine is taking issue with Cicero himself or merely reacting against the excessive formalism of the rhetors of his own time.[3]

All of these points nevertheless leave untouched the central issue of the nature and principles of the rhetorical art, and on that score scholars are virtually unanimous in asserting that Augustine remains by and large faithful to the Ciceronian tradition. Thus, in his monumental study of the influence of the Latin classics on Augustine, Professor Harald Hagendahl is able to state that he has "followed the course of Augustine's exposition with a view to showing how much it tallies with Cicero's rhetorical treatises in the general conception of rhetoric and even in words: in the division, terminology and other technicalities, whether rendered literally or by paraphrase."[4] The conclusion at which he arrives is clear and peremptory: Augustine's teaching is based on the system of rhetoric introduced into the Roman world by Cicero. That teaching "follows . . . Cicero's views so closely, often even in the minutest particulars, that it cannot make a substantial claim to novelty and originality in the doctrinal system, at most to a slight modification on this or that point."[5]

Even Professor H. I. Marrou, who has gone further than anyone else in defending the revolutionary character of the *De Doctrina Christiana*, concedes that as regards the fundamentals of rhetoric Augustine has been content to repeat the views developed by Cicero, the chief theorist as well as the greatest master of Roman eloquence.[6] The same basic position is adopted by J. Oroz, who agrees with Marrou that the themes of Christian and pagan rhetoric are worlds apart but finds that on all other important points the *De Doctrina Christiana* remains well within the boundaries defined by the Ciceronian tradition.[7] The new wine of the gospel has simply been poured into the old pagan cask without in any way causing it to be altered in the process.

Yet, when all the evidence is sifted out, one wonders to what degree full justice has been done to the subtlety of Augustine's thought; for it is still conceivable that the cribbings from Cicero have been used to formulate a notion of rhetoric which resembles that of Cicero in outward appearance more than in inner substance. With the help newly provided by A. Hus's study of *docere* and its cognates in Cicero's rhetorical works,[8] one may be in a better position to review the merits of the case and determine more accurately the extent of Augustine's originality. That originality, as far as I can tell, is much greater than anyone has yet dared to maintain.

Like the *Orator* and the *De Oratore*, the *De Doctrina Christiana* assigns to the orator the threefold duty of "teaching" (*docere*), of "pleasing" (*delectare*), and of "persuading" (*flectere*). To teach, Augustine adds, again quoting Cicero, is a matter of necessity: *docere necessitates est*. To speak in a pleasing manner adds an element of charm to the orator's words: *delectare suavitatis*. Finally, to persuade pertains to the triumph that the orator seeks for his client or his cause: *flectere victoriae*.[9] The question is whether the "teaching" to which the *De Doctrina Christiana* refers has anything at all in common with what Cicero originally intended by that term. A fresh look at the relevant texts suggests that Augustine has in fact profoundly modified the Ciceronian doctrine on two major points at least: first, by asserting the priority of the teaching function of the orator over the two other functions, and, secondly, by investing the terms *docere* and *doctrina*, which best express that function, with a meaning that could never have been ascribed to them by Cicero. We shall gain new insight into the matter if we begin by examining that "teaching" to which in Cicero's view a substantial portion of the orator's efforts must be devoted.

Cicero's remarks occur within the broad context of a discussion of the two leading forms of oratory, namely, deliberative or political and judicial oratory.[10] Before reaching any important decision in matters of public policy or rendering a verdict in a court of law, the assembly or the judges must be supplied with all of the necessary information pertaining to the issue before them. A judge, for example, should not only know what crime has been committed but, as much as possible, why and how it was committed, what the provisions of the law in regard to such a crime might be, and a host of other relevant data. The lawyer is thus faced with the initial task of apprizing his hearers of the facts of the case, or, if the facts are not contested, of establishing the validity of his case on the basis of commonly accepted principles of justice.[11] To that extent he may be said to teach. But the teaching with which he is concerned is clearly in the service of something else, which is to persuade the judge of the innocence of his client.[12] This and nothing else is the end to which all of his energies are directed. The criminal lawyer will not spare any effort to obtain a favorable verdict; the political orator, if he can help it, will not settle for anything less than a vote resulting in the adoption of the measure that he advocates. In either case, whatever teaching they may be called upon to do remains subordinate to the one goal on the attainment of which the success or failure of their respective endeavors hinges. Neither of them will have accomplished anything if the accused is convicted or if the proposal in behalf of which he pleads is defeated.

This is not to deny that the orator's teaching function is as much a part of the rhetorical art as either of the other two functions; for the outcome of the legal or juridical proceedings in which he is involved will be affected to a very large extent by the manner in which the case is presented in the first place. Not any kind of presentation will do. The speaker must see to it that his narration of the facts is not only clear but "credible."[13] This alone requires considerable skill on his part, and all the more so as the art which he brings to that "narration" must remain imperceptible to the listener.[14] The same rule applies to the *loci communes* or general principles which the orator has at his disposal and which are not equally suitable to his needs. Attention must be drawn to those principles which support his case and away from those which could conceivably weaken it. One may argue, for example, that the particular law which the accused has violated needs to be reinterpreted in the light of a higher principle which it contravenes, or, inversely, that the higher principle in the light of which the accused would appear to stand convicted is itself in need of correction by some more precise law justifying its transgression in specific instances.

One gathers therefore that the "teaching" which the orator dispenses cannot be construed as a universal teaching in the strict sense, since it has to do either with the particulars of the issue at hand or with a series of more general arguments whose usefulness depends less on their intrinsic worth than on the opinion that people commonly entertain in regard to them. What is most important in all such cases is not that the argument be defensible on rational grounds but that it seem plausible to the hearer. The orator is of necessity less concerned with the truth than with its appearance. A plausible falsehood is infinitely more valuable to him than an unlikely truth.

It should not be inferred from these remarks that Cicero had no regard for the truth in political or judicial matters but only that he was aware of the frequent impossibility of arriving at any completely objective solution to the problems that they raise. The question to which the orator addresses himself can rarely be decided on the basis of knowledge alone. If he speaks about them, it is less for the purpose of instructing his hearers than of persuading them, and passion rather than reason is the instrument par excellence of persuasion, the middle term as it were by which the orator seeks to win the assent of his audience and gain acceptance for such courses of action as practical wisdom may dictate given the nature of the case and the circumstances that surround it.[15] Hence the confidence that he inspires is as much a function of the opinion that others have formed of him as a man as it is of his competence or his ability to speak well. People will trust him if they are convinced that he is a good man and that he has their common good at heart.[16] In that regard, his own person is a better witness to the "truth" of his assertions than any of the arguments that he may be able to muster in support of them.

The deeper point of Cicero's observations could easily be missed, however, if one were to leave it at saying that opinion rather than true knowledge is the stuff of rhetoric or that the complexity of human affairs precludes any attempt to approach them with the detachment that characterizes rational or scientific discourse. One cannot point to the limitations of any rhetorical argument without at the same time raising the larger issue of the relation of rhetoric to philosophy and, more generally, of the political life to the philosophic life. What

distinguishes Cicero's works from the common run of rhetorical treatises is precisely that they are guided by an awareness of philosophy
and its ambiguous relationship to the city. For the orator that Cicero
has in mind is not just the man who combines a natural talent for public speaking with a knowledge of the rules of rhetoric but a new type
of orator in whose person the accomplishments of the statesman and
the philosopher coalesce and are brought to a higher level of perfection.[17] The consequences of this important fact will come to light if we
glance briefly at the attributes of the perfect orator as they are outlined
in the *Orator* and the *De Oratore*.

The highest form of oratory is political oratory, and political oratory deals with the greatest and best of human affairs: religion, death,
piety, patriotism, right and wrong, the virtues and vices of men, the
duties of citizens, their pleasures and pains, the passions by which
they are moved, and the evils to which they succumb.[18] One cannot
begin to speak wisely about such matters until one has achieved a true
understanding of human nature; for only the man who has a thorough
knowledge of the whole is the proper judge of the ends of human
existence and of the means by which they are best attained. It follows
that the orator must have mastered not only the art of persuasion but
all of the theoretical sciences as well.[19]

Needless to say, few men have either the capacity, or the opportunity, or for that matter the desire to engage in such pursuits. Even
the greatest orators of the past—Pericles, Demosthenes—did not con-
form to the proposed ideal and it is doubtful whether anyone could.[20]
The crucial point, however, is not whether the perfect orator has ever
existed or ever will but, assuming that the quest for theoretical wisdom
has uncovered a dimension of reality that transcends the horizon of
the political life, whether there is any common measure between the
knowledge that is ideally demanded of him and the notions of justice
by which most men are guided. If by justice one understands, as Cicero
did, not simply the rules governing the distribution or the exchange
of goods among fellow citizens but the perfect order of the soul or
the perfectly just way of life, one may come to the conclusion that the
degree of justice of which a particular society is capable at any given
moment will fall considerably short of what a wise man would regard
as truly just. To say nothing of other matters, it is doubtful whether
Cicero seriously thought that belief in the gods of the Roman Pan-
theon was compatible with justice in this loftier sense. Yet any orator

speaking in behalf of Rome would necessarily have to defer to such beliefs. Viewed in that perspective, the question is not only how much injustice a society can tolerate but how much justice it can bear without endangering its own existence.[21] Granted that all societies should strive for justice, a point is sooner or later reached at which it becomes impossible, without injustice, to enforce such measures as would be in perfect accord with the demands of theoretical reason. The counsels of the wise man will represent at best a compromise between what reason is capable of knowing about justice and the needs of the society for which they are intended.

But this can only mean that in addressing his fellow citizens the orator is compelled to adopt an ironic posture. Although his teaching does not correspond fully to what he himself knows to be true, it is essential that it be perceived as a true teaching by his hearers. He will be successful to the extent to which others remain ignorant of the fact that what he does is the one thing that he cannot claim to be doing.[22] There is an element of high comedy in the highest form of oratory. Cicero's perfect orator is a liar, not because he wants to, but because he has no choice in the matter. Between thought and speech or between theory and practice there is a necessary cleavage, of which Cicero himself, whose aim it was to bring about a fusion between Greek philosophy and Roman virtue,[23] seems to have been uniquely aware.

It is hardly surprising therefore that Cicero should have refrained from using the word *doctrina* to characterize the content of the orator's speech. As opposed to the older and more neutral *docere*, which designates the act by which knowledge or information of any kind is imparted to another person, *doctrina* refers specifically to the object of philosophic inquiry and functions most often as the equivalent of the Greek *epistêmê* in Cicero's own dialogues and treatises.[24] Philosophers qua philosophers speak to the educated for the purpose of instructing them and not for the purpose of swaying them: *docendi non capiendi causa*.[25] The proper mode of their discourses is dialectical rather than rhetorical. These discourses may have an eloquence all their own, but of a kind that is only remotely akin to that to which the typical orator is accustomed.

A vastly different picture emerges the moment we turn to Augustine's Christian adaptation of the Ciceronian doctrine. Augustine's preacher must also begin by instructing his audience, and this he does by laying before them the truths of the faith and, whenever necessary, by using arguments based on the proper authorities to clarify any difficulties that they may have in regard to them.[26] But, as might be expected, the kind of teaching in which he engages is no longer the object of the subtle depreciation that we encountered in Cicero. The substance of that teaching is the "sound doctrine" of which Saint Paul had spoken and in which the preacher has steeped himself through the assiduous reading and study of the Scriptures.[27] Its cognitive status is therefore totally different from the pagan orator. Augustine's preacher teaches in a way in which even Cicero's perfect orator could never be said to teach. It is above all the superior dignity of that "teaching" which accounts for Augustine's inversion of the order of rank of the three functions performed by the orator. The duty to teach is not merely the Christian orator's first duty, it is his highest and in a sense his only duty.[28] The preacher will have accomplished all that is essentially required of him if what he teaches is the truth. If he is to be judged at all, it is on his ability to discharge that function rather than on any natural endowments or oratorical talents that he may or may not possess. He has no other title to be heard. Hence, departing from the canon of Ciceronian orthodoxy, Augustine takes it for granted that, regardless of the style in which the preacher expresses himself, whether it be the simple, the moderate, or the grand, his primary goal is still to instruct his audience. The *munus docendi* is no longer restricted to the simple style and vice versa; it pervades all three styles and is itself the end to which they are universally ordered.[29]

The same concern for the primacy of truth is evinced by another, less conspicuous but equally significant alteration that Augustine has introduced into the Ciceronian scheme. Contrary to what Hagendahl suggests, one observes that, in paraphrasing the text of the *De Oratore*, Augustine tacitly deleted all reference to what Cicero regarded as the chief merit of any rhetorical argument, namely, its plausibility. The word *verisimiliter* does appear in the *De Doctrina Christiana*, but only in connection with the teachers of false doctrines.[30] The suggestion is not that, for Augustine, the truths (*vera*) of the faith are implausible but only that it would be misleading to describe them as plausible truths. The contrast on which the whole discussion plays is precisely between the eminently truthful character of the Christian faith and the apparent truths or merely plausible teachings of the promoters of erroneous doctrines.

This does not mean that it is not to the preacher's advantage to cultivate other qualities of a good orator if he has the ability to do so. There is surely no reason why the divine truth should not be rendered as appealing as possible to the hearer. Even a preacher has nothing to gain by boring his audience. It would be strange, to say the least, if error were to be clothed in an attractive garb by its proponents while truth is made to appear tedious and dull for lack of proper adornments.[31] Furthermore, it sometimes happens that the hearer is already familiar with the truths of the faith but cannot bring himself to act in accordance with them; in which case the preacher may be summoned to use whatever powers of persuasion he has at his command to induce him to reform his life.[32] For all of these reasons, then, one should not underestimate the benefits of eloquence. In general, the man who speaks both "wisely" and "well" will accomplish more than the one who speaks only wisely.[33]

Here again, however, the classic formula, *sapiens et eloquens*, which Augustine inherits this time from the *De Inventione*,[34] partially masks a more profound disagreement with Cicero on the relation of teaching to persuading in rhetorical discourse. The truth which the Christian is "persuaded" to accept is not a truth in any ordinary sense of the word but a beatifying or saving truth,[35] which presupposes a decision on the part of the knower and which can be said to have been fully appropriated only when it issues in those deeds to which it points as its fulfillment. In and of itself it has the power to transform the individual who apprehends it. It is in one and the same act both theoretical and practical and thus transcends the dichotomy between thought and action or between instruction and persuasion on which the classical understanding of rhetoric was predicated. As Augustine puts it elsewhere, anyone who is "taught of God"[36] has been given simultaneously both "to know what he ought to do and to do what he knows,"[37] he "not only has the power to come but does come,"[38] he "not only believes what ought to be loved but loves what he believes."[39]

It is hardly necessary to point out that such a doctrine is incommensurable with what Augustine himself once referred to as the "heartless doctrines"—*doctrinae sine corde*—of the philosophers.[40] The precise manner in which the two modes of thought are related is more complex than one might be tempted to assume on the basis of some of Augustine's well-known pronouncements on the subject.[41] The objection to philosophy from a religious point of view is not so much that its teachings are sometimes at odds with those of the faith, for in that case a measure of agreement could still be reached between the philosopher and the Christian, if not always on the solutions to the common problems with which they both deal, at least on the nature of those problems and the terms in which they might suitably be posed. The more serious difficulty arises from the philosopher's own inability to arrive at any firm conclusion concerning matters of the utmost interest for the whole of human life. The philosopher is compelled by his love of the truth to suspend his judgment about all such matters until the theoretical issues to which they give rise have been fully examined. The question is whether one can ever be satisfied that the necessary clarity about any of these fundamental issues has been reached. If the object of the investigation should prove to be more elusive than had been anticipated or the problems more readily accessible than the solutions to them, the philosopher may find it difficult to commit himself heart and soul to any position whatever. What had begun as an attempt on his part to set forth the truth about the good life has, it seems, transformed itself into an endless and hence unfulfilled quest for the nature of the good life.

It is precisely this radical character of philosophy, which refuses to take knowledge itself for granted, that constitutes the ultimate challenge to the Christian faith. The opposition in the final analysis is not so much between one set of doctrines and another but between the self-proclaimed ignorance of the philosopher and the firmly held beliefs of the religious thinker. The touchstone of one's attachment to the truth is one's willingness to die for it. But, even though philosophers have often been persecuted across the centuries, few of them have ever demonstrated any real appetite for martyrdom. It may be objected that Socrates was willing to sacrifice himself for the truth. Even this example, however, is not decisive; for there is no guarantee that what Socrates did at the age of seventy is exactly what he would have done had his trial taken place thirty years earlier.[42] The lesson that later philosophers learned from Socrates is not that they should be ready to lay down their lives for the truth but that, for their own protection, they would be well-advised to accommodate themselves to the prejudices of the society in which they happen to live. Philosophers may parade as lovers and teachers of moral virtue, but none of them seems to have been eager to place the service of his fellow men above the good of the mind.[43] Socrates's own "coldness" and aloofness from the affairs of the city is no doubt a better index of his fundamental disposition than his public declarations of piety or his professed concern for the welfare of his fellow Athenians.[44] The philosopher poses a threat to religion and society not because he knows too much but because he knows too little. By questioning all things, he undermines the consensus on which both religion and society depend for their well-being.

But even this is only half the story. If Socrates can boast of his ignorance, it is because he has learned what true knowledge is and is able to distinguish it from its opposite. His would-be ignorance is merely the obverse of a deep-seated pride which causes him to place himself above the rest of society. He speaks to his judges or to the citizens of Athens as one speaks to children, telling them only what is good for them, regardless of whether it is true or not.[45] His own speeches were more "persuasive" than genuinely truthful.[46] They were aimed as much at keeping the multitude away from the truth as they were at attracting to it the few who had proved themselves worthy of it by their ability to penetrate the disguise in which it is habitually cloaked. Between his arrogance (*praesumptio*) and his humble "confession" of the believer, it is difficult to see how any reconciliation could be effected.[47]

Even though Augustine could not accept Plato's and Cicero's views concerning the essential disproportion between theoretical reason and political reason, he was nevertheless very much aware of the need to speak differently to different audiences. It would obviously be foolish to think that everyone is capable of the same degree of understanding of the divine truth. The Scriptures themselves are often written in a manner that makes it hard for most people to grasp them without the aid of an interpreter.[48] Anyone who undertakes to explain them to the general public must first learn to express himself in a language that all men can understand and not in a language that is intelligible only to the learned.[49] Moreover, it is reasonable to suppose that there are depths of understanding to which the untrained multitude is incapable of acceding. One would perform a disservice to the simple faithful by burdening them with subtleties that exceed their powers of comprehension. Accordingly, the *De Doctrina Christiana* makes it clear that there are questions which "by their very nature are not understood or are barely understood no matter how much, how often, how clearly, or how well they are expounded, and these either should never be brought up before a popular audience or only rarely, when there is a special reason to do so."[50] By maintaining a prudent reserve on all such questions, the preacher does not commit an injustice toward anyone, since the doctrines that he passes over in silence would only be misunderstood and possibly misused by the majority of his hearers. The situation is different if one has the opportunity to deal in private conversation with individuals whose intelligence, degree of preparation, and willingness to learn can be assessed more easily and more accurately.[51]

But if the mode of presentation of the divine truth varies with each audience, its substance does not, and on this level all Christians are united in the knowledge of the same basic truth. There is only one truth, "which all men hear in the same measure when it is publicly spoken, but which each one appropriates in his own measure."[52] The wise preacher undoubtedly knows *more* than his less learned fellows, but what he knows is not something *other* than what every Christian knows.[53] To the extent to which he has achieved a more profound grasp of the divine mysteries, he can add the knowledge that others already have of them, but the foundation on which he builds is the same in all cases. There can be no question of persuading the hearer to accept any doctrine to which the speaker has not previously given his own wholehearted assent. What one knows in one way "in the world at large" is not essentially different from what one knows "in the privacy of his chambers."[54] Embroidering on the metaphor that Saint Paul had used in the First Letter to the Corinthians, Augustine explains that the milk with which the mother nourishes her suckling is the very food from which her own sustenance is derived and which has merely been transformed into a substance that is more easily absorbed by the child. It therefore makes no sense to speak, as others had done, of an "opposition" between the simple fare that is provided for beginners and the wisdom reserved for those who have attained a higher level of spiritual advancement.[55] The latter simply perceive more perfectly what the former strive to assimilate according to their own capacity.

What is even more important, however, is the conclusion regarding the need for absolute truthfulness which Augustine draws from these premises. The Christian's commitment to the truth is such that he can never publicly or privately betray it in speech even for the noblest of causes. There may be valid reasons for not revealing to others all of one's thoughts on some subjects; but it is one thing to withhold the truth from someone and quite another to lie to him.[56] The sacred writers themselves deliberately concealed certain doctrines from the multitude but without ever lying about anything: *nonnulla obtegunt, sed nulla mentiuntur.*[57] The Christian orator can do no less. One can say without exaggeration that there is no moral principle which Augustine defended with greater vehemence and on which he was least willing to compromise. Never, even under the most extreme circumstances, is one allowed to speak an untruth. The question is, Why? For it is surely not self-evident that the true interests of one's fellow men are better served by the determination to speak the truth at all times than by an occasional breach of truthfulness. To take a simple example, one has a hard time imagining that a man who perpetrates a white lie in order to save, not indeed his own life, but the life of a loved one or perhaps some other innocent person is guilty of any sin whatever. Christian charity, to say nothing of plain common sense, would seem to prescribe as much. Yet Augustine, who was prepared to make allowances for what would appear to be the much more grievous crime of adultery,[58] is adamant in his refusal to make even the slightest concession on that point.

The reason, we discover, is not unrelated to the central task of preaching the word of God which has been entrusted to the Christian orator. That reason is best illustrated by Augustine's reaction to Jerome's commentary on chapter two of the Letter to the Galatians, in which Paul gives an account of his famous altercation with Peter at Antioch.[59] It may be recalled that on the occasion Paul publicly upbraided Peter for refusing to eat with the Gentiles in order to placate the circumcision party, headed by James. Following Origen's interpretation, Jerome had attempted to remove any trace of dissension among the apostles by contending that Peter was not guilty of wrongdoing but had merely sought to accommodate himself to the prejudices of the Judaizers. Had not Paul himself done as much by circumcising Timothy and, on James's advice, by providing for the offering of sacrifices in accordance with the prescriptions of the Old Law, thereby giving credence to the belief that Christian salvation was linked to these observances?[60] It is hardly likely, then, that he should have quarreled with Peter over a similar issue. Far from finding fault with Peter, Paul actually sided with him but feigned to rebuke him lest others should interpret his conduct as signifying that the Gentiles were to be subjected to the Jewish Law.[61]

Augustine expresses utter astonishment at the fact that Jerome had chosen to endorse what would really amount to an *officiosum mendacium* on Paul's part.[62] For if what Peter did is what he was supposed to do, then Paul lied when he accused him of not being straightforward about the truth of the Gospel. That he should have done so for a good cause is beside the point. Nor does it matter that the enemies of the faith should seize upon the disagreement of which Paul speaks as a pretext for discrediting the New Testament. Nothing can justify the imputation of lies to the Bible. To suggest for one moment that the sacred writers indulged in falsehood is to jeopardize the authority of the whole of Scripture and open the door to every kind of malice. "If one were to admit in that supreme authority even one polite lie, nothing at all would be left of these books, because whenever anyone finds something difficult to practice or hard to achieve, he will follow this most dangerous precedent and explain it is the thought or practice of a lying author."[63] As long as the *veritas doctrinae* remains intact, one can always turn to it to rectify any error into which he may have fallen; but if that standard is itself subject to doubt, the very possibility of a return to the truth is destroyed forever.[64] It is therefore preferable to believe that, out of weakness, "Peter did so act as to compel the Gentiles to live like Jews."[65] Better a thousand times a cowardly Peter than a lying Paul. No immediate advantage could ever compensate for the unlimited harm that is done by calling into question even a single passage of Scripture.

What is said of the sacred writers applies, *mutatis mutandis*, to all Christian teachers as well; for what confidence should one have in a person who is of the opinion that it is sometimes permissible to lie? Could not he, too, by any chance be lying when he speaks to others about the mysteries of faith?[66] Like everyone else, the Christian orator may unwittingly err in his interpretation of the sacred text; but if what he says is conducive to the love of God and neighbor, which is the principle in the light of which all of Scripture is to be interpreted, he leads no one astray and is not himself guilty of any wicked deed.[67] What is intolerable is to think that anyone could arrogate to himself the prerogative of using evil in order to bring about a greater good among men. One puts it mildly when one says that Cicero's ideal orator had no such qualms about lying to his hearers. The road leading from the *De Oratore* to the *De Doctrina Chrstiana* may indeed be longer and more tortuous than the casual reader would ever have suspected.

It would be futile to deny that, in elaborating his views on Christian oratory, Augustine has relied extensively on the tradition of Roman rhetoric in which he had been trained. He himself certainly made no great effort to conceal his indebtedness to that tradition and to its foremost representative, Cicero. But it would be a grave misconception to think that one can give an adequate account of his thought merely by listing the numerous parallels between the two authors. One is reminded in this connection of Lord Acton's remark (to Mary Gladstone) that a disposition to detect resemblances is one of the greatest sources of error. The paradox of book 4 of the *De Doctrina Christiana* is that it is precisely when Augustine sounds most like Cicero, to the point of reproducing his own words, that he stands at the furthest remove from him. There are good reasons to believe that Augustine quoted Cicero the way Shakespeare's devil quotes the Bible—for his own purposes. The success with which he was able to do so is amply demonstrated by the difficulty that one experiences in trying to assess the originality of his thought.

Modern scholars have been guilty not so much of misreading Augustine as rashly ascribing to Cicero what is in fact a profound albeit silent transformation of Cicero's basic teaching. The pitfall might have been avoided if, before attempting to second-guess Augustine, greater pains had been taken to arrive at a satisfactory interpretation of the original Ciceronian doctrine. It should probably be added that anyone embarking upon such an endeavor would have received little direct encouragement from Augustine himself. In defending what he considered to be the cause of truth, Augustine had much to gain and little to lose by stressing the similarity rather than the dissimilarity between his position and that of Cicero. Nor was there any "special reason" for calling attention to that strategy. To discuss openly the points on which at a deeper level the divergences between the Christian and the classical views of truth become truly significant would have necessitated the public disclosure of a whole gamut of problems that are of no interest to most Christians or, as far as that goes, to most preachers.

Like all the great books on rhetoric written in antiquity, whether it be the *Gorgias*, the *Phaedrus*, the *Orator*, or the *De Oratore*, the *De Doctrina Christiana* is rhetorical in mode as well as in content. In this respect at least it remains remarkably faithful to the spirit of the classical tradition. The moderation in speech that it both advocates and displays may well be the most important lesson that Augustine learned from his revered pagan masters.

SAINT AUGUSTINE AND MARTIANUS CAPELLA
CONTINUITY AND CHANGE IN FIFTH-CENTURY LATIN RHETORICAL THEORY*

Michael C. Leff

Instead of treating Augustine's De Doctrina Christiana *and Martianus Capella's* On the Marriage of Philology and Mercury *as incommensurable, Michael Leff compares the two works. Leff argues that Augustine the Christian and Martianus the pagan wrote their rhetorical treatises in response to the same exigence: changing cultural conditions in the wake of the Roman Republic's collapse, including the rise of autocracy and an intellectual move away from practical, civic concerns and toward authoritarianism and hierarchy. Leff argues that, in spite of these changing conditions, the Ciceronian rhetorical ideal of melding eloquence and wisdom continued to hold sway, as reflected in Augustine's and Martianus's treatises. While Augustine and Martianus faced the same exigence, they appropriated the Ciceronian ideal in different ways to serve their particular goals. Like Cicero, Augustine viewed form and content as inseparable and eschewed sets of rules or precepts for rhetoric. Augustine argued that genuine eloquence arises from the soundness of thought. Leff contends that Augustine used the structure and terms of Ciceronian theory but posited Scripture as both the source and the goal of rhetoric. By contrast, Martianus was a pagan whose rhetorical theory shows the influence of Neoplatonism and Neopythagoreanism. As a result, Martianus's rhetorical theory was oriented toward a vision of immortality sharply different from that envisioned by Augustine's notion of Christianity. For Martianus, one does not learn rhetoric to improve one's effectiveness in speaking in this world. Rather, the purpose of rhetorical training is to train the mind for the next world. Leff concludes that, in order to maintain viability, rhetorical theory must adapt to cultural conditions. As such, Leff points out the continuing influence of Cicero on two opposed rhetorical theorists: Augustine and Martianus.*

* Originally published as Michael C. Leff, "St. Augustine and Martianus Capella: Continuity and Change in Fifth-Century Latin Rheteorical Theory." *Communication Quarterly* 24.4 (1976): 2–9. Headnote by Drew M. Loewe.

To many observers, the fifth century A.D. presents the simple and melancholy spectacle of the collapse of the Western Roman Empire. Close examination reveals greater complexity. The fall of the old order unleashed powerful creative forces, as thinkers were compelled to conceive a new basis for society and culture. Thus, Christopher Dawson has described the age as one of "material loss and spiritual recovery when amidst the ruins of a bankrupt order men strove . . . to rebuild the house of life on eternal foundations."[1] This spiritual revolution occurred gradually over a period of centuries. But its signs were spread throughout the literature of the fifth century and were duly reflected in the works devoted to rhetoric.

The most influential Latin rhetorical works of the fifth century were written by two North Africans, Saint Augustine and Martianus Capella.[2] Contemporary histories of rhetoric acknowledge the importance of both men, but they treat the two separately.[3] No study compares their theories. This deficiency is understandable in light of the obvious differences between Augustine and Martianius. Augustine was a Christian, a profoundly original thinker, and his rhetorical theory resulted in a creative synthesis of pagan eloquence and Christian doctrine. Martianus was a pagan, an apparently unoriginal thinker, and his rhetoric was a jejune collection of technical precepts borrowed from various classical handbooks.

Nevertheless, both men were products of their age, and the spiritualism of the fifth century affected pagans as well as Christians. Thus, in constructing a theory of rhetoric suited to the needs of their time, both Augustine and Martianus had to confront the same basic problem. The established classical theory had become an anachronism. It was premised on the concepts of practical culture and civic humanism. Late Roman thought, however, had shifted away from the pragmatic and relative toward the contemplative and absolute.[4] By the fifth century, the climate of opinion could no longer tolerate the supple humanism associated with Ciceronian rhetoric. Yet, rhetoric was too important an element in late ancient culture for it to be ignored completely. These circumstances encouraged, if they did not actually force, a philosophical reconsideration of rhetorical theory.

The purpose of this essay is to examine how Augustine and Martianus adapted Ciceronian rhetoric to the monistic presuppositions of their age. While this central problem framed the efforts of both men, it resulted in two very different responses. Augustine preserved the most valuable precepts of Cicero's rhetoric by grounding them in the fixed authority of Scripture. Martianus preserved the technical apparatus of the old rhetoric by investing it with a metaphysical significance. Both responses provide interesting case studies of the way that rhetorical theories adjust to changing cultural and intellectual conditions.

THE BACKGROUND

In order to understand the cultural revolution of the fifth century, we must first understand something about the background against which the changes took place. In the case of rhetorical theory, this background was thoroughly Ciceronian. Cicero's rhetorical works had done far more than prescribe rules for the training of public speakers. They had established the orator/statesman as the paradigm of culture. And Cicero's thought had a decisive influence on later Roman intellectual history.

Cicero clearly rejected the contemplative ideal of the Greek philosophers. Instead, he sought to define the end of education in terms of the active life of the orator. The Ciceronian orator, of course, was no ordinary advocate. He was a cultured gentleman who possessed "the broad estates of learning" and acted in accord with the dictates of civic virtue and practical wisdom.[5] As such, the orator was superior to the philosopher, since he not only mastered the content of philosophical knowledge, but also commanded the means of expressing it effectively.[6] This union of wisdom and eloquence was the central tenet of Cicero's program. Following in the civic humanistic tradition of the Greek sophists, Cicero attempted to preserve the integrity of the *logos*, to forge an unbreakable link between the art of thinking and the art of speaking, and to bring this whole system into contact with the political life of the community.

Two important corollaries emerged from this fundamental doctrine of the unity of wisdom and eloquence. The first was that style and content were inseparable. This proposition followed almost unavoidably from Cicero's basic premise, for if wisdom and eloquence were unitary, one could hardly expect to divorce the matter of discourse from its form. To Cicero, eloquent expression arose directly from the loftiness of the thoughts themselves. Furthermore, this result occurred through a process embedded in nature: "An abundant supply of matter begets an abundant supply of words, and if the subjects discussed are themselves of an elevated character, a spontaneous brilliance of style results. . . . So easily will nature of herself, given training and a plentiful supply of matter, find her way without any guidance to the adornments of oratory."[7]

This belief in natural eloquence, coupled with Cicero's pragmatism, led to the second corollary, the priority of practice and experience over theoretical instruction. Since the orator's goal entailed an almost limitless number of process and content variables, it was impossible to capture its essence in a static set of rules. In fact, at one point Cicero expressed doubt about whether an art of oratory existed, and he certainly never gave it anything more than a tentative status.[8,9] The standard rhetorical precepts did have a certain value. Nevertheless, the orator was better advised to study and imitate past masters of the art than to devote himself to theory. Consequently, Cicero's position corresponded more closely to the imitative pedagogy of Isocrates than the systematic theory of Aristotle.[10]

This program of rhetorical education defined the function of the orator in terms of his contributions to the political system. Consequently, it presumed some form of representative government. Ironically, however, Cicero had scarcely completed his theory of the orator/ statesman before the Roman Republic collapsed and an autocracy arose in its place. Even more ironically, this dramatic political change had little effect in retarding the spread of the Ciceronian ideal. The *Institutes* of Quintilian,[11] the panegyric orations of the late imperial rhetors,[12] and the late Roman law codes[13] all testified to the powerful grip that the rhetorical ideal continued to exercise over the Roman mind. Nevertheless, by the fifth century, it had become impossible to blink away political and social realities. Traditional institutions were decaying, and they could no longer disguise the gap between the old ideals and the actual conditions of society.

At the same time, a series of profound changes in conceptual life were nearing their culmination. Educated Romans were less attracted to the maneuvers of the law courts and the now decadent political assemblies. The practical and relativistic side of Roman life receded as concepts of hierarchical order became more prominent. H. P. L'Orange observes that, in the late Empire, "there is a movement away from the complex towards the simple, from the mobile towards the static, from the dialectic and relative toward the dogmatic and authoritarian, from the empirical towards theology and theosophy. There is a trend toward plain uncomplicated absolutes which are imperturbably fixed in themselves."[14] These changes affected every phase of Roman culture. But they were particularly important for rhetoric, since the ancient Latin theorists had conceived the art as the epitome of the pragmatic and relativistic aspects of intellectual life. Thus, while Augustine and Martianus were influenced strongly by the traditional theory of rhetoric, they were forced to alter the standard Ciceronian doctrines.

AUGUSTINE

The fourth book of *De Doctrina Christiana* contains Augustine's most complete statement on rhetorical theory.[15] The book is studded with references to Cicero, and modern scholars have compiled an impressive list of passages in *De Doctrina* IV that parallel Cicero's rhetorical treatises.[16] Yet, the Ciceronian influence appears so strong as to exceed a mere listing of specific citations. As Baldwin argues, the almost innumerable reminiscences of Cicero suggest a "pervasive preoccupation."[17] Augustine's rhetoric seems to breathe something of the spirit of Ciceronianism.

In the first place, Augustine shares Cicero's distaste for mechanical rules and his preference for practice over theory. Augustine specifically warns the reader of *De Doctrina* not to expect a conventional catalogue of rules.[18] These rules have some value, but they are best learned in one's youth and ought never to divert a man from more important pursuits.[19] At any rate, "those with acute minds more readily learn eloquence by reading and hearing the eloquent than by following the rules of eloquence."[20] The surest path to eloquence is through practice and imitation: "Therefore, since infants are not taught to speak except by learning the expressions of speakers, why can men not be made eloquent, not by teaching them the rules of eloquence, but by having them read and hear the expressions of the eloquent and imitate them in so far as they are able to follow them?"[21] Perhaps Augustine pushes this point farther than Cicero, but the two men certainly assume similar positions.

Augustine also supports the Ciceronian doctrine of the coalescence of style and content. Augustine conceives of genuine eloquence as that which is informed by sound thought. He demands a style that is not precious but substantial, and he clarifies his view through a highly apposite metaphor: "Just as things which are both bitter and healthful are frequently to be taken, so also a pernicious sweetness is always to be avoided. But what is better than a wholesome sweetness or sweet wholesomeness? The more eagerly the sweetness is desired, the more readily the wholesomeness becomes profitable."[22] In other words, the use of eloquence is justifiable, but only on the condition that it supports respectable ideas. Truly eloquent style has its origin in the message itself. Scripture provides sure evidence of this fact. The language of the Scriptures is perfectly suited to the content, and an almost unconscious flow of eloquence issues from them: "And in those places where by chance eloquence is recognized by the learned, such things are said that the words with which they are said seem not to have been sought by the speaker, but to have been joined to the things spoken about as if spontaneously, like Wisdom coming from her house (that is, from the breast of the wise man) followed by eloquence as if she were an inseparable servant who was not called."[23]

This passage suggests that Augustine appreciates the conceptual significance of the union of wisdom and eloquence. Other passages in the text point to the same conclusion. The terms *eloquentia* and *sapientia* (or some variant of them) appear more than a dozen times in *De Doctrina* IV.[24] Moreover, the concept seems pivotal in the development of Augustine's argument. The conjunction of wisdom and eloquence appears first at IV.7-10, just as Augustine makes a transition from his discussion of the nature and utility of eloquence to his analysis of its application in Christian literature. The section ends with the assertion that a spontaneous and natural eloquence attaches itself to Scripture. Augustine then illustrates his point by referring to Romans 5:3-5. In this passage, Paul emerges as "unlearnedly learned" in the art of expression, as a man whose wisdom is "accompanied by eloquence."[25] Thus, Augustine can describe the Apostle as a "companion to wisdom and leader of eloquence, following the first and not scorning the second."[26] The result is that we find the Ciceronian ideal of wisdom and eloquence embodied in the works of Paul, and as we learn later, in the works of other Christians as well.[27]

The similarities between Augustine and Cicero are obvious and striking. Yet, the differences are even more notable. For example, Augustine consciously abandoned the classical genres of oratory. The Ciceronian orator fulfilled his duty by speaking within the framework of forensic, deliberative, and epideictic oratory, since these genres adequately covered the public business relevant to his function. But, to Augustine, the orator's purpose had to be referred "not to the temporal welfare of man, but to his eternal welfare."[28] Thus, the Christian orator had only one legitimate objective—the spiritual salvation of his auditors. Recognition of this single, overarching goal resulted in an entirely new conception of the orator's function. To cite another example, Augustine retained Cicero's imitative pedagogy, but he established new models for imitation. Paul, Ambrose, and Cyprian replaced Cicero, Demosthenes, and Virgil as the exemplars of eloquence. In a system where form and matter were intertwined, this change was not trivial. The Christian student no longer had a need to consult pagan literature. He could become eloquent by studying the same sources that provided him with wisdom. Wisdom and eloquence were still united, but the concept of wisdom itself had been redefined in Christian terms.[29]

These specific differences, and others as well, reduce themselves to a single major discrepancy between the thinking of the two men; Cicero and Augustine adopt different phenomenologies of mind. Cicero prefers reason and action to faith and contemplation. Augustine assumes the opposite position. And their theories of rhetoric clearly reflect their differing commitments on this issue. Cicero's orator is a consummately political animal, taking his guidance from the lights of civic duty and civic virtue; his wisdom comes from the pagan philosophical schools and his models of eloquence from the oratory of Greek and Roman political leaders. Augustine, on the other hand, describes the Christian preacher whose words transcend the ambiguities of the secular order. The preacher's matter comes from Scripture, since a man speaks "more or less wisely to the extent that he has become more or less proficient in Holy Scripture."[30] Likewise, the preacher's models come from sacred literature and his task arises from the single goal of propagating the faith. Augustine, then, uses elements of Ciceronian rhetoric, but he alters and subordinates them to meet his theological purposes. To put it simply, he removes the orator from the city of man and places him in the City of God.

MARTIANUS CAPELLA

In turning from Augustine to Martianus Capella, we encounter a very different kind of scholar. Martianus is a shadowy character, known to us only through his allegorical encyclopedia, *On the Marriage of Mercury and Philology.*[31] Modern scholars generally agree that Martianus was a North African and that he composed his encyclopedia sometime between A.D. 410 and 430.[32] From the content of his work, we can infer that Martianus was a pagan strongly influenced by the mystical doctrines of Neoplatonism and Neopythagoreanism. Aside from these few facts, we can say nothing about him with certainty, although some scholars speculate that he was a lawyer and perhaps a professional rhetorician.[33]

The *Marriage of Mercury and Philology* is a strange work—a technical encyclopedia of the seven liberal arts dressed in allegorical form. The work is divided into nine books. The first two narrate the story of Philology's marriage to Mercury, the allegorical base of the encyclopedia. The remaining seven books consist of a seriatim analysis of the trivium (grammar, dialectic, and rhetoric) and the quadrivium (geometry, arithmetic, astronomy, and harmony). The literary form is the Menippean satire, a genre that intersperses prose and verse.[34] The style of the work is as peculiar as its format; neologisms are frequent, and the syntax is often clumsy and obscure.[35] Despite these defects, however, the *Marriage* proved one of the most popular books of the Middle Ages. An impressive number of manuscripts of the work still survive, and its influence in both literature and education persisted for more than a thousand years after Martianus' death.[36]

Martianus devotes his fifth book to rhetorical theory. Most historians of rhetoric isolate this book and treat it as a separate entity.[37] Yet, as Johnson points out, "for a full appreciation, the work deserves to be seen as a whole; and to be seen not as a collection of seven handbooks but as one philosophicoreligious work."[38] The admonition is particularly relevant for rhetoricians, since the central allegory tells us much about the author's conception of eloquence. For this reason, I wish to concentrate on the allegory itself rather than on the technical rhetorical precepts contained in book 5.

The allegory begins when Mercury (the god of travelers, merchants, heralds, thieves, and orators) decides to seek a wife. After following several false leads, Mercury finally enlists the assistance of Virtue and Apollo. They recommend a match with Philology, a mortal woman of great learning. Apollo and Mercury then travel high into the astral realm to seek out Jupiter and obtain his consent. A convocation of the gods ensues, and the marriage is given divine sanction.

Meanwhile, back in the regions below the moon, Philology is playing the part of the blushing bride-to-be. As it turns out, she has good reason to be nervous. The wedding is to take place in the celestial realm where no mortal can survive. Consequently, Philology must be initiated into the rites of immortality before the proceedings can begin. The first step is for her to disgorge the learning she has stored up within herself. She coughs up this material, and the resulting refuse immediately turns into publications of an incredible variety. Then Philology drinks from the cup of immortality and is removed by chariot to the heavens. Mercury greets her, and after some ado, presents his bride with a gift of seven handmaidens. These ladies-in-waiting turn out to be none other than the seven liberal arts, and the rest of the work consists of their attempt to explain themselves.[39]

While this allegory may seem trivial or even frivolous, it does involve some serious educational and theological doctrine. The twelfth century humanist, John of Salisbury, comments: "Antiquity considered that Prudence, the sister of Truth, was not sterile, but bore a wonderful daughter [Philology], whom she committed to the chaste embrace of Mercury. In other words, Prudence, the sister of Truth, arranged that [her daughter], the Love of [Logical] Reasoning and [Scientific] Knowledge, would acquire fertility and luster from Eloquence. Such is the union of Philology and Mercury [Eloquence]."[40] In effect, John is saying that Martianus' allegory symbolizes the union of wisdom and eloquence, and modern authorities agree.[41] On one level, we may view the *Marriage* as a merger of the verbal arts of the trivium with the scientific arts of the quadrivium. On another and more profound level, it indicates divine sanction for the union of wisdom and eloquence and suggests "that the curriculum of the seven liberal arts, being the means to achieve this goal, bears the same sanction; that through prowess in these studies and the benefits one thus brings to mankind, it is possible to win immortality and the fellowship of the gods."[42]

The attainment of immortality emerges as one of Martianus' main themes. The allegory is shot through with Neopythagorean eschatological doctrines. The astral setting of the wedding is perhaps the key symbol, since it allows Martianus to expound on the character of the nether regions. We find the heavens populated by deities arranged in hierarchical order; the highest beings are located above the sun, while the lesser deities, in order of their potency, descend down to the region between the moon and the earth. Man, in his corporeal existence, is confined to the earth at the bottom of the hierarchy. Nevertheless, the human soul contains a divine spark, and once liberated from the body, the soul has the potential to rise into the heavens. The possibility and degree of the ascent depends on the purity of the soul's being.[43]

Johnson notes that this form of pagan mysticism bears some similarity to the Christian doctrines of asceticism and salvation. Yet, he emphasizes some very important differences. In Martianus, the achievement of immortality rests not on personal goodness or faith, but on attainments in the arts and sciences. One rises to glory by dint of intellectual effort. Thus, "the idea that an untutored peasant, by the mere quality of his love for God and His creatures, may attain sanctity and eternal bliss, is alien to Martianus; immortality in his eyes is earned by fame won through service, not by love or innocence alone."[44] Furthermore, unlike Christian theologians, Martianus has nothing to say about personal ethics.

But if Martianus disagrees with Christian doctrine, he is even farther removed from Ciceronian humanism. The very notion of a celestial allegory leads to an intolerable distortion of Cicero's vision of the union of wisdom and eloquence. By joining wisdom to eloquence and by retaining the concept of service through intellectual effort, Martianus retains some semblance of humanistic *paideia*. Nevertheless, both the content and form of his message are set in terms totally foreign to the spirit of Ciceronianism. Martianus has his eyes set on objects that transcend Cicero's earthly sphere. One striking illustration of this point is his elimination of medicine and architecture from the liberal arts. These studies, he argues, deal with things that are mortal and earthbound. They focus attention on the mechanics of material things and detract from the life of the soul; they do not partake of the divine impracticality of genuinely liberal studies.[45] Thus, the liberal arts begin to lose their contact with practical wisdom and become important largely as a propaedeutic to cosmology.

Even a cursory glance at book 5 of the *Marriage* reveals how Martianus' cosmological assumptions are reflected in his theory of rhetoric. The book consists of an intricately organized sequence of technical rules. The material is a pastiche culled from *De Inventione* and from late Latin manuals of an even more severely mechanical nature.[46] There is not the slightest hint of advice about how to adapt these precepts to actual situations. Cicero and Augustine distrust any system of rules; they subordinate theory to the practical needs of the orator.

For Martianus, however, there is no practical application. In fact, this lack of context is a positive good, since it removes the mind from the here and now and directs it toward the heavens. One is reminded of a common type of early medieval painting in which a figure stands against a featureless background as though floating free in space. The rhetorical correlate is a theory in which the rules divorce themselves from the concrete problems of the orator. The technicalities so much despised by Cicero have found a metaphysical purpose. The student no longer learns the rules of the system in order to better his performance in actual speaking situations. Rather, he learns them in order to discipline his mind and prepare it for purposes beyond the realm of human affairs. As Brehaut notes, Martianus is less interested in the education of a gentleman than in the training of a mystic.[47]

CONCLUSION

The concept of the union of wisdom and eloquence influenced both Augustine and Martianus, but neither theorist could accept it in its original form. Consequently, they altered the Ciceronian concept by fixing it in a hierarchical system. For Augustine, the crucial step was to identify Christian literature as the authentic source for both wisdom and eloquence. He thereby retained Cicero's original terminology but attached new meanings to the terms themselves. Rhetoric became a vehicle for transmitting the truths revealed by faith. And the source for this revealed knowledge, Scripture, also provided the model for eloquent expression. Rhetoric was still a practical art, and its two essential elements were still united; but they were now united at a level that transcended Cicero's secular pluralism.

For his part, Martianus attempted a synthesis of pagan mysticism and Ciceronian doctrine. He raised the union of wisdom and eloquence to a higher level by means of a celestial allegory. This strategy allowed him to redefine the function of a liberal education in a way that was consistent with Neoplatonic eschatology. But the result was more a conflation than a genuine synthesis. The allegorical setting succeeded only in providing an external framework for the arts; it did not resolve the question of how the form and the content of a discourse were interconnected. This question was implicit in the concept of the unity of wisdom and eloquence, and the failure to deal with it stripped rhetoric of its traditional significance. Rhetoric no longer functioned to produce, integrate, or transmit knowledge. It was studied, along with a number of other arts, exclusively for the sake of mental exercise.

This study of Augustine and Martianus lends further support to the hypothesis that rhetorical theory must adapt itself to changing cultural conditions. But it should also alert us to one of the limitations of this hypothesis. Augustine and Martianus substantially altered the established Ciceronian tradition, but they did not ignore it. They were not free to construct a theory of rhetoric solely on the basis of the emerging cultural assumptions of their age. They also had to account for the traditional theory inherited from the past. And this limitation does not appear to be an accident peculiar to the circumstances of the fifth century. Like all other disciplines, rhetoric develops through conventions and traditions located within the art itself, and these internal factors often modify the effect of external circumstances. Even if traditional theory acts only as an obstacle to change, it still exerts an influence on those who attempt reform. Thus, the emergence of a new "paradigm" for rhetoric may reflect the continuity of tradition as well as the vicissitudes of changing patterns of culture.

8

SAINT AUGUSTINE'S THEORY OF LANGUAGE*

Gerard Watson

By examining Augustine's approach to language and signs in De Doctrina Christiana *and other works, Gerard Watson counters Wittgenstein's view on Augustine's
supposedly essentialist theory of language. In* Philosophical Investigations,
Wittgenstein criticizes Augustine's view of language based on a passage from his
Confessions, *a limitation in scope that Watson calls into question. Watson claims
that, in this passage, Augustine's goal is oriented toward describing the way a child
learns language, rather than offering a general theory of language (as Wittgenstein
implies). By tracing Augustine's close acquaintance with rhetoric and by analyzing
his theory of language across his body of work (particularly in* De Magistro, De
Doctrina Christiana, *and* De Trinitate*), Watson illustrates that Augustine
treats language with greater depth and sophistication than Wittgenstein's critique
acknowledges. Specifically, Watson notes that Augustine's language theory reflects
Stoic influences; Augustine discusses signs as intrinsic to human nature and demonstrates language to be part of the world of sensation and perception, with the sounds
of words corresponding to the physical realm and their meanings corresponding to
the realm of the soul. Watson also suggests that Augustine's view of the relationship
between language and knowledge acquisition is indebted to Cicero's* Academica.
*Overall, Watson illustrates that Augustine's general theory of language includes
dimensions beyond the scope of his discussion in the* Confessions *and complicates
the simple word-object correspondence that Wittgenstein attributes to Augustine's
thought. As such, Watson suggests that Augustine's theory of rhetoric is supported
by a well-developed theory of language, illustrating the depth of Augustine's rhetorical thought.*

One of the seminal works of modern philosophy begins with a criticism of "a particular picture of the essence of human language."
That work is the *Philosophical Investigations* of Wittgenstein and the

* Originally published as "St. Augustine's Theory of Language." *The Maynooth
Review* 6.2 (1982): 4–20. Headnote by Sarah L. Yoder.

particular picture that is criticized is that of Saint Augustine in the
Confessions. According to Wittgenstein, Augustine's picture is that "the
individual words in language name objects—sentences are combinations of such names." It is not my purpose in this paper to defend the
picture of the *Confessions* against the criticisms of Wittgenstein, but
rather to put it in context by considering Augustine's interest in language and his knowledge of earlier theories, and by looking at some
other passages in his works where he turns his attention to the topic.

It may seem strange at first sight that Wittgenstein should choose
Augustine of all people as the peg on which to hang his opening
remarks on language. For, as Eugenio Coseriu has pointed out in one
of the most recent histories of the philosophy of language,[1] Augustine
is normally not even mentioned as a philosopher of language, and
references to him in this connection are hardly to be found in the presentations of the history of philosophy. And so he does not appear in
Steinthal, or Lersch, or even in Bochenski.[2] This is all the more strange
given the fact that Augustine's business was with words and language
right through his life. Time and again his exposition of a particular
topic will be held up as he wonders over a word, playing with similarly
sounding words, teasing out their various meanings as if they contained some great mystery which if solved would solve the mystery of
the universe. He had been trained in the schools of the rhetoricians
and eventually became a teacher of rhetoric himself. He must have
been a very good one, and even if we had not his writings the mere
record of his career would be an indication of success: He taught at
Carthage for seven years, from 376 to 383, and then for a year at
Rome, and reached the climax of his career as a professor of rhetoric
in Milan from 384 to 386. Even when he abandoned the teaching of
rhetoric officially in 386 with his decision to become baptized, he was
not allowed to abandon the practice of it for any length of time. In
a few years (391) he was ordained priest, and then (395) bishop, and
from that until the end of his life in 430 he was a practitioner of the
art of words. Besides, as a Christian teacher he developed a further
interest in words. He saw all the world as a sacrament or sign of a
hidden reality, and among the signs the most striking were words. The
world process itself could be seen as a gradually unfolding sentence,
a sentence whose full meaning only God could see, but which by the
very fact of its fragmentary and puzzling nature stimulates us to keep
on searching for the ultimate meaning. For, as he says in a book which

is devoted to the discussion of signs, "things which are easily worked out are frequently regarded as worthless" (*DDC* 2, 6).

One could, of course, keep talking for all one's life (seventy-six years for Augustine) without ever reflecting on the nature of language. But in the case of Augustine this does not seem likely. He was by nature a philosopher. Why then is it rather the exceptional thing, as indicated by Coseriu, to look at him as a theorist of language? Part of the reason is that Augustine is thought of primarily as the theologian and pastoral bishop who was so much involved in ecclesiastical controversy and administration that he is not expected to have been able to indulge in the luxury of abstract speculation on the nature of language. The further presumption is made that he had not the necessary background which would enable him to contribute anything of value in this field. It is said that Augustine had very little, if any, formal training in philosophy, partly because he was educated in his birthplace in North Africa, Thagaste, in the neighboring town of Madaura and in Carthage, but mainly because he never mastered the language of philosophy, Greek.

Augustine reproaches himself for this gap in his education and for his sin in failing to submit himself properly to the discipline of learning Greek as a boy. He was, he says, too fond of Vergil, and wept too much for Dido dead. "But why," he asks, "did I hate Greek literature when it sang the same songs as Vergil did? For Homer, too, is skilled in weaving such fables, he too is unreal and yet charmingly unreal. Nevertheless, he was not charming to me as a boy. I suppose that even Vergil affects Greek boys in the same way when they are forced to learn him as I was forced to learn Homer. The difficulty of learning thoroughly a foreign language sprinkled bitter salt on all these sweet Greek fairy tales. For I didn't know any of these Greek words, and I was put under enormous pressure, through savage threats and punishments to learn them" (*Conf.* 1, 14, 23).

The mature Augustine obviously knew some Greek: estimates vary somewhat as to how much. But it seems clear that he never felt inclined to read Plato with his feet on the fender. Peter Brown says: "Augustine's failure to learn Greek was a momentous casualty of the Late Roman educational system: he will become the only Latin philosopher in antiquity to be virtually ignorant of Greek."[3] And yet Duchrow can say (in *Sprachverständnis und Biblisches Hören bei Augustinus*, Tübingen 1965, p. 72) that Augustine's philosophy of language in *De*

Magistro reflects the entire Graeco-Roman discussion since the *Cratylus*. If we are to evaluate this statement we must first try to ascertain the philosophical sources on which Augustine could draw if he wished to formulate a theory of language.

Theoretically, of course, he could have drawn on all the philosophies developed up to his own day: the philosophy of Plotinus, for instance, and the Neoplatonists, the Stoics, the Epicureans, the school of Aristotle, and the Academy in its different phases. But making all possible allowances I think it is safe to say that Augustine could not have done much important independent research in the purely Greek sources. In Latin translation he could have read Plato's *Timaeus*, but the *Timaeus* has little to offer for theory of language. He knew of Plato's Theory of Forms, but an attempt to make use of it to explain the phenomenon of meaningful language is another matter. Dialogues like the *Cratylus*, the *Parmenides*, and the *Sophist*, which could have been a stimulus at least to further investigation, seem to have been completely unknown to him. We can then, I think, exclude Plato as a direct influence on Augustine's theory of language. The situation with Aristotle is somewhat different. He talks with some pride in the *Confessions* (4, 16, 28) of how he read and understood the *Categories* of Aristotle when he was aged about twenty—and all this without a teacher and with no great difficulty. In that same chapter he says: "Whatever was written either of the art of rhetoric or of logic, of the dimensions of figures or music or arithmetic I understood with no great difficulty and had no need of an instructor . . . I did not discover that these matters were difficult to grasp even for the studious and intelligent, until I tried to teach them to others—and that pupil was regarded as the most excellent who could follow my exposition least laggingly." Augustine does not say whether he read the *Categories* in Greek or Latin, but I think we can take it that he read the translation. Translations of the *Categories* and Aristotle's *De Interpretatione* and of Porphyry's *Eisagōgē* had been made in the century in which Augustine was born by a man whose translations of "the books of the Platonists" were to be an important factor in Augustine's conversion to Christianity. This man was Marius Victorinus who among other things wrote commentaries on works of Cicero and wrote works of his own *On Definitions* and *On Hypothetical Syllogisms*. Aristotle therefore cannot be ruled out as a direct influence on Augustine's theory of language.

However, in the scholarly debates on signification in the tradition preceding Augustine, the center of interest was not the theory of Aristotle but the quarrel between the Epicureans and the Stoics: it was not only concerning the Highest Good that Augustine could say: "You will find the Epicureans and Stoics disputing among themselves most bitterly" (*Ep.* 118. 3, 6). The point at issue was the nature of the sign, and this naturally involved language. In keeping with their general bias, the Epicureans held that the sign was perceptible, *aisthêton*. The Stoics on the other hand maintained that the sign is intelligible, *noêton*.[4] And here perhaps we can begin to see a possible explanation of the acceptance by Augustine, even after his conversion in 386, of positions held by this allegedly completely materialist school.

If Augustine did accept Stoic influence in formulating a theory of language it would, I think, have implications for Wittgenstein's view of his picture of the essence of human language in the *Confessions*. The question is, did he? The Stoics were materialists, and Augustine could not, of course, accept that position in its entirety, certainly not in the post-386 period, and he criticized it frequently. The Stoic position did, however, provide a useful basis for comparison for his own views. So, he says, in *The City of God* 7, 6, the Stoic *pneuma*, the spirit which permeates the world, could be used at least to support monotheism, but he also says, more critically, that monotheism should be maintained and not negated by the introduction of a swarm of splinter gods (*ibid.* 4, 11). He contrasts Varro's (Stoic) position unfavourably with that of the "Platonists" who believe in a God who transcends the world and all soul (*ibid.* 8, 1).

But after that basic distinction there was much that Augustine could and did accept from Stoicism. An order such as was to be found especially in the Stoic system had always had a particular attraction for Augustine. *De Ordine* was one of his earliest works, and there and in *De Musica* VI (especially 16) his admiration for a mathematizing God under whom all develops according to the determined formulae, seminal principles, is very evident. But the Stoic notion of order is not confined to the early works: striking expressions are to be found in *De Trinitate* and *The City of God*,[5] where man is the peak of the pyramid of God's creation with beneath him the different grades of life at the animal, vegetable, and mineral level, each with their different principle of unity: in the Stoic system *hexis*, *physis*, and *psyche*.

Man is the most important seed in all these seeds of the universe. According to the Stoics, his development, like that of all things, proceeded in accordance with the principle of *oikeiôsis*, the process whereby concern for oneself is gradually extended to the whole world. The theory is again to be found throughout Augustine, with a particularly clear expression in *De Vera Religione* 41, 77. In man *oikeiôsis* develops with the development of sensation: it is the gradual extension of the *synaesthesis*, or consciousness, which the child possesses. The theory of sensation and perception in *The Greatness of the Soul* (71) uses the Stoic analogy of seeing as being like touching an object with a stick. Normally, however, Augustine refers to such theories only in passing and indirectly, with his attention fixed on another theme. So for example he will discuss the Incarnation and says that we grasp Christ's humanity there because we have an impressed knowledge (*infixam notitiam*) or idea of human nature in accordance with which we know that someone is a human being or has the form of a human being (*De Trin.* 8.4). Impressed "*notitia*" occurs very frequently in Latin accounts of Stoic teaching.[6] Judgment can be seen as an extension of *oikeiôsis*. Our mind has a certain penetrating and shaping power: its knowledge is not formed just as a heap is formed, by an accumulation of detritus over the years—see *Conf.* 10.19 and especially *De Trin.* 9.6, 10 on the presentations ("Phantasias," a central Stoic word) of corporal things drawn in through the senses of the body and in some way poured into and fixed in the memory.

I am not attempting to argue that in this area of his thinking Augustine is Stoic and nothing but Stoic. I merely wish to establish that he was in contact with a wide range of Stoic thought and could consequently draw on it for theory of language. We have to concern ourselves more particularly with the Stoic theory of meaning and its diffusion in the intellectual world into which Augustine was born. A glance at the relevant section of von Arnim's fragments from the Stoics will show that if we had to consider merely chronological possibilities, the most important witnesses were available to Augustine. One of these was, for instance, Sextus Empiricus who lived at the beginning of the third century and preserved the debate on the Stoic semantical theory. Augustine makes a few statements which look remarkably like ideas to be found in Sextus, yet once again Augustine's knowledge of Greek makes his reading of Sextus unlikely. We have to leave the possibility of common Latin sources for Sextus and Augustine open for the moment: it is always there, because, as Mates says, "the essentials of Stoic logic were brought together in handbooks not long after the time of Chrysippus. Such handbooks were commonly entitled 'Introduction to Logic' (*Eisagôgê Dialektikê*) and evidently had a very wide circulation."[7] The same handbooks could have been used by Diogenes Laertius, our next best source for this part of Stoic theory, but as with Sextus we can at best say that we are uncertain on the relation of Augustine to him or his sources: Diogenes too wrote in Greek. But while it is safer to presume no special knowledge on the part of Augustine without documentary evidence, it would nevertheless be rash to assume that we are in possession of all the sources available to him. Augustine is, for example, our main source for the reconstruction of the lost *Hortensius* of Cicero. But other portions of the work of Cicero have been lost which are more to the point for our enquiry. Augustine had an excellent knowledge of the four-book version of Cicero's *Academica*. He knew therefore the portion of *Academica* I that still survives, and although, as Hagendahl says,[8] there is nothing to suggest that he knew *Lucullus*, we are justified in assuming that the *Lucullus* that survives, corresponding to books 3 and 4 of the version Augustine knew, must be suggestive for his Stoic awareness. Let us therefore examine these writings.

A comparison of Augustine's *Contra Academicos* and Cicero's *Academica* justifies Hagendahl's contention[9] that it had a great influence on Augustine. There in *Academica* 1.40, we know that Cicero referred to Zeno's teaching on perception and had an account of *phantasia* (presentation), *phantasia katalêptikê* (convincing presentation), *synkatathesis* (assent), *epistêmê* (knowledge) and *doxa* (opinion). There also Augustine read that Zeno held the senses to be trustworthy because of the power of *katalêpsis*: "because nature had bestowed as it were a 'measuring-rod' of knowledge and a first principle of itself from which subsequently notions of things could be impressed upon the mind, out of which not first principles only but certain broader roads to the discovery of reasoned truth were opened up" (42).

In *Academica* 2.95 we have an attempt to destroy the Stoic dialectic: "the foundation of dialectic is that whatever is enunciated (this they call the *axiôma*, that is the *effatum* for us) is either true or false." Against this is raised the famous paradox of "The Liar," and the first mode of coming to a conclusion is challenged. The disjunctive proposition also comes in for attack. Finally near the end, in 145, Zeno's model of the process of knowledge is reproduced.

Did Augustine learn anything about the Stoic semantic theory from this or rather from the corresponding part we no longer possess? I suspect it, but we cannot presume it. *Axiôma* (proposition) and *lekton* (that which can be expressed, central to their theory of meaning) go closely together in Stoic theory, with truth theory and criterion and signs, but we have no clear union of the themes that we know of in Cicero's *Academica* (the *axiôma* occurs again in *Tusculans* 1.14 and *De Fato* 1.10, both of which Augustine would have known).

Let us therefore leave Cicero for the moment and see what his older contemporary Varro has to offer. Augustine knew Varro well and used him extensively. He sometimes but not, however, always *says* that he is using him: one has only to think of *The City of God*. Thus Hagendahl[10] points out that Varro's *Disciplinarum Libri* are never mentioned in Augustine in spite of their influence on the early writings: this work was, as he says, "in all probability . . . the basis of Augustine's encyclopedia on the *artes*."[11] Varro's teacher was Antiochus who had taken over many of the Stoic tenets. And there is no doubt about Stoic influence on Varro himself. *De Lingua Latina* as we have it is largely taken up with etymology, which he marks off from semantics at the beginning of book 5. The whole arrangement of the fifth book is Stoic, as Dahlmann says.[12] Varro mentions Chrysippus and Antipater as his primary authorities at the beginning of book 6, and much straight Stoicism could be quoted.

Aulus Gellius, like Augustine, admired Varro. Augustine knew Gellius and was able to use him on the distinction between *phantasia* and *synkatathesis* (CD 9.4, 5). Gellius touches on Stoic doctrine at a number of points. Section 5.15 discusses whether the *vox* is a *corpus* or *asômaton* (incorporeal): different views including the Stoic are given. Section 16.8 defines the *axiôma* as a complete *lekton* assertoric by itself, like "Hannibal was a Carthaginian." Any full or complete thought, says Gellius, which is so expressed in words that it is necessarily either true or false is called "proposition" (*axiôma*) by the logicians. Varro, he says, in the twenty-fourth book of *De Lingua Latina*, dedicated to Cicero, translated this as *proloquium*, and Cicero, in one place, as *pronuntiatum*. Gellius then discusses types of propositions, conditionals, etc. Augustine could have learned much from Gellius. He could also have learned something from his fellow countryman Apuleius to whom, among other works, is attributed a *Peri Hermeneias*, where the proposition is also discussed.

All these are authors of whom Augustine knew at least something and who must be considered possibilities for influence. Is it too daring to suggest an acquaintance with the *Introductions* of which Aulus speaks? Augustine tells us himself that he had a particular interest in logic,[13] and that among logicians he had a special admiration for the Stoics. Dialectic is the discipline of disciplines. Finally, he worked for years on an encyclopedia: how many more handbooks on philosophy like that of Celsus have we simply never heard of?[14] These are lost to us, but so too are some other of Augustine's own early works. And Duchrow mentions in particular the great loss of the sections of Augustine's *Libri Disciplinarum* on speech, which he regards as particularly important since all the statements of the later period on the word and on the Word of God can only be properly understood from the foundations laid here.[15] Augustine himself says in the *Retractationes* that he had begun to write in Milan on five disciplines other than music which were now lost to him but might still be possessed by other people (1.5).

One particular work to which Augustine may have been referring is the *De Dialectica*, which is a title he mentions and which we do not possess in its entirety (Fischer reckons that just about one eighth is completed).[16] The *De Dialectica* seems to be the reproduction of a Stoic source, and if this is so it would have important consequences for his later works: that is, if Augustine fully understood his source. And if he did understand it, did he retain it in his later writings? And if he rejected it, at what point did he do so and for what reason?

But before glancing at this work there is one prior important question which we must acknowledge, and that is the authenticity of the work. This is a question that has been disputed from the sixteenth century, and it would be tedious even to list those who have taken sides for and against. For over one hundred years now the tide has been running in favor of authenticity, and the question seems to me to have been settled by the careful and balanced study by Jackson which appeared in 1975.[17] I see no reason for rejecting it myself and shall therefore turn to it now as a work of Saint Augustine's earliest period. The *De Dialectica* is in fact a very small work, merely the beginnings of a guide to the science of effective disputation, which is how dialectic is described here at the beginning and in the Stoa.[18] There is then reference to verbs, particularly those in the first and second person which can, in Latin, here and now be listed under headings of true or false, because they can be affirmed or denied. Stoic influence is again there obvious. An example of what he calls "conjoined" words is next given: "a man walks." This makes one think of the Stoic complete *lekta*, just as again we think of Stoicism in the distinction further drawn in chapter 2 between sentences which are either true or false, and sentences on the other hand which cannot be affirmed or denied, as when we give orders, make wishes, express curses, and so on.[19]

The *axiômata* or propositions constituted the most important class of *lekta* for the Stoics, and they distinguished between the simple (or atomic) and non-simple. So too Augustine gives as an example of the simple "every human being walks," and of the conjoined "if he walks, he is in motion." Finally, at the end of chapter 3, Augustine talks of the *summa* which comes into being from a combination of *sententiae*, and this again seems to be a Stoic description of the combination of judgments to form an argument.[20]

So much by way of introduction. In chapter 4 he distinguishes the two main portions, the first "De loquendo," and the second which is again subdivided into three sections. There is nothing new in this: what is interesting about it is that there is a very similar disposition in Martianus Capella 4.335 and a reference there to Varro and his six *normae*.[21]

Chapter 5 contains definitions of *verbum*, *res*, and *signum*. The word is described as "the sign of anything, preferred by a speaker, which can be understood by the hearer." This corresponds closely to a Stoic definition of speaking given by Sextus Empiricus (*Adv. Math.* 8.80).[22] A thing is "whatever is sensed or understood or which lies hidden." A sign "is something which shows itself to the sense, and besides itself, shows something to the mind." This should be compared to Sextus' description of the Stoics' version of the process of signification (*Adv. Math.* 8.11ff.). Augustine further remarks that the word as mere sound of a word has nothing to do with dialectic: here again he seems clearly to be referring to the Stoic distinction between *lexis* and *logos*.[23]

The most interesting part of what remains is his explanation of the word *dicibile*, which would be the Latin version of *lekton*. This he explains as "what is picked up from a word not by the ears but by the mind, and which is held within the mind." And again, "What I called *dicibile* signifies a word, and nevertheless not (just) a word, but what is understood in the word and held in the mind." The five final chapters that are left to us are concerned with words and especially with a topic dear to the Stoics, the obscurity and ambiguity of words.[24]

I think enough has been said to indicate that the *De Dialectica* is a work which is very strongly Stoic-colored. If it is an early work of Augustine's, the main contemporary work for comparison is the *De Magistro* of 389 which I now turn to. But before doing so I wish to refer briefly to another work from the previous year, *On the Greatness of the Soul.* Word and meaning are simply being used there to illustrate a point about the soul. Augustine there (32.65ff.) says (and there is a very interesting parallel in his sermon on John the Baptist) that there is a difference between the sound itself and what the sound signifies; that a word consists of sound and meaning, and the sound has to do with the ears and the meaning with the mind. So in a word, just as in some living being, the sound is the body and the meaning is, as it were, the soul. The meaning is indivisible and, without being extended, animates and integrates all the letters of the word.

But this is only in passing. By far the longest treatment we have in Augustine of words, language, and meaning is the *De Magistro*, although even at the end of that he says: "at some other time, God willing, we shall investigate the entire problem of the utility of words, which, if considered properly, is not negligible." But in fact he never actually did write this special work, so the *De Magistro* is still our largest source for what Augustine thought on our topic. It is a work which can be used for and against the contention of Wittgenstein that the picture of the essence of human language given by Augustine in the *Confessions* is that "the individual words in language name objects—sentences are combinations of such names."

Chapter 2, for instance, starts from the agreement that words are signs. So far the statement "words are signs" has been allowed to remain ambiguous. But now Augustine quotes the line, from *Aeneid* 2.659: *si nihil ex tanta superis placet urbe relinqui.* It has eight words and they agree that therefore there are eight signs. The *ergo* might be a concession to ordinary language, but as it stands it could be taken to refer to a one sign-one object position. But the interpretation of the individual words that follows makes us wonder about that, and seems to be an explicit weakening of the "crude correspondence" position suggested by the eight words-eight signs statement. *Si* (if), for instance, is not easily referred even to another Latin word; it is an indication of doubt, but that is something in the mind, not a concrete object in the world. Or again, *nihil* (nothing): it is agreed that "instead of saying that this word signifies a thing which does not exist, we shall rather say that it signifies some state of the mind when it sees no reality, yet finds, or thinks that it finds, that the reality does not exist." And of *ex* it is said: "It seems to me that some sort of separation from a thing in which something had been, is signified; and that this is said to be 'from' the former." It is stated explicitly a little later (4.9) that *si* and *ex* are words but not nouns. "And there are many such examples."

What follows immediately on the discussion of *si*, *nihil*, and *ex* is that "pointing to" is possible "only in regard to nouns that signify bodies, and when those bodies are present" (3.5), and it is explained that by *corpora* (bodies) is meant *visibilia* (visible things). Questioning of this leads to a discussion of whether we ever get *beyond* signs; Adeodatus, the son of Augustine and his partner in the dialogue, remarks, "Obviously the pointing of the finger (at the wall) is not the wall, but a sign is given through it, by means of which the wall can be seen" (3.6). That is, the question is being asked, what makes a sign a sign? How are we capable of accepting it and going beyond it?

Adeodatus rounds off this section by saying, "I see nothing, therefore, that can be made known without signs." He capitulates immediately, however, when Augustine objects that if he asked, "What is walking?" and Adeodatus got up and walked, Augustine would have what he wanted without the use of words or signs. But Augustine says to him that he should not have yielded so easily. Suppose Augustine were completely ignorant of the meaning of the word "walking": how, he asks, would Adeodatus show him the difference between "walking" and "hurrying"? The words may on occasion coincide, but they have different fields of force. Once more Adeodatus gives in and says he admits that we cannot make a thing clear without a sign, if we are asked to do so while actually performing the action.

This topic is discussed on three other occasions in the dialogue, and from the variations on each occasion one has the impression that Augustine is deliberately leaving the question open, in the manner of Plato, in order to stimulate reflection. For Adeodatus here makes one exception to his concession that we cannot make a thing clear without a sign, if we are asked to do so while actually performing the action. The exception is the case of speech, *loquendo*, where apparently it can be made clear what a person is doing without any further sign. Augustine seems to accept this exception of speaking from Adeodatus. Yet one paragraph further on he says that for a human sound to be a word "it must be uttered in an articulate voice with some meaning," a statement which derives from the Stoic *lexis-logos* distinction and which is repeated three more times, twice within the next five pages. Later (10.34) he asks us to suppose that we heard the word *caput* spoken for the first time. We would not know whether this was something simply sounding or whether it was also signifying something. There are two elements in the sign—the sound and the signification—and we learn the signification of *caput* by seeing the reality which is pointed out to us: before this we had not been able to associate sign and reality. Augustine is obviously aware of the distinction between the parrot-like sounding of a word and speaking a word with meaning, as is obvious from his discussion of "sarabara" in 10.35, but he remains disappointingly inconclusive in the dialogue. "Treating of words by means of words is as complicated a business," he says (5.14), "as interlocking and rubbing the fingers of one hand with the fingers of the other, where it is scarcely discernible, except by the one doing it, which fingers are itching and which are relieving the itch."

"We feel as if we had to repair a torn spider's web with our fingers" was how Wittgenstein expressed his awareness of the same difficulty (*P. I.* 106). That Augustine's hesitations about language and meaning were due to awareness and not ignorance of some of the solutions that had been offered is shown by a few other portions of the *De Magistro* which I shall refer to before summing up on this dialogue. To support his reflections on the importance of the *nomen*, Augustine says (5.16): "As you know, the most eminent masters of argumentation teach that a noun and a verb constitute a complete *sententia* which may be said to be true or false. Cicero somewhere calls that sort of thing a *pronuntiatum*." The "most eminent masters of argumentation' are the Stoics, and the place in Cicero is the *Tusculans*. What follows is paralleled in the *De Dialectica*, and refers to the Stoic distinction between complete and incomplete *lekta*, although Augustine does not use that terminology. But he gives as examples of complete *lekta* or propositions "a man sits" or "a horse runs," whereas to "sits" or "runs" the noun "man" or "horse" must be added "to complete the proposition, that is, such a sentence as can be said to be true or false." And immediately afterwards approval is expressed of the conditional proposition "If it is a man, it is an animal"—that is, the type of proposition favored by the Stoics.

What are we to make of the *De Magistro* from the point of view of language theory? The dialogue leaves much to be desired from our point of view. But to be fair to Augustine we must realize that the whole purpose of the work is to emphasize the *limits* of signs and particularly the most important class of these, words. We must then remember that a very heavy theological bias is imposed on any philosophical theory that might be brought forward. We must consequently be careful and not be too quick to impute to him a naive object-bound theory of meaning. If one wanted to be pedantic, one could maintain that at the outset (2.3*) si nihil ex tanta superis placet urbe relinqui* is understood as one verse. Moreover, in spite of the natural prejudice in favor of a word (i.e., sign) correspondence to object, a prejudice which the Stoics shared, a word-object relation analysis is not given to the words which are considered, *si, nihil,* and *ex.* He does in fact call *si* and *est* nouns later in the work, but there he is arguing that *any* word can be used in the grammatical function of a noun.

I think that the most that can be alleged against Augustine in the *De Magistro* is a tendency to treat words as if they always referred to objects. Is there any possible explanation of this tendency *apart from* a mistaken theory of language? I suggest once again the purpose of the work. We communicate through signs, that is, we teach or remind others or ourselves of various realities. Are signs absolutely necessary for this communication? In order to decide on this, signs have to be examined closely. Consequently we have an examination of what the Stoics called the incomplete as well as the complete *lekta.* We must remember that a large part of the Stoic dialectic consisted of the analysis of incomplete *lekta.* We can see this from the remains that are left to us, and I suggest it would have been a much more striking feature of the sources available to Augustine.

What were the particular sources for *De Magistro*? Varro is always a prime suspect in a discussion of words, and the etymology of *verba a verberando, nomina a noscendo* in 5.12 is taken from him (we can see the same etymologies in Quintilian, Cassiodorus, Isidore, Donatus, and the *De Dialectica*). But, apart from Varro, behind *De Magistro* there may be grammarians and others stretching over a period of four or five hundred years. We need only glance at Martianus Capella to see that Augustine had a tradition to draw on (see M.C. 4.388 and 4.349). Given that tradition, it is remarkable how restrained Augustine is in *De Magistro* on the theory of language. We must grant that it is, regarded as a "semantic" document, disappointing. Augustine has his own thesis to make and he does so. The position he is arguing is an extreme one, backed by the dangerous combination of theology and rhetoric. He is conscious that it is extreme: if taken at its face value it would leave all discussion pointless. It is in fact all Augustine's thought writ small, signs with their pointlessness set against reality. But the dialogue is not to be taken at its face value: it is to be interpreted rhetorically. Rhetoric works partly through exaggeration, first one side, then the other: the audience must use its judgment. Speech is not getting its full due in the *De Magistro*, but to say that a *false* account of language is given is to go too far.

The next important work chronologically where Augustine touches on theory of language is the *Confessions*, where there occurs the passage to which Wittgenstein refers. But this I wish to leave to the end. At about the same time, he began writing *De Doctrina Christiana* (*On the Teaching of Christians*), and the reason it interests us particularly is that Augustine says that "All teaching concerns either things or signs, but things are learned through signs" (1.2). Coming to it as we do from *De Magistro* the prologue is particularly interesting: the core of it is the point that means, i.e. signs, are to be used even though they are not sufficient. All sorts of things could have been done through an angel, "but the condition of man would be lowered if God had not wished that men supply his word to men." After the introduction, the first big division, that into things and signs, *res* and *signa*, is made in chapter 2 of book 1. Signs are ordered to things, as use is to enjoyment. Every sign is also a thing, a reality, but not every reality is also a sign. And there are signs, he says, whose whole use is in signifying, like words. For no one uses words except for the purpose of signifying something.

But for a fuller treatment of words we have to wait until book 2, which is concerned with signs of all sorts and their interpretation. The definition of a sign given there in chapter 1 is that it is "a thing which of itself makes us think of something besides the presentation (*species*) it brings to our senses. Among signs some are natural and others are conventional. Those are natural which, without any desire or intention of signifying, make us aware of something beyond themselves, like smoke which signifies fire." The smoke does not *want* to do that, but, he says, "through observation, a memory of experience with things, *it is known* that there is an underlying fire." The "it is known" implies that there is always a knower understood.

But these natural signs, as Augustine remarks, are not his primary interest and are mentioned only for completeness. *Conventional* signs are "those which living creatures show to one another for the purpose of conveying, in so far as they are able, the motions of their spirit or something which they have sensed or understood" (2.2). The intention of signifying is important, and he is not quite sure if a cock's crowing falls under this head. Words are the most important class of signs, but, he says, because "vibrations in the air soon pass away and remain no longer than they sound, signs of words have been constructed by means of letters" (2.4). "Vibrations in the air," *verberato aere*, is a reference to an etymology of *verbum* which also occurs in the *De Magistro* and *De Dialectica*.

All possible disciplines must be turned to use for the proper interpretation of words. One of these, and most important, is the science of disputation (2.31), dialectic. For the interconnectedness of things, on which the laws of reasoning depend, is not simply a convention (2.32), and he gives as an example of necessary connection: "When the consequent is false, it is necessary that the antecedent be so also." It is interesting to note the propositional form here. He then gets involved in a discussion of truth conditions. He warns of the importance of distinguishing valid reasoning from the validity of the conclusions, and keeps on emphasizing the value of logic as a formal process. He defines the false for us: it is to give a sense to a thing when the case is not such as it is signified to be. He says there are two kinds of falsehood, the completely impossible and the simply not so, though possible, illustrating both kinds with propositions, the first if someone were to say $7 + 3 = 11$, and the second if someone were to say that it rained on the calends of January, even though it did not rain on the day.

What I wish to draw attention to in this passage is the parallel which it offers to Sextus Empiricus' discussion of the importance of the sign for the very notion of man in Stoic philosophy. Among the marks of man is the fact that "since he has a conception of logical sequence, he immediately grasps also the notion of sign because of the sequence; for in fact the sign in itself is of this form—'If this, this.' Therefore the existence of sign follows from the nature and structure of man. Also, it is generally agreed that proof is of the genus sign" (*Adv. Math.* 8.276f.). Here again it seems to me that Augustine was drawing on a Stoic handbook.

Augustine's next statement of any bulk on our topic occurs in the *De Trinitate* (399–419). He only comes to the subject at all in the *first* place because of the difficulty of language about God (1.1.1–3), a favorite theme with him. But it was inevitable that the notion of the Logos, the Word of God, should suggest the parallel of human speech. He talks in book 8 (4.7) of our image-making habit when we read or hear anything. In the course of this discussion he uses a distinction which had been used by Stoics between *phantasia* and *phantasma* (v. D.L. 7.50). But he warns of the danger of being restricted by the image, and what follows shows again that Augustine's theory of language was not naively object-bound. He says we must rise to the level of knowledge purified by love. This immediately raises the problem of how to love God: but let us first consider loving man. We love Paul because he is a "just soul." We know "soul" because we all have one, he says. But how do we know "just"? We are certainly not all just, and we do not form a *phantasia* or *phantasma* of justice. It is a truth which dwells within us that helps us to grasp the notion.

To try to confine Augustine here to Stoic influence would be foolish. But that the Stoic influence was important in the *De Trinitate* also is clear from book 9 where he talks about the formation of concepts and particularly the foundation of our judgment of true and false, right and wrong. Seeing the true internal *logos*, and assenting to it, enables us to pursue or reject certain courses of action. The internal judgment, *endiathetos*, is given expression externally in action, *proforikos*. Finally, the internal word is a central theme of book 15. When we say something which is true, we say something which is born inside us, a thought formed from the knowledge which is held in our memory. And this word is neither Greek nor Latin nor belongs to any other language—the old Stoic idea again—but when we want to bring it to the knowledge of others we have to have recourse to signs, normally sounds but sometimes gestures. One has only to read this passage to see that Augustine is not confined to a one word-one object theory of language.

I shall cite only one more passage in support of this, a passage taken from a work of roughly the same time as *De Trinitate* and somewhat later than the *Confessions*. This is *De Genesi ad litteram* (401–14). In book 8.16 of that work, the question is raised: "How could the first man have any understanding of the word 'evil' before he had any

experience of evil itself?" The question is answered by the application
of what seems again to be Stoic theory, as reported for instance by
Diogenes Laertius (7.52–53), which explains that general notions are
gained, some by direct contact, some by resemblance, some by analogy, by transposition, by composition, and by contrariety. Death for
instance is an example of a notion due to contrariety, and privation
originates notions; for instance, that of the man without hands. So
too Augustine says we understand many things from contraries and
privation: that is how we understand the word *nihil*, and *inane*, and *mors*.
And so in general: we understand from contraries or from similars the
meaning of all sorts of things we have not experienced.

We return finally to the *Confessions* and the passage which Wittgenstein criticized. Augustine is explaining there (18) how he learned
to speak. He says that as a small child, "I did not always manage to
express the right meanings to the right people. So I began to reflect.
When my elders named some object, and accordingly moved towards
something, I saw this and I grasped that the thing was called by the
sound they uttered when they meant to point it out. Their intention
was shown by their bodily movements, as it were the natural language
of all peoples: the expression of the face, the play of the eyes, the
movements of other parts of the body, and the tone of voice which
expresses our state of mind in seeking, having, rejecting, or avoiding
something. Thus, as I heard words repeatedly used in their proper
places in various sentences, I gradually learnt to understand what
objects they signified; and after I had trained my mouth to form these
signs, I used them to express my own desires."

Wittgenstein says of this: "In this picture of language we find the
roots of the following idea: Every word has a meaning. This meaning
is correlated with the word. It is the object for which the word stands.
Augustine does not say that there is any difference between kinds of
word. If you describe the learning of language in this way you are, I
believe, thinking primarily of nouns like 'table,' 'chair,' 'bread,' and
of individuals' names, and only secondarily of the names of certain
actions and properties; and of the remaining kinds of word as something that will take care of itself."

I think Wittgenstein is a little bit unfair to Augustine here. Augustine is describing how a child learns the simplest things first and these
tend to be the names of objects, animals, people he wants or which
please or displease him. But he is not setting out in the *Confessions*

to give a general picture of language. I have been trying to indicate that if he had, it would have been somewhat more sophisticated than Wittgenstein allows. As Wittgenstein also said in the *Philosophical Investigations*: "A main cause of philosophical disease—a one sided diet: one nourishes one's thinking with only one kind of example."

CHARITY, OBSCURITY, CLARITY
AUGUSTINE'S SEARCH FOR A TRUE RHETORIC*

David W. Tracy

David Tracy analyzes each of the four books of De Doctrina Christiana *and examines how they are tied together, even though Augustine's text was written in two parts. Tracy argues that* DDC *is significant as a work of rhetorical* inventio, *rather than a work of conversion, which he asserts is the case with Augustine's* Confessions. *Tracy discusses Augustine's teachings on "signs" versus "things," and on "enjoying" versus "using." He also discusses* caritas, *as well as the value of the Scriptures being obscure. Augustine's views on oral rhetoric, Christian sermons, and pagan practices and texts place him within the broader rhetorical tradition and highlight his role in promoting a Christian rhetoric that could borrow from pagan rhetoric. Tracy also addresses the historical context in which Augustine wrote* DDC, *including insights on Augustine's audience. Tracy also notes that after Augustine completed books 1, 2, and most of book 3, he stopped writing* DDC *to write* Confessions, *finally completing books 3 and 4 later in his life. While some critics argue that* DDC *feels more like two texts than one, Tracy claims that book 4 draws on what Augustine writes in books 1–3 and discusses how Christian preachers can best use rhetorical styles in order to teach, delight, and move their audiences.*

INTRODUCTION: PUZZLES AND PARADOXES

It would be difficult to name a more rhetorically informed contemporary theologian than Nathan A. Scott Jr. His contributions to the discipline of "theology and culture" are without equal. And those theological contributions are always rendered in a style that fits the mature reflections of a theologian who unites content and style. Scott's Anglican heritage, united to the more Reformed tonalities of his mentors, Paul Tillich and Reinhold Niebuhr, have given his theology a deeply

* Originally published as David W. Tracy. "Charity, Obscurity, Clarity: Augustine's Search for a True Rhetoric." *Morphologies of Faith*. Eds. Mary Gerhart and Anthony C. Yu. Atlanta, GA: Scholars Press, 1990. Headnote by Lisa Michelle Thomas.

Augustinian cast. But, unlike Tillich and Niebuhr and more like the classic Anglican tradition from the Caroline divines through T. S. Eliot, Nathan Scott has appropriated not only Augustine's profound theological vision but also his concern with rhetorical practice and theory.

Any theologian who writes as well as Augustine did and as Scott does is, ironically, always in danger of being misunderstood by theological practitioners of the "plain style" of what the ancients named dialectics. Not until the recent revival of rhetorical theory and hermeneutics have the limitations of dialectic and the persuasive power of rhetoric been readmitted to the more usual conversations of philosophers and theologians. To the purely dialectical mind, a rhetoricized theology can seem a half-way house to "true" theology. This dialectical self-deception belies both the rhetoric in all dialectical arguments and the argumentative force of all good rhetoric.

Augustine, the greatest of rhetorical theologians, is often the first victim of this widespread prejudice. Indeed, Augustine never explicated his full rhetorical theory. But he did leave us his great text *De Doctrina Christiana*. That text, I fear, is too often hurried through by many theologians anxious to move on to Augustine's more speculative (*On the Trinity*) and more anti-Pelagian writings. However, as Nathan A. Scott's remarkable oeuvre and as the recent revival of interest in rhetoric demonstrate, this will not do.

For only in *De Doctrina Christiana* does one find Augustine's clearest statement of his hermeneutics and what he left us of his rhetorical theory. Too often Augustine's theory has been read through the neo-Aristotelian eyes of many modern rhetoricians as concerned solely or, at least, principally, with style rather than with content, that is, with the need for *inventio* as discovery of true arguments and topics.[1] This reading, however familiar, is, I fear, a serious misreading. Augustine, to be sure, is deeply concerned with style. But he is equally concerned with a rhetoric of *inventio*. However, the Augustinian understanding of *inventio* can only be understood in his theological terms and not in purely philosophical terms. Augustine continues to persuade, that is, to "instruct, delight, and move," because he has also developed hermeneutical and theological principles of discovery or *inventio* by means of which he could instruct and move his readers. On the welcome occasion of a *Festschrift* for Nathan A. Scott Jr.—a theologian who has so instructed, delighted, and moved us all over the years of his remarkable career—it seems fitting to return to Augustine, the first great rhetorical theologian, and to his classic rhetorical text, *De Doctrina Christiana*. There one may find both a classic formulation of "theology and culture" as well as a rhetoric of both discovery and communication.

Before interpreting Augustine's text, however, there are three background issues worth noting: the first two suggest possible difficulties with the text itself; the third with the history of its interpretation. All three issues demand attention if an interpreter is to explicate the partly explicit, partly implicit, theory of Christian hermeneutics and rhetoric in this text of a former professor of rhetoric in the cosmopolitan capitals of Milan and Rome turned Christian bishop-rhetorician in the provincial city of Hippo.

1) The first issue is both the most obvious and, hermeneutically, the most central: the strange combination of simplicity and complexity of *De Doctrina Christiana*. On the one hand, this influential text of Augustine seems far less complex in its analysis of rhetoric than the texts of either Plato or Aristotle or even Augustine's own major mentor, Cicero. *De Doctrina* is also far less complex a text than other texts of Augustine himself: not only the *Confessions*, *The City of God*, *On the Trinity*, but also some of his great commentaries on Genesis, the Gospel of John, and the Psalms. On the other hand, as I hope to show, *De Doctrina Christiana* (henceforth *DDC*) remains a quintessential Augustinian text which can illumine all his more "complex" texts and is illuminated by them. For the hermeneutical and rhetorical theory on the relationship of theology and culture in *DDC* is often a central clue for reading other Augustinian texts.

2) The problem of the text is further complicated by the question of whether it is, in fact, a "whole." The circumstances of *DDC*'s origins and completion over a twenty-year period are not without interest here. It seems reasonably clear that after Augustine resigned as professor of rhetoric following his Christian conversion, he desired to remain a contemplative (more exactly a Christian Platonist contemplative) in the company of a few like-minded friends. He hoped to produce dialogues like those at Cassiciacum (*De Dialectica, De Musica, De Magistro, De Ordine*, etc.). It is important to recall that Augustine's Christian conversion is the final conversion in a prolonged journey of conversion. The first conversion was to philosophy itself as the search for true wisdom via Cicero's now lost *Hortensius*. The second conversion was to the realm of the "invisible," the "intelligible," the "spiritual" via "some writings of the Platonists."[2]

In his early years as Christian convert, priest, and even bishop,
Augustine never lost sight of the importance of these first two moments
in his long journey to Christian conversion. Like his rhetorical mentor,
Cicero, Augustine tried to be faithful to the search for both wisdom
and eloquence. Like his Platonist contemporaries and against his own
earlier materialist instincts, Augustine wanted, above all, to contem-
plate the truths of Christianity "spiritually." To Augustine, the great
example of the preaching of Ambrose in Milan demonstrated that
this ideal could be made actual: a spiritual ("Platonist") reading of the
Scriptures and all Christian doctrine which could "teach, delight, and
move" other like-minded searchers for wisdom and eloquence. Christian theology, as, philosophically, the true wisdom and, rhetorically,
the true eloquence, was the now available goal of the search of all true
seekers for wisdom and happiness. With this goal in mind, Augustine
intended to write reflections on all the "liberal arts" by dialogues with
his small group of Platonist friends—but except for *De Musica* and certain parts of his *De Dialectica* these texts are now lost. The extant dialogues of that early period (especially *De Ordine* and *De Magistro*) show
the promise of that desired life of communal contemplation—a life
which was not to be.

Why Augustine returned to North Africa—and especially the
"tough" provincial town of Hippo—remains something of a mystery
to his biographers. But whatever else that attempt to "go home again"
meant, Augustine still wanted to continue the *otium liberale* with a small
circle of friends in order to understand what he had come to believe.
The famous medieval motto—an ideal which shaped Western Christian thought for centuries—finds its roots in Augustine's use of both
dialectic and rhetoric throughout his life: "Believe in order to understand; understand in order to believe."

The ideal remained. But these early hopes for the *otium liberale*
proved illusory dreams. For Augustine was elected (forced seems the
more exact verb) by the acclamation of the people to become, first,
priest, and then, bishop, of Hippo. As bishop of an often unruly people,
he found himself with a whole new set of problems. Augustine was too
keen a rhetorician not to realize that he now had a very different audience: the remarkably diverse congregation of Hippo rather than the
little group of like-minded contemplative friends living the *otium liberale*.

This shift of audiences is a major impetus behind the emergence
of *DDC*. Augustine began to write this text shortly after he became

bishop in 396. But then—our problems with this text increase. For Augustine ceased writing *DDC* in 397 at book 3, paragraph 35 (i.e., in the midst of his discussion of the "rules for interpretation of the Scriptures by Tyconius"). The difficulties of interpretation of *DDC* increase when we realize that Augustine was also writing the *Confessions*—the great rhetoric of conversion—at this same period. Is this merely an historical accident of a prolific and deeply occasional writer? Or does this suggest that Augustine needed both the *Confessions* and *De Doctrina Christiana* to express his full rhetorical theology at this crucial moment of transition in his life—the transition from being a member of fellow contemplatives to becoming a bishop responsible for a congregation that, although it included the educated, was comprised principally of the uneducated? The rest of the text of *DDC*, moreover, was not completed until 427, that is, after Augustine's famous struggles and writings against, first, the Donatists and then, the Pelagians. Where, then, in the post-427 additions to *DDC* can one find the famously pessimistic Augustinian vision of the human situation: the new theological vision which emerged from the anti-Pelagian struggles, that troubled vision which has seemed to many commentators (including Pelagius and Julian of Eclanum) effectively to cancel out the relative optimism (especially on free will) of his earlier, more Platonist, dialogues?

Given the shifts from pre-Hippo Augustine to post-Hippo Augustine, it is amazing that this text (*DDC*) does form so clear a whole. In fact, there are very few references in the remainder of book 3 and book 4 to the Augustinian anti-Pelagian bleaker vision of human perversity. Nor in his famous *Retractions* at the end of his life does Augustine find it necessary to call into question the relative optimism on "pagan culture" to be found in *De Doctrina Christiana*. But the question recurs: should he have done so? In another context and on other theological questions, my claim would be the strong claim that *DDC* is a mature, indeed central, text of Augustine. For this exemplary hermeneutical text articulates the central theological vision (viz., *caritas*) that pervades Augustine's entire thought through all its remarkable twists and turns, its revisions, intensifications, exaggerations, and retractions up to and including the final bleak, even tormented, vision of the human condition surfacing in his anti-Pelagian writings. That strong claim, I admit, would be difficult to maintain given the "family quarrels" over the interpretation of the theology of Augustine in Western Christianity: Thomas vs. Niebuhr and Paul Tillich vs. the "Liberals," etc.

However, for the present question of how to read the complex text of *DDC*, my more modest claim is less controversial but, given the difficulties of the text, must also be tentative (which is to say it is also controversial). The claim is this: despite the significant interruption in the writing, the text of *DDC* nonetheless constitutes an authentic whole. *DDC* thereby discloses what we can know of Augustine's unwritten rhetorical theory even as it explicitly discloses his basic position on both biblical hermeneutics and the relationships of theology and culture. What the text of *DDC* is not fundamentally about, I believe, includes two other central Augustinian rhetorical exercises: first, although *DDC* includes apologetic elements, it is not rhetoric of Christian apologetics (here Augustine's earlier dialogues seem the more appropriate candidates); second, *DDC* is also not a rhetoric of conversion. Here his *Confessions*—which, to repeat, he was writing both before and after he broke off the writing of *DDC*—remains the central text in his extraordinary oeuvre. Indeed, some commentators have suggested that, in the course of writing *DDC* Augustine discovered that he needed a rhetoric of conversion in order to complete his Christian rhetorical essay—hence the *Confessions*. This hypothesis seems to me a fruitful guess. But even if a fuller Augustinian theory of religious (here Christian) rhetoric does also need an explicit rhetoric of conversion-confession, that fact only suggests the incompleteness of *DDC* as a theological-rhetorical theory, not the incorrectness of the theological-rhetorical theory actually rendered there. But this is to get a bit ahead of the story. We need first to see the final hermeneutical complication for any interpretation of the text *DDC* before risking an interpretation of this seemingly straightforward text.

3) The third complication is, indeed, the complex and conflictual history of effects of *De Doctrina Christiana*. Bluntly stated, given the actual conflict of readings, *DDC* might as well have been two texts, not one. As modern hermeneutics argues, the "history of the effects" of a classic text (i.e., its history of interpretations or readings) cannot be separated neatly from our present reading of the text itself.[3] Any later reading must, therefore, also address this "history of effects" problem as not simply an external problem to any good reading. In one sense, any Western Christian thinker (and a good number of post-Christian secular thinkers) are a part of the history of effects of the texts of Augustine. Indeed, one need only read any Eastern, that is, non-Augustinian, Christian thinker (e.g., Mircea Eliade) to understand the profoundly

Augustinian character in all the family quarrels of Western Christians: Catholic vs. Protestant and liberal vs. neo-orthodox.

If we attend to the history of readings of *DDC*, the problem of the unity of the text occurs on new grounds. The fact is that *DDC* has had such different readings that it almost seems to suggest that we have not one but two influential texts. The first text (books 1–3) is one of the crucial texts in Western biblical hermeneutics—that is, the text that employs Eastern allegorical methods in a Western anthropocentric (not Eastern cosmocentric) manner. This text gave the major impetus to Western theological figurative readings of the Christian classics, the Scriptures.[4] In more general cultural terms, this first text also provided the major impetus to a defense of "obscurity" as an intellectual value. For the medieval Augustinians (e.g., Bonaventure), a defense of "obscurity" was largely a defense of symbolic-religious texts. For moderns, since Petrarch, Erasmus, and Boccaccio through the Romantics and the Modernists to the hermeneutical theories of our own period, a defense of "obscurity" became a claim to the priority of the poetic and symbolic over the conceptual, the propositional, and, in that limited sense, the "literal."

It is not, of course, as if Augustine was simply an Alexandrian with a strong (indeed, too strong) emphasis on the "allegorical" sense of Scripture. Indeed, in *DDC* and elsewhere Augustine provides one of the great defenses of the "literal" sense of Scripture. This is the case even if a modern reader suspects that Augustine's heart (i.e., his Christian Platonist heart) is elsewhere: with his equally strong defense of the spiritual, allegorical sense of Scripture, Augustine, to be sure, does not strictly argue for the primacy of the "literal" sense in the manner of his later and very different admirers, Aquinas and Luther. Rather, Augustine's rhetorical sense of the importance and value of "obscurity" in *both* the literal and the spiritual senses of the Scriptures led him to employ the New Testament tradition of typological reading in a manner that could, in principle, honor both the "literal" and the "spiritual" senses of the scriptural texts. As Hans Frei justly argues, Augustine did envisage the world as formed by the history-like and realistic narratives rendered in the biblical stories as the "history of salvation."[5] In that post-Augustinian sense, Augustine could be said to accord a certain priority to the "literal" sense: i.e., as "plain sense of the Christian community." At the same time, Augustine's further rhetorical and theological interests lay elsewhere: assuming the plain sense

of Scriptures and assuming the traditional typological mode of readings, how can a Christian interpreter honor and control the reading of
both the "literal" and the "spiritual" senses of the text whenever the
"obscurity" of the text itself demanded such further reflections—as,
for Augustine, the Bible often did? Here the history of the readings
of books 1–3 fruitfully shows that Augustine's joint defense of both
obscurity in the text allied to a necessary plurality of readings is the
one sure clue to the heart of Augustinian biblical and cultural hermeneutics. This will also prove central to his rhetorical theory.

The second "text" (book 4) is often cited by historians of rhetoric
as a major influence of a different sort: viz., the narrowing of Western
rhetorical interests to concerns of style alone. On that reading, book
4 and its profound influence on Christian preaching and rhetoric is
charged with no little of the blame for the removal of philosophical
inventio from the rhetorical tradition in favor of an overconcern with
style—an overconcern which is always in danger of sliding into "mere
rhetoric." A strange charge to post to the door of the Ciceronian professor of rhetoric of Milan and Rome; or even, as I shall try to show,
to post on the door of the beleaguered bishop of Hippo!

But the charge would basically hold if all we could learn from *DDC*
on the rhetoric is found in book 4. But what if the text really constitutes a whole? What if books 1–3 effectively (if largely implicitly) give
Augustine's new suggestions for Christian theological *inventio*? What
if the hermeneutical concerns of books 1–3 constitute a new form of
philosophical-theological *inventio* suggesting new topics and new forms
of argument for the new Christian reading of both the old classics (the
liberal arts) and the new classics (the Scriptures)? Then what is really
involved in Augustinian *inventio* is a new model for the relationship of
Christianity and culture. That Augustinian model formed medieval
and Renaissance culture and continues to inform much contemporary
Christian theology, including the magisterial and here clearly Augustinian new principles for *inventio* in the oeuvre of Nathan A. Scott, Jr.
On this reading, the text of *De Doctrina Christiana* must be read as a
whole. On this reading, moreover, the Augustine of *DDC* never suffered the nightmare of his contemporary Jerome who dreamt that at
the Last Judgment he declared himself a Christian only to have Christ
condemn him as a "Ciceronian." Nor did the Augustine of *DDC* share
the belief of his North African forensic rhetorician predecessor, Tertullian, that the question "What has Athens to do with Jerusalem" was a

"merely" rhetorical question to which the implied answer is, of course, "nothing." In one contemporary language, the question of *DDC* is: what has a hermeneutics of *inventio* to do with a rhetoric of style? In Augustine's own context the question is: what have books 1–3 to do with book 4? Or even, what does the Ciceronian professor of rhetoric of Milan and Rome have to do with the bishop of Hippo?

INVENTIO AS HERMENEUTICS: BOOK 1

> There are two things necessary to the treatment of the Scriptures: a way of discovering those things which are to be understood, and a way of teaching what we have learned. We shall speak first of discovery and second of teaching (1.1).[6]

In one sense, Augustine places the reader *in media res* in a pursuit of principles of discovery (*inventio*) for interpreting the Scriptures. More exactly, we are quickly informed that in order to understand the Scriptures we must pay attention to two related realities: things (*res*) and signs (*signa*). There follow brief examples of this distinction; for example, the thing "stone" in contrast to the "stone" on which Jacob placed his head. The latter is both a "thing" and a "sign," that is, "a thing used to signify something else." As influential and complex as Augustine's theory of signs will prove to be, however, here in book 1 we principally find his characteristic insistence that in order to understand signs at all, we must first understand things.

But this typical move leads just as swiftly to another famous Augustinian distinction: between *frui* (to enjoy) and *uti* (to use). Both of these realities, in turn, are quickly related to our loves and desires. What is going on here? As the next chapters (3 to 34) suggest by their frequent if abbreviated Augustinian excursions into dialectic and rhetoric (many of the chapters are, in fact, capsule summaries of arguments from his earlier dialogues), what we find in book 1, in the most general terms, is the fundamental "discovery" (and "method of discovery") informing Augustine's entire thought: the reality of love (*caritas*). Simultaneously, we find that Augustine, the Christian convert-rhetor, has not and will not abandon his first two "conversions" (to philosophy as the search for wisdom and to the realm of the intelligible, invisible, immutable, spiritual) after his Christian conversion—even after his forced assumption of duties as bishop-preacher at Hippo.

To return, then, to the distinction between *frui* and *uti*. The distinction itself is clear: "To enjoy something is to cling to it with love for its own sake. To use something, however, is to employ it in obtaining that which you love, provided it is worthy of love" (1, 4). In the next chapter this distinction is quickly linked with the search for true things (res): "The things which are to be enjoyed are the Father, the Son, and the Holy Spirit, a single Trinity, a certain supreme thing common to all who enjoy it, if, indeed, it is a thing and not rather the cause of all things, or both a thing and a cause" (5).

This all seems clear enough, save, as Augustine knows, how are we to know God, the "supreme reality?" Augustine does not hesitate to insist that God could be discovered by us only if God gave the grace (gift-power) for the discovery. A finely Augustinian paradox ensues: God must give us the grace to discover God, and yet we are inexorably driven and called to that discovery both before and after grace comes as pure gift. *DDC* is presumably written for an audience who is already in some sense "converted" yet still needs to discover the ways to understand the supreme reality who converted them and thereby allowed them to find new principles of *inventio* ("Believe *in order to understand*").

At the same time, one cannot help noticing that another audience also seems to surface in the speculations and arguments of book 1: those not converted to Christianity as well as the always present "unconverted" aspects of converted Christians—i.e., all those who need to "understand in order to believe." What any rhetorical thinker with that kind of intellectual problem most needs is some new form of ancient rhetorical *inventio* by means of which to discover the places (*topoi*) where true arguments can be found. To provide a full rhetorical theory, Augustine's principle of rhetorical *inventio* must also prove a matter of transformational *ethos*. That *ethos* will, in the Augustinian vision, necessarily be a complex one, at one and the same time respecting our desire (*eros*) for wisdom and happiness while honoring, above all, the fact that only God (the "supreme reality") can give us the living gift of grace (*agape*) to turn us around (*conversio*) to see the truth of things and thereby to transform both our understanding and our wills by reordering both rightly. Contrary to many readings of Augustine, he does develop a rhetoric of *inventio*. But his notion of *inventio* is necessarily neither Platonic nor Aristotelian nor even Ciceronian. Augustinian *inventio* is necessarily Christian theological (which includes, but cannot be confined to, philosophical *inventio*). His principal audiences are Christian interpreters who wish to know how to interpret the Scriptures correctly. A proper hermeneutics here is, therefore, simultaneously a rhetoric of discovery or *inventio*. For only that kind of *inventio* will allow Christians to know how to find the new true topics revealed by the "supreme reality," God, in the true "signs" of the Scriptures.

Nor does Augustine disappoint his readers. Unlike some of his later writings (think of the *massa damnata* motif of the anti-Pelagian writings on sin and grace, or even *The City of God* on the "virtues" of the pagans become "splendid vices" and the Empire itself become a "robber-band writ large"), grace in *DDC* does not simply confront nature to make us recognize our perversity, habits, sins. Rather, even the occasional references to such perversity and the allusions to our human, willful genius at trapping ourselves by our habits seems to function in *DDC* as unsettling but not finally incoherent moments in a larger theologically transformational context.

That key to a true interpretation is *caritas*: the transformation of our *eros* by God's *agape* of grace.[7] This alone frees us to discover both the true wisdom of all our inexorable desires and strivings for wisdom and happiness and to discover the true way to interpret (and thereby argue from) the signs of Scriptures, the new "classics" of the converted ones. In Augustine's mature theological understanding, the fall caused a rupture between our knowledge of reality and our use of signs. Even in his earlier theories on "signs" and "things," it is clear for the rhetorical thought of Augustine that we can only read "signs" correctly if we somehow already understand the "realities" to which they refer. Hermeneutically construed, Augustine's principle can be stated clearly: we must have some preunderstanding of the subject matter in order to interpret the "signs" in texts correctly. On this reading, therefore, Augustine's position in book 1 is not dependent on either his implicit philosophical position on "sense" and "reference" or on his theological reading of the Fall as causing the rupture of "signs" from "things" that he believed he found in his own lifelong convalescence. As important as these principles are for the implications of Augustine's fuller theory of "signs" and "things," they do not determine the fundamental hermeneutics of *inventio* of book 1. For that, we need only understand initially that we must have some understanding of the *res* (the subject matter) if we are to understand "signs" at all. But how can we have a true understanding? That is Augustine's problem in book 1.

The highly abbreviated reflections of book 1 can be considered, therefore, both dialectically and rhetorically. They are rhetorical and dialectical arguments on why God alone (as true *res*) can be truly enjoyed and can only be truly enjoyed by one who has been given the grace from the same God to enjoy "that supreme thing." These arguments (most of them, to repeat, summaries of the dialectical and rhetorical arguments of his earlier Dialogues) take up familiar Christian Platonist themes. The drive to true wisdom is the drive to enjoy the invisible and the immutable and is only fulfilled if the immutable discloses itself. The drive to true happiness for our highly mutable wills meets two chief obstacles: the multiplicity (and thereby internal conflict) of our desires and the traps we set for ourselves by allowing our habits to congeal into the perversity of enjoying what we should use (all mutable things, especially ourselves) and using what we should enjoy (especially the immutable, the invisible, the eternal supreme reality, God).

These two drives to wisdom and happiness constitute the fundamental *eros* that at once impels us and traps us. Only through the gift of the self-revelation of the immutable in incarnation become grace for us could *we* discover true wisdom and true happiness. For only then could we enjoy what is to be enjoyed (viz., God) and love all else by using it for the sake of that love-enjoyment of God. For Augustine, even the neighbor is to be loved as "used," that is, for the sake of God: recall Nygren's anger at Augustine's interpretation of Christian neighbor-love as *caritas*.[8]

But faith and hope for the converted render possible a transformation of the self which allows for a new search for the true discovery of wisdom and happiness. That transformation is *caritas*: since God's grace-*agape* is sheerly given, it frees the *eros* of our necessary drive to wisdom and happiness to the new synthesis of *caritas* and, therefore, new possibilities for the discovery of true wisdom and true happiness. This transformational principle of *caritas* would seem to suggest that, for Augustine, rhetorical discovery (*inventio*) is entirely a matter of the proper *ethos*. But even aside from the notorious (or, at least, anti-Quintillian [*sic*]) problem of the preacher who does not, alas, practice what is preached (book 4), this strictly *ethos* reading does not seem to hit the mark on how *caritas* also transforms the *logos* of the Christian rhetorician for the discovery of true understanding.

Caritas is needed, to be sure, to transform the *ethos* of the rhetor. But *caritas* is also another kind of clue, and one more related to *logos* and thereby *inventio*. For *caritas*, formulated as the principle of "love of God and love of neighbor," becomes the means by which new wisdom is born. "Faith" for Augustine can now be understood as a "wisdom born of *caritas*" (B. Lonergan). *Caritas*, formulated as a transformational principle, transforms both *ethos* and *logos*. *Caritas* becomes the means to discover the true meaning (and thereby the true arguments) from the new "classics"—the Scriptures. Yet, however new these biblical classics may be for the educated of antiquity,[9] they will be classic only because they are the authoritative "signs" of the self-manifestation of the true *res*, "the supreme thing," or "cause of all things," God. These signs, as books 2 and 3 will show, will yield their true meaning (and their new topics) only to the one who has grasped (or, more accurately, been grasped by) the true *res*—that is, to the one who knows that divine reality by knowing that the central topic of both the whole Scriptures and all our desires must be "the love of God and love of neighbor." The *caritas* principle of Augustine, moreover, is clearly christomorphic but still more clearly radically theocentric.

So much is this the case that Augustine does not hesitate to state what would upset many a biblical Christian even today: "Thus a man supported by faith, hope, and charity, with an unspoken hold upon them, does not need the Scriptures except for the instruction of others. And many live by these things in solitude without books" (39). So central is the *res* of God for both *ethos* and *logos* that true Christians could live without the *signa* (the words of Scripture). And yet we have these "signs" and they will help us to discover true wisdom provided we keep clearly in mind the fundamental principle of Augustine: the love of God and love of neighbor. *Caritas*, then, as both *ethos* and *logos*, will prove to be the central hermeneutical new principle of discovery (*inventio*) for both the signs of *eros* in the search for true wisdom in the classics of the pagans and the signs of *agape* in the new classics, the Scriptures. As a transformative (and not purely confrontational) principle, moreover, Augustinian *caritas* will allow the Christian rhetor to continue to learn from the wisdom of the pagan classics even while interpreting the new wisdom of the new classics of the Scriptures. Athens (and Milan and Rome), it seems, still have a good deal to do with Jerusalem (and Hippo). For theology and culture are reunited rhetorically under the new principle of *inventio*, love of God and love of neighbor.

ON DISCERNING THE SIGNS OF THE NEW
CLASSICS: A DEFENSE OF OBSCURITY AND PLURALITY
(BOOKS 2 AND 3)

Book 1, therefore, has been concerned with "things," especially the supreme thing, God, and the principle (as both *ethos* and *logos*) by means of which Christian interpreters can find principles of discovery for true wisdom and true happiness (*caritas*). But God, we have also been informed, has revealed Godself through certain "signs." The supreme "sign" of that self-revelation (viz., the "incarnation") is mentioned in book 1. Curiously, however, Augustine does not dwell upon the incarnation when he comes to reflect upon "signs" themselves. But perhaps this strange silence is lessened if we remember that the *caritas* principle is, for Augustine, precisely what the incarnation as sign reveals about what has happened to us through incarnation. Indeed, the principle of love of God and love of neighbor is what Augustine consistently employs when he does a Christian typological (and, in that sense, christological) reading of the figurative signs of the Old Testament.

It does no injustice to Augustine's relative silence on the incarnation as the "supreme sign" of the "supreme *res*" to suggest that his fundamental theological presupposition on signs in *DDC* and elsewhere can be restated in modern theological-hermeneutical terms. That presupposition is this: for the Jew and the Christian (the Muslim is, significantly, i.e., hermeneutically, different here), the relationship of the "texts" of the Scriptures and the "events" to which those texts bear authoritative (i.e., canonical) witness is this—the revelation occurs in events of divine self-disclosure (e.g., Sinai or the incarnation) to which the biblical texts witness.[10] The "events" are both historical (e.g., Jesus of Nazareth) and trans-historical (i.e., the divine self-disclosure in Jesus the Christ). The texts, the Scriptures, are not the revelation but are the authoritative witness to the original revelation. The Christian confession is, "We believe *in* Jesus Christ *with* the apostles." The texts of the New Testament are the texts of apostolic witness to the revelation of God in the event and person of Jesus Christ. That original revelation continues, in the Christian community, by being re-presented through the primary "signs" of word (proclamation) and sacrament (which is the sign which renders present what it signified—recall Augustine on the Donatists).

To translate this theological hermeneutic into the terms of books 2 and 3: Augustine's principle concern is to discover the relationship of the authoritative signs of witness (the Scriptures) to the supreme sign (incarnation) of the supreme *res* (God). Book 1 has articulated the needed principle of discovery or *inventio* (*caritas*). For Augustine, this principle is what Christian interpreters should use to interpret the authoritative texts of the Scriptures, i.e., these word-signs of witness to that supreme sign-event of the self-disclosure of the supreme *res*. To read the scripture as Scripture is to read it theologically through the christomorphic and theocentric Augustinian principle of *caritas*. The signs of the New Testament should be read, for Augustine, typologically. Both Testaments, for Augustine, should be read both literally and spiritually, depending on the nature of the written "signs" involved and the interpreter's knowledge of "true things" through the principle of love of God and love of neighbor.

Even if we grant all these Augustinian terminological and hermeneutical-theological presuppositions, however, any reader of the Scriptures realizes, with Augustine, that the interpreter still finds a host of difficulties in interpreting the word-signs of Scripture. Some of those difficulties can be treated, as they are by Augustine, with relative ease. For example, we can distinguish, with Augustine, between "natural" and "conventional" signs. We can also take common-sense methods in dealing with many of the problems of "unknown signs." As an obvious example, we can learn the original languages: Augustine, in fact, knew Greek poorly and probably had no Hebrew at all: hence his great concern in *DDC* with the best Latin translation. Other Augustinian methods of textual discernment (e.g., his Pythagorean-like love of numbers and music) strike most contemporary interpreters of Scripture as a part of the "common sense" of Augustine's late classical culture but not of ours. Still other Augustinian methods—viz., rhetorical analyses of the "tropes" in the Scriptures—live on in new forms in contemporary historical-critical and literary-critical interpretations of the Scriptures. Still other Augustinian suggestions (e.g., the importance of "context" and the relationship of parts to the scriptural "whole") were standard *topoi* of scriptural interpretation before Augustine, and have remained so, in modified forms, ever since (e.g., form-critical analysis of context, or redactional analysis of the whole of an individual gospel in order to understand the parts). Augustine's own candidate for a theocentric principle of understanding the *res* (viz., the principle of love of God and love of neighbor) and, thereby, the signs of Scripture, survives, at best, as one candidate among several for that much disputed theological role.

These Augustinian analyses are important but familiar. However, three characteristically Augustinian positions in books 2 and 3 came to bear practically a life of their own. They demand, by their novelty, further reflection.

1) The first question is how to value and understand "ambiguous" signs of the Scriptures, especially how to discern "figurative" from "literal" senses of particular texts. To treat the latter problem first: Augustine is both clear and consistent in his use of the *caritas* principle as the principal way to distinguish the literal senses and the figurative senses of particular passages (e.g., book 3.10: "Therefore a method of determining whether a location is literal or figurative must be established. And generally this method consists in this: that whatever appears in the divine Word that does not literally pertain to virtuous behavior or to the truth of faith you must take to be figurative. Virtuous behavior pertains to the love of God and one's neighbor; the truth of faith pertains to a knowledge of God and one's neighbor").

So we do possess a principle ("generally") that can help us discover the true meaning of difficult passages. But we also have a hermeneutical principle which defends not only "figurative" meanings but also the ambiguity and obscurity often present in the Scriptures, that obscurity which gives rise to this difficult issue of what is "literal" and what is "figurative." Throughout books 2 and 3 (and, under a new form in book 4's defense of the "true eloquence" of the Scriptures) we find Augustine providing one of his most original, debatable, and influential hermeneutical moves: a defense of obscurity and ambiguity. Among several examples, consider the discussion of book 2.6. We are informed there (in the midst of Augustine's fascinating interpretation of the "teeth" and "shorn sheep" metaphors in the Song of Songs) that there are both good negative reasons for scriptural obscurity and good positive reasons. Negatively, these obscure passages help to conquer our pride by hard work. They discipline our natural disdain for what seems too obvious. Indeed, Augustine does not doubt that God has provided these obscurities for such discipline.

Positively, those obscure words and passages are wise (and, later, "eloquent") because "no one doubts that things are perceived more readily through similitudes and that what is sought with difficulty is discovered with more pleasure." This is an interesting (and debatable) hermeneutical principle—and one which will free Augustine from his earlier pre-conversion disdain for the "vulgarity" and "obscurity" of the Scriptures. In sum, for Augustine, the principle of the theological value of obscurity and ambiguity allows him to argue for the Scriptures as the new classic signs—wiser and even more eloquent (book 4) than his own beloved pagan classics. Just as *caritas* can transform human *eros*, so, it seems, scriptural "obscurity" paradoxically can transform Augustine's earlier pre-conversion assessment of the status of these scriptural signs in relationship to the "clearer" signs of the pagan classics. This same principle of obscurity as a value, as noted above, will live a strange after-life in the Augustinian humanists of the Renaissance (Petrarch, Erasmus, Boccaccio). In yet another sea change, the Augustinian principle will find another life among Romantics and Modernists under the rubric of the "priority of the symbolic" (obscure-ambiguous) over the conceptual, prepositional, literal—an ironic twist, surely, to Augustine's defense of scriptural obscurity.

2) This "defense of obscurity" can also illuminate another aspect of the Augustinian program—viz., the famous analogy (borrowed from Irenaeus) of book 2.50 on stealing "Egyptian gold." This Old Testament analogy is used by Augustine to insist that, even in the new rhetorical situation where the new classics of Scripture are not the primary classics, the Christian rhetor can still use the classics of the pagan "liberal arts." Indeed, those disciplines, like the gold and silver of the Egyptians stolen by the departing Israelites, really belong to the new Israelites because these disciplines were not invented by the pagans at all. Rather, they were discovered as already existing by the grace of God who created them. Christians need not reject these treasures (*pace* Tertullian and Jerome's nightmare) since as the new Israelites they already own them.

The classics of Scripture are for Augustine both wiser and more eloquent than the pagan classics, for the Scriptures alone are the signs or witness to the direct self-disclosures of the divine. Still, the Christian rhetor, informed by the Scriptures themselves through this new interpretation of the figurative meaning of the Israelite theft of Egyptian gold and silver, can now freely use all these treasures as their own. The original biblical image and the Christian analogical argument from it may be more than a little strained. However, if one considers the

Tertullian option and the positive history of effects of this surprising ·
theft-imagery, latter-day rhetoricians and theologians cannot but agree
that Augustine's figurative reading of scriptural obscurity allowed the
"gold and silver" of the "liberal disciplines" to find a continued life in
medieval Christianity and, through the medievals, in Western modernity. The great modern discipline of theology and culture, to which
Nathan A. Scott Jr. has made such exemplary contributions, finds its
original Western Christian impetus from the surprising imagery of
theft.

3) A final note on how to interpret the signs of the Scriptures is
also worth noting: Augustine's defense of a plurality of readings of
the Scriptures (book 3.27). What is hermeneutically interesting here is
that Augustine does not allow the author's meaning in the Scriptures
to determine the meaning of the text. God, as the supreme author,
can use the human author to state a meaning which even the author
did not understand but which some later reader (e.g., Augustine) could
then discern ("And certainly the Spirit of God, who worked through
that author, undoubtedly foresaw that this meaning would occur to the
reader or listener").

This theological principle provides for a remarkable flexibility of
meaning to the scriptural texts and for a genuine plurality of readings.
That plurality, moreover, was bound to increase once Augustine's own
principle of *caritas* was also questioned. In sum, the more one moves
into books 2 and 3, the more flexible do Augustine's hermeneutical
principles of book 1 actually become in practice: the ambiguity and
obscurity of the scriptural signs are defended; the figurative begins to
play almost as great a role as the literal sense (in contrast to Aquinas
and Luther); the pagan classics of the liberal disciplines will continue
to play a role for Christian interpreters and thereby provide more
readings still; and, finally, since God is the ultimate author of these
texts, any hermeneutical primacy accorded the "author's intention"
becomes relatively unimportant. The "signs" of books 2 and 3 will
be dependent, of course, on the *res* of book 1. But as the Augustinian
theological principle of *inventio* became more and more questionable
both within later Christian readings of the Scriptures as well as in secular interpretations on the scriptural texts, some modern hermeneutes
turned rhetoricians have been tempted to find the hermeneutical principles of books 2 and 3 as the true wisdom for rhetorical discovery in
the "signs" of Augustine's own text. This would leave books 1, 2, and 3

a theological truncated text but still a hermeneutically interesting one. That new text would bear strong family resemblance to Gadamer's hermeneutics and even to his suggestion that modern rhetorical theory needs hermeneutics for its own process of *inventio*. At the same time, modern hermeneutics may be construed as ancient rhetoric modernized (i.e., historicized). But that is, to be sure, another story—and one perhaps best entitled, "The Revenge of the Egyptians."

BOOK 4: ELOQUENCE AND CLARITY

If the claim that books 1–3 present Augustine's discussion of rhetorical and theological *inventio* for discovering true wisdom by means of correct principles of interpretation of the new classics (the Scriptures), then the familiar suggestion that the strictly rhetorical interests of *DDC* may be found in book 4 on style becomes highly unlikely. Rather, on my reading, book 4's analysis of the need for the preacher to instruct, delight, and move (i.e., persuade to action) suggests that rhetorical structure, as first, always needs principles of discovery or interpretation (*inventio*) of books 1–3. Augustine is, to be sure, greatly concerned with style (or styles subdued, temperate, and grand) and does stretch Cicero a good deal in chapter 17 to link the Augustinian styles directly to the "teach, delight, persuade" motifs of Cicero. I admit that the opening sentence of book 4.2 is somewhat disconcerting for my reading of *DDC* as providing a full rhetorical theory of *inventio* insofar as it seems to suggest a somewhat sophistic understanding of rhetoric—indeed, one which Augustine's own earlier antisophistic remarks seemed firmly to exclude. Yet even in that section, the rhetorical thrust of the whole chapter (as well as Augustine's reluctance to explicate his full rhetorical theory either here or elsewhere) suggest that Augustine's concern with a rhetoric of instruction (and thereby *inventio*) remains his central rhetorical concern. More exactly, by now familiar Augustinian motifs return, on this reading, in new guises: e.g., the true wisdom of the new classics, the Scriptures, has also become true eloquence (especially in Paul and Amos). Still, the preacher of biblical wisdom and eloquence must not try to imitate the obscurity-profundity of the Bible. But why not—especially given Augustine's own plea for preachers to "imitate" classical models of eloquence as, in effect, a partial replacement for lack of formal rhetorical training?

The reason seems clear enough: the preacher is not the inspired author of Scripture who can be used by God to speak obscure truths which even the author need not understand. Rather, the preacher is the interpreter of this true wisdom and eloquence. As interpreter, the preacher should not presume to imitate scriptural obscurity; the preacher should instead render biblical obscurity clear for the instruction, delight, and persuasion of the congregation. The preacher needs rhetorical and theological principles of interpretation of the Scriptures if he is to instruct clearly (books 1–3). The preacher also needs some knowledge of "styles" (e.g., through imitation of classical styles or through rhetorical education in style) if he or she is to delight and thereby hold the congregation's attention and to move them, i.e., persuade them to action. But above all, the preacher, as interpreter of often obscure scriptural passages, must strive for clarity. Clarity alone can instruct the kind of mixed audience every preacher finds in the true wisdom and eloquence of Scripture. And only such clear instruction can properly use whatever rhetoric is both available and necessary (e.g., to delight and to move). So Augustine is not sophistic after all: at least insofar as "delighting" and a "moving" are controlled by the demands of instruction and *inventio*—and that specified by the demands of the discovery of the rules for true interpretation of books 1–3.

Perhaps Augustine, the former professor of rhetoric, might even be able to agree that my interpretation of the rhetorical and theological theory sometimes obscure in the signs of *his* text is not forced. What the bishop of Hippo might think of his latter-day theological descendants is a more unsettling question which had best be left to another day. And yet, whatever the answer to that latter question, some of Augustine's rhetorical principles seem to live in new forms in our own rhetorical context: theological "charity" become, for example, Wayne Booth's hermeneutical model of the text as "friend"; scriptural "obscurity" become the "priority of the poetic" in modern hermeneutics and literary criticism; the divine impetus to a plurality of readings not determined by the author's meaning become the "loss of the author" of modern deconstructionists; the demand for clarity in communication become arguments over the relationships of a rhetoric of instruction to a rhetoric of delight and a rhetoric of *ethos*—and all three to a fuller rhetoric of persuasion in many contemporary rhetorical debates on the relationships of the topics and the tropes. What Augustine might add to those arguments rises or falls, I suggest, on whether we read *De Doctrina Christiana* as one text or two. If one wants Augustine's apologetic rhetoric, one should read his early dialogues. If one desires Augustine's rhetoric of conversion, one must turn to the *Confessions*. But if one wishes to find Augustine's rhetoric of *inventio* as a key moment in any Christian persuasion to action, then his deliberations on both *res et signa* for correct rhetorical-theological interpretation in *De Doctrina Christiana* makes that great text the text to read and interpret. For all the new rhetorical theologies, therefore, *tolle, lege.*

THE DIALECTIC OF ORALITY AND LITERACY
THE CASE OF BOOK 4 OF AUGUSTINE'S *DE DOCTRINA CHRISTIANA**

John D. Schaeffer

John Schaeffer critiques twentieth-century scholarship on De Doctrina Christiana *by contending that book 4 has often been misread through a lens that privileges written composition, so much a part of present consciousness but not necessarily applicable to Augustine's own time and rhetorical exigence. In contrast to scholars such as Stanley Fish and others who read book 4 as a treatise on writing sermons, Schaeffer contends that Augustine's purpose was to advise Christian preachers how to deliver extemporaneous oral sermons of the kind Augustine himself delivered: sermons that express the preacher's inner state formed by a combination of scriptural study and prayer. Schaeffer resists drawing binaries between orality and literacy and describes the early Christian practice of oral performances of scriptural texts (complete with chants, gestures, and rhythmic effects) necessary to spreading a textually based religion under circumstances of low literacy rates, but also consistent with expression of an authentic Christian self shaped by doctrine and inspired by the Holy Spirit. To best convey scriptural truth, Augustine looks to Roman rhetoric. Augustine unites the wisdom of Scripture with the eloquence of an authentic speaker who has so thoroughly absorbed, ruminated on, and digested the abundant wisdom and beauty of God's revelation that it is a part of him from which he can draw extemporaneously. This abundance also gives the preacher a source from which to make spontaneous judgments about adapting and blending the Roman conception of the low, middle, and grand styles to the preacher's present rhetorical needs, liberating the three levels of style to serve the preacher's needs to teach, please, and persuade as they develop during the sermon.*

Augustine's *De Doctrina Christiana* has been praised as a landmark text in the history of rhetoric that set the agenda for Christian education until the end of the seventeenth century.[1] And yet scholars as diverse

---

* Originally published as "The Dialectic of Orality and Literacy: The Case of Book 4 of Augustine's *De doctrina christiana.*" *PMLA* 3.5 (1996): 1133–45. Headnote by Drew M. Loewe.

as Christine M. Sutherland, Thomas O. Sloane, and Stanley Fish, who cite book 4 of the *De Doctrina* as the model for their own rhetorical and stylistic analyses, claim that Augustine is writing against the tradition of classical rhetoric.[2] Drawing parallels between the *De Doctrina* and the secular writings of seventeenth-century scientists, Sutherland asserts that both disavow rhetoric and that Augustine is "antirhetorical" (35). Sloane, who argues that Augustine abandons Ciceronian skepticism, agrees with Fish that Augustine's antirhetorical rhetoric is paradigmatic for seventeenth-century literature. In a detailed analysis meant to show that book 4 actually contradicts the prescriptions of classical rhetoric, Fish maintains that Augustine describes several stages in the achievement of eloquence only to discard each in turn. Fish's summary of the book reflects this interpretation:

> Eloquence is irrelevant, because it is an adjunct of wisdom.
>
> Wisdom is irrelevant, insofar as the speaker has any responsibility for it, since to be wise he need only remember the words of Scripture.
>
> Persuasion and all the arts of persuasion, including the three styles, are irrelevant, since the truth alone persuades and its persuasiveness is independent of the speaker's skills and even of his intentions.
>
> Considerations of time, place, and audience are irrelevant, for the same reasons. (37–38)

According to Fish, Augustine effectively declares the speaker irrelevant as well when he tells would-be preachers to pray for God to put good speeches in their mouths (38).

Fish claims that the *De Doctrina* is addressed to "the writer of sermons" (38) and, given Augustine's assertion that only God persuades, asks, "Why write sermons at all?" (39). But the *De Doctrina* is not about writing sermons; it is about delivering sermons orally and extemporaneously.[3] In 1922, Roy Deferrari proved conclusively that Augustine, like most other fourth-century preachers, delivered sermons extempore (104–6). In 1930 Thérèse Sullivan also noted that Augustine's sermons were delivered extemporaneously, and she carefully analyzed the rhythm and sound effects in book 4.[4] However, like critics who trace the influence of the *De Doctrina* on seventeenth-century English literature, most twentieth-century Augustine scholars have neglected the work's orality. Unlike Fish, Henri-Irénée Marrou finds parts of book 4 too rhetorical. Specifically, he points to Augustine's treatment of oral effects as evidence of the Second Sophistic movement's decadent influence (*Saint Augustin*, 2nd ed., 511). Though these effects would have been produced extemporaneously, Marrou apparently sees them as deliberate and studied, for he refers to them as "littéraire" 'literary' (506). In a later work, Marrou retracts the assertion that Augustine's rhetoric is decadent, but he never refers to the extempore nature of preaching in late antiquity (*retractatio*). Similarly, in a classic essay on the *sermo humilis*, Erich Auerbach alludes to Augustine's rhythmic and vocal effects but does not mention that Augustine would have produced them extemporaneously (27–66).[5]

If book 4 of the *De Doctrina* is read as advice on how to deliver an extemporaneous sermon, Augustine's recommendations suggest that he is not simply opposing classical rhetoric: he is disavowing the rhetoric of the Second Sophistic movement and returning to the orally based rhetoric of republican Rome, which he is adapting to a textually based religion attended by an emerging sense of interiority.[6] I propose to develop this alternative reading of book 4 by reviewing the scholarship on the *De Doctrina* and on literacy and orality in general; exploring the role of oral performance in Jewish and Christian worship; examining the place of orality in classical rhetoric; analyzing the three main concerns of book 4—Scripture reading, prayer, and style—as constitutive of and propaedeutic to extemporaneous oral performance; and discussing the implications of my reading for modern criticism of orality and writing.

I

Historians of rhetoric agree on the crucial role the *De Doctrina Christiana* played during the Middle Ages. The work was copied far more frequently than Quintilian's *Institutio* or Cicero's *Orator, Brutus*, or *De oratore* (Conley 82). In fact, Augustine provided a Christian justification for the continued study of Cicero (Conley 78); book 4 appears to have been viewed simply as Augustine's attempt to Christianize Cicero. Augustine's exegetical method, laid out in the first three books of the *De Doctrina*, helped stimulate the Carolingian renaissance and later entered the familiar canons of medieval exegesis. The medieval reading of the *De Doctrina* seems to have ignored extemporaneity, even though medieval preaching manuals, which provided proof texts, sample outlines, and catalogs of figures arranged thematically, were obviously reference works for writing sermons (Murphy 269–355).

During the Renaissance, the *De Doctrina* was consciously applied to written rhetoric. In examining Donne's sermon style and its antecedents, John Chamberlin traces the influence of the *De Doctrina* on humanist educational writings like Erasmus's *Ratio Studiorum* (1518) and *Ecclesiastes* (1535). The second, a manual for preaching, refers frequently to the *De Doctrina* but assumes that sermons will be written out (Chamberlin 18–25, 69–72, 126–27). As Chamberlin points out, Erasmus draws his theory of preaching more from Ciceronian forensic rhetoric than from Augustine's writings (71). Erasmus and other Renaissance humanists still saw rhetoric and writing as propaedeutic to eloquence. Yet there were few opportunities for extemporaneous performance, and writing eventually became an end even while it was still regarded as a means. Humanist rhetoric thus resulted in writing with what Walter Ong calls a strong "oral residue" ("Oral Residue").

Among modern rhetoricians, only Kenneth Burke seems to have explored Augustine's orality and its role in the development of Augustine's idea of "innerness" (51). In *The Rhetoric of Religion*, which examines how Augustine's conversion to Christianity followed his growing ability to perform the mental operations characteristic of literacy, Burke shows that Augustine found in the singing of psalms a model of spontaneous address to God (55). Moreover, in analyzing how "openness" became for Augustine the dialectical counterpart of "innerness" (58–59), Burke points out that the psychological implications of these concepts are twinned with their textual applications, for example, in opening the inner meaning of a scriptural passage (62–65). The play between orality and literacy and between textuality and conversion that Burke finds in the *Confessions* is also present in book 4 of the *De Doctrina*, but it has remained unnoticed there.

Philosophical readings of the *De Doctrina* also generally ignore Augustine's orality. Two recent examples are the studies by Edward English and by Duane Arnold and Pamela Bright. Although David Chidester has examined Augustine's use of seeing and hearing as metaphors for religious discourse, he makes no reference to the *De Doctrina* or to Burke. Thus, despite the efforts of an earlier generation of scholars, the prominence of oral performance for Augustine and for other preachers in late antiquity has been overlooked for several decades, even by literary scholars acutely interested in issues of orality and literacy. Instead, since the late 1960s, literary scholars have simply assumed that Augustine was writing about writing, perhaps because poststructuralist orthodoxy pitted writing against orality and speech in a binary opposition.

Jacques Derrida has argued successfully for the priority, both temporal and logical, of writing to speech. Objecting to Western epistemology's privileging of the oral, a position he finds enshrined in Ferdinand de Saussure's linguistics, Derrida asserts in *Of Grammatology* that signification ought to be included under the rubric of writing.[7] According to John M. Ellis, Derrida fails to perceive that Saussure's emphasis on orality is itself a response to nineteenth-century philologists' emphasis on texts as sources and an attempt to reestablish a balance between writing and orality (19–21). Ong, who has championed the primacy of orality, has called Derrida's thinking "historically unreflective" and "the most text-bound of all ideologies" (*Orality* 168–69).

Critics who see orality and literacy as a binary opposition have been challenged by Brian Street, who accuses anthropologists of using an "autonomous model" of literacy (19–65), that is, treating literacy as a discrete phenomenon independent of social or institutional contexts. Jonathan Goldberg, who has addressed the tension between writing and orality in the English Renaissance, uses close readings of sixteenth- and early-seventeenth-century calligraphy textbooks to reveal the ideologies operating in the creation of standardized forms of writing and thus to discredit the autonomous model of literacy. By arguing that the handbooks could not account for writing simply as a replication of speech, even though their authors tried vainly to do so, Goldberg ultimately asserts the uniqueness of writing and thus justifies Derrida's critique. Indeed, Fish, Sutherland, and Sloane also seem to be operating within the autonomous model. They see literacy and orality as polar opposites and approach book 4 only from the perspective of literacy. By contrast, I believe book 4 makes more sense read according to what Street calls the "ideological model"; that is, it should be read as a product of social institutions that support and incorporate a mixture of orality and literacy (95–128). Instead of asserting the hegemony of either writing or orality, such a reading reveals that a rigid distinction between orality and literacy cannot do justice to the complexity of the social context in which Augustine wrote.

II

What do scholars know about Augustine's preaching and about the milieu of late antiquity? Like other preachers of his time, Augustine delivered sermons while sitting in a chair in front of the congregation, a practice that spawned the phrase *ex cathedra* "from the chair." The sermon typically followed and commented on readings from Scripture. The congregation usually responded actively, for Augustine's sermons are filled with references to congregational weeping, groaning, shouting, and applauding. The sermons were taken down in shorthand by scribes and later transcribed in longhand (Deferrari 107, 109, 119). In the *De Trinitate*, Augustine says of a sermon he preached on the Trinity, "[M]ay our words on this subject, which we delivered in a sermon to the Christian people and afterwards transcribed, suffice in the meantime" (*Trinity* 518). G. Wright Doyle has argued that even the sermons in Augustine's *In Johannis Evangelium Tractatus*, some of the most elaborate attributed to him, were delivered orally without the aid of a written manuscript (219).

Augustine's words raise an important question: Just how literate was the Roman Empire in late antiquity? William V. Harris estimates that the overall literacy rate for the western provinces was between five and ten percent (272). Harry Y. Gamble adds that literacy in the major urban centers may have been as high as twenty percent, but certainly no higher (4). This figure must be qualified, however. Literacy among Jews was certainly much higher than among Gentiles. Jewish religious practice mandated that every male be literate enough to read the Scriptures. However, many Jewish males may have been able to read Hebrew only at a rudimentary level and Latin and Greek not at all, and Greek-speaking Jewish males of the Diaspora may have been able to read only Greek, conducting services from the Septuagint. Literacy was necessary for worship in the synagogue, and synagogue worship became the model for Christian worship. Both types of services included scriptural readings followed by a homily or commentary. Christians eventually joined this practice to the celebration of the Lord's Supper. Readings and homilies would have caused no difficulty for early Christian converts drawn from Jewish communities, but when illiterate Gentiles became Christian in large numbers, some adjustments were necessary.

Gamble has used recent discoveries of second-century Egyptian papyri to describe how the early Christian church accommodated a textually based religion to congregations that were mostly illiterate. He points out that reading was orally controlled (29–32), for even though most people could not read, they could all be read to—and generally were. Even literate people were likely to retain slaves to read to them. Oral reading was similar to what is today called oral interpretation. Those who read aloud in Christian churches were likely to chant the text, using gestures, rhythm, and intonation to interpret the work (225–28). This style of reading may have derived from synagogue practice, but it also accommodated *scripta continua*, writing without spaces between words.

In the ancient world, every text involved a performance whose effect was not just informational or cognitive but also dramatic and emotional. The reader tried to reveal the emotional significance of the text so that the significance of the words would be understood and the relevance of the message would be felt. But the predominance of oral performance in Christian churches in Augustine's time must not obscure the fact that these performances were of and about written texts. The churches existed because of sacred texts, and many of those texts, like Paul's epistles, were letters addressed to churches. As Susan Miller has observed, the *De Doctrina* was the first treatise to make rhetoric "capable of power through the authority of a text, not only through the *ethos* of its speakers" (130). The speaker was no longer proclaiming a personal message, one supported and validated through character, but instead offering the message of a text. Meaning was present in the text; that is, it was displaced from the speaker into a text.[8]

The paradox of Christianity in late antiquity is that people were taught to believe in a written teaching that most could not read but only heard. The authority of the written text was conveyed by a living voice, which gave the text an effect far beyond what silent reading affords. Augustine's *De Doctrina* aims to deal with both parts of this paradox. The first three books address how Scripture is to be read; the last indicates how the truth of the reading is to be taught. To achieve the second goal Augustine marshaled the resources of Roman rhetoric.

III

C. S. Baldwin has said that the *De Doctrina Christiana* "begins rhetoric anew" (51). Augustine saw that classical rhetoric could and should be used to preach the gospel. As a rhetor himself, he knew the advantages that his training conferred, but he also rejected the applause-seeking artificiality that he thought characterized many of his contemporaries.

To understand better Augustine's recommendations in book 4, it is necessary to differentiate rhetorical training from rhetorical performance. George Kennedy has distinguished "primary rhetoric," the qualities of eloquence that shape a discourse, from "secondary rhetoric," the rhetorical devices and pedagogical methods used to teach eloquence (*Classical Rhetoric* 4–6). One form of secondary rhetoric is *letteraturizzazione*, a codified system of literary composition (Kennedy, *Greek Rhetoric* 18). In book 4, Augustine himself distinguishes primary and secondary rhetoric:

> Even those who have learned these rules [of eloquence] and speak fluently and eloquently cannot be aware of the fact that they are applying them while they are speaking unless they are discussing the rules themselves; indeed, I think that there is hardly a single eloquent man who can both speak well and think of the rules of eloquence while he is speaking. (*Christian Doctrine* 119–20)

Moreover, Augustine introduces a distinction similar to the one Stephen Krashen and Tracy Terrell make between language acquisition and language learning. According to Augustine, some people become eloquent the way that they became fluent in their native language (through acquisition), while others need rules and drills (learning) (120). Thus, secondary rhetoric is not necessary for eloquence.[9] Primary value is ascribed to the quality of the extemporaneous performance.

During the Republic and early Empire, the goal of secondary rhetoric was extemporaneous speaking, as Quintilian indicates in his *Institutio Oratoria*:

> But the crown of all our study and the highest reward of our long labours is the power of improvisation. The man who fails to acquire this had better . . . abandon the task of advocacy and devote his powers to writing other branches of literature. . . . For there are countless occasions when the sudden necessity may be imposed upon him of speaking without preparation before the magistrates or in a trial which comes on unexpectedly. (10.7.1–2)

By Augustine's time, however, extemporaneous oral performance had ceased to play a significant role in judicial or diplomatic proceedings except in rare cases. The teaching of rhetoric still used techniques from the Republican era, but it focused on the oral delivery of a previously written, rehearsed, and memorized text, a type of performance that featured elaborate wordplay and intense emotionalism. Formal declamation on familiar topics, such as praise for the emperor, became a popular form of entertainment and imperial propaganda; as Kennedy has pointed out, during late antiquity "[n]ovelty of treatment was important, but novelty of theme was not" ("Sophists" 18). Orators of the Second Sophistic school frequently delivered speeches full of verbal display, and applause was the sure sign of success (19). Eloquence, in Augustine's time, thus meant elaborate, carefully prepared declamations, usually on stock topics, that were meant to entertain the audience and reinforce imperial power. Eloquence, in short, foregrounded the secondary rhetoric that showed through the prepared performance.

Kennedy's distinction between primary and secondary rhetoric echoes Augustine's distinction between eloquence and wisdom. Augustine says that while the speeches of the eloquent are the source of the rules of eloquence and while eloquence can be acquired by listening to these speeches, eloquence must be judged according to "wisdom," for the foolish man "thinks because he hears a thing said eloquently, it is true" (*Christian Doctrine* 121). Augustine appears to be discrediting eloquence in this passage, but he may also be condemning the studied use of figural language and ornate construction, that is, eloquence as characterized by the Second Sophistic movement's *letteraturizzazione*, which privileged formulaic expression. Wisdom, by contrast, manifests itself as the sincerity, perspicacity, and doctrinal orthodoxy of the speaker whose words come directly from a heart in which the Holy Spirit dwells. In Augustine's theory and practice, wisdom and eloquence are synthesized in an extemporaneous oral performance that emerges from the preacher's interiority, that is, from an authentic self formed by doctrine.

Scholars frequently allude to Augustine's essentially oral cast of mind. In a well-known passage in the *Confessions*, Augustine sees Ambrose standing before a lectern and almost refuses to believe that Ambrose is reading because he cannot hear Ambrose's voice (114). Orality carries over to Augustine's concept of preaching in book 4 of the *De Doctrina*:

[A]n attentive crowd eager to comprehend usually shows by its motion whether it understands, and until it signifies comprehension the matter being discussed should be expressed in a variety of ways. But this technique may not be used by those who have prepared what they have to say and memorized it word for word. As soon as it is clear that the audience has understood, the discourse should be finished or another topic taken up. (134–35)

Augustine's preaching method wove together Scripture and his own words, surrounding his theme and inserting scriptural passages into novel contexts that illuminated their figural meaning and their application to the subject. He drew on his reading of Scripture as a secular rhetor would draw on his *copia*, or fund of memorized material. The sermons proceed by associative logic, whereby a point or thesis suggests a scriptural passage that in turn suggests another, until the sermon is a quilt of scriptural quotations and exegesis. A brief quotation from one of Augustine's sermons illustrates this method. In the following passage, from tract 62 on the Gospel of John, Augustine comments on Jesus's words to Judas at the Last Supper:

For He said, "What thou doest, do quickly," not as wrathfully looking to the destruction of the trust-betrayer, but in His own haste to accomplish the salvation of the faithful; for He was delivered for our offenses, and He loved the Church, and gave Himself for it. And as the apostle also says of himself: "Who loved me, and gave Himself for me." Had not then Christ given Himself, no one could have given Him up. What is there in Judas' conduct but sin? For in delivering up Christ he had no thought of our salvation, for which Christ was really delivered, but thought only of his money gain, and found the loss of his soul. He got the wages he wished, but had also given him, against his wish, the wages he merited. (*Homilies* 313)

Augustine weaves quotations from and allusions to Scripture into his own text: "He was delivered for our offenses" he takes from Romans 4:25; "He loved the Church, and gave Himself for it" from Ephesians 5:25; and "Who loved me, and gave Himself for me" from Galatians 2:20. The final sentences develop a set of antitheses on the familiar quotation "the wages of sin is death" (Rom 6:23). These quotations and allusions share a common concern with giving oneself over.

This passage illustrates Augustine's definition of eloquence and wisdom. Figurality and erudition give the sermon eloquence, but the eloquence gains real force from extemporaneous delivery. The audience recognizes that the sermon's fusion of content and style springs not from the conscious application of secondary rhetoric to a subject but from the interior of the speaker who is making these associations and that the speaker's interior has been formed by prayer and by reading Scripture. Prayer and Scripture, not the canons of rhetoric, are the basic materials of this performance, even though the performance might not be possible without rhetorical training.

IV

In book 4 Augustine declares, "For one who wishes to speak wisely, therefore, even though he cannot speak eloquently, it is above all necessary to remember the words of Scripture" (122). Fish interprets this passage to mean that, for Augustine, wisdom is not a possession of the mind but a divinely inspired book (31–32). However, another reading of this key passage would involve the distinction between primary and secondary rhetoric. For Augustine, one who speaks wisely but without eloquence is a speaker who is able to present an interpretation of Scripture without using rhetorical technique. The wisdom of the ineloquent speaker consists precisely in the ability to formulate an interpretation extemporaneously without casting those thoughts as figures. To be able to do so, the speaker must understand the Scripture, a task to which the first three books of the *De Doctrina* are dedicated. And more simply, the preacher must remember Scripture:

> For a man speaks more or less wisely to the extent that he has become more or less proficient in the Holy Scriptures. I do not speak of the man who has read widely and memorized much, but of the man who has well understood and has diligently sought out the sense of the Scriptures. For there are those who read them and neglect them, who read that they may remember but neglect them in that they fail to understand them. Those are undoubtedly to be preferred who remember the words less well, but who look into the heart of the Scriptures with the eye of their own hearts. But better than either of these is he who can quote them when he wishes and understands them properly. (122)

Here Augustine presents a description of oral composition, not a disavowal of wisdom or eloquence. If the preacher is to rhapsodize on a topic, drawing from a *copia* informed by reading of Scripture, then Scripture and its wisdom are obviously not outside the speaker but interiorized. When Augustine asserts that "it is above all necessary to remember the words of Scripture" (122), he means it is necessary to retain them in the memory for instant recall and recitation and to retain along with them the interpretations garnered through the principles outlined in the first three books of the *De Doctrina*. As Doyle has pointed out, Augustine proposes using the Bible as a collection of *topoi* (232), for topical memory involves both understanding and remembering. Texts become *loci* that can be associated with interpretive ideas and with one another. Augustine does not mean that scriptural texts are retained the way a literate reader retains ideas from reading or that they are remembered by rote. His method aims to interiorize Scripture and to keep it available as *copia*.

In the *Confessions*, Augustine suggests how Scripture was interiorized when he writes, "The memory must be . . . the stomach of the mind" (224). Augustine is referring to the antique and medieval practice of "rumination." Mary Carruthers describes this practice, sometimes called "meditating" a text, as the continuous repetition of a text in a low murmur (162–67). The meditator ruminates a text by keeping it continuously in the mouth, chewing it over until it is digested, interiorizing it, and incorporating it into the memory. As Chamberlin shows, one of Augustine's sermons on Psalm 103 exploits rumination on the psalm to discover novel associations and new contexts for interpretation (29–33).

Augustine's remark that the preacher "should pray that God will place a good speech in his mouth" attempts to replace the inspiration of the muse with the inspiration of the Holy Spirit (*Christian Doctrine* 168). Augustine transfers the classical idea of divine afflatus to the Holy Spirit, which was usually figured as wind or breath. The Spirit, the Christian muse, inspires the speaker, but the speaker must prepare by reading and internalizing Scripture, just as the bard must internalize a repertoire of oral formulas. The Christian preacher, however, also prepares by prayer, and prayer too must be seen in the context of Augustine's attempt to bring classical rhetoric to bear on extemporaneous preaching: indeed, the Latin word for prayer, *oratio*, also means "oration."[10]

V

Late antiquity did not have a concept of meditation like that reflected in the carefully constructed dramatic monologues and dialogues of Franciscan and Ignatian spirituality or in the intensely private mental prayer that entered Christianity in the early Renaissance as the *devotio moderna*. In late Antiquity, and even in the Middle Ages, prayer was either formulaic or rhetorical; that is, it was conceived either as a recitation of memorized formulas or as an oration delivered to God. The most popular prayers among Christian communities (other than the Lord's Prayer) were those in the Psalter. A Latin translation of the Psalms, the so-called Old Psalter, antedates Jerome's Vulgate. In book 9 of the *Confessions*, Augustine relates the effect the Psalms had on him:

> My God, how I poured out my heart to you as I read the Psalms of David, those faithful songs and sounding syllables of holiness. . . . How I cried aloud to you in those psalms! How they fired me toward you! How I burned to utter them aloud, if I could, to the whole world. (189)

Clearly Augustine vocalized the Psalms, even in private reading. Book 9 incorporates quotations from the Psalms into Augustine's description of the ardor he felt immediately after his conversion. Later, Augustine recounts how the singing and chanting he heard in Ambrose's church in Milan brought him to tears (193–94). Augustine contrasts the spontaneous emotion he felt at prayer with the spurious dramatics, characteristic of the Second Sophistic school, that he had taught.[11]

As Monique Vincent points out, emotions play a central role in Augustine's view of prayer. For Augustine, prayer is interior; its place is the heart (62). Language is the primary method for exciting and expressing those emotions, but prayer is the disposition of the heart; all externals, all words and actions, are directed to exciting that disposition:

> For [Augustine], gestures, the position of the body, have value only insofar as they signify a profound reality. They are useful (but not indispensable) to prayer only insofar as they are stimulants for the heart. Ultimately, only the interior attitude counts; only love gives prayer all its value.[12] (author's trans.)

The gestures and postures used for prayer are reminiscent of the studied gestures of late antique rhetoric that orators used to stimulate their

own emotions and thus those of the audience. Augustine adapts classical rhetorical techniques to create an emotional state proper for the
condition of the soul addressing God, whether it be the state proper
for repentance, praise, petition, or gratitude. An apt analogy for this
type of prayer might be contemporary method acting. Method actors
use gestures or recall past events or words to stimulate particular emotions in a controlled theatrical setting; sometimes such emotions lead
actors to improvise onstage (Hull 82–102, 131–47; Stanislavski 46–47).
Likewise, for Augustine, formal gestures and the recitation of memorized prayers can inspire emotional states in which one may pray
extempore.

Once the proper emotional state has been attained, Vincent
observes, a Christian may engage in a dialogue with God, not merely
addressing him but also listening to his voice in the heart (74–80). Vincent's account of these aspects of prayer resembles what Lloyd Bitzer
has called "the rhetorical situation," in which an orator must sense the
audience's thoughts and feelings and adjust to them. Listening to God
may be understood as an internalization of that rhetorical situation:
God is the audience that responds, and those responses are intuited in
an internal dialogue.

Augustine clarifies this theory in his letter to Proba, his most concise treatment of prayer. In advising Proba, a widow, about meeting the
gospel injunction to "pray always," Augustine envisions formal prayer
as reciting formulas, especially the Lord's Prayer, which he says contains all that may be prayed for. He also mentions the Egyptian desert
fathers, who he says frequently recite short, ejaculatory prayers "so that
the alert attention, which is necessary in prayer, does not fade and grow
heavy through long-drawn-out periods." He advises Proba to pray at
certain set times of the day and at other times when she is free but notes
that "to pray at length does not mean, as some think, to pray with much
speaking." He adds, "To speak much in prayer is to transact a necessary
piece of business with unnecessary words . . . [;] this business is trans-
acted more by sighs than by speech, more by tears than by utterance"
("To Proba" 391). There is no mention of interior monologue; instead,
Augustine warns against prayers with "long-drawn-out periods" and
emphasizes the interior emotional state as the key to prayer.

Augustine's use of prayer to prepare for preaching or dictation is
perhaps best exemplified by his own prayers in the *Confessions*. These
prayers sometimes go on for over a hundred lines, his advice to Proba

notwithstanding, but they serve an important rhetorical purpose. In the beginning of book 5, for example, Augustine sets the theme and requests divine aid in writing the book:

> Accept the sacrifice of my confessions which my tongue sets before you. You formed the tongue and moved it to make confession to your name. *Heal Thou all my bones, and let them say, O Lord, who is like unto Thee.* When we confess to you, we do not inform you of what is happening inside us; for the closed heart does not shut out your eye, and man's hardness cannot resist your hand. You dissolve it at your pleasure, either in pity or in punishment, and *nothing can hide itself from Thy heat.* (90)

This prayer goes on for another fifty lines, during which Augustine develops the idea that confession is unnecessary for God but necessary and salvific for the confessor. The prayer includes an analysis of God's omniscience and omnipresence, themes that play major roles in book 5.

These various facets of Augustine's theory and practice of prayer provide a new context for understanding the admonitions to prayer in book 4 of the *De Doctrina.* Augustine recommends prayer as a "warm-up exercise" to be done before preaching:

> When the hour in which he is to speak approaches, before he begins to preach, he should raise his thirsty soul to God in order that he may give forth what he shall drink, or pour out what shall fill him. (140)

The preacher asks God for enlightenment about a certain doctrine or truth, and praying starts the associative process that brings to mind scriptural passages related to the sermon topic. The preacher's emotional state should also be affected; prayer may induce the sadness, joy, grief, or anger appropriate to the oratorical performance to be given.

Augustine makes clear that although preparatory prayer should decisively affect what the preacher says, it does not replace rhetorical skills; rather, it marshals them:

> [H]e who would both know and teach should learn everything which should be taught and acquire a skill in speaking appropriate to an ecclesiastic, but at the time of the speech itself he should think that which the Lord says more suitable to good thought: "Take no thought how or what

to speak; for it shall be given to you in that hour what to speak, for it is not you that speak, but the Spirit of your Father that speaketh in you." (140)

Here again, Augustine has replaced the classical muse with the Holy Spirit. But it is not fair to say, as Fish does, that the preacher need know nothing. Rather, Scripture passages come to mind from the depths of memory in the heat of performance, a heat initiated by warming up in prayer.

VI

Augustine's description of the role of prayer leads directly to his discussion of the three levels of style and their proper objects. As Baldwin has pointed out, Augustine follows Cicero in designating the three styles of oratory, the low, the middle, and the grand, appropriate to three aims, to teach, to delight, and to move (166–70). However, Augustine insists that these three functions and their corresponding styles can constitute three stages of a single sermon (Baldwin 164–66).[13] And yet Fish argues that Augustine eliminates any real distinctions among the styles (36). Augustine does attribute persuasion to the middle style (*Christian Doctrine* 161), and he does state that even discourses in the grand style should begin with the middle or moderate style (159). But Fish treats style as an attribute of a written text, whereas Augustine's concept of style is orally controlled.[14]

For Augustine, style involves elements that modern rhetoricians might classify under the rubric of delivery. He defines the periodic clause performatively: "*membra* [clauses] are held suspended by the voice of the speaker until the last one is completed" (*Christian Doctrine* 125). In analyzing a passage from 2 Corinthians, he comments several times on how clauses should be read or recited to bring out both Paul's meaning and the emotional force of the text (126–28). In fact, for Augustine, the decisive difference among the three styles seems to be tone of voice, an emphasis that reflects what Ong calls the "tenaciousness of orality" (*Orality* 115–16).

The central role of emotional tone is evident in Augustine's examples of the three styles. For the low style, the style for teaching, he selects a passage from Galatians (4:21-26) in which Paul explains bondage to the law by referring to the two sons of Abraham. The passage contains few figures of speech, but it features a kind of internal dialogue in which Paul frequently asks and then answers rhetorical questions. Augustine emphasizes this dialectical turn of thought rather than the absence of figurality:

> It is relevant to teaching not only to explain those things that are hidden and to solve the difficulties of questions, but also, while these things are being done, to introduce other questions which might by chance occur, lest what is said be rendered improbable or be refuted by them. But they should be introduced in such a way that they are answered at the same time, lest we introduce something we cannot remove. (*Christian Doctrine* 147)

Augustine also exemplifies the low style with a lengthy quotation from Ambrose's arguments for the divinity of the Holy Spirit; in discussing the quotation, Augustine asserts that "the thing discussed does not need verbal ornaments, nor motions of the affections to persuade, but evidence as proof" (154). Thus, rational argument, as well as the absence of figures, characterizes the low style.

Augustine's discussion of the middle style emphasizes rhythm and cites as examples passages containing short, balanced phrases: "An ancient man rebuke not, but treat him as a father; young men as brethren; old women as mothers; young women as sisters" (148; 1 Tim 5:1-2). The same emphasis on rhythm appears in another example of the middle style:

> And having different gifts, according to the grace that is given us, either prophecy to be used according to the rule of faith; Or ministry, in ministering; or he that teacheth, in doctrine; He that exhorteth, in exhorting; he that giveth, with simplicity. (148)

The middle style highlights rhythmic prose for praising and blaming, the usual purpose of epideictic oratory.

The grand style aims to persuade people to act, sometimes in ways contrary to their inclinations. Augustine's examples of the grand style, which bristle with vehemence, include a passage filled with questions, balanced phrases, and hyperbole: "For I bear you witness, that if it could be done, you would have plucked out your own eyes, and would have given them to me. Am I then become your enemy, because I tell you the truth?" (152; Gal 4:16). Augustine points out the absence of

formal structure in the passage: "Are contrary words set against their
contraries here, or are things arranged climactically, or are *caesa* [an
ellipsis or pause] and *membra* and *circuitus* [a circumlocution or periph-
rasis] used?" He concludes that the style is nevertheless grand: "Yet not
on that account is the grand emotion which we feel in the fervor of this
eloquence diminished" (152). It is emotional vehemence rather than
syntax that makes the passage grand.

According to Augustine, all three styles can and should appear in
the same speech:

> But no one should think that it is contrary to theory to mix these three
> manners; rather, speech should be varied with all types of style in so far
> as this may be done appropriately. . . . When those things which must be
> said in the subdued style have been interposed, we return effectively to
> those things which must be said in the grand style, so that the impetus of
> our speech ebbs and flows like the sea. (159)

Augustine even includes directions for shifting styles to produce
an effective sermon. And he argues against limiting a style to only one
effect—for example, using the low style only to teach—for each style
may create in a listener or in a whole audience any or all of the desired
effects: teaching, delighting, and persuading (162–63).

Augustine defines style performatively; he subordinates syntax
and figurality to oral effects such as rhythm. Style may embrace those
aspects of language perceptible in a written text, but it is defined in
terms of delivery, especially tone of voice. Style modulates; it has
rhythm; it moves its listeners. Indeed, Augustine's conception of style
renders the sermon analogous to prayer—and to music (Vincent
229–30). Not merely a quality of a static text, style is a dynamic of
extemporaneous oral performance. Thus, the flexibility of Augustine's
treatment enhances the freedom and effectiveness of the preacher.

In contrast to critical approaches that privilege writing as the
opposite of orality, this analysis of the dynamics of extemporaneous
oral performance in book 4 of the *De Doctrina Christiana* reveals the
complexity of Augustine's social milieu, in which orality and literacy,
public speech and private reading coexisted in an uneasy but fruitful
tension. My examination also shows that book 4 attempts to resolve a
central paradox of early Christianity by synthesizing the oral world of
public performance with a religion grounded in writing and addressed

to the inner person. What is essential in book 4 is Augustine's insistence on interior states: the states proper for understanding Scripture, for praying, and finally for preaching a sermon. Style may be adapted to the audience, to the subject, or to the effect desired, but it is always an authentic reflection of the preacher's interior state, which is achieved through a life of meditative reading and prayer.

The *De Doctrina* presents concepts of reading, praying, and style that are informed by Augustine's attempt to bring classical rhetoric, a discipline associated with extemporaneous oral performance, to bear on Christian preaching, which was grounded in the interpretation of a written text. The profound and glacial changes that occurred while European culture was adopting Christianity, a textually based religion, are documented, at least partially, in book 4 of the *De Doctrina*, where Augustine attempts to transform rhetoric into a tool for oral expression of interior states formed by reading and prayer. But even reading and prayer are still orally controlled in book 4, for Augustine has not interiorized silent reading or private meditation to the extent that modern Western subjects have. As Ong has pointed out, even the eighteenth-century Augustan poets retained a high level of orality (*Presence* 247–48). Yet Fish, Sutherland, and Sloane assume that Augustine's methods are directed toward written composition in a culture in which writing has long been interiorized.

Instead of being used to justify the antirhetorical practices of later ages, the *De Doctrina* needs to be understood in its own milieu. Book 4 marks the beginning of a process that took centuries to complete. Thus, it highlights the distance that other writers have traveled from the oral matrix of rhetoric and invites a rereading of the history of that journey and a consideration of how much they (and we) have forgotten.

PART IV

CONCLUSION

RELIGION'S RHETORIC

SAINT AUGUSTINE'S UNION OF CHRISTIAN WISDOM AND SOPHISTIC ELOQUENCE

Amy K. Hermanson

Saint Augustine composed *De Doctrina Christiana* during one of the most tumultuous times in the history of the Western world. In short, the fourth century A.D. bore witness to the fall of the Roman Empire and the dawning of a new *Holy* Roman Empire. Christianity overtook the crumbling pagan world, and the Greek and Roman learning that had developed over several centuries was threatened and challenged by Christian Church leaders. Many believed Christianity and classical pagan learning were incommensurable. However, in *DDC*, Augustine rescues extensive knowledge of rhetoric and language from the fourth-century intellectual rubble of classical learning. Augustine was able to overcome the wholesale rejection of pagan learning by uncoupling rhetoric from the pagan values Christian leaders found offensive. Moreover, Augustine adapted the rhetorician's aim of uniting wisdom and eloquence to suit Christian needs and ideals. *DDC* is, therefore, the first in-depth exploration of the relationship between rhetoric and Christianity—a relationship that we now consider endemic.

One of the greatest obstacles to creating a Christian rhetoric was the fourth-century suspicion of classical, pagan learning. James J. Murphy highlights some of the concerns early Church leaders had regarding classical rhetoric and literature in "Saint Augustine and the Debate about a Christian Rhetoric." Many were suspicious of classical rhetoric because they believed its worldly orientation nurtured vices objectionable to Christians. For example, Church leaders believed that rhetoric devalued faith in God and his Word. The fact that arguments against Christianity were often based on reason and logic prompted many early Christians to dismiss rational inquiry and to cling instead to faith as the only basis of true wisdom and knowledge. Such fideists rejected rhetoric as a vehicle of reason and logic.

312

AMY K. HERMANSON

Fideism and the general distrust of classical learning created a formidable hurdle for anyone wishing to employ rhetoric in service of Christian ends. And yet, Augustine overcomes fideist objections masterfully in *DDC*. For example, at the beginning of book 4, Augustine compares using rhetoric with taking medicine in an effort to persuade preachers that rhetoric does not reduce the power of God's Word. Augustine argues that when one is sick, one takes medicine—not because one distrusts God's healing power, but because one recognizes that although God has primary control over health, medicine is a useful tool for restoring well-being. With this example, Augustine breaks down the dichotomy between faith in God and human intervention. Augustine goes on to apply this example to the question of whether to place trust in God or in human rhetorical skill. Augustine's answer is, again, to break down the false dichotomy. He argues that using rhetoric does not challenge the authority of God's Word, but rather complements or enhances its efficacy.

In another passage in book 4 meant to convince those fearful of superimposing an inferior, human art over God's Word, Augustine argues that because human beings are sinful and imperfect, they do not always perceive God's wisdom and perfection. Augustine concludes that rhetoric ought to be engaged in order to assist humans in coming to know God's wisdom. Here again, Augustine breaks down a paradigm that threatens to hinder Christian preachers from using the full power of language. In response to those who are uncomfortable with the notion of improving upon God's (already perfect) Word, Augustine argues that it is human understanding, not God's Word, that needs improvement. With these passages, Augustine demonstrates his dexterity as a rhetorician defending rhetoric. As many have noted, Augustine's treatise was widely circulated and highly influential, both among his contemporaries and among the intellectual elite in the West for centuries thereafter. Augustine's ability to assess and reach his audience effectively reveals him to be both a skilled theoretician and an adept practitioner of rhetoric.

Fideism and anticlassical sentiments were not all that stood in the way of fourth-century acceptance of rhetoric among Christians; the pleasure-driven rhetoric of fourth-century Sophists also left many Christian Church leaders skeptical of rhetoric's merits. Rhetoricians of the Second Sophistic focused primarily on the pleasing effect their words could have on an audience (versus focusing on the accuracy and importance of the message they were delivering). Many, therefore, viewed sophistic rhetoric as deceptive, since its practitioners seemed to care little about the meaning of their words, let alone about seeking Truth. It is not difficult to understand that an orientation promoting communication skills necessary for worldly success would be disconcerting to Christian preachers, whose aim was to spread *the Word* of God.

Augustine presents himself as masterful rhetorician and skilled defender of rhetoric once more as he addresses objections to sophistic rhetoric. Augustine's tactic for combating sophistic rhetoric is similar to his tactic for addressing fideism in that he again uncouples concepts that are paired unnecessarily in the minds of his readers. Addressing those readers who associate sophism with rhetoric, Augustine gives an account of rhetoric that is decidedly anti-sophistic. For example, invoking Cicero's three *officia* (*docere, delectare, movere*), Augustine places prime importance on teaching and moving. Rhetors of the Second Sophistic are described as being primarily concerned with pleasing their audience. But in a few key passages, Augustine resurrects the concepts of teaching and moving for rhetorical consideration, relegating the delight an audience takes in an oration/sermon to a place of secondary significance. One such passage appears near the middle of book 4, where Augustine argues that precepts of style and diction *may*, and even *should*, be broken if doing so best serves the purpose of teaching one's audience.

Augustine also appropriates Cicero's three levels of style for the use of his Christian rhetor. And here again, the preacher's choice of which style to use—the subdued, the moderate, or the grand—should be dictated by which level of style will best serve the purpose of instructing his audience. Augustine's discussion of style must be seen especially as an attempt to distance his rhetoric from sophistic rhetoric, because, as Baldwin points out, sophistic rhetoric valued style for style's sake. Here, Augustine leaves almost no room for appreciation of style as an end in itself but instead adopts a highly flexible view of style aimed at moving an audience toward a clear and consistent goal. Augustine's ability to address his audience's concerns about sophistic rhetoric once again reveals his dynamism as a rhetorician.

It is within a context of Christian hostility to rhetoric and sophistic abuses of rhetoric that we can begin to appreciate the extent of Augustine's contributions to rhetorical theory and his sagacity as a rhetor. In *DDC*, Augustine resurrects the all-but-forgotten roots of classical rhetoric, and from those roots crafts a new rhetoric amenable to Christian sensibilities and goals. With *DDC,* therefore, Augustine exemplifies both his dynamism as a rhetor and the malleability of rhetoric as a discipline. His rhetoric is significant, first, because in it he demonstrates supreme rhetorical skill, and second, because it redirects and redefines the course of the rhetorical tradition in the West. By navigating a path between sophism and fideism, Augustine preserved rhetoric as a useful tool specially crafted to meet the needs of the Christian preacher. Today, we take it for granted that any socially situated understanding of religion must rely on an understanding of rhetoric and language; we owe this debt in large part to Augustine. At a time when many of the intellectual elite denied the relevance of rhetoric within a religious context, Augustine effectively argued for rhetoric's relevance and usefulness; in the process of recovering and defending rhetoric in *DDC,* Augustine crafted the first Christian union of wisdom and eloquence.

ORIGINAL FRONT MATTER TO SISTER THÉRÈSE SULLIVAN'S *DE DOCTRINA CHRISTIANA*, LIBER QVARTVS

Habemus enim iam quosdam spumeos in sermone, sed in fide sanos. non itaque desperandum est, etiam hoc in isto, quamuis sit tolerabile, si permanserit, posse tamen expurgari et temperari, atque ad integrum et solidum uel perduci, uel reuocari modum: praesertim quia iuuenis esse perhibetur, ut quod minus habet peritia, suppleat diligentia; et quod cruditas loquacitatis eructat, aetatis maturitas decoquat. illud est molestum et periculosum uel perniciosum, si cum laudatur eloquentia, persuadeatur insipientia, et in pretioso poculo bibatur pestifera potio.

S. Avgustini, De Anima 1, 3, 3.

PREFACE

As the first manual of Christian rhetoric, the fourth book of *De Doctrina Christiana* has from the very beginning attracted the attention of scholars. It has seen many editions, frequent translations, and has in several monographs been more or less carefully analysed. Up to this time, however, it has not been subjected to a unified critical, linguistic, and historical investigation. The present study has been undertaken with the view to answering this need. A commentary, revised text, and translation are here presented, with an introduction in elucidation and summary of some of the more important problems of the book. It is hoped that such a treatment may serve to systematize the study of the different phases of this treatise, and may lead to a conclusive estimate of its value in whole and in part.

The Commentary here presented is on the one hand an investigation of Augustine's rhetorical theory, and on the other a study of his own language and style. Analysis of the matter of the fourth book reveals the rare mental grasp of Augustine. The author views his subject broadly and simply as a whole, but at the same time follows it through all the ramifications of its smallest details with perfect understanding

of the relation of part to part, and of part to whole. A careful study
has been made of Augustine's rhetorical sources, and rather full quotations have been given from the same, in hope that the comparison of
classical standards and those put forward by Augustine may result in a
fuller appreciation of the value of his theory. As a systematic summary
of the similarities between the two, a table of classical and Christian
rhetorical parallels has been drawn up in the Introduction. *De Arte Rhetorica*, included by some editors among the works of St. Augustine, but
now considered by most scholars as spurious, has not been regarded in
the present study. Its differences from *De Doctrina Christiana* have been
shown[1] to be sufficient proof that these two treatises were not written
by the same pen. *De Dialectica*, on the other hand, principally because
of its agreement in theory with the present book, has been treated in
these pages as Augustine's own.

On the side of the writer's language and style, the vocabulary
and syntax of the fourth book have been studied for their deviation
from classical standards. All words rare, or not occurring, or occurring
with a different meaning in classical Latin have been noted, as have
such syntactical usages not common to classical prose. Certain ordinary ecclesiastical terms have been omitted, however, such as occur
frequently in all Late writers, and which have been treated adequately
elsewhere in the Patristic Series, and in other monographs on ecclesiastical Latin, e.g. *Trinitas, Spiritus, Prouidentia, propheta, angelus, ecclesia,
ecclesiasticus, apostolus, apostolicus, christianus, euangelium, epistola, canon,
canonicus, saeculum, saecularis, fides* (—religion), *fideles, mundus, persecutio,
mysteria, sermo, sanctus, gentes, gentilis, episcopus, presbyter*. Syntactical characteristics common to all Late Latin, when they have occurred, have
likewise merely been noted, without citation of detailed references.
The terms used throughout the Patristic Series to designate the various
periods of Latinity have also been adopted here: Early, *i.e.*, pre-Cice-
ronian Latin; Class., *i.e.*, the prose of the Golden Age; Silver, *i.e.*, post-
Augustan writers through Suetonius; Late, *i.e.*, Latin from Apuleius on.
For the common lexica and grammars the usual abbreviations have
been employed. These are indicated after the respective works in the
bibliography. Reference to the bibliography is made by author and
page only. A summary of the details of the vocabulary and syntax has
not been deemed necessary in the Introduction. Information in regard
to linguistic peculiarities can readily be found in the Commentary, by

referring to the indices. The rhetorical phase of this treatise, on the other hand, has received only scant attention in the notes, but is treated as a whole in the Introduction. The interpretation follows Norden's and Polheim's analysis of fourth-century prose. The bibliography here presented has been restricted to those works actually found useful in the preparation of this monograph. Works of Augustine other than those on rhetoric are not cited in the bibliography. Where they have been used, the references in the Commentary have been made to the *Patrologia Latina,* and to the *Corpus Scriptorum Ecclesiasticorum Latinorum* of the Vienna Academy.

The text presented is a revision of the Benedictine edition of *De Doctrina Christiana* as it is printed in volume 34 of Migne's *Patrologia Latina.* This revision has been based on the collation of nine MSS. of the ninth to the thirteenth centuries, details in regard to which are given in the Introduction. The Introduction, furthermore, takes up the problems involved in the following points: date of the treatise, sources, Biblical quotations, style, influence. The lengthy Scriptural quotations used by Augustine as models of style have been compared with the Vulgate and the Old Version, that is, the composite text of the pre-Hieronymian Latin Bible, as presented by Sabatier. Though the variant readings have been individually handled in the critical apparatus, the selections in full are given in parallel columns in the Introduction, in order to afford a more graphic comparison between Augustine's text and the Bible versions current in the fourth and fifth centuries. Accuracy and a preservation of the distinctive flavor of Augustine's style have been the principal aims in the translation. For this reason elegance of diction and the use of the modern idiom have in some passages been sacrificed, where a faithful interpretation of the original has necessitated language quaint to our modem ears in order to approximate Augustine's stylistic individuality.

I wish to express my sincere gratitude to Dr. Roy J. Deferrari, Head of the Department of Latin and Greek, for his untiring interest and assistance in this study and for the inspiration he has afforded it by his stimulating direction and criticism. To Dr. Martin R. P. McGuire, Instructor in Latin and Greek, I am also deeply indebted, especially for his careful study and criticism of the manuscript, and for the generous help and suggestions which I have received from him in every part of this work. I take this opportunity also of thanking the Reverend Adolphe A. Vaschalde, Professor of Semitic Languages, for reading the manuscript. To the Superiors of the Sisters of Notre Dame of Namur, who have made this study possible, it is offered in grateful appreciation.

Sister THÉRÈSE, S. N. D.
Trinity College,
March 25, 1930

SELECT BIBLIOGRAPHY

I. PRINCIPAL EDITIONS OF *De Doctrina Christiana*.

Editio princeps, by John Mentelinus (Strasbourg, c. 1465). This edition of the fourth book of *De Doctrina Christiana* seems to have been the first printed edition of any of St. Augustine's works. *De Doctrina Christiana* appeared thereafter in the great editions of Augustine's collected works, and in various separate editions. The principal general editions are:

> Editio Amerbachiana, Basle, 1506.
>
> Editio Erasmiana, a revision of the Amerbach edition, made by Desiderius Erasmus (Basle, 1528–29). *De Doctrina Christiana* appeared in vol. 3. In the reprint made at Venice in 1545, it appeared in Vol. 1.
>
> Editio Louaniensis, by the Theologians of Louvain (Antwerp, 1577).
>
> Editio Parisina, by the Benedictines of St. Maur, edited by J. Blampin and P. Coustant (Paris, 1679–1700). *De Doctrina Christiana* appeared in Vol. 3 (Paris, 1680). Of the later Benedictine reprints, the principal ones are by Gaume, Paris, 1836–39 (*De Doctrina Christiana*, in Vol. 3), and by J. P. Migne, *PL.*, Vols. 32–47 (Paris 1845–49). This Migne edition was frequently reprinted, unfortunately with change of pagination. In the latest reprint (Paris, 1887), *De Doctrina Christiana* is to be found in Vol. 34.

Separate editions[1] of *De Doctrina Christiana* appeared in the 15th, 16th, 17th, 18th, and 19th centuries. The principal separate Louvain reprints are those of Antwerp (1601), Wittenberg (1634), Helmstadt by George Calixtus (1629, 1655). In the 19th century C. H. Bruder

---

[1] Cf. Schoenemann, *Bibliotheca Patrum Latinorum*, II, 64, 65, 66, 68, 70, 227–34.

(Leipzig 1836, 1865) brought out a separate reprint, made from the Benedictine Edition.

II. Principal Translations of *De Doctrina Christiana.*[2]

Lichter, P., De Doctrina Christiana (German Translation). Coblenz, 1829.

Poujoulat et Raulx, Oeuvres complètes de S. Augustin, 17 vols. (*De Doctrina Christiana* in Vol. 4). Bar-le-Duc, 1865–73.

Shaw, J. F., On Christian Doctrine (Edinburg, 1877), *in* Dods, M.: The Works of St. Augustine, Bishop of Hippo, A New Translation, Vol. 9. This translation appears also in Shaff, P.: A Select Library of Nicene and Post-Nicene Fathers of the Christian Church, First Series, Vol. 2 (New York, 1887; reprinted 1907).

Storf, R., De Doctrina Christiana, *in* Bibliothek der Kirchenväter. Kempten, 1879.

Baker, W. J. V., and Bickersteth, C., De Doctrina Christiana, *in* Preaching and Teaching according to St. Augustine. London, 1907.

Belli, M., I quattro libri della dottrina cristiana, 2 vols. (nos. 185–86 in Raccolta di breviarii intellettuali), Milan, 1920.

III. Works on Rhetoric and Oratory in St. Augustine.

Baker, W. J. V., and Bickersteth, C., Preaching and Teaching according to St. Augustine. London, 1907.

Barry, Sr. M. Inviolata, St. Augustine, the Orator. Washington, D. C., 1924.

Buschick, R., Die Pädagogik Augustins. Erlangen, 1893.

Cartau, J. S., L'Esprit et la Rhétorique de S. Augustin. Bordeaux, 1876.

Christopher, J. P., De Catechizandis Rudibus, Translated with an Introduction and Commentary. Washington, D. C., 1926.

Colincamp, F., Études critiques sur la Méthode oratoire dans S. Augustin. Paris, 1848.

Deferrari, R. J., St. Augustine's Method of Composing and Delivering Sermons, in The American Journal of Philology, XLIII (1922), 97–123; 193–219.

---

[2] For early translations (16th, 17th, 18th centuries), cf. Schoenemann, *Bibliotheca Patrum Latinorum*, II, 234–35.

Eggersdorfer, F. X., Der hl. Augustinus als Pädagog. Freiburg, 1907.

Eskridge, J. B., The Influence of Cicero upon Augustine in the Development of his Oratorical Theory for the Training of the Ecclesiastical Orator. Menasha, Wis., 1912.

Francey, T., Les Idées littéraires de S. Augustin dan le *De Doctrina Christiana*. Saarbrücken, (undated).

Lezat, A., De Oratore Christiano apud S. Augustinum. Paris, 1872.

Parsons, Sr. Wilfrid, A Study of the Vocabulary and Rhetoric in the Letters of St. Augustine. Washington, D.C., 1923.

Pschmadt, J., Des hl. Augustinus Gedanken zur Theorie der Predigt im vierten Buche der Doctrina Christiana, in Theologie und Glaube, Vol. 8, 1916, pp. 830-41.

Reuter, A., Zu dem Augustinischen Fragment de Arte rhetorica. Leipzig, 1888.

Sadous, A. L. N., Sancti Augustini de Doctrina Christiana libri expenduntur seu de rhetorica apud Christianos Disquisitio. Paris, 1847.

Zurek, J., De S. Aurelii Augustini Praeceptis Rhetoricis. Leipzig, 1905.

IV. General Works on Education, Rhetoric, and Oratory.

A. *Ancient.*

Bonnell, E., M. F. Quintiliani Institutionis Oratoriae libri duodecim. Leipzig, 1903.

Bywater, I., Aristotle, On the Art of Poetry. Oxford, 1909.

Friars Minor, Doctoris Seraphici S. Bonaventurae Opera Omnia: Are Concionandi, Vol. 9, pp. 8–21 (1901). Quaracchi, 1882–1902.

Friedrich, G., M. T. Ciceronis Libri ad Herennium, et de Inuentione. Leipzig, 1893.

Halm, C., Rhetores Latini Minores. Leipzig, 1863.

Migne, J. P., S. A. Augustini Libri Contra Cresconium Donatistam, Vol. 43. Paris, 1865.

———, S. A. Augustini Liber de Catechizandis Rudibus, Vol. 40. Paris, 1865.

———, S. A. Augustini Principia Dialecticae (of doubtful authenticity), Vol. 32. Paris, 1877.

———, Cassiodori Expositio in Psalterium, Vol. 70. Paris, 1865.

————, Rabani Mauri Libri III de Institutione Clericorum, Vol. 107. Paris, 1864.

Mueller, C. F. W., et Friedrich, G., M. T. Ciceronis Opera Rhetorica: De Oratore, Brutus, Orator, De Optime Genere Oratorum, Partitiones Oratoriae, Topica. Leipzig, 1912.

Roemer, A., Aristotelis Ars Rhetorica. Leipzig, 1898.

Sandys, J. E., M. T. Ciceronis ad M. Brutum Orator. Cambridge, 1885.

Spengel, L., Rhetores Graeci. Leipzig, 1894.

Wilkins, A. S., M. T. Ciceronis de Oratore libri III. Oxford, 1895.

B. *Modern.*

Ameringer, T. E., The Stylistic Influence of the Second Sophistic on the Panegyrical Sermons of St. John Chrysostom. Washington, D. C., 1921.

Baldwin, C. S., (1) Ancient Rhetoric and Poetic. New York, 1924.

————, (2) Mediaeval Rhetoric and Poetic. New York, 1928.

Berger, J. F., et Cucheval, V., Histoire d'Éloquence Latine jusqu'à Cicéron. Paris, 1872.

Bernhard, M., Der Stil des Apuleius von Madaura. Ein Beitrag zur Stilistik des Spätlateins. Stuttgart, 1927.

Blass, F., Die attische Beredsamkeit. Leipzig, 1887–93.

Campbell, J. M., The Influence of Greek Rhetoric on the Sermons of St. Basil. Washington, D.C., 1922.

Caplan, H., A Late Mediaeval Tractate on Preaching, in Studies in Rhetoric and Public Speaking in honor of James A. Winans. New York, 1925, pp. 61–90.

Chaignet, A., La Rhétorique et son histoire. Paris, 1888.

Cucheval, V., (1) Cicéron. Analyse et extraits des Traités de rhétorique. Paris, 1896.

————, (2) Histoire de l'Éloquence Romaine depuis la mort de Cicéron jusqu'à l'avènement de l'Empereur Hadrien. Paris, 1893.

De Groot, A. W., (1) A Handbook of Antique Prose Rhythm. The Hague, 1919.

————, (2) La Prose métrique des anciens. Paris, 1926.

De Jonge, E., Les Clausules métriques dans S. Cyprien. Paris, 1905.

Gwynn, A., Roman Education from Cicero to Quintilian. Oxford, 1926.

Hendrickson, G. L., (1) The Peripatetic Mean of Style and the Three Stylistic Characters, in The American Journal of Philology, XXV (1904), 125–46.

———, (2) The Origin and Meaning of the Ancient Characters of Style, in The American Journal of Philology, XXVI (1905), 249–90.

Laurand, L., Études sur le style des discours de Cicéron, Vol. 1, 3rd ed., Paris, 1928; Vol. 2, 2nd ed., 1926; Vol. 3, 2nd ed., 1927.

Méridier, L., L'Influence de la seconde Sophistique sur l'œuvre de Grégoire de Nysse. Paris,1906.

Navarre, O., Essai sur la Rhétorique grecque avant Aristote. Paris, 1900.

Norden, E., Die antike Kunstprosa, 2 vols., 4th reprint. Leipzig, 1923.

O'Daniel, V. F., Thomas Aquinas as a Preacher, in The Ecclesiastical Review, XLII (1910), 26–37.

Polheim, K., Die Lateinische Reimprosa, Berlin, 1925.

Reynolds, G., The Clausulae in the De Civitate Dei of St. Augustine. Washington, D. C., 1924.

Roberts, W. Rhys, (1) Dionysius of Halicarnassus, The Three Literary Letters. The Greek Text, edited with English Translation, etc. Cambridge, 1901.

———, (2) Demetrius on Style. The Greek text of Demetrius De Elocutione, edited after the Paris Manuscript, with Introduction, Translation, Facsimiles, etc. Cambridge, 1902.

———, (3) Longinus on the Sublime. The Greek Text edited after the Paris Manuscript, with Introduction, Translation, Facsimiles, and Appendices. Cambridge, 1907.

———, (4) Greek Rhetoric and Literary Criticism. New York, 1928.

Steeger, T., Die Klauseltechnik Leos des Grossen in seinen Sermonen. Hassfurt, 1908.

Villemain, M., Tableau de L'Éloquence chrétienne au quatrième siècle. Paris, 1858.

Volkmann, R., (1) Die Rhetorik der Griechen und Römer in systematischer Übersicht. Leipzig,1885.

———, (2) Rhetorik und Metrik (Mueller Handbuch, II, 3). Munich, 1901.

Walsh, J., St. Thomas on Preaching, in Dominicana, V (1921), 6-14.

Zielinski, T., (1) Das Clauselgesetz in Ciceros Reden, in Philologus, Supplementband IX, 1904, 589–844.

———, (2) Das Ausleben des Clauselgesetzes in der römischen Kunst-prosa, *in* Philologus, Supplementband X, 1907, 429–66.

V. WORKS ON THE SCRIPTURES.

Bechis, M., Totius Sacrae Scripturae Concordantiae iuxta Vulgatae Editionis Exemplar. Turin,1887.

Biblia Sacra iuxta Vulgatam Clementinam, Rome-Paris, 1927.

Burkitt, F. C., The Old Latin and the Itala, Vol. IV, No. 3, *in* Texts and Studies, Contributions to Biblical and Patristic Literature. Cambridge, 1896.

Corssen, P., Bericht über die lateinischen Bibelübersetzungen, *in* Bursian's Jahresbericht, CI (1899), 1–83.

Hastings, J., A Dictionary of the Bible, 5 vols. New York, 1904.

Milne, C. H., The Old-Latin Text of the Gospels used by St. Augustine. Cambridge, 1926.

Quentin, H., La Prétendue Itala de S. Augustin in Revue Biblique, XXXVI (1927), 216–25.

Sabatier, P., Bibliorum sacrorum Latinae uersiones antiquae seu uetus Italica, 3 vols. (bound in six). Paris, 1751.

Souter, A., The Earliest Latin Commentaries on the Epistles of St. Paul. Oxford, 1927.

Vigouroux, F., Dictionnaire de la Bible, 5 vols. Paris, 1903–12.

VI. WORKS ON LANGUAGE.

Adams, Sr. Miriam Annunciata, The Latinity of the Letters of St. Ambrose. Washington, D. C., 1927.

Archiv für lateinische Lexicographie und Grammatik, 15 vols. Leipzig, 1884–1908.

Arts, Sr. M. Raphael, The Syntax of the Confessions of St. Augustine. Washington, D. C., 1927.

Benoist-Goelzer, Nouveau Dictionnaire Latin-Français, 9th ed. Paris, 1922.

Bonnet, M., Le Latin de Grégoire de Tours. Paris, 1890.

Buck, Sr. Mary Joseph Aloysius, S. Ambrosii De Helia et Ieiunio, A Commentary, with an Introduction and Translation. Washington, D.C., 1929.

Colbert, Sr. M. Columkille, The Syntax of the *De Civitate Dei* of St. Augustine. Washington, D.C., 1923.

Draeger, A., Historische Syntax der lateinischen Sprache, 2nd ed., 2 vols. Leipzig, 1878–1881.

Forcellini-Corradini-Perin (For.), Lexicon Totius Latinitatis. Padua, 1864–1887.

Gabarrou, F., Le Latin d'Arnobe. Paris, 1921.

Georges, Ausführliches Handwörterbuch, 2 vols. Leipzig, 1913–1918.

Gildersleeve-Lodge, Latin Grammar. New York, 1894.

Goelzer, H., (1) Étude lexicographique et grammaticale de la Latinité de S. Jérôme. Paris, 1884.

————, (2) Le Latinité de S. Avit. Paris, 1909.

Harper's Latin Dictionary (Lewis and Short). New York, 1879.

Juret, A. C., Étude grammaticale sur le latin de S. Filastrius. Erlangen, 1904.

Kaulen, Fr., Sprachliches Handbuch sur biblischen Vulgata, 2nd ed. Freiburg i. B., 1904.

Krebs-Schmalz (K.-Schm.), Antibarbarus der lateinischen Sprache, 7th ed. Basel, 1905–1907.

Kühner-Stegmann (K.-Steg.), Ausführliche Grammatik der lateinischen Sprache, 2nd ed. Hannover, 1912–1914.

Lane, G., A Latin Grammar. New York, 1903.

Lebreton, J., Études sur la langue de Cicéron. Paris, 1901.

Löfstedt, E., Syntactica. Studien und Beiträge zur historischen Syntax des Lateins. Erster Teil. Über einige Grundfragen der lateinischen Nominalsyntax. Lund, 1928.

McGuire, M. R., S. Ambrosii De Nabuthae, A Commentary, with an Introduction and Translation. Washington, D.C., 1927.

Meader, C. L., The Latin Pronouns, *Is, Hic, Iste, Ipse*. New York, 1901.

Merguet, H., (1) Handlexikon zu Cicero. Leipzig, 1905.

————, (2) Lexikon zu den Reden des Cicero, 4 vols. Jena, 1877–1884.

————, (3) Lexikon zu den philosophischen Schriften Ciceros. Jena, 1887–1894.

Neue-Wagener, Formenlehre der lateinischen Sprache, 3d ed. Leipzig, 1892–1905.

Quicherat, L., Thesaurus Poeticus Linguae Latinae. Paris, 1836.

Régnier, A., De la latinité des Sermons de S. Augustin. Paris, 1886.

Riemann-Ernout, Syntaxe latine, 7th ed. Paris, 1927.

Rönsch, H., Itala und Vulgata, 2nd ed. Marburg, 1875.

Salonius, A. H., Vitae Patrum. Kritische Untersuchungen über Text, Syntax, and Wortschatz der spätlateinischen Vitae Patrum. Lund, 1920.

Stolz-Schmalz (St.-Schm.), Lateinische Grammatik, 5th ed. Munich, 1928.

Thesaurus Linguae Latinae (T.L.L.), Vols. I–IV (A–C), V (D-dolor), VI (F-germen). Leipzig, 1900ff.

VII. LITERARY AND HISTORICAL REFERENCES.

Bardenhewer, O., Geschichte der altkirchlichen Literatur, Vol. IV. Freiburg, 1924.

Bertrand, L., S. Augustin. Paris, 1913.

De Labriolle, P., Histoire de la Littérature latine chrétienne, 2nd ed. Paris, 1924.

Glover, T., Life and Letters in the Fourth Century. Cambridge, 1901.

Hertling, G. von, (1) Augustin. Mainz, 1902.

———, (2) Augustin. Der Untergang der antiken Kultur. Mainz, 1911.

Jordan, H., Geschichte der altchristlichen Literatur. Leipzig, 1911.

Manitius, M., Geschichte der lateinischen Literatur des Mittelalters. Munich, 1911.

Monceaux, P., Histoire littéraire de l'Afrique chrétienne, VI, VII. Paris, 1923.

Montgomery, W., St. Augustine, Aspects of his Life and Thought. London, 1914.

Reuter, A., Augustinische Studien. Gotha, 1887.

Saintsbury, G., A History of Criticism. London, 1900.

Sandys, J. E., A History of Classical Scholarship. Cambridge, 1903.

Schanz, M., Römische Literaturgeschichte, Vol. IV, 2. Munich, 1920.

Teuffel-Kroll-Skutsch, Geschichte der römischen Literatur, Vol. 3, 6th ed. Leipzig-Berlin, 1913.

Tillemont, L., Mémoires pour servir à l'Histoire ecclésiastique, Vol. XIII. Paris, 1710.

INTRODUCTION.

1. TEXT.

The first of St. Augustine's works to be printed seems to have been the fourth book of *De Doctrina Christiana*. This was published about 1465 at Strasbourg by one John Mentelinus. The treatise as a whole was printed at Venice in 1483 by Octavianus Scotus in an edition of Augustine's shorter works. It again appeared in an edition of the collected works, published in 1489 and 1491 at Strasbourg by Martin Flach. In the succeeding centuries, *De Doctrina Christiana* was printed in the great general editions of Augustine's collected works: the Amerbach edition (Basle, 1506), the Erasmian edition, vol. 3 (Basle, 1528–1529), the Louvain edition, vol. 3 (Paris, 1680). Separate reprints of the treatise, taken from these various editions, appeared in the sixteenth, seventeenth, eighteenth, and nineteenth centuries. The most important reprints of the Benedictine edition are those of Gaume, vol. 3 (Paris, 1836-39), and of J. P. Migne, vol. 34 (Paris, 1887). *De Doctrina Christiana* has not yet been included in the *Corpus Scriptorum Ecclesiasticorum Latinorum* of the Vienna Academy.

The Benedictine edition as revised by Migne has been taken as the basis of the present text. The history of the Benedictine text as given in its preface is as follows: Thirty MSS. (Codices Vaticani, Corbeienses, Floriacensis, Vindocinensis, etc.) were compared with the most important of the preceding editions, *i.e.* with the editions of J. Badius Ascensius (Paris, 1502), John Amerbach (Basle, 1506), Desiderius Erasmus (Basle, 1528), the Theologians of Louvain (Antwerp, 1576). In his reprint of the Benedictine edition, Migne further compared a later reprint (1586) of the Louvain edition, and a still later Louvain reprint, edited by George Calixtus in 1655.

For the present text, nine MSS. have been collated from photostatic copies procured by the courtesy of Jean Malye of the Association Guillaume Budé. These are:

		Sigla
1.	From the Bibliothèque Nationale:	
	Par. lat. N. A. 1595 (9th cent.)	B
	Par. lat. 1938 (10th cent.)	C
	Par. lat. 2704 (10th cent.)	D
	Par. lat. 1909 (14th cent.)	E

2. From the Vatican Library:

Urb. lat. 67 (12th cent.)	A
Palat. lat. 188 (9th–10th cent.)	F
Palat. lat. 189 (10th cent.)	G
Palat. lat. 190 (13th cent.)	H
Vat. lat. 657 (13th cent.)	I

The relation between these MSS. may be represented as follows:

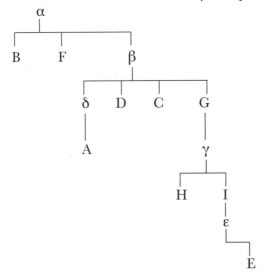

B has many emendations and variations not found in the other MSS. F, though it, too, shows frequent corrections in the form of words written over words, is in its variants more often in agreement with D, C, G, and at times with the remaining MSS., than is B. In chapter 27, after *sicut scriptum est*, it contains the quotation from Matt. 23, 2-3, *Scribae et Pharisaei . . . dicunt enim et non faciunt*, as do C, G, H, I, E. B does not contain this quotation. D is less carefully written than many of the other MSS.; it contains corrections within the text, but in many of its variants it agrees with F and B. C has some marginal corrections, and many headings and notes in the margin, amounting at times practically to an outline of the matter of the text. G contains fewest variant readings, though in these it shows relation to H and I, which themselves are closely similar, while E resembles I in many of its variants. A has frequent mistakes, and many variations, and the omission of a long quotation from Amos (*transite in Chalanne* (16) . . . *domum Israel* (17)) in chapter 7. It seems to be related to both D and C.

These MSS. have been selected and used with a view merely to improving the Migne text, and particularly to detecting any misprints, especially those of a rather subtle nature. The intention has not been to make a definitive critical text such as we must still expect from the editors of the *Corpus Scriptorum Ecclesiasticorum Latinorum*. It is hoped, however, that the critical material here presented will in some measure facilitate the making of such a text.

2. DATE AND OCCASION.

An interval of some years occurred between the composition of the first and the last parts of *De Doctrina Christiana*. In *Retractations* 2, 4, 1, Augustine gives the following information in regard to this matter: "Libris de doctrina christiana, cum imperfectos comperissem, perficere malui quam eis sic relictis ad alia retractanda transire. compleui ergo tertium, . . . addidi etiam nouissimum librum et quattuor libris opus illud impleui." That the first part was written some time shortly after 396, the date of Augustine's consecration as bishop, is evident from the place where *De Doctrina Christiana* is discussed in the order of the author's works in the *Retractions*. But *Contra Faustum* 22, 91, which is dated about 400 A.D., refers to it as having been written some time before its own date. Augustine there says in explaining a certain Scriptural passage: "Quid praefigurauerit, iam in quibusdam libris, quos de doctrina christiana praenotaui, quantum mihi tunc ocurrit, me recolo posuisse." *De Docirina Christiana* itself in 2, 40, 61 fixes the date even more definitely. St. Ambrose is there referred to as being still alive. This means that the book was written at a period before April 4, 397, the date of Ambrose's death. The early months of the year 397 A.D., therefore are the accepted date of the first three books.

Book IV followed after the lapse of some years. A.D. 426–427 seems the most probable date, since, as the author himself states in chapter 24, 53, his trip to Caesarea Mauritania occurred some eight years before its composition, and the date of this trip, according to several testimonies, is 418 A.D.[1]

Though Augustine's writings after his conversion in 386 A.D. were largely of a polemical and theological nature, it is not surprising that he turned aside in 397, and the years following, to undertake a work

[1] Cf. Commentary, 24, 53.

aiming to fit the Christian orator for his important duty of inculcating the truths of religion. Augustine himself, particularly after his consecration, was a zealous preacher. Often he spent his efforts in the pulpit for five successive days in the week. He recognized the importance of Christian teaching, and he saw that it needed all the art and training of secular speaking. He therefore set himself the task of drawing up explicit directions in regard to Scriptural interpretation, and proper style and delivery, which would enable the clergy in matter of technique, to stand on equal grounds with secular orators. Style, at first thought, seems a matter of trivial importance for the consideration of one of Augustine's station; but, as he himself says in *De Doctrina Christiana*, to him nothing was small where there was question of the service of God. Moreover, there was especial need in his day for a sane and sound formulation of stylistic theory, which would reclaim rhetoric from the odium of Sophistic excess in doctrine and practice. To show the Christian orator the need of style, and to point out its proper use was, then, the purpose of the fourth book of *De Doctrina Christiana*. Augustine's doctrine is the fruit of wide experience and of deep, sound thought. For full thirty-five years he lived out its teaching, in practice. His sermons are a proof of the utility of the *doctrina sana* set forth in *De Doctrina Christiana*.

3. ANALYSIS OF *DE DOCTRINA CHRISTIANA*.

De Doctrina Christiana is a compendium of Biblical hermeneutics, supplemented by an exposition of Christian rhetoric; it is a guide to the understanding and interpretation of Holy Scripture, and to the proper explanation of the Sacred Books in homiletic. In the opening lines of Book I the main division of the work is given. Interpretation of Scripture depends on two things: the discovery of the proper meaning of the Holy Books, and the expression of that meaning, once discovered. The first three books deal with the understanding of the proper *meaning* of the Scriptures, and make up historically the first general treatise of exegesis; the fourth, explaining *how* the Scriptures should be unfolded, is a hand-book of Christian rhetoric.

Considering realities, and the signs of realities—particularly words—as the object of knowledge, Book I, analyzing the first of these, presents a broad survey of the divine economy. The conclusion reached is that love of God and its companion virtues, faith and hope, must be

the norm for the perfect interpretation of Scripture. Book II takes up
conventional signs, *i.e.* words. Difficulties and obscurities in the Holy
Books come chiefly from unknown and ambiguous words. The light
of the Holy Spirit, and the Seven Gifts of the Holy Ghost are, here, of
first importance. As for human sciences, Greek and Hebrew, among
languages, and all the more important liberal arts and sciences are
immediately necessary for a proper understanding of strange words
and figurative language. Book III deals with ambiguities, direct and
figurative. Comparison of the various translations of Holy Scripture
with one another and with the original is the principal means of clear-
ing up direct ambiguities, *i.e.* those of punctuation, pronunciation, and
meaning. As for ambiguities through figures, knowledge of the common figures of speech is helpful, but that which is all-important is the
testing of such passages by their adherence to the law of Love.

The matter of Book IV can best be summarized by a tabular outline. This will serve to bring out the unity of the treatise, and will at
once make clear the two characteristics which most distinguish it: its
classical basis, and its Christian spirit.

BOOK IV.

I. Introduction.
    A. Aim, not to set forth rules of rhetoric.   Chap.   1
    B. Usefulness of rhetorical skill to the Christian teacher.   2
    C. Time when rules should be acquired. Method.   3

II. Christian rhetoric: its basis and ideals.

CLASSICAL PRECEPTS.   CHRISTIAN ADAPTATION
                    A. Objects of the Christian teacher.   4
                        1. To instruct to righteousness.
                        2. To conciliate to righteousness.
                        3. To stir to righteousness.
                    B. Essential qualities.
                        1. Comparative value of wisdom
                            and eloquence.   5, 6
                            Examples of eloquence united
                              to wisdom in Holy Scrip-
                            ture: Paul and Amos.   7
                            a. Obscurity of Scripture, not
                                to be imitated.   8

4. SOURCES AND PARALLELS.

Cicero is the acknowledged basis of the fourth book. St. Augustine recognized the falsity and instability of the rhetoric of his time, dominated as it was by Sophistic ideals, and for the foundation of his Christian rhetoric chose to turn back four and a half centuries to the *doctrina sana* formulated in *De Oratore* and *Orator*. These two works he found all-sufficient to guide him in the expression of a worthy theory; and in reality they do crystallize the best thought on Roman oratory, and all that is most vital and lasting in Greek rhetoric. In his acknowledgment of Cicero, therefore, Augustine manifests his allegiance to all classical authorities, and with Cicero as his intermediary, he links the fifth century A.D. even with the fifth century B.C. The following comparison of classical and Christian views will be found helpful in determining the extent of the indebtedness of *De Doctrina Christiana* to the classics.

CLASSICS	ST. AUGUSTINE
I. Division of Rhetoric	
Arist. Rhet. 3, 1, 1403 b.	De Doctr. Chris. 4, 1, 1.

CLASSICS   ST. AUGUSTINE

II. Value of Rhetoric in the orator's training
   A. *Praecepta*
      De Inuent. 1, 5, 7.   De Doctr. Chris. 4, 2, 3;
      De Orat. 1, 32, 145–46;   2, 36, 54; 4, 3, 4.
         3, 36, 146; 3, 31, 125.
   B. *Imitatio* vs. *praecepta*
      De Orat. 1, 33, 150;   De Doctr. Chris. 4, 3, 4;
         2, 23, 96; 2, 22, 90.   4, 3, 5; 4, 5, 8.
   C. Eloquence without rules
      De Orat. 1, 20, 91;   De Doctr. Chris. 4, 3, 4;
         1, 32, 146.   4, 3, 5; 4, 7, 21; 2, 36, 54.
      Quint. 2, 17, 9.
III. Traditional qualities of the parts of a speech
      Ad Her. 1, 4, 6; 1, 9, 14;   De Doctr. Chris. 4, 2, 3.
         1, 10, 18; 2, 30, 47–50.
IV. Essential qualities of an orator
   A. *Sapientia* vs. *eloquentia*
      De Orat. 1, 12, 50; 1, 12, 53;   De Doctr. Chris. 4, 5, 7;
         1, 6, 20; 1, 18, 83;   4, 28, 61.
         1, 20, 92; 3, 35, 142.
      De Inuent. 1, 1, 1.
   B. *Elegantia, compositio, dignitas*
      Ad Her. 4, 12, 17.   De Doctr. Chris. 4, 10, 24.
      Orat. 23, 79; 24, 80.
      De Orat. 3, 11, 40;
         3, 13, 48ff.
   C. Clearness
      Arist. Rhet. 3, 5, 1407 b;   De Doctr. Chris. 4, 8, 22;
         3, 2, 1404 b.   4, 9, 23; 4, 10, 24.
      De Orat. 3, 10, 37-39;
         3, 14, 52.
      Orat. 23, 77ff.
      Quint. 8, 2, 1; 8, 2, 22.
      Through Repetition
      Quint. 8, 2, 24.   De Doct. Chris. 4, 10, 25.
                        De Catech. Rud. 13, 18.

   D. Charm
      Arist. Rhet. 3, 1, 1404 a.   De Doctr. Chris. 4, 10, 25;
      De Orat. 3, 30, 121;   4, 11, 26; 4, 12, 27;
         3, 31, 125; 3, 25, 97.   4, 13, 29; 4, 14, 31.
      Orat. 6, 20; 25, 83.

CLASSICS   ST. AUGUSTINE

E. Fittingness (τὸ πρέπον)
    Arist. Rhet. 3, 2, 1404 b.   De Doctr. Chris. 4, 6, 9; 4, 7, 13;
    De Orat. 1, 32, 144;   4, 7, 17; 4, 7, 18; 4, 7, 19;
        1, 61, 260.   4, 7, 20; 4, 17, 34; 4, 20, 40;
    Orat. 21, 70–73; 35, 123;   4, 20, 42; 4, 28, 61.
        36, 124.
    Quint. 12, 10, 79–80.

V. *Officia oratoris*
  A. General
    Arist. Rhet. 1, 2, 1355 b;   De Doct. Chris. 4, 4, 6;
        1, 2, 1356 a.   4, 12, 27; 4, 17, 34.
    De Orat. 2, 27, 115;
        2, 28, 121; 2, 77, 310.
    Brut. 49, 185.
    De Opt. Gen. 1, 3; 5, 16.
    Officia as twofold
    Aris. Rhet. 1, 2, 1355 b.   De Doctr. Chris. 4, 4, 6.
    De Orat. 2, 77, 310; 2, 27, 120. Contr. Cresc. 1, 13, 16.
    Brut. 23, 89.   De Dial. 7.

  B. Particular
    1. *Docere*: its purpose and importance
    Arist. Rhet. 3, 1, 1404 a.   De Doctr. Chris. 4, 11, 26;
    De Orat. 1, 53, 229;   4, 12, 27; 4, 12, 28.
        2, 27, 115.
    2. *Delectare*: its need to *docere*
    Ad Her. 4, 11, 16.   De Doctr. Chris. 4, 11, 26.
    De Orat. 3, 11, 41.
    Orat. 25, 85; 33, 117.
    3. *Flectere*: the end of oratory
    Arist. Rhet. 1, 2, 1355 b;   De Doctr. Chris. 4, 12, 27;
        1, 1, 1354 a.   4, 12, 28; 4, 13, 29.
    De Inuent. 1, 5, 6.
    De Orat. 1, 31, 138; 1, 49, 213;
        1, 61, 260.

VI. The Styles
  A. General
    1. Definition
    Ad Her. 4, 8, 11.   De Doctr. Chris. 4, 17, 34;
    De Orat. 3, 45, 177;   4, 28, 61.
        3, 52, 199; 3, 55, 212.
    Orat. 29, 101; 21, 69.

CLASSICS   ST. AUGUSTINE

2. Variation of the styles
   a. Necessity

Ad Her. 4, 11, 16.	De Doctr. Chris. 4, 22, 51;
Orat. 29, 103.	2, 36, 54.
Quint. 12, 10, 71; 12, 10, 67.	Contr. Cresc. 1, 16, 20.
	De Dial. 7.

   b. Manner

Orat. 35, 122; 36, 124; 36, 125.	De Doctr. Chris. 4, 23, 52.

3. Union in one speech

Ad Her. 4, 8, 11ff.	De Doctr. Chris. 4, 19, 38.

B. Particular

1. *Genus submissum*
   a. Qualities

Ad Her. 4, 10, 14.	De Doctr. Chris. 4, 19, 38;
Orat. 5, 20; 23, 76; 24, 79.	4, 20, 39; 4, 22, 51.
Orat. 28, 98-9; 29, 102;	De Doctr. Chris. 4, 23, 52;
33, 116; 35, 122.	4, 24, 54; 4, 25, 55; 4, 26, 56.
Quint. 12, 10, 59.	Contr. Cresc. 1, 13, 16; 1, 16, 20.
	De Dial. 7.

   b. Examples

Ad Her. 4, 10, 14.	De Doctr. Chris. 4, 19, 38;
Orat. 29, 102.	4, 20, 39; 4, 21, 45; 4, 21, 46.
	Contr. Cresc. 1, 16, 20.

2. *Genus temperatum*
   a. Its two phases
      i. *Tertium quid*

Ad Her. 4, 8, 11; 4, 9, 13.	De Doctr. Chris. 4, 18, 35.
De Orat. 3, 52, 199;	
3, 55, 212.	
Orat. 6, 21; 26, 91.	
Quint. 12, 10, 58.	

      ii. γένος ἀνθηρόν

Orat. 12, 38; 26, 91; 27, 96.	De Doctr. Chris. 4, 20, 40;
Quint. 12, 10, 58; 12, 10, 60.	4, 20, 41.

   b. Qualities

Orat. 27, 96; 28, 98; 37, 128.	De Doctr. Chris. 4, 19, 38;
	4, 20, 40; 4, 20, 41; 4, 23, 52;
	4, 24, 54; 4, 25, 55; 4, 26, 57.

   c. Examples

Ad Her. 4, 9, 13.	De Doctr. Chris. 4, 19, 38;
Orat. 29, 102.	4, 20, 40; 4, 21, 47; 4, 21, 48.

CLASSICS	ST. AUGUSTINE
3. *Genus sublime*	
a. Qualities	
Plat. Phaedr. 271 d.	De Doctr. Chris. 4, 20, 42;
Ad Her. 4, 8, 11.	4, 22, 51; 4, 23, 52; 4, 24, 53;
Orat. 5, 20; 28, 97; 28, 99;	4, 25, 55; 4, 26, 58.
37, 128; 39, 134.	
Quint. 12, 10, 61.	
b. Examples	
Ad Her. 4, 8, 12.	De Doctr. Chris. 4, 19, 38;
Orat. 29, 102.	4, 20, 42; 4, 20, 43; 4, 20, 44;
	4, 21, 49; 4, 21, 50.

VII. *Compositio*

  A. *Iunctura*

    1. *Membrum*

Ad Her. 4, 19, 26	De Doctr. Chris. 4, 7, 11; 4, 7, 13.
Orat. 66, 221-2.	De Mus. 4, 17, 36.
Quint. 9, 4, 123; 9, 4, 125.	

    2. *Caesum*

Orat. 62, 211.	De Doctr. Chris. 4, 7, 11; 4, 7, 13.
Quint. 9, 4, 22.	
Aquila Rhet. 18.	

    3. *Ambitus*

Orat. 61, 204.	De Doctr. Chris. 4, 7, 11; 4, 7, 13.
Quint. 9, 4, 124.	
Mart. Cap. 5, 527.	

  B. *Sonus*

Orat. 49, 163.	De Doctr. Chris. 4, 20, 40.

  C. *Numerus*

    a. Nature

Orat. 20, 67; 49, 163; 53, 178;	De Doctr. Chris. 4, 20, 40;
55, 183; 70, 233.	4, 20, 41; 4, 26, 56.

    b. Laws

Orat. 58, 197.	De Doctr. Chris. 4, 20, 41.

    c. *Clausulae*

Quint. 9, 4, 61; 9, 4, 66.	De Doctr. Chris. 4, 20, 40;
	4, 20, 41.

  D. Importance of *pronuntiatio* to *compositio*

Brut. 8, 34.	De Doctr. Chris. 4, 7, 11; 4, 17,
	18; 4, 7, 19; 4, 7, 20; 4, 7, 21.

CLASSICS	ST. AUGUSTINE

VIII. *Figurae*

  A. *Figurae uerborum*

      Orat. 39, 135.   De Doctr. Chris. 4, 20, 43.

      a. *Climax*

      Ad Her. 4, 25, 34.   De Doctr. Chris. 4, 7, 11.

      Quint. 9, 3, 55.

      b. *Responsio*

      Orat. 40, 137.   De Doctr. Chris. 4, 7, 13.

      De Orat. 3, 54, 207.

  B. *Figurae sententiarum*

      Orat. 39, 136; 40, 137.   De Doctr. Chris. 4, 20, 42.

IX. Memory

  A. Of words

      De Orat. 2, 88, 359.   De Doctr. Chris. 4, 10, 25;
                                  4, 29, 62.

  B. Of things

      De Orat. 2, 88, 359.   De Doctr. Chris. 4, 20, 39.

X. Moral Requisites

  A. *Vita bona*

      Arist. Rhet. 1, 2, 1356 a. De Doctr. Chris. 4, 27, 59;

      De Orat. 2, 43, 182; 2, 20, 85.   4, 27, 60.

      Quint. 12, 1, 1; 12, 1, 2-3;
          12, 1, 29.

  B. Self-diffidence

      De Orat. 1, 26, 119;   De Doctr. Chris. 4, 15, 32.
        1, 26, 121.

XI. Oratorical ideal, and its opposite

  A. The ideal

      De Orat. 1, 15, 64; 1, 8, 31; De Doctr. Chris. 4, 4, 6;

      2, 8, 34; 1, 46, 202.   4, 28, 61.

      Orat. 2, 7-8.

  B. Sophistic

      Arist. Rhet. 3, 5, 1407 a. De Doctr. Chris. 4, 5, 8; 4, 6, 10;

      De Orat. 1, 19, 87; 1, 20, 91.   4, 6, 9; 4, 28, 61; 2, 31; 48.

      Orat. 19, 65; 69; 230ff.   Contr. Cresc. 1, 2, 3; 1, 1, 2.

      Quint. 8, 2, 18.   Conf. 1, 18, 28.

5. BIBLICAL QUOTATIONS.

Though it is generally accepted that after 400 A.D. St. Augustine regularly employed the Vulgate in his quotations from the Gospels, a study
of his use of the Epistles in such long quotations as occur in *De Doctrine
Christiana* IV does not admit of the same conclusion. The following
pages present parallel readings of *De Doctrina Christiana*, the Vulgate,
and the Old Latin Version for such Scriptural passages as are formally
quoted in the fourth book.

Before taking up the consideration of the Epistles, a review of
the other quotations will be helpful. In only one instance in this book
is the biblical source explicitly stated. Amos 7, 14-15, in chapter 7,
15, is quoted from the Vulgate, as Augustine himself states, with the
explanation that he rejects the Septuagint here because of its greater
figurativeness, and its consequent obscurity. Such an acknowledgment
is, of course, a valuable proof of Augustine's esteem for the work
of his celebrated contemporary. This, he had already manifested by
his use of the Vulgate Gospels in his critical work, *De Consensu Euan-
gelistarum* (400 A.D.), and by his letter praising the Revision, written to Jerome in 403. The same letter, however, gives evidence of
Augustine's doubts as to the expediency of the great changes made
in the Vulgate Old Testament, and expresses the desire that Jerome
should rather make an exact translation from the Septuagint, since
the different codices of the Latin text were at the time very numerous,
and were open to suspicion as possibly at variance with the Greek.
Augustine himself habitually used the Old Version in quoting from
the Old Testament. In the fourth book, besides the quotation from
Amos referred to above, the only other Old Testament quotation of
any length is that from Jeremias 5, 30-31. This, as one would expect,
agrees with the *Versio Antiqua* against the Vulgate. In regard to the
other quotations, Psalm 15, 4 and Psalm 34, 18 follow the Vulgate;
the others differ from both the Vulgate and the Old Version, probably
because quoted from memory, with the deviations usual in such cases.
The same reason, doubtless, also accounts for the variants shown in
the Gospel quotations which are found in this book. Of these, only
Matthew 10, 19-20 agrees with the Old Version and the Vulgate.

The remaining quotations—by far the longest and the most
important—are drawn from the Epistles of St. Paul. These, for the
greater part, are set down as models of the various styles, though there
are also a few short selections, scattered here and there, in illustration

of minor points. A comparison of these with the Vulgate shows complete identity between the two in only three of the short quotations. In the longer passages the *De Doctrina Christiana* rendering is sometimes nearer to the Vulgate than to the *Versio Antiqua*, but nowhere are the two entirely identical, and in some places Augustine is in evident disagreement with Jerome's text, and in agreement with the Old Version. Moreover, in 1 Corinthians 1, 17, and 1 Corinthians 3, 7, where the Vulgate and the Old Version are identical, and in Romans 5, 3-5 and Romans 12, 1; 6-16, where they are practically identical, there are many variants in the *De Doctrina* rendering which have no authority in the Vulgate and Old Version.

From these facts several inferences suggest themselves, all more or less hypothetical, and therefore to be handled guardedly until further evidence is at hand. One conclusion, however, may be safely drawn, and that is that for these quotations Augustine did not make use of a Vulgate codex, though this would seem to have often been his custom for Gospel quotations after 400. The quotations here considered may be a mosaic of Vulgate and Old Version renderings, if one would see in their mingling of Old Version and Vulgate readings a meeting in Augustine's memory of the influence of the old and the new. However, the very number and length of these passages would rather seem to preclude the idea that they are drawn from memory. A memory which could be called on to quote accurately passage after passage of ten, twelve, or sixteen verses would be no common one. Moreover, these long quotations were consciously selected and put forward as models of *style*. It seems hardly probable that Augustine would forego the exactness desirable in such a case, when he could so readily secure it by the use of a reliable codex. This view receives added favor from the fact that where Augustine, in another of his works, *Contra Cresconium* (1, 16, 20), uses one of these quotations (2 Cor. 6, 4-10), he employs the identical rendering used in *De Doctrina Christiana*. This differs considerably from the Vulgate and the Old Version taken individually, and shows some variants without foundation in either the one or the other. If this rendering occurred but once, in *De Doctrina Christiana* or *Contra Cresconium*, one might concede that it was a composite of the Vulgate and the Old Version, resembling them and differing from them as Augustine's memory suggested the one or the other; but the fact that this same individual reading appears in two different treatises, its variants identical in each, would seem rather to point to the use of a common *written* source for both. If then Augustine did use an Old Latin codex for his Epistle quotations in the fourth book, what was it? Could it have been the *Itala* which received such unstinted praise in the second book of *De Doctrina Christiana*? Whatever it was, if it really was Augustine's source, it must have been held in high repute since in this treatise where style was the point under consideration it received preference to the Vulgate, which was otherwise so widely accepted by Augustine in his later years. The readings from the Vulgate and the *Versio Antiqua* which follow are taken from *Biblia sacra iuxta Vulgatam Clementinam*, edited by the Professors of St. Sulpice (Rome, Paris, 1927), and from Sabatier: *Bibliorum sacrorum Latinae uersiones seu uetus Italica* (Paris, 1751). It should be noted that Sabatier acknowledges his indebtedness to *De Doctrina Christiana*, in his Old Version reconstruction of the following passages: Luc. 16, 10; Rom. 5, 3-5; *ibid.* 8, 28-39; *ibid.* 12, 1; 6-16; *ibid.* 13, 6-8; 12-14; 1 Cor. 6, 1-9; *ibid.* 6, 2-11; *ibid.* 11, 16-31; Gal. 3, 15-22; *ibid.* 4, 10-20; *ibid.* 4, 21-26; 1 Tim. 4, 12; *ibid.* 5, 1-2; 2 Tim. 2, 15; *ibid.* 3, 14; *ibid.* 4, 2; Tit. 1, 9; *ibid.* 2, 1-2.

De Doctr. Chris.	Vulgata	Versio Antiqua
Psal. 15, 4		
non congregabo conuenticula eorum de sanguinibus (10, 24).	non congregabo conuenticula eorum de sanguinibus.	non congregabo conuenticula eorum in sanguinibus.
Psal. 34, 18		
in populo graui laudabo te (14, 31).	in populo graui laudabo te.	in populo graui laudabo te.
Psal. 92, 5		
testimonia tua credita facta sunt ualde (26, 56).	testimonia tua credibilia facta sunt nimis.	testimonia tua credibilia facta sunt nimis.
Psal. 142, 10		
doce me facere uoluntatem tuam, quoniam tu es Deus meus (16, 33).	doce me facere uoluntatem tuam, quia Deus meus es tu.	doce me facere uoluntatem tuam, quia tu Deus meus es.
Sap. 6, 26		
multitudo sapientium sanitas est orbis terrarum (5,8).	multitudo autem sapientium sanitas est orbis terrarumm.	multitudo autem sapientium sanitas est orbis terrarum.
Ier. 5, 30-31		
pauor et horrenda facta sunt super terram; prophetae prophetabant iniqua et sacerdotes plausum dederunt manibus suis et plebs mea	stupor et mirabilia facta sunt in terra: prophetae prophetabant mendacium, et sacerdotes applaudebant minibus suis, et populus meus	pauor et horrenda facta super terram: prophetae prophetabunt iniqua, et sacerdotes plausum dederunt manibus suis: et plebs mea di-

De Doctr. Chris.	**Vulgata**	**Versio Antiqua**
dilexit sic. et quid facietis in futurum? (14, 30).	dilexit talia. quid igitur fiet in nouissimo eius?	lexit sic: et quid facietis in futurum?

Amos 6, 1-6

uae qui opulenti estis in Sion, et confiditis in monte Samariae, optimates capita populorum, ingredientes pompatice domum Israel! transite in Chalanne, et uidete, et ite inde in Emath magnam, et descendite in Geth Palaestinorum, et ad optima quaeque regna horum, si latior terminus eorum termino uestro est. qui separati estis in diem malum et appropinquatis solio iniquitatis. qui dormitis in lectis eburneis, et lasciuitis in stratis uestris; qui comeditis agnum de grege, et uitulos de medio armenti; qui canitis ad uocem psalterii. sicut Dauid putauerunt se habere uasa cantici; bibentes in phialis uinum, et optimo unguento delibuti; et nihil patiebantur super contritione Ioseph (7, 16).	uae qui opulenti estis in Sion, et confiditis in monte Samariae; optimates capita populorum, ingredientes pompatice domum Israel! transite in Chalane, et uidete, et ite inde in Emath magnam, et descendite in Geth Palaestinorum, et ad optima quaeque regna horum: si latior terminus eorum termino uestro est. qui separati estis in diem malum, et appropinquatis solio iniquitatis; qui dormitis in lectis eburneis, et lasciuitis in stratis uestris; qui comeditis agnum de grege, et uitulos de medio armenti; qui canitis ad uocem psalterii; sicut Dauid putauerunt se habere uasa cantici; bibentes uinum in phialis, et optimo unguento delibuti, et nihil patiebantur super contritione Ioseph.	uae qui despiciunt Sion, et confidunt in monte Samariae: uindemiarunt primitias gentium, et ingressi sunt sibi. domus Israel transite omnes, et uidete in Chalanem, et pertransite inde in Emath rabba: et descendite in Geth alienigenarum, optimas ex omnibus regnis his: si ampliores sunt termini eorum terminis uestris. qui uenitis in diem malum: appropinquatis et tangitis sabbata mendacia. qui dormitis in lectis eburneis, et affluitis deliciiis in stratis uestris: et comeditis haedos de gregibus, et lactentes uitulos de medio armentorum. qui concrepatis ad uocem organorum: quasi stantia putauerunt, et non quasi fugientia. qui bibitis uinum desecatum, et primis unguentis ungimini: et nihil patiebamini super contritione Ioseph.

Matt. 6, 8

scit pater uester quid uobis necessarium sit, prius quam petatis ab eo (16, 33).	scit pater uester, quid opus sit uobis, antequam petatis eum.	scit enim pater uester, quid uobis opus sit, antequam petatis ab eo.

Matt. 10, 19-20

nolite cogitare quomodo aut quid loquamini; dabitur enim uobis in illa	nolite cogitare quomodo aut quid loquamini: dabitur enim uobis in illa	nolite cogitare quomodo aut quid loquamini; dabitur enim uobis in

De Doctr. Chris.	**Vulgata**	**Versio Antiqua**
hora quid loquamini: non enim uos estis qui loquimini, sed Spiritus Patris uestri qui loquitur in uobis (15, 32).	hora quid loquamini: non enim uos estis loquimini, sed Spiritus Patris uestri qui loquitur in uobis.	illa hora, quid loquamini: non enim estis uos qui loguimini, sed Spiritus Patris uestri, qui loquitur in uobis.

Matt. 12, 34

hypocritae, quomodo potestis bona loqui, cum sitis mali? (29, 62).	progenies uiperarum, quomodo potestis bona loqui, cum sitis mali?	progenies uiperarum, quomodo potestis bona loqui, cum sitis mali?

Matt. 23, 2-3

super cathedram Moysi sederunt...quae dicunt, facite, quae autem faciunt, facere nolite. dicunt enim et non faciunt (27, 59; 29, 62).	super cathedram Moysi sederunt scribae et pharisaei. omnia ergo quaecumque dixerunt uobis, seruate, et facite; secundum opera uero eorum nolite facere: dicunt enim, et non faciunt.	super cathedram Moysi sederunt scribae, et pharisaei. omnia ergo quaecumque dixerunt uobis, seruate, et facite: secundum autem facta eorum nolite facere: dicunt enim, et ipsi non faciunt.

Luc. 16, 10

qui in minimo fidelis est, et in mango fidelis est (18, 35).	qui fidelis est in minimo, et in maiori fidelis est.	qui fidelis est in minimo, et in maius fidelis est.

Rom. 5, 3-5

gloriamur in tribulationibus, scientes quia tribulatio patientiam operatur, patientia autem probationem, probatio autem spem, spes autem non confundit: quia charitas Dei diffusa est in cordibus nostris per Spiritum sanctum qui datus est nobis (7, 11).	gloriamur in tribulationibus, scientes quia tribulatio patientiam operatur, patientia autem probationem, probatio uero spem. spes autem non confundit, quia charitas Dei diffusa est in cordibus nostris per Spiritum sanctum, qui datus est nobis.	gloriamur in tribulationibus, scientes quod tribulatio patientiam operatur: patientia autem probationem, probatio autem spem, spes autem non confundit: quia caritas Dei diffusa est in cordibus nostris per Spiritum sanctum, qui datus est nobis.

Rom. 8, 28-39

scimus, quoniam diligentibus Deum omnia cooperantur in bonum, iis qui secundum propositum uocati sunt. quoniam quos ante praesciuit, et praedestinauit conformes imaginis Filii sui, ut sit ipse	scimus autem quoniam diligentibus Deum omnia cooperantur in bonum, iis qui secundum propositum uocati sunt sancti. nam quos praesciuit, et praedestinauit conformes fieri imaginis Filii sui, ut sit ipse	scimus autem quoniam diligentibus Deum omnia procedunt in bonis, his qui secundum propositum uocati sunt. quia quos praescit, et praedestinauit conformes fieri imaginis Filii eius, ut sit ipse primogenitus

De Doctr. Chris.	**Vulgata**	**Versio Antiqua**
primogenitus in multis fratribus. quos autem praedestinauit, illos et uocauit; et quos uocauit, ipsos et iustificauit; quos autem iustificauit, illos et glorificauit. quid ergo dicemus ad haec? si Deus pro nobis, quis contra nos? qui Filio proprio non pepercit, sed pro nobis omnibus tradidit eum, quomodo non et cum illo omnia nobis donauit? quis accusabit aduersus electos Dei? Deus qui iustificat? quis est qui condemnet? Christus Iesus qui mortuus est, magis autem qui resurrexit, qui est in dextera Dei, qui et interpellat pro nobis? quis nos separabit a charitate Christi? tribulatio? an angustia? an persecutio? an fames? an nuditas? an periculum? an gladius? sicut scriptum est, 'quia propter te mortificamur tota die, aestimati sumus ut oues occisionis.' sed in his omnibus superuincimus per eum qui dilexit nos. certus sum enim quia neque mors, neque uita, neque angelus, neque principatus, neque praesentia, neque futura, neque uirtus, neque altitudo, neque profundum, neque creatura alia poterit nos	primogenitus in multis fratribus. quos autem praedestinauit, hos et uocauit; et quos uocauit, hos et iustificauit; quos autem iustificauit, illos et glorificauit. quid ergo dicemus ad haec? si Deus pro nobis, quis contra nos? qui etiam proprio Filio suo non pepercit, sed pro nobis omnibus tradidit illum, quomodo non etiam cum illo omnia nobis donauit? quis accusabit aduersus electos Dei? Deus, qui iustificat, quis est, qui condemnet? Christus Iesus, qui mortuus est, immo qui et resurrexit, qui est ad dexteram Dei, qui etiam interpellat pro nobis. quis ergo nos separabit a charitate Christi? tribulatio? an angustia? an fames? an nuditas? an periculum? an persecutio? an gladius? (scriptum est: quia propter te mortificamur tota die; aestimati sumus sicut oues occisionis) sed in his omnibus superamus propter eum, qui dilexit nos. certus sum enim, quia neque mors, neque uita, neque angeli, neque principatus, neque uirtutes, neque instantia, neque futura, neque fortitudo, neque altitudo, neque profundum, neque	in multis fratribus. quos autem praedestinauit, eos et uocauit: et quos uocauit, eos et iustificauit: quos autem iustificauit, illos et magnificauit. quid ergo dicemus aduersus haec: si Deus pro nobis, quis contra nos? qui nec Filio suo pepercit, sed pro nobis omnibus tradidit illum: quomodo non etiam cum illo omnia nobis donauit? quis aduersus excusauit electos Dei? Deus qui iustificat, quis condemnet? Christus, qui mortuus est, imo et resurrexit, qui et est ad dexteram Dei, qui etiam interpellat pro nobis. quis nos separabit a caritate Christi? tribulatio? an angustia? an persecutio? an fames? an nuditas? an periculum? an gladius? (sicut scriptum est: quia propter te morti afficimur tota die: aestimati sumus ut oues occisionis.) sed in his omnibus superamus propter eum, qui dilexit nos. certus sum enim, quia neque mors, neque uita, neque angelus, neque potestas, neque initia, neque instantia, neque futura, neque uirtus, neque altitudo, neque profundum, neque creatura alia poterit nos separare a caritate

De Doctr. Chris.	Vulgata	Versio Antiqua
separare a charitate Dei, quae est in Christo Iesu Domino nostro (20, 43).	creatura alia poterit nos separare a charitate Dei, quae est in Christo Iesu Domino nostro.	Dei, quae est in Christo Iesu Domino nostro.

Rom. 12, 1; 6-16

obsecro autem uos, fratres, per miserationem Dei, ut exhibeatis corpora uestra hostiam uiuam, sanctam, Deo placentem. . . . habentes dona diuersa secundum gratiam quae data est nobis; siue prophetiam, secundum regulam fidei; siue ministerium, in ministrando; siue qui docet, in doctrina; siue qui exhortatur, in exhortatione; qui tribuit, in simplicitate; qui praeest, in sollicitudine; qui miseretur, in hilaritate. dilecto sine simulatione; odio habentes malum, adhaerentes bono: charitate fraternitatis inuicem diligentes, honore mutuo praeuenientes, studio non pigri, spiritu feruentes, Domino seruientes, spe gaudentes, in tribulatione patientes, orationi instantes, necessariis sanctorum communicantes, hospitalitatem sectantes. benedicte persequentes uos; benedicite, et nolite maledicere. guadere cum gaudentibus, fiere cum flentibus; idipsum inuicem sentientes. non alta sapientes, sed humilibus consentientes (20, 40).	obsecro itaque uos, fratres, per misericordiam Dei, ut exhibeatis corpora uestra hostiam uiuentem, sanctam, Deo placentem, rationabile obsequium uestrum. . . . . habentes autem donationes secundum gratiam, quae data est nobis, differentes; siue prophetiam secundum rationem fidei, sine ministerium in ministrando, siue qui docet in doctrina, qui exhortatur in exhortando, qui tribuit in simplicitate, qui praeest in sollicitudine, qui miseretur in hilaritate. dilectio sine simulatione: odientes malum, adhaerentes bono; charitate fraternitatis inuicem diligentes; honore inuicem praeuenientes; sollicitudine non pigri; spiritu feruentes; Domino seruientes; spe gaudentes; in tribulatione patientes; orationi instantes; necessitatibus sanctorum communicantes; hospitalitatem sectantes. benedicite persequentibus uos: benedicite, et nolite maledicere. gaudere cum gaudentibus, fiere cum flentibus; idipsum inuicem sentientes; non alta sapientes, sed humilibus consentientes.	obsecro itaque uos fratres per misericordiam Dei, ut exhibeatis corpora uestra hostiam uiuentem sanctam, placentem Deo, rationabile obsequium uestrum. . . . habentes autem donationes secundum gratiam, quae data est nobis, differentes, siue prophetiam secundum rationem fidei, siue ministerium in ministrando, siue qui docet in doctrina, qui exhortatur in exhortando, qui tribuit in simplicitate, qui praeest in sollicitudine, qui miseretur in hilaritate. dilectio sine simulatione. odientes malum adhaerentes bono: caritate fraternitatis inuicem benigni: honore inuicem praeuenientes: sollicitudine non pigri: spiritu feruentes: Domino seruientes: spe gaudentes: in tribulatione patientes: orationi instantes: necessitatibus sanctorum communicantes: hospitalitatem sectantes. benedicite et nolite maledicere: benedicite persequentibus uos. gaudere cum gaudentibus, fiere cum flentibus: idipsum inuicem sentientes: non alta sapientes, sed humilibu consentientes.

De Doctr. Chris. **Rom. 13, 6-8; 12-14**	**Vulgata**	**Versio Antiqua**
in hoc ipso perseuerantes, reddite omnibus debita; cui tributum, tributum; cui uectigal, uectigal; cui timorem, timorem; cui honorem, honorem. nemini quidquam debeatis, nisi ut inuicem diligatis. . . . nox praecessit, dies autum appropinquauit. abiciamus itaque opera tenebrarum, et induamus nos arma lucis: sicut in die honeste ambulemus; non in comessationibus et ebrietatibus, non in cubilibus et impudicitiis, non in contentione et aemulatione; sed induite Dominum Iesus Christum, et carnis pruidentiam ne feceritis in concupiscentiis (20, 40).	in hoc ipso seuerantes. reddite ergo omnibus debita: cui tributum, tributum; cui uectigal, uectigal; cui timorem, timorem; cui honorem, honorem. nemini quidquam debeatis, nisi ut inuicem diligatis. . . . . nox praecessit, dies autem appropinquauit. abiciamus ergo opera tenebrarum, et induamur arma lucis. sicut in die honeste ambulemus, non in comessationibus et ebrietatibus, non in cubilibus et impudicitiis, non in contentione et aemulatione: sed induimini Dominum Iesum Christum, et carnis curam ne feceritis in desideriis.	in hoc ipsum seruientes. reddite ergo omnibus debita: cui tributum, tributum: cui uectigal. uectigal: cui timorem, timorem: cui honorem, honorem. nemini quicquam debeatis, nisi ut inuicem diligatis. . . . nox praecessit, dies autem adpropriauit. abiciamus ergo facta tenebrarum, et induamur opera lucis. sicut in die honeste ambulemus: non comessationibus, et ebrietatibus, non cubilibus, et impudicitiis, non contentione, et aemulatione: sed induite Dominum Iesum Christum, et carnis curam ne feceritis in desideriis.
1 Cor. 1, 17		
non in sapentia uerbi, ne euacuetur crux Christi (28, 61).	non in sapentia uerbi, ut non euacuetur crux Christi.	non in sapentia uerbi, ut non euacuetur crux Christi.
1 Cor. 3, 7		
et tamen neque qui plantat est aliquid, neque qui rigat, sed Deus qui incrementum dat (16, 33).	itaque neque, qui plantat, est aliquid, neque, qui rigat, sed, qui incrementum dat, Deus.	itaque neque qui plantat est aliquid, neque qui rigat: sed, qui incrementum dat, Deus.
1 Cor. 6, 1-9		
audet quisquam uestrum aduersus alterum negotium habens, iudicari ab iniquis, et non apud sanctos? an nescitis quia sancti mundum iudicabunt? et si in uobis iudicabitur mundus, indigni estis qui de minimis iudicetis? nescitis quoniam ange-	audet aliquis uestrum, habens negotium aduersus alterum, iudicari apud iniquos, et non apud sanctos? an nescitis, quoniam sancti de hoc mundo iudicabunt? et si in uobis iudicabitur mundus, indigni estis, qui de minimis iudicetis? nescitis quo-	audet aliquis uestrum, aduersus alterum negotium habens, iudicari apud iniustos et non apud sanctos? aut nescitis quia sancti de hoc mundo iudicabunt, et in uobis iudicabitur hic mundus? indigni estis iudiciorum minimorum. nescitis quoniam ange-

De Doctr. Chris.	Vulgata	Versio Antiqua
los iudicabimus, nedum saecularia? saecularia igitur iudicia si habueritis, eos qui contemptibiles sunt in ecclesia, hos collocate ad iudicandum. ad reuerentiam uobis dico. sic non est inter uos quisquam sapiens, qui posit inter fratrem suum iudicare? sed frater cum fratre iudicatur et hoc apud infideles. iam quidem omnino delictum est, quia uidicia habetis uobiscum. quare non magis iniquitatem patimini? quare non potius fraudamini? sed uos iniquitatem facitis, et fraudatis, et hoc fratres. an nescitis quia iniusti regnum Dei non haereditabunt? (18, 36).	niam angelos iudicabimus? quanto magis saecularia? saecularia igitur si habueritis, contemtibiles, qui sunt in ecclesia, illos constituite ad iudicandum. ad uerecundiam uestram dico. sic non est inter uos sapiens quisquam, qui possit iudicare inter fratrem suum? sed frater cum fratre iudicio contendit, et hoc apud infideles? iam quidem omnino delictum est in uobis, quod iudicia habetis inter uos. quare non magis iniuriam accipitis? quare non magis fraudem patimini? sed uos iniuriam facitis, et fraudatis: et hoc fratribus. an nescitis, quia iniqui regnum Dei non possidebunt?	los iudicamus, neque saecularia? saecularia igitur iudicia si habueritis: contemptibiles qui sunt in ecclesia, illos constutuite. ad reuerentiam uobia dico. sic non est inter uos sapiens, qui posit iudicare inter fratrem suum? sed frater cum fratre iudicio contendit: et hoc apud infideles? iam quidem omnino delictum est uobis, quia iudicia habetis inter uos. quare non magis iniuriam patimini? quare non magis fraudamini? sed sed uos fraudatis, et iniuriam facitis: et hoc fratribus. aut nescitis quoniam iniqui regnum Dei non possidebunt?

2 Cor. 6, 2-11

ecce nunc tempus acceptabile, ecce nunc dies salutis. nullam in quoquam dantes offensionem, ut non reprehendatur ministerium nostrum: sed in omnibus commendantes nosmetipsos ut Dei ministros, in multa patientia, in tribulationibus, in necessitatibus, in angustiis, in plagis, in carceribus, in seditionibus, in laboribus, in uigiliis, in ieiuniis, in castitate, in scientia, in longanimitate, in benignitate, in Spiritu sancto, in	ecce, nunc tempus acceptabile: ecce, nunc dies salutis. nemini dantes ullam offensionem, ut non uituperetur ministerium nostrum: sed in omnibus exhibeamus nosmetipsos sicut Dei ministros in multa patientia, in tribulationibus, in necessitatibus, in angustiis, in plagis, in carceribus, in seditionibus, in laboribus, in uigiliis, in ieiuniis, in castitate, in scientia, in longanimitate, in suauitate, in Spiritu sancto, in charitate non ficta,	ecce nunc tempus acceptum, ecce nunc dies salutis: nullam in nullo dantes offensionem, ut non uituperetur ministerium nostrum: sed in omnibus commendantes nosmetipsos sicut Dei ministry, in patientia multa, in tribulationibus, in necessitatibus, in angustiis, in plagis, in carceribus, in seditionibus, in laboribus, in uigiliis, in ieiuniis, in castitate, in scientia, in magnanimitate, in benignitate, in Spiritu sancto, in caritate non

De Doctr. Chris.	Vulgata	Versio Antiqua
charitate non ficta, in uerbo ueritatis, in uirtute Dei: per arma iustitiae dextra et sinistra, per gloriam et ignobilitatem, per infamiam et bonam famam; ut seductores, et ueraces; ut qui ignoramur, et cognoscimur; quasi morientes, et ecce uiuimus: ut coerciti, et non mortificati; ut tristes, semper autem gaudentes; sicut egeni, multos autem ditantes; tamquam nihil habentes, et omnia possidentes. os nostrum patet ad uos, o Corinthii: cor nostrum dilatatum est (19, 42).	in uerbo ueritatis, in uirtute Dei, per arma iustitiae a dextris et a sinistris, per gloriam et ignobilitatem, per infamiam et bonam famam: ut seductores et ueraces, sicut qui ignoti et cogniti; quasi morientes, et ecce, uiuimus: ut castigati et non mortificati: quasi tristes, simper autem gaudentes; sicut egentes, multos autem locupletantes: tamquam nihil habentes; et omnia possidentes. os nostrum patet ad uos, o Corinthii, cor nostrum dilatatum est.	ficta, in uerbo ueritatis, in uirtute Dei, per arma iustitiae a dextris, et sinistris; per gloriam in nouitatem; per infamiam, et bonam famam: ut seductores, et ueraces; ut qui ignoramur, et cognoscimus: ut morientes, et ecce uiuimus: ut tentati, et non mortificati: ut tristes, simper autem gaudentes: sicut et egentes, multos autem locupletantes: tamquam nihil habentes, et omnia possidentes. os nostrum patet ad uos, Corinthii, cor nostrum dilatatum est.

2 Cor. 11, 6

etsi imperitus sermone, sed non scientia (7, 15).	nam et si imperitus sermone, sed non scientia.	etsi imperitus sum sermone, sed non scientia.

2 Cor. 11, 16-31

iterum dico, ne quis me existimet insipientem esse; alioquin uelut insipientem suscipite me, ut et ego modicum quid glorier. quod loquor, non loquor secundum Deum, sed quasi in stultitia, in hac substantia gloriae. quoniam quidem multi gloriantur secundum carnem, et ego gloriabor. libenter enim sustinetis insipientes, cum sitia ipsi sapientes. toleratis enim si quis uos in seruitutem redigit, si quis deuorat, si quis accipit, si quis extollitur, si quis in faciem uos caedit. secun-	iterum dico (ne quis me putet insipientem esse, alioquin uelut insipientem accipite me, ut et ego modicum quid glorier): quod loquor, non loquor secundum Deum, sed quasi in insipientia, in hac substantia gloriae. quoniam multi gloriantur secundum carnem, et ego gloriabor. libenter enim suffertis insipientes, cum sitis ipsi sapientes. sustinetis enim, si quis uos in seruitutem redigit, si quis deuorat, si quis accipit, si quis extollitur, si quis in faciem uos caedit. secundum	iterum dico, (ne quis me existimet insipientem, alioquin uelut insipientem suscipite me, ut ego pusillum quid glorier) quod loquor, non loquor, secundum Dominum, sed quasi in insipientia, in hac substantia gloriae. quia multi gloriantur secundum carnem: et ego gloriabor. libenter enim suffertis insipientes: cum sapientes sitis. suffertis enim si quis uos in seruitutem redigit, si quis deuorat, si quis accipit, si quis, extollitur, si quis in faciem uos caedit. secundum ignobilitatem dico,

De Doctr. Chris.

dum ignobilitatem dico,
quasi nos infirmati si-
mus. in quo autem quis
audet (in insipientia
dico), audio et ego.
Hebraei sunt? et ego.
Israelitae sunt? et ego.
semen Abrahae sunt? et
ego. ministri Christi
sunt? (insipiens dico)
super ego. in laboribus
plurimum, in carceribus
abundantius, in plagis
supra modum, in morti-
bus saepius. a Iudaeis
quinquies, quadraginta
una minus accepti. ter
uirgis caesus sum, se-
mel lapidatus sum, ter
naufragium feci: nocte
et die in profundo ma-
ris fui; in itineribus
saepe, periculis flumi-
num, periculis latro-
num, periculis ex gene-
re, periculis ex gentibus,
periculis in ciuitate,
periculis in deserto, pe-
riculis in mari, pericu-
lis in falsis fratribus;
in labore et aerumna,
in uigiliis saepius, in
fame et siti, in ieiuniis
saepius, in frigore et
nuditate; praeter illa
quae extrinsecus sunt,
incursus in me quotidi-
anus, sollicitudo omni-
um ecclesiarum. quis
infirmatur, et ego non
infirmor? quis scanda-
lizatur, et ego non uror?
si gloriari oportet, in
iis quae infirmitatis
meae sunt, gloriabor.

Vulgata

ignobilitatem dico, qua-
si nos infirmi fuerimus
in hac parte. in quo
quis audet (in insipi-
entia dico), audeo et ego:
Hebraei sunt, et ego:
Israelitae sunt, et ego:
semen Abrahae sunt, et
ego: ministri Christi
sunt, (ut minus sapiens
dico) plus ego in labo-
ribus plurimis, in car-
ceribus abundantius, in
plagis supra modum, in
mortibus frequenter. a
Iudaeis quinquies, quad-
ragenas, una minus ac-
cepi. ter uirgis caesus
sum, semel lapidatus
sum, ter naufragium
feci, nocte et die in profundo maris fui, in
itineribus saepe, peri-
culis fluminum, pericu-
lis latronum, periculis
ex genere, periculis ex
gentibus, periculis in
ciuitate, periculis in
solitudine, periculis in
mari, periculis in fal-
sis fratribus: in labore
et aerumna, in uigiliis
multis, in fame et siti,
in ieiuniis multis, in
frigore, et nuditate,
praeter illa quae extrin-
secus sunt, instantia
mea quotidians, sollici-
tudo omnium ecclesia-
rum. quis infirmatur,
et ego non infirmor?
quis scandalizatur et
ego non uror? si glori-
ari oportet, quae infir-
mitatis meae sunt, glo-

Versio Antiqua

quasi nos infirmi fueri-
mus in hac parte. in
quo quis audet (in insi-
pientiam dico) audeo
et ego: Hebraei sunt,
et ego: Israelitae sunt,
et ego: semen Abraham
sunt, et ego: ministri
Christi sunt, (ut minus
sapiens dico) super ego:
in laboribus plurimis,
in carceribus abundan-
tius, in plagis supra
modum, in mortibus
frequenter. a Iudaeis
quinquies, quadraginta,
una minus, accepi. ter
uirgis caesus sum, se-
mel lapidatus sum, ter
naufragium feci, noctem
et diem in profundo
maris feci, itineribus
multis, periculis flumi-
num, periculis latro-
num, periculis ex gene-
re, periculis ex genti-
bus, periculis in ciui-
tate, periculis in deser-
to, periculis in mari,
periculis in falsis fra-
tribus: labore, et ae-
rumna, in uigiliis mul-
tis, in fame et siti, in
ieiuniis multis, in fri-
gore, et nuditate: prae-
ter illa, quae extrinse-
cus sunt, concursus in
me cottidianus, solli-
tudo omnium ecclesia-
rum. quis infirmatur, et
ego non infirmor? quis
scandalisatur, et non
ego uror? si gloriari
oportet: quae infirmi-
tatis meae sunt, gloria-

De Doctr. Chris.	Vulgata	Versio Antiqua
Deus et Pater Domini nostri Iesu Christi scit, qui est benedictus in saecula, quod non mentior (7, 12-13).	riabor. Deus et Pater Domini nostri Iesu Christi, qui est benedictus in saecula, scit, quod non mentior.	bor. Deus Israel, et Pater Domini nostri Iesu Christi scit (benedictus in saecula) quia non mentior.

Gal. 3, 15-22

fratres, secundum hominem dico, tamen hominis confirmatum testamentum nemo irritum acit, aut superordinat. Abrahae dictae sunt promissiones et semini eius. non dicit, 'et seminibus,' tamquam in multis sed tamquam in uno, 'et semini tuo,' quod est Christus. hoc autem dico, testementum confirmatum a Deo, quae post quadringentos et triginta annos facta est lex, non infirmat ad euacuandas promissiones. si enim ex lege haereditas, iam non ex promissione. Abrahae autem per repromissionem donauit Deus. quid ergo lex? transgressionis gratia proposita est, donec ueniret semen cui promissum est, disposita per angelos in manu mediatoris. mediator autem unius non est, deus uero unus est. lex ergo aduersus promissa Dei? absit. si enim data esset lex quae posset uiuificare, omnino ex lege esset iustitia. sed conclusit scriptura omnia sub peccato, ut promissio ex fide Iesu Christi daretur credentibus (20, 39).	fratres (secundum hominem dico), tamen hominis confirmatum testamentum nemo spernit, aut superordinat. Abrahae dictae sunt promissiones, et semini eius. non dicit: et seminibus, quasi in multis; sed quasi in uno: et semini tuo; qui est Christus. hoc autem dico, testamentum confirmatum a Deo, quae post quadringentos et triginta annos facta est lex, non irritum facit ad euacuandam promissonem. nam si ex lege hereditas, iam non ex promissione. Abrahae autem per repromissionem donauit Deus. quid igitur lex? propter transgressiones posita est, donec ueniret semen, cui promiserat, ordinata per angelos in manu mediatoris. mediator autem unius non est; Deus autem unus est. lex ergo aduersus promissa Dei? absit. si enim data esset lex, quae posset uiuificare, uere ex lege esset iustitia. sed conclusit scriptura omnia sub peccato, ut promissio ex fide Iesu Christi daretur credentibus.	fratres (secundum hominem dico), tamen hominis confirmatum testamentum nemo irritum faciat, aut superordinat. Abrahae dictae sunt promissiones, ut semini eius. non dicit: et seminibus tuis, tamquam in multis: sed sicut in uno: et semini tuo, qui est Christus. hoc autem dico, testamentum confirmatum a Deo in Christo: quae post quadringentos et triginta annos facta est lex, non irritam facit ad euacuandam repromissinem. si enim ex lege haereditas, iam non ex repromissione. Abrahae autem repromissionem donauit Deus. quid ergo lex factorum gratia posita est, quoadusque ueniat semen, cui repromissus est, dispositum per angelos in manu mediatoris. mediator autem unius non est. Deus autem unus est. lex ergo aduersus promissa? absit. si enim data est lex. quae posset uiuificare, procerto ex lege iustitia. sed conclusit scriptura omnia sub peccato, ut promissio ex fide Iesu Christi daetur eis qui credunt.

De Doctr. Chris. Gal. 4, 10-20	Vulgata	Versio Antiqua
dies obseruatis, et menses, et annos, et tempora. timeo uos, ne forte sine causa laborauerim in uobis. estote sicut et ego, quoniam et ego sicut uos: fratres, precor uos; nihil me laesistis. scitis quia per infirmitatem carnis iampridem euangelizaui uobis, et tentationem uestram in carne mea non spreuistis, neque respuistis; sed sicut angelum Dei excepistis me, sicut Christum Iesum. quae ergo fuit beatitido uestra? testimonium uobis perhibeo, quoniam si fieri posset, oculos uestros eruissetis et dedissetis mihi. ergo inimicus factus sum uobis uerum praedicans? ambulantur uos non bene; sed excludere uos uolunt, ut eos aemulemini. bonum est autem aemulari in bono semper, et non solum cum praesens sum apud uos. filioli mei, quos iterum parturio donec Christus formetur in uobis. uellem autem nunc adesse apud uos, et mutare uocem meam, quia confundor in uobis (20, 44).	dies obseruatis et menses, et tempora et annos. timeo uos, ne forte sine causa laborauerim in uobis. estote, sicut ego, quia et ego, sicut uos; fratres, obsecro uos: nihil me laesistis. scitis autem, quia per infirmitatem carnis euangelizaui uobis iampridem, et tentationem uestram in carne mea non spreuistis, neque respuistis: sed sicut angelum Dei excepistis me, sicut Christum Iesum. ubi est ergo beatitudo uestra? testimonium enim perhibeo uobis, quia, si fieri posset, oculos uestros eruissetis, et dedissetis mihi. ergo inimicus uobis factus sum, uerum dicens uobis? aemulantur uos non bene, sed excludere uos uolunt, ut illos aemulemini. bonum autem aemulamini in bono semper, et non tantum cum praesens sum apud uos. filioli mei, quos iterum parturio, donec formetur Christus in uobis. uellem autem esse apud uos modo, et mutare uocem meam, quoniam confundor in uobis.	dies obseruatis, et menses et annos, et tempora timeo uos, ne forte sine causa laborauerim, in uobis. estote sicut et ego, quia et ego sicut uos: fratres obsecro uos: nihil me laesistis. scitis quod per infirmitatem carnis euangelizaui uobis iampridem: et tentationem uestram in carne mea non spreuistis, neque respuistis: sed sicut angelum Dei excepistis me, sicut Christum Iesum. quae ergo erat beatitudo uestra? testimonium enim uobis perhibeo, quia, si fieri posset, oculos uestros eruissetis, et dedissetis mihi. ergo ego inimicus uobis factus sum, uerum dicens uobis? aemulantur uos non bene; sed excludere uos uolunt, ut eos aemulemini. aemulamini autem meliora dona. bonum est aemulari in bonis semper: et non solum cum praesens sum apud uos. filii mei, quos iterum parturio, donec formetur Christus in uobis. uellem autem adesse apud uos modo, et mutare uocem meam: quoniam confundor in uobis.
Gal. 4, 21-26		
dicite mihi, sub lege uolentes esse, legem non	dicite mihi, qui sub lege uultis esse: legem non	dicite mihi sub lege uolentes esse, legem non

De Doctr. Chris.	**Vulgata**	**Versio Antiqua**
audistis? scriptum est enim, quod Abraham duos filios habuit, unum de ancilla, et unum de libera; sed ille quidem qui de ancilla, secundum carnem natus est: qui autem de libera, per repromissionem: quae sunt in allegoria. haec enim sunt duo testamenta: unum quidem in monte Sina in seruitutem generans, quae est Agar. Sina enim mons est in Arabia, qui coniunctus est huic quae nunc est Ierusalem, et seruit cum filiis suis. quae autem sursum est Ierusalem, libera est, quae est mater nostra (20, 39).	legistis? scriptum est enim: quoniam Abraham duos filios habuit, unum de ancilla et unum de libera. sed qui de ancilla, secundum carnem natus est; qui autem de libera, per repromissionem; quae sunt per allegoriam dicta. haec enim sunt duo testamenta. unum quidem in monte Sina, in seruitutem generans, quae est Agar; Sina enim mons est in Arabia, qui coniunctus est ei, quae nunc est Ierusalem, et seruit cum filiis suis. illa autem, quae sursum est Ierusalem, libera est, quae est mater nostra.	legistis? scriptum est enim: quia Abraham duos filios habuit, unum ex ancilla, et unum de libera. sed is quidem, qui de ancilla, secundum carnem natus est: qui autem de libera, per repromissionem: quae sunt significantia. haec enim sunt duo testamenta. unum quidem a monte Sina, in seruitutem generans: quae est Agar: Agar enim mons est in Arabia, quae consonat huic quae nunc est Hierusalem: seruit enim cum filiis suis. quae autem sursum est Hierusalem, libera est; quae est mater nostra.

Philip. 1, 18

| siue occasione, siue ueritate, Christus annuntietur (27, 59). | siue per occasionem, siue per ueritatem Christus annuntietur. | siue per occasionem, siue per ueritatem, Christus annunitatur. |

1 Tim. 4, 11

| annuntia haec et doce (16, 33). | praecipe haec, et doce. | praecipe haec et doce. |

1 Tim. 4, 12

| nemo adolescentiam tuam contemnat . . . sed forma esto fidelium in sermone, in conuersatione, in dilectione, in fide, in castitate (27, 60). | nemo adolescentiam tuam contemnat: sed exemplum esto fidelium in uerbo, in conuersatione, in charitate, in fide, in castitate. | nemo tuam adolescentiam contemnat. sed figura esto fidelibus in sermone, in conuersatione, in caritate, in fide, in castitate. |

1 Tim. 5, 1-2

| seniorem ne increpaueris, sed obsecra ut patrem, iuniores ut fratres, anus, ut matres, adolescentulas ut sorores (16, 33; 20, 40). | seniorem ne increpaueris, sed obsecra ut patrem: iuuenes, ut fratres: anus, ut matres: iuuenculas, ut sorores. | seniorem ne increpaueris, sed obsecra ut patrem; iuniores ut fratres; anus, ut matres; adulescentulas ut sorores. |

De Doctr. Chris.	Vulgata	Versio Antiqua
2 Tim. 1, 13		
formam habe uerborum sanorum, quae a me audisti (16, 33).	forman habe sanorum uerborum, quae a me audisti.	forman habens sanorum uerborum, quae a me audisti.
2 Tim. 2, 14-15		
noli uerbis contendere; ad nihil enim utile est, nisi ad subuersionem audientium (28, 61). satis age, teipsum probabilem operarium exhibens Deo, non erubescentem, uerbum ueritatis recte tractantem (16, 33).	noli contendere uerbis; ad nihil enim utile est, nisi ad subuersionem audientium. sollicite cura teipsum probabilem exhibere Deo, operarium inconfusibilem, recte tractantem uerbum ueritatis.	noli uerbis contendere: in nihil enim utile est, in subuersione audientium. sollicite cura teipsum exhibere Deo operarium inconfusibilem recte tractantem uerbum ueritatis.
2 Tim. 3, 14		
tu autem perseuera in iis quae didicisti, et credita sunt tibi, sciens a quo didiceris (16, 33).	tu uero permane in iis, quae didicisti, et credita sunt tibi: sciens, a quo didiceris.	tu uero permane in his, quae didicisti, et credita sunt tibi: sciens a quibus didiceris.
2 Tim. 4, 2		
praedica uerbum, insta opportune, importune; argue, obsecra, increpa in omni longanimitate et doctrina (16, 33).	praedica uerbum, insta opportune, importune: argue, obsecra, increpa in omni patientia et doctrina.	praedica uerbum, insta opportune, importune: argue, exhortare, increpa in omni patientia, et doctrina.
Tit. 1, 9		
ut potens sit in doctrina sana et contradicentes redarguere (16, 33; 28, 61).	ut potens sit exhortari in doctrina sana, et eos, qui contradicunt, arguere.	ut potens sit et exhortari in doctrinam sanam, et contradicentes reuincere.
Tit. 1, 16		
confitentur se nosse Deum factis autem negant (29, 62).	confitentur, se nosse Deum, factis autem negant.	Deum confitentur se nosse, factis autem negant.
Tit. 2, 1-2; 15		
tu uero loquere quae decent sanam doctrinam, senes sobrios esse. . . . . haec loquere, et exhortare, et increpa cum omni imperio. nemo te contemnat (16, 33).	tu autem loquere, quae decent sanam doctrinam: senes ut sobrii sint. . . . haec loquere et exhortare, et argue cum omni imperio. nemo te contemnat.	tu autem loquere quae decet sanam doctrinam: senes sobrios esse. . . . haec loquere, et hortare, et argue cum omni imperio. nemo te contemnat.
Tit. 3, 1		
admone illos principibus et potestatibus subditos esse (16, 33).	admone illos, principibus et potestatibus subditos esse.	admone illos principibus, et potestatibus subditos esse.

6. Style.[1]

The fourth book, though itself only a manual of style, is so pervaded by the individuality of its author that it is worthy of study from the standpoint of style. Style is the individuality of an author finding expression in writing; and the style of an author is worthy of a place in literature, in as far as the author's personality is worthy to be perpetuated, and is worthily expressed. Augustine's personality is so striking that the reader is not surprised to find that it stamps with its own peculiar seal even so technical a composition as a manual of oratory. Cicero's personality has lifted *De Oratore* to a place in literature; *De Doctrina Christiana* is no less a literary work, even though it has attained its place by means of a style far different from that of Augustine's master. Van Doren[2] claims that an author, to take his place in literature, must bring to his work an attitude and a gift. Augustine, in the present treatise, has done so. He has brought to his writing the conviction of the validity of classical principles, and dominating this, an intense enthusiasm for Christian truth; he has brought the gift of a penetrating clearness of thought, and a remarkable dexterity in the manipulation of words. It is his word-power that we purpose to consider here. Augustine early enjoyed a high reputation for dialectic. It was this, along with the influence of sophistic training, that made him so clever a wielder of words. In *Contra Cresconium* he vigorously defends himself against the attack of the Donatist who accused him of a *false* use of eloquence, of being a mere dabbler in words, and a framer of fine language. Though it is true that by training, and through long years of practice Augustine was a conscious artist, familiar with his tools and skilled in their use, still it is no less a fact that he escaped what is really pernicious in Sophistic, since with him the truth of his message is ever of first importance, and a clever turn of phrase or a pleasing balance of clause is used merely to enforce the thought. His words in chapter 28 of the fourth book are literally true of himself: "nec doctor uerbis seruiat, sed uerba doctori. . . . porro qui non uerbis contendit siue submisse, siue temperae, siue granditer dicat, it agit uerbis ut ueritas pateat, ueritas placeat, ueritas moueat."

---

[1] Rhetorical qualities are alone taken up here. Vocabulary and syntax are treated in the Commentary. See index for references.

[2] *American and British Literature since 1890*, p. 215ff.

Since Book IV is a manual of style, one would not expect it to be ornately written; and it is not. Augustine's explanations are clear, and logical throughout. In places he is very consciously the dialectician; his words are chosen with simplicity and precision, and are even at times deliberately repeated in order to gain greater clearness. This is especially true when he explains the plain style, where very naturally his own manner illustrates the matter in hand. Less frequently his explanation becomes more ornate or heated; but it does so when he is dealing with the two styles that belong to rhetoric proper, the temperate and the grand. Throughout the book, however, whether when writing dialectically or rhetorically, he makes at least a moderate use of the more common figures of words, the stock-in-trade of fourth century literature. The two kinds of figures which stand out as giving particular color to his style are (1) those of parallelism, (2) those of sound. Parison, or the occurrence of two or more successive clauses of the same general structure, with its often attendant *homoioteleuton*, is especially representative of the first class; *paronomasia* and its sister-figures represent the figures of sound, wherein similarity in sound is played off in a variety of ways: by change of prefixes; by change of case, voice, mood, etc.; by coupling of derivatives of a same root; by change of a letter or a syllable in a word, etc.

The figures of parallelism are first in importance. Norden (616ff.) points these out as *the* characteristic of Christian oratory, and it may be added, of Late prose in general. He says: "Die Signatur des Stils der christlichen Predigt in lateinischer Sprache ist der antithetische Satzparallelismus mit Homoioteleuton, nicht etwa, wie der Semitist vielleicht denken konnte, jener 'parallelismus membrorum,' wie er sich in der hebräischen Poesie, den Reden der Propheten, den Reden Jesus findet, sondern derselbe, den in griechischer Rede Gorgias begründet hatte."

Quintilian (9, 3, 76ff.) explains *parison* and *homoioteleuton* thus: "Cleosteleus πάρισον existimat, quod sit e membris non dissimilibus; secundum, ut clausula similiter cadat, syllabis iisdem in ultimam partem collatis, ὁμοιοτέλευτον, similem duarum sententiarum uel plurium finem." Examples could be multiplied of this balance of structure in the present book, but a few will suffice to show how naturally, and with what variety Augustine uses this device.

1) *Simple Parison:*

    a   With *homoioteleuton* and *polysyndeton*:

        agit ut intellegenter,
            ut libenter,
            ut obedienter audiatur (15, 32).

    b) With *homoioteleuton* and *polyptoton* (a word repeated in a different inflectional form):

        illam sequens,
        istam praecedens, et sequentem
            respuens (7, 12).

    c) With *alliteration* and *antithesis*:

        sicut   autem saepe   sumenda sunt et amara salubria
        ita   semper   uitanda est perniciosa dulcedo (5, 7).

    d) With *homoioteleuton* and *epanaphora*:

        haec quando a   magistris docentur,
                  pro   magno   habentur,
                        magno   emuntur pretio,
                        magno   iactatione uenduntur (7, 14).

    Varied by the use of double-rhymed *homoioteleuton*:

        quid est ergo   non solum eloquenter,
                     sed etiam sapienter dicere,
        nisi uerba in submisso genere   sufficientia,
                 in temperato   splendentia,
                 in grandi   uehementia adhibere (28, 61).

    e) With *epanaphora* and *pleonasm*:

        nec curat quid   bene sonet,
            sed   quid   bene indicet atque
                      intimet
        quod ostendere intendit (10, 24).

    f)   With *polysyndeton* and *homoioteleuton*, followed by *asyndeton* with *epanaphora* and *homoioteleuton*:

        porro qui non uerbis contendit   siue submisse,
                                 siue temperate,
                                 siue granditer dicat,
        id agit uerbis ut ueritas pateat,
                     ueritas placeat,
                     ueritas moueat (28, 61).

2) *Double Parison:*

    a) With *polysyndeton* and *homoioteleuton*:

        et aliquando de una eademque re magna
            et submisse dicitur,   si docetur;

```
    et temperate,              si praedicatur;
    et granditer,              si auersus        ut conuertatur
                                 impellitur        (19, 38).
  non ut libeat      quod horrebat,
  aut ut fiat        quod pigebat,
  sed ut appareat    quod latebat       (11, 26).
```

And the clever adaptation of the *officia oratoris* to Cicero's
definition of the styles:

is erit igitur eloquens, qui

```
        ut doceat,          poterit parua submisse;
        ut delectet,        modica temperate;
        ut flectat,         magna granditer dicere (17, 34).
```

b)   With *polyptoton* and *homoioteleuton*:

```
ut qui     audit, uerum  audiat,
ut quod  audit,            intellegat (10, 25).
sicut enim gratus  est qui cognoscenda   enubilat,
sic onerosus       est qui cognita        inculcat    (10, 25).
```

c)   With *epanaphora, polyptoton*, and *homoioteleuton*:

```
modus inueniendi quae intellegenda  sunt et
modus proferendi quae intellecta      sunt    (1, 1).
```

d)   With *chiasmus* and *homoioteleuton*:
    (a passage imitating the grand style):

ita flectitur

```
        si amet quod polliceris,
          timeat quod arguis,
                  quod commendas, amplectatur,
                  quod dolendum exaggeras, doleat,
              cum quid laetandum praedicas, gaudeat,
misereatur eorum    quos miserandos ante oculos dicendo constituis,
    fugiat eos        quos cauendos              terrendo proponis
                                                          (12, 27).
```

Of the other devices of parallelism besides parison and homoioteleuton, *chiasmus*, or reversal in the order of words in two parallel
clauses, is also important for its frequency. Often it is combined with
parison. Examples are:

probando enim delectat, qui minus potest delectare dicendo.   (5, 8).

With *parison*:

> uerum et ipsi laudabiliter appetant, fugiantque uituperabiliter uiuere
>
> > (24, 55).
>
> sicut est autem ut teneatur ad audiendum delectandus auditor, ita
>
> > flectendus ut moueatur ad agendum   (12, 27).

A means sometimes used to heighten the effect of a parallel state-ment is *metathesis*, i.e., the repetition of two terms in two successive clauses so that in the second clause a reversal of the relation between the two is expressed, for example:

> nec doctor uerbis seruiat,
> sed uerba doctori   (28, 61).

a)   With *polysyndeton*:

> nec ipsos decet alia,
> nec alios ipsa   (6, 9).

b)   With *alliteration* and *homoioteleuton*:

> sed salubri suauitate
> uel suaui suauitate, quid melius?   (5, 7).
> non intenta in eloquentiam sapientia,
> sed a sapientia non recedente eloquentia   (7, 21).

Besides the instances noted above, *polysyndeton*, as a means to emphasize parallel structure is conspicuous in the following examples:

a)   With *pleonasm*, or word-parallelism:

> cum et iusta et sancta et bona dicit   (15, 32).

b)   With *parison*:

> ubicumque agantur haec, siue ad populum siue priuatim, siue ad unum siue ad plures, siue ad amicos siue ad inimicos, siue in per-petua dictione siue in collocutione, siue in tractibus siue in libris, siue in epistolis uel longissimis uel breuissimis, magna sunt (18,37).

Epanaphora, or the repetition of the same word at the beginning of successive phrases, clauses, or sentences, has also been noted above in connection with parison. Other striking examples are:

> et certe minus intellegantur, minus placeant, minus moueant quae dicun-tur (14, 30).
> quia ueritas sic demonstrata, sic defensa, sic inuicta delectat (26, 56).
> quid est quod sic indignatur apostolus, sic corripit, sic exprobrat, sic increpat, sic minatur? quid est quod sui animi affectum tam crebra

> et tam aspera uocis mutatione testatur? quid est postremo quod de
> rebus minimis tam granditer dicit? (18, 36)
> persuadet autem in submisso genere uera esse quae dicit; persuadet in
> grandi ut agantur quae agenda esse iam sciuntur, nec aguntur; per-
> suadet in genere temperato, pulchre ornateque se dicere (25, 55)

Hyperbaton, or the separation of words which grammatically
belong together, is another figure of structure frequent in this book as
in all of Augustine's writings. In this the writer approaches Cicero and
the classics more closely than in the figures of parallelism just noted.
Hyperbaton is used in many cases obviously for the sake of the clausulae
involved. Examples are:

> sed quia non ostentant quam nimis isti diligunt eloquentiam (7, 14).
> et fraternae ideo negligentissimos charitatis (7, 16).
> nescio utrum illa quam didicimus et docuimus arte tradatur (7, 20).

Of equal importance with the figures just considered are the figures of sound that fill this book. These are the figures which taken
to the extreme constitute in large part that word-jugglery which has
become synonymous with the name "Sophistic." They are fundamentally the balancing of words having similarity of sound but dissimilarity of sense. It is not by a sparing use of these figures that Augustine
saves himself from the reproach that belongs to this phase of Sophistic; it is through the purpose which he makes these figures serve that
he avoids the blame usually attendant upon their use. Augustine's aim
in these clever turns of expression is not, as is the Sophist's, to flaunt
his wit in terms of empty display; he uses them in order to compel the
attention of his reader, and thereby to win favor and assent for the
matter under discussion.

Paronomasia proper, occurs in words alike in sound, but different in
sense because of difference in prefix. The following are examples:

> quis ita *desipiat,* ut hoc *sapiat?* (2, 3).
> quae formam pigmentis *colorant,* uel potius *decolorant*   (21, 49).
> et bona *docere,* et mala *dedocere* (4, 6).
> uel in malis quae *pendit,* uel in bonis quae *rependit*   (7, 20).
> nos ea tanti *pendimus,* ut eis discendis iam maturos . . . aetates uelimus
> *impendi* (3, 4).
> haec tamen sic *detrahit* ornatum, ut sordes non *contrahat*   (10, 24).
> quae pectora eorum hostiliter *obsidebat,* uel potius *possidebat* (24, 53).

imperite peritus (considering the meaning, an example also of *oxymoron*, i.e., the combination of two apparently contradictory terms) (7, 11).

Polyptoton, called also *traductio*, is a kind of paronomasia produced by the repetition of a word in different case, mood, tense, etc., with the set purpose of rhetorical effect. Examples are:

> qui potuit euangelium dare *homini*, etiam non ab *hominibus*, neque per *hominem* (16, 33).
> cum uero *boni fideles bonis fidelibus* hanc operam commodant (29, 62).

Often this figure is used in dialectical passages where Augustine wishes to be particularly precise and clear, as for example:

> fit autem ut cum *incidentes quaestioni* aliae *quaestiones*, et aliae rursus *incidentibus incidentes* pertractantur atque soluuntur in eam longitudinem (20, 39).
> qui ergo *dicit* cum docere uult, quamdiu non intellegetur, nondum se existimet *dixisse quod* uult ei quem uult docere (12, 27).

Polyptoton occurs often in antithetical sentences:

> quod si etiam delectare uult eum cui *dicit*, . . . non quocumque modo *dixerit, faciet*, sed interest quomodo *dicat* ut *faciat* (12, 27).
> non quid *agendum sit* ut *sciant*, sed ut *agant* quod *agendum esse iam sciunt* (12, 27).
> qua etsi *dixit* quod ipsi *intellegit* nondum ille *dixisse* putandus est, a quo *intellectus* non est; si uere *intellectus est*, quocumque medo *dixerit, dixit* (12, 27).
> quod ergo *minimum* est *minimum* est; sed in *minimo* fidelem esse magnum est (18, 35).
> nam sine praeceptis rhetoricis nouimus *plurimos eloquentiores plurimis* qui illa didicerunt, sine lectis uero et auditis *eloquentium* disputationibus uel dictionibus, neminem (3, 5).

Paragmenon, or *deriuatio*, is another species of paronomasia, consisting of the repetition of a word in form of a derivative—an adjective from a noun, an adverb from a verb or an adjective, etc. Examples are:

> et ea sua faciunt, quae non ipsi *componere* potuerunt, qui secundum illa *composite* uiunt (29, 62).
> in sermonibus . . . *eloquentium* impleta reperiuntur praecepta *eloquentiae*, de quibus illi ut *eloquerentur* uel cum *eloquerentur*, non cogitauerunt (3, 4).

et haec se posse si potuerit . . . pietate magis *orationum*, quam *oratorum* facultate non dubitet, ut *orando* pro se . . . sit *orator* antequam dictor   (15, 32).

All three kinds of *paronomasia* are combined in the following example:

cum ex infantibus *loquentes* non fiant, nisi *locutiones* discendo *loquentium* cur *eloquentes* fieri non possint, nulla *eloquendi* arte tradita, sed *elocutiones eloquentium* legendo (3, 5).

Similarity of sound with dissimilarity of sense in words of different root is a kind of *paronomasia* called *parachesis*. The following are examples:

nec *moris* est nec *decoris* (10, 25).
tamquam *debita reddita* (20, 40).
prorsus haec est in *docendo* eloquentia, qua fit *dicendo*, etc. (11, 26).
nonnullam similitudinem, *uescentes* atque *discentes*, etc.   (11, 26).

a) With *litotes* and *hyperbaton*:
sic namque *eligit* bonam uitam, ut etiam bonam non *neglegat* famam
(28, 61).

b) With *polyptoton*:
si ergo loquitur in eis Spiritus sanctus qui *persequentibus* traduntur
    pro Christo, cur non et in eis qui tradunt *discentibus* Christum?
(15, 32).

c) With *paradox*:
qui *stertit, aduertit* (7, 12).

Alliteration occurs frequently in the fourth book, especially as a means of enhancing other figures, as noted above. Further examples are:

sua enim quaerere student, sed sua docere non audent, de loco scilicet
    superiore sedis eccelesiasticae quam sana doctrina constituit
(27, 67).

a) With *onomatopoeia* and *parachesis*:
non dicuntur ista nisi mirabiliter affluentissima fecunditate facundiae (14, 31).

b) With *assonance* (same sound in the middle or end of words) and *polyptoton*:
bonorum ingeniorum insignis est indoles, in uerbis uerum amare, non uerba (11, 26).

The figures of imagery in the fourth book may be dismissed in a few words. As would be expected in a manual of technique, only the most common *metaphors* and *comparisons* are found. The following are representative *metaphors*:

> deinde quattuor caesa decentissimo impetu profluunt   (7, 13).
> qui huius sapientiae filii et ministri sumus   (5, 7).

St. Paul is termed:

> comes sapientiae, dux eloquentiae   (7, 12).

The following *comparisons* occur:

> dum (dictio submissa) sententias acutissimas de nescio quibus quasi cauernis, unde non sperabatur, eruit et ostendit (26, 56).
> sicut autem pulchrum corpus et deformis est animus, magis dolendus est, quam si deforme est animus (28, 61). (The comparison is to oratory of empty display.)
> quasi sapientiam . . . procedere intellegas, et tamquam inseparabilem famulam . . . sequi eloquentiam   (6, 9).
> locorum nominibus tamquam luminibus ornatur eloquium (7, 17).
> totus iste quasi anhelans locus bimenbri circuitu terminatur (7, 13).

From the preceding examples it may readily be concluded (1) that on the whole Augustine's use of figures in the present treatise is a moderate one, both from the point of view of quantity and of quality; (2) that the figures most frequent, those of parallelism and of sound, while they are particularly sophistic in character, are used naturally by Augustine, wholly for the purpose of stressing the matter; and that they therefore accomplish the result of so enhancing and strengthening the thought as to raise a mere manual of technique into something literary.

In order better to appreciate the mingling of these opposite qualities, *i.e.*, artificiality and spontaneity of expression, exuberance and moderation, it may be helpful to analyze one of the chapters of the fourth book, and to test for these qualities its mingling of figures.

nam cum per artem rhetoricam et uera suadeantur et falsa (polysyndeton and hyperbaton), quis audeat dicere aduersus mendacium in defensoribus suis inermem debere consistere ueritatem (hyperbaton), ut illi qui res falsas persuadere conantur, nouerint auditorem uel beneuolum, uel intentum, uel (polysyndeton) docilem proemio facere, isti (antithesis) autem non nouerint;

illi falsa breuiter, aperte, uerisimiliter (asyndeton), et isti (antithesis) uera sic
narrent, ut audire taedeat, intellegere non pateat, credere postremo non libeat
(parison, homoioteleuton); illi fallacibus argumentis ueritatem (antithesis)
oppugnent, asserant falsitatem (chiasmus), isti (antithesis) nec uera defendere
nec (polysyndeton) falsa ualeant refutare; illi animos audientium (alliteration)
in errorem mouentes impellentesque (pleonasm) dicendo terreant, contristent,
exhilarent, exhortentur (asyndeton) ardenter (assonance), isti (antithesis) pro
ueritate lenti frigidique (pleonasm) dormitent (metaphor). quis ita desipiat, ut
hoc sapiat (paronomasia)? cum ergo sit in medio posita (hyperbaton) facultas
eloquii, quae ad persuadenda seu praua seu (polysyndeton) recta (antithesis)
ualet plurimum, cur non bonorum studio comparatur, ut militet ueritati (metaphor), si eam mali (antithesis) ad obtinendas peruersas uanasque causas in
usus iniquitatis et erroris (pleonasm) usurpant (interrogatio)?   (2, 3).

This chapter, representative as it is of the whole of Book IV, serves
to show the sanity of Augustine's expression. It is carefully written;
it abounds in figures; but these are so relatively commonplace and
natural, so thoroughly a part of the thought, that while the reader realizes that he has here something higher than the flat, bald style of the
ordinary manual, he feels too that this writing is far from the bad taste
inherent in floridity and empty display.

The clausulae of *De Doctrina Christiana* will not be taken up here.
Even the casual reader will notice that rhythm has not been ignored in
this treatise, though Augustine's care for cadences naturally is different
in a technical work from what it is in a work of the grand style, as for
example in *De Civitate Dei*. But if in other points of style, as has been
seen, *De Doctrina Christiana* is worthy to rank as literature beside *De Oratore* and *Orator*, the reader may conclude that in rhythm also the author
has been careful to teach by illustration through his own style.

7. INFLUENCE.

"The fourth book of *De Doctrina Christiana* has historical significance in
the early years of the fifth century out of all proportion to its size; for
it begins rhetoric anew. It not only ignores Sophistic; it goes back over
centuries of the lore of personal triumph to the ancient idea of moving
men to truth; and it gives to the vital counsels of Cicero a new emphasis for the urgent tasks of preaching the word of God."[1] This estimate

---

[1] Baldwin (2) 51.

of the fourth book sums up the three points which make the whole value of the treatise: its repudiation of Sophistic, its re-introduction of the classical standard, and its presentation of the Christian ideal.

The value of *De Doctrina Christiana* was early recognized, and made St. Augustine an authority for homiletic not only in his own time, but especially throughout the Middle Ages. To trace in detail his influence on rhetorical thought would be the matter for separate study, and cannot be attempted here. It is sufficient to point to a few outstanding instances where the dominance of Augustine's theory is most clearly evident. Cassiodorus appeals to *De Doctrina Christiana* in his exposition of the Psalter; Rabanus Maurus in *De Institutione Clericorum* draws almost entirely from it for his third book; St. Bonaventure, in the treatise now generally accredited to him, the *Ars Concionandi*, opens his discussion by reference to Augustine's distinction between *inuentio* and *elocutio* (modus inueniendi . . . modus proferendi, 4, 1, 1) and to 4, 12, 37, and quotes copiously from the fourth book as he proceeds in the third part of his treatise;[2] St. Thomas often recalls Augustine's position, especially in regard to the purpose of the temperate style, the qualities required in a preacher, the necessity to the ecclesiastic of a thorough knowledge of things sacred, and the power of a good life to influence an audience.

A mediaeval tractate on preaching,[3] recently found in a volume of incunabula belonging to the library of Cornell University, quotes from *De Oratore* II and *De Doctrina Christiana* IV to emphasize the importance of considering not only *what*, but also *how* to speak. It is not a mere coincidence that master and disciple are thus coupled. It shows that if for Augustine in the fifth-century "Cicero" stood for all that was best in the classical tradition, to the Middle Ages and later times "Cicero and Augustine" expressed well-rounded Latin rhetorical authority.

---

[2] Cf. references to De Doctr. Chris. 4, 2,3 ; 4, 5, 7; 4, 5, 8; 4, 9, 23; 4, 10, 24; 4, 11, 26; 4, 12, 27: 4, 28, 61; 4, 15, 32.

[3] Cf. Caplan 70–71.

NOTES

Introduction

[1] This work has been translated as both *On Christian Doctrine* and *On Christian Teaching*, thus offering somewhat different points of emphasis, as the critics in this volume demonstrate. Scholars generally agree that Augustine composed the first three books of *DDC* ca. 397 A.D., around the time he became the bishop of Hippo (396 A.D.), and that he wrote the fourth and final book in 427 A.D., three years before his death.

Part III
Chapter 4

[1] In *Patrologia latina* and in the Vienna *Corpus Scriptorum Ecclesiasticorum Latinorum*; reprinted, Missouri Lutheran Synod (St. Louis, 1882); translated (1) by Dods (M.) (Edinburgh, 1872–1875) (reprinted in Schaff's Nicene and post-Nicene Fathers); (2) by Baker (W. J. V.) and Bickersteth (C.) in *Preaching and Teaching According to St. Augustine* (Book IV only, with *De catechizandis rudibus*) (London, 1907); (3) by Sister Thérèse, S.N.D. (IV, with text and commentary) (Washington, 1928).

To the references and abbreviations at the head of chapter 1 add: Barry (Sister Inviolata), *St. Augustine the Orator*, Catholic University of America Patristic Studies VI (Washington, 1924); and Christopher (J. P.), *S. Aureli Augustini . . . de catechizandis rudibus*, translated with an introduction and commentary, Catholic University of America Patristic Studies 8 (Washington, 1926).

[2] For detailed analysis, see Barry.

[3] Even though the application of the text from Ecclus. xxxvii: 20 be questioned, the rebuke of sophistic display, whether in dialectic or in style, is none the less clear.

[4] Other allusions may be found in the passages quoted below from vi, from xiv, and from xxv.

[5] βαδιζόντων εἰς τὰς τῶν Γαλιλαίων ἐκκληίας ἐξηγησόμενοι Ματθαῖον καὶ Λουκᾶν. Julian, "Epistle 42," cited in Gibbon's twenty-third chapter.

[6] ARP 51, 56. The reminiscences of Cicero are so numerous as to show a pervasive preoccupation. See J. B. Eskredge, *The Influence of Cicero upon Augustine* (Chicago Dissertation), 1912.

[7] E.g., *De oratore* II.xxi.88.

[8] The traditional maxim for the *exordium*, *reddere auditores benevolos, attentos, dociles*, as again in iv.

[9] The traditional maxim for the *narratio*.

[10] *Exercitatione sive scribendi, sive dictandi, postremo etiam dicendi.* Cf. the close of xxi.

[11] Thus I venture to translate *sapientes*, remembering the connotation of the word both for Augustine and for his master Cicero.

[12] So toward the close "The Christian preacher prefers to appeal rather with matter than with manner, and thinks neither that anything is said better which is not said more truly, nor that the teacher must serve words, but words the teacher." (xxviii).

[13] For this sort of analysis see ARP, chapter 5, and the terms in the index. For the more elaborate sophistical analysis, see Méridier, Guignet, and the other studies of Greek fathers cited above. To suggest such further study, the Greek of the first example and the King James English of the third have been set beside. St Augustine not only confines himself to the Latin version, but disclaims competence in Greek style.

[14] The linking iteration is characteristic of climax as practiced by sophistic.

[15] Chapter 29 of book 3 relegates the study of figures to *grammatica*; but there also Augustine reminds his readers that figures, without regard to books or teaching, are a natural expression of the imaginative impulse.

[16] As to this form of *memoria*, see also chapter 29.

[17] *Docere necessitates est, delectare suavitatis, flectere victoriæ. Or.* xxi.69, with *docere* for the original *probare*.

[18] *Ante oculos dicendo constituis* (12) recalls the *De sublimitate*, and behind that the *Rhetoric* of Aristotle. Its immediate source is doubtless Cicero.

[19] The warning is repeated where Augustine is gathering the three tasks into the final and constant idea of persuasion: "But that which is handled in the way of charm . . . is not to be made an end in itself (xxv) . . . nor does it seek merely to please." Nothing is more admirable in Augustine's exposition than this expert linking of his chain of progress.

[20] *Numquid hic ornamenta et non documenta quæruntur?*

[21] *Orator*, xxix.101.

[22] Cf. xxix with the quotation from x above; and see *memoria* in the index to ARP.

[23] For his cadences, see Barry.

[24] Aristotle, *Rhetoric* I.ii.

[25] That the Scriptures enter all the three fields of oratory indicated by Aristotle in *Rhetoric* I.iii, is suggested by the language of a passage in Augustine's third book: *Non autem adserit [scriptura] nisi catholicam fidem rebus præteritis et futuris et præsentibus. Præteritorum narratio est, futurorum prænuntiatio, præsentium demonstratio,* III.x. For the last two words suggest in the context ἐπιδεικτιτός, and hence δικανικός for the first phrase of the sentence and συμβουλευτικός for the second, according to the Aristotelian division. If so, Augustine has not followed Cicero's reducing of the fields to two (ARP 47, 53).

[26] In the passage quoted above from chapter 19, and in other places, there are clear references to occasional oratory.

[27] See Eduard Norden, *Agnostos Theos: Untersuchungen zur Formengeschichte religiöser Rede* (Leipzig, 1913). But this speech, to judge from the indications of Acts 17, was as original in plan as in idea.

Chapter 5

[1] Charles S. Baldwin, *Medieval Rhetoric and Poetic* (New York, 1928), 51.

[2] S. Aurelii Augustini, *De Doctrina Christiana Liber Quartus*, trans. Sister Thérèse Sullivan, Catholic University Patristic Studies 23 (Washington, D.C., 1930), 8.

[3] Bernard Huppé, *Doctrine and Poetry: Augustine's Influence on Old English Poetry* (New York, 1959), v.

[4] Dorothea Roth, *Die mittelalterliche Predigttheorie und das Manuale Curatorum des Johann Ulrich Surgant* (Basel, 1956).

[5] Rhabanus Maurus, *De clericorum institutione*; J. P. Migne, *Patrologia Latina* [PL] 107, cols. 294–420; Alain de Lille, *Summa de arte praedicatoria* [PL] 210, cols. 110–98; Humbert of Romans, *Treatise on Preaching*, trans. Dominican Students (Westminister, Md., 1951); Robert de Basevorn, *Forma praedicandi*, in Th.-M. Charland, *Artes praedicandi*, Publications de l'Institut d'études médiévales d'Ottowa (Paris, 1936). This last work has been translated by Leopold Krul, O.S.B.: M.A. Thesis, Cornell University, 1950.

[6] E.g., *De Doctrina Christiana* IV.v.7 and IV.xxviii.61, *De catechizandis rudibus* 9, and *Confessions* IX.ii.4. Note also the careful discussion of the utility of pleasure in *De Doctrina* IV.xxv.55-58, where pleasure is made to serve the purpose of persuasion.

[7] M. Paul Lejay, quoted in Pierre DeLabriolle, *The History and Literature of Christianity from Tertullian to Boethius* (New York, 1924), 231.

[8] St. Paul, for instance said: "And my speech and my preaching was not in the persuasive words of human wisdom, but in the showing of the Spirit and the Power" (1 Cor 2:3-4). Virtually every early Christian writer stresses the difference between *sapientia huius saeculi* and *sapientia spiritualis*. John of Antioch, for instance, declares in his sermon "On the Heroes of the Faith": "But the Cross wrought persuasion by means of unlearned men; yea, it persuaded even the whole world."

[9] Lactantius, *Divinae institutiones* (*Corpus Scriptorum Ecclesiasticorum Latinorum*) CSEL 19, 400.4.

[10] Arnobius, *Adversus Nations*, CSEL 4, I.59. Arnobius helped make a watchword of a phrase of Saint Paul: "The wisdom of man is foolishness before God" (1 Cor 3:19).

[11] Gustave Bardy, *L'église et l'enseignment pendant les trois premiers siecles*, *Revue des sciences religieuses* 12 (1932): 1–28. The awful magnitude of this renunciation may easily be overlooked by a modern reader who does not recall the pervasiveness of teaching through *imitatio* in Roman schools.

[12] Titian, *Oratio*, 1–3 quoted in Gustave Combès, *Saint Augustin et la culture classique* (Paris, 1927), 88.

[13] Titian, *Oratio*.

[14] Labriolle, *History and Literature*, 17.

[15] Tertullian, *De Praescriptione*, PL 2, cols. 20a–b, 7. Centuries later Gregory the Great, reproving a clerk who taught classical literature to his classes, expressed a similar view: "The same mouth singeth not the praises of Jove and the praises of Christ." R. L. Poole, *Illustrations in the History of Medieval Thought* (London, 1884), 8.

[16] For a survey of Tertullian's views on these related subjects, see Gerard L. Ellspermann, *The Attitude of the Early Christian Latin Writers toward Pagan Literature and Learning*, Catholic University of America Patristic Studies 82 (Washington, D.C., 1949), 23–42.

[17] Labriolle, *History and Literature*, 18.

[18] Augustine, "Epistle 91," in *Select Letters of Saint Augustine*, trans. James H. Baxter, Loeb Classical Library (London, 1930), 159.

[19] Minucius Felix, *Octavius*, trans. Gerald H. Rendall, Loeb Classical Library (London, 1953), xxiv, 2, 7.

[20] Hilarius, *De Trinitate*, PL 10, vii,1.

[21] A. S. Pease, "The Attitude of Jerome toward Pagan Literature," *Transactions and Proceedings of the American Philological Association* 50 (1919):150–67.

[22] Cf. James Campbell, *The Influence of the Second Sophistic on the Style of the Sermons of Saint Basil the Great*, Patristic Studies 2 (Washington, D.C., 1922).

[23] Cyprian, *Ad Donatus*, 2, quoted in Ellspermann, *Attitude of the Early Christian Latin Writers*, 51.

[24] Augustine, *Contra Cresconium et donatistam libri* IV, *CSEL* 52, I.i.2.

[25] Combès, *Saint Augustin et la culture classique*, 97. For a survey of Basil's reactions to pagan culture, cf. Sister Mary M. Fox, *The Life and Times of Saint Basil the Great as Revealed in His Works*, Patristic Studies 57 (Washington, D.C., 1939).

[26] Basil, "Epistle 309," quoted in Fox, *Life and Times of Saint Basil*, 89.

[27] Ellspermann, *Attitude of the Early Christian Latin Writers*, 120–23.

[28] Ellspermann, *Attitude of the Early Christian Latin Writers*, 114. The idea was of course not original with Ambrose, having antecedents in pre-Christian Alexandrian thought. Cassiodorus repeated it for the later middle ages.

[29] Max W. Laistner, "The Christian Attitude to Pagan Literature," *History* 20 (1935): 49–54.

[30] Ambrose, *De officiis ministrorum*, PL 16, cols. 23–184.

[31] Jerome, "Epistle 22," *CSEL* 54, translated in Ellspermann, *Attitude of the Early Christian Latin Writers*, 159–60.

[32] The translation follows that of Labriolle, *History and Literature*, 11–12.

[33] Pease, "The Attitude of Jerome toward Pagan Literature," 150–67. Rufinus had accused Jerome of teaching the classics and of having a monk copy Cicero.

[34] Ellspermann, *Attitude of Early Christian Latin Writers*, 157.

[35] Jerome, *Liber contra Helvidium de perpetua virginitate Mariae* xii, quoted in Sister M. Jamesetta Kelly, *Life and Times as Revealed in the Writings of St. Jerome Exclusive of His Letters*, Patristic Studies 52 (Washington, D.C., 1944), 59.

[36] Jerome, "Epistle 59," *CSEL* 54, quoted in Ellspermann, *Attitude of Early Christian Latin Writers*, 147. Interestingly enough, he also recommends Lysias and the Gracchi. The rest of the list (e.g., for poetry, Homer, Vergil, Menander, and Terence) is reminiscent of the typical Roman grammar school curriculum.

[37] Cf. *De Doctrina* II.xl.60–xlii.63, where Augustine compares useful pagan learning to the gold and silver which the Israelites took away from Egypt in the Exodus.

[37] Ellspermann, *Attitude of Early Christian Latin Writers*, 167.

[39] For other discussions, see Max Laistner, *Christianity and Pagan Culture in the Later Roman Empire* (Ithaca, N.Y., 1951), 49–73; Franz Maier, *Augustin und das antike Rom* (Stuttgart, 1955), esp. 17–36 and 206–14; E. K. Rand, *Founders of the Middle Ages* (rpt. New York, 1957), 1–134; and Labriolle, *History and Literature*, 6–32.

[40] Thomas E. Ameringer, *The Stylistic Influence of the Second Sophistic on the Panegyrical Sermons of St. John Chrysostom*, Patristic Studies 6 (Washington, D.C., 1921); Sister M.

Albania Burns. *St. John Chrysostom's Homilies on the Statues: A Study of Rhetorical Qualities and Form*, Patristic Studies 22 (Washington, D.C., 1930); and Campbell, *The Influence of the Second Sophistic*. Sample homilies are printed in a number of anthologies, including those of Guy Lee, David Brewer, and Mabel Platz.

[41] Gregory Naziensus. For a revealing biography of the notorious Prohaeresius, perhaps the best single exemplar of the Second Sophistic, see Philostratus and Eunapius, *Lives of the Sophists*, trans. Wilmer C. Wright, Loeb Classical Library (London, 1922).

[42] Portions of the following have appeared in *Western Speech* 22 (1958): 24–29.

[43] To the best of this writer's knowledge, the texts of the sermons preached at the University of Paris during the academic year 1230–1231 provide the earliest evidence of a new sermon mode. See the Latin texts in M. M. Davy, *Les sermons universitaires parisiens de 1230–31: contribution a l'histoire de la prédication médiévale* (Paris, 1931). The earliest extant manuals of the new style are of an even later date. Cf. Ray C. Petry, *No Uncertain Sound: Sermons that Shaped the Pulpit Tradition* (Philadelphia, 1948), 4ff.

[44] *S. Aurelii Augustini de doctrina christiana libros quattor*, ed. H. J. Vogels, Florilegium Patristicum 24 (Bonnae, 1930). For an easily available translation, see *Saint Augustine on Christian Doctrine*, trans. D. W. Robertson, Library of Liberal Arts 80 (New York, 1958). The fourth book is edited with translation and commentary by Sister Thérèse Sullivan in Patristic Studies 23. Charles S. Baldwin supplies a brief summary of book 4 in his *Medieval Rhetoric and Poetic*, chap. 2.

[45] *De Doctrina* II.i.1.

[46] *De Doctrina* II.xxxix.58. In the same book he refers to "rules of eloquence" as desirable, II.xxxvi.54.

[47] *De Doctrina* IV.v.8. The reference to "wisdom. . . . eloquence" is to the opening passage of Cicero's *De inventione.*

[48] *De Doctrina* IV.2.3. The *officia* of the exordium of a speech in Roman rhetorical theory was to render the audience "attentive, docile, and well-disposed." Cf. *Rhetorica ad Herennium* I.iv.6 and *De inventione* I.xv.20.

[49] *De Doctrina* IV.iii.3. He expresses the same idea elsewhere: II.xxvi.54, and *Contra Cresconium* I.i.2.

[50] *De Doctrina* IV.vi.9. Sections 18 through 26 of book 4 provide numerous examples, especially from Saint Paul. It is interesting to note that when Saint Bede wished to provide examples of the tropes and schemes of the Latin grammarian Donatus, he was able to produce 122 scriptural passages to illustrate them. Bede, *Liber de scematibus et tropis*, in *Rhetores Minores Latini*, ed. Carolus Halm (Lipsiae, 1863), 607–18.

[51] Roman rhetorical training followed three major methods: the teaching of rules (*praecepta*), the imitation of models (*imitatio*), and free composition on a theme (*declamatio*). Augustine in book 4 seems to favor *imitatio* as a method of acquiring eloquence (cf. IV.iii.4–5), but it must be noted that earlier he recommends study of *praecepta* (II. xxxix.58). For a comment on Augustine's possible larger uneasiness later about his recommendation, cf. Laistner, "The Christian Attitude to Pagan Literature," 51.

[52] *De Doctrina*, IV.xv and IV.xxx. For an analysis of an earlier treatment of the same problem, see Jean Daniélou, *Origen*, trans. Walter Mitchell (New York, 1955), 102ff.

[53] Marie Comeau, *La rhétorique de Saint Augustin d'apres les Tractatus in Joannem* (Paris, 1930), xv.

Chapter 6

[1] Cf. Harald Hagendahl, *Augustine and the Latin Classics* (Göteborg, 1967), 558.

[2] De Doctr. Christ. IV.3, 4.

[3] Cf. [H.] I. Marrou, *Saint Augustin et la fin de la culture antique* (Paris, 1938), 524ff.; C. Morhmann, *Études sur le latin des chrétiens* I (Rome, 1958), 359.

[4] Hagendahl, *Augustine and the Latin Classics*, 565.

[5] Hagendahl, *Augustine and the Latin Classics*, 567. For a somewhat more balanced view, see M. Testard, *Saint Augustin et Cicéron* I (Paris, 1958), 235–36, 261, 268–69, 279, 330. Also, among the other studies, C. S. Baldwin, *Medieval Rhetoric and Poetic* (New York, 1928), 52: ". . . and now scarcely an edition or translation of Augustine's works is published which, by cross references and footnotes, does not so stress the 'classical elements' in Augustine's rhetoric that the reader is led to believe that only minor differences distinguish the rhetorical doctrines of Cicero and Augustine." M. Comeau, *La rhétorique de saint Agustin d'après les Tructatus in Ioannem* (Paris, 1930), 21: "Ainsi le livre du *De doctrina Christiana*, en dépit de quelques vues personnelless à son auteur, se place-t-il naturellement dans la longue série de rhétoriques que les écrivains latins publièrent à l'envi jusqu'aux invasions barbares. La théorie du style et de l'éloquence n'y présente aucune nouveacauté." Further references in Hagendahl, *Augustine and the Latin Classics*, 565, n. 1. A stronger emphasis on the newness of Augustine's position is to be found in L. D. McNew, "The Relation of Cicero's Rhetoric to Augustine," *Research Studies of the State College of Washington* 25:1 (1957): 5–13.

[6] Marrou, *Saint Augustin et la fin de la culture antique*, 520. See also Marrou's review of Hagendahl's book in *Gnomon* 41 (1969): 282–85.

[7] J. Oroz, "El *De Doctrina Christiana* o la retorica cristiana," *Estudios Clasicos* 3 (1956): 452–59. Idem., "La retorica augustiniana: Clasicismo y Cristianismo," *Studia Patristica* 6 (1962): 490: "Por lo dicho hasta ahora, podemos affirmar que la obra de san Augustin sobre la retorica es notamente clasicista, es decir sigue la linea ortodoxa de los autores clasicós, y sobre todo de Ciceron."

[8] A. Hus, *Docere et les mots de la jamille de docere: Etude de semantique latine* (Paris: 1965).

[9] De Docr. Christ. IV.12, 27. Cf. Cicero, *Orator* 69; *De Oratore* 11, 310; also *Brutus* 185; *De Optimo Genere Or.* 3.

[10] On the lesser importance of epideictic rhetoric, cf. *Orator* 207; *De Oratore* II.43ff.

[11] Cf. *Orator* 120 ff.; *De Oratore* II.307ff.

[12] On persuasion as the goal of rhetoric, cf. *Orator* 128; *De Oratore* I.60; II.214; *Brutus* 279.

[13] Narrationes credibiles: *Orator* 124. Cf. Aristotle, *Rhetoric* III.16, 1417a.

[14] Cf. *Orator* 78, 208–9; *De Oratore* II.153, 156, 177; *De Doctr Christ.* IV.6, 10.

[15] Cf. *Orator* 15; *De Oratore* II.185 ff., 201ff.; *Tusc. Disp.* IV.55.

[16] On the orator as *vir bonus dicendi peritus*, see A. S. Wilkins's introduction to the *De Oratore* (Oxford: 1888), 47.

[17] Cf. *De Oratore* I.48, 60; II.337.

[18] *Orator* 118.

[19] *Orator* 14ff.

[20] *Orator* 3, 7, 19, 101.

[21] On the whole question of the necessity and feasibility of justice, see esp. Cicero, *De Republica* III.

[22] *De Oratore* II.310–11.

[23] *De Oratore* III.137.

[24] Cf. A. Hus, *Docere et les mots de la jamille de docere*, 283ff.

[25] *Orator* 63.

[26] De Doctr. Christ. IV.4, 6.

[27] De Doctr. Christ. IV.21, 45; 27, 59; 31, 64.

[28] De Doctr. Christ. IV.12, 28.

[29] De Doctr. Christ. IV.17, 34; 25, 55. Cicero, *Orator* 69 and 101.

[30] Compare *De Doctr. Christ.* IV.2, 3 with *De Oratore* II.80; *probabiliter* is substituted for *verisimilis* in *Orator* 122.

[31] *De Doctr. Christ.* IV.2, 3; 14, 30.

[32] *De Doctr. Christ.* IV.12, 28.

[33] *De Doctr. Christ.* IV.5, 7; cf. IV.5, 8; 6, 9; 25, 55; 26, 56; 27, 59. See Augustine's defense of his own use of rhetoric in *Contra Cresconium* I.1.

[34] *De Doctr. Christ.* IV.5, 7. Cicero, *De Inventione* I.1.

[35] *De Doctr. Christ.* IV.21, 35: *rerum divinarum atque salubrium scientia.*

[36] Isaiah 54:13; John 6:45.

[37] *De Gratia Christi* 13, 14 (PL 44, 367).

[38] *De Gratia Christi* 14, 15 (PL 44, 368).

[39] *De Gratia Christi* 12, 13 (PL 44, 367).

[40] *Confessions* VIII.8, 19.

[41] e.g., *De Doctr. Christ.* II.40, 60.

[42] Cf. *Critio* 53d.

[43] Cf. *Apol. of Socrates* 31b.

[44] *Apol. of Socrates* 31d.

[45] Cf. *Gorgias* 521e

[46] *Apol. of Socrates* 17a–b, 20d–e, 22b et passim.

[47] Cf. *Confession* VII.20, 26.

[48] *De Doctr. Christ.* IV.21, 45.

[49] *De Doctr. Christ.* IV.8, 22; cf. *De Gen. contra Manichaeos* I.1.1; *De Mor. Eccl.* I.1.

[50] *De Doctr. Christ.* IV.9, 23.

[51] *De Doctr. Christ.* IV.9, 23.

[52] *Tractatus in Joan.* 98, 2 (PL 35, 1881).

[53] *Tractatus in Joan.* 98, 7 (PL 35, 1884); italics in original.

[54] *Tractatus in Joan.* 98, 2 (PL 35 1881).

[55] *Tractatus in Joan.* 98, 6 (PL 35, 1883).

[56] Cf. *contra Mendacium* 10, 23; D*e Mendacio* 10, 17.

[57] *De Vera Religione* 28, 51.

[58] Cf. *De Sermone Doinini in Monte* 1, 16.

[59] See especially Augustine, "Epistles," 28, 40, and 82.

[60] Cf. Acts 16:3 and 21:17-26.

[61] See Jerome's letter to Augustine in Augustine, "Epistles," 75:3, 4 (PL 33, 252).

[62] *Officiosum mendacium*: "Epistles" 28:3, 4; 40:3, 3; 82:2, 21.

[63] "Epistles," 28.3, 3.
[64] Cf. *De Mendacio* 19, 40.
[65] "Epistles," 82.3, 3.
[66] Cf. *De Mendacio* 8, 11.
[67] *De Doctr. Christ.* I.36, 40.

Chapter 7

[1] "St. Augustine and His Age," in *Saint Augustine* (New York: Meridian Books, 1957), 16.

[2] The influence of Augustine's *De Doctrina Christiana* is too well known to require comment. Martianus devotes a book of his encyclopedia, *On the Marriage of Mercury and Philology*, to rhetoric. The *Marriage* enjoyed widespread popularity during the Middle Ages. See n. 36 below.

[3] See, for example, Charles Sears Baldwin, *Medieval Rhetoric and Poetic (to 1400): Interpreted from Representative Works* (New York: Macmillan, 1928; rpt Gloucester, Mass., 1959); and James J. Murphy, *Rhetoric in the Middle Ages: A History of Rhetorical Theory from St. Augustine to the Renaissance* (Berkeley: University of California Press, 1974). Baldwin devotes the whole of his second chapter to Augustine. He briefly discusses Martianus in the second section of the next chapter, pages 91–94. Murphy deals with both Augustine and Martianus in his second chapter, pages 44–64. But comparison of the two is limited to a single and very general comment on page 64.

[4] See H. P. L'Orange, *Art Forms and Civic Life in the Late Roman Empire* (Princeton: Princeton University Press, 1975), 126–29.

[5] *De Oratore* III.122. All quotations from *De Oratore*, trans. by E. W. Sutton and H. Rackham, Loeb Classical Library (London: William Heineman, 1942).

[6] *De Oratore* I.54, and III.142.

[7] *De Oratore* III.125.

[8] *De Oratore* I.107.

[9] *De Oratore* I.109, II.89, and Brutus, 184–200, esp. 187.

[10] For a more complete analysis of Ciceronian theory, see Donovan J. Ochs, "Cicero's Rhetorical Theory," in *A Synoptic History of Classical Rhetoric*, ed. James J. Murphy (New York: Random House, 1972), 90–150; George Kennedy, *The Art of Rhetoric in the Roman World* (Princeton: Princeton University Press, 1972), 205–30, 239–59; Alain Michael, *Rhétorique et philosophie chez Cicéron: essais sur les fondements philosophique de l'art de parler* (Paris: Presses Universitaires de France, 1960); and A. D. Leeman, *Orationis Ratio: The Stylistic Theories and Practice of the Roman Orators, Historians, and Philosophers*, vol. 1 (Amsterdam: Adolf M. Hakkert, 1963), 91–111.

[11] See George Kennedy, "An Estimate of Quintilian," *American Journal of Philology* 83 (1962): 130–46; and J. Cousin, *Études sur Quintilian*, vol. 1 (rpt. Amsterdam: P. Schippers, 1967), 787.

[12] Eumenius' speech, "Pro instruendis scholis," (esp. 8–14) provides a particularly good example. For analysis of this speech, see Henri I. Marrou, *A History of Education in Antiquity*, trans. George Lamb (New York: Mentor, 1964), 414–15; and C. E. Van Sickle, "Eumenius and the Schools of Autun," *American Journal of Philology* 55 (1934): 236–43.

[13] See, for example, *Theodosian Code* XIII.3.1, 11, 16, and XIV.9.3. The code is available in an English translation by Clyde Pharr (Princeton: Princeton University

Press, 1952). Concerning the influence of rhetoric in late classical rhetoric in general, see Ferdinand Lot, *The End of the Ancient World and the Beginning of the Middle Ages*, trans. Philip and Mariette Leon (New York: Harper & Row, 1961), 163–67; M. L. Clarke, *Rhetoric at Rome: A Historical Survey* (London: Cohen & West, 1953), 142; and H. O. Tayler, *The Classical Heritage of the Middle Ages*, 3rd ed. (New York: Macmillan, 1929), 34–35.

[14] *Art Forms and Civic Life*, 128.

[15] For Augustine's rhetoric, see James J. Murphy, "Saint Augustine and the Debate about a Christian Rhetoric," *Quarterly Journal of Speech* 46 (1960), 400–10; and *Rhetoric in the Middle Ages*, 57–64; Sister Thérèse Sullivan, *S. Aureli Augustini Hipponiensis Episcopi de Doctrina Christiana Liber Quartus: A Commentary with a Revised Text, Introduction, and Translation*, The Catholic University of America Patristic Studies 23 (Washington, D.C.: Catholic University of America, 1930), 1–42; Charles S. Baldwin, *Medieval Rhetoric and Poetic*, 52–73; Clark, *Rhetoric at Rome*, 150–54; J. B. Eskridge, "The Influence of Cicero upon Augustine in the Development of his Oratorical Theory for the Training of the Ecclesiastical Orator," Diss., University of Chicago, 1912; and Maurice Testard, *Saint Augustine et Cicéron, I: Cicéron dans la formation et dans l'oevre de Saint Augustin* (Paris: Études Augustiniennes, 1958), 189–92.

[16] See Sullivan, *S. Aureli Augustini Hipponiensis Episcopi de Doctrina Christiana Liber Quartus*, 8–12; J. Zurek, "De S. Aureli Augustini Preceptis Rhetoricis," in *Dissertationes philologiae Vindobonesis* 8 (Viennes-Leipzig: 1905), 91–108; and Testard, *Saint Augustin et Cicéron, II: Repertoire de textes* (Paris: Études Augustinennes, 1958), 27–29.

[17] Baldwin, *Medieval Rhetoric and Poetic*, 55, n. 7. See also Testard, *Augustin I*, 190, n. 1. Sullivan, *S. Aureli Augustini Hipponiensis Episcopi de Doctrina Christiana Liber Quartus*, 8, calls Augustine's position a return to the *doctrina sana* of Cicero's *Orator* and *De Oratore*.

[18] Saint Augustine, *On Christian Doctrine*, trans. D. W. Robertson. Jr. (Indianapolis: Bobbs-Merrill, 1958), IV.2. All quotations from *De Doctrina Christiana* are taken from Robertson's translation.

[19] *De Doctrina* IV.2.

[20] *De Doctrina* IV.4.

[21] *De Doctrina* IV.5.

[22] *De Doctrina* IV.8.

[23] *De Doctrina* IV.10.

[24] *De Doctrina* IV.7, 8 (several times), 9, 10, 11, 12 (several times), 21, 55, and 61.

[25] *De Doctrina* IV.11.

[26] *De Doctrina* IV.12.

[27] At *De Doctrina* IV.15–21, Augustine analyzes the eloquence of Amos, and at IV.45–50 he attempts to demonstrate the eloquence of Cyprian and Ambrose.

[28] *De Doctrina* IV.35.

[29] Augustine departs from Cicero in a number of other important respects. For example, at IV.35, Augustine rejects Cicero's dictum that the style of a speech ought to vary as a function of the magnitude of the subject. (His argument is that since the Christian orator always deals with the welfare of the soul, all of his speeches are of the same importance.) In this paragraph and the next, I present a very simplified statement about Augustine epistemology and his view of the contemplative life. Lack of space prevents a more detailed analysis. For a good introduction to these subjects, see

Fr. Robert J. O'Connell, "Action and Contemplation," in *Augustine: A Collection of Critical Essays*, ed. R. A. Markus (Garden City, N.Y.: Doubleday, 1972), 38–58.

[30] *De Doctrina* IV.7.

[31] The standard editions of this work are by F. Eysenhardt (Leipzig: Teubner, 1866) and Adolph Dick (Leipzig: Teubner, 1925). James Willis is currently preparing yet another edition for Teubner. Book 5 (on rhetoric) is included in Halm's *Rhetores Latinines Minores* (Leipzig: Teubner, 1866; rpt. Frankfurt: Minerva, 1964), 449–91. There is no published English translation of the *Marriage* as a whole. A translation of the introduction to book 5 is found in Baldwin's *Medieval Rhetoric and Poetic*, pages 93–94. Earlier secondary works are largely supplanted by William Harris Stahl, *Martianus Capella and the Seven Liberal Arts*, vol. 1: *The Quadrivium of Martianus Capella*, with a study of the allegory and verbal disciplines by Richard Johnson and E. L. Burge (New York: Columbia University Press, 1971). (Hereafter cited as *Martianus*). The book includes an extensive bibliography, pages 253–63.

[32] Stahl, *Martianus*, 12. See also Percival Cole, *Later Roman Education in Ausonius, Capella, and the Theodosian Code* (New York: Columbia University Press, 1909), 16ff.; and H. Parker, "The Seven Liberal Arts," *English Historical Review* 5 (1890): 444ff.

[33] Stahl, *Martianus*, 16–20.

[34] Stahl, *Martianus*, 27.

[35] Stahl, *Martianus*, 28–39.

[36] The manuscript evidence is collected in Claudio Leonardi, "I codici di Marziano Capella," *Aevum* 33 (1959: 433–89; 34 (1960): 1–99, 411–524. For an analysis of Martianus' influence, see Stahl, *Martianus*, 55–71 et passim.

[37] See, e.g., Murphy, *Rhetoric in the Middle Ages*, 44–46.

[38] Richard Johnson, "The Allegory and the Trivium," in *Martianus*, 120.

[39] For more detailed summaries of the contents of books 1 and 2, see Eleanor Shipley Duckett, *Latin Writers of the Fifth Century* (New York: Henry Holt, 1930), 224–30; and Percival R. Cole, *Later Roman Education*, 19–22. As Cole indicates, Philology's "disgorging" is literally performed for cosmetic purposes (to reduce the size of her bust). But this act obviously has an important allegorical function in terms of the ceremony as a whole.

[40] *The Metalogicon*, trans. Daniel D. McGarry (Berkeley: University of California Press, 1962), II.

[41] Stahl, *Martianus*, 24–25.

[42] Johnson, *Maritianus*, 83. The analysis of the allegory that follows is based on Johnson, 88–89.

[43] See, Johnson, *Martianus*, 88.

[44] Johnson, *Martianus*, 88.

[45] *De nuptiis Philologiae et Mercurii* IV.13. For the influence of Martianus on Isidore of Seville in this respect, see Ernest Brehaut, *An Encyclopediast of the Dark Ages, Isidore of Seville* (New York: Columbia University Press, 1912; rpt. New York: Burt Franklin, n.d.), 81, note.

[46] Two dissertations study the sources of book 5: Hans Fischer, *Untersuchungen über die Quellen des Rhetorik des Martianus Capella* (Breslau: 1936); and David A. G. Hinks, *Martianus Capella on Rhetoric* (Cambridge: 1935). Fischer (37ff.) stresses the influence of Fortunatianus' *Ars rhetorica* on Martianus much more than does Hinks. But the differ-

ences between the two are not significant for my purposes here. Johnson's analysis, pages 118–19, is based on Hinks.

[47] Brehaut, *Isidore of Seville*, 82, note.

Chapter 8

[1] E. Coseriu, *Die Geschichte der Sprachphilosophie von der Antike bis zur Gegenwart*, vol. 1 (Tübingen: 1975), 123.

[2] H. Steinthal, *Geschichte der Sprachwissenschaft bei den Griechen und Römern*. 2 vols. (Berlin: 1890–1891); L. Lersch, *Die Sprachphilosophie der Alten*. 3 vols. (Bonn: 1838); J. M. Bochenski, *Ancient Formal Logic* (Amsterdam, 1951).

[3] *Augustine of Hippo* (London: 1967), 36.

[4] *Stoicorum Veterum Fragmenta*, ii.222.

[5] *De Trin.* IV.16, 21; *C.D.* V.11; XXII.24.

[6] See Pease's note on Cicero n.d., i.44.

[7] B. Mates, *Stoic Logic* (Berkeley: 1953), 8.

[8] H. Hagendahl, *Augustine and the Latin Classics* (Göteborg, 1967), 498.

[9] Hagendahl, *Augustine and the Latin Classics*, 498.

[10] Hagendahl, *Augustine and the Latin Classics*, 590.

[11] Hagendahl, *Augustine and the Latin Classics*, 627.

[12] H. Dahlmann, *Varro und die hellenistische Sprachtheorie* (Berlin: 1932), 16.

[13] See *83 Questions* and *Contra Academicos* iii.29. Read A. Solignac in *Augustinus Magister* (Paris: 1954), 307–15, on Chrysippean logic in *83 Questions*.

[14] Cf. A. Solignac, "Doxographies et manuels dans la formation philosophique de St. Augustin," *Rech. Aug.* 1 (1958). 147.

[15] Ulrich Duchrow, *Sprachverständnis und Biblisches Hören bei Augustinus* (Tübingen: 1965), 30.

[16] B. Fischer, *De Augustini Disciplinarum Libro qui est De Dialectica* (Jena: 1912).

[17] B. D. Jackson, *Augustine De Dialectica* (Dordrecht: 1975). Jackson bases his conclusions on parallels in language, ideas, and semantic theory between *De Dialectica* and other works of Augustine and on a computer-assisted statistical study of *De Dialectica*. He also gives a detailed history of the work, as well as Penborg's text, a translation, and notes. One reason for doubting the authenticity of the work was a manuscript attribution of the work to Chirius Fortunatius. Jackson concludes: "The negative conclusion that Fortunatius did not write *De Dialectica* is as close to certain as statistical reasoning can take us. The same reasoning allows the positive conclusion that Augustine wrote *De Dialectica*. There seems to be no sufficient reason to reject that conclusion" (71).

[18] See *SVF* iii.267. Cf. Cicero *De Oratore* ii.157, Quintilian 2.15.34, and Diogenes Laertius vii.42. Augustine gives a mixture of Diogenes' definitions of rhetoric and dialectic.

[19] See Diogenes Laertius vii.67–68; Sextus Empiricus, *Adv. Math.* viii.71–72. Augustine uses "sententia" here: Varro had defined *axiôma* as "sententia in qua nihil desideratur" (Aulus Gellius n.a. 16.8.6.).

[20] Rendering *symperasma*; see Mates, *Stoic Logic*, 135. Cf. Cicero, *De Or.* ii.158, and see Jackson's note on the word.

[21] See Fischer, *De Augustini Disciplinarum Libro qui est De Dialectica*, 28f., and Diogenes Laertius vii.63. Cf. K. Barwick, *Probleme der Stoischen Sprachiehre und Rhetorik* (Berlin: 1957), 10.

[22] "To speak is, as the Stoics say, to utter the sound capable of signifying the object conceived."

[23] See Diogenes Laertius vii.56–57.

[24] Chapter 9 opens: "Itaque rectissime a dialecticis dictum est ambiguum esse omne verbum." Cf. Aulus Gellius n.a. 11.12: "Chrysippus ait omne verbum ambiguum natura esse."

Chapter 9

[1] On the discussion of the relationships of Augustine's rhetoric to Greek and Roman models, see James J. Murphy, *Rhetoric in the Middle Ages: A History of Rhetorical Theory from St. Augustine to the Renaissance* (Berkeley: University of California Press, 1974); Richard McKeon, "Rhetoric in the Middle Ages," *Speculum* 1 (1926): 1–32; Maurice Festard, *St. Augustine et Ciceron*, 2 vols., Etudes Augustiniennes (Paris: Aubier, 1958). For the Greek and Roman models, see George Kennedy, *The Art of Persuasion in Greece* (Princeton: Princeton University Press, 1963); idem., *The Art of Rhetoric in the Roman World* (Princeton: Princeton University Press, 1972).

[2] Robert O'Connell, *St. Augustine's* Confessions*: The Odyssey of Soul* (Cambridge: Harvard University Press, 1969); idem., *St. Augustine's Early Theory of Man, A.D. 386–391* (Cambridge: Harvard University Press, 1968).

[3] Hans Georg Gadamer, *Truth and Method* (New York: Crossroad, 1976).

[4] James Preus, *From Shadow to Promise: Old Testament Interpretation from Augustine to Young Luther* (Cambridge: Belknap Press of Harvard University Press, 1969); Henri de Lubac, *Exégèse Médiévale*, 3 vols. (Paris: Aubier, 1968).

[5] Hans Frei, *The Eclipse of Biblical Narrative: A Study of Eighteenth- and Nineteenth-Century Hermeneutics* (New Haven: Yale University Press, 1974), 1–3.

[6] Saint Augustine, *On Christian Doctrine*, trans. D. W. Robertson Jr. (Indianapolis: Bobbs-Merrill, 1958). The translations throughout are Robertson's. I have used the book, chapter (1.1) in the text itself to facilitate use of both Robertson's fine English translation and the original Latin. The latter may be found in J. B. Migne, ed., *Patrological cursus completus. Series Latina* 34.1 (Paris), and in S. Aurelei, *Augustini De Doctrina Christiana Libros Quatuor*, ed. H. J. Vogels, *Floridegium Patristicum* 24 (Bonn, 1930). The necessary citations are, therefore, in the text of this essay rather than in the footnotes.

[7] The best modern study of *caritas* is John Burnaby, *"Amor Dei": A Study of the Religion of St. Augustine* (London: Hodder & Staughton, 1938).

[8] Anders Nygren, *Agape and Eros* (New York: Harper & Row, 1969), 449–563, esp. 539–43.

[9] The classic study is Henri-Irénée Marrou, *Saint Augustin et La Fin de La Culture Antique* (Paris: De Boccard, 1949); see also Ragnar Holte, *Béatitude et Sagesse: St. Augustin et le problème de la fin l'homme dans la philosophie ancienne* (Paris: Etudes Augustiniennes, 1962). These works should be read in conjunction with the fine biography by Peter Brown, *Augustine of Hippo: A Biography* (Berkeley: University of California Press, 1969).

[10] For an analysis here, see David Tracy, *The Analogical Imagination: Christian Theology and the Culture of Pluralism* (New York: Crossroad, 1981), 233–339; Robert M. Grant

with David Tracy, *A Short History of the Interpretation of the Bible* (London: SCM Press, 1984), 174–87.

Chapter 10

[1] Major studies of Augustine's influence on Western culture include those by Charles S. Baldwin, Ernest L. Fortin, Erich Auerbach, Henri-Irénée Marrou, and James J. Murphy.

[2] In the 1960s Joseph Mazzeo argued that book 4 of the *De Doctrina*, especially its theories of style and signs, foreshadows seventeenth-century poetics (*Renaissance and Seventeenth-Century Studies* [New York: Columbia University Press, 1964], 1–16).

[3] *Extemporaneously* means unrehearsed but not unprepared. The preacher prepared by reading and meditation but did not write out a text or memorize prepared phrases or passages. The preacher improvised the sermon in front of the audience, and improvisational skill was part of the appeal of the performance.

[4] Walter Ong has shown how strongly the Latin literary tradition was tied to oral performance (*The Presence of the Word* [New Haven: Yale University Press, 1967], 55–59; *Orality and Literacy* [London: Methuen, 1982], 112–17).

[5] James Murphy likewise takes little notice of Augustine's orality, although he does cite Deferrari and other scholars who acknowledge it (*Rhetoric in the Middle Ages*, 57–63).

[6] For a description of the rhetorical theory and practice of the Second Sophistic school, see George Kennedy, *Classical Rhetoric and Its Christian and Secular Tradition from Ancient to Modern Times* (Chapel Hill: University of North Carolina Press, 1980), 37–40; idem., *Greek Rhetoric under Christian Emperors* (Princeton: Princeton University Press, 1983), 133–80. For an account of Augustine's role in the controversy about rhetoric's place in the newly liberated Christian church, see Murphy, *Rhetoric in the Middle Ages,* 47–63. For a discussion of orality, literacy, and interiority, see Ong, *Orality and Literacy,* 71–74 and *Presence of the Word* 117–21, 124–26, 146–47, 309–10.

[7] Paul de Man has articulated a new account of reading that challenges naive assumptions about how the mind encounters a text.

[8] Miller too fails to note that Augustine's theory is directed toward extemporaneous performance.

[9] Marrou remarks on Augustine's innovation here, pointing out that in late antiquity eloquence was always associated with the application of techniques learned by the formal study of rhetoric. It was a truism to say, as Cicero did, that formal training was not sufficient to produce the orator; it was revolutionary to say, as Augustine did, that such training was not necessary (*Saint Augustin et la fin de la culture antique*, 2nd ed. [Paris: Boccard, 1949], 514–16).

[10] The relation of rhetoric to prayer has been studied very little, and Augustine's concept of prayer has been the subject of only one recent study (Monique Vincent, *Saint Augustin maître de prière: D'après les* Enarrationes in Psalmos [Paris: Beauchesne, 1990]).

[11] Even Cicero in the *De Oratore* laments that "the whole of this department [delivery] has been abandoned by the orators who are the players that act real life, and has been taken over by the actors, who only mimic reality" (3.57.215). Methods of delivery by which a speaker can arouse an audience's emotions are treated in *Rhetorica*

ad Herennium (*Ad C. Herennium* 3.2.19–27) and in Quintilian's comprehensive *Institutio Oratoria* 11.3.1–137.

[12] "Pour [Augustin], les gestes, les attitudes du corps, n'ont de valeur que dans la mesure où ils signifient une réalité profonde. S'ils sont utiles (mais non indispensables) à la prière, c'est en tant que stimulants pour le coeur. En définitive, seule compte l'attitude intérieure, seul l'amour donne toute sa valeur à la prière" (Vincent, *Saint Augustin maître de prière*, 67).

[13] Debora Shuger has argued that Augustine's treatment of style differs from his predecessors' because of his emphasis on emotional force, particularly on the vehemence of the grand style (*Sacred Rhetoric: The Christian Grand Style in the English Renaissance* [Princeton: Princeton University Press, 1988], 43–44). Moreover, as Erich Auerbach points out, Augustine rejects the Ciceronian view that subject matter determines style (*Literary Language and Its Public in Late Latin Antiquity and in the Middle Ages* [Princeton: Princeton University Press, 1993], 35–39); for Augustine, no subject is low or unworthy, so long as it relates to the gospel.

[14] Shuger maintains that the three styles are distinct for Augustine, although she does not attend to their oral or extemporaneous qualities (*Sacred Rhetoric*, 42–46). Sister Thérèse Sullivan mentions the oral qualities of Augustine's treatment of style and finds classical precedents for them in Cicero, but she does not place those qualities in the context of extemporaneous performance (*Augustini De Doctrina Christiana Liber Quartus* [Washington, D.C.: Catholic University of America Press, 1930], 94, 136, 138–43).

BIBLIOGRAPHY

Roger Thompson and Lisa Michelle Thomas

Ad C. Herennium de ratione dicendi [Rhetorica ad Herennium]. Translated by Harry Caplan. Loeb Classical Library. Cambridge: Harvard University Press, 1954.

Ando, Clifford. "Signs, Idols, and the Incarnation in Augustinian Metaphysics." *Representations* 73 (2001): 24–53.

Arnold, Duane W. H., and Pamela Bright, eds. *De Doctrina Christiana: A Classic of Western Culture*. Notre Dame: University of Notre Dame Press, 1995.

Auerbach, Erich. *Literary Language and Its Public in Late Latin Antiquity and in the Middle Ages*. Translated by Ralph Manheim. Bollingen Series 74. Princeton: Princeton University Press, 1993.

Augustine. *The Confessions of St. Augustine*. Translated by Rex Warner. New York: NAL, 1963.

———. *Homilies on the Gospel of John*. Translated by John Gibb and James Innes. A Select Library of the Nicene and Post-Nicene Fathers of the Christian Church 7. Edited by Phillip Schaff. New York: Christian Literature, 1888. Translation of *In Johannis Evangelium Tractatus*.

———. *On Christian Doctrine*. Translated by D. W. Robertson, Jr. Library of the Liberal Arts. Indianapolis: Bobbs-Merrill, 1976. Translation of *De Doctrina Christiana*.

———. "To Proba." *St. Augustine: Letters 83–130*. Translated by Wilfrid Parsons. The Fathers of the Church: A New Translation 10. Washington: Catholic University of America Press, 1953. 376–401. Translation of *Ad Probam*.

———. *The Trinity*. Translated by Stephen McKenna. The Fathers of the Church: A New Translation 45. Washington: Catholic University of America Press, 1963. Translation of *De Trinitate*.

Ayres, Lewis. "Augustine on the Rule of Faith: Rhetoric, Christology, and the Foundation of Christian Thinking." *Augustinian Studies* 36.1 (2005): 33–49.

Baer, Helmut David. "The Fruit of Charity: Using the Neighbor in *De Doctrina Christiana*." *Journal of Religious Ethics* 24.1 (1996): 47–64.

Baldwin, Charles Sears. "St. Augustine on Preaching. (*De Doctrina Christiana*, IV)." In *Medieval Rhetoric and Poetic (to 1400): Interpreted from Representative Works*. 1928. Gloucester: Peter Smith, 1959. 51–73. See also: "St. Augustine on Preaching." In *Essays on the Rhetoric of the Western World*. Edited by Edward P. J. Corbett, James L. Golden, and Goodwin F. Berquist. Dubuque, Iowa: Kendall/Hunt, 1990. 195–206.

Bedos-Rezak, Brigitte Miriam. "Medieval Identity: A Sign and a Concept." *American Historical Review* 105.5 (2000): 1489–1533.

Bergvall, Ake. "The Theology of the Signs: St. Augustine and Spenser's Legend of Holiness." *Studies in English Literature, 1500–1900* 33.1 (1993): 21–42.

Bernard, Robert W. "The Rhetoric of God in the Figurative Exegesis of Augustine." In *Biblical Hermeneutics in Historical Perspective*. Edited by Mark S. Burrows and Paul Rorem. Grand Rapids: W. B. Eerdmans, 1991.

Bitzer, Lloyd. "The Rhetorical Situation." *Philosophy and Rhetoric* 1 (1968): 1–14.

Bizzell, Patricia, and Bruce Herzberg, eds. *The Rhetorical Tradition*. 2nd ed. Boston and New York: Bedford/St. Martins, 2001 (1st ed., 1990).

Bonner, Gerald. *Augustine and His Critics*. London: Routledge, 2000.

Booth, Edward. "St. Augustine's Neo-Platonists." *Augustiniana* 27 (1977): 70–132.

Boyle, Marjorie O'Rourke. "A Likely Story: The Autobiographical as Epideictic." *Journal of the American Academy of Religion* 57 (1989): 23–51.

Brinton, Alan. "St. Augustine and the Problem of Deception in Religious Persuasion." *Religious Studies* 19 (1983): 437–50.

Burke, Kenneth. *The Rhetoric of Religion: Studies in Logology*. Berkeley: University of California Press, 1970.

Caplan, Harry. "The Decay of Eloquence at Rome in the First Century." In *Studies in Speech and Drama in Honor of Alexander M. Drummond*. Edited by Herbert A. Wichelns. Ithaca: Cornell University Press, 1944. 295–325.

———. *Of Eloquence: Studies in Ancient and Medieval Rhetoric*. Ithaca: Cornell University Press, 1970.

Carruthers, Mary J. *The Book of Memory: A Study of Memory in Medieval Culture*. Cambridge: Cambridge University Press, 1990.

Cavadini, John C. "The Sweetness of the Word: Salvation and Rhetoric in Augustine's *De Doctrina Christiana*." In *De Doctrina Christiana: A Clas-*

sic of Western Literature. Edited by Duane W. H. Arnold and Pamela
   Bright. Notre Dame: University of Notre Dame Press, 1995.

Chamberlin, John S. *Increase and Multiply: Arts-of-Discourse Procedure in the Preaching of Donne.* Chapel Hill: University of North Carolina Press, 1976.

Chidester, David. *Word and Light: Seeing, Hearing, and Religious Discourse.* Urbana:
   University of Illinois Press, 1992.

Cicero, Marcus Tullius. *De Oratore.* Translated by E. W. Sutton and H. Rackham. Loeb Classical Library. Cambridge: Harvard University Press,
   1929.

Colish, Marcia L. "Augustine: The Expression of the Word." In *The Mirror of
   Language: A Study in the Medieval Theory of Knowledge.* Rev. ed. Lincoln:
   University of Nebraska Press, 1983. 7–54.

———. "St. Augustine's Silence Revisited." *Augustine Studies* 9 (1978): 15–24.

Condon, Matthew G. "The Unnamed and the Defaced: The Limits of Rhetoric in Augustine's *Confessions.*" *Journal of the American Academy of Religion* 69.1 (2001): 43–63.

Conley, Thomas M. *Rhetoric in the European Tradition.* Chicago: University of
   Chicago Press, 1990.

Corrigan, Kevin. "Love of God, Love of Self, and Love of Neighbor: Augustine's Critical Dialogue with Platonism." *Augustinian Studies* 34.1
   (2003): 97–106.

Curtius, Ernst Robert. *European Literature and the Latin Middle Ages.* New York:
   Bollingen Foundation, 1953.

Deferrari, Roy. "St. Augustine's Method of Composing and Delivering Sermons." *American Journal of Philology* 43 (1922): 97–123, 193–220.

Deems, Mervin Monroe. "Augustine's Use of Scripture." *Church History* 14.3
   (1945): 188–200.

de Man, Paul. *Allegories of Reading: Figural Language in Rousseau, Nietzsche, Rilke,
   and Proust.* New Haven: Yale University Press, 1979.

De Rijk, Rudolf P. "St. Augustine on Language." In *Studies Presented to Professor
   Roman Jakobson by His Students.* Edited by Charles E. Gribble. Cambridge, Mass.: Slavica. 91–104.

Derrida, Jacques. *Of Grammatology.* Trans. Gayatri Chakravorty Spivak. Baltimore: Johns Hopkins University Press, 1976.

Dieter, Otto Alvin, and William Charles Kurth. "The *De Rhetorica* of Aurelius
   Augustine." *Communication Monographs* 35 (1968): 90–108.

DiLorenzo, Raymond D. "Rational Research in the Rhetoric of Augustine's
   Confessio." In *From Cloister to Classroom.* Edited by E. Rozanne Elder.
   Kalamazoo: Cistercian Publications, 1986. 1–26.

Doyle, Daniel Edward. *The Bishop as Disciplinarian in the Letters of St. Augustine*. New York: P. Lang, 2002.

Doyle, G. Wright. "Augustine's Sermonic Method." *Westminster Theological Journal* 39 (1977): 213–38.

Eden, Kathy. "The Rhetorical Tradition and Augustinian Hermeneutics in *De Doctrina Christiana*." *Rhetorica* 8 (1990): 45–63.

Ellis, John M. *Against Deconstruction*. Princeton: Princeton University Press, 1989.

English, Edward D., ed. *Reading and Wisdom:* De Doctrina Christiana *of Augustine in the Middle Ages*. Notre Dame: University of Notre Dame Press, 1995.

Eskridge, James B. *The Influence of Cicero upon Augustine in the Development of His Oratorical Theory for the Training of the Ecclesiastical Orator*. Menasha, Wis.: Collegiate Press, George Banta, 1912.

Fish, Stanley E. *Self-Consuming Artifacts: The Experience of Seventeenth-Century Literature*. Berkeley: University of California Press, 1972.

Fortin, Ernest L. "Augustine and the Problem of Christian Rhetoric." *Augustine Studies* 5 (1974): 85–100.

Freccero, John. "Logology: Burke on St. Augustine." In *Representing Kenneth Burke*. Edited by Hayden White and Margaret Brose. Baltimore: Johns Hopkins University Press, 1982. 52–67.

Gamble, Harry Y. *Books and Readers in the Early Church: A History of Early Christian Texts*. New Haven: Yale University Press, 1995.

Gerli, E. Michael. "The Greeks, the Romans, and the Ambiguity of Signs: *De Doctrina Christiana*, the Fall, and the Hermeneutics of the *Libro de Buen Amor*." *Bulletin of Spanish Studies* 79.4 (2002): 411–28.

Goldberg, Jonathan. *Writing Matter: From the Hands of the English Renaissance*. Palo Alto: Stanford University Press, 1990.

Hanby, Michael. *Augustine and Modernity*. London: Routledge, 2003.

Hannam, Walter A. "*Nodo Unitatis et Caritatis:* The Structure and Argument of Augustine's *De Doctrina Christiana*." *Florilegium* 15 (1998): 145–65.

Harpham, Geoffrey Galt. "The Fertile Word: Augustine's Ascetics of Interpretation." *Criticism* 28.3 (1986): 237–54.

Harris, William V. *Ancient Literacy*. Cambridge: Harvard University Press, 1989.

Hilgendorf, M. D. "St. Augustine: The Original Homiletician." *Concordia Journal* 17 (1991): 164–75.

Hull, S. Lorraine. *Strasberg's Method as Taught by Lorrie Hull*. Woodbridge, Conn.: Ox Bow, 1985.

Jackson, Darrell B. *Semantics and Hermeneutics in St. Augustine's* De Doctrina Christiana. New Haven: Yale University Press, 1967.

———. "The Theory of Signs in St. Augustine's *De Doctrina Christiana.*" *Revue des Etudes Augustiniennes* 15 (1969): 9–49.

Jamieson, Kathleen. "Jerome, Augustine, and the Stesichoran Palinode." *Rhetorica* 5 (1987): 353–67.

Johnson, W. R. "Isocrates Flowering: The Rhetoric of St. Augustine." *Philosophy and Rhetoric* 9 (1976): 217–31.

Kannengiesser, Charles. "Local Setting and Motivation of *De Doctrina Christiana.*" In *Collectanea Augustiniana: Augustine-Presbyter Factus Sum.* Edited by Joseph T. Lienhard, Earl C. Muller, and Roland J. Teske. New York: Peter Lang, 1993. 331–39.

Kennedy, George. *Classical Rhetoric and Its Christian and Secular Tradition from Ancient to Modern Times.* Chapel Hill: University of North Carolina Press, 1980.

———. *Greek Rhetoric under Christian Emperors.* Princeton: Princeton University Press, 1983.

———. "The Sophists as Declaimers." In *Approaches to the Second Sophistic.* Edited by G. W. Bowersock. University Park, Penn.: American Philological Association, 1974. 17–22.

Kleinberg, Aviad M. "De Agone Christiano: The Preacher and His Audience." *Journal of Theological Studies* 38 (1987): 16–33.

Krashen, Stephen D., and Tracy Terrell. *The Natural Approach: Language Acquisition in the Classroom.* Oxford: Pergamon, 1983.

Leff, Michael C. "St. Augustine and Martianus Cappella: Continuity and Change in Fifth-Century Latin Rhetorical Theory." *Communication Quarterly* 24.4 (1976): 2–9.

Levenick, Christopher D. "Exceptis Igitur Iocis: Augustine on Lying, Joking, and Jesting." *Augustinian Studies* 35.2 (2004): 301–323.

Luecke, Richard. "The Rhetoric of Faith." *Word and World* 6.3 (1986): 304–12.

Markus, Robert Austin, ed. *Augustine: A Collection of Critical Essays.* New York: Doubleday, 1972.

———. *Saeculum: History and Society in the Theology of St. Augustine.* Cambridge: Cambridge University Press, 1970.

Marrou, Henri-Irénée. *The Resurrection and Saint Augustine's Theology of Human Values.* Trans. Maria Consolata. Villanova: Villanova University Press, 1966.

———. *St. Augustine and His Influence through the Ages.* Translated by Patrick Hepburne-Scott; texts of St. Augustine trans. Edmund Hill. Men

of Wisdom, No. 2. New York: Harper Torchbooks; London: Long-mans, 1957.

Marrou, Henri-Irénée. *Saint Augustin et la fin de la culture antique.* 1938. 2nd ed. Paris: Boccard, 1949.

———. *Saint Augustin et la fin de la culture antique: Retractatio.* Paris: Boccard, 1949.

———. *St. Augustine et la fin de la culture antique.* 4th ed. Paris: Éditions E. De Boccard, 1958.

Marshall, Donald G. "Making Letters Speak: Interpreter as Orator in Augustine's *De Doctrina Christiana.*" *Religion and Literature* 24.2 (1992): 1–17.

Martin, Thomas F. "'An Abundant Supply of Discourse': Augustine and the Rhetoric of Monasticism." *Downside Review* 116 (1998): 7–25.

———. *Our Restless Heart: The Augustinian Tradition.* Maryknoll, N.Y.: Orbis, 2003.

Mazzeo, Joseph A. "St. Augustine's Rhetoric of Silence." *Journal of the History of Ideas* 23 (1962): 175–96.

———. *Renaissance and Seventeenth-Century Studies.* New York: Columbia University Press, 1964.

McWilliam, Joanne, Timothy Barnes, Michael Fahey, and Peter Slater, eds. *Augustine: From Rhetor to Theologian.* Waterloo, Ont.: Wilfrid Laurier University Press, 1992. 109–20.

Miller, Susan. *Rescuing the Subject: A Critical Introduction to Rhetoric and the Writer.* Carbondale: Southern Illinois University Press, 1989.

Mohler, James A. *Late Have I Loved You: An Interpretation of Saint Augustine on Human and Divine Relationships.* Brooklyn: New City Press, 1991.

Monfasani, John. "The *De Doctrina Christiana* and Renaissance Rhetoric." In *Reading and Wisdom: The* De Doctrina Christiana *of Augustine in the Middle Ages.* Edited by Edward D. English. Notre Dame: University of Notre Dame Press, 1995. 172–88.

Mountford, Roxanne. "Aurelius Augustinus." In *Classical Rhetorics and Rhetoricians: Critical Studies and Sources.* Edited by Michelle Ballif and Michael G. Moran. Westport, Conn. and London: Praeger Publishers, 2005: 74–85.

Murphy, James J., ed. *Medieval Eloquence: Studies in the Theory and Practice of Medieval Rhetoric.* Berkeley: University of California Press, 1978.

———. *Rhetoric in the Middle Ages: A History of Rhetorical Theory from St. Augustine to the Renaissance.* Berkeley: University of California Press, 1974.

———. "Saint Augustine and the Debate about a Christian Rhetoric." *Quarterly Journal of Speech* 46 (1960): 400–410.

Nichols, Stephen G. "Prophetic Discourse: St. Augustine to Christine de Pizan." In *The Bible in the Middle Ages: Its Influence on Literature and Art*. Ed. Bernard S. Levy. Binghamton, N.Y.: Medieval and Renaissance Texts and Studies, 1992. 51–76.

O'Meara, John J. "Augustine's *Confessions*: Elements of Fiction." In *Augustine: From Rhetor to Theologian*. Edited by Joanne McWilliam, Timothy Barnes, Michael Fahey, and Peter Slater. Waterloo, Ont.: Wilfrid Laurier University Press, 1992. 77–95.

———. "The Neoplatonism of St. Augustine." *Neoplatonism and Christian Thought*. Edited by Dominic J. O'Meara. Norfolk: International Society for Neoplatonic Studies, 1981. 34–41.

Ong, Walter J. *Orality and Literacy: The Technologizing of the Word*. London: Methuen, 1982.

———. "Oral Residue in Tudor Prose Style." In *Rhetoric, Romance, and Technology: Studies in the Interaction of Expression and Culture*. Ithaca: Cornell University Press, 1971. 23–47.

———. *The Presence of the Word: Some Prolegomena for Cultural and Religious History*. New Haven: Yale University Press, 1967.

Patton, John H. "Wisdom and Elegance: The Alliance of Exegesis and Rhetoric in Augustine." *Communication Studies* 28 (1977): 96–105.

Penticoff, Richard. "Augustine, Saint, Bishop of Hippo (354–430 C.E.)." In *Encyclopedia of Rhetoric and Composition: Communication from Ancient Times to the Information Age*. Edited by Theresa Enos. New York: Garland, 1996. 50–2.

Portalié, Eugène. *A Guide to the Thought of Saint Augustine*. Chicago: H. Regnery, 1960.

Press, Gerald A. "The Content and Argument of Augustine's *De Doctrina Christiana*." *Augustiniana* 31 (1981): 165–82.

Protevi, John. "*Inventio* and the Unsurpassable Metaphor: Ricoeur's Treatment of Augustine's Time Meditation." *Philosophy Today* 43.1 (1999): 86–94.

Pulsiano, Phillip. "Language Theory and Narrative Patterning in *De Civitate Dei*, Books XV–XVIII." In *The City of God: A Collection of Critical Essays*. Edited by Dorothy F. Donnelly. New York: Peter Lang, 1995. 241–52.

Quillen, Carol E. "A Tradition Invented: Petrarch, Augustine, and the Language of Humanism." *Journal of the History of Ideas* 53.2 (1992): 179–207.

Quintilian. *The Institutio Oratoria of Quintilian.* Translated by H. E. Butler. 4 vols. Loeb Classical Library. Cambridge: Harvard University Press; London: Heinemann, 1980.

Ray, Roger D. "Christian Conscience and Pagan Rhetoric: Augustine's Treatises on Lying." *Studia Patristica* 22. Edited by Elizabeth A. Livingstone. Leuven, Belg.: Peeters Press, 1987.

Reinsma, Luke. "Rhetoric in England: The Age of Aelfric, 970–1020." *Communication Monographs* 44 (1977): 390–403.

Schaeffer, John D. "The Dialectic of Orality and Literacy: The Case of Book 4 of Augustine's *De Doctrina Christiana.*" *PMLA* 111.5 (1996): 1133–45.

Schildgen, Brenda Deen. "Augustine's Answer to Jacques Derrida in the *De Doctrina Christiana.*" *New Literary History: A Journal of Theory and Interpretation* 25.2 (1994): 383–97.

Scott, Jamie S. "From Literal Self-Sacrifice to Literary Self-Sacrifice: Augustine's *Confessions* and the Rhetoric of Testimony." In *Augustine: From Rhetor to Theologian.* Ed. J. McWilliam. Waterloo, Ont.: Wilfrid Laurier University Press, 1992. 31–49.

Shuger, Debora K. *Sacred Rhetoric: The Christian Grand Style in the English Renaissance.* Princeton: Princeton University Press, 1988.

Sloane, Thomas O. *Donne, Milton, and the End of Humanist Rhetoric.* Berkeley: University of California Press, 1985.

Smith, James K. A. "Between Predication and Silence: Augustine on How (Not) to Speak of God." *Heythrop Journal* 41.1 (2000): 66–86.

Staley, Kevin M. "Augustine on Language and the Nature of Belief." In *Collectanea Augustiniana: Augustine-Presbyter Factus Sum.* Edited by Joseph T. Lienhard, Earl C. Muller, and Roland J. Teske. New York: Peter Lang, 1993. 305–16.

Stanislavski, Constantin. *Stanislavski's Legacy: A Collection of Comments on a Variety of Aspects of an Actor's Art and Life.* Edited and translated by Elizabeth Reynolds Hapgood. New York: Theatre Arts, 1968.

Street, Brian. *Literacy in Theory and Practice.* Cambridge: Cambridge University Press, 1984.

Sullivan, Sister Thérèse. *Augustini De Doctrina Christiana Liber Quartus.* Catholic University of America Patristic Studies 23. Washington, D.C.: Catholic University of America Press, 1930.

Sutherland, Christine Mason. "Love as Rhetorical Principle: The Relationship between Content and Style in the Rhetoric of St. Augustine." In

Grace, Politics, and Desire: Essays on Augustine. Edited by H. A. Meynell. Calgary: University of Calgary Press, 1990.

———. "Reforms of Style: St. Augustine and the Seventeenth Century." *Rhetoric Society Quarterly* 21.2 (1991): 26-37.

Toom, Tarmo. "Augustine on the 'Communicative Gaps' in Book Two of *De Doctrina Christiana.*" *Augustinian Studies* 34.2 (2003): 213–222.

Tracy, David W. "Charity, Obscurity, Clarity: Augustine's Search for a True Rhetoric." In *Morphologies of Faith.* Edited by Mary Gerhart and Anthony C. Yu. Atlanta: Scholars Press, 1990.

Trinkuns, Charles. "Erasmus, Augustine, and the Nominalists." *Archiv fur Reformationsgeschichte* 67 (1976): 5–32.

Troup, Calvin L. *Temporality, Eternity, and Wisdom: The Rhetoric of Augustine's* Confessions. Columbia: University of South Carolina Press, 1999.

Vance, Eugene. "St. Augustine: Language as Temporality." In *Mimesis: From Mirror to Method, Augustine to Descartes.* Edited by John D. Lyon and Stephen G. Nichols, Jr. Lebanon, N.H.: University Press of New England, 1992. 20–35.

Vincent, Monique. *Saint Augustin maître de prière: D'après les Enarrationes in Psalmos.* Paris: Beauchesne, 1990.

Watson, Gerard. "Imagination and Religion in Classical Thought." In *Religious Imagination.* Edited James P. Mackey. Edinburgh: Edinburgh University Press, 1986.

———. "St. Augustine's Theory of Language." *Maynooth Review* 6.2 (1982): 4–20.

Weaver, Rebecca Harden. "Reading the Signs: Guidance for the Pilgrim Community." *Interpretation* 58.1 (2004): 28–42.

Wiethoff, William E. "Obscurantism in Ancient Hellenistic Rhetoric." *Communication Studies* 30 (1979): 211–19.

———. "The Obscurantist Design in Saint Augustine's Rhetoric." *Communication Studies* 31 (1980): 128–36.

Yarbrough, Stephen R. "The Love of Invention: Augustine, Davidson, and the Discourse of Unifying Belief." *Rhetoric Society Quarterly* 30.1 (2000): 29–46.

Yoos, George E., ed. *Rhetoric Society Quarterly* 15.3–4 (1985) (double issue).

—Anderson, Floyd D. "*De Doctrina Christiana* 2.18.28: The Convergence of Athens and Jerusalem."

—Erickson, Keith V. "The Significance of '*Doctrina*' in Augustine's *De Doctrina Christiana.*"

—Fulkerson, Gerald. "Augustine's Attitude toward Rhetoric in *De Doctrina Christiana*: The Significance of 2.37.55."

—King, Andrew A. "St. Augustine's Doctrine of Participation as a Metaphysics of Persuasion."

—Wiethoff, William E. "The Merits of *De Doctrina Christiana*: 4.11.26."

Young, Archibald M. "Some Aspects of St. Augustine's Literary Aesthetics, Studied Chiefly in *De Doctrina Christiana*." *Harvard Theological Review* 62.3 (1969): 289–99.

Young, Frances. "Augustine's Hermeneutics and Postmodern Criticism." *Interpretation* 58.1 (2004): 42–55.

INDEX